New Trends in Technologies: Control, Management, Computational Intelligence and Network Systems

edited by

Prof. Meng Joo Er

New Trends in Technologies: Control, Management, Computational Intelligence and Network Systems

Edited by Prof. Meng Joo Er

Republished by InTech

Janeza Trdine 9, 51000 Rijeka, Croatia

Publishing Process ManagerJelena Marusic

Technical Editor Goran Bajac

Cover Designer Martina Sirotic

Additional hard copies can be obtained from orders@intechopen.com

New Trends in Technologies: Control, Management, Computational Intelligence and Network Systems,
Edited by Prof. Meng Joo Er
p. cm.
ISBN 978-953-307-213-5

For EU product safety concerns:
IN TECH d.o.o., Prolaz Marije Krucifikse Kozulić 3, 51000 Rijeka, Croatia,
info@intechopen.com or visit our website at intechopen.com.

Meet the editor

Professor Er Meng Joo is currently a Full Professor in Electrical and Electronic Engineering, Nanyang Technological University, Singapore. He served as the Founding Director of Renaissance Engineering Programme and an elected member of the NTU Advisory Board and from 2009 to 2012. He served as a member of the NTU Senate Steering Committee from 2010 to 2012. He has authored five books entitled "Dynamic Fuzzy Neural Networks: Architectures, Algorithms and Applications" and "Engineering Mathematics with Real-World Applications" published by McGraw Hill in 2003 and 2005 respectively, and "Theory and Novel Applications of Machine Learning" published by In-Tech in 2009, "New Trends in Technology: Control, Management, Computational Intelligence and Network Systems" and "New Trends in Technology: Devices, Computer, Communication and Industrial Systems", both published by SCIYO, 18 book chapters and more than 500 refereed journal and conference papers in his research areas of interest. Professor Er was bestowed the Web of Science Top 1 % Best Cited Paper and the Elsevier Top 20 Best Cited Paper Award in 2007 and 2008 respectively. In recognition of the significant and impactful contributions to Singapore's development by his research projects, Professor Er won the Institution of Engineers, Singapore (IES) Prestigious Engineering Achievement Award twice (2011 and 2015). He is also the only dual winner in Singapore IES Prestigious Publication Award in Application (1996) and IES Prestigious Publication Award in Theory (2001). Under his leadership, the NTU Team emerged first runner-up in the Freescale Technology Forum Design Challenge 2008. He received the Teacher of the Year Award for the School of EEE in 1999, School of EEE Year 2 Teaching Excellence Award in 2008, the Most Zealous Professor of the Year Award in 2009 and the Outstanding Mentor Award in 2014. He also received the Best Session Presentation Award at the World Congress on Computational Intelligence in 2006, Best Paper Award (First Prize) at the International Automatic Control Conference 2016 and Best Presentation Award at the IEEE International Conference on Intelligent Control, Power and Instrumentation (ICICPI) 2016. On top of this, he has more than 60 awards received at international and local competitions. Currently, Professor Er serves as the Editor-in-Chief of 3 international journals, namely International Journal of Intelligent Autonomous Systems, Transactions on Machine Learning and Artificial Intelligence and the International Journal of Electrical and Electronic Engineering and Telecommunications. He also serves an Area Editor of International Journal of Intelligent Systems Science and an Associate Editor of 14 refereed international journals, namely IEEE Transaction on Cybernetics, Information Sciences, Neurocomputing, Asian Journal of Control, International Journal of Fuzzy Systems, ETRI Journal, International Journal of Humanoid Robots, International Journal of Modelling, Simulation and Scientific Computing, International Journal of Applied Computational Intelligence and Soft Computing, International Journal of Business Intelligence and Data Mining, International Journal of Fuzzy and Uncertain Systems, International Journal of Automation and Smart Technology, International Journal of Intelligent Information Processing and an editorial board member of the Open Automation and Control Systems Journal and the EE Times. Professor Er has been invited to deliver more than 60 keynote speeches and invited talks overseas. He has also been active in professional bodies. Under his leadership, the IEEE CIS Singapore Chapter won the CIS Outstanding Chapter Award in 2012 (The Singapore Chapter is the first chapter in Asia to win the award). He was bestowed the IEEE Outstanding Volunteer Award (Singapore Section) and the IES Silver Medal in 2011. He is listed in Who's Who in Engineering, Singapore, Edition 2013.

Contents

Preface

From the metallurgists who ended the Stone Age to the shipbuilders who united the world's peoples through travel and trade, the past witnessed many marvels of engineering prowess. As civilization grew, it was nourished and enhanced with the help of increasingly sophisticated tools for agriculture, technologies for producing textiles, and inventions transforming human interaction and communication. Inventions such as the mechanical clock and the printing press irrevocably changed civilization.

In the modern era, the Industrial Revolution brought engineering's influence to every niche of life, as machines supplemented and replaced human labor for countless tasks, improved systems for sanitation enhanced health, and the steam engine facilitated mining, powered trains and ships, and provided energy for factories.

In the century just ended, engineering recorded its grandest accomplishments. The widespread development and distribution of electricity and clean water, automobiles and airplanes, radio and television, spacecraft and lasers, antibiotics and medical imaging, and computers and the Internet are just some of the highlights from a century in which engineering revolutionized and improved virtually every aspect of human life.

In this book entitled "New Trends in Technologies: Control, Management, Computational Intelligence and Network Systems", the authors provide a glimpse of the new trends of technologies pertaining to control, management, computational intelligence and network systems. The book comprised of 21 very interesting and excellent articles covers core topics ranging from "A Survey of Decentralised Adaptive Control" to "Transplant Evolution for Optimisation of General Controllers" in Control, "Technologies and Methodologies Enabling Reliable Real-time Wireless Automation" to "Inventory Management: Spare Parts and Reliability Centred Maintenance for Production Lines" in Management and "Face Recognition Under Varying Illumination to Development" of "Fuzzy Neural Networks: Current Framework and Trends". It also covers topics pertaining to network systems ranging from "EMC Aspect as Important Parameter of New Technologies" to "Methods and Tools for the Temporal Analysis of Avionic Networks". The book will serve as a unique purpose through these multi-disciplinary topics to share different but interesting views on each of these exciting topics which form the backbone of Engineering Challenges for the 21St Century.

I would like to thank all the authors for their excellent contributions in the different areas of their expertise. It is their domain knowledge, enthusiastic collaboration and strong support which made the creation of this book possible. I sincerely hope that readers of all disciplines will find this book valuable.

Editor

Professor Meng Joo Er
School of Electrical and Electronic Engineering
Nanyang Technological University

1

A Survey of Decentralized Adaptive Control

Karel Perutka
Tomas Bata University in Zlin, Faculty of Applied Informatics
Czech Republic,
European Union

1. Introduction

Systems with multi inputs and multi outputs are in common controlled by centralized controllers, multivariable controllers or by a set of single input and single output controllers. The decentralized systems dominated in industry due to the following advantages: flexibility in operation, failure tolerance, simplified design and tuning (Garelli et al., 2006).
Decentralized control techniques can be found in a broad spectrum of applications ranging from robotics to civil engineering. Approaches to decentralized control design differ from each other in the assumptions - kind of interaction, the model of the system, the model of information exchange and the control design technique (Keviczky et al., 2006).
Bakule wrote the nice paper that reviews the past and present in the area of decentralized control (Bakule, 2008). The usefulness of decentralized control is provided in a very readable way. The paper includes the description of disjoint subsystems, overlapping subsystems, symmetric composite systems and decentralized networked control. One of the useful approaches to decentralized control problems was the parametrization (Date and Chow, 1993). This paper is extended by the work of Garelli et al. (Garelli et al., 2006) who focused on the limiting interactions in decentralized control of systems. During decentralized control might appear some problems at systems composed of two subsystems. A special linear star coupled dynamical network was proposed to limit the influence of some problems (Duan et al., 2007).
During last years it was proven that it seems to be perspective to combine predictive and decentralized control, for example unconstrained networked decentralized model predictive control (Vaccarini et al., 2009) or fuzzy and neural networks, such as adaptive decentralized control using recurrent fuzzy neural networks (Hernandez and Tang, 2009). Another task is to use automatic decentralized control structure selection (Jørgensen and Jørgensen, 2000).
Adaptive control enlarges the area of usage at decentralized controllers. Adaptive control does not limit at linear systems, it can deal for example with time delay (Shah et al., 1997).
Another possibility is to use the predictive control with the combination with adaptive control (Clarke, 1996). Nice paper summarizing the results and applications at adaptive control of nonlinear systems was written by Marino (Marino, 1997).
The chapter is organized in the following way. After introduction, there is a literary research dealing with decentralized control and adaptive control. Next part of the chapter describes chosen method of multi model decentralized control with the results of experiments.

2. Decentralized control

2.1 Nonlinear systems

This subchapter deals with the following: The gap metric approach applied on nonlinear multi-unit plants, linearized model of the nonlinear chemical plant, decentralized power controllers which reduces the disturbance to the power frequency.

A gap metric approach is one of the approaches used for decentralized control (Lee at al., 2000). The plants were multi-unit and they displayed nonlinear behavior. This method has two measures that characterize stability and performance of a controller and are derived from robust control theory. In the paper written by Li at al. (Li et al., 2000), a common design strategy for decentralized control of a chemical process is given. It generates a linearized model of the nonlinear plant and then designs a decentralized robust controller based on the linearized model. Decentralized power controllers are designed in paper (Guo et al., 2000). It is an application of nonlinear decentralized robust control to large-scale power systems with the usage of nonlinear bounds of generator interconnections, which achieves less-conservative control gains. Decentralized controller design for power systems is popular (Xi et al., 2002). The paper is dealing with a multimachine power system as a Hamiltonian control system with dissipation and its decentralized excitation control solving the problem of disturbance attenuation simultaneously.

2.2 Large-scale systems

The mentioned papers of this subchapter solve the problem of continuous decentralized output feedback stabilization, decentralized holographic-structure controllers with unmatched uncertainties, linear constant decentralized controllers for such systems, decentralized state-feedback and variable structure controllers.

The problem of continuous decentralized output feedback robust stabilization is successfully solved by Yan and Dai (Yan and Dai, 1998). It was studied for time-varying nonlinear large scale systems, in which general interconnection and fully nonlinear nominal subsystems were considered. Robust decentralized holographic-structure controllers (DHSCs) are given by Yan et al. (Yan et al., 1999). In this paper, robust control for a class of nonlinear large-scale systems possessing similar subsystems is considered. In the paper written by Ni and Chen (Ni and Chen, 1996), the method for the design of linear constant decentralized robust controllers for a class of uncertain interconnected systems is presented. Ugrinovskii et al. (Ugrinovskii et al., 2000) solved the decentralized state-feedback stabilization. In the considered class of uncertain large-scale systems, the interconnections between subsystems are described by integral quadratic constraints. Variable structure controller was also used in decentralized control (Tsai et al., 2001). The introduction of two sets of switching surfaces in the sliding phase together with the new invariance conditions were given, meaning the sliding mode was used. The usage of decentralized receding horizon control was proven as useful (Keviczky et al., 2006).

2.3 Autonomous control

This subchapter solves the question of autonomous decentralized systems and swarm intelligence, provides application of such systems in Gensym G2 environment on the evaporating system or control of the bio-chemical reactor for separating a gas phase from a liquid phase.

The question of autonomous decentralized systems and swarm intelligence is solved by Koshijima et al. (Koshijima et al., 1996). In the paper, authors present the framework of processing systems design and operations on the basis of the autonomous decentralized system concept. This approach was verified in Chiyoda Corporation in Yokohama, Japan. Application of autonomous decentralized systems was also done in Gensym G2 environment on the multi-effect evaporating system (Koshijima and Toki, 1997). The authors give the realization method on control system, the autonomous decentralized chemical plant (ADChP), the special term and the design of the communication system. Decentralized autonomous control system based on computer technology of fieldbus for reducing the operative personnel in Japanese plant in practice is given by Egi (Egi, 1997).

2.4 Robust control

Robust control is a very popular approach in decentralized control. For instance, the robust exponential decentralized stabilization is solved. Moreover, the usage of RGA is mentioned as well as the J-spectral factorization in decentralized suboptimal control is discussed. The design of robust control for interconnected systems with time-varying uncertainties is also solved. The idea of combination of the decentralized and centralized control is also given. There exists also a combination of adaptive and robust decentralized control, for instance decentralized model reference adaptive control. Robust control of unstable systems is another solved task of decentralized controllers.

The question of decentralized stabilization is formulated and solved by Guan et al. (Guan et al., 2002), namely the robust exponential decentralized stabilization for a class of large-scale, time delay, and uncertain impulsive dynamical systems. Samyudia et al. (Samyudia et al., 1995) proposed a new approach to decentralized control design. In decentralized control design, interaction measures such as the Relative Gain Array (RGA) and the Block Relative Gain Array (BRGA) are commonly used, especially to screen alternative control structures, as the authors says. Another way is based on interaction measures based upon the structured singular value, μ. Decentralized global robust stabilization was also presented by Xie and Xie (Xie and Xie, 2000). The paper focuses on a class of large-scale interconnected minimum-phase nonlinear systems with parameter uncertainty and nonlinear interconnections. J-spectral factorization in decentralized controller and suboptimal controller design for two-channel systems is mentioned by Seo et al. (Seo et al., 1999). In paper by Yang and Zhang (Yang and Zhang, 1996), the decentralized robust control design for a class of interconnected systems with time-varying uncertainties. The idea of combination the decentralized and centralized control is given by Guo et al. (Guo et al., 1999). The problem of decentralized H-infinity almost disturbance decoupling for a class of large-scale nonlinear uncertain systems in the absence of matching conditions was solved. The question of global decentralized robust stabilization is solved by Liu and Huang (Liu and Huang, 2001). The stabilization was done for a class of large-scale interconnected nonlinear systems with uncertainties. Makoudi and Radouane (Makoudi and Radouane, 1999) presented the decentralized model reference adaptive control (DMRAC). The controlled subsystems are interconnected subsystems with unknown and/or time delay. The totally decentralized adaptive stabilizers are formulated by Zhang et al. (Zhang et al., 2000). The paper presents a scheme of for stabilizers for a class of large-scale subsystems having arbitrary relative degrees. The attention to the robust decentralized controller design for unstable systems is paid by Loh and Chiu (Loh and Chiu, 1997). The stable factorization approach is used for facilitating the independent design for open-loop unstable processes.

2.5 PI control

The papers dealing with PI control formulates the guide lines for the tuning and the evaluation. PI controllers might be obtained by minimizing a robust performance criterion using mu-synthesis, for instance, or might be used in HVAC control systems in buildings helping to reduce energy use.

Pomerleau and Pomerleau (Pomerleau and Pomerleau, 2001) gave the guide lines for the tuning and the evaluation of decentralized and decoupling controllers were. In particular, the design of single-input single-output (SISO) controllers for highly coupled multivariable processes often leads to poor performance because of a bad choice of manipulated variables, poor specifications and poor tuning of the controllers. One of the very interesting methods of decentralized robust control is also presented by Gagnon et al. (Gagnon et al., 1998). The PI controller tunings are obtained by minimizing a robust performance criterion and the minimized cost function is derived from the standard mu-synthesis criterion and it takes into account the process uncertainty and desired performance. The usage of decentralized control loops in HVAC control is given by Jetté and al., (Jetté and al., 1998). HVAC control systems in buildings help reduce energy use, this paper is concentrated on PI control of dual duct systems.

2.6 Automatic tuning

Automatic Tuning was described in the theoretical way. It consists of two phases. In the first, the desired critical point consisting of critical gains and a critical frequency is identified when the controllers are replaced by relays. In the second stage, the data of the desired critical point is used to tune the PID controllers by the Ziegler-Nichols rules or their modifications.

Halevi and al. (Halevi at al., 1997) presented the automatic tuning for decentralized control, namely decentralized PID control in multi-input multi-output plants, which had generalized the authors' auto-tuner. Their algorithm consists of two phases. In the first, the desired critical point consisting of critical gains and a critical frequency is identified when the controllers are replaced by relays. In the second stage, the data of the desired critical point is used to tune the PID controllers by the Ziegler-Nichols rules or their modifications. Decentralized controller is taken as a matrix main diagonal controller. The automatic tuning session is successful however the curse is very oscillating. Automating of decentralized controllers is one of the most important parts in decentralized control as it is evident from the paper written by Palmor et al. (Palmor et al., 1995), where the automatic tuning of decentralized PID controllers for TITO processes is given. In paper written by Wang et al. (Wang et al., 1997), a method for automatically tuning fully cross-coupled multivariable PID controllers from decentralized relay feedback is given together with the techniques for process frequency-response matrix estimation and multivariable decoupling design.

2.7 Other strategies

All other approaches are summarized in this subchapter named as Other strategies, for instance the linear quadratic decentralized pole location problem. The other important area is the decentralized control using neural networks or decentralized supervisory control or decentralized internal model control.

Linear quadratic decentralized pole location for singularly perturbed systems is presented (Garcia et al., 2002). The LQ control problem with pole location in a sector is solved using the LMI approach and the decentralized control problem is solved in the reduced slow system using structure constraints on the matrix variables using the state-space formulae. The decentralized control using the neural networks is given by Napolitano et al.

(Napolitano et al., 2000). The paper describes the performance of a neural network-based fault-tolerant system within a flight control system. The nonblocking decentralized supervisory control of discrete event systems is studied by Takai and Ushio (Takai and Ushio, 2002). A modified normality condition defined in terms of a modified natural projection map was introduced there. Decentralized internal model control (IMC) design method is described by Tan and Chiu (Tan and Chiu, 2001). The stability problem of symmetric state-space systems by means of decentralized control is also concerned (Yang et al., 2001). It was shown that the set of decentralized fixed modes of a symmetric system is equal to the set of uncontrollable and unobservable modes of the system. Delay-feedback control using decentralized controller is presented by Konishi and Kokame (Konishi and Kokame, 1999). It is the control of a one-way coupled ring map lattice. The paper considering a decentralized H-infinity control problem for multi-channel linear time-invariant systems with dynamic output feedback was also given (Zhai and al., 2001). The control problem was reduced to a feasibility problem of a bilinear matrix inequality (BMI) solved by using the homotopy method. Another approach to decentralized feedback control is given by El Kashlan and El Geneidy (El Kashlan and El Geneidy, 1996). It is based on eigenspectrum assignment for a large-scale system composed of symmetrically interconnected subsystems preserving the autonomy of the subsystems with sharing the global assignment process using the state space formula. Decentralization in a decentralized static output feedback framework facilitating the use of a quasi-Newton optimization algorithm is described by Corrado et al. (Corrado et al., 1999).There is given a scheme for synthesis using two controllers cascading them in the feedback loop and optimizing over the five free controller parameters, the relative degree two controller. It is important to emphasize that decentralized control as all other control strategies besides its positive features has also some drawbacks meaning that in some cases pure decentralized control becomes inadequate. One of the possible solutions is given (Cho and Lim, 1999) and is based on combination of centralized and decentralized control in supervisory control. Decentralized control dealing with the effects of recycle streams on the controllability of integrated plants and the improvement of performance by a direct compensation of the recycle was used by Scali and Ferrari (Scali and Ferrari, 1999). The global process was decomposed in two parts, one representing the process without recycle and the other one representing the recycle. The decentralized control of plants with uncertain mathematical models is studied, too (Andersson and Marklung, 2000). In particular, it is assumed that the plant is described by a continuous LTI model, which is contained in a specified family P of plant models, and in this case it is assumed that a family of decentralized controllers has been found to satisfactorily control the models contained in P.

2.8 Important areas

A methodology for decentralized control in real-time was proposed (Törgren and Wikander, 1996). An engineering methodology for evaluating different hardware structures, control-system structures and allocation approaches was outlined. It consists of the following steps: control system structuring, decentralization involving partitioning, allocation and evaluation, and execution strategy. The generalization of the concept of contractibility of decentralized control laws in the Inclusion Principle is described by Stanković and Šiljak (Stanković and Šiljak, 2001). A general definition of the contractibility of dynamic output controllers for linear dynamic systems was given together with a discussion related to different restriction and aggregation types adding the contradictory requirements for state controller and observer contractibility. Frequency domain analysis of oscillatory modes in decentralized control systems was given (Calazans de Castro, Silva de Araújo, 1998). In large systems and particularly in the case of systems with interconnected subsystems, different kinds of oscillatory modes (OM), with specific features, can occur. In decentralized control, there exists the static output feedback decentralized stabilization problem, which is solved (Cao et al., 1998). It is addressed using an iterative linear matrix inequality approach together with the derivation of sufficient condition for static output feedback decentralized stabilizability for linear time-invariant large-scale systems. The performance limitations in decentralized control have also been discussed (Cui and Jacobsen, 2002). The authors consider performance limitations from non-minimum phase transmission zeros of other subsystems across the imaginary axis. In paper by Gündes and Kabuli (Gündes and Kabuli, 1996), the reliable stabilization with integral action is studied in a linear, time-invariant, multi-input, multi-output, two-channel decentralized control system, where the plant was stable. The objective was to achieve closed-loop stability when both controllers act together and when each controller acted alone. The choice of the structure of interconnections between manipulated variables and controlled outputs is the task of another paper (Schmidt and Jacobsen, 2003). It is an important task in the design of decentralized control systems for multivariable plants. Instead of the approaches addressing the stability properties of the overall system such as the RGA, the paper focuses on performance, considering the problem of selecting control structures that enable a desired performance proposing the decentralized relative gain (dRG). The stabilization of decentralized control systems might be realized by means of periodic feedback (Lavei and Aghdam, 2008). According to Chen and Seborg (Chen and Seborg, 2003), the closed-loop stability of the decentralized systems using PI controllers can be guaranteed by Nyquist stability conditions. However, a detuning factor for each loop is established and based on a diagonal dominance index. Decomposition is an approach that is connected with decentralized or decoupling control (He and Chen, 2002), namely the structural decomposition of general single-input and single-output linear singular systems. For nonlinear interconnected systems, it is useful to have decentralized observation (Dhbaibi et al., 2009).

2.9 Integral controllability

Decentralized integral controllability (DIC) is one of the very interesting control tasks (Lee and Edgar, 2000). It concerns the existence of stable decentralized controllers with integral action having stable independent detuning. The only information needed for DIC is the steady state process gain matrix. The conditions for decentralized integral controllability were also given (Lee and Edgar, 2002). The first step in designing decentralized controllers is the pairing between manipulated variables and controlled variables. Decentralized integral controllability (DIC) addresses most of the advantages of decentralized controllers over multivariable controllers and is especially useful to eliminate unworkable pairings.

3. Applications

3.1 Industry

The paper by Bakule et al. (Bakule et al., 2002) solves the problem of influence of several different earthquakes onto the two-tower-cable-stayed-bridge. The bridge can be divided into two parts, the subsystems, which influence each other via the middle part of the flooring between the towers. The value of the horizontal forces acting upon the flooring is controlled. In paper by Watanabe (Watanabe, 2002), there is controlled the system turbine - governor in the electricity supply system. The suppression of the low-frequency oscillation in the electricity supply system is the control objective. The contribution written by Cui et al. (Cui, 1999) uses the decentralized theory of control for control of the interconnected electric supply systems with many machines. Each local controller is designed for each generator model. The control was used in the Chubu power plant in Japan. The paper by Aschemann et al. (Aschemann et al., 2002) makes use of the decentralized approach at the control of the Iveco DLK 23-12CS rotating car ladder trajectory employed e.g. by the fire brigades. There is also used the decentralized approach at the milling (Harakawa et al., 1999). The procedure came into existence because of the Nippon Steel corporation, the control system was shipped by the Toshiba company. The works which compare model predictive control with decentralized control we also performed (Lundström and Skogestad, 1995). A comparison of decentralized extended PID and model-based predictive multivariable control was also realized (Pomerleau et al., 2003). The paper is dealing with the cooling zone of an induration furnace where a moving bed of solid pellets had to be cooled for process operation requirements and energy recycling, two fans were used to force the cooling air circulation.

Heat, ventilation, and air-conditioning (HVAC) systems require control of environmental variables such as pressure, temperature or humidity and therefore it is possible to use the decoupling PID auto-tuning of such multivariable systems as presented by Bi et al. (Bi et al., 2000). The algorithm was verified on the cooling-only HVAC pilot plant system and on the air handling units of a commercial building in Singapore. Decentralized control was also used for control of retrofit heat-exchanger networks (HEN) (Uztürk and Akar, 1997). The decentralized optimal control theory allows us to use it for control of chaos in nonlinear networks (Oketani et al., 1995). It is a practical application for stabilizing any specific unstable periodic orbit embedded in a chaotic attractor extended to chaotic nonlinear networks. There was also developed a decentralized control for the Tennessee Eastman Challenge Process, so called TE problem (Rickler, 1996). The design procedure begins with the selection of the method for production-rate control, to which inventory controls and other functions are then coordinated. Nice application of robust decentralized control was also realized for the large scale web handling system, namely for the winding system, experimental set-up with 3 motors and 2 loads cells (Benlatreche et al., 2008) or decentralized robust control of boiler system (Labibi et al., 2009).

3.2 Power systems

Another method for decentralized controller design in power systems was developed by Yang (Yang et al., 1999). The proposed algorithm was applied to the decentralized design of a power-system stabilizer for a model of 10-machine power system. Nonlinear adaptive closed-loop decentralized stabilizing control of multimachine systems is given by Hu et al. (Hu et al., 2002). The system is with unknown parameters and the method is used for the excitation control of power systems. The verification was realized on a 6-machine 22-bus system. A robust decentralized excitation nonlinear control is devoted by Wang et al. (Wang et al., 1997). It was designed for mutimachine power system transient stability enhancement. Nice application of multimachine power system was realized by De Tuglie et al. (De Tuglie et al., 2008), the feedback-linearization and feedback-feedforward decentralized control was used.

3.3 Social sciences and economy

A decentralized control of a two-level distribution system with one central warehouse and *N* non-identical retailers is a control task of the multi-echelon arborescent system (Andersson and Marklund, 2000). Such a system is a member of the supply chain and is decomposed for easily control. The usage of decentralized control in economy and management appears to be adequate at the large. The mathematical model of this multi-level stochastic system with from time to time emerging variable time delay was created. The objective is to optimize the cost in all parts of the system and for that purpose the method of approximate cost evaluation with a modified cost-structure at the warehouse is used. A systematic approach of the analysis of the minimum control requirements that are imposed on power producing units in the Netherlands, in the case when decentralized production increases are studied (Roffel and de Boer, 2003). First, an overview of the amount and type of power production is given. Then the UCTE (Union pour la Coordination de la Transport de l'Electricity) power system model is introduced and tested against frequency and power measurements after failure of a 558 MW production unit. An application of decentralization in production, manufacturing and logistics is given by Jørgensen and Kort (Jørgensen and Kort, 2002). There is studied an optimal control problem of pricing and inventory replenishment in a system with serial inventories, centralized and decentralized decision making is realized. A setup in management of two stocks is decentralized such that pricing decisions are made by the store manager.

3.4 Nature and ecology

Decentralized control is used in branches of the sciences and practical application. The paper written by Bottura and Cáceres (Bottura and Cáceres, 2002) uses the decentralized algorithm for control of the oxygen demand and biochemical oxygen demand with usage of the water works in each parts of the river bed, and thereby the water quality control in the river. The watercourse can be divided into the set of the serially interconnected subsystems. The decentralization phenomenon can also be observed in the open air, e.g. at the behavior of the one type of the animals group. Tian et al. (Tian et al., 1999) are interested in the fish school. The fish school is a typical example of the autonomous decentralized system and self-organizing system typical for the open air because it shows the high level of coordinated behavior in the leader absence. The authors created the mathematical models of heterogeneous fish school and verified it during the repeated forced modification of the school fish movement direction.

4. Adaptive control

The strategies employing the decentralized adaptive control for motion control of uncertain electrically-driven manipulators have also been presented (Colbaugh and Glass, 1996). One of the approaches ensures semi-global asymptotic convergence of the error to an arbitrary small neighborhood of zero in the presence of bounded disturbances the other one ensures the arbitrarily accurate tracking in the presence of bounded disturbances. These approaches were verified on the six DOF terrestrial manipulators and on the free-flying space manipulators consisting of one or more arms mounted on a space vehicle. The problem solution of completely decentralized adaptive control of large-scale systems is also described (El Adel et al., 1999).Each subsystem is modelled by an orthonormal Laguerre network put in state-space form and decentralized predictive control. Decentralized adaptive control is also used in the problem of controlling the motion of nonholonomic mechanical systems in the presence of incomplete information concerning the system model and state as presented by Colbaugh and Glass (Colbaugh and Glass, 1998). The integrator backstepping approach together with an adaptive law using parameter projection is employed to design robust decentralized adaptive controllers in paper (Wen and Soh, 1997). There is a quite interesting task to use decentralized adaptive control at systems with nonlinearities at the input, such as dead-zone. This was solved for example by Zhou (Zhou, 2008).

Nice summary paper about the adaptive control was written by Anderson and Dehghani (Anderson and Dehghani, 2008). The paper was written with respect to three types of challenges to adaptive control in the view of the authors. The paper has more than one page of interesting references. Mainly two challenges are interesting and should be mentioned – difficulties that have frequently been overlooked and issues to which researchers look nowadays. The mentioned difficulties or problems of adaptive control according to the authors are: impractical control objectives, transient instability, suddenly unstable closed loops, changing experimental conditions. Another fact is the following - the adaptive algorithm works only under given assumptions. The question is what happens if the assumption is not fulfilled, for instance the controller has frozen parameters and the plant-controller closed loop is unstable or if it is necessary to divide in the algorithm by value close to zero – the signals will be enormous and have to be limited. Another question is the possibility of adaptive control to overcome the unexpected instabilities such as the component failure. However, too fast changes in adaptive controllers are dangerous, the adaptive control needs certain time to overcome the instabilities and sometimes it is not enough. It is always useful to have some a priori information about possible instabilities and failures. Next chapter of the paper discuss the permanent and future of adaptive control. It provides information about multiple model adaptive control, model-free adaptive control and formulates and verifies the method of validating controllers via closed-loop data. Multiple model adaptive control provides nice alternative to pure adaptive control especially in the case of linear plants but it can be used in the case of nonlinear systems control, too. This approach has incorporated the supervisor which is responsible to switch among the controllers in the case the performance is not satisfactory. But there are also problems with the implementation of supervisor, for example the destabilising controller cannot be switched instead of the controller with low performance but stabilizing. Each controller has to be tested before it is switched. Model-free adaptive control does not require the identification of the model, it simultaneously forecasts the performance of all controllers before one is chosen. This strategy leads to the unfalsified adaptive control.

Historically, robust and adaptive control was two approaches competing with each other, but it turned out that it was useful to join the results from both approaches for example for plant model identification in closed loops (Landau, 1999). According to this paper, adaptive control is used for reducing the uncertainty level of the model by using appropriate plant model identifier and robust controller deals with designing the controller in the presence of plant uncertainties. Landau provides the list of necessary needs for a high-performance control system and enlarges it by the detailed description of each one. He mentions important fact from practice that the same data can be used for identification of the model and for the controller validation and that the major improvement in performance occurs after the first identification in a closed loop.

There are many processes in practice that are not linear. Special attention was aimed at systems with time-delay. For such processes, the nice algorithm was proposed (Shah et al., 1997) and it is called as simple adaptive control. The paper provides interested summary of classical adaptive control schemes, such as model reference adaptive control (MRAC), self-tuning regulator (STR) and generalized predictive control (GPC).

5. Decentralized adaptive multi model control

5.1 Theoretical background

This approach is based on the combination of two methods previously published by Perutka (Perutka, 2009, Perutka and Dostalek, 2009). In one paper, there was published the real-time control of rewinding machine by self-tuning decentralized controllers (STC) and initial data for on-line identification were obtain before, using so called pre-identification procedure (Perutka, 2009). Another paper employed simple nonlinear controller (SNC) and added it into adaptive procedure (Perutka and Dostalek, 2009). This method used higher order of plant than classical self-tuning.

Now, we combined these two methods together using the supervisor. The real system is partly identified before the control using the pre-identification. After that, the real-time control is performed. In each time instant, the system is identified by on-line identification twice - for model using STC and SNC, because SNC uses higher order of subsystems models than STC. There is counted 4 time instants of control error after the actual time instant and weighted for both methods, the lower control error says which model and controller is used. This runs for every subsystem simultaneously with one exemption - time around the changes of set-point values, during that time runs only simple nonlinear controller without identification.

5.2 Apparatus description

Laboratory apparatus CE108, coupled drives apparatus manufactured by TecQuipment Ltd., see Fig. 1, simulates several practical tasks of tension and speed of material during continuous processes. In CE108, the flexible belt is mounted on three wheels. The belt forms the isosceles triangle and the wheels are in the corners of the triangle. Two of the wheels are

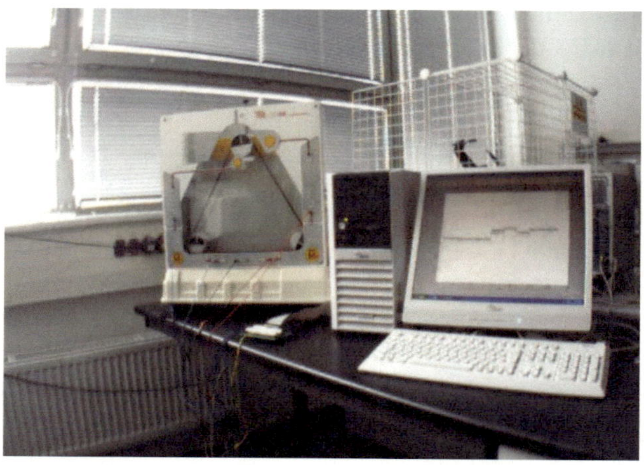

Fig. 1. Photography of CE108 laboratory apparatus connected to PC

connected to the amplifiers of two servomotors and these wheels are fixed. Third wheel, on the top of the apparatus, is mounted on the jib that is connected to the spring. This wheel simulates the workstation. Two servomotors control the speed of all wheels and the belt tension. The speed of the wheels is from the interval 0 - 3000 rpm, which corresponds with the voltage 0 - 10 V. Two control inputs of the apparatus are the control voltages of the servo motors amplifiers, both drives are bidirectional. There are four controlled outputs, the voltage corresponding to the speed of all 3 wheels and the voltage corresponding to tension of the belt. It can be chosen which outputs and how many of them are controlled. The apparatus is connected to the PC via technological card Advantech and via the screw terminal board. The real-time control is realized in MATLAB using Real Time Toolbox. (Perutka and Dostalek, 2009).

5.3 Results of control

The results of control using the method described hereinfore are depicted in figure 2, where sub index 1 is connected with the first subsystem and 2 with second subsystem, u is action signal, y is output signal from the subsystem and w is reference signal.

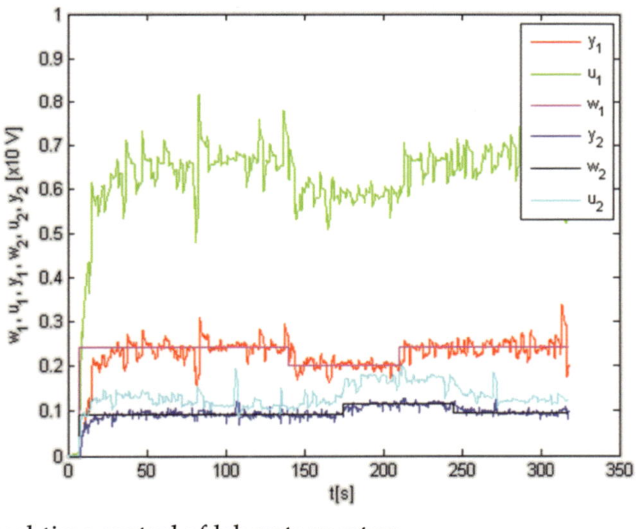

Fig. 2. Results of real-time control of laboratory setup

6. Acknowledgement

The author would like to mention the grant MSM7088352101 from which the work was supported.

7. References

Anderson, B.D.O. & Dehghani, A. (2008). Challenges of adaptive control-past, permanent and future. *Annual Reviews in Control*, Vol. 32, pp. 123-135.

Andersson, J. & Marklund, J. (2000). Decentralized inventory control in a two-level distribution system. *European Journal of Operational Research*, Vol. 39, pp. 483-506.

Aschemann, H.; Sawodny, O.; Bulach, A. & Hofer, E.P.: (2002). Model Based Trajectory Control of a Flexible Turntable Ladder, *Proc. American Control Conference 2002*, Anchorage, Alaska, U.S.A., pp. 921-926.

Bakule, L. (2008). Decentralized control: An overview. *Annual Reviews in Control*, Vol. 32, pp. 87-98.

Bakule, L.; Paulet-Crainiceanu, F. & Rodellar, J. (2002). Decentralized Control Design for a Cable-Stayed Bridge Benchmark, *Proc. American Control Conference 2002*, Anchorage, Alaska, U.S.A., pp. 3046-3051.

Benlatreche, A.; Knittel, D. & Ostertag, E. (2008). Robust decentralized control strategies for large-scale web handling systems. *Control Engineering Practice*, Vol. 16, pp. 736-750.

Bi, G.; Cai, W.J.; Wang, Q.G.; Hang, C.C.; Lee, E.L.; Sun, Y.; Liu, K.D.; Zhang, Y. & Zou, B. (2000). Advanced controller auto-tuning and its application in HVAC systems. *Control Eng. Practice*, Vol. 8, pp. 633-644.

Bottura, C.P. & Cáceres, A.F.T. (2002). Decentralized Control of Serial Interconnected Systems for River Water Quality via Subspace Identification, *Proc. American Control Conference 2002*, Anchorage, Alaska, U.S.A., pp. 3338-3342.

Calazans de Castro, J. & Silva de Araújo, C. (1998). Frequency Domain Analysis of Oscillatory Modes in Decentralized Control Systems. *Automatica*, Vol. 34, pp. 1647-1649.

Cao, Y.Y.; Sun, Y.X. & Mao, W.J. (1998). Output feedback decentralized stabilization: ILMI approach. *Systems & Control Letters*, Vol. 35, pp. 184-194.

Chen, D. & Seborg, D.E. (2003). Design of decentralized PI control systems based on Nyquist stability analysis. *Journal of Process Control*, Vol. 13, pp. 27-39.

Cho, K.H. & Lim, J.T. (1999). Mixed centralized/decentralized supervisory control of discrete event dynamic systems. Automatica, 35, pp. 121-128.

Clarke, D.W. (1996). Adaptive predictive control. *Annual Reviews in Control*, Vol. 20, pp. 83-94.

Colbaugh, R. & Glass, K. (1996). Decentralized Adaptive Control of Electrically-driven Manipulators. *Computers Elect. Engng*, Vol. 22, pp. 383-401.

Colbaugh, R. & Glass, K. (1998). Decentralized Adaptive Control of Nonholonomic Mechanical Systems. *Computers & Electrical Engineering*, Vol. 24, pp. 135-136.

Corrado, J.R.; Haddad, W.M. & Bernstein, D.S. (1999). H2 – optimal synthesis of controllers with relative degree two. *Automatica*, Vol. 35, pp. 1169-1173.

Cui, H. & Jacobsen, E.W. (2002). Performance Limitations in Decentralized Control. *Journal of Process Control*, Vol. 12, pp. 485-494.

Cui, S.; Ukai, H.; Kando, H.; Nakamura, K. & Fujita, H. (1999). Decentralized Control of Large Scale Power System by H-infinity Based Excitation Control System, *IFAC World Congress 1999 Proceedings*, Beijing, P. R. China. CD-ROM, O-7c-06, Elsevier Science.

Date, R.A. & Chow, J.H. (1993). A Parametrization Approach to Optimal H_2 and H_∞ Decentralized Control Problems. *Automatica*, Vol. 29, No. 2., pp. 457-463.

Dhbaibi, S.; Tlili, A.S.; Elloumi, S. & Braiek, N.B. (2009). H_∞ decentralized observation and control of nonlinear interconnected systems. *ISA Transactions*, Vol. 48, pp. 458-467.

Duan, Z.; Wang J. & Huang L. (2007). Special decentralized control problems in discrete-time interconnected systems composed of two subsystems. *Systems & Control Letters*, Vol. 56, pp. 206-214.

Egi, N. (1997). New bio-process control scheme: decentralized autonomous control system. *Journal of Biotechnology*, Vol. 52, pp. 283-288.

El Adel, M.; Makoudi, M. & Radouane, L. (1999). Decentralized adaptive control of linear interconnected systems based on Laguerre series representation. *Automatica*, Vol. 35, pp. 1873-1881.

El Kashlan, A. & El Geneidy, M. (1996). Design of Decentralized Control for Symmetrically Interconnected Systems. *Automatica*, Vol. 32, pp. 475-476.

Gagnon, E.; Pomerleau, A. & Desbiens, A. (1998). Simplified, ideal or inverted decoupling? *ISA Transactions*, Vol. 37, pp. 265-276.

Garcia, G.; Daafouz, J. & Bernussou, J. (2002). The infinite time near optimal decentralized regulator problem for singularly perturbed systems: a convex optimization approach. *Automatica*, Vol. 38, pp. 1397-1406.

Garelli, F.; Mantz, R.J. & De Battista, H. (2006). Limiting interactions in decentralized control of MIMO systems. *Journal of Process Control*, Vol. 16, pp. 473- 483.

Guan, Z.H.; Chen, G.; Yu, X. & Qin, Y. (2002). Robust decentralized stabilization for a class of large-scale time-delay uncertain impulsive dynamical systems. *Automatica*, Vol. 38, pp. 2075-2084.

Gündes, A.N. & Kabuli, M.G. (1996). Reliable Stabilization with Integral Action in Decentralized Control Systems. *Automatica*, Vol. 32, pp. 1021-1025.

Guo, Y.; Hill, D.J. & Wang, Y. (2000). Nonlinear decentralized control of large-scale power systems. *Automatica*, Vol. 36, pp. 1275-1289.

Guo, Y.; Jiang, Z.P. & Hill, D.J. (1999). Decentralized robust disturbance attenuation for a class of large-scale nonlinear systems. *Systems & Control Letters*, Vol. 37, pp. 71-85.

Halevi, Y.; Palmor, Z.J. & Efrati, T. (1997). Automatic tuning of decentralized PID controllers for MIMO processes. *Journal of Process Control*, Vol. 7, pp. 119-128.

Harakawa, T.; Kano, R.; Ogai, H.; Nakamura, R.; Sekiguchi, K. & Kurosawa, R. (1999). Development of Strip Tension Stabilization by Decentralized Control Strategy Based on Advanced Mill Drive System Suppressing Resonant Vibrations in Hot Strip Finisher Mill, *IFAC World Congress 1999 Proceedings*, Beijing, P. R. China. CD-ROM, O-7b-04, Elsevier Science.

He, M. & Chen, B.M. (2002). Structural decomposition of linear singular systems: the single input and single output case. *Systems & Control Letters*, Vol. 47, pp. 327-334.

Hernandez, M. & Tang, Y. (2009). Adaptive output-feedback decentralized control of a class of second order nonlinear systems using recurrent fuzzy neural networks. *Neurocomputing*, Vol. 76, pp. 461-467.

Hu, W.; Mei, S.; Lu, Q.; Shen, T. & Yokoyama, A. (2002). Nonlinear adaptive decentralized stabilizing control of multimachine systems. *Applied Mathematics and Computations*, Vol. 133, pp. 519-532.

Jetté, I.; Zaheer-Uddin, M. & Fazio, M. (1998). PI-control of Dual Duct Systems: Manual Tuning and Control Loop Interaction. *Energy Convers. Mgmt*, Vol. 39, pp. 1471-1482.

Jørgensen, J.B. & Jørgensen, S.B. (2000). Towards automatic decentralized control structure selection. *Computers and Chemical Engineering*, Vol. 24, pp. 841-846.

Jørgensen, S. & Kort, P.M. (2002). Optimal Pricing and Inventory Policies: Centralized and decentralized decision making. *European Journal of Operational Research*, Vol. 138, pp. 578-600.

Keviczky, T.; Borelli, F. & Balas, G.J. (2006). Decentralized receding horizon control for large scale dynamically decoupled systems. *Automatica*, Vol. 42, pp. 2105-2115.

Konishi, K. & Kokame, H. (1999). Decentralized delayed-feedback control of a one-way coupled ring map lattice. *Physica D*, Vol. 127, pp. 1-12.

Koshijima, I. & Toki, A. (1997). Design of Autonomous Decentralized Multi-effect Evaporating Systems. *Computers chem. Engng*, Vol. 21, pp. S107-S112.

Koshijima, I.; Niida, K. & Umeda, T. (1996). A micro module approach to the design and control of autonomous decentralized chemical plant. *Journal of Process Control*, Vol. 6, pp. 169-176.

Labibi, B.; Marquez, H.J. & Chen, T. (2009). Decentralized robust control of a class of nonlinear systems and application to a boiler system. *Journal of Process Control*, Vol. 19, pp. 761-772.

Landau, I.D. (1999). From robust to adaptive control. *Control Engineering Practice*, Vol. 7, pp. 1113-1124.

Lavei, J. & Aghdam, A.G. (2008). Stabilization of decentralized control systems by means of periodic feedback. *Automatica*, Vol. 44, pp. 1120-1126.

Lee, J. & Edgar, T.F. (2000). Computational method for decentralized integral controllability of low dimensional processes. *Computers & Chemical Engineering*, Vol. 24, pp. 847-852.

Lee, J. & Edgar, T.F. (2002). Conditions for Decentralized Integral Controllability. *Journal of Process Control*, Vol. 12, pp. 797-805.

Lee, P.L.; Li, H. & Cameron, I.T. (2000). Decentralized control design for nonlinear multi-unit plants: a gap metric approach. *Chemical Engineering Science*, Vol. 55, pp. 3743-3758.

Li, H.; Lee, P.L., Bahri, P. & Cameron, I.T. (2000). Decentralized control design for nonlinear plants: a ν-metric approach. *Computers & Chemical Engineering*, Vol. 24, pp. 273-278.

Liu, X. & Huang, G. (2001). Global decentralized robust stabilization for interconnected uncertain nonlinear systems with multiple inputs. *Automatica*, Vol. 37, pp. 1435-1442.

Loh, E.J. & Chiu, M.S. (1997). Robust decentralized controller design for unstable systems. *Chemical Engineering Science*, Vol. 52, pp. 2299-2311.

Lundström, P. & Skogestad, S. (1995). Opportunities and difficulties with 5x5 distillation control. *Journal of Process Control*, Vol. 5, pp. 249-261.

Makoudi, M. & Radouane, L. (1999). Robust decentralized adaptive control for non-minimum phase systems with unknown and/or time varying delay. *Automatica*, Vol. 35, pp. 1417-1426.

Marino, R. (1997). Adaptive Control of Nonlinear Systems: Basic Results and Applications. *Annual Reviews in Control*, Vol. 21, pp. 55-66.

Napolitano, M.R.; An, Y. & Seanor, B.A. (2000). A fault tolerant flight control system for sensor and actuator failures using neural networks. *Aircraft Design*, Vol. 3, pp. 103-128.

Ni, M.L. & Chen, Y. (1996). Decentralized Stabilization and Output Tracking of Large-scale Uncertain Systems. *Automatica*, Vol. 32, pp. 1077-1080.

Oketani, N.; Ushio, T. & Hirai, K. (1995). Decentralized control of chaos in nonlinear networks. *Physics Letters A*, Vol. 198, pp. 327-332.

Palmor, Z.J.; Halevi, Y. & Krasney, N. (1995). Automatic Tuning of Decentralized PID controllers for TITO processes. *Automatica*, Vol. 31, pp. 1001-1010.

Perutka, K. (2009). Pre-identification for Real-time Control. *Lecture Notes in Computer Science*, Vol. 5717, pp. 626-632.

Perutka, K. & Dostalek, P. (2009). Simple decentralized autonomous adaptive nonlinear real-time controller with controller source code optimization: Case study, *Proceedings of IEEE International Symposium on Autonomous Decentralized Systems ISADS 2009*, Athens, Greece, pp. 87-92.

Pomerleau, D. & Pomerleau, A. (2001). Guide lines for the tuning and the evaluation of decentralized and decoupling controllers for processes with recirculation. *ISA Transactions*, Vol. 40, pp. 341-351.

Pomerleau, D.; Pomerleau, A., Hodouin, D. & Poulin, É. (2003). A procedure for the design and evaluation of decentralized and model-based predictive multivariable controllers for a pellet cooling process. *Computers & Chemical Engineering*, Vol. 27, pp. 217-233.

Ricker, M.L. (1996). Decentralized Control of the Tennessee Eastman Challenge Process. *Journal of Process Control*, Vol. 6, pp. 205-221.

Roffel, B. & de Boer, W.W. (2003). Analysis of power and frequency control requirements in view of increased decentralized production and market liberalization. *Control Engineering Practice*, Vol. 11, pp.367-375.

Samyudaia, Y.; Lee, P.L.; Cameron, I.T. & Green, M. (1995). A new approach to decentralised control design. *Chemical Engineering Science*, Vol. 50, pp.1695-1706.

Scali, C. & Ferrari, F. (1999). Performance of control systems based on recycle compensators in integrated plants. *Journal of Process Control*, Vol. 9, pp. 425-437.

Schmidt, H. & Jacobsen, E.W. (2003). Selecting control configurations for performance with independent design. *Computers & Chemical Engineering*, Vol. 27, pp. 101-109.

Seo, J.H.; Jo, C.H. & Lee, S.H. (1999). Decentralized H_∞ - controller design. *Automatica*, Vol. 35, pp. 865-876.

Shah, S.; Iwai, Z.; Mizumoto, I. & Deng, M. (1997). Simple adaptive control of processes with time-delay. *Journal of Process Control*, Vol. 7, No. 6, pp. 439-449.

Stanković, S.S. & Šiljak, D.D. (2001). Contractibility of overlapping decentralized control. *Systems & Control Letters*, Vol. 44, pp. 189-200.

Takai, S. & Ushio, T. (2002). A modified normality condition for decentralized supervisory control of discrete event systems. *Automatica*, Vol. 38, pp. 185-189.

Tan, G.T. & Chiu, M.S. (2001). A multiple-model approach to decentralized internal model control design. *Chemical Engineering Science*, Vol. 56, pp. 6651-6660.

Tian, Y.; Sannomiya, N. & Matuda, K. (1999). A simulation study on self-organization in the behavior of a heterogeneous fish school, *IFAC World Congress 1999 Proceedings*, Beijing, P. R. China. CD-ROM, L-5a-04, Elsevier Science.

Törgren, M. & Wikander, J. (1996). A decentralization methodology for real-time control applications. *Control Eng. Practice*, Vol. 4, pp. 219-228.

Tsai, Y.W.; Shyu, K.K. & Chang, K.C. (2001). Decentralized variable structure control for mismatched uncertain large-scale systems: a new approach. *Systems & Control Letters*, Vol. 43, pp. 117-125.

Tuglie, E. D.; Iannone, S.M. & Torelli, F. (2008). Feedback-linerization and feedback-feedforward decentralized control for multimachine power systems. *Electric Power Systems Research*, Vol. 78, pp. 382-391.

Ugrinovskii, V.A.; Petersen, I.R.; Savkin, A.V. & Ugrinovskaya, E.Y. (2000). Decentralized state-feedback stabilization and robust control of uncertain large-scale systems with integrally constrained interconnections. *Systems & Control Letters*, Vol. 40, pp.107-119.

Uztürk, D. & Akar, U. (1997). Centralized and decentralized control of retrofit heat-exchanger network. *Computers chem. Engng*, Vol. 21, pp. S373-S378.

Vaccarini, M.; Longhi, S. & Katebi, M.R. (2009). Unconstrained networked decentralized model predictive control. *Journal of Process Control*, Vol. 19, pp. 328-339.

Wang, Q.G.; Zou, B.; Lee, T.H. & Bi, Q. (1997). Auto-tuning of Multivariable PID Controllers from Decentralized Relay Feedback. *Automatica*, Vol. 33, pp. 319-330.

Wang, Y.; Guo, G. & Hill, D.J. (1997). Robust Decentralized Nonlinear Linear Controller Design for Multimachine Power Systems. *Automatica*, Vol. 33, pp. 1725-1733.

Watanabe, T. (2002). Robust Decentralized Turbine-Governor Control Subject to Saturation Nonlinearity, *Proc. American Control Conference 2002*, Anchorage, Alaska, U.S.A., pp. 1948-1953.

Wen, C. & Soh, Y.C. (1997). Decentralized Adaptive Control Using Integrator Backstepping. *Automatica*, Vol. 33, pp. 1719-1724.

Xi, Z.; Cheng, D., Lu, Q. & Mei, S. (2002). Nonlinear decentralized controller design for multimachine power systems using Hamiltonian function method. *Automatica*, Vol. 38, pp. 527-534.

Xie, S. & Xie, L. (2000). Decentralized global robust stabilization of a class of interconnected minimum-phase nonlinear systems. *Systems & Control Letters*, Vol. 41, pp. 251-263.

Yan, X.G. & Dai, G.Z. (1998). Decentralized Output Feedback Robust Control for Non-linear Large-scale Systems. *Automatica*, Vol. 34, pp. 1469-1472.

Yan, X.G.; Lam, J. & Dai, G.Z. (1999). Decentralized robust control for non-linear large scale systems with similarity. *Computers & Electrical Engineering*, Vol. 25, pp. 169-179.

Yang, G.H. & Zhang, S.Y. (1996). Decentralized Robust Control for Interconnected Systems with Time-varying Uncertainties. *Automatica*, Vol. 32, pp. 1603-1608.

Yang, G.H.; Wang, J.L. & Soh, Y.C. (2001). Decentralized Control of Symmetric Systems. *Systems & Control Letters*, Vol. 42, pp. 145-149.

Yang, T.C.; Zhang, J.H. & Yu, H. (1999). A new decentralised controller design method with application to power-system stabilized design. *Control Engineering Practice*, Vol. 7, pp. 537-545.

Zhai, G.; Ikeda, M. & Fujisaki, Y. (2001). Decentralized H_∞ - controller design: a matrix inequality approach using a homotopy method. *Automatica*, Vol. 37, pp. 1275-1289.

Zhang, Y.; Wen, C. & Soh, Y.C. (2000). Robust decentralized stabilization of interconnected systems with guaranteed transient performance. *Automatica*, Vol. 36, pp. 907-915.

Zhou, J. (2008). Decentralized adaptive control for large-scale time-delay systems with dead-zone input. *Automatica*, Vol. 44, pp. 1790-1799.

2

Intelligent Technologies in Modelling and Control of Turbojet Engines

Ladislav Madarász, Rudolf Andoga and Ladislav Főző
Technical University of Košice
Slovakia

1. Introduction

The state of present technologies in technical and also non-technical practice is represented by growing complexity of systems. A turbojet engine as a complex system is multidimensional highly parametric system with complex dynamics and strong non-linear behavior with stochastic properties. Its particular property is operation in a wide spectrum of changes of its operating environment (e.g., temperatures from -60 to +40 °C, different humidity, different pressures, etc.). If we want to secure optimal function of such system, it is necessary to develop models and control systems implementing the newest knowledge from the areas of automation, control technologies preferably with elements of artificial intelligence (AI). The present control systems and dynamic models are often limited to control or modeling of a complex system in its certain (operational) states. However, in practice the turbojet engine finds itself in very different operating conditions that influence its parameters of operation and characteristics. To create progressive control algorithms for a turbojet engine, it is necessary to design models in the whole dynamic spectrum of the modeled system including its erroneous states. Furthermore we need to design a control system that will secure operation converging towards optimality in all eventual states of working environment and also inner states of the system represented by its parameters. This leads to the need of having increased intelligence of control of turbojet engines that reduces workload of a pilot and also increases safety of operation. Safety represents a decisive factor in design of control systems of turbojet engines and is presently bound with increasing authority of them. The present trend designates such control systems as FADEC - Full Authority Digital Engine Control, however in reality such control systems have different levels of authority, intelligence and come in very different implementations. These are often not presented as they are intellectual properties of commercial companies. The article will be aimed on description of some present trends in development of FADEC systems and own proposals of methodologies leading towards design and implementation of a FADEC system with high level of intelligence able to solve all operational situations of a turbojet engine. This is strictly bound with presentation of modern methods of modeling of turbojet engines and the use of advanced methods of mainly sub-symbolic artificial intelligence. The proposed methods are all tested in real-world environment using a small turbojet engine MPM-20 in our laboratory setup. Therefore the article will also deal with approaches in digital real-time measurement of state parameters of this engine and design of control algorithms from engineering standpoint.

2. Modern control systems of turbojet engines

The main global aim of control of turbojet engines is similar to other systems and that lies in increasing their safety and effectiveness by possible reduction of costs. This requires application of new technologies, materials and new conceptual solutions. One mean to achieve that is the development in systems of control and regulation of the engines themselves and processes ongoing in them.

Demands for control and regulation systems result mainly from specific properties of the object of control - a turbojet engine. The basic functions of control systems of a turbojet engine are the following ones - manual control, regulation of its parameters and their limitation. Manual control and therefore choice of regime of the engine is realized by a throttle lever according to a flight situation or expected maneuver. By regulation of a turbojet engine we understand such a kind of control where the chosen parameters of the engine are maintained on certain set levels, thus keeping its regime.

In the past, the classical control systems of turbojet engines were implemented mainly by hydro-mechanical elements, which however suffered from deficiencies characteristic for such systems. Among such deficiencies were, high mass of such systems, inaccuracies due to mechanical looses and low count of regulated parameters. However development of electronic systems and their elements is ongoing, which will allow to increase precision of regulation of parameters of turbojet engines and their count to secure more complex and precise control of turbojets.

Use of electronics and digital technologies in control systems of turbojet engines has brought: (Lazar, 2000):

- lowering of mass of control system
- higher complexity of control - The count of regulated parameters used to be 3 to 7 by hydro-mechanical systems, however the digital systems operate with 12 to 16 parameters;
- increasing of static precision of regulation of different parameters (for example, precision of rotations from ±0.5 % to ±0.1 %, precision of regulation of temperature from ±12K to ±5K
- increase in reliability, service life and economics of operation of the driving unit of an aircraft;
- easier backup, technology of use and repairs, possibility of use of automatic diagnostics.

By design of solution of a control system for a turbojet engine, it is necessary to build an appropriate mathematical model of the engine. The ideal approach to design of electronic systems is a modular one, from hardware or software point of view. This implies use of qualitative processing units that are resistant to noises of environment and also realization of bus systems with low delays is very important in this approach. Further improvement in quality of control can be achieved by implementation of progressive algorithms of control, diagnostics and planning in electronic systems. These algorithms have to be able to asses the state of the controlled system (turbojet engine in our case), then parameterize action elements and they have to be able to control the engine under erroneous conditions represented in outer environment or as errors in subsystems of the engine itself. Prediction of such states represents an area to incorporate predictive control system. Methods of situational control bound with elements of artificial intelligence supply many robust tools for solution of afore mentioned problems and sub-problems.

From the point of view of use of electrical and electronic systems in controls the turbojet control systems can be roughly hierarchically divided into following sets (Lazar, 2000):

1. Electronic limiters,
2. Partial Authority Flight Control Augmentation (PAFCA,
3. „High Integration Digital Electronic Control" (HIDEC); „Digital Engine Control" - (DEC); „Full Authority Digital Engine Control" - (FADEC)).

The division of control systems into these three levels is not absolutely distinct, as systems on higher level as for example HIDEC system can utilize control mechanisms as electronic limiters. For example FADEC systems are often realized as single or double loop control systems with utilization of PI control algorithms or electronic limiters with estimation filters (Jonathan, 2005; Sanjay, 2005). Example of such FADEC algorithm is shown in figure 1 (Jonathan, 2005).

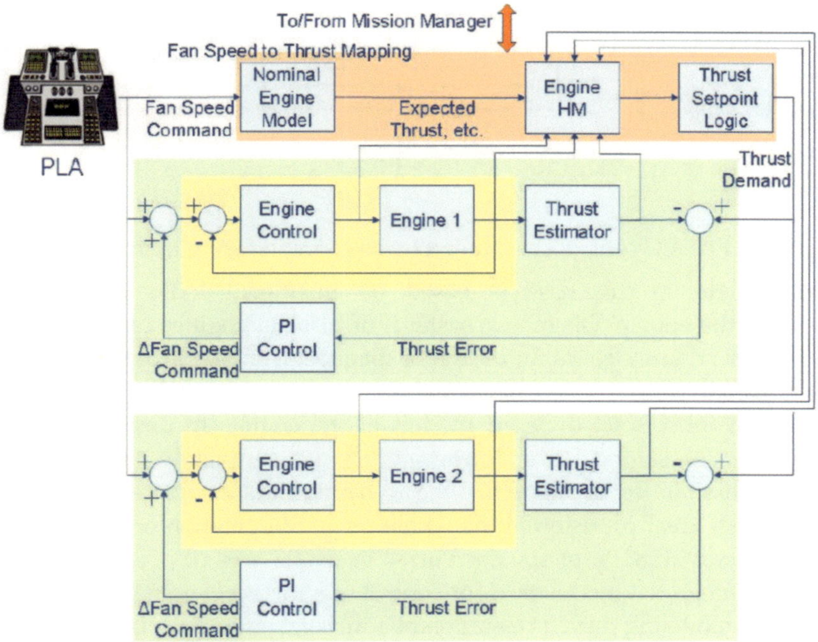

Fig. 1. FADEC control system with implemented PI electronic controllers

Such engine control systems are often integrated into the whole framework of an aircraft control system.

3. Full authority control systems

There are of course many possibilities and methodologies applicable to control systems of turbojet engines, which are FADEC compliant. Such application has to cope with strong non-linearity and changing structure of models and constants during operation of a turbojet engine. Such intelligent system should also be able to form decisions and predict faults either in control circuit or the object of turbojet engine itself. Therefore intelligent turbojet engine control is often bound with design of intelligent diagnostics systems (Wiseman, 2005) that also deal with control of an engine during its long-term deterioration. Example of such control based on diagnostics modules is shown in figure 2.

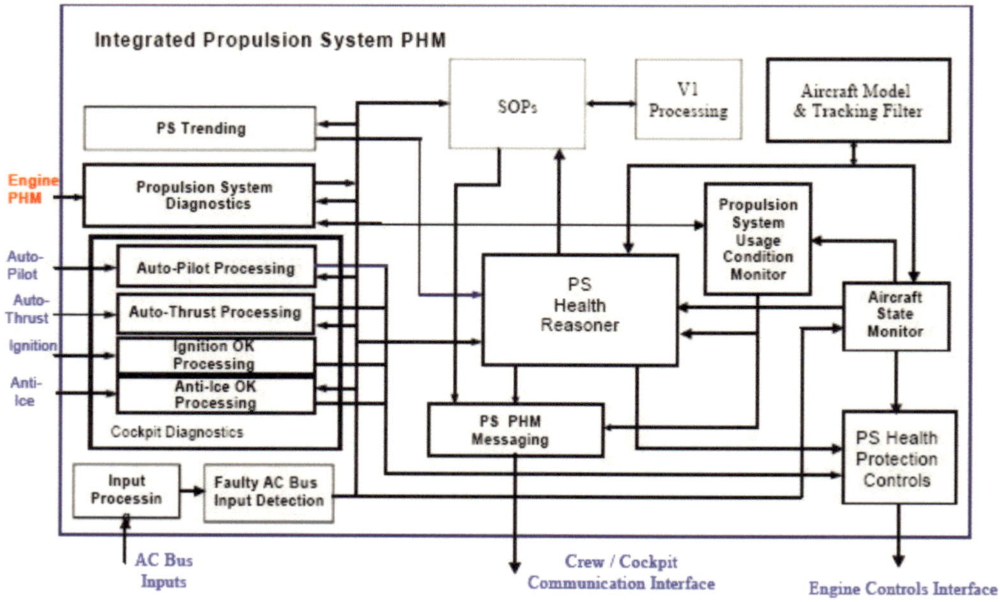

Fig. 2. Diagnostic FADEC control system of a turbojet engine (Wiseman, 2005)

The control system in this case is based on intelligent PHM (Prognostics Health Management) of the engine. Diagnostic systems of turbojet engines can be further realized by means of artificial intelligence. In design of diagnostic and control system which would control the engine in its erroneous states and act long before actual critical states develops itself; we need to form exact dynamic models of the engine. In design of classic control systems only first to second order linear models are commonly used. Methods of AI however offer possibilities of modeling the dynamic parameters of an engine in multi variable space with great precision in the whole range of operation of engine. Such models can have precision within 2% of standard error in whole area of operation of a jet engine (Andoga, 2006). Integrated model used for control of a turbojet engine can be seen in figure 1. Importance of modeling during operation of a turbojet engine can be further extended to fault detection of sensors and other parts of control system and the engine itself. In design of control system, the architecture also plays a significant role. Two common architectures can be presently found in design of turbojet engine FADEC control systems (Sanjay, 2007). The first one is the centralized one, which is reliable and well understood, but on the other hand has many drawbacks like inflexibility, high weight, complicated fault detection, etc. This architecture is shown in the figure 3.

The other usable architecture for design is the distributed architecture (fig. 4). Its main advantage is high flexibility, easier fault detection and isolation, its cons are mainly higher complexity, communication unknowns and deterministic behavior and it requires new technologies, i.e. high temperature electronics for use in turbojet engines.

The basic element of the FADEC control system is the electronic engine control (EEC) unit that represents the main computer (outlined in black, in the previous figures). Such systems that are presently used to control common commercial airliners' engines can be schematically depicted in the following figure 4 (Linke-Diesenger, 2008).

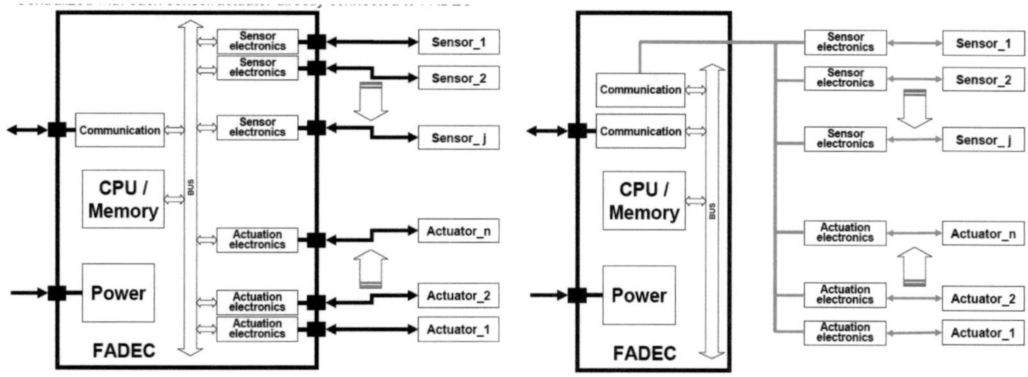

Fig. 3. Centralized (left) and decentralized (right) FADEC architectures (Sanjay, 2007)

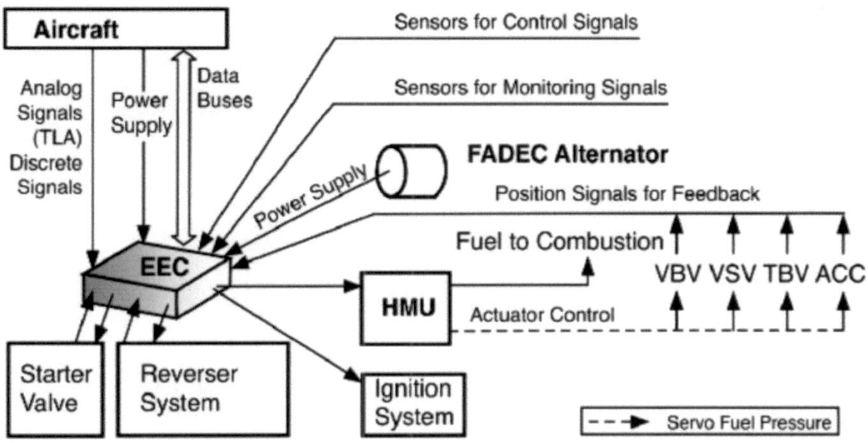

Fig. 4. The system architecture of a FADEC system with the centralized arrangement of servo valves in an HMU (Linke-Diesenger, 2008)

4. Small turbojet engine – MPM 20

The experimental engine MPM 20 has been derived from the TS - 20 engine, which is a turbo-starter turbo-shaft engine previously used for starting engines AL-7F and AL-21F. The engine has been rebuilt to a state, where it represents a single stream engine with radial compressor and a single stage non-cooled turbine and outlet jet. The basic scheme of the engine is shown in the figure 5

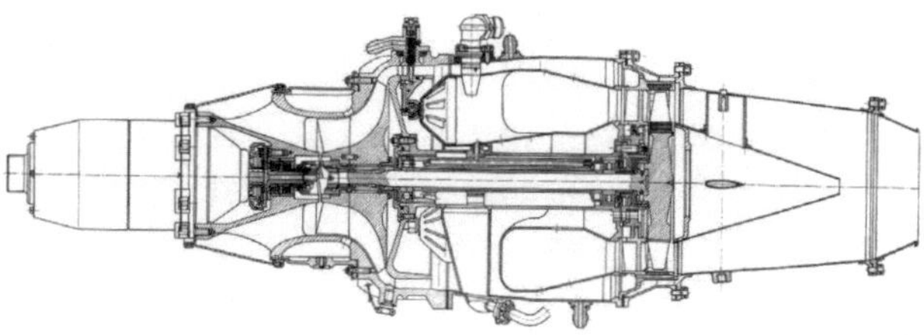

Fig. 5. The basic scheme of MPM 20 engine

All sensors, except fuel flow and rotations sensor, are in fact analogue and have voltage output. This is then digitalized by a SCXI measurement system and corresponding A/D converters and sent through a bus into computer. Every parameter is measured at the sampling rate of 10 Hz. The data acquisition has been done in LabView environment. The digital measurement of parameters of MPM-20 engine in real time is important to create a model and control systems complying with FADEC definition („Full Authority Digital Electronic Engine Control"). Moreover we needed to change the engine from static single regime engine into a dynamic object, what was done by regulation of pressure beyond the compressor according to which the current fuel supply actuator changes actual fuel supply for the engine in real time. The system has been described in (Andoga, 2006). The graph in figure 6 shows dynamic changes of parameters of the engine to changes of fuel supply input.

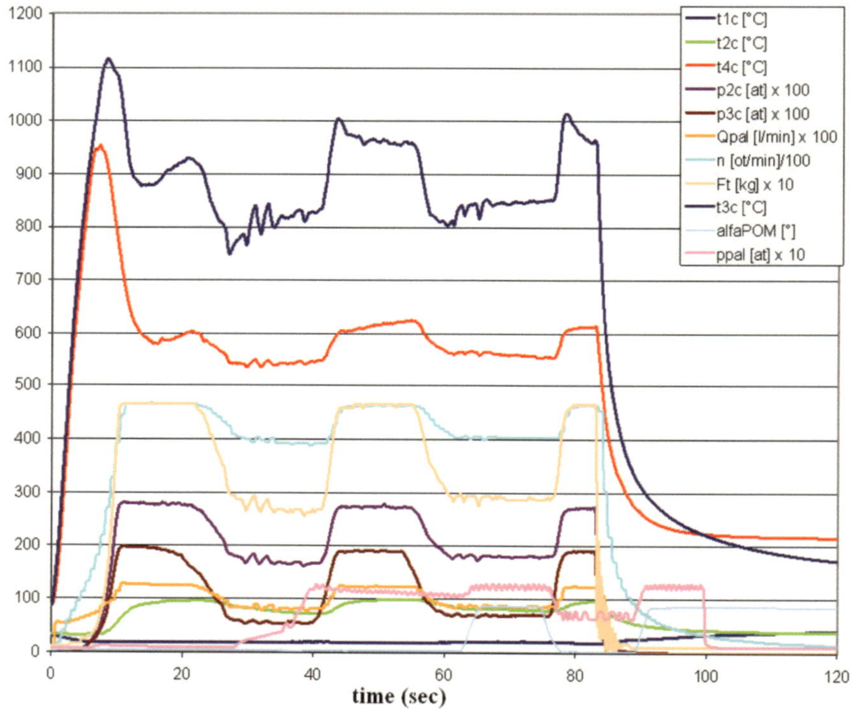

Fig. 6. One run of the engine with changes in fuel flow supply

The following basic parameters are measured:

- air temperature at the outlet from the diffuser of the radial compressor - T_{2C} [°C];
- gas temperatures in front of the gas turbine - $\mathbf{T_{3C}}$ [°C];
- gas temperature beyond the gas turbine - T_{4C} [°C];
- static pressure of air beyond the compressor P_2 [Ata];
- static pressure of gases in front of the gas turbine P_3 [Ata];
- static pressure of gases beyond the gas turbine P_4 [Ata];
- fuel flow supply Q_{pal} [l/min];
- thrust Th [kg];
- rotations of the turbine/compressor, n_1 [rpm].

5. Modeling of turbojet engines

5.1 Basic approaches in modeling of turbojet engines

In order to design and develop a control system for a turbojet engine, its mathematical model has to be constructed. In mathematical modeling of technical systems, many approaches can be used for different purposes. Specifically in the area of turbojet engines modeling two basic can be used. The first one is the analytic one that is usually developed under equilibrium conditions and uses physical relations and formulas to model usually static characteristics of different areas of an engine like inlet system, compressor, combustion chamber, etc. Such model is mainly used in design of the engine itself and to estimate basic operating parameters and envelopes in different environments. Basic control laws can be also estimated from such model. The second approach used mainly in design of control algorithms and diagnostic systems lies in creation of dynamic experimental models that model the engine or its parts as black boxes as transfer functions between input and output parameters (Harris, et. al, 2006). These models are aimed on simulation of dynamic behavior and regimes of an engine. To create a complex and intelligent control system both approaches have to be used and the further sections of this chapter will show some of these approaches to create precise computational models with use of elements of artificial intelligence. The authors of the paper deal with both approaches in modeling and as a real-world object a small turbojet engine MPM-20 is used.

5.2 Analytic modeling

Static and dynamic properties of turbojet engines (MPM-20) can also be described by a mathematical model of operation single stream engine under equilibrium or non-equilibrium conditions. This will allow modeling the thrust, fuel consumption, pressures and temperatures of the engine by different altitudes and velocities in the chosen cuts of the engine.

The steady operation of the engine is such a regime, where in every element of the engine same thermodynamic processes are realized. Operation of an engine in its steady operation can be described by:

1. algebraic equations of balance of mass flow of working materials through nodes of the engine, equations of output balance, equations of regulation rules and equations describing particular oddities of an engine. A system of equations expresses that for given outer conditions of operation of an engine, characteristics of all nodes of an engines and preset values of control parameters (fuel supply, cross section of the output nozzle, angle of compressor blades), operation of the engine will settle itself on one and only one regime (Ružek, Kmoch, 1979) .
2. graphically by utilization of knowledge of characteristics of all parts (output, compressor, turbine, etc) of the engine and their preset curves of joint operations (e.g. lines of stable rations of T_{3c}/T_{1c} in compressor). Designation of all curves of the engine is done in a way that we will try to fulfill continuity conditions for all parts of the engine and characteristics of all these parts are given. These characteristics can be found by direct measurement, computation, etc.

Any regime of the turbojet engine has to fulfill the continuity equation which designates dependencies between mass flow of air through the compressor, turbine, combustion chamber and exhaust system (Považan, 1999):

$$Q_{VS} = Q_k = Q_{SK} = Q_T = Q_{tr} = Q \qquad (1)$$

and a condition of no distortion of the shaft

$$n_k = n_T = n \qquad (2)$$

where

Q_{VS} – mass flow of air through input system,
Q_k – mass flow of air through the compressor
Q_{SK} – mass flow of air through combustion chamber,
Q_T – mass flow of gases through the turbine,
Q_{tr} – mass flow of gases through exhaust nozzle,
n_k – revolutions of compressor,
n_T – revolutions of turbine.

Another condition for steady operation of the engine has to be fulfilled – the engine doesn't change its revolutions in time.

$$\frac{dn}{dt} = 0 \qquad (3)$$

This condition will be fulfilled when output of the turbine will be the same as output taken by the compressor and accessories of the engine

$$W_{KC} = \eta_m W_{TC} \qquad (4)$$

where

η_m – mechanical effectiveness of the engine,
W_{KC} – technical work of the compressor,
W_{TC} – technical work of the turbine.

A detailed algorithm of designation of operational points of steady operation of a single stream engine is described in (Főző, 2008).

Non steady operation of an engine is a regime of its operation, where in every element of the engine time changing thermodynamic processes occur. Function of the engine in such non steady regimes can be described by a system of differential and algebraic equations. Such system of equations describes transient processes by change of regime of the engine, when thrust lever is moved or other change of flight regime occurs.

Such non-steady regime occurs when work of the turbine and compressor isn't equal, this means that rotation moments of the turbine M_T and compressor M_K aren't equal. Acceleration of the engine is dependant upon this difference equation:

$$M_T - M_K - M_{ag} = J\frac{d\omega}{dt} \qquad (5)$$

where

$\frac{d\omega}{dt}$ - angular acceleration of the engine,
J - moment of inertia of all rotating masses reduced to the shaft of the engine
M_{ag} - moment needed for actuation of aggregates and overcoming of friction.

As the angular velocity of the MPM-20 engine is given by the equation $\omega = \frac{\pi n}{30}$ and output is given by equation $P = M\omega$, after incursion of mechanical effectiveness, the basic equation of non-steady operation of the engine is obtained:

$$P_T \eta_m - P_k = J \frac{\pi^2}{900} n \frac{dn}{dt} \tag{6}$$

Stable operation of the engine is then computed which gives us the initial conditions. Differences of revolutions are then computed in a given time space Δt and we repeat this algorithm until the end of the transient process.

Analytic mathematical model of the engine is based on physical rules which characterize properties and operation of different nodes of the engine, thermodynamic and aerodynamic processes obtained by temperature cycle. While we have to take in account range of operation of turbojet engines which give changes of thermodynamic properties of working material.

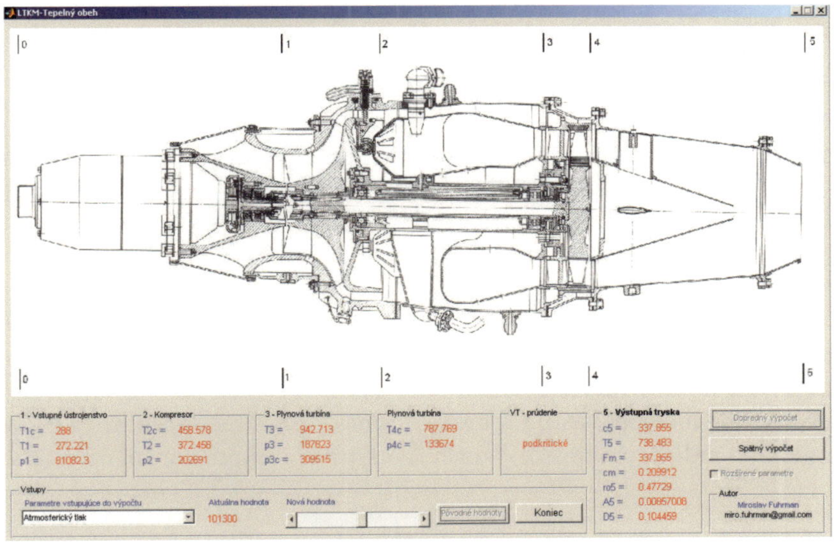

Fig. 7. Temperature circuit calculation implemented in Matlab GUI

Contrary to the experimental one, the analytical model of the engine allows us to compute parameters of the engine that cannot be simply simulated by models built upon the experimental data, which use only known parameters. This way we can compute engine surge lines, workloads on shafts, different internal temperatures and also parameters, which are measured and can be used for checking the results of the model. The analytic model allows us to compute parameters of our engine also by different values of outer pressure and temperature of air, different speed of flight and height. Complexity of the model is out of scope of this paper, the figure 8 illustrates computed curve of steady state of operation for the MPM 20 engine. X-axis denotes the air flow through the engine, Y-axis the compression ratio, red line represents surge line, green lines represent different speeds (reduced RPM's), and the dark red line represents acceleration of the engine with fast geometry of the exhaust nozzle.

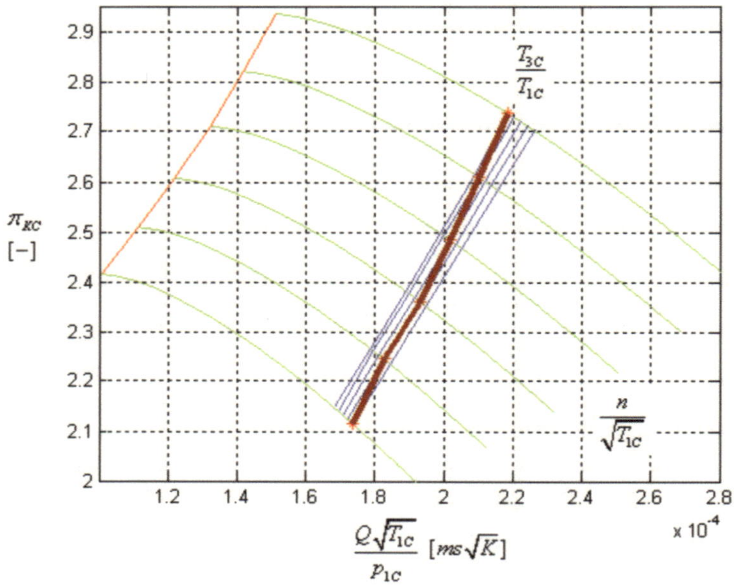

Fig. 8. The steady state line of operation of the MPM-20 engine

5.3 Methods of artificial intelligence in analytic modeling of the MPM-20 engine

Resulting from practical expertise of the data and created analytic models we found that adaptive fuzzy inference systems are well suited for replacing the complex equations found in analytic modelling. We used the ANFIS - Adaptive-Network-based Fuzzy Inference System (Roger Jang, 1993).

This system is based on network architecture just like the neural networks that maps input on the bases of membership fuzzy functions and their parameters to outputs. The network architecture is of feed-forward character.

To verify the ANFIS method, we are showing a simple physical dependency expressing the pressure ratio of a radial compressor, which is a type of compressor found on the MPM 20 engine.

$$\Pi_{KC} = \left[1 + \frac{u_2^{\,2}(\mu + \alpha)}{c_p T_{1C}} \eta_{KC}\right]^{\frac{\kappa}{\kappa - 1}} \tag{7}$$

The equation can be understood as a static transfer function with two inputs - the temperature T_{1c} and circumferential speed u_2 (speed of the compressor) and one output in the form of the pressure ratio. The surface shown in the figure 9 is equal to numeric computation of the equation 12.

The obtained results have confirmed that the chosen method ANFIS is suitable for modelling of mathematic - physical equations with very low computational demands (trained FIS system is computationally very simple) with very fine sampling periods (by very fine division of interval of values of input parameters). Therefore we will further be oriented on improvement of the complex and highly computationally demanding analytic model of the MPM 20 engine by use of AI methods, with ANFIS in particular.

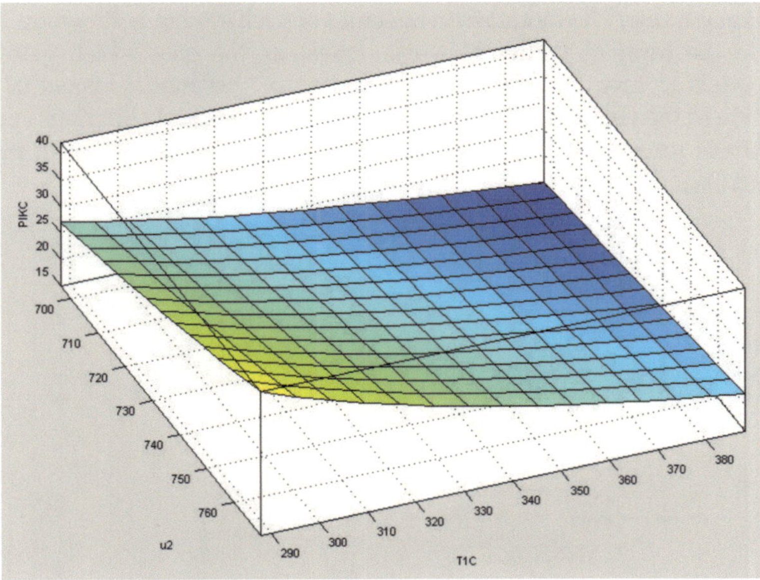

Fig. 9. The equation (7) modeled by ANFIS

5.4 Situational modeling of the MPM-20 engine

Individual dynamical dependencies of parameters of a turbojet engine are more complex than they can be depicted by static analytic models. In experimental modeling we will consider T_{2c}, T_{4c}, P_{2c}, n input parameters on Q_{pal} parameter in the figure 6. The other arising problem is that these dependencies are not stationary and are changing during course of turbojet's engine operation. In such case it isn't possible to easily set operating points in multi-dimensional non linear parametric space. The operating point will lie on a functional of the following parameters:

$$O_p = f\,(Qp, N1, T4, T2, P2) \tag{8}$$

To decompose the model into subspaces, we will use the methodology of situational modeling and decompose the model into sub-models representing certain operating points of the engine.

$$O_{pi} = f_i\,(N1, T4, T2, P2),\ i=1\ldots n \tag{9}$$

where n is the regimes count. This decomposition can be done by expert knowledge or with use of some clustering algorithm. We propose the decomposition of the model into a set of three operating points ($n=3$), or in terms of situational modeling into three distinct situations (Andoga, 2006). That is the startup of the engine, stable operation of the engine and its shutdown. Every situational model is further decomposed into a set of non equivalent sub-models, which are interconnected according to the basic physical dependencies in the engine and are treated as black box systems. Every one of these sub-models is then represented by a neural network or fuzzy inference system, which models the individual parameter dependencies and further decomposes the operating points into local operating points which are then represented as local neural or fuzzy models. Furthermore all models have to be put in an adaptive structure that will be able to decide, which model to use for certain situational frame. The modular architecture of such system is shown in the figure 10. A classifier in the form of neural network represents the gate which gates outputs of individual models to give a correct prediction. Use of this model allows us to simulate whole operation of the engine with also highly non-linear atypical situations such as startup and shut down of the engine. The model has only a single input parameter in the form of fuel flow input Q_{pal}.

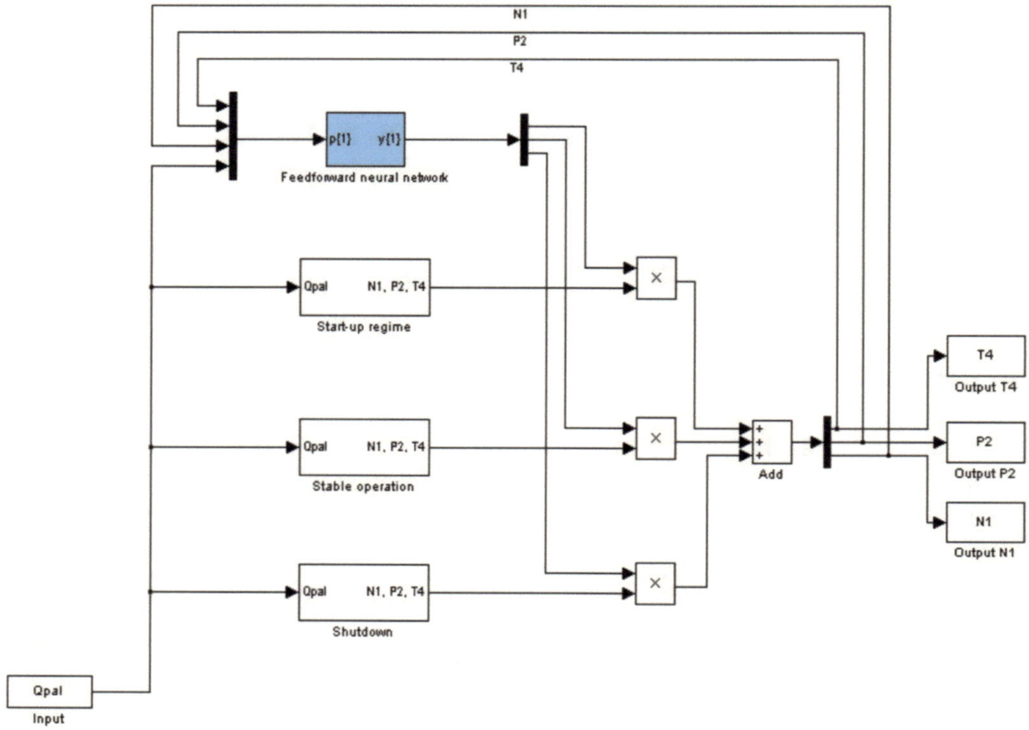

Fig. 10. Modular architecture of the dynamic engine model

The inputs for the classifier neural network are state variables resulting from the model, the only input to the model is the fuel flow parameter. The output of the network will be defined as a vector:

$$O_u = [x_1, \dots, x_n] \quad (11)$$

where n is the number of situational model frames and $x_i = \{0;1\}$,in our case $n=3$.

5.5 Simulations with the situational model of the MPM-20 engine

We can evaluate the situational model in terms of simulating the start-up of the engine, its stable regime of operation and its run down, together with the whole operation. The figure 12 shows the plot of speed (rpm) of the engine during its startup with three different startup levels of fuel flow input. The individual sub-models for this frame are in the form of neural networks trained by scaled conjugate gradient algorithm (Moller, 1993) with the modification of time delayed inputs. The individual models are shown in the following figure.

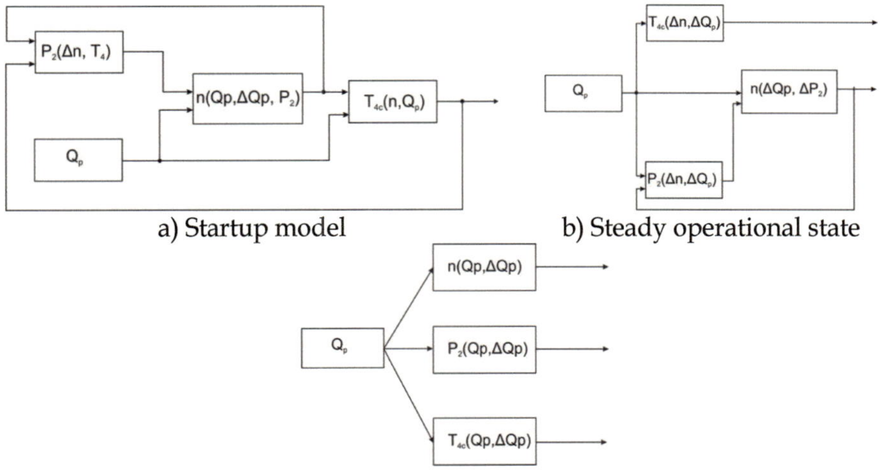

Fig. 11.Structure of the models for three situational frames of operation of the engine.

All models were tested separately with fuel supply inputs measured by different runs of the engine and tests were also done with the whole model with 15 different consecutive runs defined by measured fuel flow supply. The model does not take in account environmental conditions as they are kept constant in the laboratory. The startup model uses time delayed feedforward neural networks with two hidden layers trained by SCG algorithm, the steady operational state model uses Takagi Sugeno (TSK) fuzzy inference systems to model individual parameter dependencies and the shut-down model uses neural networks of identical structure as the startup model trained with other data.

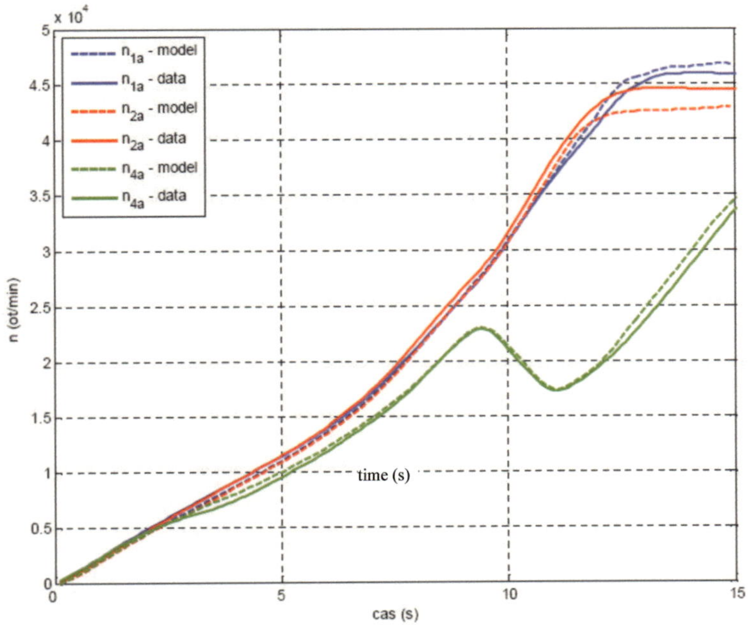

Fig. 12. The results of the start-up model for different levels of input signal

Figure 13 shows simulation of a stable operation of the engine with individual models in the form of TSK fuzzy inference systems (FIS).

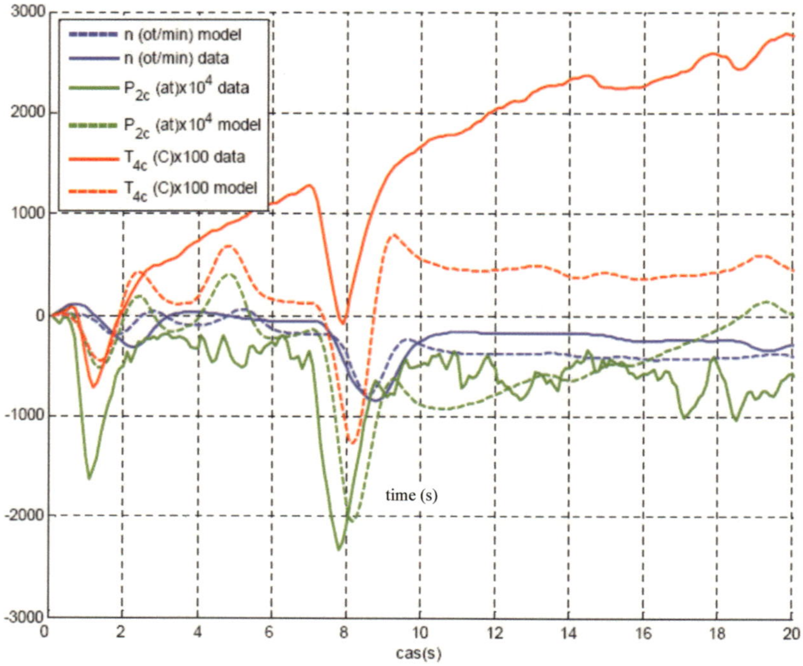

Fig. 13. One run of the engine in simulation of differences of all variables in the stable regime.

The problematic area in this case is temperature T_{4c}, because by use of the FIS TSK model we aren't able to simulate overheating of the engine as time of operation isn't the input parameter. Simulation of the whole operation of MPM20 engine is shown in the figure 13. The errors of simulation of 15 different measured runs of the engine in its whole operation are summarized in the table 1. The table shows means of mean absolute (MAE) and the maximum absolute error (MAAE).

Parameter	$MAE_{i=1...15}$	$MAAE_{i=1...15}$	$MAPE_{i=1...15}$	$MAAPE_{i=1...15}$
N(rpm)	67	275	0.14	0.61
T_{4C}(°C)	13	56	1.1	2.7
P_{2C}(at)	0.065	0.071	1.7	1.88

Table 1. A summary of the MPM-20 model simulations

We can see that the maximum absolute percentage error is about 1.7% for P_{2C} parameter in the whole dynamic range and the maximum percentage absolute error is by 2.7% which gives way more accurate predictions than linear dynamic models. One exemplar run of the model is shown in the figure 14.

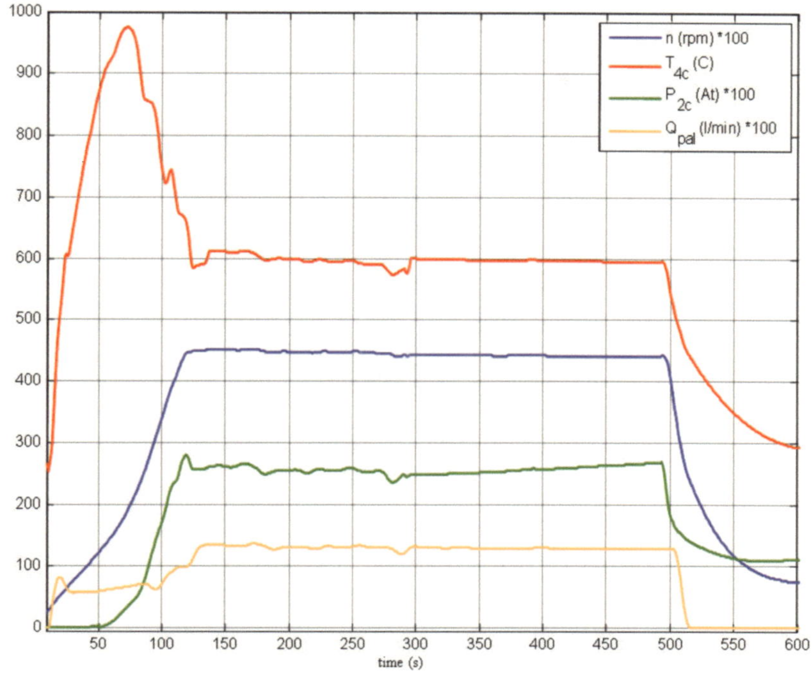

Fig. 14. One run of the engine simulated by the situational model

6. Situational control algorithms for turbojet engines

6.1 Situational control algorithms of large scale systems

Methods of artificial intelligence may offer new quality into control systems. Situational control was designed for the control of complex systems, where the traditional cybernetic models weren't sufficient (Pospelov, 1986). The model proposed in (Pospelov, 1986) wasn't sufficient to control systems characterized by features like unique dynamics, incompleteness and indeterminacy of description, ambiguity and presence of a free will.

More general approach to situational control is the following structural scheme of formatter control of complexes shown in the figure 15. Formatter control of a complex means not only the control of its parameters, but also the control of the form of the complex system.

The central element of this system is the control component, which is represented by a structure of a control component (fig 16) using methods of situational control. This means that it is a system, which makes situational classification and chooses the appropriate control strategy upon the basis of incoming signals from analyzers ANX, ANY, ANR and ANZ. The following figure shows the functional scheme of situational control of a complex system.

The control process is composed of two phases, the decision and the control phase, where every of them is divided into classification and the action phase. Processed situation is analyzed in the selection part of the decision phase (classification). According to analysis of results, the actual situation is then assigned to one of the prepared situations. Every standard situation has a certain file of control algorithms which are stored in memory or an algorithm has a file of situations that can be handled by it. During the action period of the decision-making phase, the most suitable file of algorithms is being activated to process the given situation.

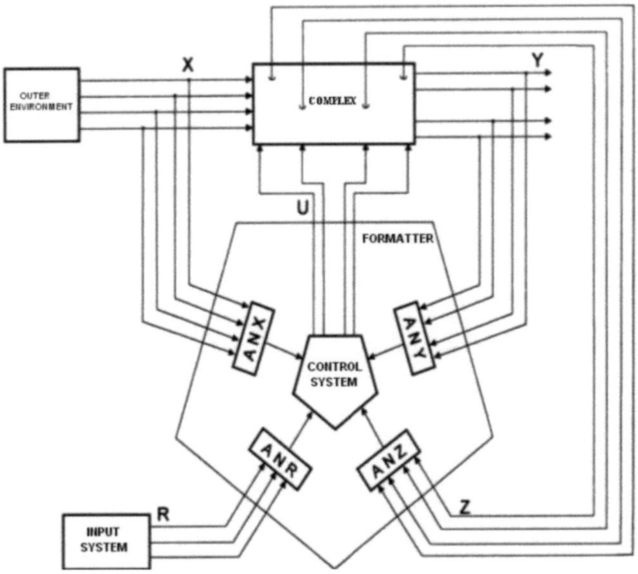

Fig. 15. Formatter control of a complex system (Beneš, 1974)

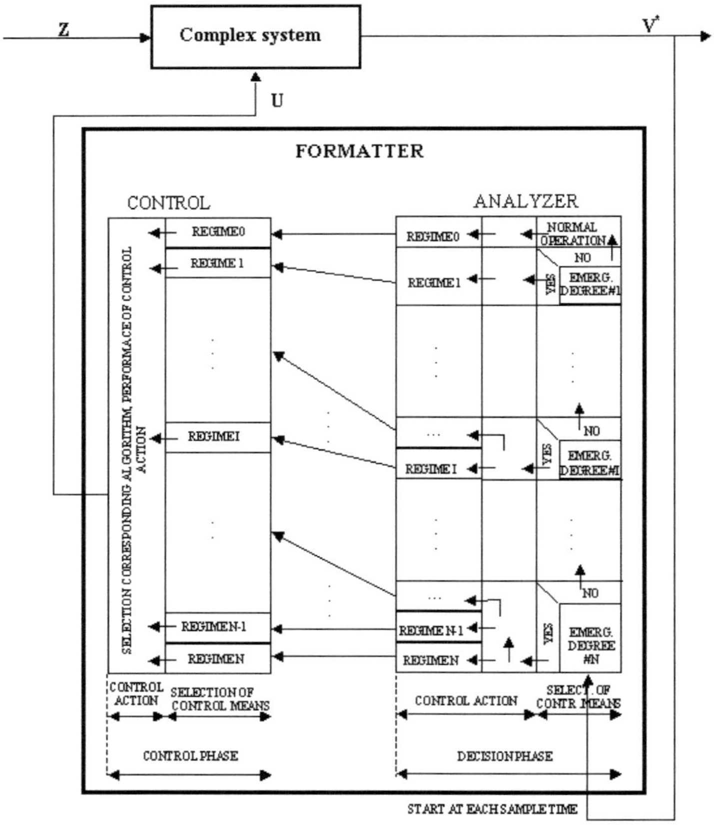

Fig. 16. Functional scheme of situational control system (Madarász, 1994)

During the selection interval of the control phase, these algorithms adapt themselves for solution of the given situation (parameterization and other adaptation connected with activation). Realization of control activity occurs in the action period of the control phase, this control activity is passed to action elements that manipulate with the system.
For the design of a system respecting the requirements of control in anytime, the following algorithm is proposed (Madarász, 1994):

a. description of the structure and function of the controlled complex system,
b. global goal designation,
c. classification of erroneous operational states and their causes,
d. classification and description regimes functions of the control, that are assigned to individual erroneous states,
e. algorithmization of individual regimes of control,
f. implementation.

By algorithmization and design of regimes of control and also by the design of a classification mechanism, it is today necessary to consider use of robust intelligent methods for these tasks. In the past methods of multi-criteria decision making, expert systems, or catastrophe and chaos theory have been used for situational classification. A suitable approach lies today in the use of adaptive learning systems that will be covered further.

6.2 Situational control system design for a turbojet engine

Methods of artificial intelligence may offer new quality into control systems. However they can bring such benefits only after a careful model based analysis of a system where they should be applied with regards to simplicity and error free operation of such control system. Because on the lowest level of control we deal mostly with data and raw numbers, the approaches of sub-symbolic AI are appropriate to be used in design of intelligent FADEC control systems. However, on higher level of integration some symbolic concepts could also be used. From the area of symbolic AI three basic approaches can be successfully used:

- neural networks,
- fuzzy inference systems,
- genetic algorithms.

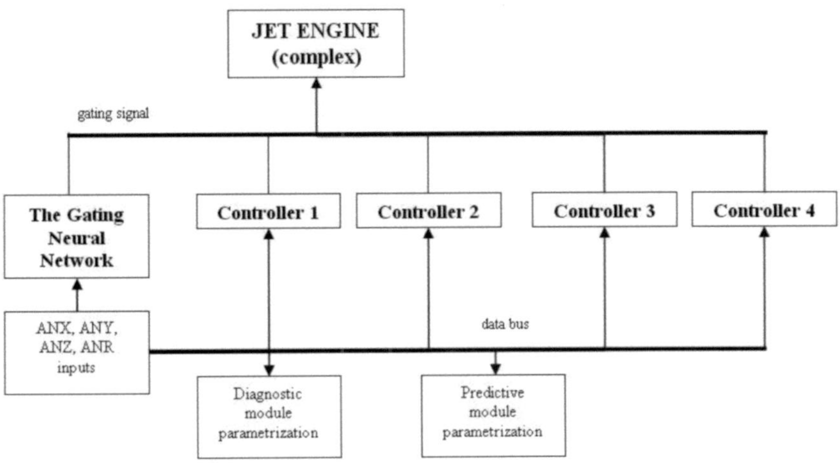

Fig. 17. General situational control system scheme to be used in turbojet engines

All three approaches offer a vast number of methods and their combinations in hybrid architectures. Feed-forward topologies can be successfully employed mainly in modeling of non linearity of a jet engine and as decision elements in control circuits, for example as a gating neural network in general jet engine situational control formatter scheme designed by authors as shown in the figure 17.
The whole concept of the situational control system is decomposition of operational states into time spaced situational frames (classes) and every situational frame has at least one corresponding control algorithm (or controller) assigned to handle it. Special attention is put on handling of critical states. The exemplar system in the figure 17 handles only four basic situational frames.

6.3 Situational control system of the MPM-20 engine

In development and design of FADEC (Full Authority Digital Engine Control) compliant control system, situational control methodology approach has been used. It is similar in to the one described in previous chapter, what means we use a gating neural network as a classifier of situational frames and system of controllers to handle those situational frames. We use concepts of traditional situational control and formatter control of complex systems. The resulting physical architecture including analyzers of input (X), state (Z), output (Y) and desired (R) parameters is shown in the figure 18

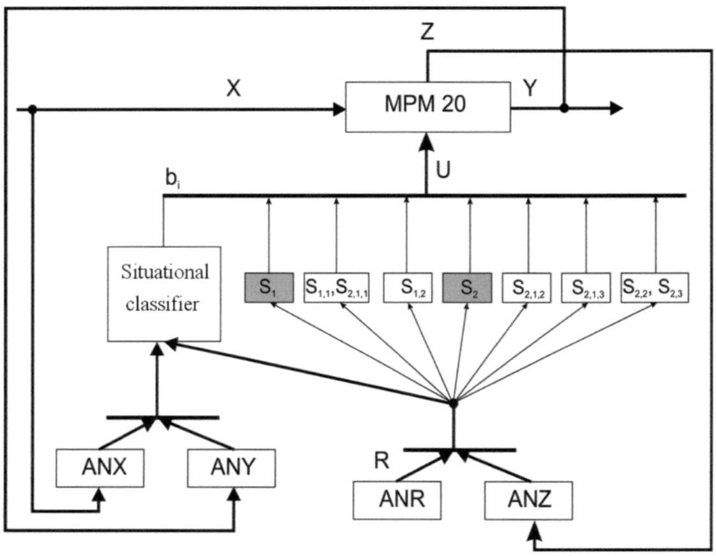

Fig. 18. Implementation of situational control system with decomposition into situational frames

Blocks designated as $S_{i,j,k}$ represent controllers for different situational frames, which result from the situational decomposition of operation of the engine in three levels:

- start-up of the engine – situational frame S_1
- steady operational state – situational frame S_2
- shut down – situational frame S_3

The whole decomposition is done with use of expert knowledge in the area and data clustering algorithms. Full situational decomposition of states is shown in the figure 18.

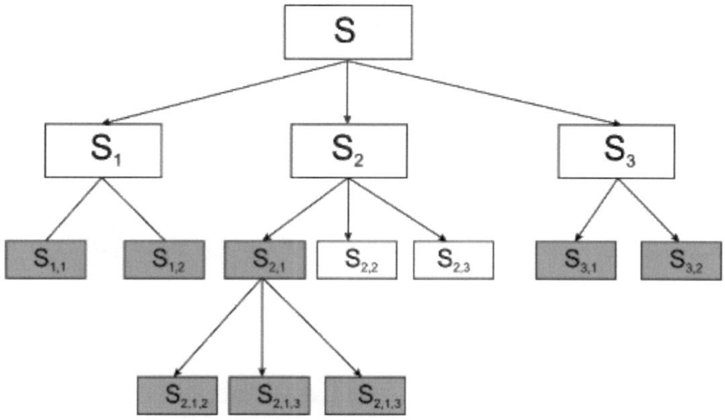

Fig. 19. Situational decomposition into situational frames

The blocks in the figure 18 have the following meaning:

S_1 - startup of the engine:

$S_{1,1}$ -temperature problem, $S_{1,2}$ -pressure $P_{2c\ problem}$

S_2 - steady state of operation:

$S_{2,1}$ - atypical state :

$S_{2,1,1}$: low compression, $S_{2,1,2}$ - low fuel flow, $S_{2,1,3}$ - unstable speed,

$S_{2,2}$ - acceleration, $S_{2,3}$ - deceleration

S_3 - shutdown

$S_{3,1}$ - stall of the engine

$S_{3,2}$ - error by run-down

The grey blocks in the figure 19 represent atypical situational frames and every frame has defined control strategy while the switching element is done by feed-forward neural network with time delays on input, trained by scaled conjugate gradient algorithm. The next chapter will cover design of one controller that handles situational frames S_1 and $S_{1,1}$.

6.4 Start-up controller design for the MPM-20 engine

In design of control algorithms as elements of an integrated control circuit fuzzy inference systems can be successfully used. Such system has been used to design a startup controller for MPM 20 - the experimental small turbojet engine. This controller is acting only by startup of the engine and its aim is to decrease the temperature overshoot by startup that decreases life cycle of the engine and in certain cases can lead to turbine engine damage. The present startup techniques are mainly time based, what means that the fuel flow input is increased in a time based function rather than parameter based. The control algorithm can be seen as controller S_1 in the figure 18 and is bound with digitally controlled servo vent for fuel supply control.

The basic idea is to decompose the startup process of the engine into model micro-situational frames, where one rule of the inference system would correspond to one micro-situational frame in the start-up macro-situational frame.

Each rule in the form of <IF> … <THEN> … postulate has a corresponding output value of fuel supply assigned. In this way we can handle not only the classical situations at startup, but also emergency situations like flameout of the engine or fire in the engine at startup. Three inputs and one output were chosen for the rules so the rule looks like this:

IF *T4c* IS *L{T4c}* AND *dT4c* IS *L{dT4c}* and *n* IS *L{n}* THEN Qpal IS *L{Qpal}* (10)

where
T_{4c} – temperature of gases behind the turbine
dT_{4c} – derivation of temperature of gases behind the turbine
n – speed of the engine
Q_{pal} – fuel flow supply to the engine
L – function that assigns fuzzy membership function in corresponding universe of the afore mentioned parameters
In this way the fuzzy controller handles 60 micro-situations with a small excerpt shown in the following table.

29	if	n	is PS	and	T_4	is PB	and	dT_4	is PS	THEN	Q_{pal}	is PS	
30	if	n	is PS	and	T_4	is PB	and	dT_4	is PM	THEN	Q_{pal}	is PS	Critical T_4
31	if	n	is PM	and	T_4	is PS	and	dT_4	is NM	THEN	Q_{pal}	is Z	Flameout
32	if	n	is PM	and	T_4	is PS	and	dT_4	is NS	THEN	Q_{pal}	is Z	Flameout
33	if	n	is PM	and	T_4	is PS	and	dT_4	is Z	THEN	Q_{pal}	is Z	Flameout
34	if	n	is PM	and	T_4	is PS	and	dT_4	is PS	THEN	Q_{pal}	is PB	
35	if	n	is PM	and	T_4	is PS	and	dT_4	is PM	THEN	Q_{pal}	is PS	
36	if	n	is PM	and	T_4	is PM	and	dT_4	is NM	THEN	Q_{pal}	is PB	
37	if	n	is PM	and	T_4	is PM	and	dT_4	is NS	THEN	Q_{pal}	is PB	
38	if	n	is PM	and	T_4	is PM	and	dT_4	is Z	THEN	Q_{pal}	is PB	Final rule
39	if	n	is PM	and	T_4	is PM	and	dT_4	is PS	THEN	Q_{pal}	is PM	
40	if	n	is PM	and	T_4	is PM	and	dT_4	is PM	THEN	Q_{pal}	is PS	
41	if	n	is PM	and	T_4	is PB	and	dT_4	is NM	THEN	Q_{pal}	is PM	
42	if	n	is PM	and	T_4	is PB	and	dT_4	is NS	THEN	Q_{pal}	is PM	
43	if	n	is PM	and	T_4	is PB	and	dT_4	is Z	THEN	Q_{pal}	is PS	Critical T_4
44	if	n	is PM	and	T_4	is PB	and	dT_4	is PS	THEN	Q_{pal}	is Z	
45	if	n	is PM	and	T_4	is PB	and	dT_4	is PM	THEN	Q_{pal}	is Z	Fire
46	if	n	is PB	and	T_4	is PS	and	dT_4	is NM	THEN	Q_{pal}	is Z	Flameout
47	if	n	is PB	and	T_4	is PS	and	dT_4	is NS	THEN	Q_{pal}	is Z	Flameout

Table 2. Rules for the start-up controller of the MPM-20 engine

Where rules in yellow color represent critical temperature states, blue color represent stall of the engine, red color represents rule handling fire of the engine and green color represents the final rule after execution of which control is handled to another controller and engine transits from startup macro-situation into another macro situational frame. The last figure shows the control surfaces of the startup macro-situation for MPM-20 engine.
The proposed controller for the start-up of the MPM-20 will be included into the whole situational control system and is awaiting further testing in laboratory conditions. Although the controller is used only for specific situational frame, it can be further developed and used on normal sized engines of similar type.

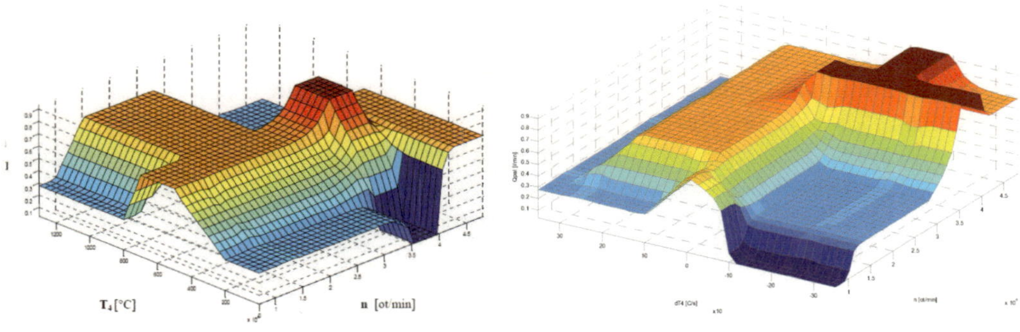

Fig. 20. Control surfaces of the startup controller

7. Conclusion

The article presented some basic approaches in modeling and control of turbojet engines in general and applied for the object of the MPM-20 engine. This engine gives us an ideal test bed for research of methods in the areas of non-linear dynamic systems modeling and design of advanced control algorithms. Further research will be done in the area of situational modeling that will be headed towards broadening of input parameters of the situational model of the engine and further refinement situational classes. In this area we will be aimed at use of automatic algorithms to find boundaries between situational frames within multivariate space of parameters contrary to their setting by an expert. This also applies for situational control algorithm with the main aim lying in research of adaptive situational classifier systems that will be able to create classes and automatically assign controllers for them. All research in the areas of situational modeling, situational control should bring new quality of control and modeling in the area of turbojet engines and we expect this knowledge to be also expanded to other areas of technical systems.

8. Acknowledgement

The work described in this chapter has been supported by VEGA num. 1/0394/08 „Algorithms of situational control and modelling of complex systems "and KEGA no. 001-010TUKE-4/2010 - Use of intelligent methods in modelling and control of aircraft engines in education.

9. References

Andoga, R., Madarász, L., Főző, L. (2006). *Situational modeling and control of a small turbojet engine MPM 20*, IEEE International Conference on Computational Cybernetics, 20.-22. August, 2006, ISBN. 1-4244-0071-6, pp. 81-85., Tallinn, Estonia

Beneš, J. (1974), *Teorie systémů (řízení komplexů)(Theory of systems)*, 200 pp. Academia, nakladatelství ČSAV, 1974, Czech. Rep.

Főző, L.(2008). *Use of mathematical model of steady and nonsteady operation of MPM20 turbojet engine by design of anytime control algorithms* (in Slovak), Dissertation thesis, Dept. of Cybernetics and AI, Faculty of Electrical Engineerin and Informatics, Technical University of Košice, 144 p., September 2008., Slovakia

Harris, Ch., Hong, X., Gan, Q. (2006) Adaptive Modelling, *Estimation and Fusion from Data*, Springer, ISBN 3-540-42686-8, pp. 323, 2006.

J.-S. Roger Jang. (1993). *ANFIS: Adaptive-Network-Based Fuzzy Inference Systems*," IEEE Transactions on Systems, Man, and Cybernetics, Vol. 23, No. 03, pp 665-685

Jonathan S., L., Turso, J., A., Shah, N., Sowers., T., S., Owen, K., A. (2005) *A Demonstration of a Retrofit Architecture for Intelligent Control and Diagnostics of a Turbofan Engine*, NASA/TM -2005-214019, USA

Lazar, T. et al. (2000), *Tendencie vývoja a modelovania avionických systémov*, Ministerstvo Obrany SR, pp.160, ISBN 80-8842-26-3., Slovakia

Linke-Diesenger, A. (2008). *Systems of commercial turbofan engines: an introduction to systems functions*, Springer, ISBN 978-3-540-73618-9

Madarász, L., Andoga R., Főző, L., Lazar. T. (2009). Situational control, modeling and diagnostics of large scale systems, In: *Towards Intelligent Engineering and Information Technology*, Rudas I.J., Fodor, J., Kacprzyk, J. (Ed.), p. 153-164., ISBN 978-3-642-03737-5, Springer-Verlag, Berlin.

Madarász, L. (2004).: *Intelligent technologies and their applications in large scale systems*. University Press, elfa s.r.o. Košice, 368 pp., ISBN - 89062 - 41 - 5

Madarász, L., Holečko, P. (1994), *Methodology of Situational Control Creation and its Applications*. 1st IFAC Workshop, New Trends in Design of Control Systems, pp. 155 - 162. Smolenice, Slovakia

Moller, M. F. (1993), *A scaled conjugate gradient algorithm for fast supervised learning*, Neural Networks, vol. 6, pp. 525-533, 1993.

Pospelov, D.A (1986), *Situacionnoje upravlenije. Teoria i praks. Nauka*, 284 pp., Moskva

Považan J (1999).: *Konštrukcia matematických modelov leteckých turbokompresorových motorov (Construction of mathematic models of aircraft engines)*, VLA M.R.Š. v Košiciach, ISBN 80-7166-030-2., Slovakia

Ružek, J., Kmoch, P.(1979), *Teorie leteckých motoru I.*, 373 pp, 1979, Czech Rep.

Sanjay, G.(2005). *NASA Glenn Research in Controls and Diagnostics for Intelligent Propulsion Systems*, NASA/TM 2005-214036, USA

Wiseman, M. (2005). *Intelligent Engine Systems*, NASA CR/-2005-213964, USA

3

Software Implementation of Self-Tuning Controllers

Radek Matušů and Roman Prokop
Department of Automation and Control Engineering
Faculty of Applied Informatics
Tomas Bata University in Zlín
Nad Stráněmi 4511, Zlín 76005
Czech Republic

1. Introduction

Real control of industrial processes is almost always burden with various perturbations, disturbances and changes in process parameters or dynamics due to varying operational conditions, plant properties themselves, etc. Furthermore, an acceptable a priori mathematical model does not have to be known. In spite of it, such processes have to be controlled.

A possible solution to this task represents an area of control theory known as adaptive control or more specifically usage of self-tuning controllers (Åström & Wittenmark, 1973); (Åström et al., 1977); (Clarke & Gawthrop, 1979); (Åström & Wittenmark, 1989); (Wellstead & Zarrop, 1991); (Isermann et al. 1992); (Hang et al., 1993); (Bobál et al., 1999); (Bobál et al., 2005). Main idea consists in modification of control law according to the changing plant parameters obtained via recursive identification. Their advantage is some kind of "intelligent" behaviour, but on the other hand these regulators are quite complex and not easily applicable.

This chapter deals mainly with software implementation of selected digital self-tuning control algorithms into the Matlab and Pascal environment for the purpose of possible industrial utilization. The work was motivated by co-operation with a manufacturer of aluminium-based rolled products and packaging materials. His project has supposed primarily the application of discrete-time adaptive compensator to control of a metal smelting furnace. Other requirements were the plant model with "a2b3" structure and final implementation in Borland Pascal (because of integration into the existing system). However the paper presents not only derived relations applicable to Pascal environment but also program for simulative purposes and testing created under Matlab and some preliminary simulation results. In the first stage, the applied methods have included a polynomial approach to discrete-time control design and recursive least-squares identification algorithm LDDIF, but subsequently also two alternative techniques, namely control using continuous-time regulator with fixed parameters and use of delta approach in self-tuning control, have been verified. Although all the tasks were motivated by our

specific problem, the whole chapter tries to present them in more or less generally applicable way.
The chapter is organized as follows. In Section 2, basic theoretical background of digital self-tuning controllers using polynomial synthesis and applicable relations are provided. The Section 3 then contains the fundamentals of related recursive identification algorithm LDDIF. Next, the Section 4 describes the preliminary software implementation and demonstrates its facilities on an application-oriented example. Furthermore, design and utilization of fixed continuous-time controller along with self-tuning control using delta models as two various alternative approaches are presented in an extensive Section 5. And finally, Section 6 offers some conclusion remarks.
The preliminary version of this work has been presented at conferences (Matušů & Prokop, 2009), (Matušů et al., 2009).

2. Discrete-time polynomial synthesis

In the first instance the digital self tuning controllers were intended to be implemented. Their very basic principle consists in consecutive identification of the controlled process using a recursive algorithm (see the following Section) and application of obtained plant parameters in computing the control law. The control design itself has been based on algebraic approach and pole placement (Kučera, 1979); (Kučera, 1993); (Wellstead et al., 1979); (Åström & Wittenmark, 1980).
Despite the existence of more complex control configurations, just the very basic single-input single-output (SISO) control loop with one degree of freedom has been assumed. This classical feedback connection in a discrete-time sense is shown in Fig. 1.

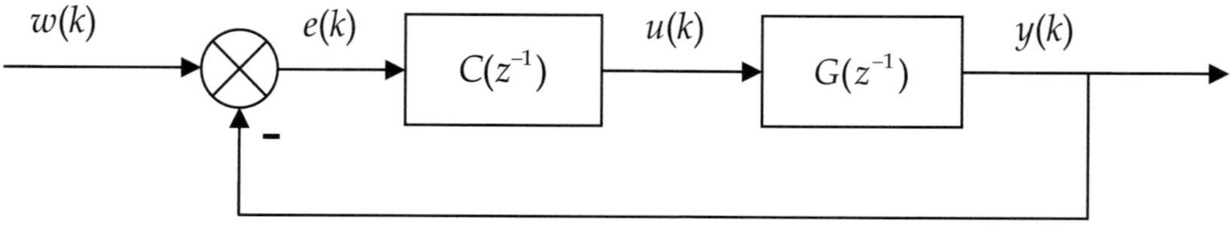

Fig. 1. Basic closed control loop

The signals $w(k)$, $e(k)$, $u(k)$ and $y(k)$ from Fig. 1 represent reference value, tracking (control) error, actuating (manipulated) signal and controlled (output) variable, respectively, and blocks $C(z^{-1})$ and $G(z^{-1})$ mean discrete-time transfer functions of a controller and controlled system.
According to project requirements a controlled plant is supposed to has an "a2b3" structure, i.e. its transfer function is:

$$G(z^{-1}) = \frac{b(z^{-1})}{a(z^{-1})} = \frac{b_1 z^{-1} + b_2 z^{-2} + b_3 z^{-3}}{1 + a_1 z^{-1} + a_2 z^{-2}} \tag{1}$$

A suitable controller which ensures stabilization of the whole control circuit (Fig. 1) and asymptotic tracking of stepwise reference variable can be obtained by solution of Diophantine equation (Kučera, 1979); (Kučera, 1993):

$$a(z^{-1})f(z^{-1})p(z^{-1})+b(z^{-1})q(z^{-1})=m(z^{-1}) \tag{2}$$

where $a(z^{-1})$, $b(z^{-1})$ are from the controlled system (1), and $p(z^{-1})$, $q(z^{-1})$ from discrete-time controller:

$$C(z^{-1})=\frac{q(z^{-1})}{f(z^{-1})p(z^{-1})}=\frac{q_0+q_1z^{-1}+q_2z^{-2}}{f(z^{-1})\left(p_0+p_1z^{-1}+p_2z^{-2}\right)} \tag{3}$$

and where $f(z^{-1})$ is the denominator of image of stepwise reference signal:

$$W(z^{-1})=\frac{h(z^{-1})}{f(z^{-1})}=\frac{h(z^{-1})}{1-z^{-1}} \tag{4}$$

Moreover, right-hand polynomial $m(z^{-1})$ from (2) is a stable polynomial of appropriate order. Thus the equation (2) takes here the specific form:

$$\begin{aligned}&\left(1+a_1z^{-1}+a_2z^{-2}\right)\left(1-z^{-1}\right)\left(p_0+p_1z^{-1}+p_2z^{-2}\right)+\left(b_1z^{-1}+b_2z^{-2}+b_3z^{-3}\right)\left(q_0+q_1z^{-1}+q_2z^{-2}\right)=\\&=m_0+m_1z^{-1}+m_2z^{-2}+m_3z^{-3}+m_4z^{-4}+m_5z^{-5}\end{aligned} \tag{5}$$

Obviously, the aim is to calculate coefficients of $p(z^{-1})$, $q(z^{-1})$ to get the controller (3). A simple method for finding the particular solution of Diophantine equation (5) grounds in the comparison of coefficients with the same power and consequent transformation of (5) into the set of six equations with six unknowns. This set can be written in a matrix form as follows:

$$\begin{pmatrix}1 & 0 & 0 & 0 & 0 & 0\\ a_1-1 & 1 & 0 & b_1 & 0 & 0\\ a_2-a_1 & a_1-1 & 1 & b_2 & b_1 & 0\\ -a_2 & a_2-a_1 & a_1-1 & b_3 & b_2 & b_1\\ 0 & -a_2 & a_2-a_1 & 0 & b_3 & b_2\\ 0 & 0 & -a_2 & 0 & 0 & b_3\end{pmatrix}\begin{pmatrix}p_0\\ p_1\\ p_2\\ q_0\\ q_1\\ q_2\end{pmatrix}=\begin{pmatrix}m_0\\ m_1\\ m_2\\ m_3\\ m_4\\ m_5\end{pmatrix} \tag{6}$$

Solving the equation system (6) would be an easy task in many software packages. However, the final implementation of control algorithm in Borland Pascal environment was required by assignment and so the analytical solution of (6) had to be derived in order to be easily programmable. Thus, the utilizable controller parameters are computed according to:

$$\begin{aligned}q_0&=x_{13}/x_{12}\\ q_1&=x_{14}/x_{12}\\ q_2&=x_{15}/x_{12}\\ p_0&=m_0\\ p_1&=x_2-b_1q_0\\ p_2&=\left(q_2b_3-m_5\right)/a_2\end{aligned} \tag{7}$$

where auxiliary variables are:

$$
\begin{aligned}
x_1 &= (a_2 - a_1)b_3 + b_2 a_2 \\
x_2 &= m_1 + (1 - a_1)m_0 \\
x_3 &= \left[a_2 m_4 + a_2^2 x_2 + (a_2 - a_1)m_5\right]/x_1 \\
x_4 &= \left(a_2^2 b_1\right)/x_1 \\
x_5 &= (a_2 b_3)/x_1 \\
x_6 &= m_0(a_2 - a_1) + x_2 a_1 - x_2 \\
x_7 &= -b_1 a_1 + b_1 + b_2 \\
x_8 &= m_2 - x_6 + m_5/a_2 \\
x_9 &= -b_1 a_2 + b_1 a_1 + b_3 \\
x_{10} &= (b_3 a_1)/a_2 - b_3/a_2 + b_1 \\
x_{11} &= m_3 + m_0 a_2 - h_2 a_2 + h_2 a_1 + (m_5 a_1)/a_2 - m_5/a_2 \\
x_{12} &= x_4 b_1 x_{10} + x_7 b_2 + x_9 x_5 (b_3/a_2) - b_1 x_9 - (b_3/a_2) b_2 x_4 - x_{10} x_5 x_7 \\
x_{13} &= x_3 b_1 x_{10} + x_8 b_2 + x_{11} x_5 (b_3/a_2) - b_1 x_{11} - (b_3/a_2) b_2 x_3 - x_{10} x_5 x_8 \\
x_{14} &= x_4 x_8 x_{10} + x_7 x_{11} + x_9 x_3 (b_3/a_2) - x_8 x_9 - (b_3/a_2) x_{11} x_4 - x_{10} x_3 x_7 \\
x_{15} &= x_4 b_1 x_{11} + x_7 b_2 x_3 + x_9 x_5 x_8 - x_3 b_1 x_9 - x_8 b_2 x_4 - x_{11} x_5 x_7
\end{aligned}
\tag{8}
$$

The coefficients of the polynomial $m(z^{-1})$ can be used for controller tuning and thus for influencing the closed-loop control behaviour. The suitable choice of the roots of the closed-loop characteristic polynomial $m(z^{-1})$ is known as pole placement problem. Anyway, this case of fifth order $m(z^{-1})$ can be easily "degraded" to the lower order ones by equalling the appropriate coefficients to zero. Moreover, the special events are represented by so-called dead-beat control for $m(z^{-1}) = 1$ or by linear quadratic (LQ) control for $m(z^{-1})$ given by means of minimizing the LQ criterion (Hunt et al., 1993); (Bobál et al., 1999).

Finally, the calculated parameters (7) are applied to programmable control law which corresponds to the controller (3) and which generates the control signal $u(k)$. It can be formulated as:

$$u(k) = \left[(p_0 - p_1)u(k-1) + (p_1 - p_2)u(k-2) + p_2 u(k-3) + q_0 e(k) + q_1 e(k-1) + q_2 e(k-2)\right]/p_0 \tag{9}$$

Interested reader can find more information on algebraic methods and their application in analysis and synthesis of control systems e.g. in (Kučera, 1979); (Kučera, 1993); (Vidyasagar, 1985); (Doyle et al., 1992).

3. Recursive identification algorithm

A LDDIF routine has been used as plant parameters identification technique for combination with algebraic synthesis from the previous Section in order to obtain self-tuning controller. It is recursive least-squares algorithm with exponential and directional forgetting (Kulhavý & Kárný, 1984). Moreover, the corrections influencing the covariance

matrix $\boldsymbol{P}(k)$ of the estimated parameters by adding some multiple of identity matrix, which have been suggested in (Bittanti et al., 1990), are implemented to improve the tracking performance.
The algorithm can be described by equations (Čirka et al., 2006):

$$\begin{aligned}
&\varepsilon(k) = \boldsymbol{y}(k) - \boldsymbol{\Phi}(k)^T \boldsymbol{\theta}(k-1) \\
&r(k) = \boldsymbol{\Phi}(k)^T \boldsymbol{P}(k-1)\boldsymbol{\Phi}(k) \\
&\boldsymbol{\kappa}(k) = \frac{\boldsymbol{P}(k-1)\boldsymbol{\Phi}(k)}{1+r(k)} \\
&\beta(k) = \begin{cases} \varphi - \dfrac{1-\varphi}{r(k)} & \text{if } r(k) > 0 \\ 1 & \text{if } r(k) > 0 \end{cases} \\
&\boldsymbol{P}(k) = \boldsymbol{P}(k-1) - \frac{\boldsymbol{P}(k-1)\boldsymbol{\Phi}(k)\boldsymbol{\Phi}(k)^T \boldsymbol{P}(k-1)}{\beta(k)^{-1} + r(k)} + \delta \boldsymbol{I} \\
&\boldsymbol{\theta}(k) = \boldsymbol{\theta}(k-1) + \boldsymbol{\kappa}(k)\varepsilon(k)
\end{aligned} \tag{10}$$

where $\boldsymbol{\Phi}(k) = \left[-y(k-1) \quad -y(k-2) \quad u(k-1) \quad u(k-2) \quad u(k-3)\right]$ is observation vector, $\theta(k) = \left[a_1(k) \quad a_2(k) \quad b_1(k) \quad b_2(k) \quad b_3(k)\right]$ is vector of parameters and φ is exponential forgetting. The initial values for the algorithm are usually preset to $\varphi = 0.985$, $\boldsymbol{P}(0) = 10^6 \boldsymbol{I}$ and $\delta = 0.01$.
The main complication from the implementation point of view has been the arduousness in working with matrices.

4. Software implementation of self-tuning controllers

As it was adumbrated before, Borland Pascal had to be assumed for final application in real industrial conditions because of easy implementation into the existing system. However, several preliminary tests, algorithm verifications and simulations were done in Matlab environment due to better convenience for these testing purposes. As a result, a simple program has been created. Its main window is shown in fig. 2.
Initial real control and identification experiments for sampling time T = 45s have led to parameters of controlled system (1):

$$\begin{aligned}
a_1 &= -1.04 \\
a_2 &= 0.139 \\
b_1 &= -0.327 \\
b_2 &= 1.079 \\
b_3 &= 0.763
\end{aligned} \tag{11}$$

The closed-loop characteristic polynomial has been supposed as:

$$m(z^{-1}) = 1 - 2.45z^{-1} + 2.22z^{-2} - 0.907z^{-3} + 0.1601z^{-4} - 0.008925z^{-5} \tag{12}$$

which means that the poles of the closed loop transfer function (Fig. 1) have been placed to:

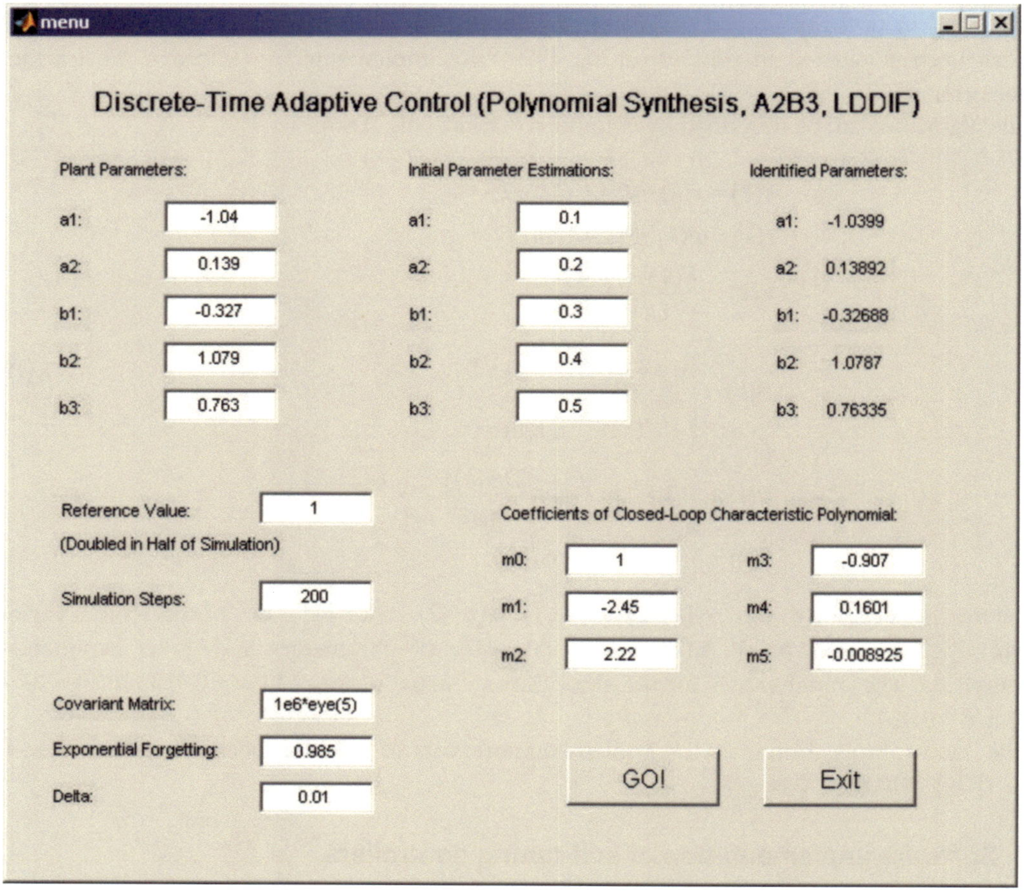

Fig. 2. Main window of the preliminary simulation program in Matlab

$$\begin{aligned} r_1 &= 0.85 \\ r_2 &= 0.7 \\ r_3 &= 0.5 \\ r_4 &= 0.3 \\ r_5 &= 0.1 \end{aligned} \tag{13}$$

Simulation result of control behaviour is depicted in Fig. 3. The huge overshoot in the beginning of the process is caused by not completed identification stage. The parameters of the controlled system were assumed to be unknown and preset to random starting values (as demonstrated in Fig. 2). The progress in identification of these parameters during control is shown in Fig. 4 with zoomed x-axis. As can be seen the plant parameters was properly identified after several initial steps and thanks to this the control response from Fig. 3 is much better at middle step change of reference signal.

However, one must emphasize that horizontal axis from Fig. 3 represents steps while each step takes 45 seconds. Unfortunately, such sampling time turned out not to be admissible to the submitter of the task because of psychological aspects for staff during operational changes. Thus, also other approaches without long-term sampling periods have been verified.

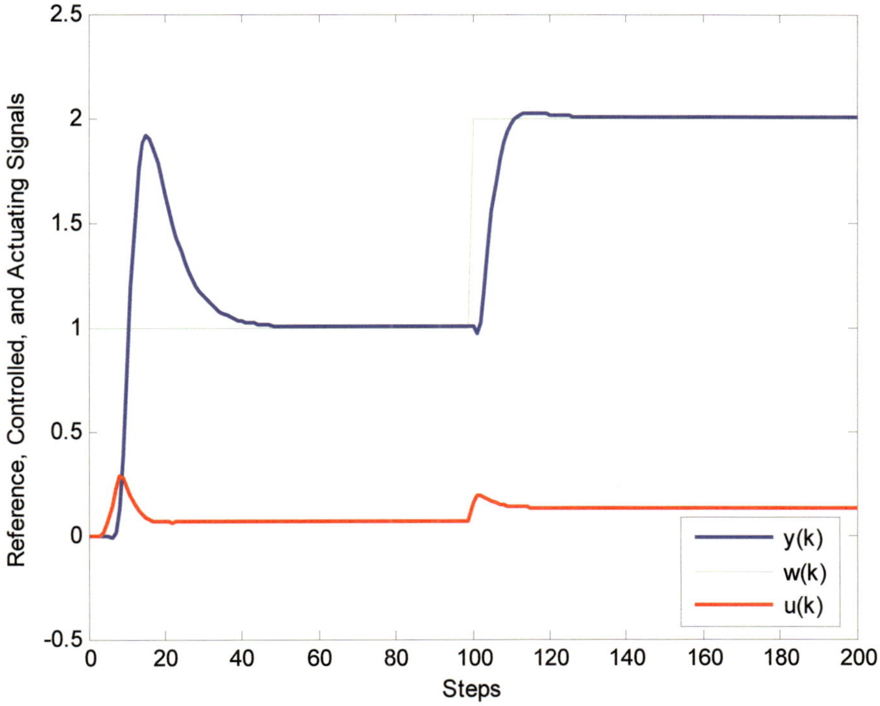

Fig. 3. Control of plant using discrete-time self-tuning controller - simulation

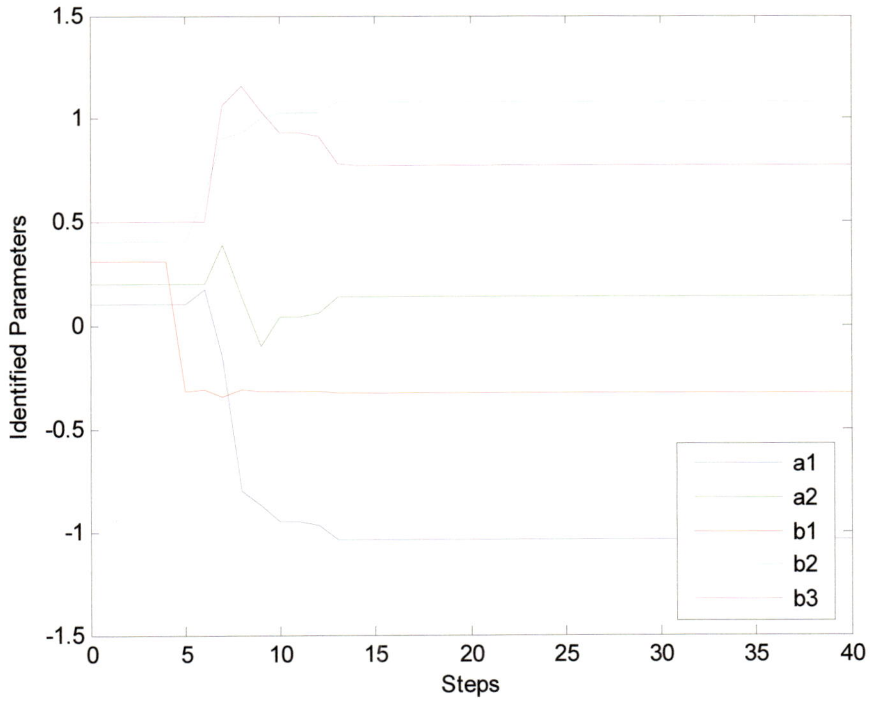

Fig. 4. Development of the identified parameters

5. Alternative approaches

5.1 Fixed continuous-time controller

First alternative technique to control synthesis has been based on the similar algebraic tools as described in Section 2 (Kučera, 1993), but now in continuous-time representation. Moreover, one off-line controller with fixed parameters has been tuned and due to this fact no recursive identification for adaptation reasons was needed anymore.

Primarily, the discrete-time model (1) with identified parameters (11) had to be transformed into continuous-time model suitable for linear Diophantine equations using first order Taylor approximation of time-delay term in denominator:

$$G(z^{-1}) = \frac{b_1 + b_2 z^{-1} + b_3 z^{-2}}{1 + a_1 z^{-1} + a_2 z^{-2}} z^{-1} \Rightarrow \frac{-0.327s^2 - 0.0289s + 0.001746}{s^2 + 0.04385s + 0.0001141} e^{-45s} \approx$$
$$\approx \frac{-0.007267s^2 - 0.0006423s + 0.0000388}{s^3 + 0.06607s^2 + 0.001089s + 0.000002535} = G(s) \qquad (14)$$

Correspondence of $G(z^{-1})$ and $G(s)$ is demonstrated in Fig. 5 where step responses of both models are compared.

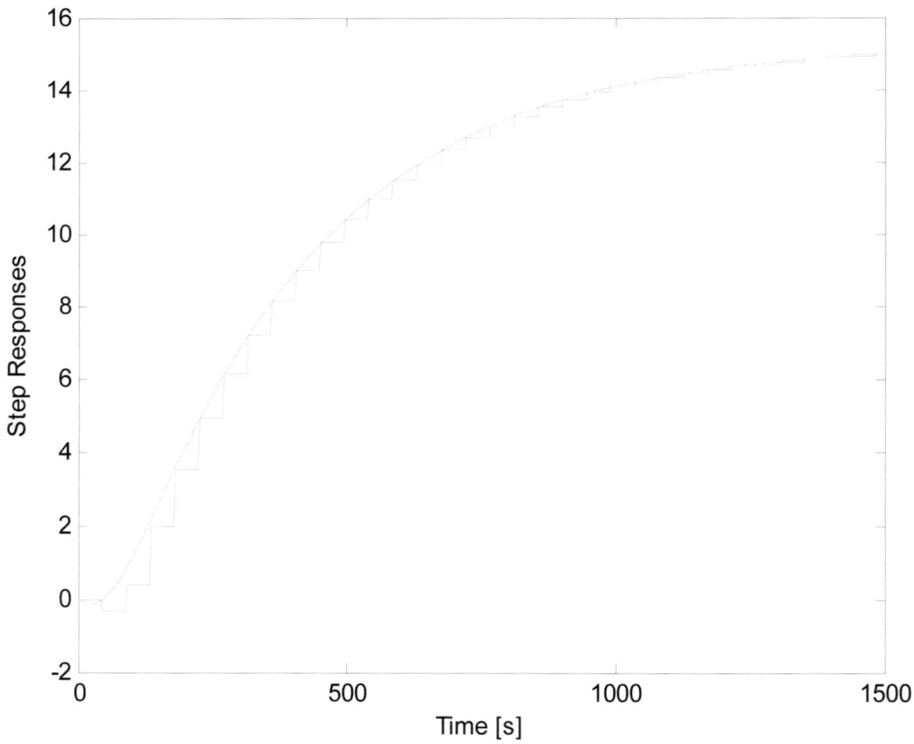

Fig. 5. Comparison of step responses of discrete-time and continuous-time models

The control design itself starts from continuous-time version of Diophantine equation (2):

$$a(s)f(s)p(s)+b(s)q(s)=m(s) \tag{15}$$

where analogically to Section 2:

$$\begin{aligned} a(s) &= s^3+0.06607s^2+0.001089s+0.000002535 \\ b(s) &= -0.007267s^2-0.0006423s+0.0000388 \\ f(s) &= s \end{aligned} \tag{16}$$

and where closed-loop characteristic polynomial has been assumed:

$$m(s)=s^6+0.133s^5+0.006765s^4+0.0001689s^3+2.14925\cdot10^{-6}s^2+1.26\cdot10^{-8}s+2.25\cdot10^{-11} \tag{17}$$

i.e. its roots are:

$$\begin{aligned} r_1 &= -0.003 \\ r_2 &= -0.05 \\ r_3 &= -0.02 \\ r_4 &= -0.02 \\ r_5 &= -0.025 \\ r_6 &= -0.015 \end{aligned} \tag{18}$$

The final continuous-time controller has been calculated as:

$$\mathrm{C}(s)=\frac{q(s)}{f(s)p(s)}=\frac{0.2591s^3+0.01549s^2+0.0002423s+5.799\cdot10^{-7}}{s^3+0.06881s^2+0.001409s} \tag{19}$$

Supposing the derivative approximation (e.g. here for tracking error e):

$$\frac{de(t)}{dt}\approx\frac{e(k)-e(k-1)}{T} \tag{20}$$

leads to "emulation" of continuous-time (19) suitable for Borland Pascal environment. Thus, the control law can be accomplished by relation:

$$u(k)=\left.\begin{bmatrix} q_3\left(e(k)-3e(k-1)+3e(k-2)-e(k-3)\right)+\cdots \\ \cdots+Tq_2\left(e(k)-2e(k-1)+e(k-2)\right)+T^2q_1\left(e(k)-e(k-1)\right)+\cdots \\ \cdots+T^3q_0e(k)+3u(k-1)-3u(k-2)+u(k-3)-\cdots \\ \cdots Tp_2\left(-2u(k-1)+u(k-2)\right)+T^2p_1u(k-1) \end{bmatrix}\right/\left(1+Tp_2+T^2p_1\right) \tag{21}$$

Symbol T in (20) and (21) represents sampling time, usually very short one, because the shorter sampling period means the closer approximation of continuous-time controller (19) by the equation (21). From the practical point of view, the sampling time must be adjusted according to available hardware possibilities.

Results of control simulation are visualized in Fig. 6.

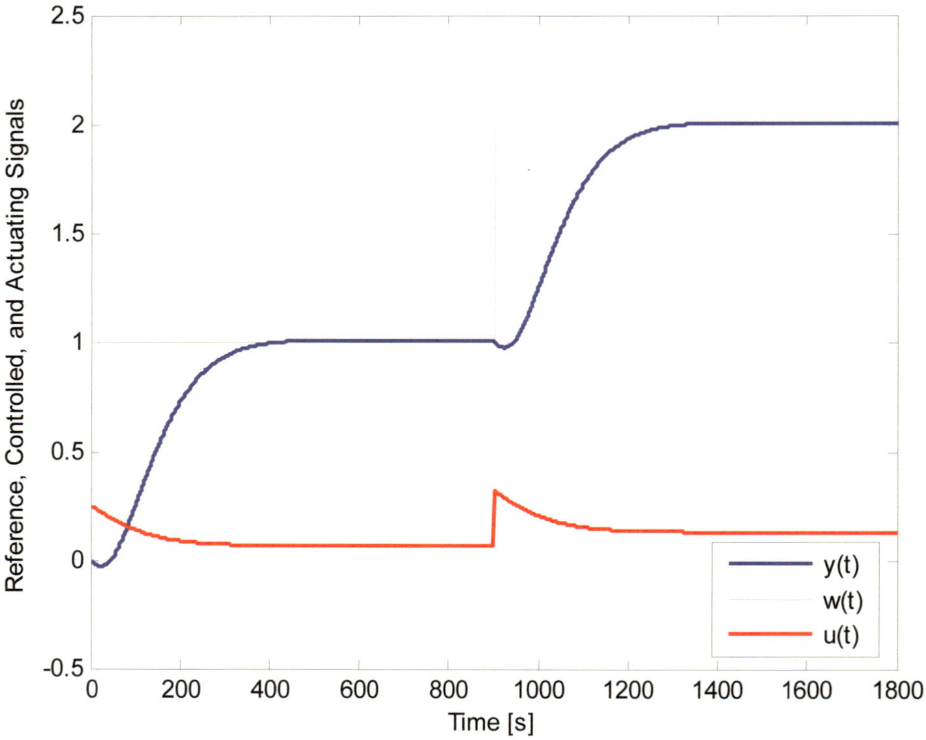

Fig. 6. Control of plant using continuous-time controller - simulation

5.2 Control design using delta models

Another alternative to avoid potential problems with long sampling periods consists in usage of delta models. They act as a bridge between discrete-time and continuous-time representations and eliminate objectionable numerical properties of discrete-time models under short sampling times. Originally, the delta operator has been defined in (Middleton & Goodwin, 1989):

$$\delta = \frac{z-1}{T} \tag{22}$$

Consequent generalization of such models with complex variable γ has been published in (Mukhopadhyay et al., 1992). It has proved that all operators:

$$\gamma = \frac{z-1}{\lambda T z + (1-\lambda)T}; \quad 0 \le \lambda \le 1 \tag{23}$$

converge to derivation. Three most common cases are for $\lambda = 0$ (forward model):

$$\gamma = \frac{z-1}{T} \tag{24}$$

$\lambda = 1$ (backward model):

$$\gamma = \frac{1 - z^{-1}}{T} \tag{25}$$

and $\lambda = 0.5$ (Tustin approximation):

$$\gamma = \frac{2}{T}\frac{z-1}{z+1} \tag{26}$$

The PID-B2 controller (Bobál et al., 1999); (Sysel, 2001) has been utilized in this method. It is based on structure developed in (Ortega & Kelly, 1984) which is shown in Fig. 7.

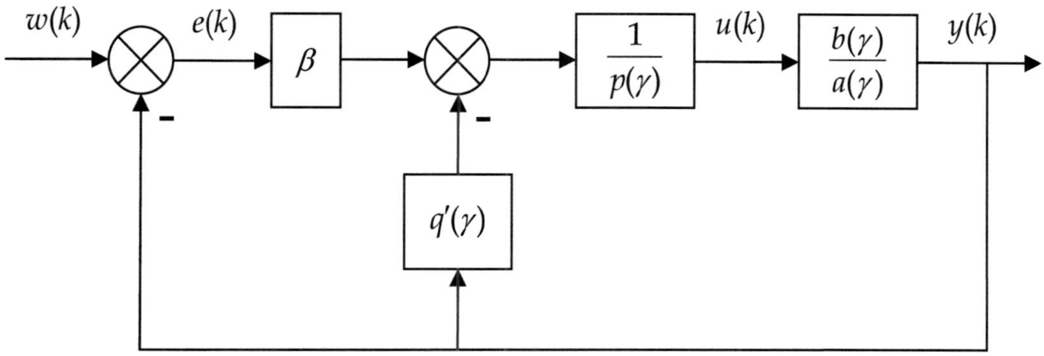

Fig. 7. Closed loop with PID-B controller

The controlled plant from Fig. 7 is supposed as:

$$\frac{b(\gamma)}{a(\gamma)} = \frac{b_1\gamma + b_0}{\gamma^2 + a_1\gamma + a_0} \tag{27}$$

and controller polynomials are:

$$\begin{aligned} p(\gamma) &= \gamma(\gamma + \lambda) \\ q'(\gamma) &= \gamma(q'_2\gamma + q'_1) \end{aligned} \tag{28}$$

Generally, closed-loop characteristic polynomial of the connection in Fig. 7 is:

$$a(\gamma)p(\gamma) + b(\gamma)\left[q'(\gamma) + \beta\right] = m(\gamma) \tag{29}$$

And more specifically, it is assumed to have the form:

$$m(\gamma) = (\gamma - \alpha)^2\left[\gamma - (\alpha + j\omega)\right]\left[\gamma - (\alpha - j\omega)\right] \tag{30}$$

The parameter α can serve for changing speed of control process and "aggressiveness" of actuating signal, while ω is useful for selecting size of overshoot.

However, for the sake of control loop stability, roots of the polynomial (30) must always lie inside the circle with centre in $-1/T$ and the same radius (the circle goes through the origin of the complex plane).

Thus, adjusted characteristic polynomial can be written as (Sysel, 2001):

$$\begin{aligned}&\gamma^4+\gamma^3\left[a_1+\lambda+b_1\left(q_2'+\beta\right)\right]+\gamma^2\left[a_0+a_1\lambda+b_1\left(q_1'+\frac{2\beta}{T}\right)+b_0\left(q_2'+\beta\right)\right]+\\&+\gamma\left[a_0\lambda+\frac{\beta}{T^2}b_1+b_0\left(q_1'+\frac{2\beta}{T}\right)\right]+\frac{\beta}{T^2}b_0=\\&=\gamma^4-4\gamma^3\alpha+\gamma^2\left(6\alpha^2+\omega^2\right)+\gamma\left[-2\alpha\left(2\alpha^2+\omega^2\right)\right]+\alpha^2\left(\alpha^2+\omega^2\right)\end{aligned} \tag{31}$$

More convenient matrix form is:

$$\begin{pmatrix} b_1 & 0 & b_1 & 1 \\ b_0 & b_1 & b_0+\dfrac{2b_1}{T} & a_1 \\ 0 & b_0 & \dfrac{2b_0}{T}+\dfrac{b_1}{T^2} & a_0 \\ 0 & 0 & \dfrac{b_0}{T^2} & 0 \end{pmatrix}\begin{pmatrix} q_2' \\ q_1' \\ \beta \\ \lambda \end{pmatrix}=\begin{pmatrix} -4\alpha-a_1 \\ 6\alpha^2+\omega^2-a_0 \\ -2\alpha\left(2\alpha^2+\omega^2\right) \\ \alpha^2\left(\alpha^2+\omega^2\right) \end{pmatrix} \tag{32}$$

Analytical solution suitable for Pascal implementation can look like:

$$\begin{aligned}&\beta=\frac{x_{r4}}{x_{l3}}\\&q_1'=\frac{a_0x_{r5}-\left(b_1a_1-b_0\right)x_{r6}}{a_0b_1^2-\left(b_1a_1-b_0\right)b_0}\\&\lambda=\frac{x_{r6}-b_0q_1}{a_0}\\&q_2'=\frac{x_{r1}-b_1\beta-\lambda}{b_1}\end{aligned} \tag{33}$$

where auxiliary variables are:

$$\begin{aligned}&x_{l1}=b_0+\frac{2b_1}{T}\\&x_{l2}=\frac{2b_0}{T}+\frac{b_1}{T^2}\\&x_{l3}=\frac{b_0}{T^2}\\&x_{r1}=-4\alpha-a_1\\&x_{r2}=6\alpha^2+\omega^2-a_0\\&x_{r3}=-2\alpha\left(2\alpha^2+\omega^2\right)\\&x_{r4}=\alpha^2\left(\alpha^2+\omega^2\right)\end{aligned} \tag{34}$$

and

$$\begin{aligned}&x_{r5}=-b_0x_{r1}+b_1x_{r2}+b_0b_1\beta-b_1x_{l1}\beta\\&x_{r6}=x_{r3}-x_{l2}\beta\end{aligned} \tag{35}$$

The final control law is then generated by:

$$\begin{aligned} u(k) &= \beta e(k) - q_2'\left[y(k) - 2y(k-1) + y(k-2)\right] - q_1'T\left[y(k-1) - y(k-2)\right] - \cdots \\ &\cdots \lambda T\left[u(k-1) - u(k-2)\right] + 2u(k-1) - u(k-2) \end{aligned} \tag{36}$$

while the vector of parameters $\theta(k) = \left[a_1(k) \quad a_0(k) \quad b_1(k) \quad b_0(k)\right]$ is identified using the same recursive algorithm as described in Section 3. The only modifications necessary because of delta representation are that measured output $y(k)$ is replaced by the ratio $\left[y(k) - 2y(k-1) + y(k-2)\right]/T^2$; and that the observation vector has the form $\boldsymbol{\Phi}(k) = \left[-(y(k-1) - y(k-2))/T \quad -y(k-2) \quad (u(k-1) - u(k-2))/T \quad u(k-2)\right]$.

6. Conclusion

This chapter has been focused mainly on preliminary software implementation of digital self-tuning controllers into the Matlab (for simulative and testing purposes) and Pascal (for real application) environment. The motivation to this task as well as basic conditions and restrictions have been based on technical assignment of a manufacturer of aluminium-based products related to control of a metal smelting furnace. In the first instance, the applied techniques have comprised a polynomial approach to discrete-time control design and recursive least-squares identification algorithm LDDIF. On top of that, continuous-time controller with fixed parameters and delta approach in self-tuning control have been utilized. The future work should eventually lead to complete real-time industrial application.

7. Acknowledgements

The work was supported by the Ministry of Education, Youth and Sports of the Czech Republic under Research Plan No. MSM 7088352102. This assistance is very gratefully acknowledged. Moreover, the authors would like to thank Jaromír Kovář for his intense and enthusiastic co-operation on the project connected with content of this chapter.

8. References

Åström, K. J. & Wittenmark, B. (1973). On self-tuning regulators. *Automatica*, Vol. 9, No. 2, pp. 185-199, ISSN 0005-1098.

Åström, K. J. & Wittenmark, B. (1980). Self-tuning controller based on pole-zero placement. *IEE Proceedings*, Vol. 127, No. 3, pp. 120-130.

Åström, K. J. & Wittenmark, B. (1989). *Adaptive Control*, Addison-Wesley, Reading, Massachusetts, USA.

Åström, K. J.; Borisson, U.; Ljung, L. & Wittenmark, B. (1977). Theory and applications of self-tuning regulators. *Automatica*, Vol. 13, No. 5, pp. 457-476, ISSN 0005-1098.

Bittanti, S.; Bolzern, P. & Campi, M. (1990). Exponential Convergence of a Modified Directional Forgetting Identification Algorithm. *Systems & Control Letters*, Vol. 14, No. 2, pp. 131-137, ISSN 0167-6911.

Bobál, V.; Böhm, J.; Fessl, J. & Macháček, J. (2005). *Digital Self-tuning Controllers: Algorithms, Implementation and Applications*, Springer-Verlag London, ISBN 1-85233-980-2.

Bobál, V.; Böhm, J.; Prokop, R. & Fessl, J. (1999). *Practical Aspects of Self-Tuning Controllers: Algorithms and Implementation*, (*Praktické aspekty samočinně se nastavujících regulátorů:*

algoritmy a implementace), Brno University of Technology, VUTIUM, ISBN 80-214-1299-2, Brno, Czech Republic. (In Czech).

Čirka, Ľ.; Fikar, M. & Petruš, P. (2006). IDTOOL 4.0 - A Dynamical System Identification Toolbox for Matlab/Simulink, *Proceedings of Technical Computing Prague 2006*, Prague, Czech Republic.

Clarke, D. W. & Gawthrop, P. J. (1979). Self-tuning control. *IEE Proceedings*, Vol. 126, No. 6, pp. 633-640.

Doyle, J. C.; Francis, B. A. & Tannenbaum, A. R. (1992). *Feedback Control Theory*, Macmillan, New York, USA.

Hang, C. C.; Lee, T. H. & Ho, W. K. (1993). *Adaptive Control*, Instrument Society of America, North Carolina, USA.

Hunt, K. J.; Šebek, M. & Kučera, V. (1993). H_2 Control Problems, In: *Polynomial Methods in Optimal Control and Filtering*, Hunt, K. J. (Ed.), pp. 29-55, Peter Peregrinus Ltd., ISBN 0-86341-295-5, Stevenage, United Kingdom.

Isermann, R.; Lachmann, K.-H. & Matko, D. (1992). *Adaptive Control Systems*, Prentice Hall, Englewood Cliffs, New Jersey, USA.

Kučera, V. (1979). *Discrete Linear Control: The Polynomial Equation Approach*, John Wiley, Chichester, UK.

Kučera, V. (1991). *Analysis and Design of Discrete Linear System*, Prentice Hall, Englewood Cliffs, New Jersey, USA.

Kučera, V. (1993). Diophantine Equations in Control - A Survey. *Automatica*, Vol. 29, No. 6, pp. 1361-1375, ISSN 0005-1098.

Kulhavý, R. & Kárný, M. (1984). Tracking of Slowly Varying Parameters by Directional Forgetting, *Proceedings of the 9th IFAC World Congress*, pp. 79-83, Budapest, Hungary, 1984.

Matušů, R. & Prokop, R. (2009). Software Implementation of Discrete-Time Adaptive Control, *Proceedings of 13th International Research/Expert Conference "Trends in the Development of Machinery and Associated Technology"*, Hammamet, Tunisia, 2009, pp. 785-788, ISSN 1840-4944.

Matušů, R., Prokop, R. & Pekař, L. (2009). Polynomial Approach to Discrete-Time Adaptive Control: Software Implementation for Industrial Application, *Annals of DAAAM for 2009 & Proceedings of the 20th International DAAAM Symposium*, Vienna, Austria, pp. 523-524, ISBN 978-3-901509-70-4, ISSN 1726-9679.

Middleton, R. H. & Goodwin, G. C. (1989). *Digital Control and Estimation: A Unified Approach*, Prentice Hall, Englewood Cliffs, New Jersey, USA.

Mukhopadhyay, S.; Patra, A. & Rao, G. P. (1992). New class of discrete-time models for continuous-time systems. *International Journal of Control*, Vol. 55, No. 5, pp. 1161-1187.

Ortega, R. & Kelly, R. (1984). PID self-tuners: Some theoretical and practical aspects. *IEEE Transactions on Industrial Electronics*, Vol. 31, No. 4, pp. 332-338.

Sysel, M. (2001). *Application of delta models to process control*, (*Využití delta modelů pro řízení procesů*), Ph.D. Thesis, Faculty of Technology, Tomas Bata University in Zlín, Czech Republic. (In Czech).

Vidyasagar, M. (1985). *Control System Synthesis: A Factorization Approach*, MIT Press, Cambridge, Massachusetts, USA.

Wellstead, P. E. & Zarrop, M. B. (1991). *Self-Tuning Systems*, Wiley, New York, USA.

Wellstead, P. E.; Prager, D. I. & Zanker, P. M. (1979). A pole assignment self-tuning regulator. *IEE Proceedings*, Vol. 126, No. 8, pp. 781-787.

4

Graphical Languages for Enterprise Control

Charlotta Johnsson
Lund University
Sweden

1. Introduction

The market for many industrial production companies is getting tougher as the global competition is increasing. The collaborative manufacturing model, see Figure 1 (Gorbach & Nick, 2002), reflects the fact that companies today need to collaborate both externally and internally to reach success on the market. The external collaboration is presented through the two horisontal axis'. The value chain axis highlights the need for cooperation with suppliers and customers, and the lifecycle axis that goes from design to support often includes third parties and thereby also calls for external collaborations. The vertical axis, the enterprise axis, represents the need for internal cooperation from the business side to the production side, sometimes expressed in statements such as "shop floor to top floor", "sensor to boardroom" or "Plant to enterprise". The internal cooperation is, in this article refered to as Enterprise Control.

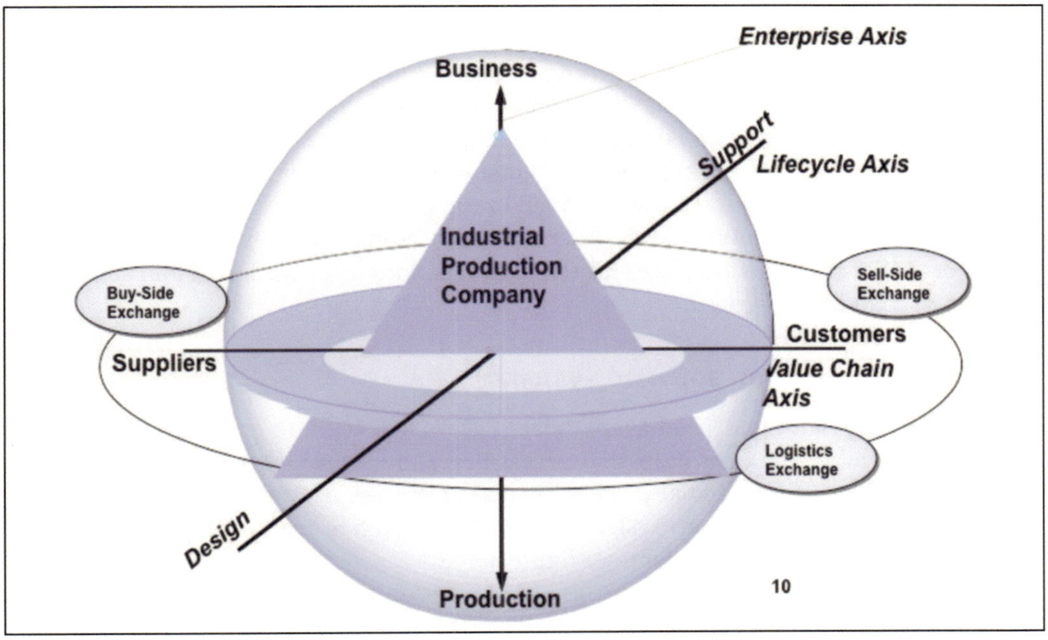

Fig. 1. A variant of the Collaborative Manufacturing Model developed by ARC (Gorbach & Nick, 2002).

Enterprise control includes different aspects of control, monitoring, supervision and data and information management. Taking care of these aspects has become increasingly important and today there are several products out on the market dealing with these issues. From the operator's perspective they can be supported via different means such as implementation through textual languages, or implementation through graphical languages etc.
The usage of graphical languages has many advantages such as giving the user a good visual interpretation of what is happening (compare "a picture says more than a thousand words"), the user often believe it is easier to program by graphical means then by textual means, increased possibility to use colours, etc. In this spirit, the possibility to have one common graphical language for Enterprise Control is very appealing. A well developed graphical language should have support for formal analysis, have a well defined and limited number of graphical elements, good abstraction facilities, and a solid base in it syntax, semantics and pragmatics.
The aim if this paper is to present trends, similarities and differences in the usage of graphical languages within Enterprise Control. The paper also gives ideas of how a common language could be used to increase the internal collaboration and what advantages this could bring.

2. Production systems

Industrial production can be classified in many various ways. One natural way is to classify them according to the industrial sector they are acting within. Example of such sectors are; Food& Beverage, Pharmaceutical, Metal, Pulp&Paper, Chemical and PetroChemical, Refining, Automotive, Fine chemicals, Biotechnology, Machine parts etc (Martin & Hale, 2010).
Another way of classifying industrial production is according to the main manufacturing process that they have. Three types of manufacturing processes exists; continuous, discrete and batch. There are industrial production systems that include all three types of processes and there are others that operates only one of them. It is common to refer to an industrial production system according to the dominant type of process (Brandl, 2006).
Many and various decisions related to production have to be taken. The decisions can be divided in several layers ranging from long-time strategic decisions to real-time decisions. This is true for all types of industrial production companies. The decisions concern various types of issues ranging from long-time financial issues, planning, and procurement, through tactical decisions down to operative and real time decisions associated to automated control and human actions, see figure 2.

3. Industrial production software systems

In order to help with the production related decisions, various software systems are available. Generally speaking, industrial production software systems can be divided into three layers. Closest to the actual process/plant, the process control systems (PCS) reside, with a manufacturing operations system (MOS) often on top of this, and a business system (BS) constituting the superior system, see figure 3.
At the BS level, the system needs to be able to perform reasoning. The system is e.g., responsible for modifying the basic plant production schedule for orders received, based on resource availability changes, energy sources available, power demand levels, and maintenance requirements, etc.

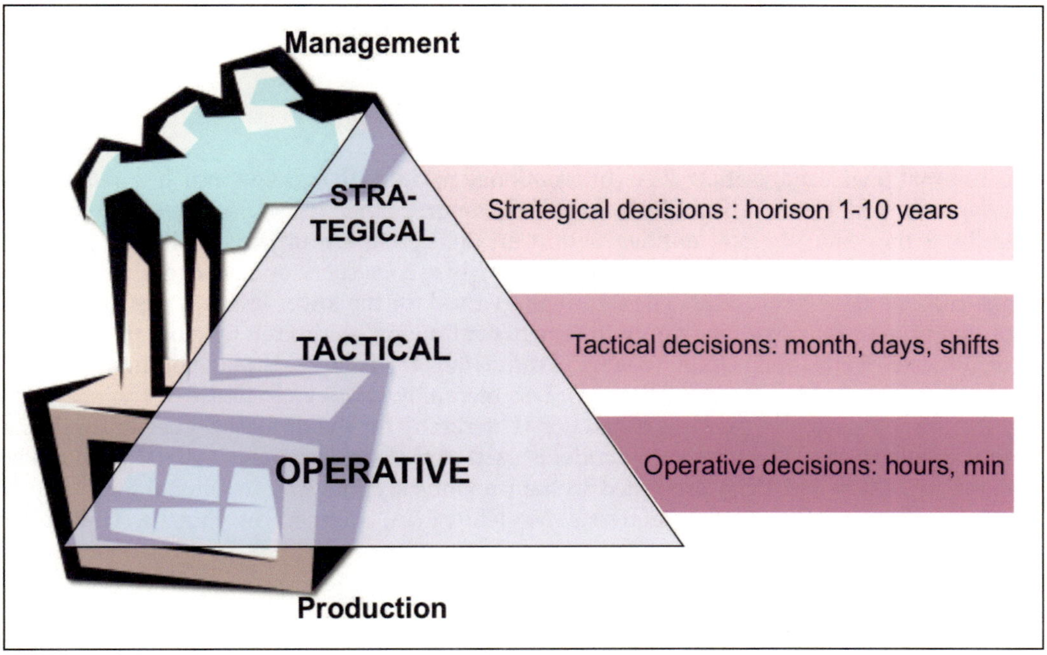

Fig. 2. Various decisions within an enterprise and their respective time horizon.

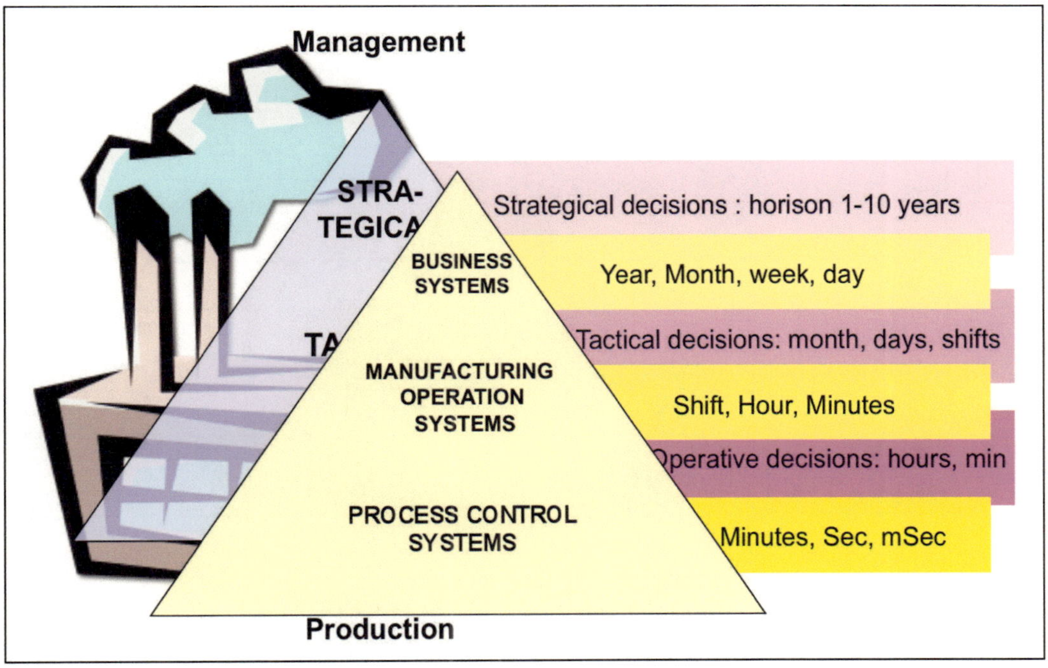

Fig. 3. Various decisions and their respective industrial production systems.

At the MOS level, the system should e.g., calculate the detailed production schedule, perform data collection, calculate various production performance measurements, and assure tracking and traceability.

The PCS level assures classical process control functions such as sensor readings and setting of actuator setpoints and PID control of various variables.

4. Hierarchies

The international organisation ISA (International Society of Automation) has released a standard, named ISA 95 (ISA, 2000), in which, among other things, a physical hierarchy describing how the physical entities within an enterprise are organised. In the physical model, the highest level is the Enterprise, an enterprise consists of one or several Sites, a site consists of one or several Areas. The terminology used for the lower levels varies depending upon the type of industry they apply to (batch, continuous, or discrete). Below the Area we have Process Cells and Units (batch), Production Units and Units (continuous) and Production Line and Work Cells (discrete). This hierarchy is shown in figure 4.
The ISA 95 standard also presents a functional hierarchy for the different types of functions within an enterprise. The functional model is used as the basis for the industrial production systems (BS, MOS and PCS) presented in the previous section. The functional hierarchy is based on Purdue Enterprise Reference Model, PERA, defined at Purdue University (Williams, 1992).

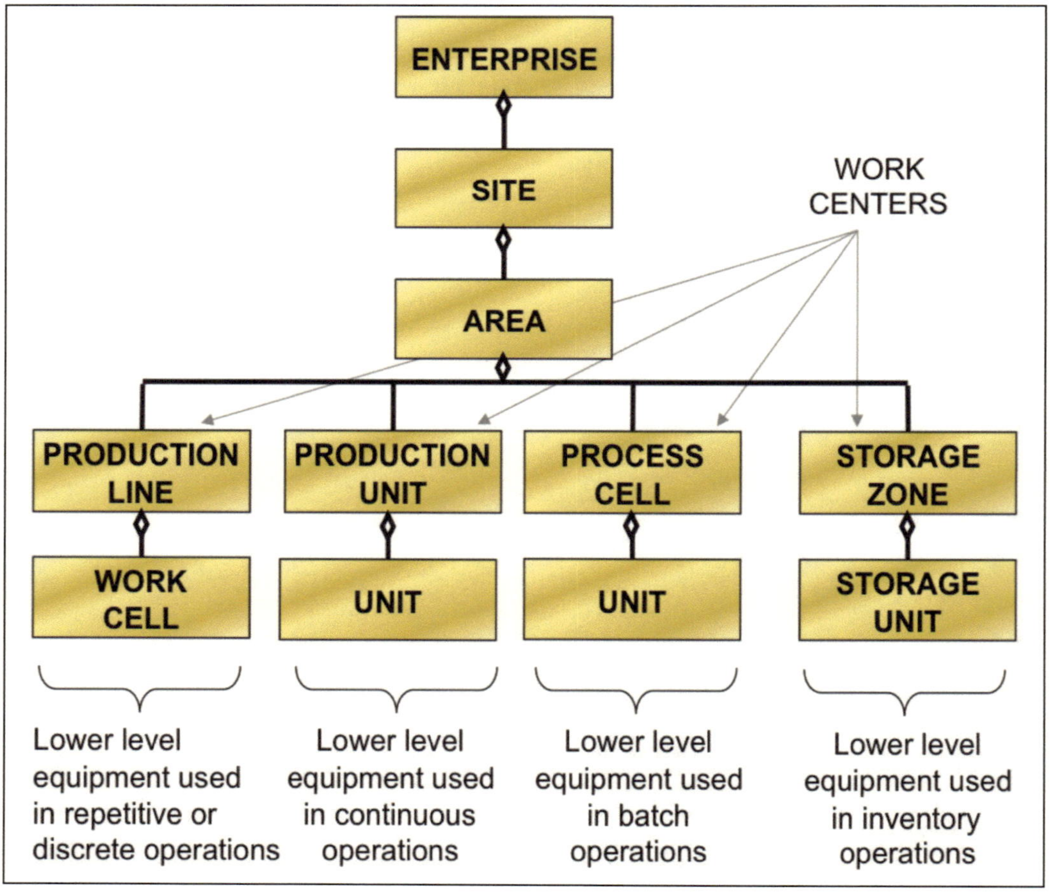

Fig. 4. Equipment hierarchy according to the standard ISA 95 (IEC 62264).

5. Current usage of graphical languages

Roughly speaking one could say that the PCS system should effectuate control of the equipment at the level of and the level below the unit and work cell level. The MOS system should assure the control of the activities residing at the work center, area and/ or site level, and the BS system should have control of the activities at the site and enterprise level. (Johnsson, 2008). This is highlighted in figure 5.

5.1 Graphical languages at the PCS level

The process control system should assure that basic control issues are taken care of, i.e., control issues that are dedicated to establishing and maintaining a specific state of equipment or process condition, and/or simple on/off control. The process control system often depends on the type of industry where it is applied; discrete, continuous or batch.

- Continuous processes are characterized by the production of material in a continuous flow e.g., bulk chemicals, pulp and paper production. In continuous industries the basic control consists of running a system in steady state.
- Discrete processes are characterized by production of a specific quantity of material, where each element of the material can be uniquely identified, e.g., production of cars. In discrete processes the basic control includes the control of start up, transition and shut down phases.
- Batch processes are characterized by generation of finite quantities of material, called a batch, at each production cycle. Material is produced by subjecting specific quantities of input materials to a specified order of processing actions using one or more pieces of equipment. One example could be the production of cookies, in which several cookies are produced in the same batch. The cookies produced in the same batch can not be uniquely identified, but the cookies produced by different batches can be identified. Basic control for batch processes includes characteristics from both continuous and discrete processes.

IEC 61131-3 is a global standard for industrial control programming at the PCS level (IEC, 1993). The standard specifies the syntax and semantics of a five programming languages; Instruction List, Structured Text, Ladder Diagram, Function Block Diagram and Sequential Function Chart (SFC). Two of the languages are textual; Instruction List and Structured Text, and two are graphical; Ladder Diagram and Function Block Diagram. In addition, the graphical language Sequential Function Chart (SFC) is defined with the purpose of structuring the internal organization of a program.

IEC 60848 is another international standard that specifies Grafcet. Grafcet was proposed in France in 1977 as a formal specification and realization method for logical controllers. During several years Grafcet was tested in French industries. It soon proved to be a convenient tool for representing small and medium scale sequential systems at the PCS level. In 1988 Grafcet, with minor changes, was adopted as an international standard known as IEC 60848 (IEC, 1988).

The basic building blocks in Grafcet and SFC are steps and transitions. An example of a Grafcet/SFC is shown in Figure 6.

In discrete and batch manufacturing, graphical languages such as Grafcet or SFC (Sequential Function Chart) are commonly used. These languages are both based on a state/transition model and can therefore be used in order to express the sequential order in which actions should be carried out. Due to their intuitive nature and their ease of use, they have become very popular. Within continuous industries, textual languages are still most frequently used, however, a sequential language such as Grafcet or SFC can be used for certain tasks.

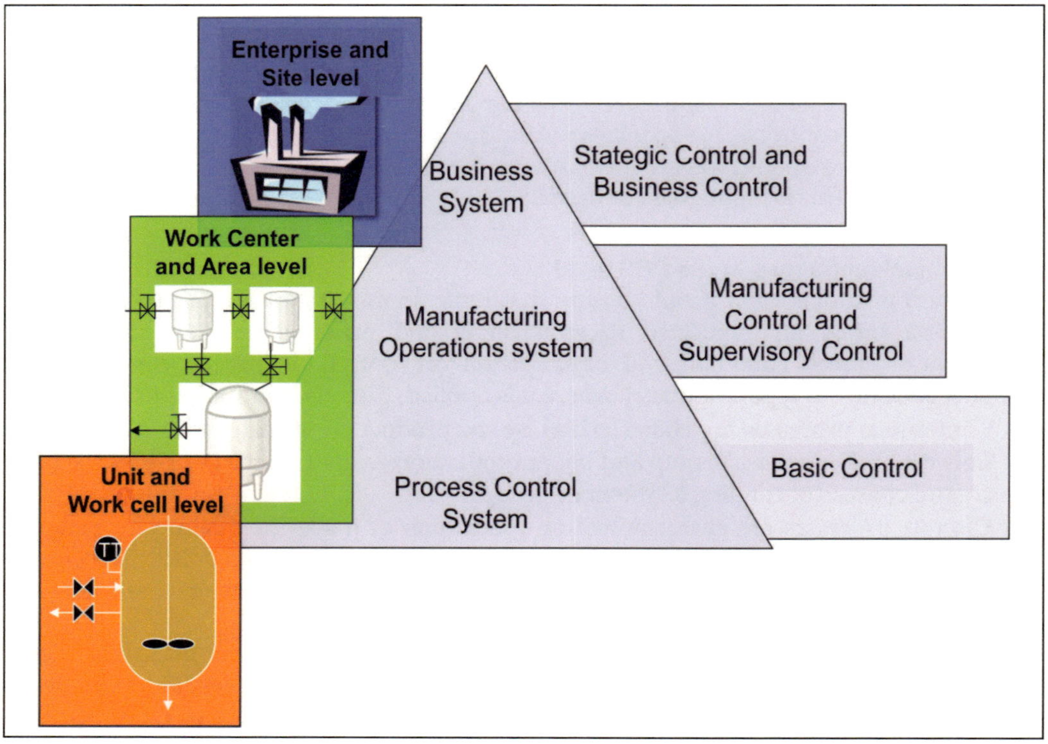

Fig. 5. The three control levels and their respective approximate equipment levels.

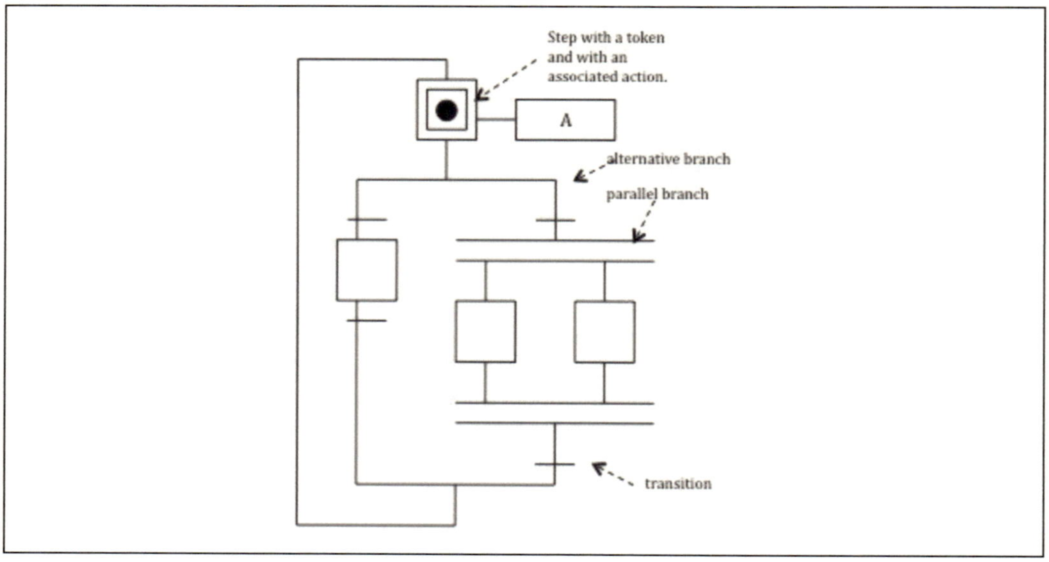

Fig. 6. An example of a Grafcet.

The traditional user of a PCS system is a person that is highly technically skilled, he/she has a good understanding of the production process and is used to various programming languages.

5.2 Graphical languages at the MOS level

At the MOS level there is a need for both supervisory control at the work cell level and for, what could be called, "manufacturing control" at the area and site level.

Within the batch community a language called Procedural Function Chart (PFC), aimed at supervisory control, has been proposed and included in the ISA standard for batch control called ISA 88.01 (ISA, 1995). This standard has also been accepted as an international standard referred to IEC 61512-1 (IEC, 1997). The PFC takes care of the control of activities at the process cell level. PFC is highly influenced by Grafcet/SFC regarding its syntax. PFC is becoming popular also in the discrete industry.

Another graphical language developed recently and aimed at supervisory control applications at the process cell level is Grafchart (Johnsson, 1999). Grafchart has been developed at Lund Institute of Technology, Sweden since 1991 (Arzén, 1991). Grafchart is based on Grafcet/SFC. It contains support for step with actions, transitions, parallel and alternative branching, and macro steps. An entire chart can be encapsulated within a Grafchart process and sequences that are executed in more than one place can be represented as Grafchart procedures. In addition to this there is additional support for procedural programming (procedural step) and for separate execution threads (process steps). These two new graphical elements together with the fact that Grafchart is object-oriented and that it has support for parameterization and methods and message passing highly facilitates the reusability of an implementation. Grafchart served as a source of inspiration for PFCs.

An example of a Grafchart, used for structuring a batch recipe at the process cell level, is shown in Figure 7.

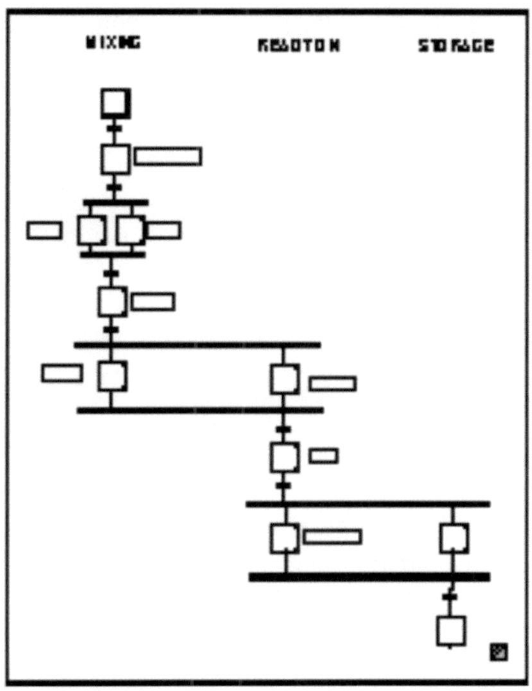

Fig. 7. An example of a Grafchart.

The typical user of a MOS system is an operator working in the production plant and/or its production manager. Both persons have a good understanding of the production process and are often technically skilled. In case the production plant is executed by manual actions, the operator might use the graphical language for visualizing the sequential order of the operations he/she should perform. If the production plant is run automatically by various equipments and machines, the operator might use the graphical language for looking at the sequential progress of the execution taking place in the production plant.
The manufacturing operation systems have lately received a lot of interest form the industries. The reason being that there is a need for a clear definition of activities at this level as well as a desire of a more sophisticated and advanced coordination control at this level, let's call it "manufacturing control". At this level, activities at the area and/or site level should be taken care of, this could for example be the synchronization of a batch process cell followed by a discrete packaging line.

5.2 Graphical languages at the BS level

At the Business Systems level, the interest in depicting business processes has increased. Business Process Managment has been identified as a top business priority (Recker et al., 2006).
Within a producing enterprise, the ultimate level depicts the overall process of going from a customer order to delivery, or from customer need to customer satisfaction. The overall business process consists of one or several sub-process, one of them is certainly manufacturing.
The overall process description is used for off-line visualization of the business process for the management and board of the company.
The manufacturing process, being a sub-part of the overall business process, can also be visualized. Figure 8 shows an example of a manufacturing process, i.e., how to go from internal order to produced order. The manufacturing process could span over one or many areas, e.g., the production area and the packaging area.

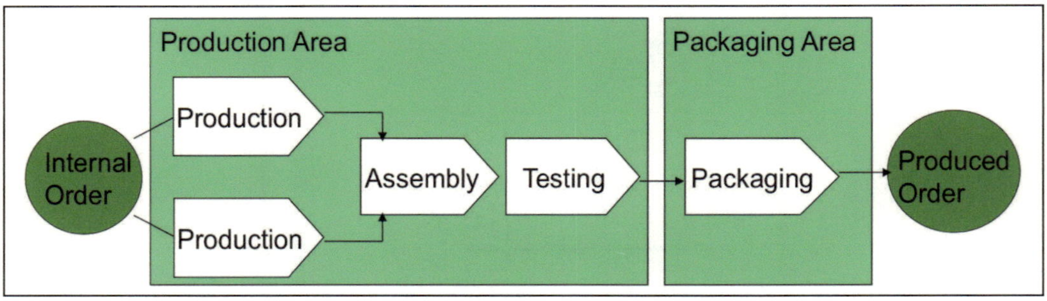

Fig. 8. The manufacturing business process.

In many cases, the language used at this level is most often local to the company and the processes visualized are only used as off-line tool for organization improvements.
In general, process models at the BS level, serve two main purposes.
First, intuitive business process models are used for scoping the project, and capturing and discussing business requirements and process improvement initiatives with subject matter experts. The recent introduction of legislative frameworks such as the Sarbanes-Oxley Act (Nielsen & Main, 2004) further contributed to the increasing interest in business process

modeling as a way of capturing and graphically documenting the processes of an organization (Recker et al., 2006).
Second, business process models are used for process automation, which requires their conversion into executable specifications, i.e., turning the depicted processes into an on-line workflow management system (Recker et al., 2006).
The graphical languages for processes are being harmonized, one example of such an initiative is The Business Process Modeling Notation (BPMN) developed by Business Process Management Initiative (BPMI), (BPMI, 2007).
The typical person interested in the business processes are management, i.e., usually persons without a deep technical knowledge of the production process. In addition, the management does more often have a strategic or economic interest in looking at the processes.

5.4 Situation at present

The The situation concerning the usage of graphical languages could be summaries in the following way, see also figure 9:

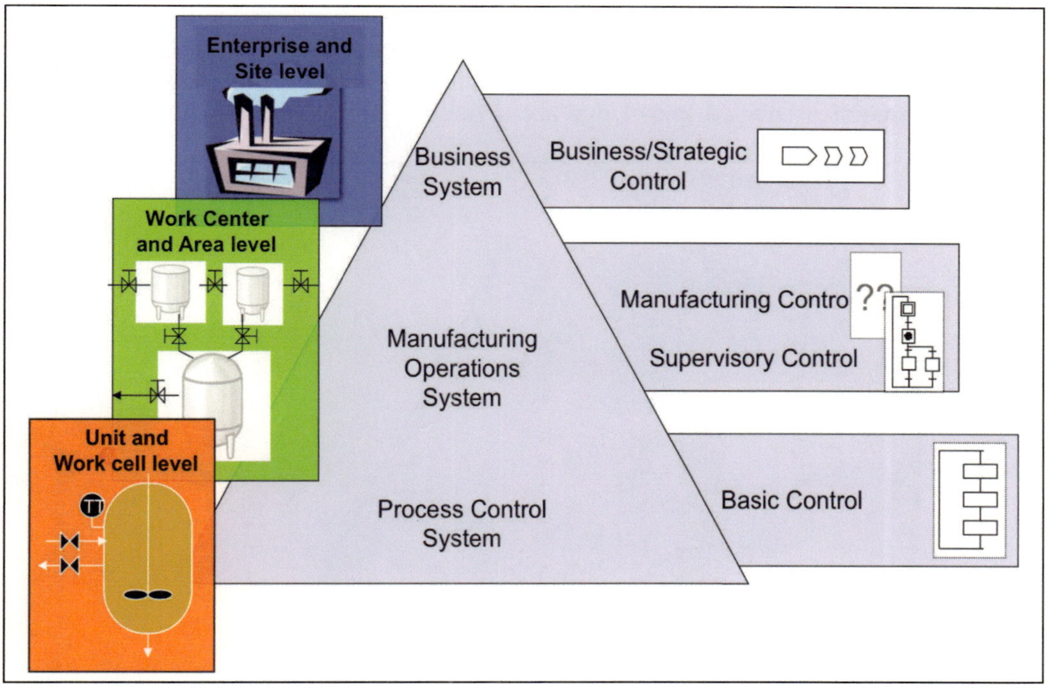

Fig. 9. The manufacturing business process.

- PCS level: Standardized graphical languages are used for basic control issues.
- MOS level: Standardized graphical languages exist and are, together with some proprietary graphical control languages, used for supervisory control issues. None or only local graphical control languages are used for "Manufacturing control" issues.
- At the PCS and MOS level, the languages are use for executing control over the production process. The graphical language has a bi-directional communication with the plant, i.e., data can be collected from the plant and visualized for the user by the

means of a graphical language, or data can be sent to the plant through the graphical language.
- The syntax and semantics of the languages used at the PCS and MOS level are very similar.
- BS level: Local graphical languages are used for visualising the business processes. Initiatives exist striving to standardize the language used for visualization of business processes.
- At the BS level, the languages are used for presenting the business processes. The languages do not have a communication with the production plant.
- The syntax of the languages used at the BS level is different from the one used at the PCS and MOS level.

6. Integration

As global competition in manufacturing has increased, trends within industry have been to increase the level and amount of control and automation at all three levels. The requirement to increasing the integration between the three levels is also notable, being driven by business needs and business processes, see figure 10.
There are always some business processes that needs information from production or needs to exercise control over production. Typical business drivers of today are; Just in time production (requires detailed knowledge about the available capacity in the plant), asset

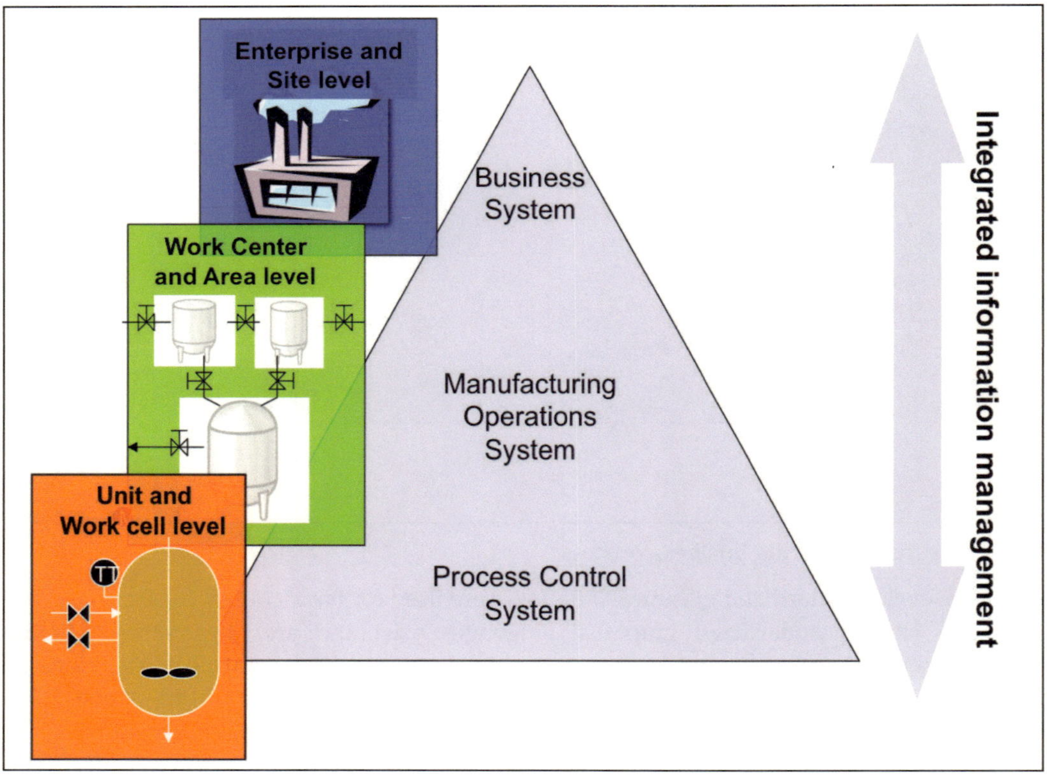

Fig. 10. The manufacturing business process.

efficiency and overall equipment efficiency (requires detailed knowledge of actual use), reduced cycle time (requires detailed knowledge about start and stop times), new regulations for tracabilty (requires better logging and tracking possibilities), finding hidden potentials (requires the collection and analysis of previously unknown data), etc.
Another approach to integration is Unified Enterprise Modeling Language, UEML. However, UEML is not intended as a programming language by itself but rather as an intermediate language, or a hub, through which different languages can be connected (UEML, 2007).

7. Grafchart

Grafchart is the name of graphical language for sequential control applications (Johnsson, 1999). The language of Grafchart is, like any other programming language, fully defined by its syntax, semantics and pragmatics, (Turbak et al., 1995). The syntax defines the notations used, the semantics defines the meaning of the syntax, and the pragmatics focuses upon how the semantics is implemented.
Grafchart is based on Grafcet/SFC. There are strong similarities beween Gracfet and Grafchart regarding both the syntax, semantics and pragmatics (Johnsson 2000).

- Syntax: The graphical syntax of Grafchart and Gracet is very similar. Both are based on steps and transitions with support for macro steps, parallell and alternative branches, see figure 6 and 7. The Grafchart language contains more graphical elements (building blocks) than Grafcet. The new building blocks introduced in Grafchart are: Grafchart process, Grafchart procedure, process step, Procedure step and exception transition. However, the new building blocks does not extend the functionality of Grafchart compared to Grafcet, but they facilitates the implementation of more advanced sequence structure. The development of Grafchart from Grafcet can be compared to the evolution of assembler languages to a high-level programming language like e.g., Java.
- Semantics: The firing rules that apply to Grafchart are similar to those of Grafcet. Rule 1: All fireable transitions are immediately fired - this rule applies to Grafcet and Grafchart. Rule 2: Several simultaneously fireable transitions are simultaneously fired - for Grafcet this is true in all situations, for Grafchart this is true for all situations except in an ordivergence. Rule 3: When a step must be simultaneously activated and deactivated, it remains active - this rule apply to Grafcet but not to Grafchart. In Grafchart, the step will first be deactivated and then activated again.
- Pragmatics: the actual implementation of the language transformes the language from being a model to being a toolbox/framework. There are several software systems implementing Grafcet. Grafchart exists in two versions; one version is implemented in G2, an expert system from Gensym corporation, and one version is implemented in Java and refered to as JGrafchart (Arzen, 2002).

Thanks to the strong connection between Grafchart and Grafcet a user of one of the langauges would easily recognize him/her self in the other language.
Grafchart is also influenced by ideas from Petri nets, high-level Petri Nets and object-oriented programming. By adding new features to the language, Grafchart is suitable for supervisory control applications at the MOS level. The new features are;

- Parameterization: Macro steps, and steps may have attributes acting as parameters. The parameters can be accessed from within the step actions and the transition receptivities using a special notation "sup.attribute". The parameters are given their actual values when the procedure is called.

- Methods and message passing: The method feature denotes the possibility to have Grafchart procedures as methods of general objects. From the body of the Grafchart procedure realizing the method it is possible to reference the attributes of the object that the method belongs to using a special "self.attribute" notation. A method is called through a procedure step. The method that will be called is determined by an object reference and a method reference.

At the MOS level, there is an international well accepted standard, IEC 62264, also refered to as ISA95. The standard has several parts, the first ones are published whereas the later ones are still under development. The standard recognized the need for support for presenting Manufacturing control applications, possibly through a graphical language (ISA, 2005).

The advantages of graphical programming languages are simplicity and declarativeness, this is true at all levels; PCS, MOS and BS. The graphical languages often allow programming in a style that closely mimics the style that people model problems. Examples of mental models that are naturally represented graphically include fault trees, organization charts, programflowcharts, and block diagrams. Graphical languages fit users' existing perception of problem, making the application easier to build, debug, document, and maintain. An added benefit is the possibility to use colour and animation to provide feedback as the program executes.

As the vertical integration between the levels becomes more and more important it would be challenging to see, if and what, a unified common graphical language for BS, MOS and PCS level, could bring.

One future scenario could be to connect the business processes to the Manufacturing Operations Systems. This would imply that the business processes could get data directly from the plant, and thereby directly visualize various key performance indicators (KPIs) for the management, see figure 11.

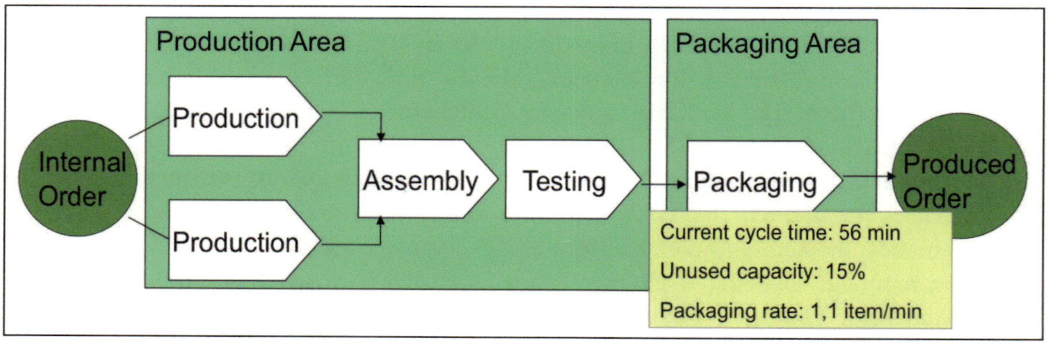

Fig. 11. The manufacturing business process with visualized key performance indicators.

9. Conclusions

The focus for this article is graphical languages used at companies in the producing and manufacturing sector and to issues related to production. The production systems used within the companiy can be divided in three hierarchical levels; Process Control Systems, Manufacturing Operations Systems and Business Systems. The trends, similarities and differences in the usage of graphical languages at these three levels are examined.

There are strong similarities between the languages used at the PCS level for basic control and the languages used at the MOS level for supervisory control. At these levels, the activities at the unit level and below are taken care of, and there is a very close connection to the production occurring in the plant.

There is currently no standardized graphical language for "manufacturing control", i.e., for coordinating and synchronizing the activities between various work centers and area.

At the BS level, the business processes are modelled and executed. Initiatives exist that strive to standardize the graphical language used at this level. The syntax is different from the one used at the PCS and MOS level. The business processes seldom has a connection to the production plant. Various KPIs and aggregated data from the plant are, rarely presented by the mean of a graphical language.

A future trend within Enterprise control will certainly be to further investigate, if, to what extent and how, the graphical languages used at the three levels could be harmonized, and to explore the advantages this could bring to its user.

10. References

Arzén, K.-E. (1991), Sequential Function Charts for knowledge-based, real-time applications. In Proc. Third IFAC workshop on AI in Real-time control. Rohnert Park, California, USA.

Arzén, K.-E. (2002), Jgrafchart: Sequence Control and procedure handling in Java. In Proceedings of Reglermote, May 2002.

BPMI (2007), http://www.bpmi.org/

Brandl D., (2006), Design patterns for flexible manufacturing. Instrumentation, ISA, ISBN/ID 978-1-55617-998-3, Research Triangle Park, NC, USA, 2006.

IEC (1988), IEC 60848: Preparation of function charts for control systems. Technical report. International Electrotechical Commission.

IEC (1993), IEC 61131: Programmable controllers - part 3: Programming languages. Technical report. International Electrotechical Commission.

IEC (1997), IEC 61512-1: Batch Control, Part 1: Models and Terminology. Technical report. International Electrotechical Commission.

ISA (1995), ISA-S88.01, Batch Control, Part 1: Models and Terminology. Instrumentation, Systems and Automation Society.

ISA (2000), ISA-95.00.01, Enterprise-Control System Integration Part 1: Models and Terminology. Instrumentation, Systems and Automation Society.

ISA (2005), ISA-95.00.03, Enterprise-Control System Integration Part 3: Models of Manufacturing Operations Management. Instrumentation, Systems and Automation Society.

Gorbach G., Nick R. (2002), Collaborative Manufacturing Management Strategies" ARC Advisory Group, November 2002. Ed. E. Bassett & A. Chatha.

Johnsson, C. (1999), A Graphical Language for Batch Control. PhD-thesis, Lund Institute of Technology, Lund, Sweden.

Johnsson, C. (2000), Grafcahrt and Grafcet: A comparison between two graphical languages aimed for sequential control applications. In procedings IFAC world congress 2000. Beijing, China.

Johnsson, C. (2008), Graphical Languages for Business Processes and Manufacturing Operations. In proceedings IFAC world-congress 2008. Seoul, South Korea.

Martin P.G., Hale G., (2010), Automation made easy. Everything you need to know about automation - and need to ask. International Society of Automation, Research Triangle Park, NC, USA 2010.

Nielsen and Main, (2004), Company Liability After the Sarbanes-Oxley Act, Insights (18) 10, pp. 2-12.

Recker J., Rosemann M., Indulska M. and Green P. (2006), http://is.tm.tue.nl/staff/wvdaalst/BPMcenter/reports/2006/BPM-06-20.pdf BPM Center Report BPM-06-20, BPMcenter.org.

Turbak, F., D. Gifford, and B. Reistad (1995), Applied semantics of programming languages. Unpublished Draft.

UEML (2007), http://is.uib.no/wiki/UEML/UEML

Williams, T. (1992), The Purdue Enterprise Reference Architecture--A Technical Guide for CIM Planning and Implementation, ISA, Research Triangle Park, NC, USA.

5

Two-Level Transplant Evolution for Optimization of General Controllers

Roman Weisser, Pavel Ošmera, Jan Roupec, and Radomil Matousek
University of Technology VUT in Brno
European Polytechnical Institute Kunovice
Czech Republic

1. Introduction

The aim of this paper is to describe a new optimization method that can create control equations of general regulators. For this type of optimization a new method was created and we call it Two-Level Transplant Evolution (TLTE). This method allowed us to apply advanced methods of optimization, for example direct tree reducing of tree structure of control equation. The reduction method was named Arithmetic Tree Reducing (ART). For the optimization of control equations of general controllers it is suitable to combine two evolutionary algorithms. The main goal in the first level of TLTE is the optimization of the structure of general controllers. In the second level of TLTE the concrete parameters are optimized and the unknown abstract parameters in the structure of equations are set. The method TLTE was created by the combination of the Transplant Evolution method (TE) and the Differential Evolution method (DE). The Transplant Evolution (TE) optimizes the structure of the solution with unknown abstract parameters and the DE optimizes the parameters in this structure. The parameters are real numbers. The real numbers are not easy to find directly in TE without DE. Some new methods for evaluation of the quality of the found control equation are described here, which allow us evaluate their quality. These can be used in the case when the simulation of the control process cannot be finished. Some practical applications are shown in the results. In all calculation of TLTE the control equation had a better quality of the control process, than the classical PSD controllers and Takahashi`s modification of the PSD controller.

2. Transplant Evolution

Transplant Evolution (TE) was inspired by biological transplantation. It is an analogy to the transplant surgery of organs. Every transplanted organ was created by DNA information but some parts of an ill body can be replaced by a new organ from the database of organs. The description parts of individual (organs) in the database are not stored on the level DNA (genotype). In Transplant Evolution (TE) every individual part (organ) is created by the translation of grammar rules similar to Grammatical Evolution (GE), but Transplant Evolution (TE) does not store the genotype and the grammatical rules are chosen randomly. The newly created structure is stored only as a tree. This is like Genetic Programming (GP).
The Transplant Evolution algorithm (TE) combines the best properties of Genetic Programming (GP) [2] and Grammatical Evolution (GE) [4]. The Two-Level Transplant

Evolution (TLTE) in addition to that uses the Differential Evolution algorithm (DE). Optimization of the numerical parameters of general controllers in recurrent control equations of general controllers is a very difficult problem. We applied the second level of optimization by the Differential Evolution method (DE). The individuals in TE and TLTE are represented only by a phenotype in the shape of an object tree. During the initialization of population and during the creation of these phenotypes, similar methods are used as in GE. In Grammatical Evolution the numerically represented chromosomes are used. The codons of these chromosomes are used for the selection of some rule from a set of rules. In Transplant Evolution the chromosomes and codons are not used, but for the selection of some rule from a set of rules randomly generated numbers are used. These numbers are not stored in the individual chromosome. The new individuals in the population are created with the use of analytic and generative grammar and by using crossover and mutation operators. These operators are projected for work with the phenotype of an individual, similarly as in GP. Because the individuals of TE and TLTE are represented only by phenotype, it was possible to implement these? advanced methods in the course of evolution:

- an effective change of the rules in the course of evolution, without the loss of generated solutions,
- a difference of probability in the selection of rules from the set of rules and the possibility of this changing during the evolutionary process,
- the possibility of using methods of direct reduction of the tree using algebraic operations,
- there is a possible to insert some solutions into the population, in the form of an inline entry of phenotype (for example: $U_{k-1} + E_k + E_{k-1} * num$),
- new methods of crossover are possible to use, (for example *crossover by linking trees*)
- etc.

2.1 Initialization of individual

During the initialization, the generative grammar rules are used. These rules are selected randomly from the set of rules by the following equation:

$$rule = random(0, \max\text{Int}) \% rules\_count \tag{1}$$

Where: *random* is a pseudo-random number generator, *maxInt* is a high number, % is the remainder operator (modulus), and *rules_count* denotes the number of possible rules to transcribe a given non-terminal symbol.

The algorithm TE which is described by equation 1 differs by the way of initialization of individual in Grammatical Evolution (GE).The Original initialization algorithm GE uses forward processing of grammatical rules. In the Grammatical Evolution the method of crossover and mutation are made on the genotype level. The phenotype is created by a later translation of this genotype. This way of mutation and crossover does not allow the using of advanced method in crossover and mutation operators, which does not destruct the already created parts of the individual (O'Neill M. and Ryan C., 2003). During the evolution of this algorithm the Backward Processing of Rules (BPR) arose (Popelka, O., 2007). The BPR method uses gene marking. This approach has the hidden knowledge of tree structure. Due to the BPR the advanced and effective methods of crossover and mutation can be used. Anyhow the BPR method has some disadvantages. Due to these disadvantages the new method Transplant Evolution (TE) was created. The TE method does not store genotype information. The equation 1 is used for the selection of a rule from rules base. The advantage of TE is the possibility to use both types of grammatical processing (forward and backward)

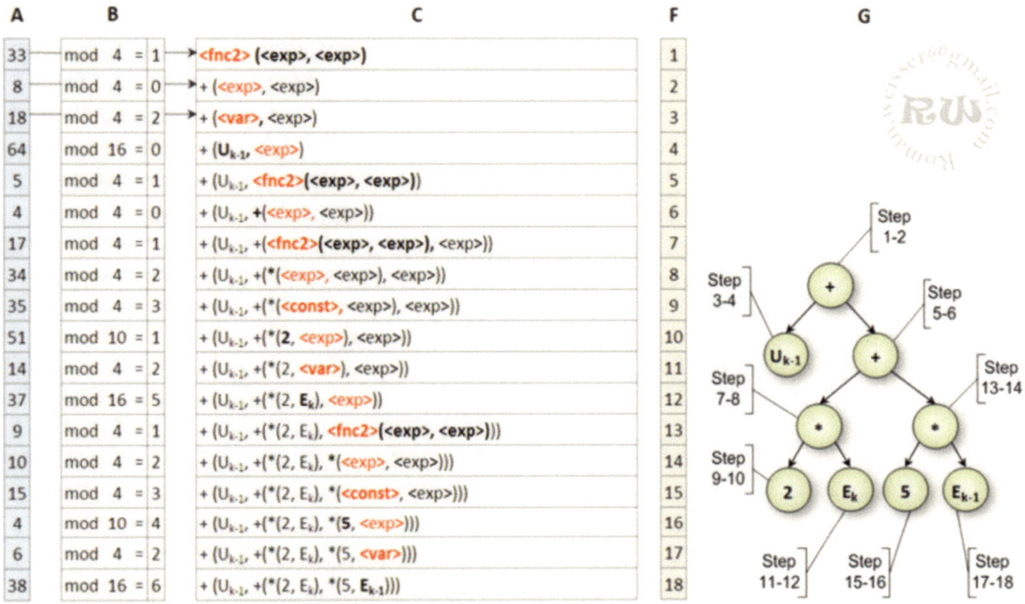

Fig. 1. Translation in TE (forward processing)

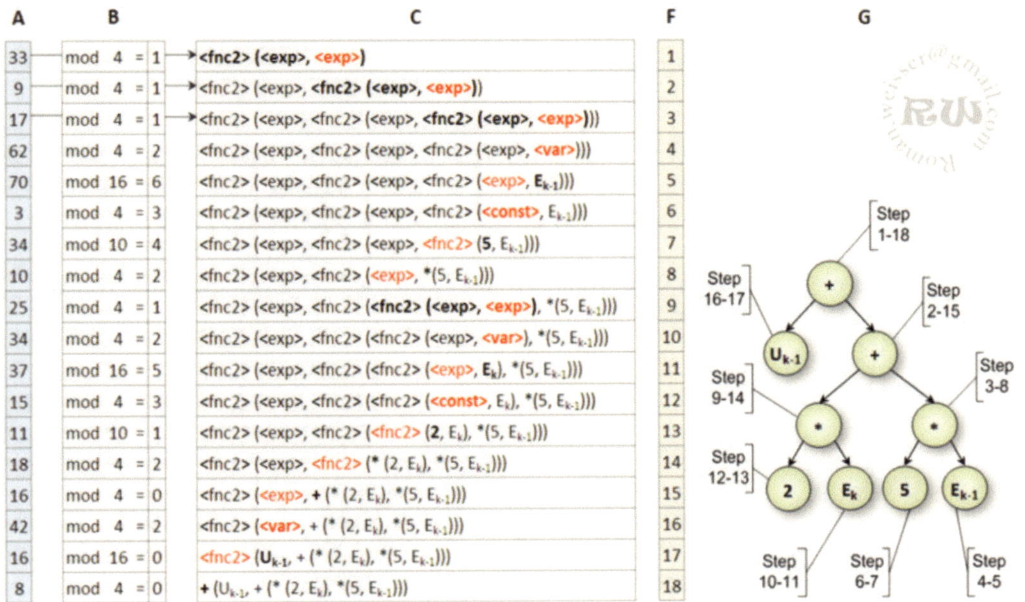

Fig. 2. Translation in TE (backward processing)

with the same results, because TE works only with the phenotype and the procedure of phenotype creation is not important. Some examples of forward and backward initializations are shown in Fig. 1 and Fig. 2. The phenotype in these cases has the following structure $U_{k-1} + 2^* E_k + 5 * E_{k-1}$.
In *column A* are shown the randomly generated values. These values are not stored anywhere! The values are generated only when is necessary to select from more grammatical rules. In *column B* is shown the arithmetic operation. In *column C* is shown a state of rules translation, but it must be remembered that the translation rules is done at the tree (in the nodes of the phenotype). In *column F* is the order of operations. These numbers are used for a description of the tree nodes initialization order. The tree initialization is shown at *column G.* Each node of the tree in *column G* is described by a number in the form *Step X-Y.* In the ***Step X-Y***, *X* represents the step in which the node was created. *Y* represents the step in which the node was fully initialized (after initialization all of its subnodes).
As you can see, the finite tree structures are the same, but they have a different order of fully initialization. The generated numbers in column A were changed too.
Both the examples of initialization of the individual expected generative grammar rules (productive rules) are in prefix form. The generative grammar is defined in Table 1. The rules in this table are written in Backus Naur Form (BNF) (BACKUS, J. W., et al., 1997).

$\langle S \rangle$	::=	$\langle exp \rangle$
$\langle exp \rangle$	::=	$\langle fnc1 \rangle \langle exp \rangle \mid \langle fnc2 \rangle \langle exp \rangle \langle exp \rangle \mid \langle var \rangle \mid \langle const \rangle$
$\langle fnc1 \rangle$	::=	$U+ \mid U-$
$\langle fnc2 \rangle$	::=	$+ \mid - \mid * \mid /$
$\langle var \rangle$	::=	$U_{k-1} \mid U_{k-2} \mid U_{k-3} \mid U_{k-4} \mid U_{k-5} \mid$ $E_k \mid E_{k-1} \mid E_{k-2} \mid E_{k-3} \mid E_{k-4} \mid E_{k-5} \mid$ $dE_k \mid dE_{k-1} \mid dE_{k-2} \mid dE_{k-3} \mid dE_{k-4}$
$\langle const \rangle$	::=	$1 \mid 2 \mid 3 \mid 4 \mid 5 \mid 6 \mid 7 \mid 8 \mid 9 \mid 0$

Table 1. Generative grammar

The main principle of the initialization of individual in Transplant Evolution is described by the recurrent pseudo-code in Fig. 3. In this pseudo-code it can be seen that some rules can be disabled or the probability of selection can be changed. This possibility can be seen on row 2 in Fig. 3. The random selection of rule from rule base are shown on row 9. This approach is realized by the method called Get_ random_rule. The method CreateSubTree on row 11 creates the subtree of present tree.

2.2 Crossover

The crossover is a distinctive tool for genetic algorithms and is one of the methods in evolutionary algorithms that are able to acquire a new population of individuals. The crossover is realized in a similar way as in Genetic Programming (GP) [2].
The TE uses three types of crossover. The first type of crossover is named *crossover the parts of trees,* the second type is named *crossover of nodes,* and the third type is named *crossover by linking trees.* The nodes or subparts of trees in the individuals for crossover are selected randomly.
In the case of the method *crossover of nodes it* is neccessary to keep change of the same types of nodes. This request is possible to express by this relationship:

```
Input: G – context-free grammar; P – array of rules; L_max – max nodes count
Result: individual
if length[this] ≥ L_max then
  | Disable_rules('function') ;
end
for i ← length[P] to i ≥ 1 do
  | if P[i] is terminal symbol then
  |   | rule ← P[i]
  | else
  |   | P_temp ← array of rules for the nonterminal P[i] in G indexed from zero;
  |   | rule ← Get_random_rule(P_temp) ;
  | end
  | sub_tree ← CreateSubTree(G; rule; L_max) ;
  | this ← add child sub_tree ;
end
if P[0] is terminal then
  | this.terminal = P[0] ;
else
  | sub_tree ← CreateSubTree(G; P[0]; L_max) ;
  | this.terminal ← sub_tree;
end
return this;
```

Fig. 3. Pseudo-code of initialization of individuals

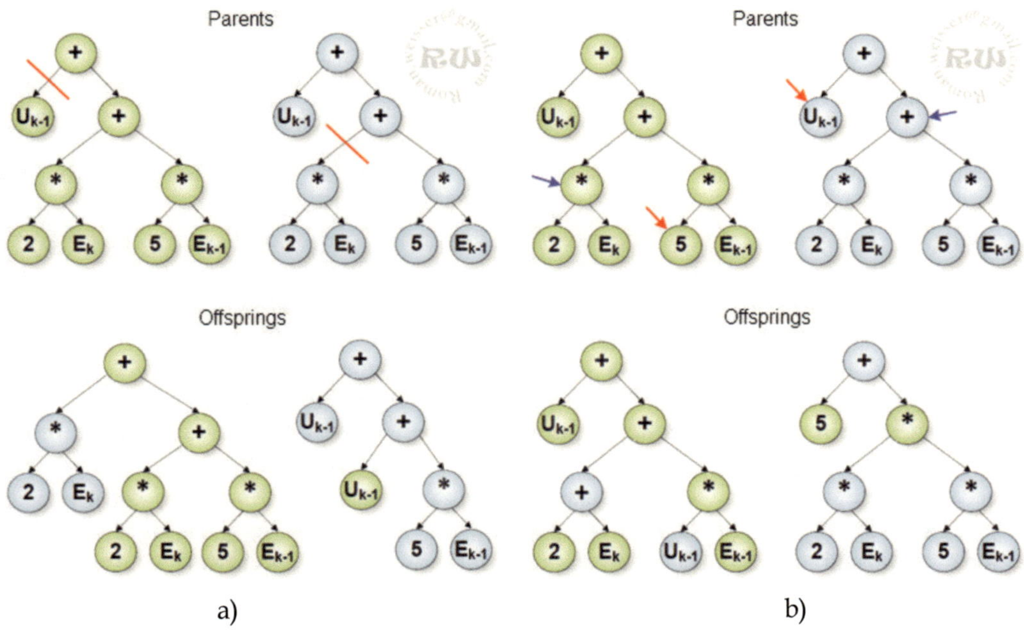

Fig. 4. Crossover: a) crossover the parts of trees, b) crossover of nodes

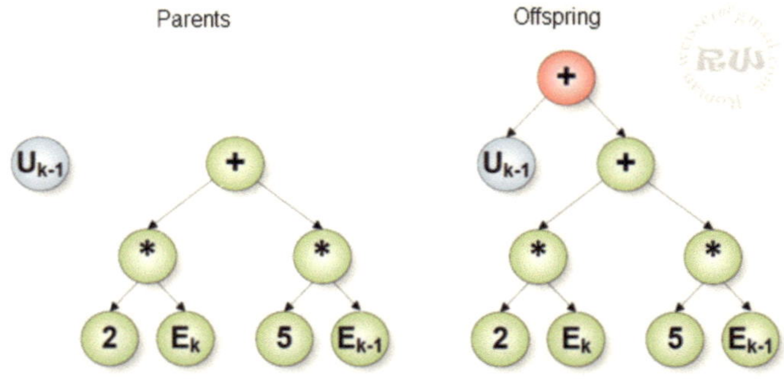

Fig. 5. Crossover by linking trees

$$\langle fnc1 \rangle \nLeftrightarrow \langle fnc2 \rangle \nLeftrightarrow \{\langle \mathrm{var} \rangle \Leftrightarrow \langle const \rangle\} \tag{2}$$

The method of *crossover by linking trees* is a new method. This method creates one offspring from two parents. The parts of the parents are linked by the newly generated node. The newly generated node has two subparts. The first one of them is the tree of the first parent and the second one of them is the tree of the second parent.

2.3 Mutation

Mutation is the second operator to obtain new individuals. This operator can add new structures, which are not included in the population so far. Mutation is performed on individuals from the old population. The nodes in the individuals for mutation are selected randomly. The mutation operator can be subdivided into two types. The first type of mutation is *non-structural mutation* and second type is *structural mutation*. Structural mutation can be divided into shortening structural mutation and extending structural mutation. The mutation operator uses analytic grammar and generative grammar rules.

Non-structural mutation does not affect the structure of the already generated individual. In the individual that is selected for mutation, the chosen nodes of the object sub-tree are further subjected to mutation. The mutation will randomly change the chosen nodes, whereas the used grammar is respected. For example it means that the mutated node, which is a function of two variables (i.e. + - × ÷) cannot be changed by the node representing the function of one variable (unary minus, etc.) or only a variable (Ek, etc.), etc. See Fig. 6.

The selected node in the tree G1 is marked by an orange color (or a different level of gray). The tree after mutation is marked G2 and the mutated node is marked an orange color (or different level of gray) too. The mutation was made by the using of generative and analytic grammar. The operations with this grammar are marked in columns A, B, C, and F. The randomly generated value for rule selection are shown in column A. The modulus operations are shown in column B. The processing of rules is shown in column C.

This example assumes the generative grammar rules in Table 1 and the analytic grammar rules in Table 2.

Structural mutations, unlike non-structural mutations, affect the tree structure of individuals. Changes of the sub-tree by extending or shortening its parts depend on the method of structural mutations. Structural mutation can be divided into two types: Structural mutation which is *extending an object tree structure* and structural mutation which is *shortening a tree structure*. In the case of the **extending structural mutation**, a randomly selected node is replaced by a part of the newly created sub-tree that respects the rules of the defined grammar (see Fig. 7). Conversely the **shortening structural mutation** replaces a randomly selected node of the tree, including its child nodes, by a node which is described by a terminal symbol (i.e. a variable or a number). This type of mutation can be regarded as a method of indirectly reducing the complexity of the object tree (see Fig. 7).

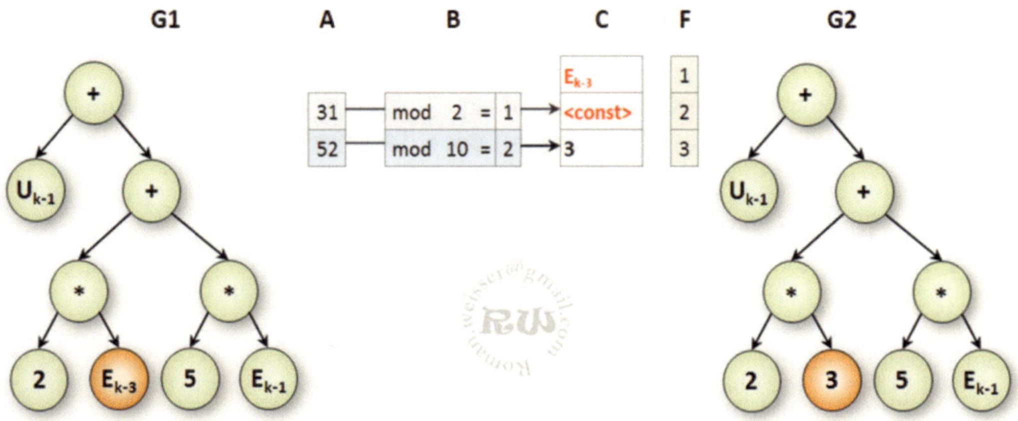

Fig. 6. Non-structural mutation

$U_{k-1} \mid U_{k-2} \mid U_{k-3} \mid U_{k-4} \mid U_{k-5}$	$::=$	$\langle var \rangle \mid \langle const \rangle$
$E_k \mid E_{k-1} \mid E_{k-2} \mid E_{k-3} \mid E_{k-4} \mid E_{k-5}$	$::=$	$\langle var \rangle \mid \langle const \rangle$
$dE_k \mid dE_{k-1} \mid dE_{k-2} \mid dE_{k-3} \mid dE_{k-4}$	$::=$	$\langle var \rangle \mid \langle const \rangle$
$decimal$	$::=$	$\langle var \rangle \mid \langle const \rangle$
$U+ \mid U-$	$::=$	$\langle fnc1 \rangle$
$+ \mid - \mid * \mid /$	$::=$	$\langle fnc2 \rangle$

Table 2. Analytic grammar (non-structural mutation)

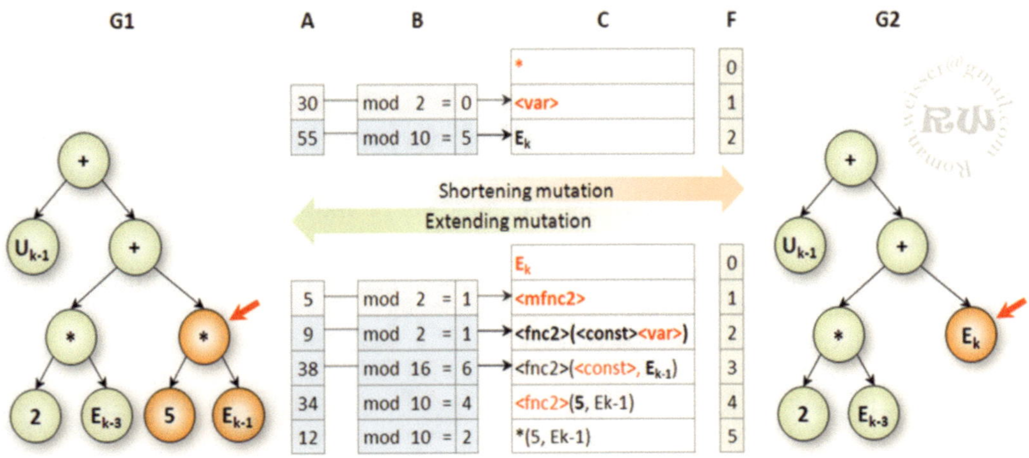

Fig. 7. Structural mutation (Shortening, Extending)

On this figure there are presented two trees, which are marked G1 and G2. In the case of the shortening mutation the mutation is done from tree G1 to tree G2, through the operations which are shown in columns A, B, C, and F (above the arrows). In the case of the extending mutation the mutation is done from tree G2 to tree G1, through the operations which are shown in columns A, B, C, and F (under the arrows). The randomly generated values for selection of the rules are shown in column A, the arithmetic operation modulus is shown in column B, the processing of rules is shown in column C, and the order of operation is shown in column F.

The operator of the structural mutation in Fig. 7 assumes the analytic grammar and generative grammar rules from tables Table 3, Table 4, Table 5 and Table 1.

$U_{k-1} \mid U_{k-2} \mid U_{k-3} \mid U_{k-4} \mid U_{k-5}$	$::=$	$\langle mfnc1\rangle \mid \langle mfnc2\rangle$
$E_k \mid E_{k-1} \mid E_{k-2} \mid E_{k-3} \mid E_{k-4} \mid E_{k-5}$	$::=$	$\langle mfnc1\rangle \mid \langle mfnc2\rangle$
$dE_k \mid dE_{k-1} \mid dE_{k-2} \mid dE_{k-3} \mid dE_{k-4}$	$::=$	$\langle mfnc1\rangle \mid \langle mfnc2\rangle$
$U+ \mid U-$	$::=$	$\langle mfnc2\rangle$

Table 3. Analytic grammar (extending structural mutation)

$U+ \mid U-$	$::=$	$\langle var\rangle \mid \langle const\rangle$
$+ \mid - \mid * \mid /$	$::=$	$\langle var\rangle \mid \langle const\rangle$

Table 4. Analytic grammar (shortening structural mutation)

$\langle mfnc1\rangle$	$::=$	$\langle fnc1\rangle\langle var\rangle \mid \langle fnc1\rangle\langle const\rangle$
$\langle mfnc2\rangle$	$::=$	$\langle fnc2\rangle\ \langle var\rangle\langle var\rangle \mid \langle fnc2\rangle\langle const\rangle\langle var\rangle$

Table 5. Generative grammar (expansion for analytic grammar)

3. Two-level Transplant Evolution

The Two-Level Transplant Evolution (TLTE) is a new type of evolutionary algorithm that performs the optimization of structure in the first level and the parameters in the structure are optimized in the second level of optimization. The optimization of structure is realized by the Transplant Evolution (TE) and the optimization of abstract numerical parameters are realized by the Differential Evolution (DE) [6], or some other algorithm for numerical parameters optimization. Joining the two evolution algorithms has the goal to eliminate the very hard optimization of the numerical parameters by the grammar based evolutionary algorithms. The DE method was chosen for high power of optimization of the real number parameters.

The generative grammar and analytic grammar rules are needed to be modified for the generation or mutation of abstract numerical parameters. To these grammar rules it is necessary to add these expansion rules

$\langle var\rangle$	$::=$	num

num	$::=$	$\langle var\rangle$

Table 6. Generative and analytic grammar (expansion for TLTE)

Some early defined rules are possible to delete. For example non-terminal <const>, etc.

3.1 Architecture

From the implementation viewpoint, the joining of the two evolutionary algorithms is the most difficult process. For the best flexibility the interconnecting of three separate computational modules that are join by an interlayer were chosen. The interlayer mediates a communication among the modules and prepares data in the required form. With this implementation it is possible to use each module separately for another optimization problem, or similarly to change some module by another module.

3.1.1 Transplant Evolution Module

The transplant Evolution Module (MTE), see Fig. 8 ensures optimization of the structure of controllers. The principle of this algorithm was described in the article TLTE. Its task is to create a population of individuals which uses generative grammar G and analytic grammar G^{-1}. This module can make a numerical optimization of parameters in the structure solutions too, but the quality is not so good as in the case of the two-level structure. Optimization of the parameters is provided by the Differential Evolution Module (MDE). The agent for the communication between these layers is the Interlayer, which is responsible for preparing the data in the desired form for each module.The input parameters for the MTE are the generative grammar rules P and the analytic grammar rules P^{-1}, which leads to the evolution of individuals (solutions). The output parameter of the MTE is a fully optimized solution that includes both the appropriate structure, and its parameters.

3.1.2 Differential Evolution Module

The Differential Evolution Module (MDE), see Fig. 8 ensures the optimization of abstract parameters in the structure of the individual. The principle function of *Differential Evolution* (DE) is explained for example in [4]. This module is activated by the *Interlayer*, which gives it the vector of variables $\overrightarrow{num} = (num_1, ..., num_n)$ as one of the input parameters. The number of parameters of this vector is equal to the number of variables, which was included in the structure of the solutions that came from the MTE. The output parameter MDE is the optimized vector of parameters that is sent into the *Interlayer*.

3.1.3 Fitness Module

The fitness Module (FM), see Fig. 8, provides an evaluation of the models. The model is some structure of the solutions, including some parameters. This model, together with the controlled system is the input of simulation. For a given controller and controlled system, the simulation of regulation is started. The quality of model is included in the fitness function after the finishing of the simulation. The evaluated model is send to the *Interlayer*.

3.1.4 Interlayer

The Interlayer, see Fig. 8 is the most important part in the whole architecture of Two-Level architecture. The Interlayer is the main module, which holds instances of all the computational modules. The *interlayer* provides communication among the computational modules through the communication interface. This module contains the knowledge about the strategy of optimization so this means what to be optimized and how to optimize it. The *interlayer* controls the parameters of all the computational modules (MTE, MDE, and FM), for example: size of populations TE or DE, number of generations, type of selection methods, set of probability of crossover and mutation, etc. The *interlayer* makes the communication with an Output Module (OM). The OM is a graphical output, which shows the evolution outputs, simulation of control outputs, etc. The most important task of the *interlayer* is data preparation in the correct form during the communication among the computational modules, for example during the request for fitness evaluation, see Fig. 8. From this perspective, the tasks can be divided as follows:

- To create the vector of symbolic variables for MDE during the communication with MTE.
- The abstract variables will be set by concrete optimized parameters in abstract variables after the finishing of the optimization.
- To send a full model of the solution (structure + parameters) to the FM, during the request of the MTE for the calculation of the quality of an individual, which does not include any abstract parameter.

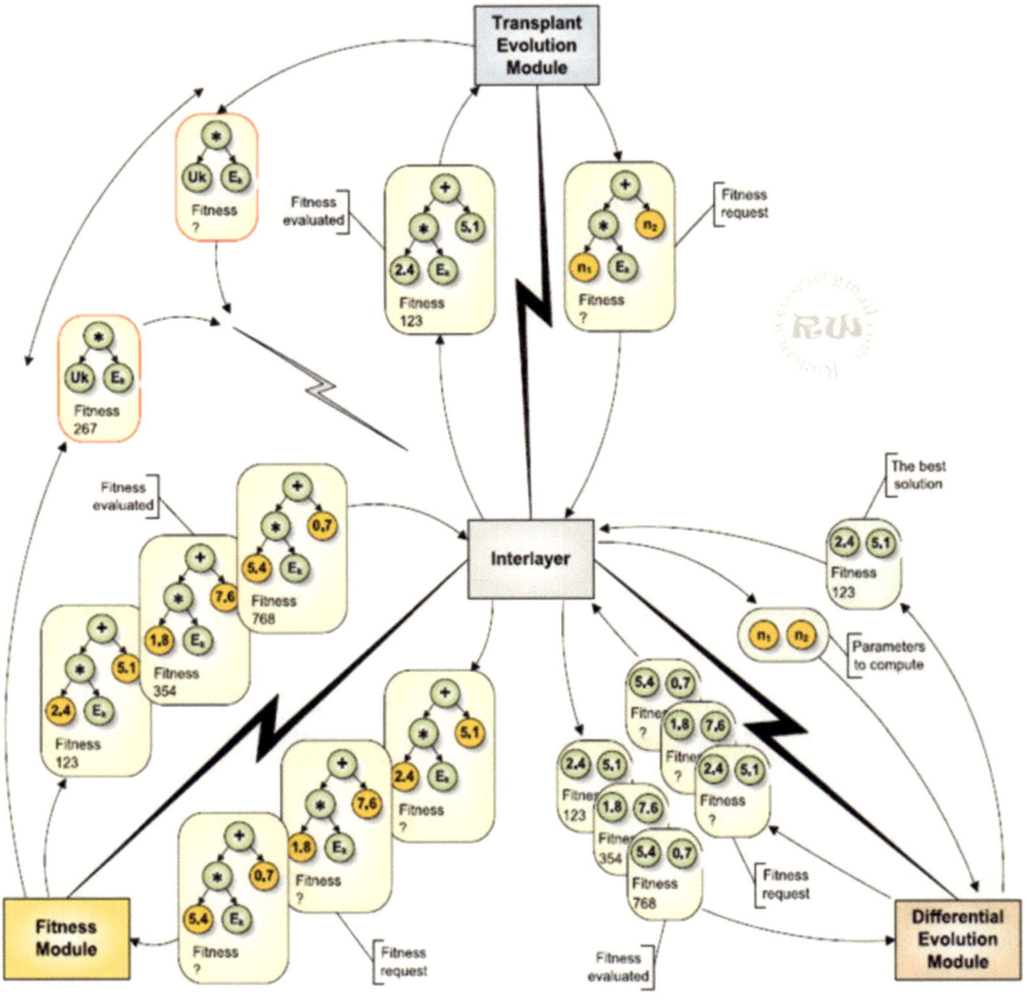

Fig. 8. Architecture and data flow in TLTE

3.2 Arithmetic tree reducing

By penalizing the part of the individual fitness which contains a complex object tree, the method of targeted *shortening structural mutation* of individual, or the direct shortening of the tree using algebraic adjustments - Algebraic Reducing Tree (ART).

- By penalizing the part of the individual fitness which contains a complex object tree,
- Method of targeted *shortening structural mutation* of individual,
- The direct shortening of the tree using algebraic adjustments - Algebraic Reducing Tree (ART).

The last-mentioned method can be realized by the TE, where all of the individuals do not contain the genotype, and then a change in the phenotype is not affected by treatment with the genotype. The realization of the above mentioned problem with an individual, which uses the genotype would be in this case very difficult. This new method is based on the algebraic arrangement of the tree features that are intended to reduce the number of functional blocks in the body of individuals (such as repeating blocks "unary minus", etc.).
In view of the object tree complexity of the individual and also for the subsequent crossover it is preferable to have a function in the form of $x = 3 \times a$, *rather* than $x = a + a + a$, or more generally $x = n \times A$. Another example is the shortening of the function $x = -(-a)$, where the form $x = a$ is preferable (it is removing the redundant marks in the object tree individual). The introduction of algebraic modifications of the individual phenotype leads to a shorter result of the optimal solution and consequently to a shorter presentation of the individual and the shortening of the time of calculation of the function that is represented in the object tree and also to finding optimal solutions faster because of the higher probability of crossover in the suitable points with a higher probability to produce meaningful solutions. The essential difference stems from the use of the direct contraction of trees, which leads to a significantly shorter resulting structure than without using this method.
The arithmetic tree reducing method is shown on Fig. 9. The tree on the beginning of the process of ART is shown under the number 1, the resulting tree after the use of ART is shown under number 4.

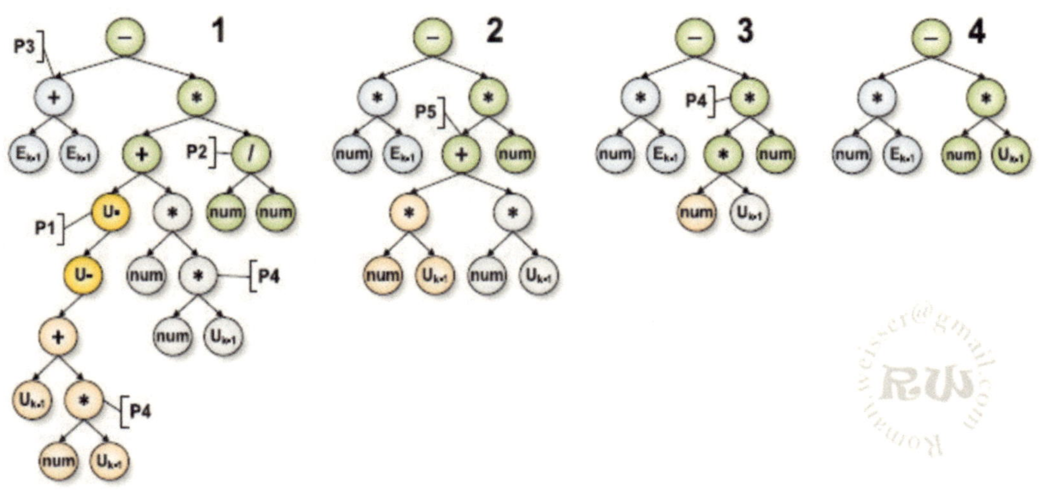

Fig. 9. Arithmetic tree reducing

$f_{2s}, f_{2m}, a, a_1, a_2$ Substitutional symbols of terminals

$f_{2s} \in \Sigma^{2s}$

$f_{2m} \in \Sigma^{2m}$

$\Sigma^{2s} \in \{+,-\}$

$\Sigma^{2m} \in \{*,/\}$

$(a, a_1, a_2) \in \Sigma^{rv}$

$a = a_1 = a_2$

$\Sigma^{re} = \Sigma^{2s} \cup \Sigma^{2m} \cup \Sigma^{rv}$

$e \in \Sigma^{re}$

$pair(a) = f_{2m}(num, a) \mid f_{2m}(a, num)$

P1	U+(*e*)	::=	*e*
	U-(U-(*e*))	::=	*e*
	U-(U+(*e*)) | U+(U-(*e*))	::=	U-(*e*)
P2	$f_{2m}(num, num) \mid f_{2s}(num, num)$	::=	*num*
P3	$+(a_1, a_2)$	::=	$*(num, a)$
	$-(a_1, a_2)$	::=	*num*
	$/(a_1, a_2)$	::=	*num*
P4	$f_{2m}(num, pair(a)) \mid f_{2m}(pair(a), num)$	::=	$*(num, a)$
	$f_{2s}(num, pair(a)) \mid f_{2s}(pair(a), num)$	::=	$*(num, a)$
P5	$f_{2s}(pair(a), pair(a))$	::=	$*(num, a)$

Fig. 10. Dictionary of arithmetic tree reducing method (ART)

The ART method uses a dictionary by which searches in the trees of individuals the subtrees contained in the dictionary, that reduces to the shape defined in the dictionary. The dictionary of ART method is shown on Fig. 10.

4. Fitness criterions

Considering the uses of the transplant evolution for the optimizing of the general controller, the fitness function was experimentally defined as the multi-criteria function of:

- Integral criterions: $I = \int_0^\infty e(t)dt$, $I = \int_0^\infty |e(t)|dt$, $I = \int_0^\infty [e(t)]^2 dt$, $I_{ITAE} = \int_0^\infty t|e(t)|dt$, $I_{ITSE} = \int_0^\infty t[e(t)]^2 dt$
- The count of extremes of controlled variable
- Average control error at the end of desired value interval
- A ratio of the number of points in the control error tolerance to the total number of points
- A ratio of the length of the curve of the controlled variable to the length of the curve of the desired variable
- Maximal absolute overshoot of controlled variable

Maximal absolute overshoot of manipulated variable

The target of optimization is to minimize the ITAE, minimize the count of extremes of controlled variable, to maximize the number of points within the control error tolerance, minimize the maximal overshoot of the manipulated variable and controlled variable.

The fitness criterions are shown on Fig. 11.

5. Evaluation of the simulation process in the case of error during simulation

In order to evaluate the simulation control according to the criteria set out in chapter 0, it is necessary to complete the whole process simulation. If the simulation process will not be completed for any reason (for example: divide by zero, ± ∞, etc.), the algorithm must be able

to evaluate the simulation by another way. These criteria will vary depending on the optimized problem. In the event of PSD controller optimization, the fitness is evaluated according to the calculated number of cycles of the recurrent equations of the PSD controller. More precisely, the ratio C_C / C_{CP}, where C_C is the actual calculated number of cycles and the C_{CP} is the expected number of cycles.
Example: simulation time is *10s*, sampling period is *0.1s*. It follows that the total expected number of calculations of the recurrent equation PSD controller is *100*. If the simulation will be interrupted for any reason during the calculation of recurrent equations at *8 seconds*, the ratio C_C / C_{CP} = 79 = 100 = 0.79 (79 successfully completed calculations).
If the optimization of the recurrent equation of the general controller is started, the fitness is evaluated according to successfully evaluated nodes in the tree structure of the individual during the simulation of the control. This is described by the ratio (C_N/C_{NC}), where C_N is the count of successfully evaluated nodes, and C_{NC} is a number of all the nodes in the structure of the recurrent equation of the controller.

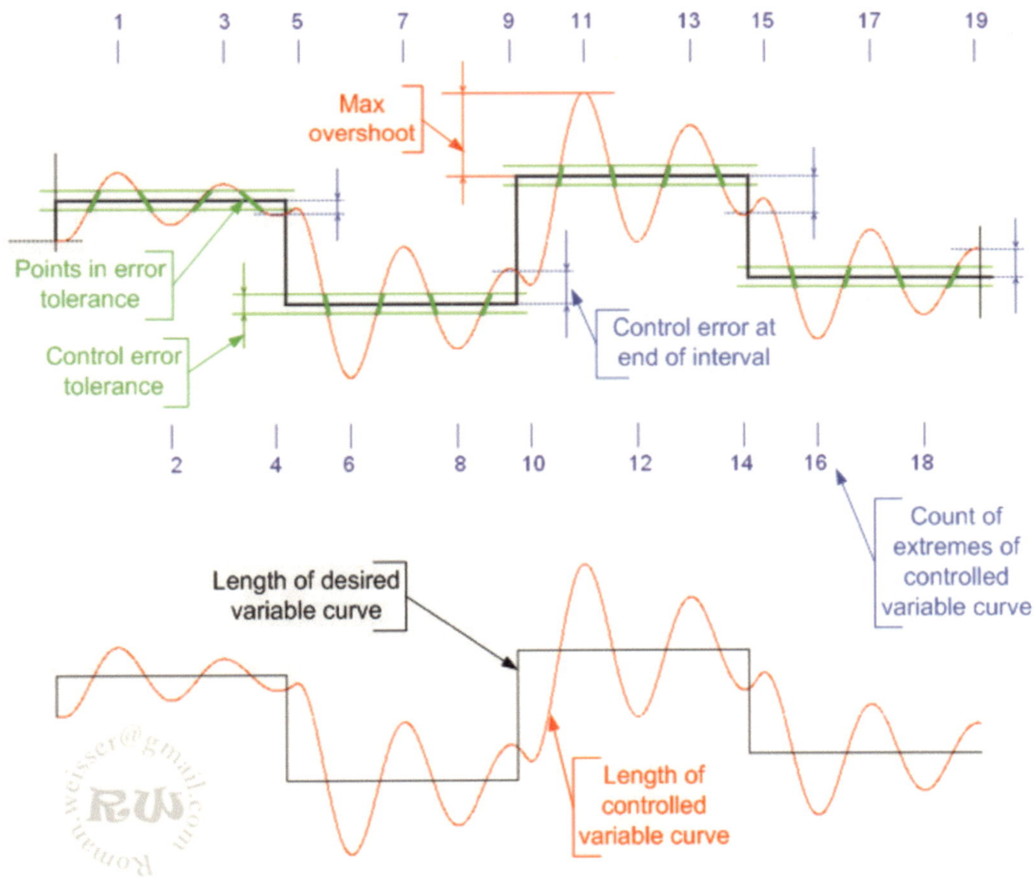

Fig. 11. Fitness criterions of control process

Example: simulation time is *10s*, sampling period is *0.1s*, the equation of the controller is in the form Uk = 3 * Ek. This equation shows that the function tree has 3 nodes (C_{NC} = 3). With each successive calculation of the recurrent equation only three nodes will be calculated. If the simulation will be interrupted for any reason during the calculation of the recurrent equations at 8 seconds, when calculating the product of the nodes 3 and Ek the resulting number of units is calculated by 79 * 3 +1 * 2 (79 times was successfully completed the calculation of three nodes and in the latter calculation were calculated only 2 nodes). This means, the ratio is: CN/CNC = 239/3 = 79.66. In the case where the ratio is divided by the length of simulation and the size of the sampling period, we receive the same ratio as in the case of optimization of PSD controller (79.66/100 = 0.7966). The counting of successfully calculated nodes of recurrent equation of general controllers is more precise. It can be seen in the previous example. If the simulation is finished, it does not mean that the fitness will be successfully evaluated. Whereas that the fitness function make multi-criterion fitness evaluation of simulation, it can occur $\pm \infty$. In this case the fitness is evaluated by the successfully calculated number of criterions. It means that the evaluation of simulation can be done by three ways:

1. The simulation was not successfully finished. In this case the fitness is calculated from the ratio C_C/C_{CP}, or C_N/C_{NC}.
2. The simulation was successfully finished. In this case the fitness is calculated from the successfully finished criterions.
3. The simulation and evaluation of fitness were successfully finished.

This means that way of evaluation 3 is every time better than evaluation 2, and the way of Evaluation 2 is every time better than evaluation 1 ($fi_3 < fi_2 < fi_1$).
The evaluation of the successfully calculated fitness criterions are now shown in the picture Fig. 12. This type of evaluation is very important during the optimization of the general controller. If those criterions would not be added, the optimal solution could not be found. In some cases the successful solution was found after 3000 generations of DE!

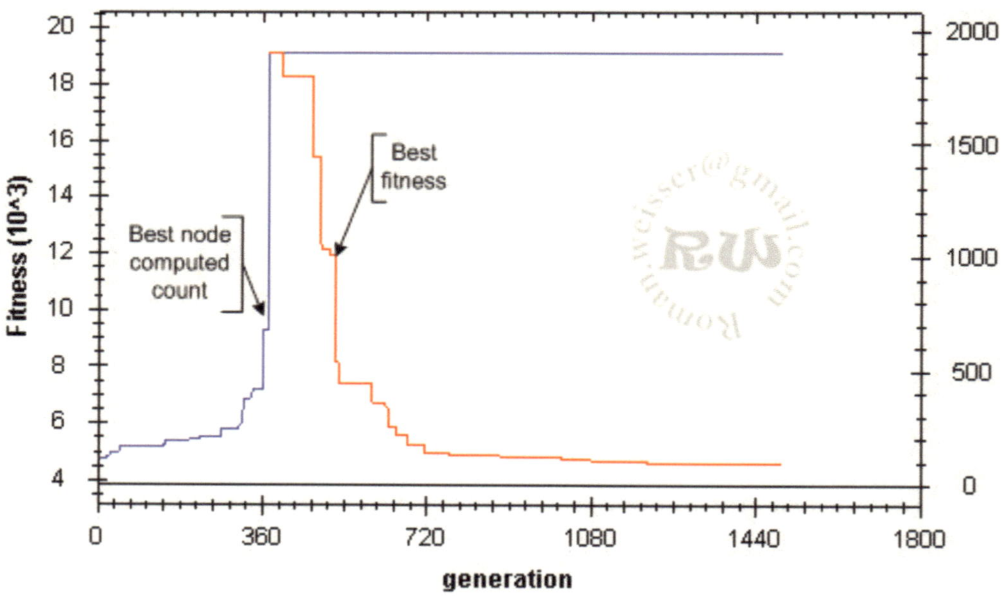

Fig. 12. Two types of fitness evaluation

6. Results

We tested the TLTE method for the optimization of the recurrent equation of general controllers. Here there are some results of the optimization for following two systems.

6.1 Integral system with a transport delay

$$G_S(S) = \frac{5}{s(9s+1)} e^{-2s} \tag{2}$$

In Fig. 13 we compare 3 types of controllers. There is one PSD controller marked PSD_DE and two general controllers marked General_DE and General_TLTE. The curve marked PSD_DE is the PSD controller. The parameters (Kr, Ti, Td) of this controller were optimized by Differential Evolution (DE). The curve marked General DE is for the general controller which has the control equation in PSD equation form, but the parameters q0, q1, q2 were optimized directly by DE. The relation between q0, q1, q2 and Kr, Ti, Td are shown in Table 7. The curve marked General_TLTE is for the general controller with a general control equation that was optimized by Two-Level Transplant Evolution (TLTE). As you can see, the best result is given by the General_TLTE. In this case we receive the recurrent control equation with the following form:

```
Uk = (Ek_5+(((-((Ek_5*(-4,69210604912152))-(-((((Yk*5,14847786853854)*
     Yk_3*1,59643919322167))+((Ek_5+22,2867094434306)*Ek_2))*
     (Uk_2*(-3,80995100289523E-06))))))+((11,9436857350138*Ek)+
     (((-0,322492294234783)*Uk_3)+((-18,5463669625012)*Ek_2))))+
     (Ek_1+(-0,00399257533723234))))
```

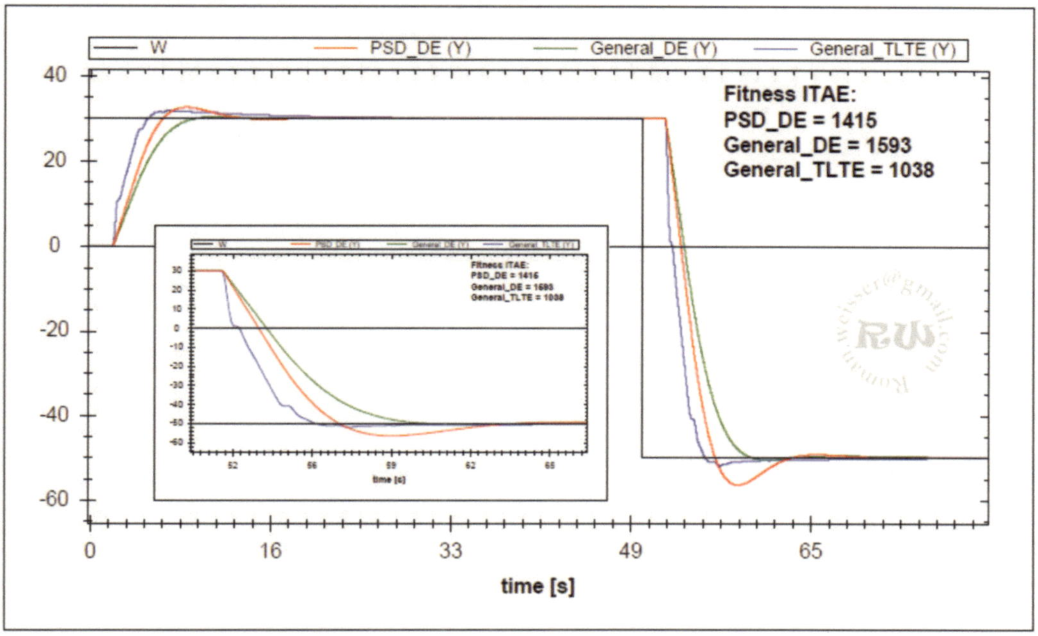

Fig. 13. Step response for integration system with time delay

	q_0	q_1	q_2
ZOBD	$k_R\left(1+\frac{T_D}{T}+\frac{T}{T_I}\right)$	$-k_R\left(1+2\frac{T_D}{T}\right)$	$k_R\frac{T_D}{T}$
DOBD	$k_R\left(1+\frac{T_D}{T}\right)$	$-k_R\left(1+2\frac{T_D}{T}-\frac{T}{T_I}\right)$	$k_R\frac{T_D}{T}$
LICHO	$k_R\left(1+\frac{T_D}{T}+\frac{T}{2T_I}\right)$	$-k_R\left(1+2\frac{T_D}{T}-\frac{T}{2T_I}\right)$	$k_R\frac{T_D}{T}$

Table 7. Examples of calculation of reccurent equation parameteres (q0, q1, q2) or (Kr, Ti, Td)

6.2 Second order system with time delay

$$G_S(S)=\frac{k_S}{T_0^2 s^2+2\xi T_0 s+1}e^{-T_d s} \tag{3}$$

where $k_s = 1$, $T_0 = 1$, $\xi = 0.1$, $T_d = 1$

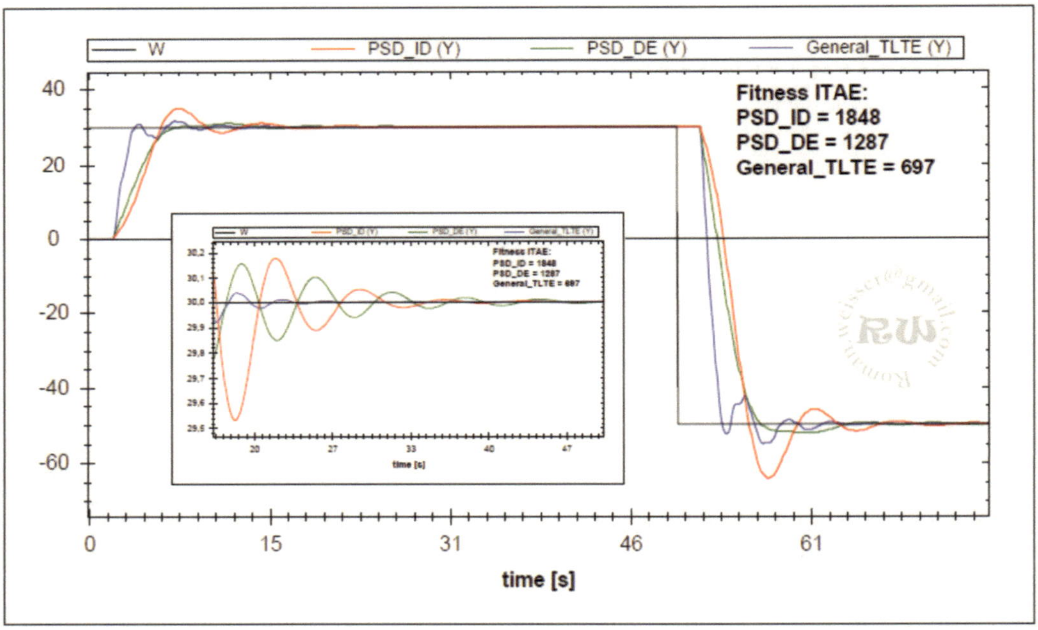

Fig. 14. Step response for oscilating proportionate second order system system with time delay

In Fig. 14 we compare 3 types of controllers. There are two types of PSD controllers marked PSD_ID, PSD_DE, and one general controller marked General_TLTE. The curve marked PSD_ID is for the PSD controller that was set by the method of inverse dynamics.

As you can see, the best result is given again by the General_TLTE. In this case we receive the recurrent control equation with following form:

```
Uk=(((Yk_3*15,3645727059621)+(((Ek*3,80273057221998)-
   ((Ek-0,000331083646885983)+((Uk_5*0,571665466205751)+
   (Yk_4*13,7928925600503))))-(Ek_3*0,958174106578814)))-Ek_4)
```

7. Conclusion

The Two-Level Transplant Evolution (TLTE) was successfully used for the automatic generation of control programs of general controllers. We tested this algorithm on many problems, only two examples were described in this paper. We hope that this new method of controller design will be used in practice, not only for simulation.

This work has been supported by the Czech Ministry of Education No: MSM 00216305529 Intelligent Systems in Automation and GA ČR No: 102/09/1668.

8. References

BACKUS, J. W., et al. ALGOL-like Languages. Volume 1. Cambridge, MA, USA: Birkhauser Boston Inc., 1997. Revised report on the algorithmic language ALGOL 60, p. 19-49.

Koza J.R., Genetic Programming: On the Programming of Computers by Means of Natural Selection, The MIT Press, 1992

Kratochvíl O., Ošmera P., Popelka O. 2009: Parallel grammatical evolution for circuit optimization, in Proc. WCECS, World Congress on Engineering and Computer Science, San Francisco, 1032-1040.

Li Z. and Halang W. A. and Chen G. 2006: Integration of Fuzzy Logic and Chaos Theory; paragraph: Osmera P.: Evolution of Complexity, Springer, 527 - 578.

O'Neill, M., Brabazon, A.: Grammatical Differential Evolution, In Proc. International Conference on Artificial Intelligence (ICAI'06) CSEA Press Las Vegas, Nevada.

O'Neill M. and Ryan C. 2003: Grammatical Evolution: Evolutionary Automatic Programming in an Arbitrary Language Kluwer Academic Publishers.

Ošmera P. and Šimoník I. and Roupec J. 1995: Multilevel distributed genetic algorithms. In Proceedings of the International Conference IEE/IEEE on Genetic Algorithms, Sheffield, 505–510.

Ošmera P. and Roupec J. 2000: Limited Lifetime Genetic Algorithms in Comparison with Sexual Reproduction Based GAs, Proceedings of MENDEL, Brno, Czech Republic, 118 - 126.

Popelka, O.: Parallel Grammatical Evolution for Circuit Optimization. In: Proceedings of MENDEL 2007, Prague, Czech Republic, pp. 88–92 (2007)

Price K. Differential evolution: a fast and simple numerical optimizer, Biennial Conference of the North American Fuzzy Information Processing Society, 1996, NAFIPS, IEEE Press, New York, NY, 524-527.

Rukovanský I., Evolution of Complex Systems. 8th Joint Conference on Information Sciences. Salt Lake City. Utah. July 21-25, 2005.

Rukovanský I. Optimization of the throughput of Computer Network Based on Parallel EA. In Proceedings of the World Congress on Engineering and Computer Science WCECS 2009, San Francisco, CA, Oct. 20-22, 2009, Vol. II, pp. 1038-1043

Rukovanský I., Popelka O. Increasing Performance of Computer Networks Via Node to Node throughput Optimization. In : Proceedings of the Information Conference on Soft Computing Applied in Computer and Economic Environments, ICSC 2008, Kunovice : EPI, Ltd. Czech Republic, January 25, 2008, pp. 171-175

Weisser R., Ošmera P., Matoušek R., Transplant Evolution with Modified Schema of Differential Evolution : Optimization Structure of Controllers. In International Conference on Soft Computing MENDEL. Brno : MENDEL, 2010.

Weisser R., Ošmera P., Šeda, M., Kratochvíl, O. Transplant Evolution for Optimization of General Controllers. In European Conference on Modelling and Simulation. 24th. Kuala Lumpur (Malaysia) : ECMS 2010. s. 250 -- 260.

Weisser R., Ošmera P., Two-level Tranpslant Evolution, In East West Fuzzy Colloquium, 17th Zittau Fuzzy Colloquium 2010

Weisser R., Ošmera P., Two-level Tranpslant Evolution: Optimization of General Controllers, In East West Fuzzy Colloquium, 17th Zittau Fuzzy Colloquium 2010

Zelinka I., Oplatkova Z. Nolle L., Analytic Programming - Symbolic Regression by Means of Arbitrary Evolutionary Algorithms, In: Special Issue on Inteligent Systems, International Journal of Simulation, Systems, Science and Technology, Volume 6, Issue 9, August 2005, pp 44 - 56, ISSN 1473-8031

6

Technologies and Methodologies Enabling Reliable Real-Time Wireless Automation

Mikael Björkbom, Lasse M. Eriksson and Joni Silvo
Aalto University School of Science and Technology
Finland

1. Introduction

Wireless automation is an emerging field of research, engineering and industrial development that aims at significant savings in installation times and costs of cabling in automation systems, while providing a new level of flexibility for system design, reconfiguration, and agility. It is applicable to both new automation systems and retrofit applications. The use of wireless technologies is rather common in consumer applications, consider, for example, cellular phones, cordless desktops, etc., but the strict real-timeliness and reliability requirements of automation systems have limited the use of wireless technology in industrial environments. There are, however, a variety of existing industrial applications of Bluetooth, ZigBee and WLAN networks, but very rarely these are used in time-critical applications. The bulletproof wireless technologies are few, and hence the technologies have not yet spread to wide use in industrial automation. The main concerns in this respect are related to the problem of how the reliability and real-timeliness of wireless communications could be guaranteed.

Wireless automation considers a wide range of technologies that are used in an automation system to enable wireless communications on one or several levels of the system, including factory, automation system, and field device levels. The wireless communications are used to deliver measurements and control values, device configuration information and other process data between the devices, control rooms and servers. This chapter reviews the wireless automation standards and related technologies, but also certain medium access control (MAC) and routing protocols and control design approaches are discussed that together could solve the problem of achieving a reliably working real-time wireless automation system. We will also consider simulation of wireless automation systems, which is essential for the network and automation system co-design validation, and evaluate some candidate system designs with a suitable simulator. The focus is on the field device level, and hence the technologies used for device to device wireless communication for control purposes are addressed.

The main contributions of this chapter include a review of current technologies used in wireless automation. We also discuss and propose a new MAC and mesh routing protocol (limited broadcast protocol, LBP) to enhance the reliability and real-time performance of wireless automation systems. We will also demonstrate how the modelling and simulation of packet drops could be done and integrated in the co-design procedure of wireless automation systems. Finally, we will investigate some practical control solutions and designs for wireless automation with a full-scale simulator to validate the proposed designs.

1.1 Wireless automation

Wireless automation and the related field of wireless sensor networks (WSN) are currently attracting researchers and industry world-wide. The progress of development has emerged into two industrial wireless automation standards, namely WirelessHART (2007) and ISA100.11a (2009). In the current phase, these standards consider mainly monitoring applications without guarantees of real-time performance. However, in automation systems, it is possible to handle the missing data and variable time-delays induced by the somewhat non-deterministic wireless communications by proper design of the system, especially via appropriate control design.

The primary benefit of wireless control technology is the reduced installation cost, as a considerable investment is made in the wiring of factories, both financially and in labor (Brooks, 2001). The use of wireless technology is not only a replacement of cables; the benefits go beyond that. With wireless devices, increased flexibility is gained, as sensors can be placed more freely, even on rotating machines. Robustness is increased, as the communication can be done over several paths in a mesh network and failure of cables is eliminated (TSMP, 2010). Finally, there are the opportunities for new applications that are enabled by wireless control. Some existing or emerging applications are remote control of devices, for example cranes or dexterous and mobile robots, mobile applications, and wireless monitoring of large plants for fault detection, maintenance, production quality monitoring, and compliance to environmental regulations (Gungor & Hancke, 2009).

There is a strong aim (Moyne & Tilbury, 2007) to develop and deploy wireless networked control systems (WiNCS), where a control system communicates over a wireless network, in factory and home automation. In a related field, sensor network applications have as well received much attention (Akyildiz et al., 2002; Baronti et al., 2007). Today, wireless automation technologies are mostly used in monitoring applications, because in these applications the operational requirements can be satisfied with the current technology. The industry is cautious in applying wireless to closed-loop control, due to the inherent unreliability of wireless communications. Next we summarize the main research activities on WiNCS to enable wireless automation.

1.2 Research on wireless networked control systems

A networked control system (NCS) is a distributed real-time control system consisting of the plant, sensors, controllers, actuators, and a shared data network that is used for communication between the components of the system (Antsaklis & Baillieul, 2004). A general NCS layout is depicted in Fig. 1. In WiNCS, wireless networks are used for transferring data.

One of the benefits of NCS is reduced cabling cost (Neumann, 2007), which is removed completely by the introduction of wireless devices. Other advantages include ease of adding field devices, introducing two-way communication with field devices for remote configuration and device health monitoring, and more advanced control strategies are possible because of improved availability of field level data (Gungor & Hancke, 2009; Neumann, 2007). Wireless control systems deliver more benefits than NCSs as there are no wires, but also more problems, mainly because of the unreliable shared communication medium. The main concern against deploying wireless networks for control is the uncertainty of communication and inability to guarantee a sufficient quality of service for the control system. The network must provide real-time and continuous operation, as controlling a physical system is a continuous task (Moyne & Tilbury, 2007). This real-timeliness may not always be guaranteed, which causes problems for the control system design (Lian et al., 2006). Soft real-time operation is enough, if it is taken into account in the control design as shown later on. Another concern hindering the adoption of wireless technologies is security, since the wireless medium is open for eavesdropping and interference (Mustard, 2006). The security issue is solved by authentication and encryption methods (Karlof et al., 2004).

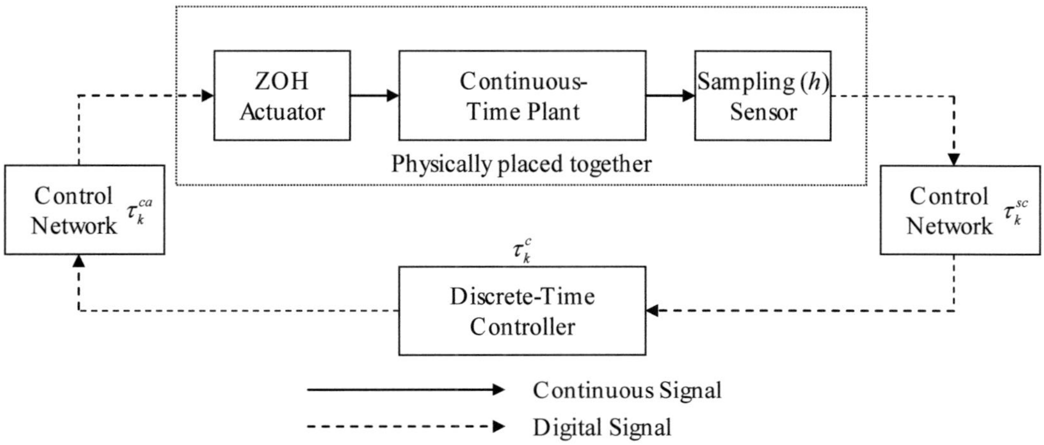

Fig. 1. The (Wi)NCS model, modified from (Nilsson, 1998).

Ethernet networks are becoming regularly used in control applications (Moyne & Tilbury, 2007). Similarly the "Industrial Ethernets" (Neumann, 2007), which allow for real-time operation, where an operation is guaranteed to be executed in a given time, are gradually being applied. The same benefits are also available by means of wireless technology, such as WLAN, with the addition of accessing the data wirelessly using a handheld device, enabling in-situ inspection of the process (Brooks, 2001). An overview of NCSs can be found in (Antsaklis & Baillieul, 2004) and (Hespanha et al., 2006).

The field of WiNCS is multidisciplinary: the network, the control system and their interactions need to be taken into account. Traditionally, either the network or the control system has been studied separately. As such there has been relatively little research focusing on both aspects at the same time. Current wireless control system research has its roots in networked control system theory, as the issues of a shared communication medium are the same, mainly related to variable communication time-delays and packet losses, and system architecture design, see (Willig, 2008). Both fields deal with network protocols (Akkaya & Younis, 2005; Marco et al., 2010), transmission scheduling (Weiss et al. 2009), communication and control co-scheduling (Samii et al., 2009), traffic reduction (Lian et al., 2002), congestion control (Velasco et al., 2004), estimation (Nebot et al., 1999), LQG control with packet drop (Gupta et al., 2007), Kalman filtering (Sinopoli et al., 2004), controller tuning (Eriksson, 2008), control performance (Lian et al., 2001), and control stability (Cervin et al., 2004; Gupta et al., 2007; Kao & Lincoln, 2004; Weiss et al., 2009). The main difference between NCSs and WiNCSs is that wireless communication is less deterministic because of interference and finite communication range, but problems with wiring and failing connectors are eliminated.

2. Technologies in wireless automation – A review

The physical properties of the radio, such as frequency, antenna and modulation, determine the range and bit rate of the network. The medium access control (MAC) determines the delay a message experiences before the transmitter gains access to the wireless medium and the message can be transmitted. In a large control system, there are many small packets, containing, for instance, measurements from a sensor or control values to actuators, to be transmitted in a short timeframe. The particular communication attributes and the need for a real-time WiNCS set special requirements on the MAC protocol, which among other things, affects the packet delay and collision probability. The MAC protocol is thus one of the most important network design issues in WiNCS.

2.1 Medium access and networking protocol

The main categorization of MAC protocols is between deterministic (contention free) and random access (contention based). In random access MACs, no guarantees that a certain node gets access to the medium in a given time can, in general, be given. Most of the random access MACs used in wireless sensor networks are based on the carrier sense multiple access (CSMA) protocol. In deterministic MACs, a communication slot (either in frequency, time or with code division, or a combination of them) is assigned to each node. This assignment has the advantage that the communication is deterministic in the sense that the access to the medium can be guaranteed in a predetermined time. Networks using time-scheduled MAC are typically controlled by a centralized network manager, and they require tight time-synchronization of the whole network.

The advantage of random access MAC is that in low traffic conditions (low sampling rate), any node can transmit immediately if the medium is idle. In high traffic conditions (large number of control loops or high sampling frequency), a packet might experience collisions and random back-off times. The non-deterministic exponential back-off is not suitable for wireless control applications, since the communication delay, which is important for the control stability (Cervin et al., 2004), cannot be bounded and packet drop due to congestion decreases the performance (Liu & Goldsmith, 2003). Therefore, deterministic MAC protocols are often desired in control applications to overcome the problem of variability in transmission times. Although deterministic MAC protocols might not always provide the optimal use of resources, they are used in WiNCS as one solution to support real-timeliness. In current wireless automation standards, the trend is also to use deterministic MAC protocols, which enable a reliable communication schedule for periodic measurements and control packets.

The original IEEE 802.15.4 standard defines two operation modes. In the beacon mode, it is possible to utilize both reserved time slots (scheduled MAC), and contention based slots (random access). However, most of the shipped radios nowadays come only with CSMA random access MAC, which is due to the complexity of the beacon mode protocol and its known performance problems (Werb et al., 2005). The WirelessHART protocol (WirelessHART, 2010), aimed at industrial applications, defines both token passing and scheduled MAC. The protocol allows frequency-time slots to be dedicated to links. Some slots can also be reserved for contention based access using CSMA. Another industrial wireless automation standard is ISA100.11a, which uses a similar MAC protocol to WirelessHART. These industrial standards are further discussed in Section 3.

As in any realistic large-scale sensor network, not all the nodes are able to communicate directly with each other due to the limited radio range and dynamic nature and other challenges posed by the environment. Hence routing protocols are needed to ensure that the data could be transmitted from any node to any other node at all times in the network. The aim of a routing protocol is to setup the routes in the network in an energy-efficient manner and to reliably relay the data from the source to the sink node (Akkaya & Younis, 2005). Typically in monitoring applications, the data are eventually collected into one of the nodes, i.e. the sink node, having the capability to store the data for offline analysis and/or visualize the data for the system user.

Many of the proposed routing protocols can be divided into data-centric, hierarchical or location-based, but some of them also consider e.g. network quality of service (QoS). For a more detailed review of routing protocols in WSN, see (Akkaya & Younis, 2005).

It should be noticed that especially in networks having real-timeliness constraints, the MAC and routing protocols are tightly coupled. For example, an intermediate node on the route should be able to forward a message once the node receives it as fast as possible to the next node along the path to reduce the end-to-end communication delay. In WirelessHART networks the routes are either predetermined by the network manager (graph routing) or determined by the nodes themselves (source routing for ad hoc communications) (Song et al., 2008).

2.2 Radios for wireless automation

Wireless networks for control applications are currently envisioned to use existing standard wireless technologies, such as Bluetooth, ZigBee (based on IEEE 802.15.4 radio) (Baronti et al., 2007), and WLAN (IEEE 802.11). Nevertheless, it should be noted that the traditional computer networks, such as Ethernet and WLAN, use CSMA type medium access control with exponential back-off in case of collisions, which is not always applicable in wireless control as already discussed above. The wireless network design problems are further discussed, for instance, in (Kumar, 2001).

Wireless networks are already used in control. The preferred solution is to use deterministic networks, using polling (e.g. Bluetooth) or scheduling (WirelessHART and ISA100.11a), but standard wireless networks are also used in control applications. Using standard wireless hardware for automation is considered in (Pellegrini et al., 2006), where two application layer protocols suitable for real-time control are designed and evaluated. Some early adoptions of wireless devices as cable replacements are listed in (Koumpis et al., 2005). The first wireless deployments have been mostly cable replacements using Bluetooth. Bluetooth has, however, given way to ZigBee, as ZigBee has lower power consumption and more flexible networking.

An overview of ZigBee/IEEE 802.15.4 can be found in (Baronti et al., 2007). ZigBee has rightfully been criticized for being unreliable, lacking techniques to mitigate the communication problems, and unsuitable for industrial control (Lennvall et al., 2008). ZigBee is more suitable for small applications, and there are separate industrial standards for wireless automation. ZigBee is used, for example, for home and building automation as an enabling technology to create smart home and smart energy applications.

WLAN networks provide such high data throughputs that they could be well used in automation systems from the data rate point of view. The problem with WLAN is the high energy consumption of the radio. Obviously, a standard WLAN network does not support real-time communications, but the radio technology itself is useful for creating high-

bandwidth real-time systems. Nevertheless, it is challenging to create purely wireless WLAN networks for automation due to the high energy consumption of the nodes. For cable replacement, though, if power is available from the process, the WLAN radios can be well used for single hop wireless communication.
The use of heterogeneous networks spanning the whole automation system from low level devices to high level functions, such as production monitoring, is considered in (Moyne & Tilbury, 2007; Neumann, 2007), where the applicability of different networks at the different levels and tasks are evaluated. For the higher level functions, such as plant monitoring and production planning, trend analysis, or gathering of batch information, real-time operation is not necessary, and office grade wireless networks are suitable for these tasks. In the current wireless automation standards only field device level wireless networks, where sensor devices report their measured values and possible health data to a gateway and the rest of the automation system, are considered. The network is thus used only at the lowest device level in the whole automation system (Steigmann & Endresen, 2006). In practice, also plant wide wireless networks with proprietary protocols based on the office grade IEEE 802.11 standard are used.

3. Standards and applications

Currently, there are two standards for industrial wireless automation: WirelessHART and ISA100.11a. Both industrial standards are based on the IEEE 802.15.4 radio (ZigBee, 2006). The IEEE 802.15.4 standard is suitable for building automation (Kintner-Meyer, 2005), industrial monitoring, and control applications (Wheeler, 2007). The main characteristics are low bit rate and low power consumption. The WirelessHART standard and some implementation details are discussed in (Song et al., 2008). ISA100.11a is in practice very similar to WirelessHART, as both have similar design goals, but the two standards are not compatible. Furthermore, it should be noted that the WISA system (Scheible et al., 2007) is a complete solution for a reliable wireless cell in industrial manufacturing.
The architecture of both industrial wireless automation standards includes sensor nodes, wireless routers communicating with each other, and a gateway, which is connected to the automation fieldbus and the rest of the automation system. Mesh networking is possible for reliability, but all communication between devices in the wireless network is routed via the gateway. This routing constraint makes the network scheduling and routing easier.
WirelessHART is by now in use (WirelessHART, 2010) and several manufacturers have released devices for WirelessHART. The ISA100.11a standard (ISA100, 2010) was published in September 2009, and is submitted for ANSI and IEC standard approvals. Hence, the field of industrial wireless control has taken its first steps. The standards are designed for determinism, such that traditional control can readily be applied. Although determinism is the main design goal, this is never fully assured. Wireless networks are inherently non-deterministic, and no network design can make it fully dependable, because of interference in the open communication media.
The WirelessHART protocol is designed for deterministic communication and interference resistance, satisfying the real-time requirements of a wireless control system. WirelessHART uses a combination of time division multiple access (TDMA) and frequency division multiple access (FDMA) MAC protocol. The TDMA slot length is 10 ms, in which the data packet with sensor or control information and an acknowledgement are exchanged between two nodes. The network and transport layers are based on the Time Synchronized Mesh

Protocol (TSMP) originally developed by Dust Networks (TSMP, 2010). Each node pair is assigned a unique time/frequency slot for contention free communication by a centralized network manager. Some slots can be reserved for contention based access using CSMA, for communicating rare event messages. Additionally frequency hopping is used to mitigate interference on some channels. A more detailed presentation of WirelessHART can be found in (Song et al., 2008).

The benefits of WirelessHART and how to accommodate the control system to the wireless network, and meet the required control performance, is discussed in (Nixon et al., 2008). ISA100.11a uses similar techniques and both network standards can be applied where the application can tolerate a delay jitter in the order of 100 ms. The delay jitter stems from packet drop due to interference. In laboratory setting, the TSMP combined with frequency hopping over the 16 available channels of the IEEE 802.15.4 radio has been reported to achieve carrier grade reliability for a low data rate wireless sensor network (Werb et al., 2005).

Due to the determinism of the TDMA approach with a pre-determined schedule, fixed bounds on the communication can be advertized, although not guaranteed. In the case of packet drops due to interference or fading, retransmission is needed, which may cause the information to exceed the delay bound. Retransmission slots must thus be incorporated into the schedule, which reduces the bandwidth usage and unavoidably introduces delay jitter. Retransmission can take place on the slots allocated for random access, or on extra slots allocated in the schedule. Current research related to the standards is, for instance, communication and controller scheduling (Samii et al., 2009) and the optimality of the time/frequency-slot scheduling and routing (Weiss et al., 2009).

Despite the wireless communication, the devices may still have wired power, because of large power requirements of the sensor or, usually, the actuator. For truly wireless devices, the power source must be local. A battery contains a finite amount of energy, and thus either the device lifetime is limited, or energy must be gathered during operation from the environment with energy harvesting techniques. Sources of auxiliary energy are, for example, electromagnetic waves, light, vibration, or temperature differences (Paradiso & Starner, 2005). Another solution to completely get rid of cables is wireless power transportation. An existing solution is inductive power transfer to devices located inside a cage by the ABB WISA system (Scheible et al., 2007). The cage walls induce a rotating magnetic field that solenoids in the devices convert to current. Typical power transfer ranges from 10 to 100 mW (Steigmann & Endresen, 2006).

4. Design challenges and solutions

The wireless roadmap, with the needed technological and social development for the adoption of wireless technology in automation, is summarized in (Koumpis et al., 2005). A comprehensive overview of current technologies, future issues, and research topics of wireless industrial networking is given in (Gungor & Hancke, 2009) and (Willig, 2008). Several wireless standards are presented and the anticipated promising research topics are introduced. Some of them are: network architecture and scalability, network standards, quality of service measures, provisioning and analysis of wireless industrial networks, real-time and reliability, security, and energy efficiency.

There are many other papers giving an overview of the current wireless technologies and networks for control, e.g. (Gungor & Hancke, 2009; Pellegrini et al., 2006), and (Willig et al.,

2005). Gungor & Hancke (2009) review the challenges, design goals, and technical solutions for industrial wireless sensor networks. Willig et al. (2005) discuss several properties and challenges of using wireless in real-time control applications. Some of the network related issues are: interference, path loss, timing and timeliness, co-existence of other wireless networks, and connection to an existing wired automation system. Pellegrini (2006) discusses the requirements and features for using wireless at the device level in an automation system, including power consumption, security, and connection to the wired control system. The necessity of wireless protocols aimed specifically at control applications is also pointed out.

4.1 Radio environment challenges in wireless automation

The use of wireless technologies in automation also introduces new challenges, as cable replacement does not simply mean unplugging a wire and using a wireless device instead. The radio channel is a shared medium, and thus subject to interference from co-channel transmissions. Wireless communication is usually less reliable than wired solutions. Radio propagation conditions in industrial setting can be harsh. Measurement results in factories indicate that the channel is subject to frequency selective fading due to multipath propagation. Furthermore, errors tend to appear in bursts in which several consecutive packets are lost (Willig & Mitschke, 2006). The unreliability and interference problems of the wireless networks can be addressed in the different protocol layers. These design choices have an impact on the used control methods, which also need to be redesigned to cope with the problems of wireless communication.

In the current wireless automation applications, the radios typically operate in the open 2.4 GHz ISM frequency band. The ISM band is quite crowded, as also the office networks (WLAN, Bluetooth) operate at the same frequencies. The existence of other networks in the same band does not mean that the wireless automation network could not be used. The reliability of communications depends then on the activity of the interfering network. To avoid collisions and interference, frequency hopping and channel blacklisting are useful techniques. In the future, a separate frequency band should be reserved world-wide exclusively for industrial automation applications, to enable proper, interference free wireless control operation.

There are several studies of the performance of IEEE 802.11 networks, e.g. (Prasad et al., 2001), where the network design is also discussed. In industrial or factory environments the radio propagation signal deviates considerably from the ideal free space propagation models used in most network simulator models. Besides the free space model there exists many other fading models for wireless communication (Goldsmith, 2004). Metal and obstacles, typically present in a factory, cause shadowing and multipath effects that amplify or attenuate the radio signal strength. The radio environment in a factory can be harsh with motors radiating interfering electromagnetic waves and moving machinery temporarily blocking links of the wireless network. Reflections of radio waves, causing multipath fading, can in these environments be an advantage, because shadowed locations can obtain a strong signal through reflections.

There are some reports on studies of measurements done in industrial environments. The received signal strength in a chemical pulp factory, cable factory and a nuclear power plant was measured with an IEEE 802.11 network at the 2.4 GHz ISM radio band (Kjesbu & Brunsvik, 2000). The conclusions of the experiments were that the radio environment is not as harsh as initially thought; multipath improves the signal strength in shadow areas. While many locations are improved by multipath fading, communication in some locations is impossible, due to no signal or destructive interference, even if the distance is short (Björkbom et al., 2010). Another study presents measurements of the bit-error-rate and more importantly, the error pattern, of an IEEE 802.11 network in an industrial environment (Willig et al., 2002). Interesting findings were that the packet losses are correlated, error burst and packet loss burst lengths fluctuate several orders of magnitude with time. This means that the outages due to consecutive packet drops may be long in some instants and hard to eliminate, for various physical reasons caused by the environment and the radio. On the other hand, error free periods also vary and can be long. Packet loss rates vary from the high 80 % to less than 10 % in generous situations.

Next, we present a method for modelling packet drop probability in an industrial environment, such that the models could be used in wireless automation network and control design. The measurements done in a real industrial hall show the challenge of wireless communication in harsh environments. When packet drop occurs, feedback information for the controller is not available and the real-time operation of a wireless automation network is endangered. Suitable control design to cope with this problem is presented in Section 5.

4.2 Measurements and models for radio environments

In order to study and design WiNCS, realistic packet drop models of networks are needed, since information loss affects the control performance. The physical properties of an existing radio environment can be assessed by carrying out actual measurements at the target site, as described next. Our interest is to use IEEE 802.15.4 radios in a particular industrial environment and hence the tests are performed with such radios. To efficiently collect packet drop data from an environment of interest, we propose the following hardware setup to be used for the tests. The transmitter device is connected to two monopole WLAN antennas, with a spatial separation of 12.5 cm. Similarly four receivers are arranged in an array, placed 6.25 cm from each other, which is half the wavelength at 2.4 GHz. The purpose of having multiple antennas at the transmitter and receiver is to implement and test diversity techniques (both temporal and spatial diversity).

The sensor nodes are equipped with Texas Instruments CC2431 radio modules. Transmission power is set to 0 dBm and measurements are taken for several different distances and locations. The transmitter switches between the two antennas for every consecutive packet, thus eight different signal paths are recorded. A total of 15000 packets of size 119 bytes are transmitted for each location at an interval of 0.1 seconds. In the tests, we use the channel 26 of the IEEE 802.15.4 radio, which has the least frequency overlap with the IEEE 802.11 radio, to mitigate packet drop due to WLAN interference and other devices.

Packets are recorded with their RSSI value (Received Signal Strength Indicator) and an indication if the packet was correctly received with no bit errors, or dropped. These measurements differ from other similar measurements, e.g. (Kjesbu & Brunsvik, 2000), as the packet reception is measured, not only the received signal strength. Here, the same hardware as would be used in a real application is used, not a specialized measurement device, which could differ significantly from the signal reception capabilities of the actual device.

As an example, measurements performed in an industrial assembly hall are presented. In the industrial hall there are machines, racks of tools, and open spaces. Measurements are made in different parts of the hall, which can be categorized as light: open space, medium: mostly open with machines standing on the floor, and heavy: racks of tools obstructing the line-of-sight. The distances between the transmitter and receiver for the different measurements are in the range of 25-35 m.

The packet drop results from the industrial hall case are shown in Fig. 3. The packet drop probability varies from location to location and there is significant variation between the antenna pairs. This implies that the signal strength is very sensitive to the antenna location, due to multipath fading.

A common way to model a network with packet drops is the Gilbert-Elliott (G-E) model (Elliott, 1963; Gilbert, 1960), which is based on the Markov-chain. The G-E model has two states: one corresponding to good (G) and the other to bad (B) conditions, with separate packet drop probabilities in the good and bad state, $P(drop|G)=d_G$ and $P(drop|B)=d_B$, respectively. The transitions between the states follow a two-state Markov model. The state-transition matrix is given by

$$\mathbf{P}=\begin{bmatrix} p_{GG} & p_{GB} \\ p_{BG} & p_{BB} \end{bmatrix}, \quad \begin{matrix} p_{GB}=P(X(k)=B\,|\,X(k-1)=G), & p_{GG}=1-p_{GB} \\ p_{BG}=P(X(k)=G\,|\,X(k-1)=B), & p_{BB}=1-p_{BG} \end{matrix}, \tag{1}$$

where p_{GG} and p_{BB} are the state-holding, and p_{GB} and p_{BG} are the state-transition probabilities as illustrated in Fig. 2. The state residence time of state i is given by

$$T_{GE,i}=\frac{h}{1-p_{ii}}, \tag{2}$$

where h is the time-step of the Markov-chain. The average state probabilities of the G-E model are

$$\pi_G=\frac{p_{BG}}{p_{BG}+p_{GB}}, \quad \pi_B=\frac{p_{GB}}{p_{BG}+p_{GB}}, \tag{3}$$

and the mean packet drop is (Hohlfeld et al., 2008)

$$d_{GE}=\pi_G d_G+\pi_B d_B. \tag{4}$$

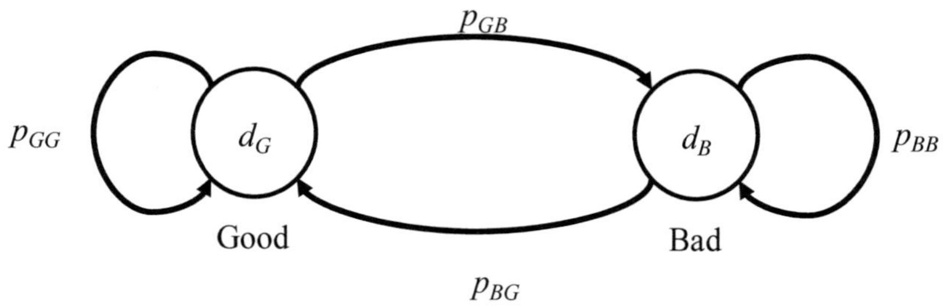

Fig. 2. Gilbert-Elliot model with states Good and Bad. State-transitions and probabilities indicated.

Based on the measurements performed in the industrial hall, Gilbert-Elliott packet drop models are identified from the data. The models are implemented to the ns-2 network simulator and they are later used in simulations to evaluate the effect of the radio environment to the control system performance. The model identification is a Hidden Markov Model fitting problem (Hohlfeld et al., 2008), where the observations, in this case the packet drops, are available and the underlying states and emission probabilities are estimated. The data from all the links are individually fitted to separate G-E models using the Baum-Welch algorithm (Baum et al, 1970).

Some identification results are illustrated in Fig. 4. In general, packet drop probability of the good state is low whereas the drop probability of the bad state is high and the time spent in the good state is longer than in the bad state. There are, however, large variations among the different links. Similar results are obtained for the other locations in the industrial hall. The radio environment for wireless automation is thus challenging and special protocols are needed to meet the real-time requirements.

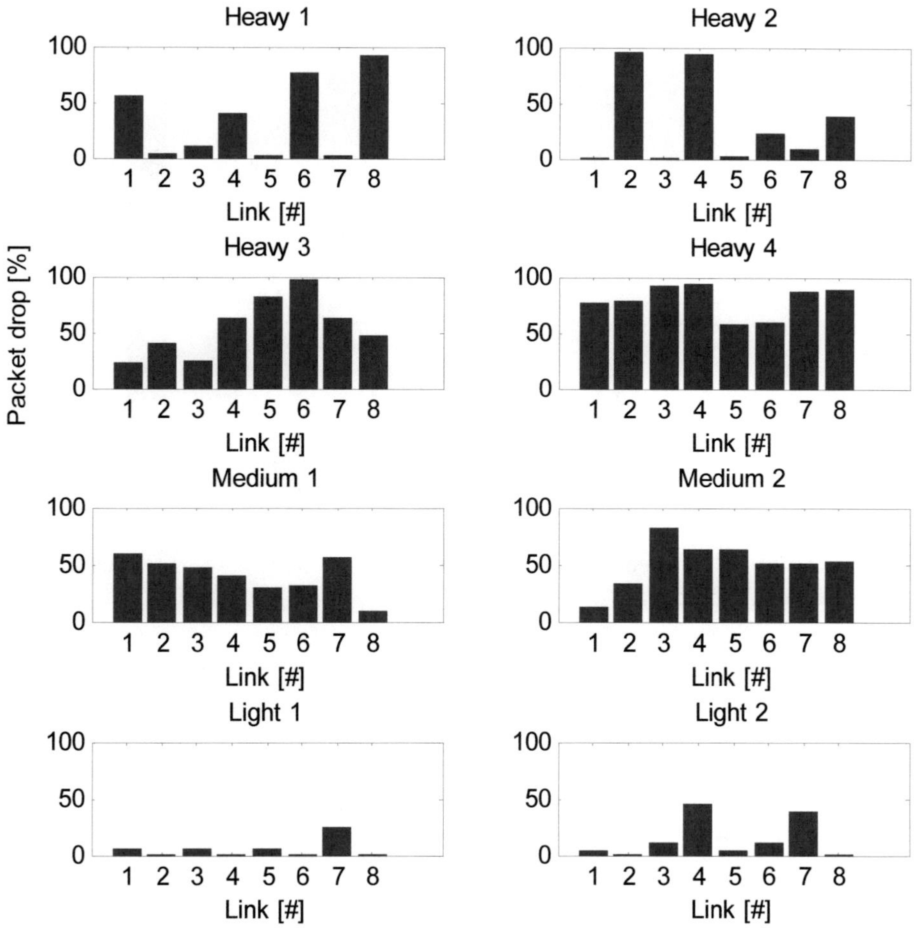

Fig. 3. Measured packet drop probability for different locations in an industrial hall. The probability is given for every antenna pair, ordered such that every odd numbered link represents a transmission from antenna 1.

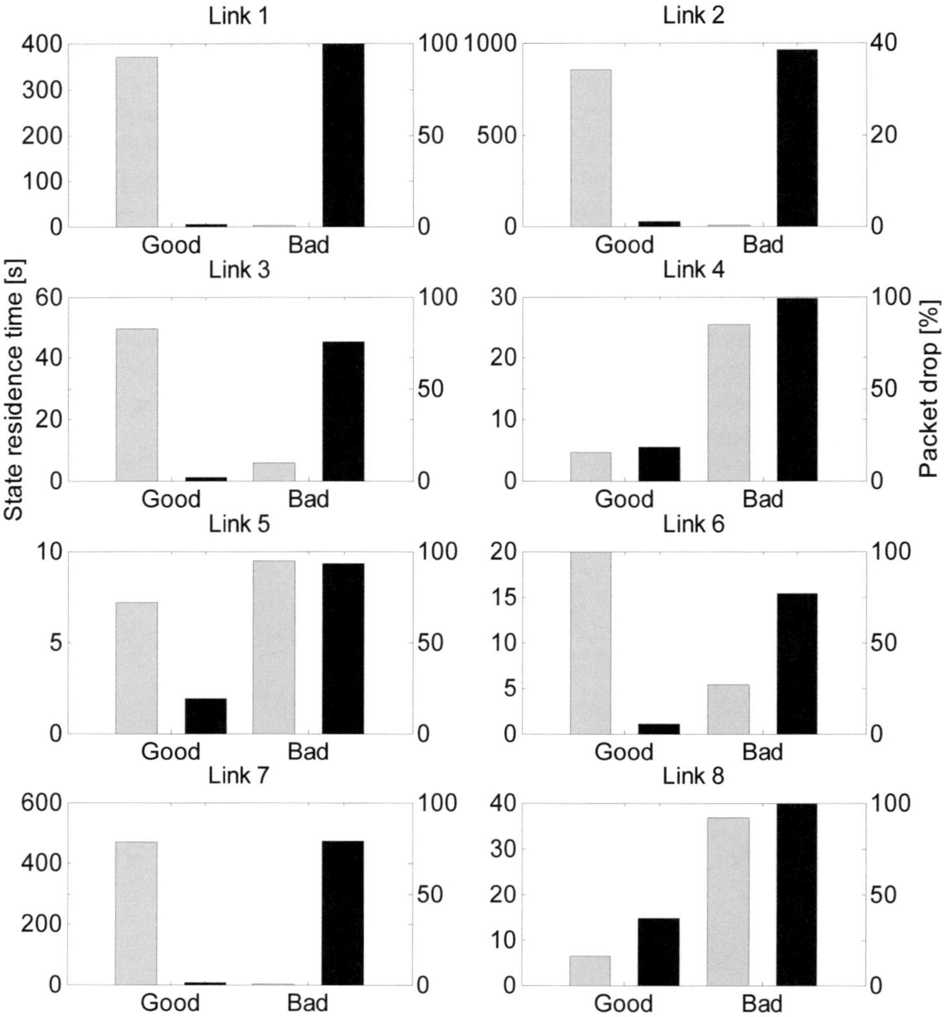

Fig. 4. Gilbert-Elliott model for each link. Grey bar indicates mean state-residence time (2) and black bar packet drop probability.

4.3 Enhancements to MAC and routing protocols for real-time communication

There are several methods to design the network protocols such that real-time requirements of the control application can be met. In general, to enable real-time operation, the handling of packet drop should be such that the retransmission has the highest probability to succeed. This is achieved with diversity: if the packet drop was caused by interference, it is likely that interference will continue and therefore retransmission is wise to do on another frequency. In general, the following diversity methods are available: frequency (channel hopping), time (retransmission), code, spatial (send to different node or with different antenna), which all should be optimally used.

Reliability and real-timeliness of wireless communication can be improved in many ways. Reliable hardware with powerful enough radio is the base for all wireless technology. However, reliable hardware itself does not guarantee reliable nor real-time communication, and instead the communication must be controlled and organized for optimal performance. The interest in using wireless sensor networks for real-time applications, such as process control, has grown during the recent years. Therefore, considerable research effort has been put into developing reliable real-time routing protocols, which also consider the computational limitations and energy constraints of the wireless devices. Some protocols, such as SPEED (He et al., 2003) and MM-SPEED (Felemban et al., 2006), are based on geographic routing mechanism. Both the protocols rely on position information of the nodes, which they receive via GPS. Optimal route is determined based on the distance between the source and destination and the time left to deliver the packet. In indoor situations, the location information should obviously be obtained by other means than the GPS. RTLD (Adel & Norsheila, 2008) takes a similar approach, but the localization of the nodes is done based on the RSSI-values and a path loss model of the environment. Yet, another similar protocol is proposed in (Abinash et al., 2006), the main difference being a prioritized MAC, where real-time packets have shorter backoffs and inter frame spaces (IFS) than other packets. Real-time and non-real-time packets also have different transmission queues and the real-time packets are sorted by an urgency factor. These sorts of solutions are suitable for large scale WSN, where the nodes are spread over a large area and distances between the nodes are long.

Another way to approach the problem is to make modifications on the MAC layer. Black Burst (BB) contention has been studied in (Sheu et al., 2004; Sobrinho & Krishnakumar, 1999). In BB contention the nodes jam the channel with pulses of energy, the duration of the pulse is relative to the time the nodes have been waiting for the access to the channel. The node which has been waiting for the longest time transmits a longer pulse than any of the other nodes and thus gains access to the channel. In (Sheu et al., 2004), additional modifications have been made to the MAC to deal with situations where several nodes have packets with same priority. After the BB contention a unique ID is given to each node and then the nodes transmit in a round robin manner based on the IDs. This sort of solution can be easily implemented on top of CSMA by substituting random backoffs with BB. However, the downside is that both energy and time are wasted for contending over the channel.

Both ODMRP (Lee et al., 2002) and AMRoute (Xie et al., 2002) take advantage of a multicast scheme. They are designed to be robust and reliable communication protocols for wireless ad hoc networks. In addition to multicast communication, both protocols utilize a mesh topology instead of a conventional tree type of network for improved reliability. Improved reliability is a result from the fact that even if the network topology changes, a mesh is more likely going to maintain some functional links between the nodes unlike a tree, where even one broken link will obstruct the communication. However, neither of the two protocols focuses on the network latency or real-timeliness and is therefore not suitable for control applications.

Since wireless control networks are typically limited in the number of nodes and the amount of data needed to be transmitted, the communication protocols need not to be ultimately scalable nor support high data rates. From this perspective, we have developed a robust communication protocol for real-time control applications called Limited Broadcast Protocol, which will be presented next. It has been implemented and tested on IEEE 802.15.4 compatible wireless sensor nodes, but it could also be applied on different radio network platforms after some adjustment of communication parameters.

4.4 Limited Broadcast Protocol

Limited Broadcast Protocol (LBP) is a wireless communication protocol designed for real-time control applications with limited size networks. It is designed for a scenario, where the

gateway needs to repeatedly collect new measurements from the nodes of a sensor network in a predefined time, which could be in the order of 50-500 ms. LBP takes advantage of mesh networking and broadcasting. In a dynamic environment a mesh network is relatively robust, since there could be several links between the different nodes. If one link fails then alternative routes can be used for delivering packets with minimal additional delay. All transmissions in LBP are broadcasted and in an ideal case every node is capable of receiving and forwarding any packet in the network. In this way, occasional link failures do not deteriorate the performance of the network. To meet the real-time requirements all transmissions are scheduled in time in order to avoid packet collisions and unnecessary retransmissions. Reliability is achieved by a smart retransmission system in addition to packet forwarding, piggybacking and multi-hop communication.
The protocol uses dedicated time slots for communication (i.e., TDMA). All communications between the nodes occur during a superframe (Fig. 5). The length of the superframe is determined by the maximum delay that can be tolerated in the system, i.e. the time in which all sensor values need to be collected by the gateway node. The superframe further consists of several repeating frames. Consequently, the length of a frame is determined by the number of nodes in the network and the length of the slot reserved for each of them. At the end of each frame, one extra slot is reserved for receiving late replies possibly generated by the CSMA as described below. A frame is repeated, within a superframe, as many times as necessary to receive a reply from all the nodes. However, if a superframe expires before all nodes have replied, there will be no more retransmissions and the data are lost. When all the nodes have replied a new superframe can be initiated.

<table>
<tr><td>GW</td><td>2</td><td>3</td><td>4</td><td>5</td><td></td><td>GW</td><td>2</td><td>3</td><td>4</td><td>5</td><td></td><td>GW</td><td>2</td><td>3</td><td>4</td><td>5</td><td></td><td>GW</td><td>2</td><td>3</td><td>4</td><td>5</td><td></td></tr>
<tr><td colspan="6">FRAME</td><td colspan="6">FRAME</td><td colspan="6">FRAME</td><td colspan="6">FRAME</td></tr>
<tr><td colspan="12">SUPERFRAME</td><td colspan="12">SUPERFRAME</td></tr>
</table>

Fig. 5. The superframe structure used in LBP. Numbered slots are reserved for particular nodes, and in the end of a frame, there is space for contention based communications.

This TDMA-like protocol can be implemented either on the top of a CSMA/CA MAC or the communications can be purely time-slotted (TDMA), in which case, though, the contention based slot in the end of a frame would be removed. If the protocol is implemented on the network layer on top of a CSMA/CA MAC, the collision avoidance, which ensures that the channel is free before attempting a transmission, of the underlying CSMA handles some packet collisions. This might be necessary if there are coexisting wireless networks operating in the same environment. Downside to this is that, occasionally, the CSMA can generate unwanted behaviour by delaying the transmission of a packet for such a long time that it overlaps the subsequent node's transmission slot. Therefore, backoff exponent and maximum number of backoffs should be tuned depending on the size of the network, in order to optimize the operation of the protocol in terms of performance and reliability. Also the transmission slot size has significant impact on the performance of the protocol.
The gateway (GW) starts a superframe by transmitting a command packet. Command packet contains operational instructions to all the nodes in the network. Every node that receives this packet replies by transmitting its latest measurement in the dedicated time slot. It needs to be emphasized that all transmissions are broadcasted so that each node can

receive all the information available in the network. Thus within the limits of maximum packet size, all available data that have not yet reached the gateway can be forwarded in the same packet by any node. This type of packet will be referred to as a status packet. If a node misses the first command packet from the gateway then any of the received status packets can be used as a reference (Fig. 6). All the replies are scheduled in time in order to minimize the possibility of collisions and the resultant packet drops. A node, including the gateway, is always either in receiving state or transmitting a packet. This ensures that critical data are not lost unless there are serious connectivity problems. The final time slot in each frame is reserved for contention based communications. This slot can be used by a node that has missed its own time slot during the frame, e.g., if it has no direct link to the gateway. Such nodes may transmit in this slot, and hence they do not need to wait for the next frame and their own slot in that.

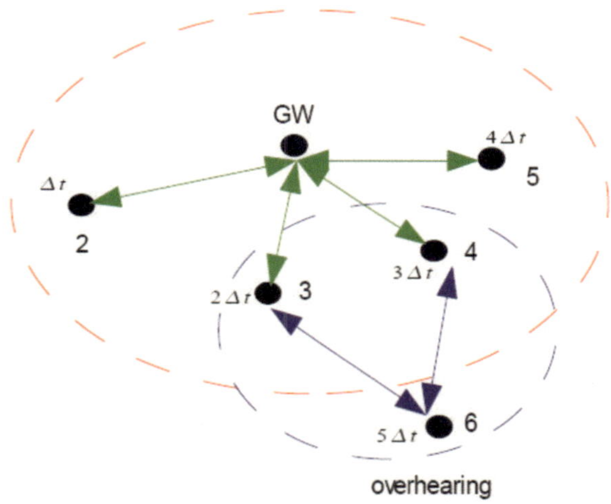

Fig. 6. In the case a node does not have direct link to the gateway, other nodes deliver the information in two ways by piggybacking.

If the gateway does not receive a reply from all the nodes during a frame, it initiates a retransmission cycle (second frame). It could be that momentarily one of the nodes is in a bad location, for example heavy machinery is obstructing the transmissions, so that it cannot receive any packets directly (as in Fig. 6). In this case, the gateway transmits a new command packet and the nodes react as described above. On the other hand, if some packets have reached other nodes, but have not yet been forwarded to the gateway, then the gateway requests the missing data from these nodes. The retransmission cycles are repeated until all data have reached the gateway or a superframe expires and the missing data are considered to be outdated and will be lost.

The LBP protocol was implemented on Sensinode's Micro series node, which is an IEEE 802.15.4 compatible wireless sensor node with CC2420 radio and MSP430 microcontroller. The protocol was tested in an industrial hall (20 m x 40 m) for two weeks with gateway unit and four other nodes. Some of the nodes were mobile, the environment was continuously changing and the time limit for the superframe was set to 500 ms. Furthermore, one of the nodes was located in a difficult position so that it could not always communicate directly with the gateway. Fig. 7 shows an example of a reply time histogram of this node (taken from a two hour operational period). It is seen in the figure that the gateway receives the measurements from this node most often in 14 - 45 ms. Such variance in the reply times indicates that the measurements are transmitted over some other nodes in the network due to the lack of direct connectivity. In the figure, replies received in 14 - 20 ms are the ones that are received directly, but the rest are dynamically routed over the mesh network.

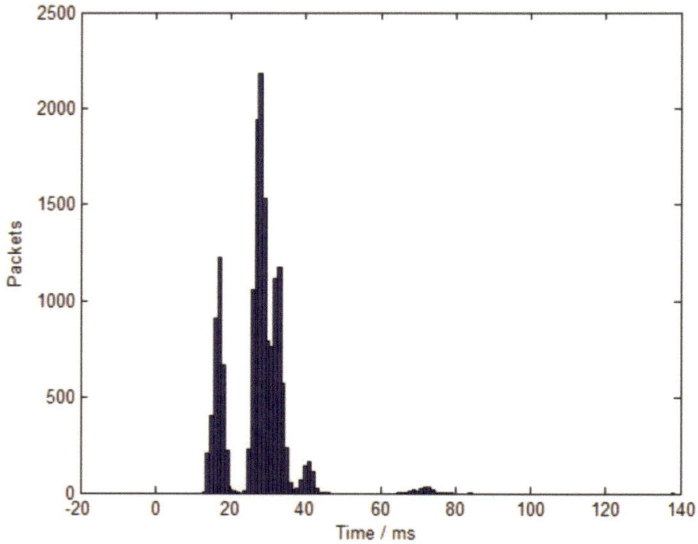

Fig. 7. Example histogram of the reply times of a particular node in a difficult location (node 6 in Fig. 6). Most of the replies go through other nodes.

During the test period, the protocol was run for approximately 750000 superframes. The gateway was able to receive the measurements from all the nodes in >99.91 % of the cases in <100 ms. Furthermore, it could receive all the data in >99.96 % of the cases in <500 ms. During the whole test period, over 6 % of all measurements from one of the nodes were transmitted through other nodes because of the lack of direct connectivity. Clearly the proposed protocol contributes to the reliability and real-timeliness required in wireless control systems, but further developments, such as integration of temporal, frequency and spatial diversity techniques, are needed to attain 100 % reliability.

5. Control design for wireless automation

Because of the networking challenges described previously, wireless real-time control is not straight-forward. In this section we describe some methods to compensate for the deficiencies of the network at the control layer. The main problem is to guarantee stability of the control system, even if the real-time operation of the network is occasionally compromised.

The schedule and retransmissions of the network used in wireless automation determine when information is available to the control system, and hence affect the control operation. There exists work where the actual network MAC protocol and related functions such as duty-cycle (Marco et al., 2010), or routing and schedule (Samii et al., 2009; Weiss et al., 2009) are taken into account in the control stability proof. These rely on a predetermined schedule, whereupon the controller stability is proven. Wireless communication is to some degree stochastic, so control stability proofs for randomly varying feedback delay are needed, such as the jitter margin presented next.

5.1 Jitter margin

Control with packet drops and varying delay stemming from a network is a complex case to be analyzed, because of the stochastic and time-varying nature of the problem. Ensuring stability of NCS has been under much research lately (Hespanha et al., 2006). Some results deal with optimal control (Lincoln & Bernhardsson, 2000), jump-linear Markov models (Xiao et al., 2000) and the jitter margin (Cervin et al., 2004; Kao & Lincoln, 2004).

The jitter margin defines the amount of additional delay that a control system can tolerate without becoming unstable. The delay may vary in any way, provided that it is bounded by the jitter margin δ_{max}. By selecting a tuning of a conventional controller such that the control loop has a positive jitter margin, the control loop is stable for network induced delay jitter and packet drop given by the jitter margin.

The jitter margin theorem states that in the continuous-time case, the closed-loop system with process $G(s)$ and controller $G_c(s)$ is stable for any additional delay $0 \le \delta(t) \le \delta_{\max}$ in the loop, if (Kao & Lincoln, 2004)

$$|G_{cl}(s)| = \left| \frac{G(j\omega)G_c(j\omega)}{1+G(j\omega)G_c(j\omega)} \right| < \frac{1}{\delta_{\max}\omega}, \quad \forall \omega \in [0,\infty[. \tag{5}$$

In the discrete-time case the criterion becomes

$$\left| \frac{G(e^{j\omega})G_c(e^{j\omega})}{1+G(e^{j\omega})G_c(e^{j\omega})} \right| < \frac{1}{N_{\max}\left|e^{j\omega}-1\right|}, \quad \forall \omega \in [0,\infty[\tag{6}$$

where

$$N_{\max} = \delta_{\max} / h \tag{7}$$

is the jitter margin in terms of sampling intervals N_{max} and h is the sampling interval of the controller. The mixed discrete-continuous-time case is the same as (6), provided that the sampling interval is chosen properly, i.e. sufficiently small, to prevent aliasing.

The jitter margin is in essence an extension to the phase margin (Kao & Lincoln, 2004). In case of only packet drop, the delay follows a sawtooth shape, and the Mirkin's lemma (Mirkin, 2007), which makes the jitter margin 57 % less conservative, can be used.

The jitter margin can be used in controller tuning to guarantee stability of a control loop with a varying delay. The above condition may be considered as a constraint in the controller parameter optimization problem, when the optimal controller parameters must satisfy the given jitter margin *requirement*, or then the jitter margin theorem can be formulated as an objective function, which leads to the maximization of the jitter margin. Alternatively, the controller tuning may be based on some known process parameters, and certain fixed tuning rules may be applied, but then it is important to study the obtained jitter margin with the specific tuning. Examples of such tuning rules and methods for the widely used PID controller are given in Table 1, based on the work in (Eriksson, 2008). It should be noted that many of these tuning rules and methods have the preferred property that the desired jitter margin is an input to the rules. The tuning adapts the PID gains to ensure a stable control system with individual packet drops, as far as the length of losses is less than δ_{max}. By increasing the jitter margin, the control becomes generally more conservative. The tuning rules allow the delay to vary in any way, which might introduce some conservativeness to the control design.

6. Co-design validation by simulation

In addition to the theoretical results, the simulation of WiNCSs is important and necessary for several reasons. Little is said in the literature about the practical implementation, behaviour, and performance of the wireless control systems. Simulations are a feasible way to test and evaluate the practical benefits of the developed theory and algorithms, where the critical properties and behavior of the network, and the impact on the control system can be analyzed. These issues, in particular the protocol specific ones, are hard to approach analytically. Simulation studies will, hopefully, unravel these matters and lead to a coherent theory, best practices knowledge, and design expertise of WiNCSs. To enable the simulation study of WiNCS, the network and control co-simulator PiccSIM has been developed. In the following section PiccSIM is described in more detail and some simulation cases are presented, that show the capabilities of PiccSIM and the benefits of co-simulation for WiNCSs design. The simulation cases involve multiple control loops, which cannot be studied without co-simulation.

6.1 PiccSIM

PiccSIM stands for *Platform for integrated communications and control design, simulation, implementation and modelling* (Nethi et al., 2007) and is developed at Aalto University School of Science and Technology (PiccSIM, 2010). PiccSIM integrates two simulators to achieve an accurate and versatile simulation system at both the communication and control level for WiNCSs.

It has the unique feature of delivering a whole chain of tools for network and control modelling and design, integrated into one package with communication and control co-simulation capabilities (Kohtamäki et al., 2009). The tools in PiccSIM range from the design of the system, through simulation and system testing, to implementation of a wireless control system.

The PiccSIM simulator is an integration of Matlab/Simulink where the dynamic system is simulated, including the control system, and ns-2 (ns-2, 2010) where the network simulation is done. The PiccSIM Toolchain (Kohtamäki et al., 2009), is a graphical user interface for network and control design, realised in Matlab. It is a front-end for the PiccSIM simulator and delivers the user access to all the PiccSIM modelling, simulation and implementation tools.

There are several reasons to build a co-simulation platform consisting of Matlab and ns-2. Matlab and Simulink are widely employed research tools used in dynamic system simulation, providing efficient tools for control design. Control engineers are accustomed to working in this environment. Ns-2, on the other hand, is the de facto standard tool for network simulation in the communication research community. Ns-2 simulates the network on a per packet basis, with models for physical layer, MAC, routing and transport protocols.

Method	Description	Process model	Tuning
Optimization	Jitter-aware controller tuning by constrained optimization	Any linear	$Min\ J(x)$ $s.t.\ \delta_{\max}(x) > \delta_0$
Optimization	Jitter-aware controller tuning by multi-objective optimization	Any linear	$Min\ \mathbf{J}(x)$ $\mathbf{J}(x) = \left[J(x) \quad 1/\delta_{\max}(x)\right]^T$
ACC rules	Simple tuning rules for stable processes. Process model possibly obtained by a simple step experiment.	The KLT model: $G(s) = \frac{K_p}{Ts+1}e^{-sL}$, $L,T \in [0.1, 10]$	$k_p = \frac{1}{K_p}\left(\frac{0.4T-0.04}{L}+0.16\right)$, $k_i = \frac{1}{100K_p}\left(\frac{-0.11T^3+1.5T^2-1.5}{L^2}+\frac{0.35T^2-4T+50}{L}\right)$, $k_d = \frac{1}{100K_p}\left(0.4T^2+11T\right)$.
Extended plant approach	Measurement filter re-design based on desired jitter margin, and standard AMIGO tuning on the extended plant.	The KLT model: $G(s) = \frac{K_p}{Ts+1}e^{-sL}$	$T_f = \begin{cases} \frac{1}{3}\delta_{\max}, & n=1 \\ \frac{1}{3\sqrt{n}}\left(\frac{n}{n-1}\right)^{(1-n)/2}\delta_{\max}, & n>1, \end{cases}$ for measurement filter time-constant T_f and order n.
Integrating processes	Optimal PID controller gain for a given jitter margin.	The FOLIPD model: $G(s) = \frac{k_v}{s(T_f s+1)}e^{-sL}$	$k_p = \frac{a}{k_v L},\ k_i = 0,\ k_d = \frac{aT_f}{k_v L}$, $a = \frac{0.947362L}{\delta_{\max}+0.634629L}$
Integrating processes	Maximized jitter margin and ITAE performance simultaneously.	The FOLIPD model: $G(s) = \frac{k_v}{s(T_f s+1)}e^{-sL}$	$k_p = \frac{10^{p(L,T_f)}}{k_v L},\ k_i = 0$, $k_d = \frac{T_f^{q(L,T_f)}}{k_v}10^{r(L)}$ $p(L,T_f) = 0.0027(T_f/L)^2 - 0.0794T_f/L - 0.34$, $q(L,T_f) = 0.02 + \left(0.51 - 0.076\log_{10}(T_f)\right)L^{0.15}$, $r(L) = 0.97 - 1.48L^{0.15}$.

Table 1. PID controller tuning methods for (wireless) networked control systems.

6.2 Other co-simulation tools

There are also other suitable simulators for WiNCSs, such as TrueTime (Cervin et al., 2003) and Modelica/ns-2 (Branicky et al., 2003). Perhaps the most well-known Simulink network blockset is TrueTime, which is actively developed at the Lund University, Sweden. It supports many network types (Wired: Ethernet, CAN, TDMA, FDMA, Round Robin, and switched Ethernet, and wireless: 802.11b WLAN and IEEE 802.15.4) and it is widely used to simulate wireless NCS (Andersson et al., 2005). TrueTime simulates only the physical and MAC layers. Besides the dynamic system simulation offered by Simulink, network node simulation includes simulation of real-time kernels. The user can write Matlab m-file functions that are scheduled and executed on a simulated CPU. Even ultrasound network and node battery simulation are included. In recent work, the simulation of a WirelessHART network is made possible by an extension of TrueTime (Biasi et al., 2008). The simulation uses frequency hopping and TDMA MAC protocol, but time-synchronization is not simulated and it is assumed to be perfect. The device table, routing, and communication schedule are specified by the user, so no network manager functionality is implemented.

The most relevant tool for WiNCS simulation besides PiccSIM, appears to be Modelica/ns-2 (Al-Hammouri et al., 2007). It is a very similar platform developed at the Case Western Reserve University (USA). As in PiccSIM, the network simulation is done in ns-2, but the plant dynamics and the control simulation are done in Modelica. Modelica is a general purpose dynamic system simulation software (Modelica, 2010).

Optimized Network Engineering Tool (OPNET) is a commercial package for general purpose detailed simulation and analysis of many different networks (Chang, 1999; OPNET, 2010). It is widely used and generally regarded as one of the best network simulator packages, and supports simulation of the physical link and the antennas. OPNET can be customized using the Proto-C language, but dynamic system simulation is not easily done. For other network simulators, mostly aimed at sensor networks, see e.g. (Curren, 2005).

6.3 PiccSIM architecture

The PiccSIM simulator consists basically of two computers on a local area network (LAN): the Simulink computer for system simulation, including plant dynamics, signal processing and control algorithms, and the ns-2 computer for network simulation. For further details see (Nethi et al., 2007), where the integration of ns-2 and Simulink is reported, and (Kohtamäki et al., 2009; Pohjola et al., 2005).

Packets sent over the simulated network are routed through the ns-2 computer, which simulates the network in ns-2 according to any TCL script specification generated automatically by a network configuration tool. Simulation time-synchronization is performed between the computers. To close the gap between the simulators, a data exchange mechanism is implemented, which can pass information from one simulator to the other. This enables the simulation of cross-layer protocols that take advantage of information from the other application layers. An example where the data exchange mechanism can be used is with mobile scenarios, where the location of the nodes and further the network topology depends on the application operation, for instance, in applications of robotics and moving machinery.

6.4 Crane control simulation case

In this section the communication and control co-simulation is demonstrated with PiccSIM, where the impact of the network protocol on the control performance is shown. The benefits of the LBP protocol presented above are demonstrated in a real-time control case, where we simulate an operator driving a trolley crane. The operator gives the velocity reference for the crane with a wireless handheld device. The control messages are routed over a local wireless IEEE 802.15.4 network installed on the crane.

The laboratory scale crane model presented in (Eriksson et al., 2006) is scaled up by a factor of ten and used in the simulation cases. The crane control system consists of PID controllers for the trolley and hoist motors, which operate the actuators based on the velocity reference given by the operator through the wireless handheld device. For simulation purposes the operator is represented by PID controllers for the vertical and horizontal movement of the load. For load swing compensation, the human transfer function identified in (Tervo et al., 2009) is used. The load of the crane is moved according to a predefined trajectory, given as reference to the "operator controllers". In the case of packet drop, the velocity reference is set to zero at the receiving side. The above presented Gilbert-Elliot packet drop models that have been identified based on extensive tests in a real industrial hall are used in the simulations.

To assess the impact of the network QoS on the control performance, simulations with different network QoS parameters are made. Several load movement trajectories are simulated with different Gilbert-Elliott network model parameters. The resulting control performances, each averaged over ten runs, are shown in Fig. 8. Obviously, at high packet drop rates the control performance is significantly decreased, but the results also show that it is extremely difficult to predict the effects of packet drops on the control performance without extensive simulations that include the network and dynamical system models.

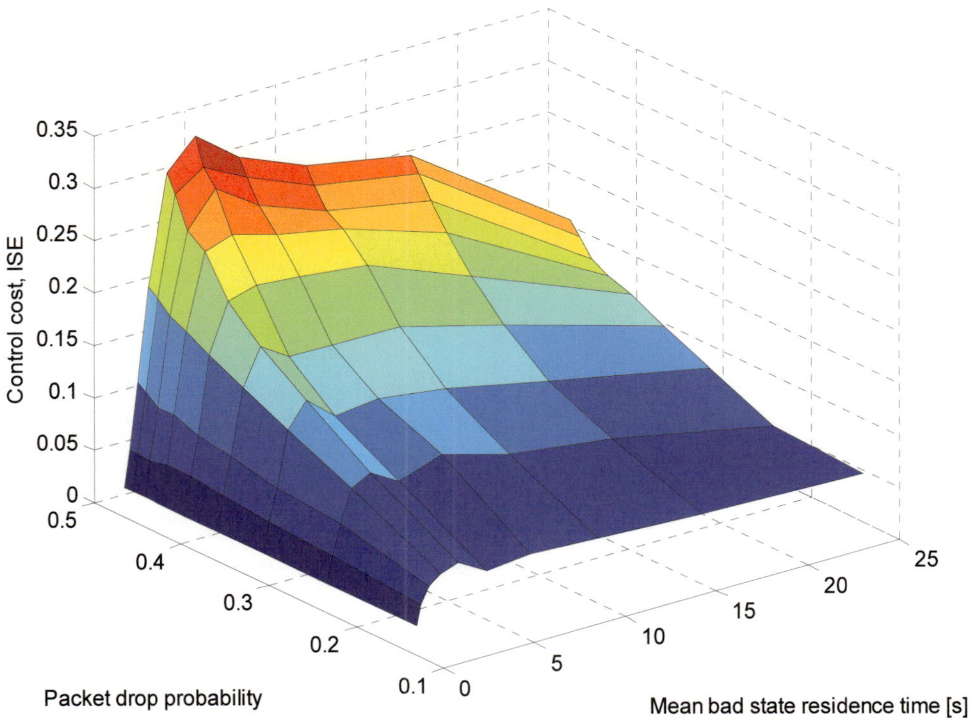

Fig. 8. Integral square error of load swing as function of Gilbert-Elliot parameters.

Then the control result when using the LBP is compared to the case of single transmission and no retry. In the simulations, to model the packet drop, data gathered during the LBP tests in the industrial hall is used. An example of the load angle swing is given in Fig. 9, where the swing is clearly compensated better when LBP is used compared to the case of single transmissions. The oscillations are due to control packet drop, when trying to compensate for the swing. This shows how the wireless control performance can be evaluated by using network simulation and data from real environments. The specific network protocol issues can be studied and design for real-time wireless control can be made with co-simulation using PiccSIM.

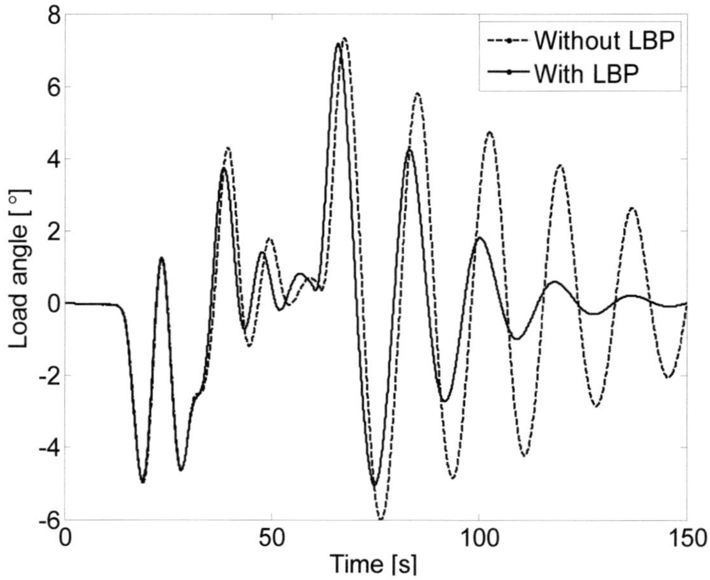

Fig. 9. Load angle swing when moving load. Communication when using LBP and without.

7. Conclusions

In this chapter, we have discussed the different technologies and methodologies enabling reliable and real-time wireless automation. The industrial environment is difficult for the use of wireless technologies, but there are currently many serious efforts in trying to achieve the level of reliability of wired communications by wireless networks. Some of these efforts have emerged recently into standards of wireless automation, e.g. WirelessHART and ISA100.11a. Besides the technology review, we proposed a communication protocol LBP for real-time networking in limited size wireless networks. The protocol can effectively take advantage of mesh networking and hence change the routing dynamically upon link failures. This is a prerequisite when operating in harsh industrial environments with real-time applications. In the end of the chapter, we presented the PiccSIM co-simulation platform and demonstrated the benefits and capabilities of such a simulator. In WiNCS, analytical results are rarely available regarding the stability of a large-scale system and hence co-simulation may reveal the problems in the design of either networking or control. Furthermore, via simulation greater insight into the behaviour and interactions of communications and control could be obtained.

8. References

Abinash, M.; Kumar, A. & Dharma, P.A. (2006). QoS and energy aware routing for real-time traffic in wireless sensor networks. *Computer Comm.*, Vol. 29, pp. 437-445

Adel, A.A. & Norsheila, F. (2008). A real-time routing protocol with load distribution in wireless sensor networks. *Computer Comm.*, Vol. 31, pp. 3190–3203

Akyildiz, I.F.; Weilian, S.; Sankarasubramaniam, Y. & Cayirci, E. (2002). Wireless sensor networks: A survey. *Computer Networks*, Vol. 38, Iss. 4

Al-Hammouri, A.T.; Liberatore, V.; Al-Omari, H.; Al-Qudah, Z.; Branicky, M.S. & Agrawal, D. (2007). A co-simulation platform for actuator networks, *Proceedings of ACM Conference on Embedded Networked Sensor Systems*, Sydney

Akkaya, K. & Younis, M. (2005). A survey on routing protocols for wireless sensor networks. *Ad Hoc Networks*, Vol. 3, Iss. 3, pp. 325-349

Andersson, M.; Henriksson, D.; Cervin, A. & Årzén, K.-E. (2005). Simulation of wireless networked control systems, *Proceedings of 44th IEEE Conference on Decision and Control and European Control Conference*, Seville, Spain

Antsaklis, P. & Baillieul, J. (Eds.) (2004). Special issue on networked control systems, *IEEE Transactions on Automatic Control*, Vol. 49, No. 9, pp. 1421–1597

Baronti, P.; Pillai, P.; Chook, V.W.C.; Chessa, S.; Gotta, A. & Hu, Y.F. (2007). Wireless sensor networks: A survey on the state of the art and the 802.15.4 and ZigBee standards. *Computer Comm.*, Vol. 30, Iss. 7, pp. 1655-1695

Baum, L. E.; Petrie, T.; Soules, G. & Weiss, N. (1970). A maximization technique occurring in the statistical analysis of probabilistic functions in Markov chains. *The Annals of Mathematical Statistics*, Vol. 41, No. 1, pp. 164–171

Biasi, M. De; Snickars, C.; Landernäs, K. & Isaksson, A.J. (2008). Simulation of process control with WirelessHART networks subject to packet losses, *Proceedings of IEEE International Conference on Automation Science and Engineering*

Björkbom, M.; Nethi, S.; Eriksson, L.M. & Jäntti, R. (2010). *Wireless control system design and co-simulation*, submitted manuscript

Branicky, M.S.; Liberatore, V. & Phillips, S.M. (2003). Networked control system co-simulation for co-design, *Proceedings of American Control Conference*, Vol. 4, pp. 3341-3346

Brooks, T. (2001). Wireless technology for industrial sensor and control networks, *Proceedings of Sensors for Industry Conference*, Rosemount, Illinois, USA

Cervin, A.; Henriksson, D.; Lincoln, B.; Eker, J. & Årzén, K.-E. (2003). How does control timing affect performance? *IEEE Control Systems Magazine*, Vol. 23, Iss. 3, pp. 16-30

Cervin, A.; Lincoln, B.; Eker, J.; Årzén, K.-E. & Buttazzo, G. (2004). The jitter margin and its application in the design of real-time control systems, *Proceedings of 10th International Conference on Real-Time and Embedded Computing Systems and Applications*, Göteborg, Sweden

Chang, X. (1999). Network simulations with OPNET, *Proceedings of 1999 Winter Simulation Conference*, Vol. 1, pp. 307-314, Phoenix, AZ, USA

Curren, D. (2005). *A survey of simulation in sensor networks*, Project report, University of Binghamton

Elliott, E.O. (1963). Estimates of error rates for codes on burst-noise channels. *Bell System Technical Journal*, No. 42, pp. 1977–1997

Eriksson, L.; Hölttä, V. & Misol, M. (2006). Modeling, simulation and control of a laboratory-scale trolley crane, *Proceedings of 47th Conference on Simulation and Modelling*, Helsinki, Finland

Eriksson, L. (2008). *PID controller design and tuning in networked control systems*, Doctoral thesis, Helsinki University of Technology, Finland

Felemban, E.; Lee, C. & Ekici, E. (2006). MMSPEED: Multipath multi-SPEED protocol for QoS guarantee of Reliability and timeliness in wireless sensor network. *IEEE Trans. Mobile Comput.*, Vol. 5, No. 6, pp. 738–754

Gilbert, E.N. (1960). Capacity of a burst-noise channel. *Bell System Technical Journal*, No. 39, pp. 1253–1265

Goldsmith, A. (2004). *Wireless communication*, Cambridge University Press, Cambridge, UK

Gungor, V.C. & Hancke, G.P. (2009). Industrial wireless sensor networks: challenges, design principles, and technical approaches. *IEEE Transactions on Industrial Electronics*, Vol. 56, No. 10

Gupta, V.; Hassibi, B. & Murray, R.M. (2007). Optimal LQG control across packet-dropping links. *Systems & Control Letters*, Vol. 56, Iss. 6, pp 439-446

He, T.; Stankovic, J.; Lu, C. & Abdelzaher, T. (2003). SPEED: a stateless protocol for real -time communication in sensor networks, *Proceedings of ICDCS*, pp. 46–55

Hespanha, J.; Naghshtabrizi, P. & Xu, Y. (2006). A survey of recent results in networked control systems. *Proceedings of the IEEE*, Special Issue on Networked Control Systems Technology, Vol. 95, No. 1, pp. 138-162

Hohlfeld, O.; Geib, R. & Haßlinger, G. (2008). Packet loss in real-time services: Markovian models generating QoE impairments, *Proceedings of 16th International Workshop on Quality of Service*, pp. 239–248

ISA100 (2010). *Wireless Systems for Automation*, online: http://www.isa.org/isa100/

Kao, C.-Y. & Lincoln, B. (2004). Simple stability criteria for systems with timevarying delays. *Automatica*, Vol. 40, pp. 1429-1434

Karlof, C.; Sastry, N. & Wagner, D. (2004). TinySec: a link layer security architecture for wireless sensor networks, *Proceedings of 2nd International Conference on Embedded Networked Sensor Systems*, pp. 162 - 175, Baltimore, MD, USA

Kintner-Meyer, M. (2005). Opportunities of wireless sensors and controls for building operation. *Journal of Energy Engineering*, Vol. 102, Iss. 5, pp 27-48

Kjesbu, S. & Brunsvik, T. (2000). Radiowave propagation in industrial environments, *Proceedings of 26th Annual Conference of the IEEE Industrial Electronics Society*, Vol. 4, Nagoya, Japan

Kohtamäki, T.; Pohjola, M.; Brand, J. & Eriksson, L.M. (2009). PiccSIM Toolchain - Design, simulation and automatic implementation of wireless networked control systems, *Proceedings of IEEE International Conference on Networking, Sensing and Control*, Okayama, Japan

Koumpis, K.; Hanna, L.; Andersson, M. & Johansson, M. (2005). Wireless industrial control and monitoring beyond cable replacement, *Proceedings of PROFIBUS International Conference*, Coombe Abbey, Warwickshire, UK

Kumar, P.R. (2001). New technological vistas for systems and control: the example of wireless networks. *IEEE Control Systems Magazine*, Vol. 21, Iss. 1, pp. 24-37

Lee, S.-J.; Su, W. & Gerla, M. (2002). On-Demand Multicast Routing Protocol in Multihop Wireless Mobile Networks. *Mobile Networks and Applications*, Vol. 7, pp. 441–453

Lennvall, T.; Svensson, S. & Hekland, F. (2008). A comparison of WirelessHART and Zigbee for industrial applications, *Proceedings of 7th IEEE International Workshop on Factory Communication Systems*

Lian, F.-L.; Moyne, J.R. & Tilbury, D.M. (2001). Performance evaluation of control networks: Ethernet, ControlNet, and DeviceNet. *IEEE Control Systems Magazine*, Vol. 21, No. 1, pp. 66–83

Lian, F.-L.; Moyne, J. & Tilbury, D. (2002). Network design consideration for distributed control systems. *IEEE Transactions on Control Systems Technology*, Vol. 10, No. 2

Lian, F.-L.; Yook, J.K.; Tilbury, D.M. & Moyne, J. (2006). Network architecture and communication modules for guaranteeing acceptable control and communication performance for networked multi-agent systems. *IEEE Transactions on Industrial Informatics*, Vol. 2, No. 1

Lincoln, B. & Bernhardsson, B. (2000). Optimal control over networks with long random delays, *Proceedings of 14th International Symposium on Mathematical Theory of Networks and Systems*, Laboratoire de Théorie des Systèmes, University of Perpignan

Liu, X. & Goldsmith, A. (2003). Wireless medium access control in networked control systems, *Proceedings of 42nd Conference on Decision and Control*

Marco, P. Di; Park, P.; Fischione, C. & Johansson, K. H. (2010). TREnD: a timely, reliable, energy-efficient and dynamic WSN protocol for control applications, *Proceedings of IEEE International Conference on Communications*, Cape Town, South Africa

Mirkin, L. (2007). Some remarks on the use of time-varying delay to model sample-and-hold circuits. *IEEE Transactions on Automatic Control*, Vol. 52, Iss. 6, pp. 1109-1112

Modelica (2010). Modelica and the Modelica Association, online: http://www.modelica.org.

Moyne, J.R. & Tilbury, D.M. (2007). The emergence of industrial control networks for manufacturing control, diagnostics, and safety data. *Proceedings of the IEEE*, Vol. 95, Iss. 1

Mustard, S. (2006). Security of distributed control systems: the concern increases. *The IEE Computing & Control Engineering*, Vol. 16, Iss. 6

Nebot, E.M.; Bozorg, M. & Durrant-Whyte, H.F. (1999). Decentralized architecture for asynchronous sensors. *Journal of Autonomous Robots*, Kluwer Academic Publishers, Boston, Vol. 6, No. 2, pp. 147-164

Nethi, S.; Pohjola, M.; Eriksson, L. & Jäntti, R. (2007). Platform for emulating networked control systems in laboratory environments, *Proceedings of 8th International Symposium on a World of Wireless, Mobile and Multimedia Networks*, Helsinki, Finland

Neumann, P. (2007). Communication in industrial automation—What is going on? *Control Engineering Practice*, Special Issue on Manufacturing Plant Control: Challenges and Issues, Vol. 15, Iss. 11, pp. 1332-1347

Nilsson, J. (1998). *Real-time control systems with delays*, Ph.D. dissertation, Lund Institute of Technology

Nixon, M.; Chen, D.; Blevins, T. & Mok, A.K. (2008). Meeting control performance over a wireless mesh network, *Proceedings of 4th IEEE Conference on Automation Science and Engineering*, Washington DC, USA, pp. 540-547

ns-2 (2010). The Network Simulator,
online: http://www.isi.edu/nsnam/ns/ and
http://nsnam.isi.edu/nsnam/index.php/Main_Page.

OPNET (2010). OPNET Technologies.
Online: http://www.opnet.com.

Paradiso, J.A. & Starner, T. (2005). Energy scavenging for mobile and wireless electronics. *IEEE Pervasive Computing*, Vol. 4, No. 1, pp. 18-27

Pellegrini, F. De; Miorandi, D.; Vitturi, S. & Zanella, A. (2006). On the use of wireless networks at low level of factory automation systems. *IEEE Transactions on Industrial Informatics*, Vol. 2, Iss. 2, pp. 129-143

PiccSIM (2010). Online:
http://autsys.tkk.fi/en/Control/PiccSIM

Pohjola, M.; Eriksson, L.; Hölttä, V. & Oksanen, T. (2005). Platform for monitoring and controlling educational laboratory processes over Internet, *Proceedings of 16th IFAC World Congress*, Prague, Czech Republic

Prasad, A.R.; Prasad, N.R.; Kamerman, A.; Moelard, H. & Eikelenboom, A. (2001). Performance evaluation, system design and network deployment of IEEE 802.11. *Wireless personal communications*, Vol. 1, Iss. 19, pp. 57 - 79

Samii, S.; Cervin, A.; Eles, P. & Peng, Z. (2009). Integrated scheduling and synthesis of control applications on distributed embedded systems, *Proceedings of ACM IEEE Design, Automation & Test in Europe*, pp. 57–62

Scheible, G.; Dacfey, D.; Endresen, J. & Frey, J.-E. (2007). Unplugged but connected - design and implementation of a truly wireless real-time sensor/actuator Interface. *IEEE Industrial Electronics Magazine*, Vol. 1, No. 2, pp. 25-34

Sheu, J-P.; Liu, C-H.; Wu, S-L. & Tseng, Y-C. (2004). A Priority MAC Protocol to Support Real-Time Traffic in Ad Hoc Networks. *Wireless Networks*, Vol. 10, pp. 61–69

Sinopoli, B.; Schenato, L.; Franceschetti, M.; Poolla, K.; Jordan, M.I. & Sastry, S.S. (2004). Kalman filtering with intermittent observations. *IEEE Transactions on Automatic Control*, Vol. 49, Iss. 9, pp. 1453-1464

Sobrinho, J.L. & Krishnakumar, A.S. (1999). Quality-of-Service in Ad Hoc Carrier Sense Multiple Access Wireless Networks. *IEEE J. on Selected Areas in Comm.*, Vol. 17, No. 8, pp. 1353–1368

Song, J.; Han, S.; Mok, A.K.; Chen, D.; Lucas, M.; Nixon, M. & Prat, W. (2008). WirelessHART: Applying wireless technology in real-time industrial process control, *Proceedings of IEEE Real-Time and Embedded Technology and Applications Symposium*

Steigmann, R. & Endresen, J. (2006). *Introduction to WISA*, White Paper, V2.0, ABB

Tervo, K.; Bocca, M.; Eriksson, L.M. & Manninen, A. (2009). Wireless joystick control for human adaptive mechatronics applications: case trolley crane, *Proceedings of IEEE International Conference on Networking, Sensing and Control*, pp. 19-24, Okayama, Japan

TSMP (2010). Technical overview of time synchronized mesh protocol (TSMP), Dust Networks, online:
http://www.dustnetworks.com/docs/TSMP_Whitepaper.pdf

Velasco, M.; Fuertes, J.M.; Lin, C.; Marti, P. & Brandt, S. (2004). A control approach to bandwidth management in networked control systems, *Proceedings of 30th Annual Conference of IEEE Industrial Electronics Society*, Vol. 3

Weiss, G.; D'Innocenzo, A.; Alur, R.; Johansson, K.H. & Pappas, G.J. (2009). Robust stability of multi-hop control networks, *Proceedings of Joint 48th IEEE Conference on Decision and Control and 28th Chinese Control Conference Shanghai*, P.R. China

Werb, J.; Newman, M.; Berry, V.; Lamb, S.; Sexton, D. & Lapinski, M. (2005). Improved quality of service in IEEE 802.15.4 mesh networks, *Proceedings of International Workshop on Wireless and Industrial Automation*, San Francisco

Wheeler, A. (2007). Commercial applications of wireless sensor networks using ZigBee. *IEEE Communications Magazine*, Vol. 45, Iss. 4, pp. 70-77

Willig, A.; Kubisch, M.; Hoene, C. & Wolisz, A. (2002). Measurements of a wireless link in an industrial environment using an IEEE 802.11-compliant physical layer. *IEEE Transactions on Industrial Electronics*, Vol. 49, Iss. 6

Willig, A.; Matheus, K. & Wolisz, A. (2005). Wireless technology in industrial networks. *Proceedings of the IEEE*, Vol. 93, Iss. 6, pp. 1130-1151

Willig, A. & Mitschke, R. (2006). Result of bit error measurements with sensor nodes and casuistic consequences for the design of energy-efficient error control schemes, *Proceedings of 3rd European Workshop on Sensor Networks*, Lecture Notes in Computer Science, Vol. 3868, pp. 310-325

Willig, A. (2008). Recent and emerging topics in wireless industrial communications: A selection. *IEEE Transactions of Industrial Informatics*, Vol. 4, Iss. 2

WirelessHART (2010).
online: http://www.hartcomm2.org/hart_protocol/
wireless_hart/wireless_hart_main.html

Xiao, L.; Hassabi, A. & How, J. P. (2000). Control with random communication delays via a discrete-time jump system approach, *Proceedings of American Control Conference*, Chicago, Illinois

Xie, J.; Talpade, R. R.; Mcauley, A. & Liu, M. (2002). AMRoute: Ad Hoc Multicast Routing Protocol. *Mobile Networks and Applications*, Vol. 7, pp. 429–439

ZigBee (2006). IEEE 802.15.4-2006, IEEE Standard for Information Technology, Telecommunications and information exchange between systems - Local and metropolitan area networks - Specific requirements, Part 15.4: wireless medium access control (MAC) and physical layer (PHY) specifications for low-rate wireless personal area networks (WPANs), IEEE Computer Society, New York, USA. ZigBee Alliance online:
http://www.zigbee.org.

Erp Concept for Enterprise Management and Knowledge Management Era

Ivona Vrdoljak Raguž
University of Dubrovnik
Croatia

1. Introduction

Development of information and communication technologies has influenced the evolution of all kinds of computer applications in the organization. At the same time external environment and phenomenon of globalisation have become more complex with new requires and conditions for enterprises. In that context, effective information system has become necessity for every organization in order to increase competitiveness by cutting down costs through better logistics. In these circumstances enterprises have two challenges: to create and implement an infrastructure for information technologies with applications for storing and sharing information and to effectively use these information for decision making process. Success for enterprises depends upon a significant flow of information and goods in the supply chain, client relationship and the ability to perform e-business (Vuković et al., 2007). E-business is concerned specifically with information systems solution packages used by enterprises for e-business transaction purposes for meeting customer requirements in Business-to-Business (B2B) and Business-to-Consumer (B2C) exchanges. Popular among the e-business applications for B2B are Supply Chain Management (SCM) and Enterprise Resource Planning (ERP) systems and may include online purchase or procurement between customer and supplier. For B2C e-business application the best example is Customer Relationship Management (CRM) system.

Information technology includes all matters concerned with the computer science and technology, design, development, installation and implementation of information systems and applications. IT is a framework for achieving strategic goals of an enterprise that incorporates a variety of commercial software packages that are related to various areas of an organisation such as finance, accounting, human resources, inventory, procurement and customer service. It is recognized that the ability to provide right information at the right time brings a great advantage to the world of complex business relationships and competitiveness.

ERP as an enterprise-wide set of management tools that balance demand and supply, having the ability to link customers and suppliers into a complete supply chain, to employ proven business processes for decision-making, and to provide high degrees of cross-functional integration among sales, marketing, manufacturing, operations, logistics, purchasing, finance, new product development, and human resources, thereby enabling people to run their business with high levels of customer service and productivity, and to simultaneously lower costs and inventories, while providing the foundation for effective e-commerce (Wallace & Krezmar 2001).

ERP as an e-business application for B2B allow the organisation to better understand its business, resources and plan for the future (the popular ERP packages in the market are: SAP, BAAN, Oracle Financials JD Edwards and People soft).
The purpose of this paper is to explore ERP concept and its implementation in enterprises. The research framework examines importance of ERP concept and its implementation as a main factor for competitiveness for large Croatian enterprises. The result of the research reveals that the ERP systems are not insufficiently used in large Croatian enterprises. Details of the results, implications of the findings, and conclusions are presented and discussed. The present study provides a starting - point for further research of implementation process of ERP systems in Republic of Croatia.

2. ERP historical perspectives

The evolution of ERP systems is a reflection of added layers of functionality to its germ-cell Materials Requirements Planning (MRP) of the 70's. Manufacturing Resource Planning (MRP II) emerged in the 80's and then followed by Enterprise Resource Planning (ERP) systems in the 90's and ERP II in the 2000's (see Table 1). ERP offers one integrated solution that aligns information technology and business processes into one repository. The ERP progression parallels the development of the economy, which was considerably instituted on the tangible assets during the 70's. But, over time this dependency gradually skewed towards the intangible assets and intellectual capital.

1960s Enterprise Resource Planning (ERP) is born in the early 1960s from a joint effort between J.I. Case, the manufacturer of tractors and other construction machinery, and partner IBM. Material Requirements Planning or MRP is the initial effort. This application software serves as the method for planning and scheduling materials for complex manufactured products.
1970s Initial MRP solutions are big, clumsy and expensive. They require a large technical staff to support the mainframe computers on which they run.
1972 Five engineers in Mannheim, Germany begin the company, SAP (Systemanalyse und Programmentwicklung). The purpose in creating SAP is to produce and market standard software for integrated business solutions.1975 Richard Lawson, Bill Lawson, and business partner, John Cerullo begin Lawson Software. The founders see the need for pre-packaged enterprise technology solutions as an alternative to customized business software applications.1976 In the manufacturing industry, MRP (Material Requirements Planning) becomes the fundamental concept used in production management and control.
1977 Jack Thompson, Dan Gregory, and Ed McVaney form JD Edwards. Each founder takes part of their name to create the company moniker. Larry Ellison begins Oracle Corporation.
1978 Jan Baan begins The Baan Corporation to provide financial and administrative consulting services.
1979 Oracle offers the first commercial SQL relational database management system.
1980 JD Edwards begins focusing on the IBM System/38 in the early 1980s. MRP (Manufacturing Resources Planning) evolves into MRP-II as a more accessible extension to shop floor and distribution management activities.
1981 Baan begins to use Unix as their main operating system.
1982 Baan delivers its first software product. JD Edwards focuses on the IBM System/38.

1983 Oracle offers both a VAX mode database as well as a database written entirely in C (for portability).
1984 Baan shifts the focus of their development to manufacturing.
1985 JD Edwards is recognized as an industry-leading supplier of applications software for the highly successful IBM AS/400 computer, a direct descendant of the System/38.
1987 PeopleSoft is founded by Dave Duffield and Ken Morris in 1987.
1988 PeopleSoft's Human Resource Management System (HRMS) is developed.
1990 Baan software is rolled out to 35 countries through indirect sales channels. The term ERP (Enterprise Resource Planning) is coined in the early 1990's when MRP-II is extended to cover areas like Engineering, Finance, Human Resources, and Project Management.
1991 PeopleSoft sets up offices in Canada. This leads the way to their presence in Europe, Asia, Africa, Central and South America, and the Pacific Rim.
1995 Baan grows to more than 1,800 customers worldwide and over 1,000 employees.
1999 JD Edwards has more than 4,700 customers with sites in over 100 countries. Oracle has 41,000 customers worldwide (16,000 U.S.). PeopleSoft software is used by more than 50 percent of the human resources market. SAP is the world's largest inter-enterprise software company and the world's fourth largest independent software supplier overall. SAP employs over 20,500 people in more than 50 countries. To date, more than 2,800 of Baan's enterprise systems have been implemented at approximately 4,800 sites around the world.
2001 - 9/11 occurs creating a drop in demand for new ERP systems
2002 Most ERP systems are enhancing their products to become "Internet Enabled" so that customers worldwide can have direct access to the supplier's ERP system.
2004 - Services Oriented Architecture (SOA) becomes a standard that ERP vendors work towards. This software architecture allows different systems to communicate between one another.
2003-2005 Industry consolidation occurs: Oracle - E-Business Suite, JD Edwards, Peoplesoft, and Seibel Microsoft - Navision, Axapta, Great Plains, and Solomon Infor - Baan, Mapics, and a slew of other products Sage - Best Software is acquired The consolidations continue to occur and the key players (SAP, Oracle, Infor and Microsoft) continue to build out their products. The next phase of ERP systems will be the merged products, including Oracle's Fusion and Microsoft's project green's end product.

Table 1. ERP history (www.erpandmore.com)

2.1 Phase 1: Manufacturing integration (MRP)

MRP systems were developed in the '70s. MRP is connected with simple production operations. It represents a more advanced concept of earlier efforts to process the bill of materials. The inventors of MRP were looking for a better method for ordering material, and they found it in that concept. The basic concept for planning material requirements is based upon the four questions which represent its logic (Vuković et al., 2007):

- What are we going to make?
- What does it take to make it?
- What do we have?
- What do we have to get?

These four questions are called the universal manufacturing equation. It has a logic that is applied in production enterprises. MRP simulates the universal manufacturing equation. It uses the master schedule to answer the question what are we going to make, the bill of material to answer the question what does it take to make it, and inventory records to answer the question what do we have, and to determine future requirements, thus answers the question what do we have to get. The main function of MRP is to guarantee the availability of a required material. MRP is used for planning the supply and production of materials for internal use, assembly, production or distribution, and it has to be available at the right time and in the right quantity. The planning process includes monitoring of stock size, automatic creation of orders for materials, intermediate production or its divisions. By functioning in that way, MRP attempts to maintain a balance between the minimum safe inventory size and the costs. Classic inventory management treats every single material, element or product separately, not taking account of the frequency of use and consumption of one part or another. The MRP approach is different because a lot of customers order individual products in packages, so that demand is not entirely independent. There must be a connection between demand of nuts and bolts, paint and brushes, etc. MRP recognizes this connection and attempts to balance demand and supply (Vuković et al., 2007).

MRP becomes a formal mechanism for priority management in changing production surroundings. The changes in production surroundings are not possible or probable—they are inevitable. The function of MRP that is directed at keeping deadlines and on changes in the production of enterprises is called the Priority Planning. Capacity is a factor that is of equal importance when compared with the previous two factors (Wight, 1993).

Tools for capacity planning in the production enterprise, as related to the MRP computer system are:

- Sales and operations planning,
- Master scheduling,
- Demand management,
- Rough-cut capacity planning.

The total development of these tools has led to the next step of planning evolution. Due to the above MRP shortcomings in the 1970's, the Manufacturing Resource Planning system (MPR II) has emerged in the 1980's. Sadagopan (1998) stated that, unlike MRP, MRP II addresses the entire manufacturing function and not just a single task. The increased functionality enabled MRP II to check the feasibility of a production schedule taking into account the constraints, and to adjust the loading of the resources, if possible, to meet the production schedule. While Siriginidi (2000) added the possibility of the integration with other shops , MRP II has certain extensions like rough cut capacity planning and capacity requirements planning for production scheduling on shop floor as well as feedback from manufacturing shops on progress of fabrication. This last functionality requires a more integrated system.

MRP II is more than a material management tool as indicated by Koch (2001) and within the logistic vision, the technology of MRP II, manufacturing resource planning offers an interpretation of both the main problems of manufacturing as material flow, and the tools and procedures needed to solve these problems by realizing a full control system. However, Swan et al (2000) observed that MRP II has been widely promoted by technology suppliers as the definitive "best practice" solution for production management and control. But, enterprises have encountered many problems in implementing MRP II - including organizational not just software. However, prior to these findings, Foxlow (1994) reported that there is a need for new knowledge-based manufacturing software, incorporating artificial intelligence techniques, offers benefits to companies whose products are complex, highly varied, or made-to-order. However, these are precisely the areas where conventional MRP II systems are widely perceived as having failed.

2.2 Phase 2: Enterprise resource planning (ERP)

With the evolution of concepts like MRP and MRP II, we arrive at the currently used concept of enterprise resource planning or ERP. The foundation for ERP is the same as in MRP II. ERP has developed as a set of business processes, thanks to the development of information and communication technologies, while its conceptual development is just one step in the evolution of enterprise management (Vuković et al., 2007).

The ERP systems were also faced with their own implementation and integration problems. The major difficulties with integration, however, appeared during the augmentation of core ERP systems with legacy systems.

The main reasons to implement the ERP concept are (Vuković et al., 2007):

- Integration of financial information.
- Integration of clients orders.
- Standardization and speed of production processes.
- Stock sizing.
- Human resources information standardization.

It is essential is to draw a difference between the concept of ERP and the ERP system. ERP systems enable the realization of the ERP concept.

2.3 Phase 3: Customer-centric Resource Planning (CRP)

The range of ERP functions was further expanded at the end of the 1990s to include "front office" functions such as sales, marketing and e-commerce. E-commerce applications needed to be connected to back-end systems and thus forced many ERP software providers including SAP, PeopleSoft and BAAN_ to reinvent themselves as CRP providers. While traditional ERP solutions were equipped to support the "make-to- stock configure-to-order business model", CRP systems are able to meet the e-commerce "build-to-order fulfil-to-order" requirement. Effective manufacturing and service delivery in the e-commerce model require customer-centric, continuous planning instead of the classic ERP assumption of long planning cycles (Bosilj-Vukšić & Spremić, 2005).

2.4 Phase 4: Inter-enterprise Integration (XRP) or ERP II

Since the world of the 2000s has become one of interconnected enterprises creating global information systems, the scope of ERP systems comprises the entire value chain of the enterprise, its customers, suppliers and trading partners. The main goal of the XRP system is to provide intelligent decision-support capabilities in order to reduce inventory, foster strategic pricing, improve cycle times and increase customer satisfaction throughout the supply chain management and selling chain management. To achieve this goal, an XRP model must support the integration of external and internal business activities with the suppliers and customer's information and processes (Bosilj Vukšić & Spremić, 2005). ERP systems were also faced with their own implementation and integration problems. The major difficulties with integration, however, appeared during the augmentation of core ERP systems with legacy systems. Themistocleous and Irani (2001) stated that ERP systems were then introduced to overcome integration problems. However, organizations did not abandon their existing systems when adopting an ERP solution, as ERP systems focus on general processes and initially did not allow much customization. The problems of integration within the core of ERP systems have resulted in multiple shortcomings as reported by DeSisto (1997) that poor ERP integration resulted in high order error rates, incorrect billing and shipping addresses, misquoted pricing and discounts, and misquoted "out of stock" inventory.

3. ERP defined

There are a numerous definitions of ERP but in this paper the most popular definitions will be presented. Wallace and Krezmar define ERP as an enterprise-wide set of management tools that balance demand and supply, having the ability to link customers and suppliers into a complete supply chain, to employ proven business processes for decision-making, and to provide high degrees of cross-functional integration among sales, marketing, manufacturing, operations, logistics, purchasing, finance, new product development, and human resources, thereby enabling people to run their business with high levels of customer service and productivity, and to simultaneously lower costs and inventories, while providing the foundation for effective e-commerce.

An enterprise resource planning system is a business management system that comprises integrated sets of comprehensive software that can be used, when successfully implemented, to manage and integrate all business processes and functions within an organization. They usually include a set of mature business applications and tools for financial and cost accounting, sales and distribution, management of materials, human resources, production planning and computer integrated manufacturing, supply chain, and customer information (Žabjek et al., 2008).

Klaus, Rosemann and Gable define ERP as a logical and compact software solution which strives toward the integration of all processes in an organization, in the aim of presenting a comprehensive view of the organization through singularity of information and IT architecture (Roseman & Gable 2000), whereas Yen, Chou and Chang (Yen et al., 2002), describe ERP as a software which can be used to integrate information through all functions of organization in order to automate all business processes. Rao (2000) described an ERP system as a software solution to produce the right product on the right place, at the right time, and for the right price, containing the best industrial and management practice captured in those solutions. It is necessary to emphasize that ERP is not a software, software package or set of computer applications. Software packages of ERP systems, or ES, provide support for efficient resource planning or ERP. The main function of ERP is to integrate operational procedures within the department, along with the MIS, and to relocate organizational resources in changing surroundings. ERP systems are integrated software solutions which are used for resource management of the organization. ERP systems are used for resource planning, and also for the concept of combining unique departments systems and utilizing the methods which are most appropriate for problem solving.

The main goal of ERP is to implement the best practices for all business processes. It may be said that ERP is a key business strategy today, and the greatest advantage of its implementation is the ability to fundamentally eliminate multiple systems within an organization, with no more redundancy. Implementing ERP on platforms is not always easy because of the massive re-engineering process that involves security, quality assurance, and training for members of the organization entrusted to use the ERP systems. In addition to maximizing the operational effectiveness of the ERP, IT managers, system security officers, and system developers will find themselves challenged on security and control issues (Vuković et al. 2007).

4. Characteristics of ERP systems

When most people refer to the "core" ERP applications or "modules," they mean the back-office capabilities to manage human resources, accounting and finance, manufacturing, and project-management functions. However, major ERP suites from Oracle, PeopleSoft, and SAP now provide much more—including modules for sales force automation, business intelligence, customer relationship management, and supply chain management (Musaji, 2002).

There are some significant differences between ERP and non-ERP systems. These differences are (Musaji, 2002):

- In ERP systems, certain control procedures leave no documentary evidence of performance. For some other procedures, the evidence of performance is indirect; it may be included in the program logic or in the operator's instructions. Therefore, compliance tests may have to be structured differently in an ERP environment and observation of the client's procedures may become more important.
- In ERP systems, information is often recorded in a form that cannot be read without the use of a computer.
- Financial and business information is often generated automatically by ERP systems based on data previously entered, without further human instructions.
- Errors that might be observed in non-ERP systems may go undetected because of the reduced human involvement in computerized processing. There is a danger that errors in processing may be applied to a large number of transactions without being noticed.
- With proper controls, ERP systems can be more reliable than non-ERP systems. This is because ERP systems subject all data to the same procedures and controls. Non-ERP systems are subject to random human error. Although computer processing will usually be consistent, errors may still occur; for example, if the computer is incorrectly programmed.
- It is difficult to make changes after an ERP system has been implemented. Therefore, we should be aware of the organization's plans to introduce significant new systems or to make major modifications to existing systems. It is advisable to review new systems or modifications before implementation so that a preliminary assessment can be made of the adequacy of control procedures, in order to ensure an adequate audit trail, and to plan any necessary changes in the audit approach.

ERP systems vary from the simplest, batch-controlled type to complex integrated applications that perform a number of functions simultaneously.

4.1 Implementation of ERP systems

Parry and Graves (2008) noted that implementation of an ERP system does not end with the system "going live" (Markus et al. 2000). It is an ongoing process where new functionality, modules, updates, and corrections need to be carried out in conjunction with changes in organisational processes (Kremmergaard & Moller 2000). These software and process changes continue throughout the lifetime of an ERP system as it evolves in parallel with the organisation. Many publications have described the ERP lifecycle as having different phases (Markus *et al.* 2000, Markus & Tanis 2000, Ross & Vitale 2000, Parry & James-Moore 2005);

however, Markus and Tanis's (2000) ERP lifecycle model has been widely accepted. They refer to an "enterprise systems experience cycle", and describe four distinct phases within this journey: the "Chartering" phase during which decisions leading to the funding of an enterprise systems will be made; the "Project „phase where the ERP software is configured and rolled out to the organisation; the „Shakedown" phase where the company makes a transition from go-live to normal operations; the "Onward and Upward „phase during which the company captures the majority of business benefits from the ERP system and plans further steps of technology implementation and business improvement. This final phase refers to the management of ERP systems that covers ERP operations, ERP upgrades, and ERP maintenance such as error fixing and minor enhancements (Markus *et al.* 2000, Markus & Tanis 2000, Nah & Lau 2001). Following initial implementation, there are subsequent revisions, re-implementations, and upgrades that transcend what is normally considered as management of ERP system (Chang 2004). Management activities for software systems are commonly classified as one of the four distinct types: (1) corrective, (2) perfective, (3) adaptive, and (4) preventive (Pressman 1992).
The figure 1 below shows how ERP can support IT process. It shows Modules in an ERP based integration approach.

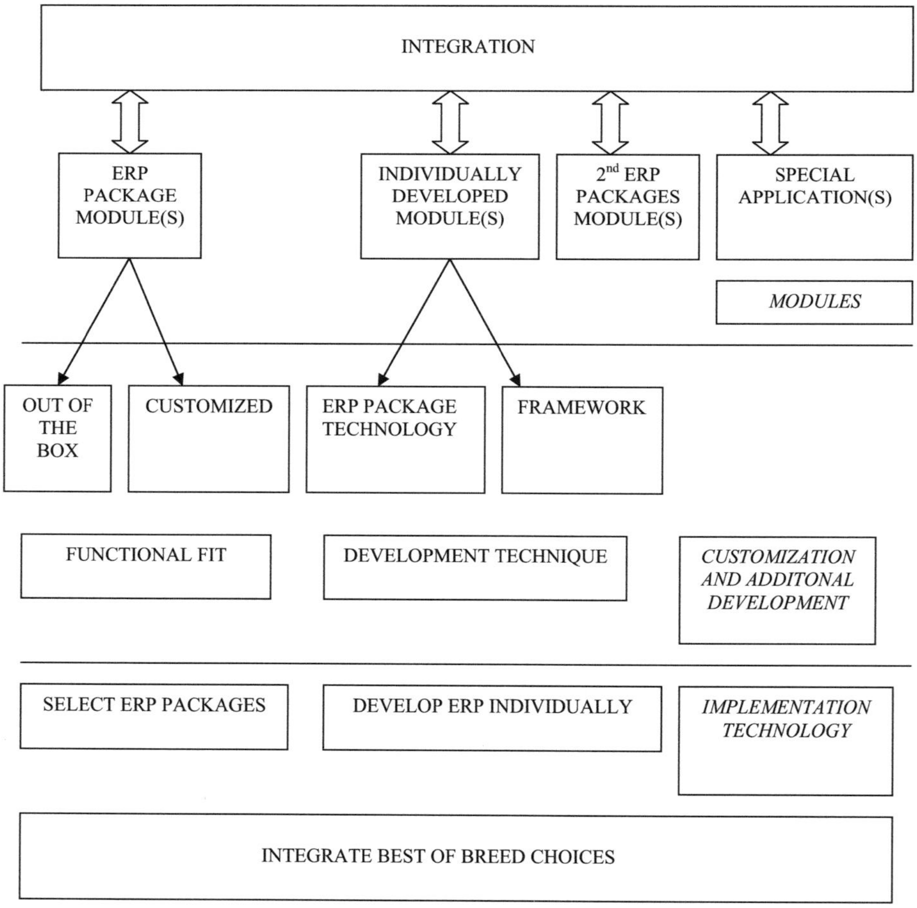

Fig. 1. Modules in an ERP based integration approach (Thomas Herzog, 2006)

4.2 Critical success factors in ERP implementation

Table 2 presents the main factors revealed from the literature review and that are found to be vital for successful ERP implementation: top management support, business plan and vision, re-engineering business process, effective project management and project champion, teamwork and composition, ERP system selection, user involvement, education and training (AL-Fawaz et al., 2008).

Critical Success Factor	References
Top management support	Al-Mashari et al. (2003); (Umble et al., 2003); Zhang et al. (2002)
Business plan and vision	Loh and Koh (2004); Schwalbe, (2000); Somers and Nelson (2004); Nah (2003)
Re-engineering business process	Davison (2002); Hammer and Champy (2001); Somers and Nelson (2004); Nah (2003); Murray and Coffin (2001)
Effective project management and project champion	Zhang et al.,(2002); Somers and Nelson (2004); Remus (2006); Loh and Koh, (2004)
Teamwork and composition	Loh and Koh (2004); Al-Mashari et al., (2006); Remus (2006); Nah (2003); Rosario (2000)
ERP system selection	Wei and Wang (2004); Shehab et al., (2004); Everdingen et al. (2000); Sprott (2000)
User involvement	Esteves et al., (2003); Zhang el at (2002)
Education and training	(Woo 2007); Nah et al., (2003); Zhang et al. (2002)

Table 2. Critical success factors in ERP implementation ((AL-Fawaz et al., 2008).

Žabjek, Kovačić and Indihar Štemberger have given more complex literature reviewed when a factor in ERP implementation (table 3) is about critical success.

Top management support.	Al-Mashari et al., 2003; Al-Sehali, 2000; Akkermans and Van Helden, 2002; Esteves-Souza and Pastor-Collado, 2000; Gargeya and Brady, 2005; Gattiker, 2002; Gupta, 2000; Harrison, 2004; Holland and Light, 1999; Jarrar et al., 2000; Mabert et al., 2003; Magnusson et al., 2004; Parr and Shanks, 2000; Skok and Legge, 2002; Somers and Nelson, 2004; Somers and Nelson, 2001; Sternad et al., 2007; Umble et al., 2003; Yen et al., 2002; Zhang et al., 2003.
Clear goals and objectives.	Al-Mashari et al., 2003; Al-Sehali, 2000; Akkermans and Van Helden, 2002; Gargeya and Brady, 2005; Holland and Light, 1999; Mabert et al., 2003; Magnusson et al., 2004; Parr and Shanks, 2000; Reif, 2001; Somers and Nelson, 2004; Somers and Nelson, 2001; Sternad et al., 2007; Umble et al., 2003.

Project team organization and competence.	Akkermans and Van Helden, 2002; Esteves-Souza and Pastor-Collado, 2000; Gargeya and Brady, 2005; Jarrar et al., 2000; Mabert et al., 2003; Magnusson et al., 2004; Parr and Shanks, 2000; Reif, 2001; Skok and Legge, 2002; Somers and Nelson, 2004; Somers and Nelson, 2001; Sternad et al., 2007; Umble et al., 2003.
User training and education.	Al-Mashari et al., 2003; Al-Sehali, 2000; Akkermans and Van Helden, 2002; Gupta, 2000; Jarrar et al., 2000; Mabert et al., 2003; Magnusson et al., 2004; Skok and Legge, 2002; Somers and Nelson, 2004; Somers and Nelson, 2001; Sternad et al., 2007; Umble et al., 2003; Zhang et al., 2003.
Business Process Reengineering.	Al-Mashari et al., 2003; Akkermans and Van Helden, 2002; Esteves-Souza and Pastor-Collado, 2000; Gargeya and Brady, 2005; Gattiker, 2002; Harrison, 2004; Jarrar et al., 2000; Magnusson et al., 2004; Skok and Legge, 2002; Somers and Nelson, 2004; Somers and Nelson, 2001; Sternad et al., 2007; Zhang et al., 2003.
Change Management.	Aladwani, 2001; Al-Mashari et al., 2003; Al-Sehali, 2000; Akkermans and Van Helden, 2002; Esteves-Souza and Pastor-Collado, 2000; Gargeya and Brady, 2005; Holland and Light, 1999; Jarrar et al., 2000; Magnusson et al., 2004; Parr and Shanks, 2000; Skok and Legge, 2002; Somers and Nelson, 2004; Somers and Nelson, 2001; Sternad et al., 2007; Umble et al., 2003; Yen et al., 2002.
Communication.	Aladwani, 2001; Al-Mashari et al., 2003; Al-Sehali, 2000; Akkermans and Van Helden, 2002; Esteves-Souza and Pastor-Collado, 2000; Gargeya and Brady, 2005; Holland and Light, 1999; Mabert et al., 2003; Magnusson et al., 2004; Somers and Nelson, 2004; Somers and Nelson, 2001; Sternad et al., 2007; Yen et al., 2002.
User involvement and participation.	Aladwani, 2001; Al-Sehali, 2000; Esteves-Souza and Pastor-Collado, 2000; Gattiker, 2002; Magnusson et al., 2004; Skok and Legge, 2002; Somers and Nelson, 2004; Sternad et al., 2007; Yen et al., 2002; Zhang et al., 2003.
Legacy system management.	Al-Sehali, 2000; Akkermans and Van Helden, 2002; Gattiker, 2002; Reif, 2001; Somers and Nelson, 2004; Somers and Nelson, 2001; Sternad et al., 2007; Umble et al., 2003; Zhang et al., 2003.

Consulting services.	Al-Mashari et al., 2003; Al-Sehali, 2000; Akkermans and Van Helden, 2002; Harrison, 2004; Magnusson et al., 2004; Skok and Legge, 2002; Somers and Nelson, 2004; Somers and Nelson, 2001; Sternad et al., 2007
Project Management.	Al-Mashari et al., 2003; Al-Sehali, 2000; Akkermans and Van Helden, 2002; Esteves-Souza and Pastor-Collado, 2000; Magnusson et al., 2004; Reif, 2001; Somers and Nelson, 2004; Somers and Nelson, 2001; Sternad et al., 2007; Umble et al., 2003; Yen et al., 2002; Zhang et al., 2003.
Sponsorship.	Akkermans and Van Helden, 2002; Esteves-Souza and Pastor-Collado, 2000; Parr and Shanks, 2000; Skok and Legge, 2002; Somers and Nelson, 2004; Somers and Nelson, 2001; Sternad et al., 2007.
System, technological.	Al-Sehali, 2000; Akkermans and Van Helden, 2002; Gargeya and Brady, 2005; Gattiker, 2002; Jarrar et al., 2000; Parr and Shanks, 2000; Somers and Nelson, 2004; Somers and Nelson, 2001; Sternad et al., 2007; Zhang et al., 2003.
Minimal Customization	Esteves-Souza and Pastor-Collado, 2000; Gargeya and Brady, 2005; Mabert et al., 2003; Somers and Nelson, 2004; Somers and Nelson, 2001; Sternad et al., 2007.

Table 3. Critical success factors in ERP implementation. Source: Adjusted and updated upon Sternad et al., 2007 in Žabjek et al. 2008.

5. Knowledge management era

Knowledge has become the most important input implemented in business organisations. Numerous books, articles and special editions of journals have already been devoted to explaining concept of knowledge and its management in organisations. It is not necessary to dwell on these, except to iterate that the key components of successful knowledge management are strategy, culture, technology, organisation and people (Drew, S., 2000). Different authors are bound to put different definitions of the knowledge management. For example, Wiig sees knowledge management as a process of facilitating and managing knowledge-related activities such as creation, capture, transformation and use (Wiig, 1997). Brooking understands knowledge management as an activity, which is concerned with strategy and tactics to manage human-centred assets (Brooking, 1997). On the other hand Bair defines it as a set of policies, organisational structures, procedures, applications and technologies intended to improve the decision-making effectiveness of a group or a firm (Bair, 1997). Finally according to Harris, knowledge management is a discipline that promotes a collaborative and integrated approach to the creation, capture, organisation, access and use of an enterprise's information assets (Harris, 1998).

Knowledge management comprises information, communication, human resources, intellectual capital, brands, etc. Knowledge Management (KM) has tactical and operational perspectives. KM is more detailed and focuses on facilitating and managing knowledge-related activities such as creation, captures, transformation and use (e.g. Wiig et.al,). Enterprises tend to pursue one or several of five basic knowledge-centred strategies (Wiig, K. M., 1997):

- Knowledge strategy as business strategy - emphasises knowledge creation, capture, organisation, renewal, sharing, and use in all operations;
- Intellectual asset management strategy - emphasises enterprise-level management of specific intellectual assets such as patents, technologies, operational and management practices, customer relations, organisational arrangements, and other structural knowledge assets;
- Personal knowledge strategy - emphasises personal responsibility for knowledge-related investments, innovations and competitiveness, renewal, effective use and availability to other or knowledge assets within each employee's area of accountability;
- Knowledge creation strategy - emphasises organisational learning, basic and applied research and development, and motivation of employees to innovate and capture lessons learned to obtain new and better knowledge that will provide improved competitiveness;
- Knowledge transfer strategy - emphasises systematic approaches to transfer knowledge to points of action where it will be use to perform work. This strategy includes knowledge sharing and adopting best practices.

Since the importance of knowledge rapidly grows, there is a growing need for knowledge management, especially the management of processes in which knowledge is created and used (Quintas & Geoff, 1997). Most authors observe human capital as a system consisted of three elements. The first element is intellectual capital. It refers to fundamental individual attributes such as cognitive complexity and the capacity to learn, together with the tacit and explicit knowledge, skills and expertise an individual builds over time (Gratton & Ghoshal, 2003). The second element of human capital is social capital - which is about who one knows, and how well one knows them. The third element is emotional capital based on a self-esteem, courage and resilience. These three different elements are highly inter-related. Social capital helps individuals to develop intellectual capital by accessing the knowledge and skills that those people possess. Emotional capital brings the integrity and self-awareness to build open and trusting relationships, which underpin the creation of social capital. As an example of the world leading company at the field of intellectual capital, it is mentioned Swedish insurance company, "Skandia", which has comprehended the importance of knowledge and intellectual capital, ten years ago. For better insight of their business accomplishments, usually observation and furtherance, "Skandia" has developed the scheme for intellectual capital (intellectual capital is composed of several important following components): IC was seen as the sum of human and structural capital. Human capital was defined as the knowledge, skill and experience of employees. Structural capital, however, was the extension and manifestation of human capital into innovations, business processes and relationships with dealers and others (Roos, 1998).

Intellectual capital management (ICM) and knowledge management (KM) are multidimensional and cover most aspects of an enterprise operation. There is overlap but there are also major differences. For example, KM has tactical and operational aspects and is more detailed. The ICM and KM role is to keep and sustain the present and future body of knowledge in order to guarantee the firm's long-term viability and profitability. Management of knowledge is becoming a new business philosophy and is treated as a source of power and together with Intellectual Capital represent the enterprise's future

potential. There is considerable overlap in the scope of intellectual capital management and knowledge management. ICM focuses on building and governing intellectual assets from strategic and enterprise governance perspectives with some focus on tactics. Its function is to take overall care of the enterprise's intellectual capital.
The management of intellectual capital is a strategic activity which positively modification efficiency of enterprises and means that the enterprise (Tipurić, D., 1999):

- Apprehended the role and importance of employees in resumption of competitive advantages;
- Defined its key competence in economic surroundings;
- Developed the system for creating necessity know-how;
- Installed the system of rewarding;
- Developed the specific culture for encouragement of experimenting and expanding total knowledge.

6. ERP concept and enterprise knowledge

ERP packages led to better production planning, quality and inventory control, expense management and more efficient distribution. The primary objective of ERP systems is to seamlessly improve the internal efficiency through order fulfilment. However, information on just one side of the business equation is ineffective in achieving a competitive advantage in the new global economy. The new market demands a distributed knowledge network, which necessitates the participation of the entire value chain from customer to supplier, and in some cases, even from competitors. Enterprises that strategically maximize the impact of these new knowledge flows will be in a position of competitive advantage in the emerging networked economy. This requires synergetic relationships between CRM, KM, and supply chain within one system (Mirghani, 2005). According to Thompson and Close (2001) since the beginning of 1997, the major ERP vendors (e.g., SAP, PeopleSoft and Oracle) have attempted to expand their dominant position in the financial, manufacturing and human capital management enterprise applications markets into the increasingly lucrative customer relationship management (CRM) market. Until recently, these attempts have mostly failed to meet client expectations. However, their labours are beginning to pay off.
Although ERP systems interconnect different departments through the various modules, but to some extent, ERPs initially created functional silos by enforcing the business process workflow through single technology. This silo effect needs to be counterbalanced by implementing KM initiatives that promote the communication and knowledge sharing among various value network collaborators. The KM initiative as supportive mechanism for ERP will reveal different kinds of knowledge to different stakeholders. The conventional ERP systems have tremendously improved order fulfilment and intra-organization business process workflow, but fell short to address the inter-enterprise business process complexities. The latter requires a full collaboration ecosystem that attracts valued customers and shareholders from all directions to share the pertinent business knowledge.
The leverage of human intellectual capabilities has been the focus of ERP. Directing and maintaining intellectual energy while attempting a restructuring or re-engineering program is seen as a typically difficult example of this much overlooked area. Gartner defined ERP as "a business strategy and a set of industry-domain-specific applications that build customer and shareholder value by enabling and optimizing enterprise and inter-enterprise collaborative operational and financial processes". This definition transformed the

traditional back-office ERP system from internal transactional system into a complete value network system that incorporates the front-office functionalities for various partner communities. Integrating the front office with ERP indisputably offers an information visibility strategy that pushes the right information to the right people at the right time through the right communications channels (Mirghani, 2005).

From systems point of view, ERP and KM systems need to be implemented simultaneously in the framework of integrated enterprise information systems. Simultaneous implementation of ERP and KM systems requires incorporation of both KM and ERP into enterprise business processes and incorporation of KM into ERP system development. Despite the different focus of ERP and KM systems, the two systems, to some extent, have common goals. Both ERP and KM aim at improving business processes to achieve better business performance, with tasks based on data, information and knowledge.

ERP systems emphasize the efficiency of business processes in enterprises. To achieve the goals, ERP systems maintain mechanism for data/information consistency through high degrees of standardization, formalization and specialization. KM systems devote to the knowledge processes of enterprises such as knowledge creating, storing, transferring and sharing. In perspectives of enterprises, the ultimate goals of the two systems are helping enterprise survive in the global market by improving their performance. In summary, ERP and KM systems manage the business from the point of views of physical and knowledge assets, respectively.

With a proper framework in which ERP and KM can cooperate with each other, an enterprise can benefit from the advantages of ERP and KM and be successful in global competition.

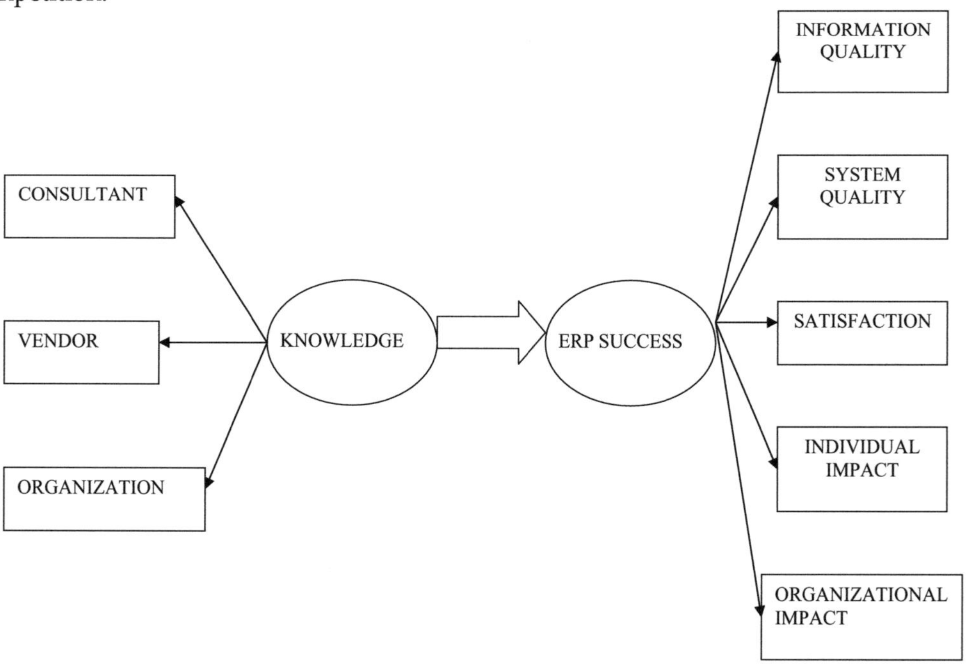

Fig. 2. Knowledge management for ERP success model (Sedera et al. 2003)

The interrelation between Knowledge Management and ERP has two facets (Hosain et. al., 2002):

- On the one side, implemented Enterprise Systems can serve as a main source for Knowledge Management. As Enterprise Systems support various areas of a company such as procurement, manufacturing, warehousing, sales, distribution, and accounting, an analysis of a run-time data can provide the knowledge manager cost-effectively with useful data about the current process performance. This perspective characterizes Enterprise Systems as a knowledge repository and can be described as "Enterprise Systems for Knowledge Management".
- On the other side, the management and especially the implementation of an ES solution requires a substantial amount of specific knowledge and expertise. Thus, a separate ES-related Knowledge Management can be identified that covers the entire management of knowledge in an ES project. This perspective can be characterized as "Knowledge Management for Enterprise Systems"

In 2003 Sedera with his colleagues has proposed a model of Knowledge Management that is crucial for ERP success.

In this study knowledge was identified as a key driver of ERP success but also needs further analysis to understand the complete influence of knowledge and other possible dimensions of knowledge.

7. ERP systems and its implementation in large Croatian enterprises

ERP systems can be considered as a "standard tool" for every large enterprise in a global economy and in the time of large competitiveness at the international market. For example "Supply Chain Management" includes e-procurement, payment and organizational optimization and without ERP as a integral source of data, ERP system will be impossible to implement.

The analysis *"Enterprise Resource Planning Systems and competitiveness of large Croatian enterprises" conducted by Nikša Alfirević from the Faculty of Economics Split, Croatia in 2003* that has been accessible from the secondary source of research and has shown that the users of SAP information system in large Croatian enterprises can be divided in two main categories:

- Enterprises with a foreign proprietary - they buy ERP systems to follow standards of "mother-companies"
- Small group of progressive domestic companies that are oriented to export and international business.

This research (Alfirević, 2003) has been conducted at the end of 2002 and the beginning of 2003. The summary of the most important conclusions of that research will be presented in this paper.

The source for analysis has been 200 leading domestic enterprises (ranked by the income) and published in a study "Privredni vjesnik" in 2002. Although the analysis of 200 enterprises cannot show all trends at the ERP market, the fact is that this source presents the majority of potential ERP users and that from this analysis all relevant indicators of market situation can be measured.

The analysis has shown that 68% of the surveyed enterprises do not have implemented ERP system and that ERP systems are not used enough. There is a large gap when is about investment in ERP systems in Croatia and in the rest of the world. This study has also shown that there is a significant correlation among ERP systems and relative performance measures ROA and Net profit margin (Spearman coefficient of correlation).

Conducted analysis has also shown that in Republic Croatia there is a relatively low level of investment in ERP technologies but that enterprises that implement ERP achieve better

business results (it can be concluded that implementation of ERP systems is very important for competitiveness). It is possible to connote that the situation of ERP systems implementation in large Croatian enterprises has not change much in the years that have accompanied from the conducted research because all trends that are presented at the professional journals in Republic Croatia show this trend.
Further researches and practice has to be oriented to adaptation of ERP systems to specifics of Croatian economy which will help to improve export capabilities and competitiveness of Croatian economy.

8. Conclusion

To adapt to today's challenging and competitive business environment, organizations are implementing ERP systems to achieve a capability to plan and integrate enterprise and to be more responsive to customer demands.
Today, ERP is still evolving, adapting to developments in technology and the demands of the market. Four important trends are shaping ERP's continuing evolution: improvements in integration and flexibility; extensions to e-business applications, a broader reach to new users; and the adoption of Internet technologies. Taking a closer look at each will help you understand where ERP is headed.
Despite the fact that ERP integrates and optimises the flow of information across the entire organization's supply chain, the implementation of such software packages can be costly, and may even require reengineering the entire business operations. Combinations of factors have to be considered when undertaking an ERP implementation including: top management support, business plan and vision, Re-engineering business process, effective project management and project champion, careful package selection process, teamwork and composition, user involvement and education and training (Al-Fawaz et al., 2008).
ERP and KM systems emphasize different characteristics, but the primary goal of the both systems is to improve the competitiveness of enterprises in global markets. From systems point of view, ERP and KM systems need to be implemented simultaneously in the framework of integrated enterprise information systems. Simultaneous implementation of ERP and KM systems requires incorporation of both KM and ERP into enterprise business processes and incorporation of KM into ERP system development. Despite the different focus of ERP and KM systems, the two systems, to some extent, have common goals. Both ERP and KM aim at improving business processes to achieve better business performance, with tasks based on data, information and knowledge.
In this paper study of implementation of ERP systems in Republic Croatia has been shown. Analysis has shown that in Republic Croatia there is a relatively low level of investment in ERP technologies but that enterprises that implement ERP achieve better business results.
It can be said that in the future enterprises in Republic Croatia and especially large Croatian enterprises have to orient more to advantages of IT especially when is about role of IT in improvement of export capabilities of large enterprises and in general when is about competitiveness of Croatian economy.

9. References

Al-Fawaz, K., Al-Salti, Z., Eldabi, T. (2008). Critical Success Factors in ERP implementation: a review, European and Mediterranean Conference on Information Systems 2008, May 25-26 2008, Dubai

Alfirević, N. (2003). ERP sustavi nedovoljno iskorišteni u Hrvatskoj, SAP MAG, 05. listopada 2003. URL www.sap mag.com.hr

Alfirević, N. (2003). ERP sustavi nedovoljno iskorišteni u Hrvatskoj, SAP MAG, 06. listopada 2003. URL www.sap mag.com.hr

Al-Mashari M, Ghani S,W Al-Rashid W. (2006), 'A study of the Critical Success Factors of ERP implementation in developing countries'. *Internet and Enterprise Management,* 4(1): 68-95.

Bosilj Vukšić, V. & Spremić, M. (2005). ERP system Implementation and Business Process Change: Case Study of a Pharmaceutical Company, *Journal of Computing and Information Technology* - CIT 13, No. 1., 11–24.

Chang, S. I., 2004. ERP life cycle implementation, management and support: implications for practice and research. Paper presented on Track 8 organizational systems and technology, ERP/EAI (ERPII) systems issues & answers (OSERP), at 37th Hawaii international conference on system sciences, 2004 Hawaii, 80227c.

DeSisto, R. (1997). *ERP Integration Strategies for TES Systems.* Gartner: Research Note: TU-724-344

Esteves J Pastor J Casanovas J 2003, 'A goal/question/metric research proposal to monitor user involvement and participation ERP implementation projects', Information Resources Management Association Conference (IRMA), Philadelphia (USA) 325-327

Foxlow, T. (1994). Knowledge-based Manufacturing: The Key to Recovery. *Logistics Information Management,* Vol. 7, No. 4., 23-26.

Hammer, M. & Champy, J. (2001). *'Reengineering the Corporation: A Manifesto for Business Revolution'*, Harper Business, New York, NY, USA

Koch, C. (2001). Enterprise resource planning: Information technology as a steamroller for management politics? *Journal of Organizational Change Management* 14: (1): 64-8.

Kremmergaard, P. & Moller, C. (2000), A research framework for studying the implementation of enterprise resource planning systems. Proceedings of the 23rd information systems research seminar in Scandinavia, Lingatan, Sweden, 139–162.

Loh T. C. & Koh S. C. (2004), 'Critical elements for a successful enterprise resource planning implementation in small- and medium-sized enterprises', *International Journal of Production Research,* 42(17) 3433–3455.

Markus, M.L., et al., (2000), Learning from adopters' experiences with ERP: problems encountered and success achieved. *Journal of Information Technology,* 15 (4), 245–265.

Markus, M. L. & Tanis, C. (2000). The enterprise systems experience - from adoption to success. In: R.W. Zmud, ed. Framing the domains of IT research: glimpsing the future through the past. Cincinnati: Pinnaflex.

Mirghani M., ERP II: Harnessing ERP Systems with Knowledge Management Capabilities, *Journal of Knowledge Management Practice, June 2005*

Musaji, Y. F. (2002). *Integrated Auditing of ERP systems,* John Wiley & Sons, Inc., New York

Nah, F. F.-H. & Lau, J.L.-S. (2001), Critical factors for successful implementation of enterprise systems, *Business Process Management Journal,* 7 (3), 285–296.

Nah, F. F-H., Zuckweiler, K.M., et al. (2003) 'ERP implementation: chief information officers' perceptions of critical success factors', *International Journal of Human-Computer Interaction,* 16(1):5–22.

Parry, G. C., Price, P., & James-Moore, M. (2003). ERP: implementation and maintenance in a lean enterprise. London:

Society of British Aerospace Companies [SBAC] & DTI.

Parry, G. & Graves, A. (2008) "The importance of knowledge management for ERP systems", *International Journal of Logistics: Research and Applications*, Vol. 11, No. 6, December 2008, 427–441

Pressman, R. S. (1992). Software engineering, a practitioner's approach. 3rd ed. NewYork: McGraw-Hill Book Co.

Rosemann, K. H. & Gable, G.G. (2000). What is ERP?. Information System Fronters, Vol. 2, No. 2., 141-162.

Rao, S.S. (2000), "Enterprise resource planning: business needs and technologies", *Industrial Management & Data Systems*, Vol. 100, No. 2, pp. 81-88.

Remus U. (2006). 'Critical Success Factors of Implementing Enterprise Portals'. Proceedings of the 39th Hawaii International Conference on System Sciences

Ross, J.W. & Vitale, M.R. (2000), The ERP revolution: surviving vs. thriving. *Information Systems Frontiers,* 2 (2), 233–241.

Sadagopan, S. (1998). *The World of ERP*. ERP 98 Top Management Workshop. Bangalore. IIM

Shehab, E., Sharp, M., Supramaniam, L. & Spedding, T. (2004), 'Enterprise resource planning: An integrative review'. *Business Process Management Journal,* 10 (4): 359-386.

Sedera, D., Gable, G, & Chan, T. (2003). "Knowledge management for ERP success", 7th Pacific Asia Conference on Information Systems, 10-13 July 2003, Adelaide, South Australia, 1405-1420

Siriginidi, S. R. (2000). Enterprise Resource Planning in Reengineering Business. *Business Process Management Journal,* Vol. 6., No. 5., 376-391.

Schwalbe K. (2000). 'Information Technology Project Management, Cambridge, MA.

Somers T. M. & Nelson K. G. (2004), 'A taxonomy of players and activities across the ERP project life cycle', *Information and Management,* 41(3):257–278.

Swan, J., Newell, S. & Robertson, M. (2000). The diffusion, design and social shaping of production management information systems in Europe. *Information Technology & People* Vol. 13., No. 1., 27-46.

Themistocleous, M. & Irani, Z. (2001). Benchmarking the benefits and barriers of application integration. *Benchmarking: An International Journal,* Vol. 8., No. 4., 317-331.

Thompson, E. & Close, W. (2001). "ERP Vendors Are a Safe Choice for CRM, but Not for All". Gartner Research Note: Markets, M-13-3257

Vuković, A., Džambas, I. & Blažević, D., (2007). Razvoj ERP koncepta i ERP sustava, *Eng. Rev.* Vol. 27., No. 2., 37-45

Wallace, T. F. & Krezmar, M. H. (2001). *ERP: Making It Happen,* John Wiley & Sons, Inc., New York

Wei, C. & Wang, M. (2004), 'A comprehensive framework for selecting an ERP system'. *International Journal of Project Management,* 22: 161–169.

Wight, O. W. (1993). *The Executive's Guide to Successful MRP II,* John Wiley and Sons, New York

Woo H. 2007. 'Critical success factors for implementing ERP: the case of a Chinese electronics' manufacturer. *Journal of Manufacturing Technology Management,* 18 (4), 431-442

Yen, D. C., Chau, D. C. & Chang, J. (2002). Synergetic Analysis for Web-based Enterprise Resource Planning Systems, *Computer Standards and Interfaces,* No. 24., 337-346.

Zhang L, K. O. Lee K. O, Banerjee P (2002). 'Critical Success Factors of Enterprise Resource Planning Systems Implementation Success in China'. Proceedings of the 36th Hawaii International Conference on System Sciences

Žabjek, D., Kovačić, A., & Indihar Štemberger, M. (2008), Business process management as an important factor for a successful ERP system implementation, *Ekonomska istraživanja,* Vol 21., No. 4., 1-18.

8

New Strategies for Technology Products Development in HealthCare

Maximiliano Romero[1], Paolo Perego[2],
Giuseppe Andreoni[2] and Fiammetta Costa[1]
[1]*Health Care Design, Campus point Lecco, INDACO, Politecnico di Milano*
[2]*Sensibilab, Campus point Lecco, INDACO, Politecnico di Milano*
Italy

1. Introduction

HealthCare Product Design, and in particular the development of bio-electronic device for diagnosis and monitoring, is usually very complex because it concerns many different disciplines (eg. Medicine, Electronics, Computer Science, Product Design, etc.). Moreover Healthcare products are almost always used by many different actors, for example caregivers, physicians, patients and their relatives. They can be therefore defined as multidisciplinary products. This implies great difficulties during the design and development of new products because it is necessary to consider many different points of view, in particular without forgetting the diverse users' needs.

Healthcare products can be structured as the sum of two components: the front-end layer i.e. the visible part of them, and the back-end layer that is the hidden part of the products. The back-end layer allows the device to work reliably and efficiently from a the technical point of view, on the other hand, the front-end layer is related to user's acceptability and functioning, so it is probably the most important characteristic to avoid usage errors.

As front-end and back-end layers are strongly related, their parallel development is needed in order to test each development step with final users. This activity is only possible through fast prototyping of both components. Both Back-end and Front-end Layers can be subdivided in hardware and software.

	Back-end Layer (Engineering development)	**Front-end Layer** (Interaction design)
Hardware	• Electronic Design • Structural Product Design • CPU programming	• Product Design • Haptic interfaces
Software	• Protocols • Signal processing	• Graphic User Interface

Table 1. Structure of product development and involved agents

The possibility to test the different design options along the development process is not only useful to check the acceptability but also to reduce the economic impact of changes in the product development itself.

Bandini Buti (2001) proposed that, from the ergonomic point of view, user tests are more efficient when the products are in an advanced phase of development, in order to offer a more realistic experience to the users involved in the test sessions. On the other hand, when products are on the final stages of development, modifications to the prototypes, models and products are more expensive. So we argue that to apply fast prototyping to anticipate as much as possible user tests.

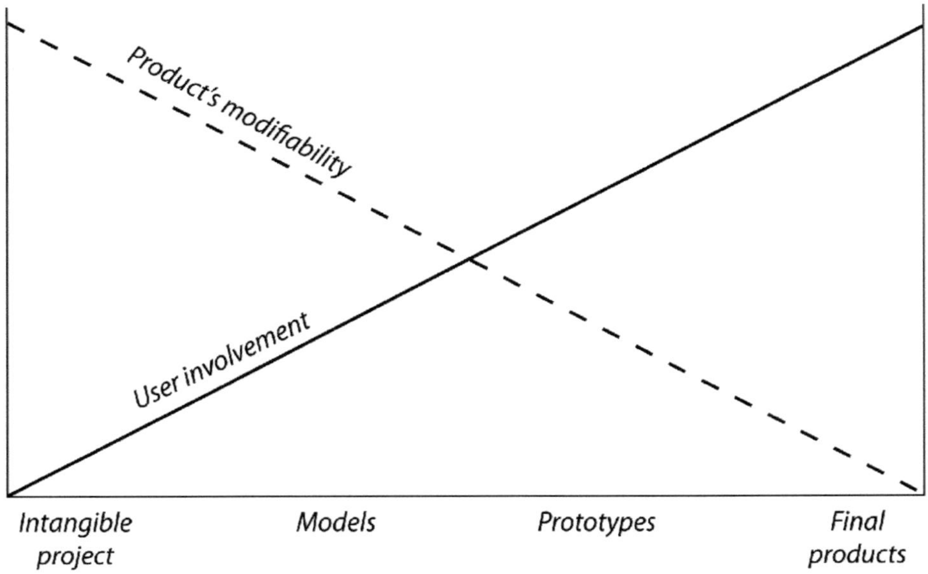

Fig. 1. Curves of User Involvement, Modifiability in a classical standard project process.

2. Multidisciplinary approach

If to develop good products in healthcare design requires a complex knowledge, then a multidisciplinary team is needed.

According with Martin (2008), "medical devices are technology driven rather than resulting from an identified un-meet need". For this reason in the set-up phase of the process, the definition of a complexity map is absolutely necessary; we define this step as "problem" (i.e. the first block of the flow chart in figure 2). If theoretically many methods can be proposed to correctly and completely set-up the problem for healthcare products (Nam et al. 2009), generally in the real world the problem is defined by marketing office of the Company (and in this case and in the next of this paper we will assume this option), or by the medical team as the result of everyday work experience.

In this condition, the first step is to define the design requirements of the system and to select with the team some fixed points. Fixed points are fundamental in order to allow concurrent engineering development process. In this process two teams develop in parallel the back-end and front-end layers of the system. For back-end layer development, engineers are the key figures to solve the technical problems identified in fixed points.

Instead, Front-end concept is designed according to the user needs collected directly from in-field ethnographic observations. Actually, in this stage, the involvement final users for proposal evaluation is difficult.

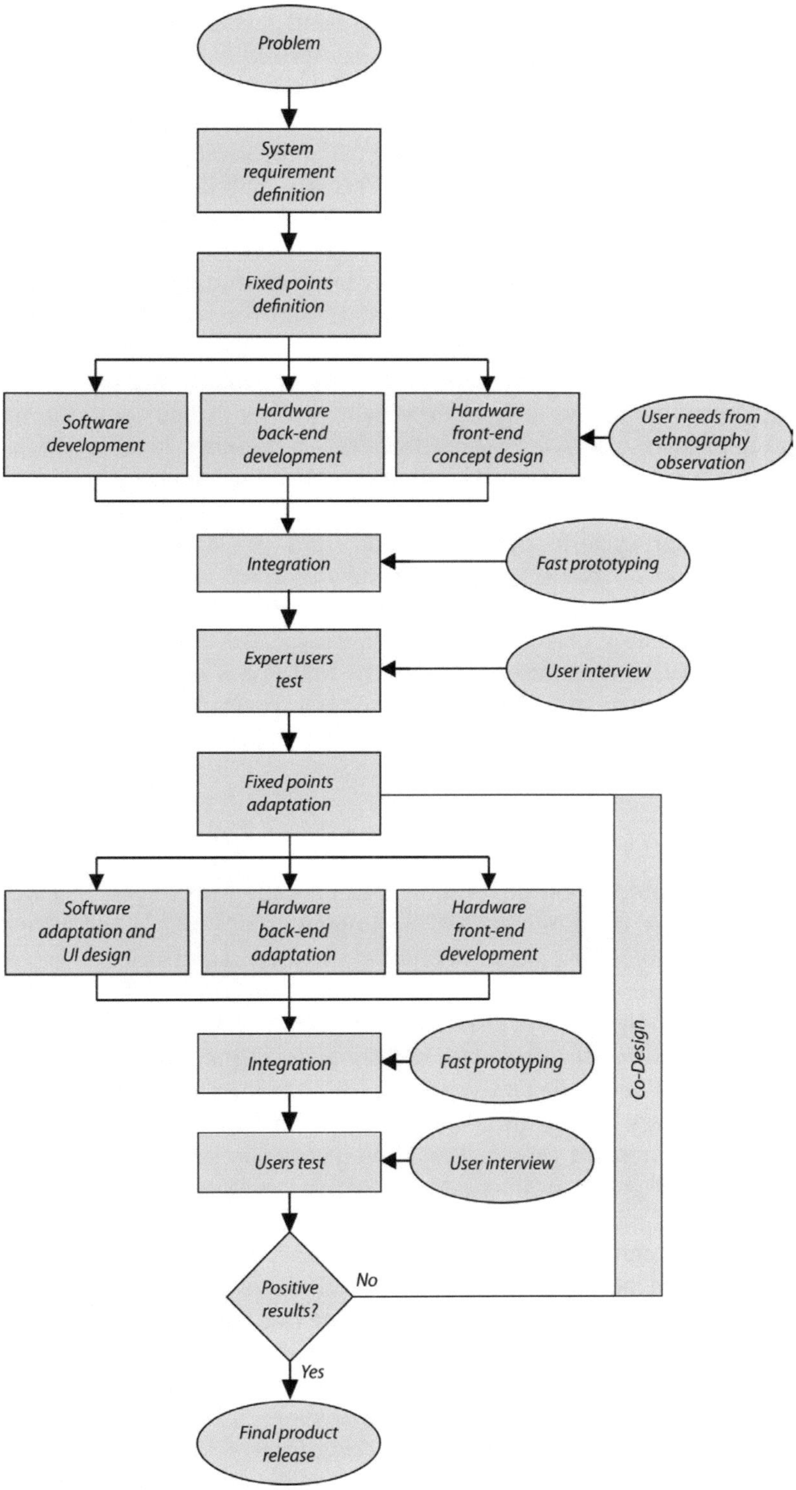

Fig. 2. Flow-chart description for multidisciplinary approach

The next step is the integration of back and front-end layers. This integration is possible thanks to fast prototyping technologies (as deeper described in the next paragraph).
As Moggridge (2006) describes "Early and often Prototyping makes each iterative step a little more realistic. At some point you are likely to experience that feeling that comes with a creative leap, but that is only an indication that you have moved forward in the detail of the aspect of the design that you are focusing on. You will only know that the design is good when you have tried it out with the people who will use it and found that they are pleased, excited, motivated, and satisfied with the result."
The first phase in this context is an "expert user test". At this stage the prototypes are not enough defined and the perception of the standard end-user could be not significant and reliable; for this reason it's not possible to have a real "User Experience" but only tests carried out by experts. Anyway, in some cases it is possible to perform an "Oz Wizard" experience in order to simulate a "real experience test" with end-users through partially operating prototypes that anyway seems to have all working functionalities. Then it is possible to collect the user's opinion about their experience using normal interviews.
Thanks to the answers obtained from the interviews, the previous fixed points can be re-defined and the design cycle (both for back and front-end layers) can start again. In this second loop, back-end developers and front-end designers can build up new proposals based on the first results of previous experimentation. These new proposals will be integrated again with fast prototyping techniques for the user involvement tests. The difference between this second "user test" and the first one is related to the interactivity of the prototypes. At this stage, prototypes are closer to a working product and for this reason users' involvement in a real experience test is possible. A co-design process could start until the team arrives to positive results.

3. Fast prototyping

The design, test and production of a robust and operating prototype is a work that can require a huge quantity of resources, both in human efforts and in time: for HealthCare products, this step could be also longer because of the several and strict rules governing this area for safety requirements: bio-compatibility, electrical safety, electromagnetic compatibility tests are only a typical example of the technical requirements to be satisfied.
Sometimes time-to-market needs becomes critical: a so long amount of resources and time could be incompatible with market's law and can bring to the premature closure of a project. Therefore an Exit Strategy is to be always defined and verified at each step of the project.
To speed up the development process Fast Prototyping can play a fundamental role. Fast prototyping is a useful tool in product design making it possible to evaluate the interaction between final users and objects in an early stage of the development process. (Erickson 1995). Concerning product design it is possible anticipate even more the evaluation of usability and satisfaction using formal models and Wizard of Oz techniques. (Maudsley et al 1993).
Fast Prototyping, also called evolutionary prototyping (for the reason that the prototype will eventually be refined to create the real product) (Crinnion 1990) is a term taken from the last years trend in software engineering in which the use of this method bring to a rapid creation of new and efficient software, compatible with the dynamic aspect of software market.
This kind of prototyping involve creating a working foretype at a very early stage, after a relative fast investigation. The method used for the realization of this prototype is usually quite informal; in fact the most important factor in fast prototyping is not the quality of the

final product but the speed with which the prototype is developed so as to involve users in the shortest possible time. Now technology also offer 3.D ABS printers or stereo-lithography builders, that just from the 3D draft drawings in a proper format (.dxf, .stl, ect.) can directly realize in a few hours the formal prototype. This first prototype will became the starting point from which, through the use of expert- and end-user tests, the developer can re-examine their expectations and clarify the requirements. But also technology developers could verify all the dimensional and mechanical issues related to the back-end layer.
For a profitable adoption of Fast Prototyping techniques in order to collect significant data from the users, the prototype has to be:

- functional even with a minimum effort;
- a means for providing users a real-like application, thanks to a faithful physical representation of the main parts of the system even before final and real product implementation;
- flexible, that is modifications require minimal effort and could be done in short time, in case tests evidence an immediate feedback for some physical features changes;
- according to the previous point, not necessarily representative of the complete expected final product.

For all the above, we can divide the Fast Prototyping phase in two parts (Figure 2):

- Back-End layer development;
- Front-End Concept Design.

4. Back-end layer development

The Back-End part consists of all the technological components of the system, i.e. specifically the hardware and the software/firmware parts.
In the hardware we include electronic circuits, electro-mechanical subsystem, mechanism, connectors, fixing components and all the things that are „hard"; the software and firmware are instead the computer programs (generally embedded or "mounted" onto a microprocessor which can be considered the core of the system itself) that manage all the operations carried out by the hardware, pre-process data and communicate or deliver or receive information/commands to the new software layer beyond the Front-end part.
Circuit simulation tools are now available to support the development through early debugging sessions; their function is similar to the fast prototyping techniques previously described for the physical shape development phase.
Sometimes technological solutions can be offered or retrieved from an open-source community; in the last decade, this "free market" has demonstrated to grow up above all among academics and since a couple of years also companies are looking with interest to these solutions about open and free hardware and software tools, and about circuit realization examples that this huge community provides.
In the next paragraph, we present some examples (both for software and for hardware components) that can be useful during fast prototyping experimentation. In particular, regarding the development of healthcare devices, we show some examples focusing on available tools that can be useful in designing for electronic biomedical devices.

4.1 Opensource and free tools for hardware design

gEDA: gEDA is a set of free software applications used for electronic design and released under the GPL license(Brorson 2006). gEDA suite includes different programs through which the developer can design a circuit device starting from drawing the electronics circuit to the realization of the printed circuit board (PCB). The suite encloses schematic software, a PCB layout software, a Spice software for analogue and digital circuit simulation and other software tools that can help in the development of an electronic device.

EAGLE CadSoft: EAGLE (Easily Applicable Graphical Layout Editor) is a schematic capture and PCB layout tool; it contains a schematic editor, for designing circuit diagrams. Even though Eagle is commercial software, CadSoft offers also a freeware limited license. One of the features relevant for fast prototyping is the presence of different plug-in that can be used, with Eagle, for example to create 3D Model of the electronic circuit which can be used during the definition of package and model.

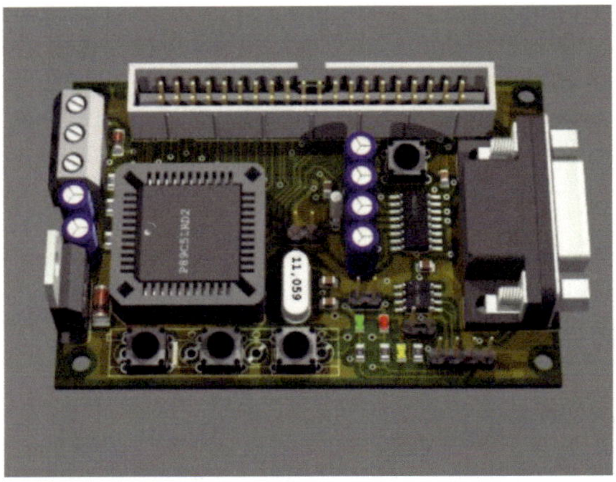

Fig. 3. Example of 3D Model generated from 3DEagle plug-in.

ARDUINO: Arduino is an open-source electronics prototyping platform based on flexible hardware and software specially developed for artists, designers, hobbyists and anyone interested in creating rapidly interactive projects (Thompson 2008). Arduino is a piece of open source hardware, free for anyone to use, modify, or sell so that can be also used in real commercial project. The "power" of Arduino is the online community created in the last years around this open source hardware. Today we can find a huge variety of different project with schematic or already mounted electronic circuits which can be easily used to create prototype with different characteristics. Nevertheless we can also find numerous libraries to program the ATMega microcontroller mounted on Arduino; in this way the time needed to design the firmware controlling all the hardware parts is considerably reduced.

4.2 Opensource for software/firmware design

A software platform for biomedical data display and processing (BCI++): BCI++ is a free and open-source (GPL) framework dedicated to biomedical data display and processing, and easy creation of User Interfaces. Originally it was designed with specific application to the development and fast prototyping of Brain Computer Interface (Wolpaw et al. 2002) systems, PC-driven protocols for different bio-signal acquisition paradigms and BCI- based applications (Perego et al. 2009). BCI++ framework is composed of two main modules that communicate via TCP/IP connection. The first module, the Hardware Interface Module (HIM) is dedicated to signal acquisition, storage and visualization, real-time execution and management of algorithms (developed both in C++ and Matlab®). The second module is the Graphics User Interface (AEnima); this module is dedicated to create and manage pc-driven

protocols based on a high level 2D/3D Graphic Engine. This structure is thought in order to split the development of a system into two parts: the part regarding signal and algorithms (the Back-End) from the graphic interface (the Front-End).
The HIM module allows interfacing the product with many commercial medical devices (Perego et al. 2009) and, with the use of express Visual Studio® wizard presents in the framework, to easily connect new devices. This module allows also to test Real-Time algorithms for bio-signal processing developed in Matlab®, and rapidly convert into C/C++ language with C4M library which can be found in the framework.
The Aenima module is based on a open source high performance real-time 3D C++ graphics engine (Irrlicht) and an open source audio engine (IrrKlang) which allow the easy and rapid creation of immersive environment with an high level of multimedia contents. Figure 4 shows an example of high multimedia contents graphics interface for a videogame used for disabled people software testing. The Aenima module is particularly useful and used for User Interfaces development.

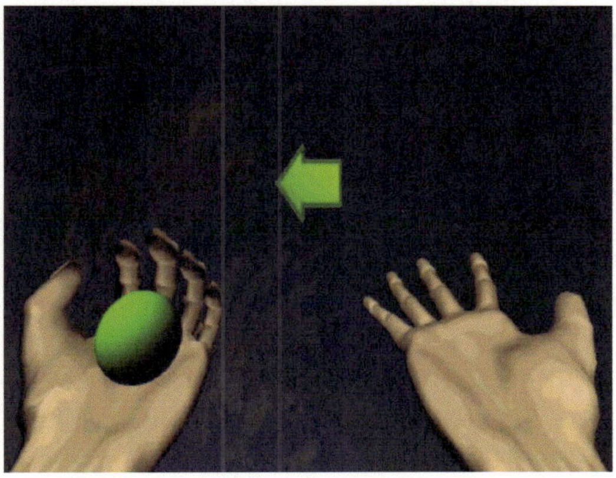

Fig. 4. Example for BCI++ Graphics Interface for imagination/simulation of grasping tasks in BCI.

GOOGLE™ CODE: Google™ Code is a Google™ site for developers; it includes several development tools, APIs created and provided by Google™ but also technical resources and open source projects that can be freely read and download. In this way Google™ Code Project Hosting allows to different developers to interact each other and exchange opinions and information to improve their experience and the quality of the project prototype. Google™ Code contains also more and more code example for developer, but also electronics schematics and 3D models, as well as extensive documentation about library and source code that developers can download and use in their project.

5. Front-end layer concept design

The Front-End layer consists in all the parts that will be in contact with the user and with which the user will interact, both physically and cognitively (interfaces, commands, buttons, icons, ...).
In most cases the role of the designer in a project is to humanize the interaction between user and technological device, to engender trust, to offer control and to minimize risk from clinician and patient perspective. Design for intuitive interfaces is the leading philosophy.

As for the technological point of view, also user interaction needs to be early tested. In this process, users are involved to evaluate the first three steps of the hierarchy of users constrains: anthropometrics, physiology and psychology (Moggridge, 2006). Users involvement is again obtained through tests with models or prototypes.
Users' interactions could be expected or real. At the beginning, designers could imagine how users will interact with the product and represent this interaction in a storyboard and then, with a real session of test, modify the interaction paradigms refining the user needs.

5.1 Early user test

As said before only the methodologies of "Oz Wizard" or Fast Prototyping (with some real functions working) could support this step to obtain significant information about concept assessment. Usually paperboard prototypes, foam or wood mock-ups are used to evaluate anthropometrics interaction in order to define general characteristics and dimensions of the packaging. Evaluating physiological aspect, as range of movement, the importance of the product weight and the accessibility of commands is also possible. Storyboards or movie scenarios (video prototyping) could be used to present a complex situation in order to immerse the user in a virtual context before evaluate the interaction with models. These kinds of tools are particularly used in service design.

5.2 Advanced (late) user test

In a second stage, front end prototype is developed with more sophisticated methods: 3D Models could be done using open-source software like Blender and physical prototypes can be built with ABS printer or stereo-lithography as previously reported; Graphical User Interfaces (GUI) can be simulated using FlashDevelop, PROCESSING, or the BCI++ platform already presented. Normally a quite final product can be necessary in order to evaluate also the physical/mechanicals issues of the product in a normal condition of use.
Those prototypes can already contain electronic circuits and boards and the test are performed directly in-field (Erdmann at al. 1971). Also the user interfaces is almost complete: LEDs, buttons and connectors are built and present at this level of realization, while colours and icons could be integrated in a very short time even if not in their final configuration. Thus, in this advanced stage thank to the availability of a well detailed prototype it is easier to evaluate also cognitive and psychological aspects of the user-product interaction.

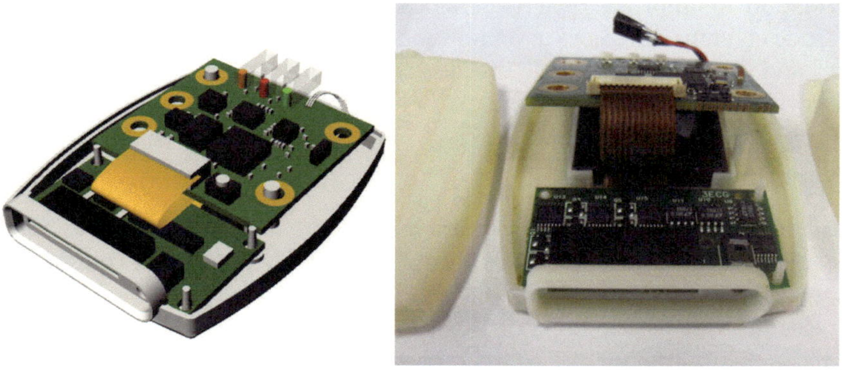

Fig. 5. Example 3D model render and ABS 3D print

BLENDER: Blender is an open source 3D graphics application that can be used for modelling, simulating and creating interactive 3D applications, including animated film, or visual effects. This software can be very useful in fast prototyping because it can create and export 3D model that can be used through 3D printer to create a prototype of the product package.

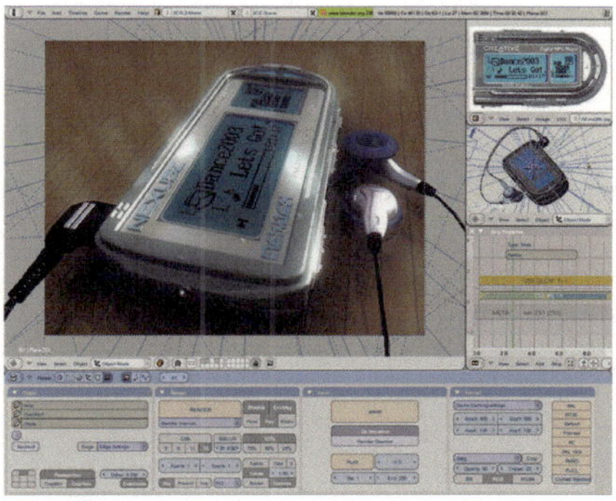

Fig. 6. Example of Blender screenshot

FlashDevelop: FlashDevelop is a free and open source code editor for general purpose project. It is an alternative open source to Flash (Adobe©) and it can be easily integrated with Flash and command line compilers. For the Graphical content of the User Interface could be used Tango Desktop that offers an open source vector-based icon set, available also for HealthCare field. Tango Desktop was used, as example, to develop Medesphere (a provider of open-source healthcare enterprise solutions).

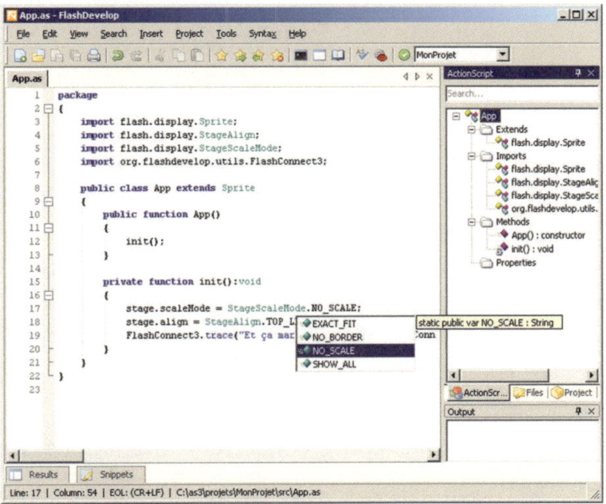

Fig. 7. Example of Flashdevelop screenshot

PROCESSING: Processing is an open source programming language and integrated development environment (IDE) for people who want to easily create user interfaces. One of the main features of Processing is the presence of a huge online community where to find a great number of libraries or already tested small software that can be rapidly included into programs.

Processing was initially developed from the idea that "programming is not only for engineers" for this reason the creation of software is very simple, nevertheless processing permits to use and interact with images, videos, sound and so on.
Another fundamental aspect of this programming language is the fact that it is cross-platform. Processing is based on Java™ programming language, the entire IDE software run on Java™ Virtual Machine and allow to the users/programmers to create and export their software in different packages so that can be used under Windows© Os, Linux Os and Mac© Os.
A Spin-Off for prototyping software in mobile phones exists (Mobile Processing) and allows designer to create small software for smart-phone and cellular phone supporting JavaME.

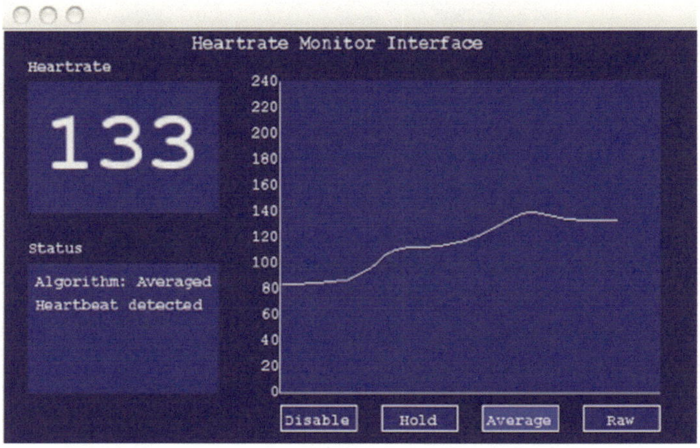

Fig. 8. Example of Heart-rate software with Processing

6. Risks in fast prototyping

Rapid prototyping is basically an analysis technique through which the designer can rapidly discover the true and complete set of formal and functional requirements for a proposed product. In classical product development, the user usually cannot view rough physical representation of the final product until the testing phase; this is critical in projects with very long development times results in a very low probability of producing an acceptable product. Nonetheless „all that glitters ain't gold!"; the wrong use of Fast Prototyping can bring to worse result than classical development, there are in fact some risks the user can fall:

- Mistake concepts of rapid prototyping concerning definitions, objectives and correct application of technique;
- Disagreements with users and costumers regards methodology, standards, tools and so on;
- Out of order test user who want to interact and evolve a prototype into a system that does everything for everyone all of the time;
- Budgets slashes and efforts shortcuts dictated by the word „fast";
- Premature delivery of a prototype indeed of final;
- Over fitted prototype substituting elegance and efficiency for flexibility.

7. Conclusion

As discussed, using fast prototyping techniques from the early steps of product design process is fundamental, especially in healthcare field, where usability can strongly affect safety during clinical processes (diagnosis, monitoring, etc.) and errors in these issues are not acceptable by definition.
In the previous paragraphs we presented and discussed different steps in a process for product design in the healthcare environment. For each of those steps we showed also some examples of new prototyping technologies and tools.
We explained how the introduction of tools for anticipating user involvement and tests (Figure 9) could produce a significant improvement in both time-to-market, and user satisfaction together with costs and resources savings.

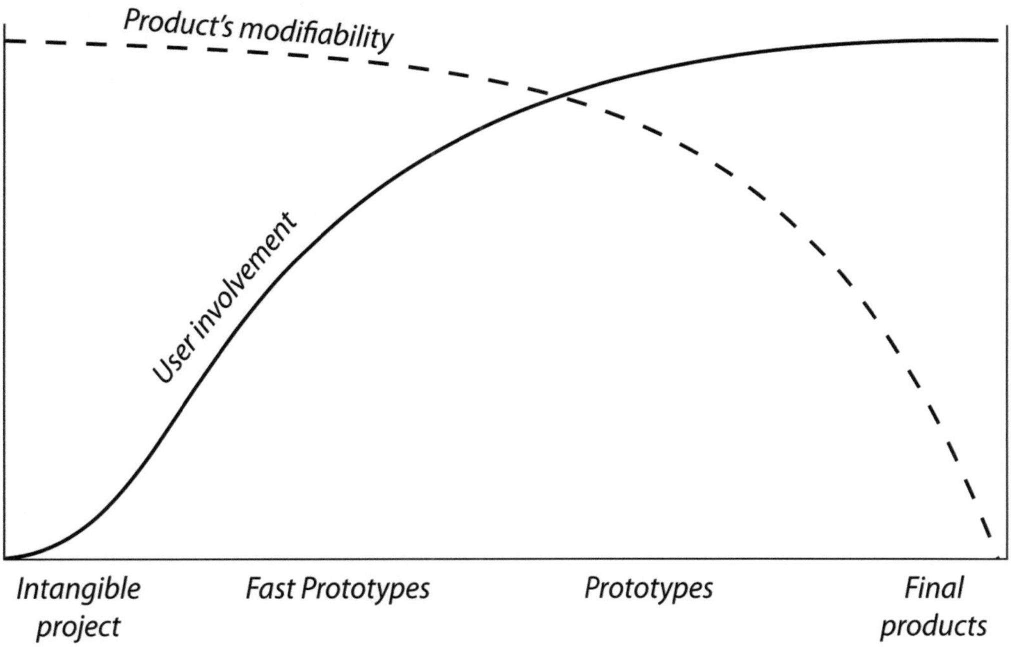

Fig. 9. Curves of User Involvement, Modifiability and project price for the proposed project procedure.

An early prototype or model with the purpose of made early user test can be very useful to create a product built no more only around technology but above all around the user. A product designed in this way will be a more a more satisfactory and useful product. In one word a well-design product.
User compliance and patient's device acceptability are increased too. Going towards a home care and monitoring future of the clinical assistance, only through this kind of process new technologies can be successfully introduced in healthcare practice.

8. References

Agostini, A., G. De Michelis, V. Susani, 2000. "From User Participation to User Seduction in the Design of Innovative User-Centered Systems". In R. Dieng, et al. (Eds.),

Designing Cooperative Systems: The Use of Theories and Models. Proceedings of the 5th International Conference on the Design of Cooperative Systems (COOP'2000, Sophia Antipolis, France, 23-26 May 2000), IOS Press, 2000, pp. 225-240.

Bandini Buti, L., 2001, Progettazione ergonomia di prodotti: i metodi e i mezzi d'indagine da utilizzare nelle varie fasi di sviluppo del progetto, in Società Italiana di Ergonomia, L'ergonomia nella società dell'informazione. VII Congresso Nazionale, 26-28 settembre 2001, Firenze.

Brorson, S., 2006. Circuit design on your Linux box using gEDA. *Linux Journal*, (141), 7.

Crinnion, J., 1990, *Evolutionary Systems Development: A Practical Guide to the Use of Prototyping Within a Structured Systems Methodology*, Springer.

Erdmann, R.L. Neal, A.S., 1971, Laboratory vs. field experimentation in human factors. An evaluation of an experimental self-service airline ticket vendor. Human Factors, 13, pp 521-531.

Erickson, T., 1995, Notes on design practice: Stories and prototypes as catalyst for communication in J. in Carroll, (ed.) (1995). Scenario-based design, Wiley & Sons: New York.

Maudsley, D., Greenberg, S. & Mander, R., 1993, Prototyping an intelligent agent through Wizard of Oz. in INTERCHI '93 Conference Proceedings, pp. 277-284.

Moggridge, B., 2006, *Designing interactions*, The MIT press, Cambridge.

Nam, H. et al, 2010, Proactive design of a hospital environment with multifaceted ergonomic considerations, AHFE proceedings, Miami, 18-21 July 2010.

Perego, P., Maggi, L. & Parini, S., 2009, BCI ++: A new framework for brain computer interface application, in Proceeding of *SEDE - ISCA*. Las Vegas (NV), pp.1- 6.

Sharp H., Y. Rogers and J. Preece, 2001, Interaction Design, Wiley.

Thompson, C., 2008, Build It. Share It. Profit. Can Open Source Hardware Work? *Wired Magazine*.

Wolpaw, J.R. et al., 2002, Brain-computer interfaces for communication and control. *Clinical neurophysiology: official journal of the International Federation of Clinical Neurophysiology*, 113(6), 767-91. Available at: http://www.ncbi.nlm.nih.gov/pubmed/12048038.

9

Perspectives of the On-line Engineering Office

Gorazd Hlebanja
University of Ljubljana
Slovenia

1. Introduction

Internet environment and internet based tools enable numerous opportunities of establishing new enterprises even without any actual, physical office. Such enterprises are already functioning in many services, e.g. language, banking, trading, to full extent. This is also true in various engineering activities. Such an environment is also beneficial in case of multinational companies, since it enables new, powerful means of communication throughout the world as a part of their distributed collaboration environment, as well as in small firms where the primary benefit lies in possibilities of the joint virtual collaboration.

On the other hand, emerging design and production systems are characterised by their atomisation. This is true for huge international enterprises, establishing their branch offices and production units in expenses and resources optimized manner. And it is also true in case of specialised small and micro enterprises. Namely, due to high tech product complexity, the latter can be competitive mostly in combined efforts. Such companies operate in a distributed production and design environment. It should be also stated that the role of the innovative design in economic growth of companies is crucial. Therefore, a distributed development environment must introduce a new working paradigm, adapted to permanent design innovation and sustainable product development.

The proposed chapter deals with the On-line engineering office (OLEO) concept. Its basis and structures will be discussed in detail, and several possible scenarios and advantages will be presented to illustrate the proposed concept. It is our belief that such a concept can importantly support not only SMEs but micro companies as well. Particularly in small economies it can be difficult to maintain and develop prosperous small specialised engineering business, thus it is necessary to spread such an enterprise over the borders. And the proposed concept seems to be a feasible solution.

Contemporary information and communication technologies (ICT) enable different means and methods for e-collaboration. The key requirements for implementation of the design and development collaboration framework are functional and resource integration; synchronous and asynchronous communication; data, file and document management; project management; and common cooperation space in a distributed environment. Besides, the ICT platform has to assure a high level of privacy, safety, and reliability, which all are essential building blocks of the OLEO. It relies on service oriented architecture and virtual portal technology and on virtual coordination unit in organisational sense.

The crucial advantage of the proposed concept is that it is lean. Lean companies are well known organisational issue. Large companies tend to "leanify" their production. And let diverse costly tasks outsource. In this context the particular OLEO consists of its basic competence, e.g. space trusses design, special gearing design, PLC planning and deployment, automatic production line design, etc. Necessary regulatory and financial tasks are outsourced. Despite its specialisation, such a business needs particular knowledge or routine at its boundaries. Or a design project appears to exceed human resources. It is efficient to find other specialists, provided a common platform can be established. No employment is needed, no additional administration, just necessary human force for the limited time period. Of course, such cooperation is based on particular competences of the involved partners. This can include human specialisation, software tools and machine operation.

The OLEO is therefore characterised as a web based on-line accessible engineering facility with sufficient competence and abilities in at least one main engineering development and design area and ability to form or adjoin another corresponding facilities based on their and collected competence. Functionalities then depend on design and development tasks that the OLEO is competent in. The proposed formation uses an adaptable ad/hoc networked development environment collecting human expertise, engineering tools, web tools and methods, data and knowledge bases, and communication and collaboration tools.

2. Mechatronic product development

Mechatronic product development is centred on discipline-specific specialisation of sub-processes, methods and tools, and the apparent need for cross-disciplinary harmonisation. The later is a prerequisite for reliable project assessment and control. It is also a foundation for efficient cooperation of individual specialists, teams and disciplines. It is a challenging task within a cross-enterprise or individual OLEOs cooperation leading to efficient task solution.

Problem discussed in this chapter relates mechatronic product or system design and development in small and medium size enterprises (SME), which have only limited resources to develop such products. However, their market position and competitiveness strongly depend on new innovative, creative goods, which basically consist of a mechanical structure, electronic and micro-processing devices, as well as programs or even intelligent software for the implementation of the operations control. This means that the complexity of the mechatronic product development, design and manufacturing requires a number of highly competent and knowledgeable subjects in different fields. It also implies usage of the newest methods, tools, and variety of data and knowledge bases. At last, results of fundamental and applied research are indispensable in development of new artefacts. On the other hand, SMEs are performing excellently in their specialised domain. To become and remain in such state they should continuously optimise their development and work systems to their production. Problems are lack of knowledge, experience and man-power in other fields, e.g. development of promising new products or systems, technologies, factory automation, etc. Thus, questions raised here from the SMEs viewpoint are

1. about definition of a new product itself and its production technology and
2. search for competent developers and developing tools.

Yet another aspect in engineering design is that designers are dealing with uncertainty starting from inexact specifications and only the degree of their competence makes possible convergence towards an improvement or new product. It is necessary to gain new information, to decide upon and build a model and possibly incorporate this in a particular

design. This could be regarded as innovation process. Only LMC have sufficient resources enabling continuous innovation.
In order to explore mechatronic product development, several aspects should be discussed. First of all the vital resources of the development process, represented in Fig. 1, should be debated. As one can see in the figure, the first are people with their particular skills and knowledge, who are trained for special tasks and who might be certified to do some (design) tasks and not less important, they should be properly motivated. Then, there are particular tools and equipment, mostly computer software and hardware, enabling such tasks. And at last, each design process is project based and self contained are procedures and methods defining interrelationships between tasks necessary for the project to converge to a mechatronic product.

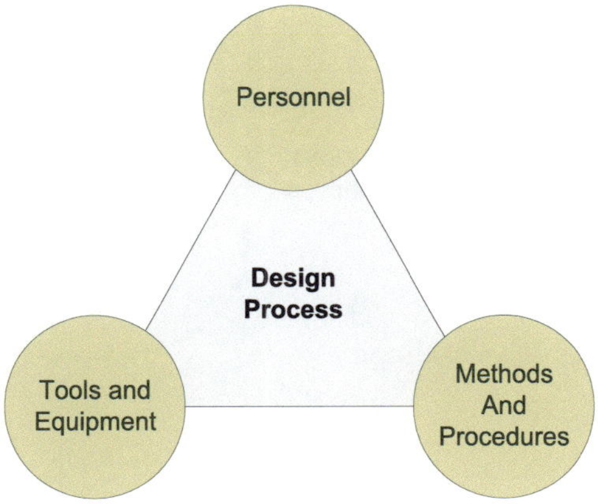

Fig. 1. Design process resources.

Another aspect is the design and development process, gradually proceeding in iterative manner from initial requirements to a mature product, as illustrated in Fig. 2. Design cannot rely only on creativeness and innovativeness. Due to complexity of intended artefacts, mechanical design systematic has been developed and put into practice especially in Germany in the second half of the last century, which is thoroughly founded in work of Pahl and Beitz from 1980 and gradually improved up to day (Pahl and Beitz, 2007). Since then, other, more abstract approach, aiming to mathematically formulate and analyse mappings from the customer needs, through the functional structure up to the design and the process domain following axiomatic rules was developed by Suh in 90-ties (Suh, 2001). Yet another approach, gaining importance, is TRIZ - Theory of inventive problem solving. TRIZ was developed mainly using knowledge acquired from engineering patents awarded in all engineering domains and is based on the concept that every superior invention is the result of resolving a contradiction and that technical systems follow generic tendencies throughout their existence, which have been named as the laws of technical system evolution (Altshuller, 1984). TRIZ aims to problem solving in computer aided innovation (Leon, 2009 and Verhaegen et al., 2009).
However, a new paradigm was necessary for mechatronic system design. Mechatronic systems could be defined as a composition of sensors and actors in a mechanical core, whereas informational structure makes possible its process(es). At first, mechatronic system development was organised in separated mechanical, electronic, control and informational domains. The first guideline in mechatronics was VDI-2422 (VDI, 1994) intended for

contemporary microcontroller based systems, where mechanical structure, circuit layout and software were developed separately, with no interdisciplinary linkage during embodiment design phase. This was overcome by a domain integration approach defined in VDI-2206 (VDI, 2004), which declares a V-model of systems engineering as a development approach in a multi-disciplinary development environment with inter and cross-domain interaction and concurrent approach. This trend towards more complex products also puts impact on more sophisticated management of product development processes. Resolution of conflicts and interferences among them became critical in such environment.

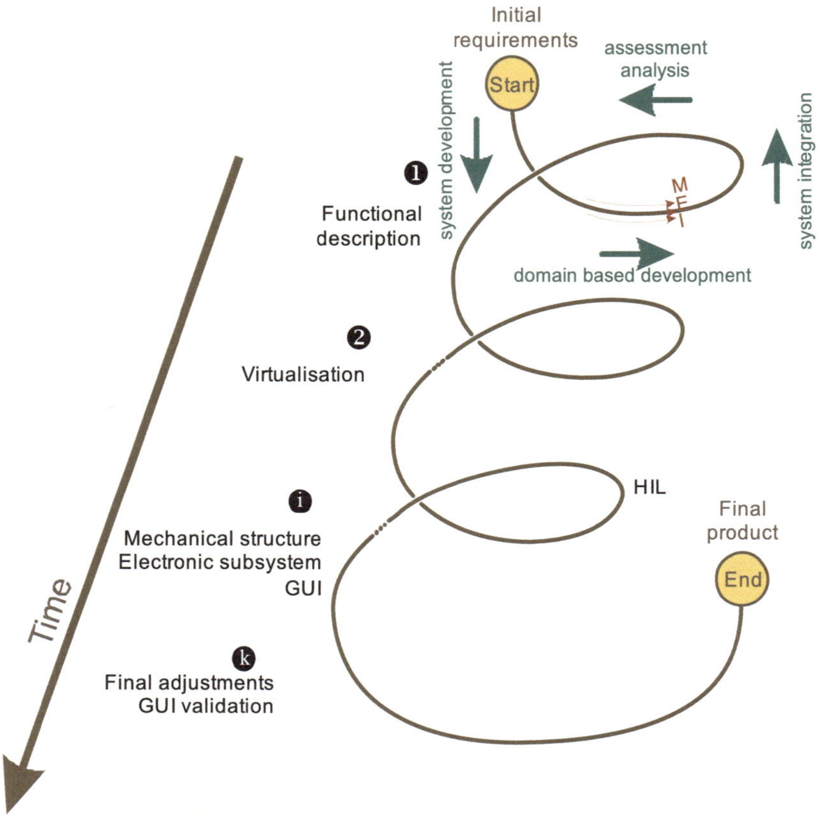

Fig. 2. Design from initial requirements to a final, mature mechatronic product.

Yet another important viewpoint is a product from its life cycle perspective. The recent advances of information technology radically changed the way product development is done. First breakthrough was achieved by CAD tools, especially by 3D modellers, which made possible effective geometric and product data generation and exchange. There would not have been any modern product development without various technical information systems like CAE, PDM and CAM, ERP and PLM which facilitate to a high extent data flow of complex digital artefacts in distributed environments. Fig. 3, adapted from (Nieman, Tichkiewitch and Westkämper, 2009), illustrates the complexity of modern product model domain complexity, due to the product life cycle perspective. Such a model is not only about a core product and its characteristics, materials, accessories, but as well about financial aspects, after sales maintenance, product service systems and recycling and safe disposal.

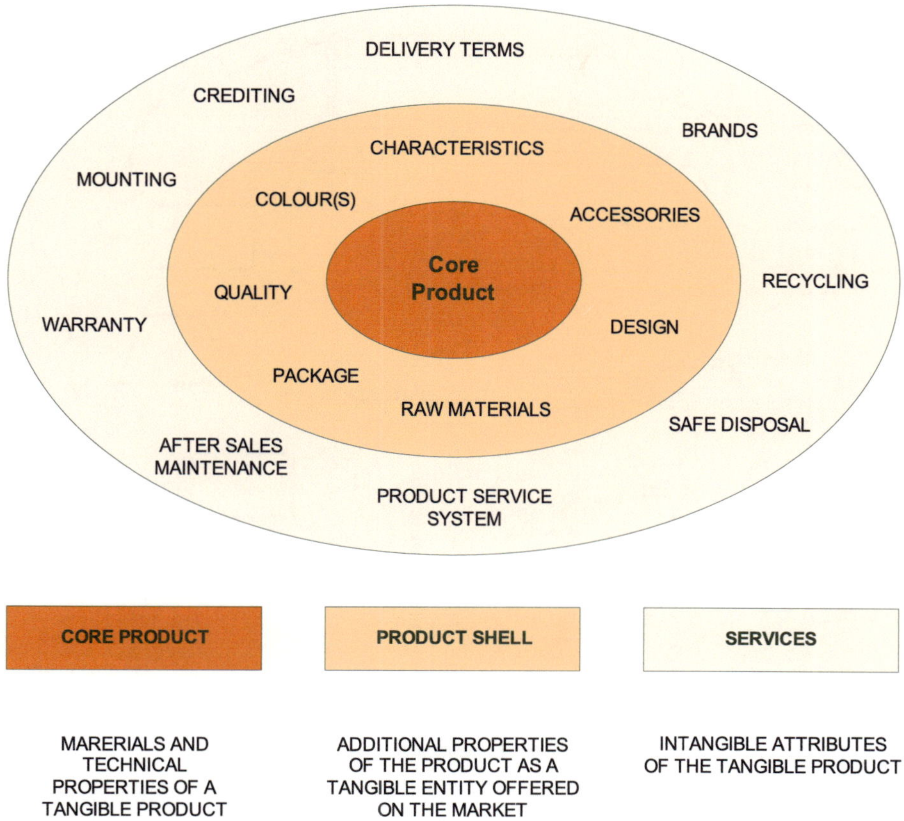

Fig. 3. Extended product model due to life cycle management.

As already stated, a mechatronic system design requires methods, tools and expertise in several engineering fields, namely mechanical, control, electronics engineering as well as various level programming. Since project based organisation of such development is evident, collective competence should be defined, composed of all individual knowledge and experience, necessary for successful implementation of a design task. Variety of tools, methods and "over-informed" staff make recognition of good design choices more difficult and again competence is of vital importance.

Therefore, a new design and development paradigm, suitable for growing market demands and coping increasing product and system complexity, should be established. Such an innovative design and development (D&D) structure has been proposed by Peklenik and reported upon in detail in (Peklenik, 2004, 2006) and is resumed here briefly. The D&D process thus starts from a product specification proceeds through the innovative development and design, prototype and manufacturing technology elaboration to a working prototype. Both processes, namely design and prototyping are conducted by specialised engineering teams. Since collected engineering knowledge might be insufficient, additional training should be available. In order to access additional less focused, broader knowledge on design and technology applied and manufacturing research teams are employed. Efficient cooperation of all teams and individuals collaborating in product formation is of crucial importance. In this context a virtual coordination unit (VCU) was developed (Peklenik, 2004), Fig. 4.

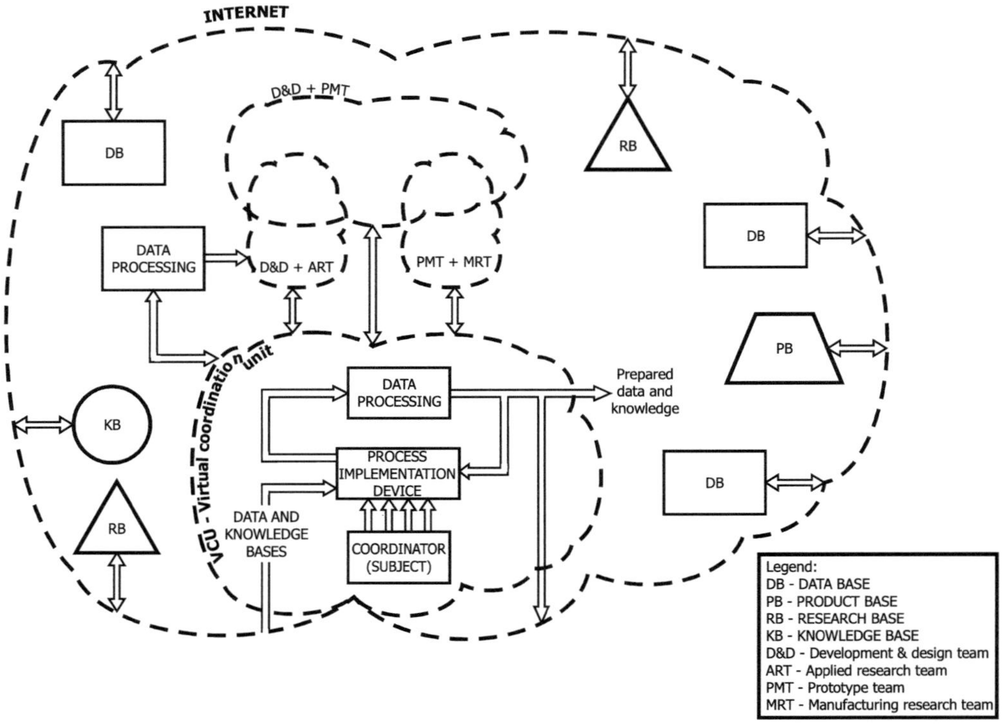

Fig. 4. Virtual coordination unit (Peklenik, 2004)

The basic tasks of the VCU are a) organisation and management of the data stored in various data and knowledge bases, on different locations; b) maintenance of effective communication, coordination and control of the activities performed by the subjects of various teams and the teams as a whole; c) communication with the innovation management, reporting on every significant aspect in the development and design of the HT-product; various aspects of patent management; d) organisation of additional training courses on-line for the subjects working in development and design prototyping teams; e) survey of the research activities of various research teams at universities, research institutes, companies: manufacturing capacities of the SME participating in the production of HT-products: etc. The term team can as well apply to the OLEO.

The VCU-function of coordination and control includes a fast and reliable communication with the manager, various teams and team subjects, the researchers of the in- and outside the R-units, the training bodies, patent office etc. The IT with the Internet and LAN-structures are the most capable means for realization of the virtual coordination function.

Whereas the coordination of processes is performed by the virtual coordination unit (VCU), a virtual competence centre (VCC) has been introduced for communication, teamwork and cooperation support (Sluga et al., 2005). It provides communication among team members, teams and VCU. The communication is carried out over the VCC portal. The portal enables access to data and knowledge bases, applications and web services that are intended for common usage. The portal also provides a common electronic workspace in order to support communication and asynchronous cooperation.

Contemporary information and communication technologies (ICT) enable different means and methods for e-collaboration. The key requirements for implementation of the D&D

collaboration framework are functional and resource integration; synchronous and asynchronous communication; data, file and document management; project management; and common cooperation space in a distributed environment. Besides, the ICT platform should assure a high level of privacy, safety, and reliability.

3. On-line engineering office

As market circumstances - i.e. growing product complexity and functionality, less predictable market, demands on higher quality, etc. - influence production companies, this reflects design and development as well. So as companies develop organizational forms enabling prompt adaptation and much higher flexibility, similar transformation is necessary in design and development domain. Goals of such an adaptation should be faster response, flexibility, ability to collaborate in a distributed environment, mastering increased complexity, cross-domain collaboration, mastering information flow, improving mutual communication to avoid misunderstandings. D&D tasks in such environment are becoming more complex and more diverging in general; time spans to accomplish such tasks are narrowing.

This also essentially influences organizational structure. In the chapter proposed formation uses an adaptable ad/hoc networked development environment collecting:

- human expertise,
- engineering tools,
- web tools and methods,
- data and knowledge bases, and
- communication and collaboration tools.

E.g. human expertise is valuable, however, it is very often hidden, it is difficult to discover information even if someone would have paid for it and previously stated environment makes it available. Thus, such an environment, collecting tools and human knowledge and coordination through internet enables better design and development possibilities also for SME.

Fig. 4 reveals the structure of the proposed on-line engineering office (OLEO) first proposed during work for European Framework Programme 6 project "Virtual Research Lab for a Knowledge Community in Production) VRL KCiP", (Peklenik et al., 2008). The general idea of the VRL KCiP is to collect human skills, tools and equipment in a virtual manner and evolved to Emiracle (Emiracle, 2010).

The OLEO environment backbone is a VCC portal assuring access to its particular elements Hlebanja et al., 2008, Hlebanja, 2009). Experts, competent professionals, use engineering tools on everyday basis. They also use data bases needed in design process, e.g. parts and assemblies, collected by TraceParts (TraceParts, 2010). Communication and collaboration tools in OLEO are of crucial importance. Rules regarding special design features (die casting, moulding, etc.) could be to some extent part of engineering tools (integrated in CAD systems), however many special methods and knowledge are systemized in additional tools, services or knowledge bases. Supplementary, even competing or complementary tools, services and methods are accessible through internet, as well work systems implementing prototypes and even labs, when experimental research is needed.

Production SMEs are usually in the position of customers; they require information, service or finished design. In this context the OLEO could be regarded as a special type ADMS (adaptive distributed manufacturing system) (Sluga et al., 2005), where design assumes the role of a product.

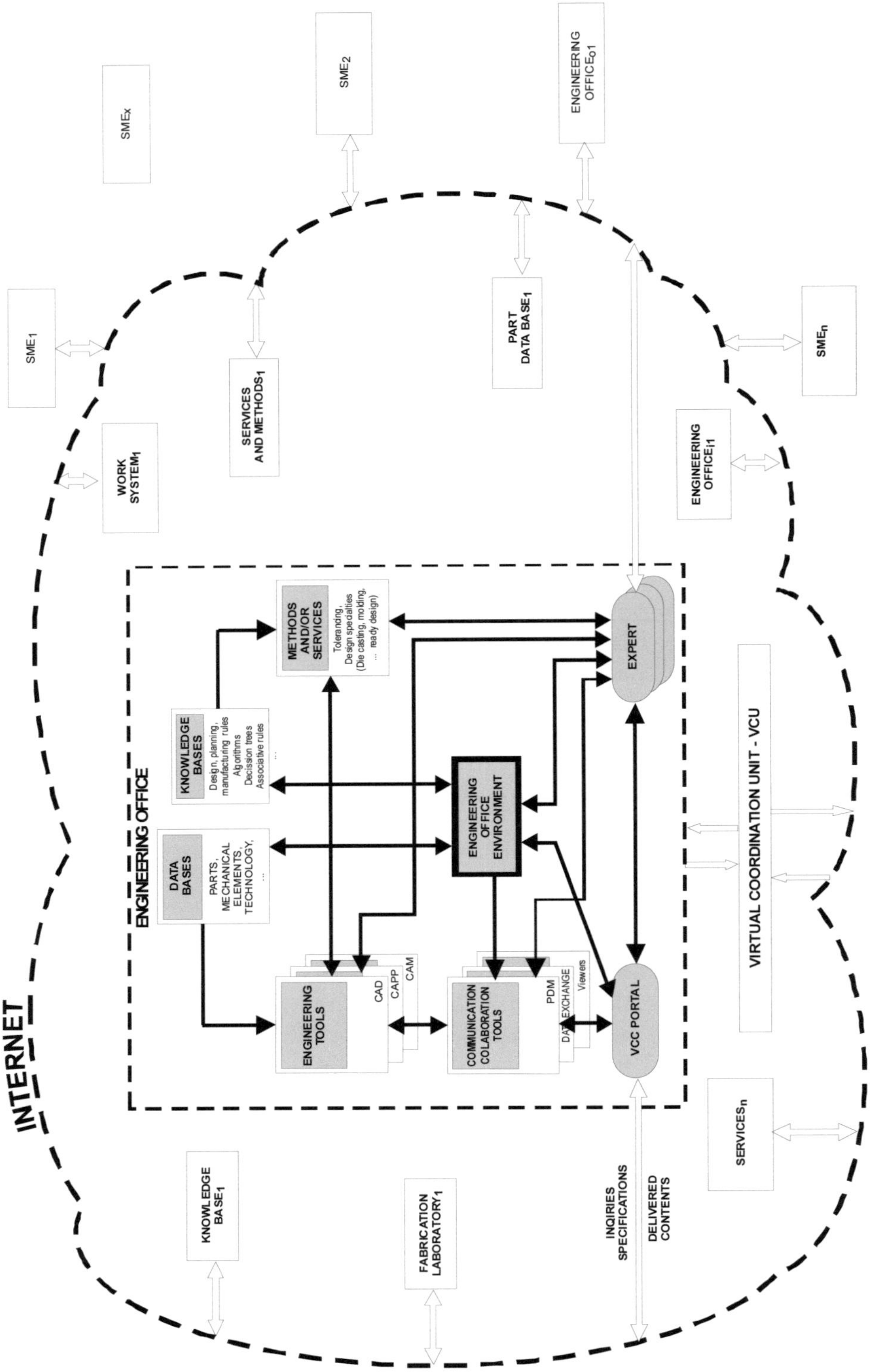

Fig. 5. The OLEO structure

An accomplished project could even result in mutual efforts of several OLEOs, which could be in a long term cooperation or in an ad-hoc connection, some tasks could be even outsourced. The ability of an ad-hoc grouping in a case of necessity is advantageous. There are almost unlimited scenario combinations. However, this is true only, if collected knowledge and experience (i.e. competence) and design process coordination lead to the objective to be accomplished.
The OLEO is therefore characterized as a web based on-line accessible engineering facility with sufficient competence and abilities in at least one main engineering development and design area and ability to form or adjoin another corresponding facilities based on their and collected competence. Functionalities then depend on design and development tasks that the OLEO is competent in. Fig. 5 reflects its structure.

Tools

High-tech or mechatronic systems - innovative products in general - development and design require interdisciplinary combination of mechanical, electronic, control and information engineering development in a concurrent manner, so called cross-domain engineering to build the underlying mechanical and electrical structure, and its control and programming environment to accomplish the system integration. Traditional engineering sequences could not result in an optimal solution.

Mechanical development tools	FEM, mechanical 3D modelling, assembly, mechanical simulations, drafting, …
Specialised tools	sheet-metal development, moulding, …, pipelines, ..
Electronic development tools	Orcad, Eagle
Control system modelling tools	Simulink/ Matlab, Matrixx/SystemBuild
System simulation	Modelica/Dymola
Software development tools	programming languages C++, C#, Java μprocessor libraries
Common services	Data exchange protocols (STEP, VDA, IGES, SET, …, xml, …)
System modelling	UML, Fujaba, …
Methods	Machine part calculations, special calculations (e.g. non-involute gears, CMM ready tolerancing, …
Data bases	Proprietary parts, WEB data bases (TraceParts, …)
Knowledge bases	Design rules, manufacturing/assembly ready design, …
Collaboration tools	Smarteam, WindChill, …

Table 1. Tools of the OLEO

Innovation lies prevailingly in early design phases, regardless of the design methodology in use, structured (Pahl&Beitz, 2007, VDI, 2004) or axiomatic design (Suh, 2001), which are basically not fundamentally different (Meijer, 2006). It appears that VDI systematics (VDI, 2004) helps to position tools and methods used in product development in a particular spot. Several interacting sub-models should be developed during HT product design already in the principal solution phase:

a. demands,
b. environment,
c. target system,
d. working structure,
e. shape,
f. functions,
g. scenarios,
h. working characteristics (e.g. dynamic response, digital logic, etc.) (Krause& Gausemeier, 2007).

Table 1 contains characteristic examples of tools used in the OLEO.

Communication, collaboration and coordination

Communication, collaboration and coordination are essential in an efficient OLEO:

1. communication between engineering office and customer, i.e. SME,
2. collaboration among developers, regardless it is intra- or inter-offices or customers,
3. coordination of development and design project.

Means of communication could be categorized in

- asynchronous tools (e.g. mailers, task organizers, file exchange, etc.),
- videoconferencing, web dialogs (e.g. Unyte),
- model visualization tools,
- tools enabling collaborative functional use of a CAD system,
- project oriented collaboration using PDM systems, and
- VCC as access point communication tool.

Collaborative engineering is facing several problems, namely: lack of collaboration tools integration, incompatibility of tools, ad-hoc collaboration, failing standards, data security, etc. Despite that, the collaborative environment is a field with a steep increase rate due to its growing importance. If someone puts search for "virtual collaboration" in Google the response is plentiful. There are free or payable solutions, project management solutions, etc. Communardo (Communardo, 2010) is a company providing appropriate innovative solutions in this field for many years.

The VCU in an OLEO gains additional role. The problem is as already said, collaboration. Design tasks are project based and the VCU should coordinate such project in two cases, depending on project ownership. In the first scenario our OLEO is the project owner and the VCU coordinates:

a. the project as such,
b. all tasks delivered to the owner and
c. all tasks delivered to other entities,

which might be SMEs, another OLEO or manufacturing facilities - autonomous work systems (Sluga et al., 2005). The opposite scenario is that our OLEO is a contractor of some company, which might also be an OLEO or SME or even LSE. The project owner is the other party in this case, so our OLEO is subordinated. The problem faced here is that each partner runs his own processes. And at this point there are two possibilities the data or process integration. Regarding the first, the coordination is about how to coordinate data transmission and transformation in such a way that the partner could accurately interpret the data and vice versa. The process oriented collaboration of a particular task is illustrated in Fig. 6. Depending on whether our OLEO is the owner or the subordinated party, it is in the left or right side in the figure. Such, task (process) based collaboration emerges in numerous scenarios, and especially in engineering change management (ECM) processes, which are of particular importance due to design process complexity and iterative procedure. The latter led to VDA recommendation, (VDA, 2010).

When there is a customer/supplier relationship between two partners, there are typically dependencies between the private ECM processes of the individual partners. At different times in the engineering change management process, one of the partners proposes a change or one partner must be integrated in the other partner's own process in order to permit activities such as technical elaboration, evaluation or decision-making. This is generally achieved by sending suitable messages to the partner (VDA, 2010), as illustrated in Fig. 6.

However, the collaborative environment could gain quite complex forms. And the VCU acquires a new role - that is coordination of such processes subordinated to a particular project.

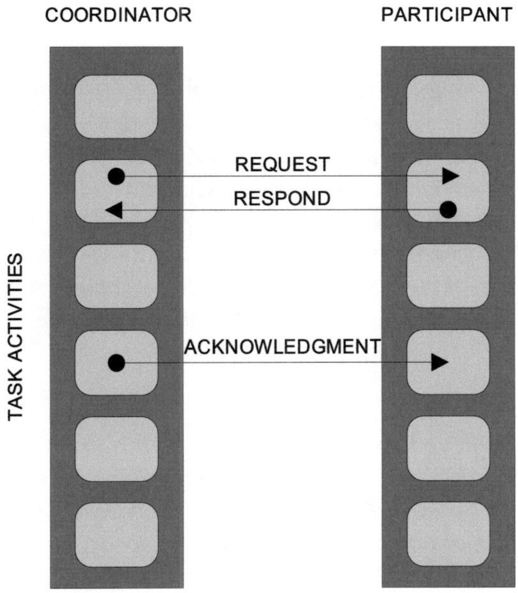

Fig. 6. Process oriented collaboration between two partners.

Services

Complex design and development tasks are usually effectively conducted in a collaborative environment, governing by a PDM system. However, this is not true for more specialized methods, which might even not be feasible for computerization or implementation on the web. On the other hand many particular methods are web accessible and could provide an important improvement in the OLEO's performance. E.g. special gear design methods (Hlebanja et al., 2005, Hlebanja et al. 2009) could have been organized in this way. Thus, it is necessary to develop

1. an evaluation procedure to facilitate selection in the web plenitude, and
2. a means of access in an OLEO.

Methods of this type should be organized as services.

Service is an activity that the service provider offers to the service receiver in a service environment and generates values for the service receivers (Tomiyama, 2004).

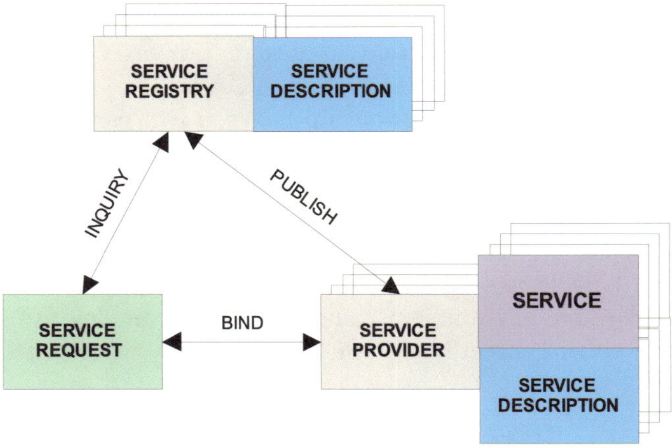

Fig. 7. Service search engine.

Web services are founded on the Service-Oriented Architecture (SOA). This concept is based on an architectural style that defines an interaction model between three primary parties: the service provider, who publishes a service description and provides the implementation for the service, a service consumer (receiver), who can either use the uniform resource identifier (URI) for the service description directly or can find the service description in a service registry and bind and invoke the service, Fig. 7. The service broker provides and maintains the service registry (Arsanjani, 2004). The registry in a web community is in principle public. However, it should be kept in a domain of the OLEO in this case.

3. Design scenario

A design scenario is employed as an illustration of the OLEO concept, in this case an automated testing rig for observation of slow speed rolling sliding contacts, developed at the Faculty of Mechanical Engineering in Ljubljana (Hlebanja&Peklenik, 2003). Many heavy duty machines, final stages of power transmissions, etc. incorporate such contacts, which are particular in their properties, possible damage forms, etc. Experimental work contributes to the development of a useful contact model of such processes, thus improving design of such contacts.

Normally the D&D process would have been started with the market research, affirming state of the art, market needs and perspectives, continues with specification, in depth iterative (system) development, and a working prototype development (system integration) (Peklenik, 2004, 2006), which also includes product testing, its acceptance and certification (if feasible). Manufacturing technology, assembly and quality control considerations would be also required in case of anticipated serial production (Iserman, 2008).

In this particular case an equivalent to the mechatronic product specification process (Peklenik, 2004) was necessary. The scientific research on feasibility and industrial relevance of such experimentation and its results had to be conducted in the first place. Upon acquired information some decisions could be derived.

The consequent pre-project phase aims

a. to define a task specification, and
b. to form a D&D team in which a mechanical designer, electronic engineer and a scientist contribute.

The situation analysis should answer questions regarding experimental conditions. In this early development stage, several aspects, influences and preliminary sub-models should be worked out. These include environmental conditions and influences, experimental strategies (scenarios) elaboration, definition of functional structure and functional units, working structure elaboration, and preliminary shaping (Gausemeier, 2005).

The above analysis implied testing rig boundary conditions, that is

- cylindrical convex-convex rolling-sliding contact,
- speed range according to Stribeck's curve between 0,035 and 0,2 m/s,
- Hertzian pressure up to 1400 N/mm^2,
- experiment duration up to 500 hours (fatigue cycles),
- sliding circumstances, etc.

Consequently, the machine size can be defined, i.e. normal force up to 10000 N. Several aspects were considered afterwards, e.g. long term experiment stability, assurance of automatic and punctual stop in case of damage (scuffing), etc. The result in this phase was redefinition of demands, confirmation of a functional model, experimental scenarios elaboration, etc. Based on above, a so called "semi-operational" scheme was developed, Fig. 8. Based on the pre-project information review and evaluation of expenses it was decided to proceed with the project.

The mechanical structure was produced and assembled in an external facility and the machine integration, revival and testing took part prior to final delivery.

The testing rig made possible slow speed rolling-sliding contact experiments, thus enabling research on cold scuffing, wear and pitting phenomena.

The testing rig was developed using computer tools. Experiments have been controlled and monitored by a computer. However, the development environment was not integrated to the extent prevailing today, communication being physical, by phone or by e-mail and file based.

How could an OLEO benefit to the above or any project?

- First of all there is the necessity for the integrated development environment, which enables better coordination, on-line accessible data, easier communication, etc.;
- the role of the VCU is expanded over the initial tasks defined by (Peklenik, 2004);
- using video-conferencing and visualisation tools for brainstorming, clarifying technical details;
- employing new collaboration tools, e.g. EVO (EVO, 2010), which enable audible and visual communication as well as sketching tools, or Unyte (Unyte, 2010), which makes public the entire desktop;
- less or no transportation time and expenses, and this way ecologically suitable;
- better prepared meetings;
- particular specialists enter D&D process only and if necessary for the time needed to accomplish their task, which is the characteristic of a lean organisation;
- efficient project management;

- better efficiency in general due to wise usage of resources.

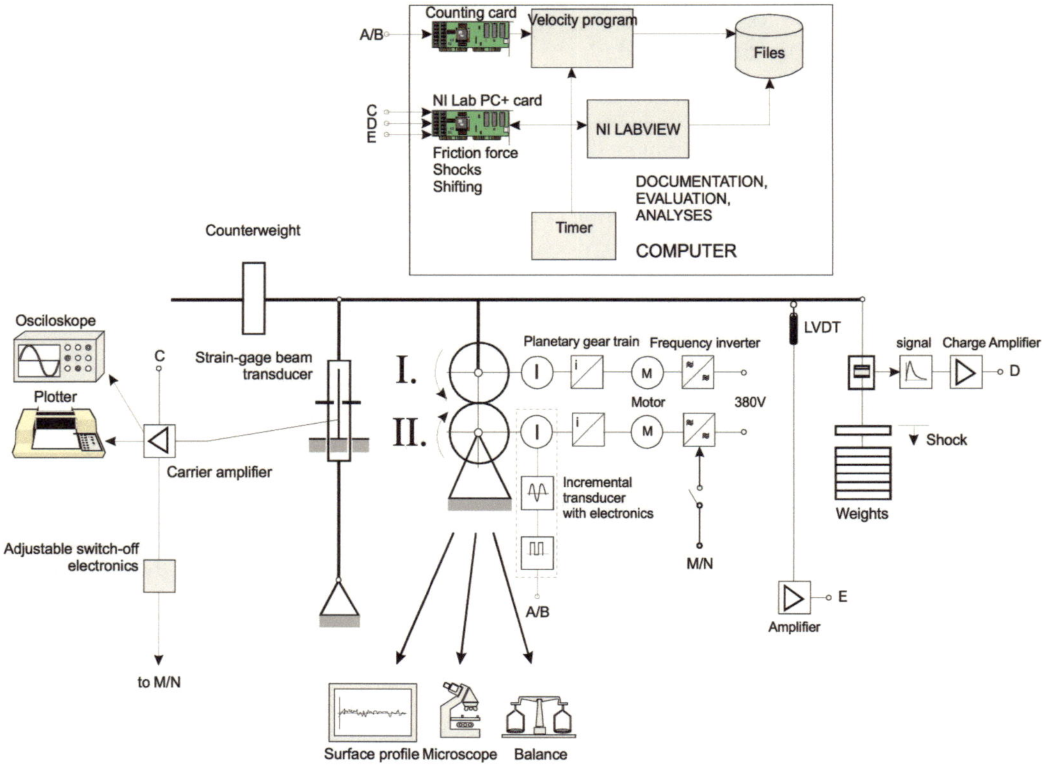

Fig. 8. Semi-operational schema of the testing rig.

4. Conclusion

The need to restructure basic characteristics of emerging design and production systems was exposed in the chapter. The concept of the adaptable and competent network structures for D&D process innovation has been summarized and the role of the virtual coordination unit explained. Furthermore, an on-line engineering office (OLEO) structure has been proposed in order to facilitate distributed development of innovative high tech products and mechatronic systems. The OLEO could be feasible structure for individual entrepreneurs as well as for SMEs. The structure of OLEO has been explored with regard to necessary human expertise, engineering tools, web tools and methods, data and knowledge bases, and communication and collaboration tools. Through the illustrative D&D scenario, the importance of web based integration was pointed out.

However, at present time this task appears to be of extreme complexity. Therefore the aim should be narrowing the OLEO domain to a controllable extent. Furthermore, methods capable of implementation as web service should be defined and evaluated, to gain their competence in the OLEO domain.

And finally it should be stated, that an OLEO is a step towards a flexible flat organization, where each partner contributes according to his expertise. Thus, in case of a complex project, many contributing partners can combine their competences in order to accomplish the common goal. However, the virtual coordination unit (VCU) should coordinate the project processes. In comparison to research and design departments there is no need to continually assemble an organized form.

And tools enabling such virtual enterprises - virtual portals are becoming more and more sophisticated each day. Activities like interpreting and proofreading can already fully rely in virtual platforms. Importance and potential of such "virtual" organization has also been widely recognized in several European FP6 projects, e.g. already mentioned VRL KCiP, which recently transformed to Emiracle (Emiracle, 2010). The flexibility of an OLEO and its ability to use resources in a lean manner and wisely makes it feasible also in sustainable product development and disposal.

5. References

Altshuller, G. (1984). *Creativity as an Exact Science.* Science Publishers, Inc., Gordon and Breach.

Arsanjani, A. (2004), Service-oriented modeling and architecture. On-line source: http://www.ibm.com/developerworks/library/ws-soa-design1/

Communardo (2010). http://www.communardo.de/home/. Accessed July 5th, 2010.

Emiracle (2010). http://www.vrl-kcip.org/spip.php?page=sommaire. Accessed, July 5th., 2010.

EVO (2010). The World Wide Collaboration Network. http://evo.caltech.edu. Accessed July 5th, 2010.

Gausemeier, J., Frank, U., Schulz, B. (2005). Domänenübergreifende Spezifikation der Prinziplösung selbstoptimierender Systeme. In: Mechatronik 2005 - Innovative Produktentwicklung, VDI-Berichte, Nr. 1892.1, VDI Düsseldorf.

Hlebanja, G. An approach to mechatronic system design process - the on-line engineering office. Machine design, 2009, str. 11-16.

Hlebanja, G., Hlebanja, J., Čarman, M. (2009). Cylindrical wormgearings with progressively curved shape of teeth flanks. Stroj. vestn., 2009, vol. 55, no. 1, p. 5-14.

Hlebanja, G., Peklenik, J. (2003). Characterization of slow rolling-sliding contact process. CIRP j. manuf. syst. Vol. 32, No.5, p.357-366.

Hlebanja, G., Peklenik, J., Sluga, A. (2008). The role of the virtual coordination unit in design process - on-line engineering office. Conf. on Knowledge Management in Product Development, University of Twente, The Netherlands, April 9-11, 26 p.

Hlebanja, J., Hlebanja, G. (2005). Anwendbarkeit der S-Verzahnung im Getriebebau : Nichtevolventische Verzahnungen weiterentwickelt. Antriebstechnik (Mainz, 1982), vol.44, No.2, p. 34-38.

Iserman, R. (2008). *Mechatronische Systeme.* 2. volst. neu bearb. Auflage. Springer, Berlin, Heidelberg.

Krause, F.-L., Franke, H.-J., Gausemeier, J., (Eds.), (2007). *Innovationspotenziale in der Produktentwicklung.* Hanser, München.

Leon, N. (2009). The future of computer-aided innovation. Computers in Industry 60, no. 8 (October 2009): 539-550.

Meijer, B. R. (2006). Self Organization in Design, In: ElMaraghy, H.A., ElMaraghy, W.H. (Eds.). *Advances in Design.* Springer, London, p.49-59.

Niemann, J., Tichkiewitch, S. and Westkämper, E. (Eds.) (2009). *Design of Sustainable Product Life Cycles.* Springer, Berlin, Heidelberg.

Pahl, G., Beitz, W., Feldhusen, J., Grote, K.-H. (2007). *Konstruktionslehre, 7. Auflage.* Springer, Berlin, Heidelberg.

Peklenik, J. (2004). Adaptive and Competent Network Structures for the Development and Design of High-tech Products. In Tichkiewitch, S. (Ed.), Brissaud, D. (Ed.). *Methods and Tools for Co-operative and Integrated Design,* p. 183-194. Kluwer.

Peklenik, J. (2006). Adaptable Network Manufacturing System - ANMS, A New Paradigm for Structuring of an Innovative Industrial Production. In 39th CIRP ISMS; June 7-9, p.9-16, Univ. of Ljubljana.

Peklenik, J., Hlebanja, G., Mitrouchev, P., Sluga, A., Butala, P. (2008) The virtual research lab for a knowledge community in production, Deliverable No. D27-48 on new working methods for knowledge and communication management, for the support of designers and engineers in design synthesis: VRL-KCiP-WP No. 3: JRA-WP3. Ljubljana: Faculty of Mech. Eng.; FP6 Prog., 2008. 25 p.

Sluga, A., Butala, P., Peklenik J. (2005). A Conceptual Framework for Collaborative Design and Operations of Manufacturing Work Systems. Annals of the CIRP, 54(1):437-440

Suh, N.P. (2001). *Axiomatic Design, Advances and Applications.* Oxford University Press, Oxford.

Tomiyama, T., Shimomura, M., Watanabe, K., (2004). A note on service design methodology. *Proceedings of DETC' 04, ASME 2004 Design Engineering Technical Conferences and Computer and Information in Engineering Conference,* 28.9-2.10 2004, Salt Lake City.

Traceparts (2010). http://www.tracepartsonline.com. Accessed, July 5th, 2010

Unyte (2010). IBM Lotus Sametime Unyte Web Conferencing Services. www.unyte.net. Accessed July 5th, 2010.

VDA (2010). ECM Recommendation. Part 0. VDA 4965, v.3.0. Verband der Automobilindustrie e.V., Berlin.

VDI (1994). *Entwicklungsmethodik für Geräte mit Steuerung durch Mikroelektronik.* VDI-Richtlinie 2422. VDI - Verlag, Düsseldorf.

VDI (2004). *Design methodology for mechatronic systems.* VDI Richtil.-2206. VDI Verlag, Düsseldorf.

Verhaegen, P.-A., J. D'hondt, J. Vertommen, S. Dewulf, and J.R. Duflou. (2009). Relating properties and functions from patents to TRIZ trends. CIRP Journal of Manufacturing Science and Technology 1, no. 3. p. 126-130.

10

Inventory Management, Spare Parts and Reliability Centred Maintenance for Production Lines

Fausto Galetto
Politecnico di Torino
Turin
Italy

1. Introduction

1st Premise: Ever since he was a young student, at the secondary school, Fausto Galetto was fond of understanding the matters he was studying: ***understanding for learning*** was his credo (φιλομαθης συνιημι); for all his life he was keeping this attitude, studying more than one ton of pages: as manager and as consultant he studied several methods invented by professors, but never he used the (many) wrong ones; on the contrary, he has been devising many original methods needed for solving the problems of the Companies he worked for, and presenting them at international conferences [where he met many bad divulgers, also *professors "ASQC **certified** quality auditors"*]; after 25 years of applications and experience, he became professor, with a dream "improve future managers (students) quality": the incompetents he met since then grew dramatically (also with documents. F.Galetto got from students ERASMUS, (Fijiu Antony et al., 2001, Sarin S. 1997). 2nd Premise: *"The wealth of nations depends increasingly on the quality of managers."* (A. Jay) and "Universities grow future managers." (F. Galetto) Entailment: due to that, the author with this paper will try, again, to provide the important consequent message: *let's, all of us, be scientific in all Universities*, that is, *let's all use our rationality*. *"What I want to teach is: to pass from a hidden non-sense to a non-sense clear."* (L. Wittgenstein). END [see the Galetto references]
"In my university studies …, in most of the cases, it seemed that students were asked simply to regurgitate at the exams what they had swallowed during the courses." (M. Gell-Mann "The Quark and the Jaguar..." [1994]). Some of those students later could have become researchers and then professors, writing "scientific" papers and books … For these last, another statement of the Nobel Prize M. Gell-Mann is relevant: *"Once that such a misunderstanding has taken place in the publication, it tends to become perpetual, because the various authors simply copy one each other."*...., similar to "Imitatores, servum pecus" [Horatius, 18 B.C.!!] and "Gravior et validior est decem virorum bonorum sententia quam totius multitudinis imperitiae" [Cicero]. When they teach, "***The result is that hundreds of people are learning what is wrong. I make this statement on the basis of experience, seeing every day the devastating effects of incompetent teaching and faulty applications.*** [Deming (1986)]", because those professors are unable to practice maieutics [μαιευτικη τεχνη], the way used by Socrates for teaching [the same was for Galileo Galilei in the *Dialogue on the Two Chief World Systems*]. Paraphrasing P. B. Crosby,

in his book Quality is free, we could say "Professors may or may not realize what has to be done to achieve quality. Or worse, they may feel, mistakenly, that they do understand what has to be done. Those types can cause the most harm."

What do have in common Crosby, Deming and Gell-Mann statements? The fact that professors and students betray an important characteristic of human beings: rationality [the "Adult state" of E. Berne (see fig. 1)]. Human beings are driven by curiosity that demands that we ask questions ("why?. ..., why?") and we try to put things in order ("this is connected with that"): curiosity is one of the best ways to learn, but "learning does not mean understanding"; only twenty-six centuries ago, in Greece, people began to have the idea that the "world" could be "understood rationally", overcoming the religious myths: they were sceptic [σκεπτομαι=to observe, to investigate] and critic [κρινω=to judge]: then and there a new kind of knowledge arose, the "rational knowledge".

Till today, after so long time, we still do not use appropriately our brain! A peculiar, stupid and terrific non-sense! During his deep and long experience of Managing and Teaching (more than 40 years), F. Galetto always had the opportunity of verifying the truth of Crosby, Deming and Gell-Mann statements.

Before proceeding we need to define the word "scientific".

A document (paper or book) is "scientific" if it "scientifically (i.e. with "scientific method") deals with matters concerning science (or science principles, or science rules)". Therefore to be "scientific" a paper must both concern "science matters" and be in accordance with the "scientific method".

The word "science" is derived from the Latin word "scire" (to know for certain) {derived from the Greek words μαθησις, επιστημη, meaning learning and knowledge, which, at that time, were very superior to "opinion" [δοξα], while today opinion of many is considered better than the knowledge of very few!}; knowledge is strongly related to "logic reasoning" [λογικος νους], as it was, for ages, for Euclid, whose Geometry was considered the best model of "scientificness". Common (good) sense ***is not*** science! Common sense does not look for "understanding", while science looks for "understanding"! "Understanding" is related to "intelligence" (from the Latin verb "intelligere" ([intus+legere: read into]: "intellige ut credas" i.e. understand to believe. Unfortunately "*none so deaf as those that won't hear*".

Let's give an example, the Pythagoras Theorem: *In a right triangle, the square of the length of the hypotenuse equals the sum of the squares of the lengths of the other two sides.* Is this statement scientific? It could be scientific because it concerns the science of Geometry and it can be proven true by mathematical arguments. It is not-scientific because we did not specify that we were dealing with the "Euclidean Geometry" (based, among others, on the "parallel axiom": from this only, one can derive that the sum of the interior angles of a triangle is always π): we did not deal "scientifically" with the axioms; we assumed them implicitly.

So we see that "scientificness" is present only if the set of statements (concerning a given "system") are non-contradictory and deductible from stated principles (as the rules of Logic and the Axioms).

Let's give another example, the 2nd law of Mechanics: *The force and the acceleration of a body are proportional vectors:* ***F****=m****a****, (m is the mass of the body).* Is this statement scientific? It could be scientific because it concerns the science of Mechanics and it can be proven "true" by well designed experiments. It is not-scientific because we did not specify that we were dealing with "frames of reference moving relatively one to another with constant velocity" [inertial frames (with the so called "Galilean Relativity": the laws of Physics look the same for inertial systems)] and that the speed involved was not comparable with the "speed of light in the vacuum [that is the same for all observers]" (as proved by the Michelson-Morley experiment: in the Special Relativity Theory, **F**=d(m**v**)/dt is true, not **F**=m**a**!) and not involving atomic or subatomic particles. We did not deal "scientifically" with the hypotheses; we assumed them implicitly. From the laws of Special Relativity we can derive *logically* the conservation laws of momentum and of energy, as could Newton for the "Galilean Relativity". For atomic or subatomic particles "quantum Mechanics" is needed (with Schrödinger equation as fundamental law).

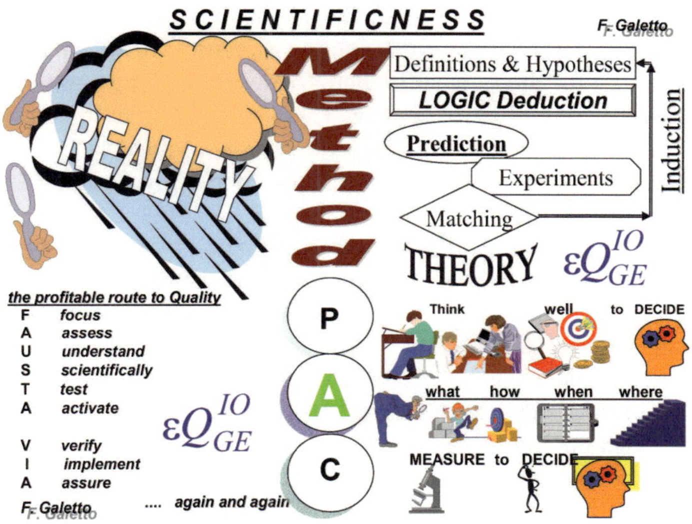

Fig. 1. Scientificness

So we see that "scientificness" is present **only** if the set of statements (concerning a given "system") do not contradict the observed data, collected through well designed experiments ["scientific" experiments]: only in the XVII century, due to Galilei, Descartes, Newton, ... we learned that. Since that time only, science could really grow.

When we start trying to learn something, generally, we are in the "clouds"; reality (and truth) is hidden by the clouds of our ignorance, the clouds of the data, the clouds of our misconceptions, the clouds of our prejudices; to understand the phenomena we need to find out the reality from the clouds: we make hypotheses, then we deduct logically some consequences, predicting the results of experiments: if predictions and experimental data do match then we "confirm" our idea and if many other are able to check our findings we get a theory. To generate a theory we need Methods. Eric Berne, the psychologist father of "Transactional Analysis", stated that everybody interacts with other people trough three states P, A, C [Parent, Adult, Child, (not connected with our age, fig. 1)]: the Adult state is the one that looks for reality, makes questions, considers the data, analyses objectively the data, draws conclusions and takes logic decisions, coherent with the data, methodically. Theory [θεωρια] comes from the Adult state! Methods [μεθοδος from μετα+οδος = the way through (which one finds out…)] used to generate a Theory come from the Adult state!

People who take for granted that the truth depends on "Ipse dixit" [αυτος εφα, "he said that"], behave with the Parent state. People who get upset if one finds their errors and they

do not consider them ["we are many and so we are right", they say!!] behave with the Child state. [see the books of the Palo Alto group]
To find scientifically the truth (out of the clouds) you must **F**ocus on the problem, **A**ssess where you are (with previous data and knowledge), **U**nderstand **S**cientifically the message in the data and find consequences that confirm (or disprove) your predictions, Scientifically design **T**est for confirmation (or disproval) and then **A**ctivate to make the Tests. If you and others **V**erify you prediction, anybody can **I**mplement actions and **A**ssure that the results are SCIENTIFIC (FAUSTA VIA): all of us then have a THEORY. SCIENTIFICNESS is there (fig. 1).
From these two examples it is important to realise that when two people want to verbally communicate, they must have some common concepts, they agree upon, in order to transfer information and ideas between each other; this is a prerequisite, if they want to understand each other: what is true for them, what is their "conventional" meaning of the words they use, which are the rules to deduce statements (Theses) from other statements (Hypotheses and "previous" Theses): **rigour is needed for science**, not opinions!!!
Many people must apply *Metanoia* [μετανοια=change their mind (to understand)] to find the truth.
Here we accept the rules of LOGIC, the *deductive* logic, where the premises of a valid argument contain the conclusion, and the truth of the conclusion follows from the truth of the premises with certainty: any well-formed sentence is either true or false. We define as *Theorem* "a statement that is proven true by reasoning, according to the rules of Logic"; we must therefore define the term *True*: "something" (statement, concept, idea, sentence, proposition) is true when there is *correspondence* between the "something" and the facts, situations or state of affairs that verify it; the *truth* is a relation of *coherence* between a thesis and the hypotheses. Logical validity is a relationship between the premises and the conclusion such that if the premises are true then the conclusion is true. The validity of an argument should be distinguished from the truth of the conclusion (based on the premises). This kind of truth is found in mathematics.
Human beings evolved because they were able to develop their knowledge from inside (the *deductive* logic, with analytic statements) and from outside, the external world, (the *inductive* logic, with synthetic statements), in any case using their intelligence; the *inductive* logic is such that the premises are evidence for the conclusion, but the truth of the conclusion follows from the truth of the evidence only with a certain probability, provided the way of reasoning is correct.
The scientific knowledge is such that any valid knowledge claim must be verifiable in experience and built up both through the *inductive* logic (with its synthetic statements) and the *deductive* logic (with its analytic statements); in any case a clear distinction must be maintained between analytic and synthetic statements.
This was the attitude of Galileo Galilei in his studies of falling bodies. At first time he formulated the tentative hypothesis that "the speed attained by a falling body is directly proportional to the distance traversed"; then he deduced from his hypothesis the conclusion that objects falling equal distances require the same amount of elapsed time. After "Gedanken Experimenten", Designed Experiments made clear that this was a false conclusion: hence, logically, the first hypothesis had to be false. Therefore Galileo framed a new hypothesis: "the speed attained is directly proportional to the time elapsed". From this he was able to deduce that the distance traversed by a falling object was proportional to the

square of the time elapsed; through Designed Experiments, by rolling balls down an inclined plane, he was able to verify experimentally his thesis (it was the first formulation of the 2nd law of Mechanics). [fig. 1]

Such agreement of a conclusion with an actual observation does not itself prove the correctness of the hypothesis from which the conclusion is derived. It simply renders that premise much more plausible.

For rational people (like were the ancient Greeks) the criticism [κρινω = to judge] is hoped for, because it permits improvement: asking questions, debating and looking for answers improves our understanding: we do not know the truth, but we can look for it and be able to find it, with our brain; to judge we need criteria [κριτεριον]. In this search Mathematics [note μαθησις] and Logic can help us a lot: Mathematics and Logic are the languages that Rational Managers must know! Proposing the criterion of testability, or falsificability, for scientific validity, Popper emphasized the *hypothetico-deductive character of science*. Scientific theories are hypotheses from which can be deduced statements testable by observation; if the appropriate experimental observations falsify these statements, the hypothesis is refused. If a hypothesis survives efforts to falsify it, it may be tentatively accepted. No scientific theory, however, can be conclusively established. A "theory" that is falsified, is **NOT** scientific.

"Good theories" are such that they **complete** previous "good" theories, in accordance with the collected new data. [fig. 1]

A good example of that is **Bell's Inequality**. In physics, this inequality was used to show that a class of theories that were intended to "complete" quantum mechanics, namely local hidden variable theories, are in fact inconsistent with quantum mechanics; quantum mechanics typically predicts probabilities, not certainties, for the outcomes of measurements. Albert Einstein [one of the greatest scientists] stated that quantum mechanics was incomplete, and that there must exist "hidden" variables that would make possible definite predictions. In 1964, J. S. Bell proved that all local hidden variable theories are inconsistent with quantum mechanics, first through a "Gedanken Experiment" and Logic, and later through Designed Experiments. Also the great scientist, A. Einstein, was wrong in this case: his idea was falsified. We see then that the ultimate test of the validity of a scientific hypothesis is its *consistency* with the totality of other aspects of the scientific framework. This inner consistency constitutes the basis for the concept of causality in science, according to which every effect is assumed to be linked with a cause. [fig. 1]

The scientific community as a whole must judge [κρινω] the work of its members by the ***objectivity and rigour*** with which that work has been conducted; in this way the scientific method should prevail.

In any case the scientific community must remember: ***Any statement (or method) that is falsified, is NOT scientific.***

Here we assume that the subject of a paper is concerning a science (like Mathematics, Statistics, Probability, Quality Methods); therefore to judge [κρινω] if a paper is scientific we have to look at the "scientific method": if the "scientific method" is present, i.e. the conclusions (statements) in the paper follow logically from the hypotheses, we shall consider the paper scientific; **on the contrary**, if there are conclusions (statements) in the paper that do not follow logically from the hypotheses, we shall NOT consider the paper scientific: a ***wrong conclusion (statement) is NOT scientific***. [fig. 1 vs Franceschini 1999]

"To understand that an answer is wrong you don't need exceptional intelligence, but to understand that is wrong a question one needs a creative mind." (A. Jay). "Intellige ut credas".

Right questions, with right methods, have to be asked to "nature" (fig. 1). "Intellige ut credas".
It is easy to show that a paper, a book, a method, is not scientific: it is sufficient to find an example that proves the wrongness of the conclusion. When there are formulas in a paper, it is not necessary to find the right formula to prove that a formula is wrong: an example is enough; to prove that a formula is wrong, one needs only intelligence; on the contrary, to find the right formula, that substitutes the wrong one, you need both intelligence and ingenuity. I will use only intelligence and I will not give any proof of my ingenuity: this paper is for intelligence ... For example, it's well known (from Algebra, Newton identities) that the coefficients and the roots of any algebraic equation are related: it's easy to prove that $\pm\sqrt{-c/a}$ is not the solution (even if you do not know the right solution) of the parabolic equation $ax^2+bx+c=0$, because the system $x_1+x_2=-b/a$, $x_1x_2=c/a$ is not satisfied (x_1 and x_2 are the roots). [Montgomery 1996 and ....]
The literature on "Quality" matters is rapidly expanding. Unfortunately, nobody, but me, as far as I know, [I thank any person that will send me names of people who take care ...], takes care of the ***Quality of Quality Methods used for making Quality*** (of product, processes and services). "Intellige ut credas". [O' Connor 1997, Brandimarte 2004]
I am eager to meet one of them, fond of Quality as I am. [fig. 1, and Galetto references]
If this kind of person existed, he would have agreed that "***facts and figures are useless, if not dangerous, without a sound theory***" (F. Galetto), "**Management need to grow-up their knowledge because experience alone, without theory, teaches nothing what to do to make Quality**" (Deming) because he had seen, like Deming, Gell-Mann and myself "***The result is that hundreds of people are learning what is wrong. I make this statement on the basis of experience, seeing every day the devastating effects of incompetent teaching and faulty applications.***" [Deming (1986)] (Montgomery 1996 and ...., Franceschini 1999)
During 2006 F. Galetto experienced the incompetence of several people who were thinking that only the "Peer Review Process" is able to assure the scientificness of papers, and that only papers published in some magazines are scientific: one is a scientist and gets funds if he publishes on those magazines!!! Using the scientific method one can prove that the referee analysis does not assure quality of publications in the magazines of fig. 2.

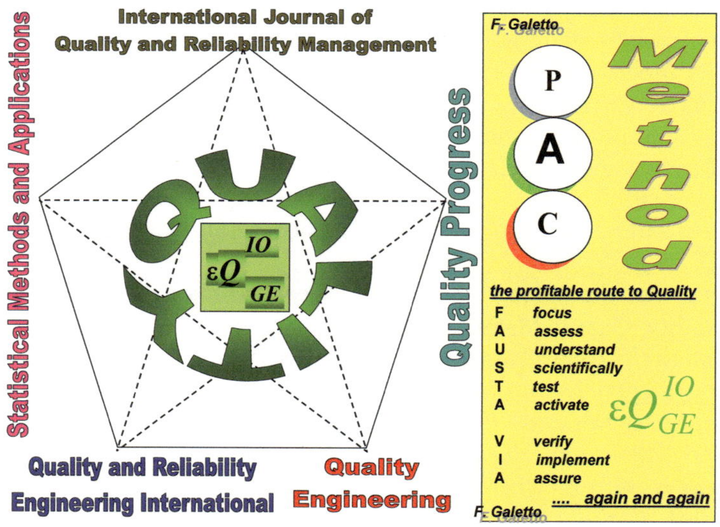

Fig. 2. The "pentalogy"

The symbol εQ_{GE}^{IO} [which stands for the "***epsilon Quality***"] was devised by F. Galetto to show that ***Q***uality depends, at any instant, in any place, at any rate of improvement, on the ***I***ntellectual h***O***nesty of people who always use experiments and think well on the experiments before actually making them (***G***edanken ***E***xperimenten) to find the truth" [*Gedanken Experimenten* was a statement used by Einstein; but, if you look at Galileo life, you can see that also the Italian scientist was used to "mental experiments", the most important tool for Science; Epsilon (ε) is a greek letter used in Mathematics and Engineering to indicate a very small quantity (actually going to zero); ***epsilon Quality*** conveys the idea that Quality is made of many and many prevention and improvement actions].
The level of knowledge F. Galetto could verify (in 40 years experience and a lot of meetings) is given in table 1.

	Logic	Management	Mathematics	Physics	Quality Management	Probability	Stochastic Processes	Statistics	Applied Statistical Methods	Parameter Estimation	Test of Hypotheses	Decision Making	System Reliability Theory	Maintainability	Design Of Experiments	Control Charts	Sampling Plans	Quality Engineering	Quality Practice
Professors	1 H	VL 95	VL 98	VL 98	VL 99	VL 99	VL 99	VL 99	VL 99	VL 99	VL 99	VL 95	VL 99	VL 99	VL 99	VL 99	VL 99	VL 99	VL 99
Managers	VL 95	VL 95	VL 98	VL 98	VL 99	VL 99	VL 99	VL 99	VL 99	VL 99	VL 99	VL 95	VL 99	VL 99	VL 99	VL 99	VL 99	1 VH	1 VH
Consultants	VL 99	VL 95	VL 98	VL 98	VL 99	VL 99	VL 99	VL 99	VL 99	VL 99	VL 99	VL 95	VL 99	VL 99	VL 99	VL 99	VL 99	1 VH	1 VH

Legenda : VL90=probability 90% that knowledge is lower than Very Low;
5VH=probability 5% that knowledge is higher than Very High
Scale: None, Very Low, Low, Medium, High, Very High, Perfect

Table 1. Level of Knowledge (based on 40 year of experience, in companies and universities)

Many times F. Galetto spoiled his time and enthusiasm at conferences, in University and in Company courses, trying to provide good ideas on Quality and showing many cases of wrong applications of stupid methods [see references]. He will try to do it again ... by showing, step by step, very few cases (out of the hundreds he could document).... in order people understand that QUALITY is a serious matter. The Nobel price R. Feynman (1965) said that *for the progress of Science are necessary experimental capability, honesty in providing the results and the intelligence of interpreting them... We need to take into account of the experiments **even though** the results are different from our expectations.* It is apparent that Deming and Feynman and Gell-Mann are in agreement with εQ_{GE}^{IO} ideas of F. Galetto. Once upon a time, A. Einstein said "*Surely there are two things infinite in the world: the Universe and the Stupidity of people. But I have some doubt that Universe is infinite*". Let's hope that Einstein was wrong, this time. Anyway, before him, Galileo Galilei had said [in the *Saggiatore*] something similar "*Infinite is the mob of fools* ". [see references]

All the methods, devised by F. Galetto, were invented and have been used for preventing and solving real problems in the Companies he was working for, as Quality Manager and as Quality Consultant: several million € have been saved.[see Galetto references]
Companies will not be able to survive the global market if they cannot provide integrally their customer the Quality they have paid for [fig. 5, Management Tetrahedron]. So it is of paramount importance to define correctly what Quality means. Quality is a serious and difficult business; it has to become an integral part of management.
The first step is to define *logically* what Quality is.
Let's start with some ideas of Soren Bisgard (2005) given in the paper Innovation, ENBIS and the Importance of Practice in the Development of Statistics, *Quality and Reliability Engineering International*. He says: "*Since the early 1930s industrial statistics has been almost synonymous with quality control and quality improvement. Some of the most important innovations in statistical theory and methods have been associated with quality.*" .... "*Quality Management also provides an intriguing example. Its scientific underpinning is greatly inspired by statistics, a point forcefully set forth by Shewhart. Quality is typically interpreted narrowly by statisticians as variance and defect reduction. However these efforts should be viewed more broadly as what economist call* ***innovation****. When we engage in statistical quality control studies ... we are engaged in* ***process innovation*** *and ... in* ***product innovation****.*" Two paragraphs of his paper are entitled: 2. Quality as innovation, and 3. Quality as systematic innovation.
One must say that the paper does not provide the definition of the term Quality, such as "Quality is ..."; however he realises that statisticians have a narrow view of Quality, as "Quality is *variance and defect reduction*."
As a matter of fact, D. C. Montgomery defines: "*Quality is the inverse of variability*" (saying "*We prefer a* ***modern*** *definition of quality*") and adds "*Quality Improvement is the reduction of variability in processes and products*". To understand the following subject the reader has to know Reliability and Statistics. Let's consider two computers (products A and B): after 3 years, A experiences $g_A(3)=9$ failures, while B experiences $g_B(3)=5$ failures; which product has better quality? B, because it experienced less failures! BUT, which product has lower variability? A, because it experienced more failures!
Generally, statisticians (and professors) do not understand this point: they are Gauss-drugged with the "normal distribution"! Let's assume, for the sake of simplicity, that two items have constant increasing failure rate (IFR, they do wear and do not have infant mortality); form the data we can estimate the MTTF (Mean Time To Failure), the Reliability R(t) and the probability density of failures f(t): B is more reliable and has more variability [the upper curve]! Therefore according to D. C. Montgomery definition B (that is more reliable) has lower "quality"! Fig 3 provides a hint for understanding ....

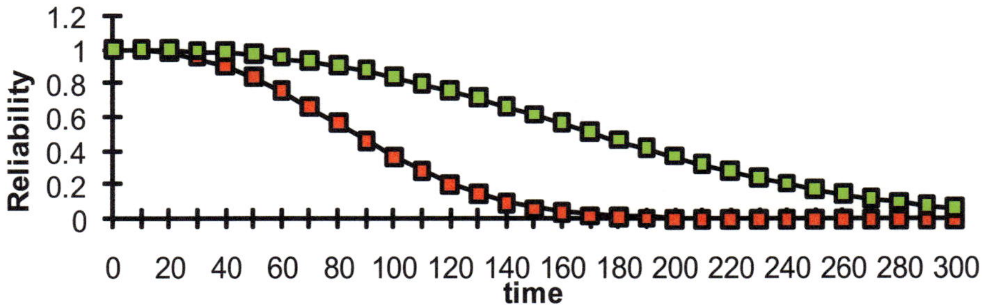

Fig. 3. An item with more variability B, has better Quality

If one thinks to the Formula One Championship and applies Montgomery's definition he finds that if the two Red Bull arrive 1st and 2nd they have lower quality than the two Ferrari that arrive 7th and 8th!!!!! Can you believe it?

There are a lot of "quality definitions; let's see some of the latest definitions of the word "Quality" that can be found in the literature (some of them existed before the date here given; the date shown refers to the latest document I read):

"conformance to requirements" (Crosby, 1979), "fitness for use" (Juran ,1988), "customer satisfaction" (Juran, 1993), "the total composite product and service characteristics of marketing, engineering, manufacture and maintenance through which product or service in use will meet the expectations by the customer" (Feigenbaum, 1983 and 1991), "totality of characteristics of an entity that bears on its ability to satisfy stated and implied needs" (ISO 8402:1994), "a predictable degree of uniformity and dependability at low cost and suited to the market" (***falsely** attributed to* Deming, 1986; I read again and again Deming documents and I could not find that), "Quality is inversely proportional to variability" (Montgomery, 1996), "degree to which a set of inherent characteristics (3.5.1) fulfils requirements (3.1.2)" [**ISO 9000:2000, Quality management systems - Fundamentals and vocabulary,** (definition 3.1.1)]

The ISO definition is very stupid; it is like confounding two very different concepts: energy and temperature; "temperature" provides the *degree* of "energy" [=Quality]; therefore *Quality* must be "the set of characteristics".

Quality definition must have Quality in it!

In order to provide a practical and managerial definition, since 1985 F. Galetto was proposing the following one:

Quality is the set of characteristics of a system that makes it able to satisfy the *needs* of the Customer, of the User and of the Society. It is clear that none of the previous eight definitions highlights the importance of the ***needs*** of the three actors: **the Customer, the User and the Society**. They are still not considered in the latest document, the ISO 9000:2008, Quality management systems - Fundamentals and vocabulary.

Some important characteristics are stated in the Quality Tetrahedron of ten characteristics Safety, Conformity, Reliability, Durability, Maintainability, Performance, Service, Aesthetics, Economy, Ecology; each characteristic has an "operational definition" that permits to state goals and verify achievement [according to FAUSTA VIA]. "Customer/User/Society ***needs*** satisfaction" must be converted from a slogan to real practice, if companies want to be competitive. Today, many managers show their commitment with customer satisfaction, but they are not prepared to invest time and money in NEEDS Satisfaction; they do not put the theory into practice; they do not speak with the facts, but only with words.

Unfortunately *management commitment to Quality is not enough*; managers must understand and learn Quality ideas: too many companies are well behind the desired level of Quality management practices. [fig. 5]

The Quality Tetrahedron shows that Management must learn that ***solving problems is essential but it is not enough***: **they must prevent future problems and take preventive actions**: Safety, Reliability, Durability, Maintainability, Ecology, Economy can be tackled rightly only through preventive actions; the PDCA cycle is useless for prevention; it very useful for improvement. Several of the Quality characteristics [in the Quality Tetrahedron] need prevention; reliability is one of the most important: very rarely failures can be attributed to blue collar workers. Failures arise from lack of prevention, and prevention is a fundamental aspect and responsibility of Management. The same happens for safety, durability, maintainability, ecology, economy, ...

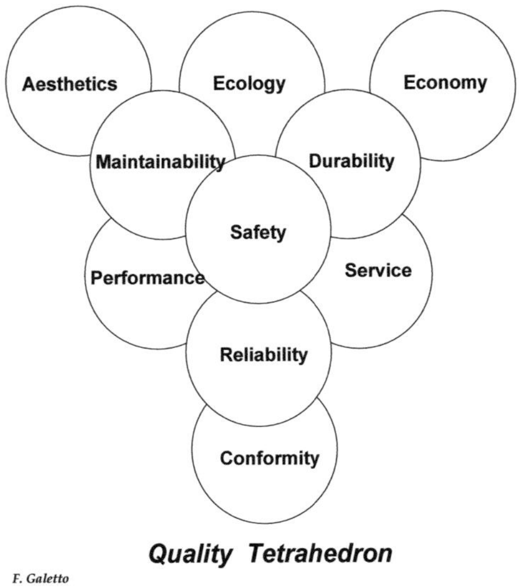

Fig. 4. The Quality Tetrahedron for the Quality definition

So we see that Quality entails much more than "innovation": you can innovate without Quality! Few decades ago electronic gadgets entered into cars; electronics was an innovation in cars, but the cars failed a lot: innovation did not take into consideration ***prevention***! The essence of Quality is prevention. Innovation is a means for competition, rarely for Quality. (see the "Business Management System" in figure 5).

We are in a new economic age: long-term thinking, prevention, Quality built at the design stage, understanding variation, waste elimination, knowledge and scientific approach are concepts absolutely needed by Management , if they want to be good Managers. In this paper, Manager is the person who *achieves the Company goals, economically, through other people, recognise existing problems, prevents future problems, states priorities, dealing with their conflicts, makes decisions thinking to their consequences, with rational and scientific method, using thinking capability and knowledge of people.* These kind of Managers behave according to the "Business Management System".

The customer is the most important driving force of any company. Companies will not be able to survive the global market if they cannot provide integrally their customer the Quality they have paid for. It is important to stress that "Customer Needs Satisfaction" is absolutely different from "Customer Satisfaction". Moreover, the previous analysis show that for a good definition of Quality there are other people involved: the user and the Society.

Prevention... We said that the essence of Quality is prevention. Innovation is a means for competition, rarely for Quality. (see the "Business Management System"). Quality is essential for any product (services are defined as products in the ISO 9000:2000 terminology). The measurement of Quality (of product and services) is important if we want to improve and better if we want to prevent problems [F. Galetto from 1973]. Quality depends on effective management of problems prevention and correction (improvement). Effective management needs effective measurement of performance and results, the absolute condition to achieve Business Excellence. A Company that wants to become "excellent" has to find the needs of Customers/Users/Society and to measure how much they are achieved. Moreover that Company has to be "sure" that all its processes are "in

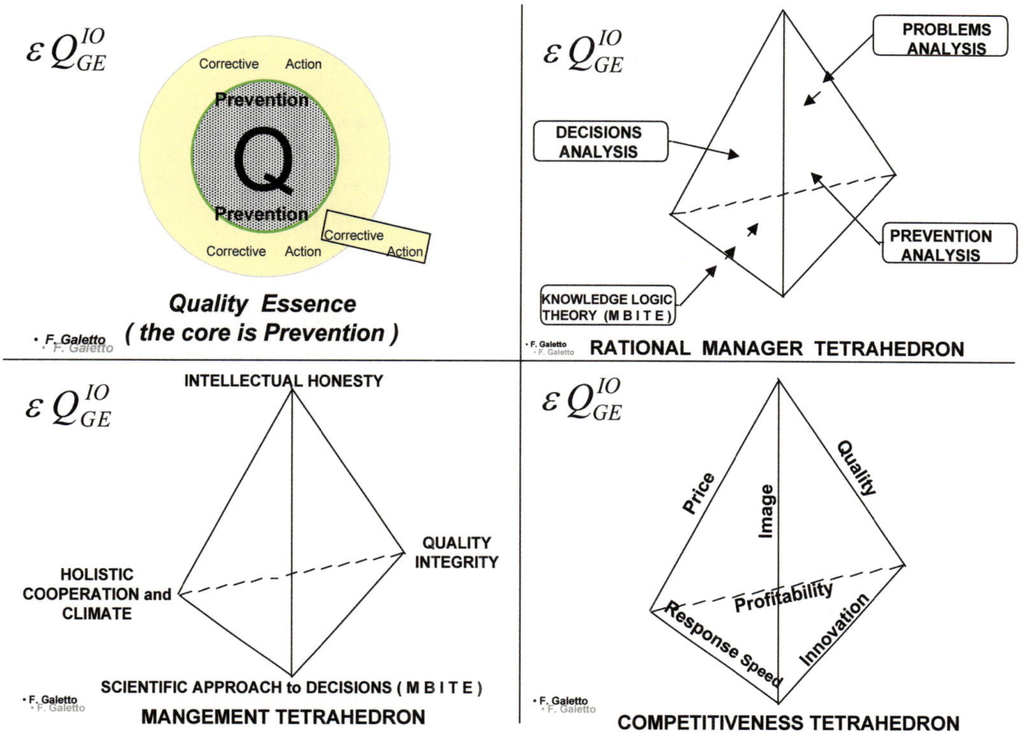

Fig. 5. The Business Management System

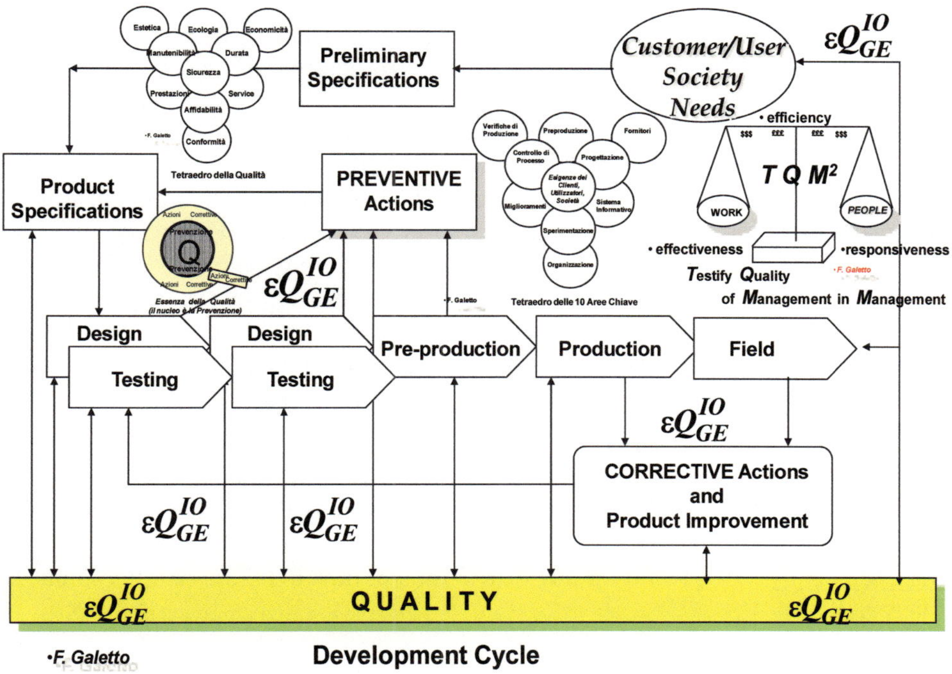

Fig. 6. The Development Cycle

control". If data are available (through properly designed method of collection), statistical methods are the foundation stone for good data analysis and "management decisions" [F. Galetto from 1973].
Prevention is very important and must be considered since from the first stages of product development as shown in figure 6; corrective actions come later.
Reliability is important in all the stages of product development. Reliability tests are essential during product development; collected data have to be analysed by scientific methods that involve Engineering, Statistics and Probability Methods. Reliability is important for preventive maintenance and for the so called RCM (Reliability Centred Maintenance). Let's for example consider the methods for data analyses and maintenance planning, as given in the papers "Total time on test plotting for failure data analyses", (1978), *SAAB-SCANIA,* and "Some graphical methods for maintenance planning", (1977), *Reliability & Maintainability Symposium.* They are connected with similar ideas of Barlow.
Let' consider a sample made of n "identical" items (n=sample size), that are neither repaired nor replaced after failure. We can view the tested sample as a system ("in parallel") that can be represented as in the graph, where state "i" indicates that "i" items are failed; g indicates the last failure observed during the test. When g=n we can apply the TTT-plot.

At any time instant x, some of the n units can be still alive (survived up to time x), while the other are failed, before x; the sum of all the "survival times" of the n items put on test is denoted TTT(x) [and named the Total Time on Test, up to the time instant x]; the duration of the test depends on the failure of the last item (out of the n) that will fail. If the items fail at times t_1, t_2, ..., t_n, then TTT(t_1) is the Total Time on Test until the 1st failure, TTT(t_i) is the Total Time on Test until the ith failure and TTT(t_n) is the Total Time on Test until the ith failure. If T_i is the *random variable* "Time to the ith failure" then TTT(T_i) is the *random variable* "Total Time on Test until the ith failure": the distribution of the *random variable* TTT(T_i) depends on the distribution of the *random variable* T_i, which depends on the distribution of the *random variable* T "Time to Failure" of any of the n "identical" items put on test. The n-1 *random variables* U_i=TTT(T_i)/TTT(T_n), the *scaled TTT*, have a distribution that depends on the *random variable* T "Time to Failure" of any item; since the distribution $F_T(t)$ of the r.v. T depends on the failure rate, one can plot a curve $F_U(t)$ [named TTT-transform] versus $F_T(t)$: the curve is contained in the square unit of the Cartesian plane and its shape depends on the type of the failure rate [constant, IFR (increasing), or DFR (decreasing)]. Therefore the TTT-plotting allows understanding the type of failure rate.
The evolution of the system depends from the functions $b_{i,i+1}(s|r)ds$, probability of the transition i⇒i+1 (i.e. the $(i+1)^{th}$ failure) in the interval s---s+ds, given that it happened into the state "i" at the time instant r; the functions $b_{i,i+1}(s|r)$ [named "kernel of the stochastic process" of failures] (Galetto, ...) allow to get the probability $\overline{W_i}(t|r)$ that the system remains in the state i for the period r---t and the probability $R_i(t|r)$ [reliability relative to state i] that the system does not be in the state g at time t (given that it entered in i at time instant r). $R_0(t|0)$ is then the probability that the system, in the interval 0---t, does not reach the state g, i.e. it experienced less than g failures: G(t)<g. We have then the fundamental system of Integral Theory of Estimates [valid for any distribution of time to failure of tested units, i.e. for any "kernel"]

$$R_i(t|r)=\overline{W_i}(t|r)+\int_r^t b_{i,i+1}(s|r)R_{i+1}(t|s)ds \quad ,i=0, ... g-1 \quad e \quad b_{g-1,g}(s|r)=0$$

For g=n we get the probability of n failures 1- $R_0(t\,|\,0)$ and the Total Time on Test.
If the items on test have constant failure rate λ, then $b_{i,i+1}(s\,|\,r) = n\lambda \exp[-n\lambda(s-r)]$, when failed items are replaced or repaired, while $b_{i,i+1}(s\,|\,r) = (n-i)\lambda \exp[-(n-i)\lambda(s-r)]$, when failed items are *not* replaced or repaired.
After the test one has the data. Let's suppose n=7 and the time to failure (in the sample) are 60, 105, 180, 300, 400, 605, 890. One can estimate $F_U(t_i)$ and $F_T(t_i)$, and plot the 7 points $[F_U(t_i),F_T(t_i)]$, obtaining the "empirical" curve.
Now Statistics Theory enters the stage. When the reliability of the items is exponential (constant failure rate), the TTT-transform $F_U(t)$ versus $F_T(t)$ is the diagonal of the unit square (the bisector of the coordinate axes). Plotting the "empirical" curve. $[F_U(t_i),F_T(t_i)]$ one finds a line "near" the bisector (β=1), and concludes that a constant failure rate is adequate. When the reliability of the items is IFR, the TTT-transform $F_U(t)$ versus $F_T(t)$ is a convex curve above the diagonal of the unit square. Figure 7 provides some curves depending on the "shape parameter β".
To practitioners this can be fantastic. They collect data, elaborate them and then they compare the "empirical" curve with the "Theoretical Curve" given in figure 7; then they "*know*" the failure distribution and take decisions. Perhaps the situation is more complex ....

- And ... what you do if you do not have the figure 7? Are you able to generate it?
- Now let's suppose that we, as managers, decide to save time for decision and we replace the items failed and we continue the test. Can we use the same figure 7?
- Now let's suppose that we, as managers, decide to save time for decision and we repair the items failed and we continue the test. Can we use the same figure 7?
- Now let's suppose that we, as managers, decide to save time for decision and we test more items (e.g. 28) and we stop the test at the 7th failure. Can we use the same figure 7?
- Now let's suppose that we, as managers, decide to save time for decision and we test more items (e.g. 50) and we stop the test at the time instant t=200. Can we use the same figure 7?

IF one is a *sensible Manager* he will answer: "I do not know. I have to study a lot; I have also to be careful if I go to some consultant". IF one is a NOT*sensible Manager* he will answer: "Yes, absolutely".
Let's see now how a problem is dealt in the paper "Total time on test plotting for failure data analyses"; in Section 5 "SYSTEM FAILURE DATA" we read [verbatim] "*It is also possible to use the TTT-plotting technique for analysing failure data from a repairable system. In this case* $TTT(T_i)$ *shall be defined as the time generated by the system until the* i^{th} *failure. If n-1 failures have been obtained until time T*, the time during which the system was observed, then we substitute T* to* T_n *and perform the plotting as before. Also the interpretation of the plot remains unchanged. The TTT-transform has, however, no counterpart. The statistical tests described in Section 4 are still applicable.*" [end of Section]. In Section 4 "STATISTICAL TESTS" we read [verbatim] "*Based on the ideas behind the TTT-plotting some statistical test may be obtained. These tests also provides us with some insight in the stochastic properties of the TTT-plot. ....* "
Now let's use Logic, as we said before. IF *The TTT-transform* does not exist how can one consider "*The statistical tests described in Section 4 are still applicable.*"? They are "*Based on the ideas behind the TTT-plotting ...*" which "*has, however, no counterpart.*" !!!! From the TTT-plot one can only have some hints of the non-applicability of "constant failure rate"!!! Nothing more! Moreover, IF one does not know TTT-transform for repairable systems, he should say "I do not know how to find the TTT-transform" and not "*The TTT-transform has, however, no counterpart.*"

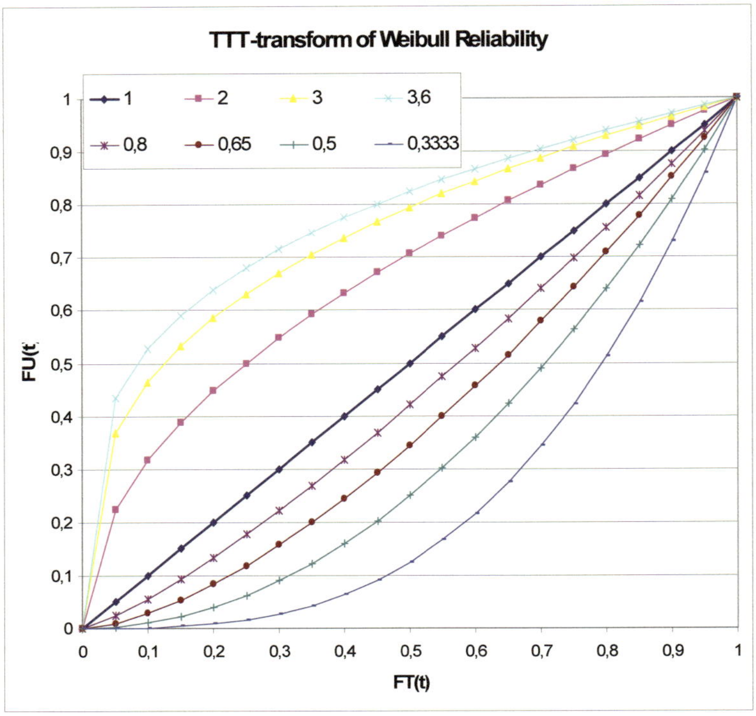

Fig. 7. Weibull TTT-transform [with "shape parameter β"]

As a matter of fact, in 1977, at the *Reliability & Maintainability Symposium*, Philadelphia, F. Galetto provided the Reliability Integral Theory that solves the problem, with his paper "SARA (System Availability and Reliability Analysis)". The theory did exist, not the single formulae: any scholar could have found them. The same theory Reliability Integral Theory, is applicable to maintenance problems, as those presented in "Some graphical methods for maintenance planning"; we will deal with this point in a successive paragraph related to preventive maintenance.

2. Logistics and inventory

Inventories are stockpiles of raw material, supplies, components, work in progress and finished goods that appear at numerous points throughout a firm's production and logistic channel. Having these inventories on hand cost at least 20% of their value per year, therefore, carefully managing inventory levels makes good economic sense, because in recent years the holding of inventories has been roundly criticised as unnecessary end wasteful. Actually good management of inventories improve customer service and reduce costs. Inventory plays a key role in the logistical behaviour of all manufacturing systems. The classical inventory results are central to more modern techniques of manufacturing management, such as material requirement planning (MRP), just-in-time (JIT) and time based competition (TBC).

1st step: the case of "constant (fixed)" demand Let's consider the oldest, and simplest, model - the Economic Order Quantity - in order to work our way to the more sophisticated ReOrder Level (ROL) model. One of the earliest applications of mathematics to factory management was the work of F. W. Harris (1913) on the problem of setting manufacturing lot sizes. He made the following assumptions about the manufacturing system: 1) production is instantaneous, 2) delivery is immediate, 3) a production run incurs a fixed setup cost, 4) there is no interaction between different products, 5) demand is deterministic, 6) demand is constant over time.

Let's consider the problem of establishing the order quantity Q [lot size] for an inventory system, dealt in **"Logistics courses"** and related books. In this field the assumptions are very similar: a single item is subject to "constant (fixed)" demand "λ" [demand rate, in units per year], there is a fixed cost A [ordering cost, in euro] of placing an order and a carrying charge "h" [holding cost, in euro per unit per unit time allotted (often year) to each item in inventory]. If no stockouts are permitted and lead time is zero (i.e. orders arrive immediately) there is a quantity Q (named EOQ: Economic Order Quantity), given by the famous Wilson lot-size formula $Q=\sqrt{2A\lambda / h}$ that minimise the "total cost per year". The inventory can be depicted as a system that starts with Q units (the level, I, of the inventory): we are certain that λt units are sold (delivered) in any interval of duration t; when the level inventory is zero, I=0, Q products are ordered and arrive immediately... and the system starts again from scratch.

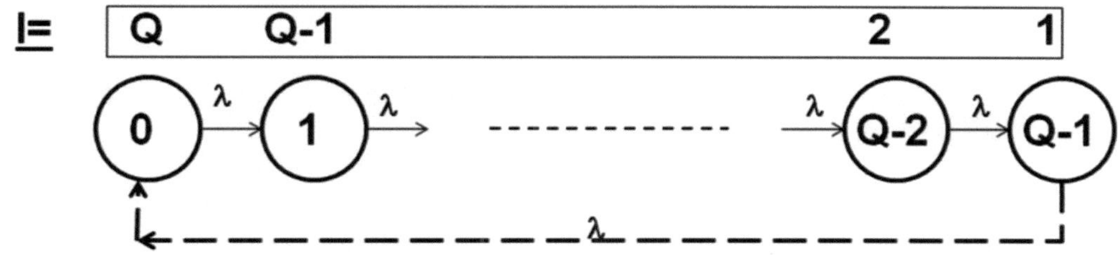

Fig. 8. System inventory states, with fixed and constant demand; state i means i products dispatched

The function depicting the curve of the inventory level I(t) is a saw-tooth line, with constant distance between peaks.

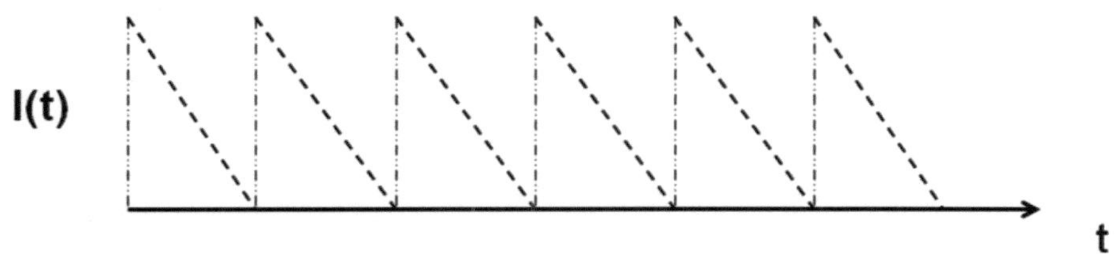

Fig. 9. Level of inventory versus time t

The production cost does not influence the solution and therefore in not considered in the "total cost per year" Y(Q)= hQ/2+Aλ/Q. Taking the derivative of Y(Q), and using elementary concepts of calculus, one gets easily the Wilson formula $Q=\sqrt{2A\lambda / h}$. In this particular case, I repeat, in this particular case, the number of lots ordered per year is N=λ/Q and the optimal time between orders is T=Q/λ, i.e. T=1/N.

Let's now see what happened in a MASTER (after 5 years of Engineering courses) on Maintenance and Reliability, in the lessons for RCM [Reliability Centred Maintenance]:

Wilson formula $Q = \sqrt{2A\lambda / h}$, which holds only in the hypotheses we said just before, was provided to student for buying the spare parts, which obviously depend on the number of failures, which obviously depend on the unreliability, which obviously depend on the time failure, which obviously is a **random variable**!!! ***A serious teacher should have proved that the formula holds true, before teaching it to students !!!!***

2nd step: the case of random demand with "constant" demand rate and steady state of the stochastic process We are going now to consider the demand as a random variable, so introducing the need of the use of probability theory. If we maintain all the previous hypotheses, but the number 5 and 6: 1) production is instantaneous, 2) delivery is immediate, 3) a production run incurs a fixed setup cost, 4) there is no interaction between different products, 5) *demand is random*, 6) *demand rate is constant over time*. We can depict the system as before [and in fig. 10]

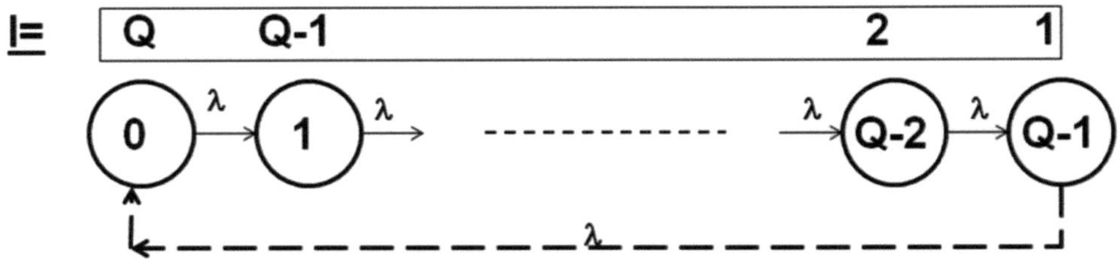

Fig. 10. System inventory states, with random demand and constant demand rate; state i means i products dispatched

where now the "time to sell a new unit (time between demands)" is a random variable exponentially distributed.

The function depicting the curve of the inventory level I(t) is a saw-tooth line, with variable [randomly] time distance between peaks.

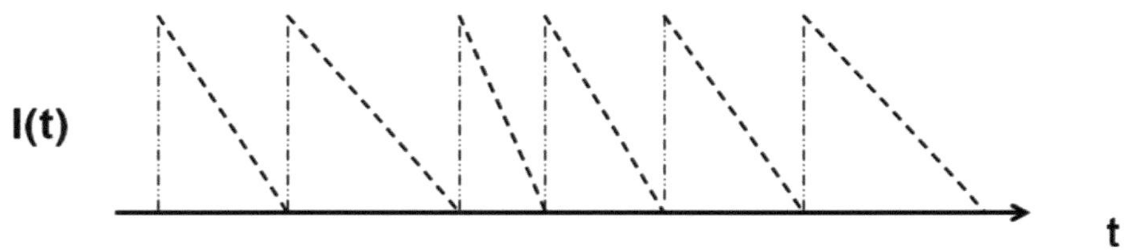

Fig. 11. Level of inventory versus time t

Therefore the probabilistic structure of the inventory system is a Markov process, periodic with period Q. The mean time (holding time) in any state is $m=1/\lambda$, the steady-state transition probability from one state i, to the next state i-1 is constant $\varphi_i = \varphi_{i-1} = 1/Q$ [use Markov chains theory]. The "reward structure" is such that the order cost A is associated with the transition from state Q-1 to 0, while the holding cost, per unit time, for state i is $y_i = (Q-i)*h$, i=2 to Q, and $y_1 = h+\lambda A$; the average cost per unit time, g (cost rate), for operating the system in the steady state is $g = [\lambda A + hQ(Q+1)/2]/Q$

The value Q that optimise the cost rate, in the steady state of the stochastic process, i.e. when the time is tending to infinity, is found as the solution of the previous equation. If Q is large, we can ignore the discrete nature of Q [Q is an integral number], assuming it can be considered as a continuous variable: so we can differentiate and set the derivative equal to zero; the solution is (the famous Wilson lot-size formula) $Q=\sqrt{2A\lambda/h}$. If Q is small, we cannot ignore the discrete nature of Q [Q is an integral number], and the solution has to be find numerically.

<u>3rd : the case of random demand with "variable" demand rate and steady state of the stochastic process</u> We are going to consider again the demand as a random variable, (need probability theory), maintaining all the previous hypotheses [as in the 2nd case], but the number 6, : 1) production is instantaneous, 2) delivery is immediate, 3) a production run incurs a fixed setup cost, 4) there is no interaction between different products, 5) *demand is random*, 6) *demand rate is **NOT** constant over time, but it varies with time, identically after any transition from a state to the following one.*

We can depict, again, the system as before [and in fig. 12]

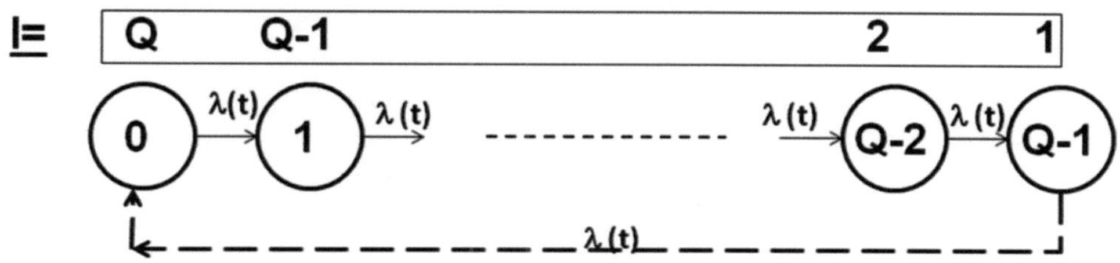

Fig. 12. System inventory states, with random demand and variable demand rate; state i means i products dispatched

where now the "time to sell a new unit (time between demands)" is a random variable "identically" [but not exponentially] distributed; let indicate the probability density of the time between transitions as f(t) [related to the "rate" λ(t), with cumulative distribution F(t)]; its mean is m.

The mean number of state transitions in the interval 0------t, M(t) is the solution of the integral equation

$$M(t)=F(t)+\int_0^t f(r)M(t-r)dr \tag{1}$$

The related intensity of state transitions, at time t, is m(t)=dM(t)/dt, the solution of the integral equation

$$m(t)=f(t)+\int_0^t f(r)m(t-r)dr \tag{2}$$

In the process steady state we have M(t)≅t/m and m(t))≅1/m, for $t \to \infty$. The function depicting the curve of the inventory level I(t) is a saw-tooth line, with variable [randomly] time distance between peaks, too. [fig. 13]

Therefore the probabilistic structure of the inventory system is a semi-Markov process, periodic with period Q. The mean time (holding time) in any state is m [the mean of the distribution] identical for all the states; then the steady-state transition probability from one state i, to the next state i-1 is constant $\varphi_i = \varphi_{i-1} = 1/Q$ [use semi-Markov processes theory]. The "reward structure" is such that the order cost A is associated with the transition from

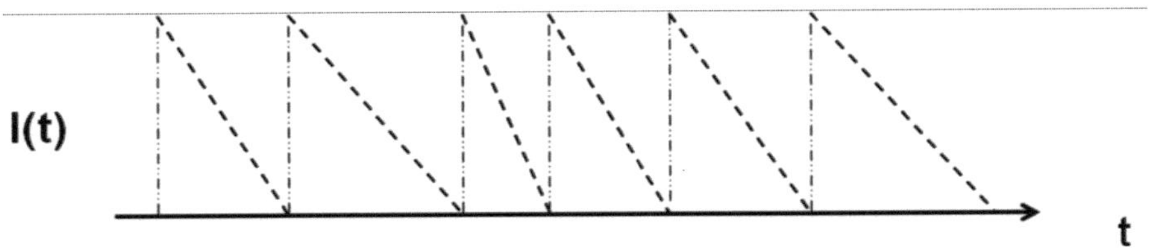

Fig. 13. Level of inventory versus time t

state Q-1 to 0, while the holding cost, per unit time, for state i is y_i = (Q-i)*h, i=2 to Q, and y_1 = h+A/m; the average cost per unit time, g (cost rate), for operating the system in the steady state is the same, as before, $g = [A/m + hQ(Q+1)/2]/Q$.

The value Q that optimise the cost rate, in the steady state of the stochastic process, i.e. when the time is tending to infinity, is found as the solution of the previous equation. If Q is large, we can ignore the discrete nature of Q [Q is an integral number], assuming it can be considered as a continuous variable: so we can differentiate and set the derivative equal to zero; the solution is $Q = \sqrt{2A/(mh)}$ (similar to the famous Wilson lot-size formula); if different types of distributions are used, but with the same mean, one gets the same optimum g. If Q is small, we cannot ignore the discrete nature of Q [Q is an integral number], and the solution has to be find numerically.

Notice that we can manipulate the formula, obtaining the following $g = \frac{A}{mQ} + \frac{hmQ(Q+1)/2}{mQ}$ that shows very clearly a fundamental fact of renewal processes: the gain rate, **<u>in the steady state of a process</u>**, is the ratio of the cost during a renewal cycle and the length of the cycle [mQ, that is the mean sum of Q random variables, identically distributed]; we will find the same idea in the formulae of preventive maintenance.

Notice that nobody says that the formulas in the various books and papers are to be considered only for the **<u>steady state</u>**.

It is very interesting noting that, after a long time t*, at which the stochastic process reaches "almost surely" its steady state, the cost for the interval t*------t*+t is

$$gt = \frac{1}{Q}\left[At/m + Q(Q+1)ht/2\right] \tag{3}$$

which shows that t/m is the mean number of orders for the interval t*------t*+t (in the steady state) and Q(Q+1)ht/2 is the mean number of products, for holding which we pay, for the interval t*------t*+t (in the steady state).

<u>4th step: the case of random demand with "constant" demand rate and steady state of the stochastic process</u> We are going to consider the demand as a random variable, so introducing the need of the use of probability theory, but we consider a lead time different from 0, we maintain some of the previous hypotheses, but the number 2, 5 and 6: 1) production is instantaneous, 2) ***delivery takes a constant time L, named Lead Time, after the order,*** 3) a production run incurs a fixed setup cost, 4) there is no interaction between different products, 5) *<u>demand is random</u>*, 6) *<u>demand rate is constant over time</u>*. We can no longer depict the system as before; we need to distinguish between the net inventory I(t) and the inventory position IP(t). The net inventory I(t) is the actual number of products we have on hand that we can send to our customers, after a time L, form their order. The inventory position IP(t) is the sum of I(t), the actual number of products we have on hand, the outstanding orders not yet arrived at time t, minus the products backlogged.; the order of Q products is placed, at any time t_0, when IP(t_0) equals the ROL (the Re-Order Level); unfortunately, in the meantime [duration L] a stockout might occur: while we wait for the lot arrival (replenishment of the inventory), at time t_0 + L, the net inventory I(t) and the inventory position IP(t) decrease because of selling (and dispatching) products. If it happens that I(t_{STO})=0, at a time t_{STO}, we face an inventory STockOut, that generates a cost: customers are unsatisfied...; we lose to sell products, a case named "Lost Sales". The cost involved in this case are: the order cost A, the cost of holding the inventory (that varies with time), and the "penalty cost" due to stockout. The "time to sell a new unit (time between demands)" is a random variable exponentially distributed. The function depicting the curve of the Inventory Position level IP(t) is a saw-tooth line, with variable [randomly] time distance between peaks, exponentially distributed. [fig. 14]

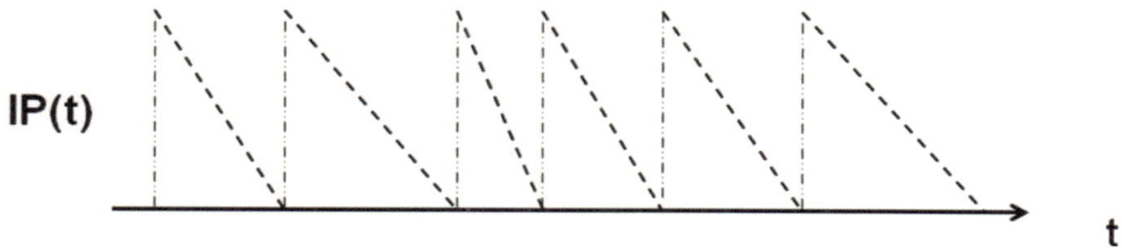

Fig. 14. Level of the inventory position versus time t

Therefore the probabilistic structure of the inventory system is a Markov process, periodic with period Q. The mean time (holding time) in any state is m=1/λ, the steady-state transition probability from one state IP=i, to the next state IP=i-1, ***in the process steady state***, is still constant $\varphi_i = \varphi_{i-1} = 1/Q$ [use Markov chains theory and fig. 15].

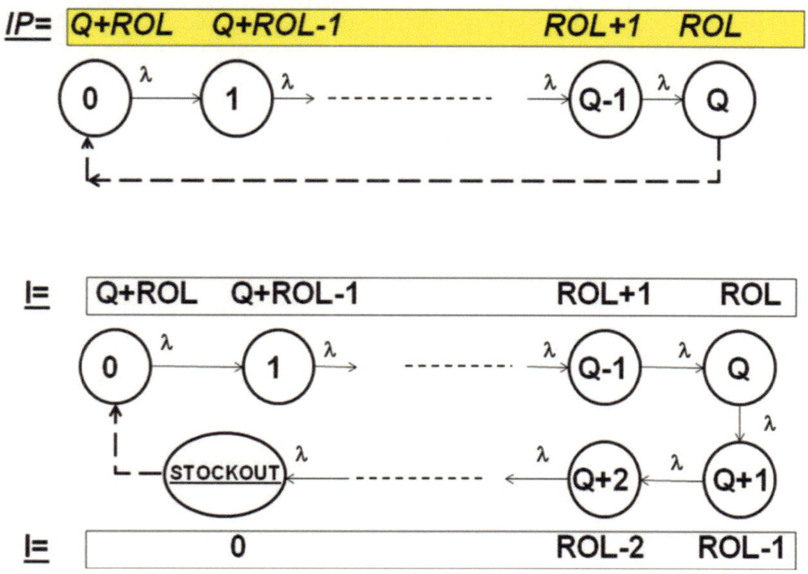

Fig. 15. System inventory states, with random demand and constant demand rate; state i means i products dispatched

The "reward structure" is such that the order cost A is associated with the transition from state Q+ROL and ROL; the carrying inventory cost is associated with the mean number of products on hand times the time they are in the inventory, while the stockout cost is related to the probability that happens the event I(t)=0, in spite that we have ROL product when we order the lot of Q products. [we will use, for short, R for the ROL, ReOrder Level]
Let t_0 be the time instant when $IP(t_0)=R$; the net inventory $I(t_0+L)$ = R - demanded quantity X_L, during the lead time L, is a random variable with the same type of distribution as Inventory Position $IP(t_0+L)$;, for any interval t_0------$t_0+\Delta t$ the holding cost is a random variable as well

$$h\int_{t_0}^{t_0+\Delta t} I(u)du = hTTI(t_0 {}^{----} t_0+\Delta t) \tag{4}$$

where we name "total time of inventory", TTI(t_0------$t_0+\Delta t$), for any interval t_0------$t_0+\Delta t$, the time for which we have to pay for the products we have on hands [net inventory] and for the time they are on hands.
The mean of this random variable is

$$h\int_{t_0}^{t_0+\Delta t} E[I(u)]du = hE[TTI(t_0 {}^{----} t_0+\Delta t)] \tag{5}$$

Being I(t)=IP(t)-Q, for any time t, the "total time of inventory", TTI(t_0------$t_0+\Delta t$) depends on the transitions between the states 0, 1, 2, ..., Q and the related probabilities. Therefore the mean of TTI is

$$E[TTI(t_0 {}^{----} t_0+\Delta t)] = \frac{\Delta t}{\lambda}\{(R+Q)+(R+Q-1)+(R+Q-1)+....+(R+1)\} - Q\Delta t \tag{6}$$

Using simple concepts of Algebra, we get

$$E[TTI(t_0 {}^{----} t_0+\Delta t)] = \frac{\Delta t}{2\lambda}\{(R+Q)(R+Q+1)-R(R+1)\} - Q\lambda\Delta t/\lambda \tag{7}$$

Letting T_Q be the random time for selling Q products, and so reorder a new lot of products, we have, for any planning cycle t_0------t_0+T_Q

$$E[TTI(t_0 {}^{----} t_0+T_Q)] = \frac{Q}{\lambda}\{R+(Q+1)/2-\lambda L\} \tag{8}$$

Therefore the expected cost of inventory is

$$h\frac{Q}{\lambda}\{R+(Q+1)/2-\lambda L\} \tag{9}$$

We proved this formula using probability theory; in all the books I read **never** there was the proof! Why?
The quantity ss=R - λL is the safety stock that we hold in order to prevent stockouts.

If t_0 is the time instant when $IP(t_0)=R$; the stockout happens when the net inventory $I(t_0+L)$ = R - demanded quantity X_L, during the lead time L, which is a random variable, falls below zero: $P_{STO}=P[I(t_0+L) \leq 0]$; it means that, at some instant, $t_{STO} \leq t_0+L$, $I(t_0+ t_{STO}) =0$. Letting T_R be the random time for selling R product, we have $P_{STO}=P[T_R \leq L]$.
If $T_R > L$ the system is able to provide products, we have on hand (net inventory), to all customers asking for them, filling their demands; that's why the probability $S(R,L) = P[T_R > L] = 1-P_{STO}$, is named Service Level (type 1), or Fill Rate.
Noting that $P[T_R > L]$ is the "reliability of a stand-by system of R products" failing with failure rate equal to λ, one can take advantage of the use of all the ideas of Reliability Theory for the field of Inventory Management.
Here we are doing that.
Let T_{STO} be the random variable "Time To Stock Out" of the inventory system and $N_{STO}(t)$ be the random variable "Number of Stock Outs" of the system, in the interval 0-----t; at time t the system has a "residual life" $\rho(t)$ until the next Stock Out, $\rho(t) = T_{N_{STO}(t)} - t$; since the transitions depend on the exponential distribution $\rho(t)$ is independent from the Number of the experienced Stockouts. Let $S(R, t+x \mid t) = P[\rho(t) > x]$ be the type 1 Service Level, related to the interval t-----t+x; F. Galetto proved [chapter 6 of *Affidabilità, Volume 1: Teoria e Metodi di Calcolo*, (1995) CLEUP, Padova. Italy] that the type 1 Service Level $S(R,t+x \mid t) = P[\rho(t) > x]$ is the solution of the integral equation

$$S(R,t+x \mid t) = S(R,t+x \mid 0) + \int_0^t f_{STO}(s) S(R,t+x \mid s) ds \tag{10}$$

where $f_{STO}(t)$ is the probability density function of the 1st T_{STO}, with mean denoted as MTTSTO and named Mean Time To STockOut.
If $t \to \infty$ the type 1 Service Level $S(R,t+x \mid t)$ depends only on x; F. Galetto proved [chapter 6 of *Affidabilità, Volume 1: Teoria e Metodi di Calcolo*, (1995) CLEUP, Padova. Italy] that $S(R, x) = P[\rho(\infty) > x]$ is related to the density of stock outs $f_{STO}(x \mid \infty)= S(R, x \mid 0)/MTTSTO$.
Therefore, after a long time t that the inventory system is running, the steady state type 1 Service Level S(R, L) is

$$S(R,L) = \int_L^\infty S(R,s) ds \tag{11}$$

3. What one can find in documents

The following excerpts are copied directly from books; it is not important to report the names of the authors! None of the authors say that their formulae hold only in the ***steady state*** of the process. Notice that a lot of attention is needed in order to find the correspondence between the different notations.
From a book one can find, where d is the random demand, LT is the lead time, $F_{dLT}(R)$ is the cumulative probability of sales during LT, p is the cost (penalty) of stock out. Notice that there is no proof of this formula in the book.

Under these assumptions the total cost is

$$C_{tot} = C_{or} + C_{in} + C_{so}$$
$$= A \cdot \frac{E(d)}{Q} + h \cdot (R + Q/2 - E(d) \cdot LT) \quad (5.15)$$
$$+ p \cdot \frac{E(d)}{Q} \cdot (1 - F_{d_{LT}}(R)). \quad (5.16)$$

From another book one can find, where CSL is the Cycle Service Level [i.e. the fraction of replenishment cycles that end with all customer demand being met (a replenishment cycle is the interval between two successive replenishment deliveries). The CSL is equal to the probability of not having a stockout in a replenishment cycle, H is the cost of holding one item for one unit of time, C_u is the cost of one item, D is the average demand for one unit of time.

In the notations of the previous book D_L=E(d), H=h, ROP=R, replenishment cycle is equal LT, CSL is then $F_{dLT}(R)$, ss=R - λL (safety stock).

Desired cycle service level = CSL,
Mean demand during lead time = D_L,
Standard deviation of demand during lead time = σ_L.

From Equation 11.3, recall that $ROP = D_L + ss$. The store manager needs to identify safety inventory ss such that the following is true:

Probability(demand during lead time ≤ $D_L + ss$) = CSL.

Demand During Stockout Is Lost

For the case where unfilled demand during the stockout period is lost, the optimal cycle service level CSL^* is given as follows:

$$CSL^* = 1 - \frac{HQ}{HQ + DC_u} \quad \textbf{(12.7)}$$

In this case we have assumed that C_u is the cost of losing one unit of demand during the stockout period. In Example 12.4, we evaluate the optimal cycle service level if demand is lost during the stockout period.

From another book, again, one can find, where G(r)=S(Q, r) is the Service Level (type 1), I(Q, r) is the average net inventory, D is the expected demand per year (in units), k is the cost per stockout.

In the notations of the previous book D=D_L=E(d), h=H=h, r=ROP=R, S(Q, r)=CSL=$F_{dLT}(R)$, k=p.

Notice that that the three books provide to the students (or the managers) **three different formulae** ***for the same concept***, the type 1 Service Level!!!

Book	Formula for Service Level	Equivalence **only IF**	Equivalence **only IF**
1	$F_{dLT}(R)$	$F_{dLT}(R) = 1 - HQ/(HQ + DC_u)$	$F_{dLT}(R) = kD/(kD + hQ)$
2	$CSL = 1 - HQ/(HQ + DC_u)$	$DC_u = kD$	$1 - HQ/(HQ + DC_u) = F_{dLT}(R)$
3	$G(r) = kD/(kD + hQ)$	$kD/(kD + hQ) = F_{dLT}(R)$	$kD = DC_u$

It is very clear that it is very improbable that the cost per stockout is equal to the cost per unit.

Stockout Cost Approach. As an alternative to the backorder cost approach, we can make verbal formulation (2.32) into a mathematical model by writing the sum of the annual setup or purchase order cost, stockout cost, and inventory carrying cost as

$$Y(Q,r) = \frac{D}{Q}A + kD[1 - S(Q,r)] + hI(Q,r) \tag{2.50}$$

Going through the usual optimization procedure (taking the derivative with respect to r, setting the result equal to zero, and solving for r) yields the following expression for the optimal reorder point:

$$G(r^*) = \frac{kD}{kD + hQ} \tag{2.52}$$

<u>A case from Fctory Physics</u>

"*Jack, the maintenance manager, has collected historical data that indicate one of the replacement parts he stocks has annual demand (D) of 14 units per year. The unit cost c of the part is $150, and since the firm uses an interest rate of 20 percent, the annual holding cost h has been set at 0,2*($150)=$30 per year. It takes 45 days to receive a replenishment order, so average demand during a replenishment lead time is* $\theta = \frac{14}{365} \cdot 45 = 1,726$" [units/lead time] "*The part is purchased from an outside supplier, and Jack estimates that the cost of time and materials required to place a purchase order A is about $15. The one remaining cost required by our model is the cost of either a backorder or stockout. Although he is very uncomfortable trying to estimate these, when pressed, Jack made a guess that the annualized cost of a backorder is about $100 per year, and the cost per stockout event can be approximated by k=$40. Finally, Jack has chosen to model demands using the Poisson distribution.*

[...] The order quantity is computed by using " [the Economic Order Quantity formula],

"*which yields* $Q^* = \sqrt{\frac{2AD}{h}} = \sqrt{\frac{2 \cdot (15) \cdot (14)}{30}} = 3,7 \approx 4$ *units.*"

Let's provide clearly the relevant data: annual demand D=14. NOTICE *"estimated from historical data"*, without any confidence interval!, Lead time L = 45 days cost of order A = 15 $, holding cost h = 30 $ per unit per year stockout cost k= 40 $, demand distribution: Poisson. Since the demand distribution is Poisson, the time between demand is exponentially distributed, and the system can be modelled with a Markov chain in the steady state of the process.
On the contrary, the Factory Physics authors *"approximate the Poisson by the normal, with mean 1.726 and standard deviation σ=1.314"*; then they compute Q=3.7 (≅4) and r=2.946 (≅3) [with the formula G(r) = kD/(kD + hQ)].
Using "reliability theory", we draw the transition diagram, with transition (selling) rate λ [solid lines] and replenishment [dotted lines]; in the steady state we can write the steady transition probability matrix P that provides us with the MTTSTO, the Cost per Unit Time, the Service Level. We compared our findings with the ones of the Factory Physics authors who *"approximate the Poisson by the normal,..."*: while the Factory Physics authors found a type 1 Service Level = 0.824, we found 0.903 a better value. We considered also other couples of values for Q and R and we found again better results; we provide the readers all the transition diagrams (fig. 16, 17, 18, 19).

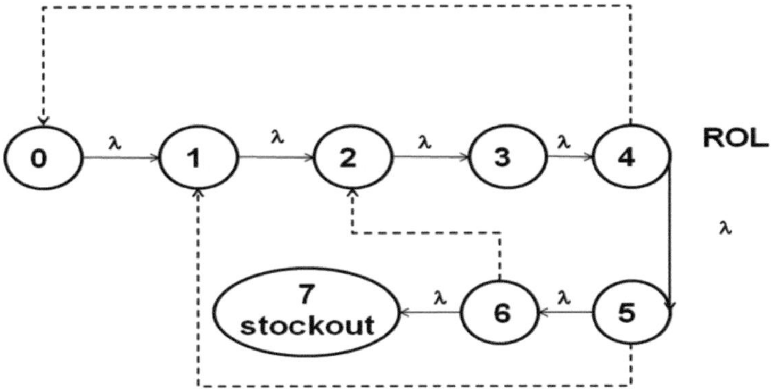

Fig. 16. System inventory states (random demand at constant rate); case Q=4, R=3 [Factory Physics]

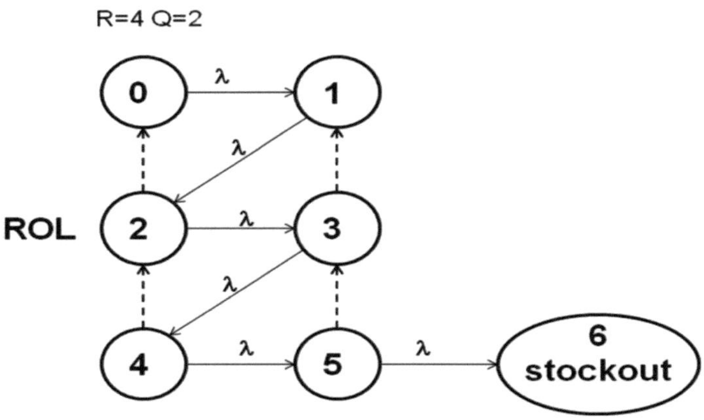

Fig. 17. System inventory states (random demand at constant rate); case Q=2, R=4 [Factory Physics]

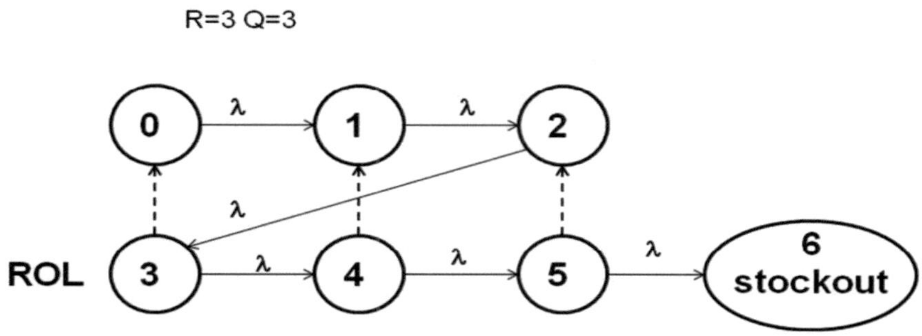

Fig. 18. System inventory states (random demand at constant rate); case Q=3, R=3 [Factory Physics]

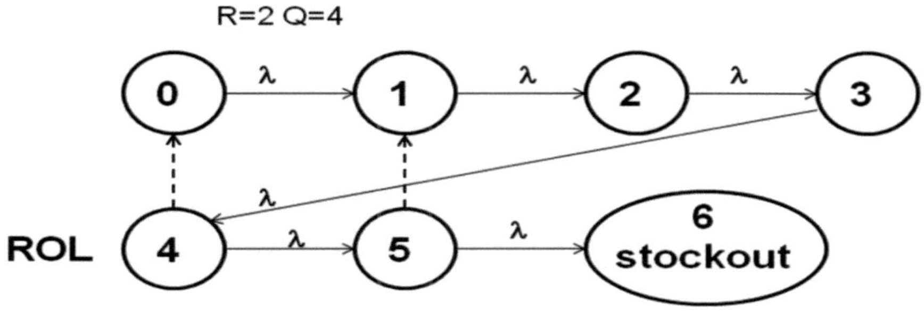

Fig. 19. System inventory states (random demand at constant rate); case Q=4, R=2 [Factory Physics]

The results are, in the steady state,

R=	4	3	2	3
Q=	2	3	4	4
Cost rate ($/year)	**230.58**	**203.24**	**178.30**	**167.32**
Service Level	**0.969**	**0.903**	**0.750**	**0.903**

It is easily seen that Q=2 and R=4 provide better Service Level (97% vs 82% found by FP) at a higher cost per year, in the steady state. In case of failures in a production line the cost of unavailability is much higher than 40$ ... !
It is interesting to notice that the Factory Physics authors did not find that Q=2 and R=4 is the best solution, provided that 97% of Service Level is considered adequate. In any case it is really better than the solution given to students by the Factory Physics authors.
We used the exponential distribution because we accepted that the "arrival of failures" was according a Poisson distribution: this implies that the reliability of each item is exponential with failure rate λ/N, where N is the number of items in use; the "Mean Number of Failures in the interval 0------t", M(t), is equal to λt and the variance is λt, as well.
The distribution of the time to failure of the items was assumed exponential; many times it is not so.
Therefore we are going to develop a method adequate for any distribution.
In order to do that we will use the following distribution of the "time to sell one item"; we do so because it is related to the normal distribution of the items sold during the time;

therefore the inventory I(t) is a normal stochastic process, during the lead time L: this is the standard assumption in all the books I read.
The probability density of the time to sell one product is (μ_1 is the mean time to sell one product)

$$f(t\,|\,1,\mu_1) = e^{-\frac{(t-\mu_1)^2}{2t\mu_1^2}} / \sqrt{2\pi t^3} \tag{12}$$

If we consider the time to sell Q products, T_Q, this has a distribution of the same type, as a result of the convolution of Q f(t|1,μ); we indicate it as $f_Q(t\,|\,\eta,\mu)$ (where we have $E[T_Q]=\mu$ and $Var[T_Q]=\mu^3/\eta$. Besides $\eta=Q^2$.)

$$f_Q(t\,|\,\eta,\mu) = \sqrt{\frac{\eta}{2\pi t^3}}\, e^{-\eta\frac{(t-\mu)^2}{2t\mu^2}} \tag{13}$$

The mean holding time in a state m_i, and steady state transition probabilities, p_{ij} are found in the same manner as in the case of the Poisson process [not with the same formulae].
Using this distribution for the previous cases, as obvious, we get quite different **steady state results**

R=	4	2
Q=	2	4
Cost rate ($/year)	**182.27**	**148.10**
Service Level	**0.959**	**0.584**

The best solution for the **steady state** cost rate is Q=4 and R=2, while for the service level is Q=2 and R=4 (as before).

4. 5th step: the case of random demand with "constant" demand rate BUT NOT steady state of the stochastic process

We maintain some of the previous hypotheses, but the number 2, 5 and 6: 1) production is instantaneous, 2) ***delivery takes a constant Lead Time, after the order,*** 3) a production run incurs a fixed setup cost, 4) there is no interaction between different products, 5) *demand is random,* 6) *demand rate is constant over time*.
Before we considered the process in its steady state, i.e. after a long time [$t\rightarrow\infty$]; now we consider the case of finite time t.
As in the previous paragraph, we distinguish between the net inventory I(t) and the inventory position IP(t). If, at some instant of time t_{STO}, $I(t_{STO})=0$, we face an inventory STockOut, that generates a cost: customers are unsatisfied...; we lose to sell products, a case named "Lost Sales": as before, the costs involved are the order cost A, the cost of holding the inventory (that varies with time, and the "penalty cost" due to stockout.
We assume again that the "time to sell a new unit (time between demands)" is a random variable exponentially distributed, with rate λ; so the Inventory Position level IP(t) is a saw-tooth line, with variable [randomly] time distance between peaks, exponentially distributed [Poisson Process]. Therefore the probabilistic structure of the inventory system is a Markov

process, periodic with period Q. Letting Pi(t)=P[process in the state i, at time t], be the probability that process in the state i, at time t, we can write a system of differential equation; in order to make the system simple we consider the case R=2 and Q=4. [fig. 21]

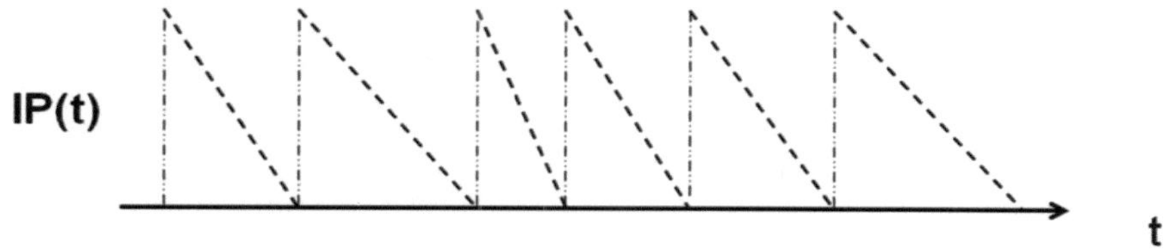

Fig. 20. Level of the inventory position versus time t

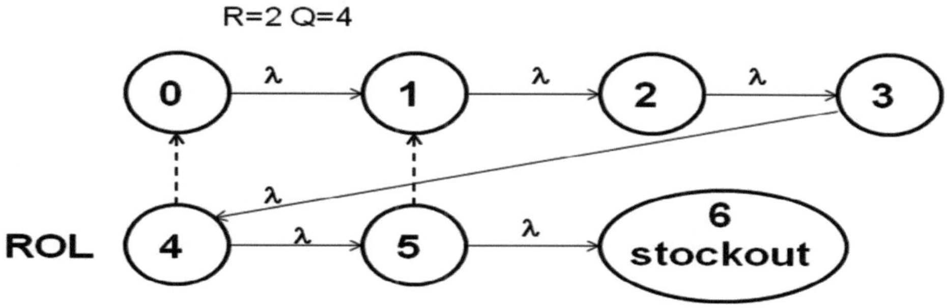

Fig. 21. System inventory states (random demand at constant rate); case Q=4, R=2 [Factory Physics]

The equations

$$P_0'(t) = -\lambda P_0(t) + \delta(t-L)P_4(t) \qquad P_1'(t) = \lambda P_0(t) - \lambda P_1(t) + \delta(t-L)P_5(t)$$
$$P_2'(t) = \lambda P_1(t) - \lambda P_2(t) \qquad P_3'(t) = \lambda P_2(t) - \lambda P_3(t) \qquad P_4'(t) = \lambda P_3(t) - \lambda P_4(t) \tag{14}$$
$$P_5'(t) = -\lambda P_5(t)$$

can be written in matrix form as

$$P'(t) = AP(t) \tag{15}$$

where we have the vector P(t) [its derivative P'(t)] and the matrix A of the transition rates, λ and δ(t-L) ["Dirac impulse"].

The Service Level S(t, L), i.e. no stockout for the interval 0------t, and Lead Time L (for replenishment) is S(t, L)=P(t)u, dot product of the vector P(t) and the vector u=[1,1,1,1,1,1].

The instantaneous Inventory Level I(s, L), for any time s of the interval 0------t, and Lead Time L (for replenishment) is

$$I(s,L) = \sum_0^5 (R+Q-i)P_i(s) \tag{16}$$

The cost of Inventory, for the interval 0------t is $I(t,L) = h\int_0^t I(s,L)ds$

The Number of Orders is the number of times [random variable] the system enters the state 4; its expected value M(t) is the mean number of orders. The probability of stockout is the probability of entrance in to the state 6.
Putting all together we have the relationship that provides the cost C(t, L) of the system; the cost rate, usually used in books, is here C(t, L)/t; it is in the following figure 22.
As we can see the cost rate increases and, after 6 months decreases. The cost rate is lower in the case Q=4 and R=2 with lower service level, as we found in the steady state analysis; both curves decrease very slowly to their steady state rate.

R=	4	2
Q=	2	4
Cost rate ($/year) at 6 months	**643.69**	**378.11**
Service Level at 6 months	**0.974**	**0.861**

If the service level 0.86, due to the consequences of downtime, is not adequate, we have to choose ...

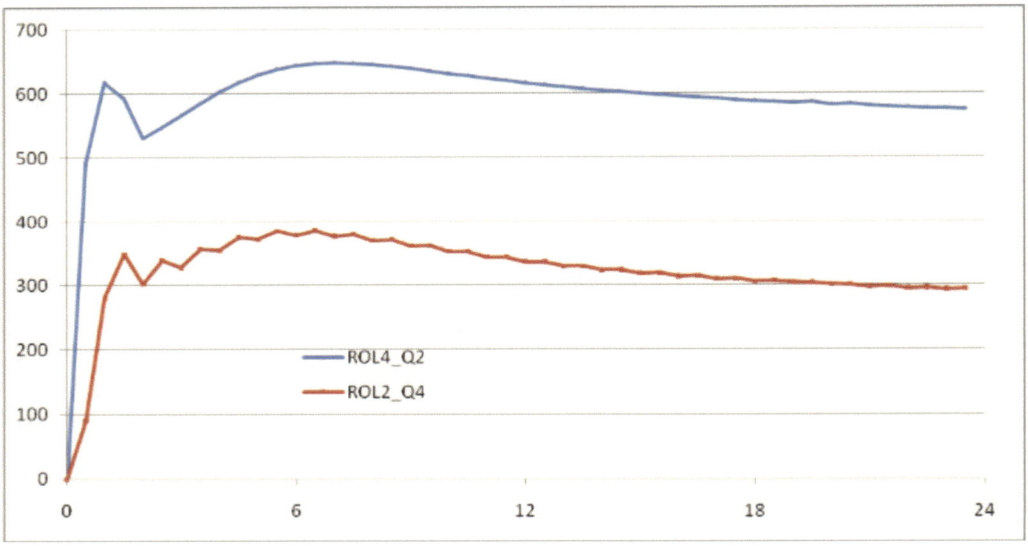

Fig. 22. Cost rate of two inventory systems (random demand at constant rate): Q=4, R=2 vs Q=2, R=4 [Factory Physics]

It is therefore very important to consider the interval in which we want to optimise.
This subject has been pointed out many times by F. Galetto, in relation with the Preventive Maintenance. We are going to show it because it has an amazing similarity with inventory management.
When the values Q and R increase the dimension of the vectors and matrices $P'(t) = AP(t)$ increase accordingly.

5. Preventive maintenance and RCM, an analogy with inventory management

We said before that it is very important the interval in which we want to optimise and that this subject has been pointed out many times by F. Galetto, related to the Preventive

Maintenance. We are now going to show it because it has an amazing similarity with inventory management, and shows that there is no need of Poisson processes.
In 1977, at the *Reliability & Maintainability Symposium*, Philadelphia, F. Galetto, with his paper "*SARA (System Availability and Reliability Analysis)*", provided the Reliability Integral Theory that solves various reliability problems that cannot be dealt through Markov processes. The theory did exist, not the single formulae: any scholar could have found them.
The same theory Reliability Integral Theory, is applicable to maintenance problems, as those presented in "Some graphical methods for maintenance planning"; in that paper, mentioned before, following ideas of Barlow, the optimum replacement interval is found, by B. Bergman, minimising the formula, *cost ratio* (given in Barlow; c_1 is the cost of preventive replacement, c_2 is the cost due to failures, while c [Bergman] is the cost of preventive replacement, assuming 1 the cost due to failures: $c= c_1 / c_2$)

$$C(t_p)=\frac{cF(t_p)+R(t_p)}{\int_0^{t_p} R(x)dx}, \quad \text{very similar to} \quad C(t_p)=\frac{c_1F(t_p)+c_2R(t_p)}{\int_0^{t_p} R(x)dx},$$

Barlow and Bergman say that those formulas are valid "in the long run": that means after an infinite time, that is after an infinite number of failures! But for a finite time span 0---t? The cost ratio is computed as the ratio of the mean cost for one cycle divided by the mean duration of one cycle, as it can be done for renewal processes, in the steady state!
The same is found in logistics books, ... but they do not say ... that it is valid ONLY in the steady state!!!! [see the cases ...]
One can understand this problem through the F. Galetto papers presented in 1977, SARA at the *Reliability & Maintainability Symposium*, Philadelphia, and CLAUDIA, *21st EOQC Conference*, Varna (Bulgaria).
Some hints are given here, for preventive maintenance:
Let $N_0(t, t_p)$ be the number of replacements of unfailed items and $N_1(t, t_p)$ be the number of failed items over the interval 0---t. They are random variables; their expectations are indicated as $M_0(t, t_p)$ and $M_1(t, t_p)$.
Let $C(t, t_p)$ be the total expected cost over the interval 0---t, when the unfailed items are "renewed" [at cost c_0] at their life t_p, and failed items are replaced [at cost c_1; c_1 includes the cost of the consequences of the failure] with new items. It is

$$C(t, t_p) = c_0 M_0(t, t_p) + c_1 M_1(t, t_p) \tag{17}$$

Let $R(t, t_p)$ be the reliability for the interval 0---t, when unfailed items are "renewed" at their life t_p, and $b(t, t_p)$ the related probability density function. To optimise the cost over the interval 0---t, we need either to compute $M_0(t, t_p)$ and $M_1(t, t_p)$ or to compute $C(t, t_p)$ from the following ***integral equation***

$$C(t,t_p)=c_0\sum_{i=1}^{n} R^i(t_p)+\int_0^t\left[c_1+C(t-s,t_p)\right]b(s,t_p)ds \tag{18}$$

where n is such that $nt_p \le t \le (n+1)t_p$ and $R(t_p)$ is the reliability of the item for the period of duration t_p. [formula derived using the "Integral Theory of Reliability" devised by F. Galetto in 1971]

In the formula the 1st term gives account of unfailed items during the interval 0--t: it excludes that any failure happens. The failures are considered in the integral from 0 to t; let the 1st failure occur in a interval s--s+ds, with probability $b(s,t_p)ds$, and cost c_1; the other failures occur in the remaining interval s--t, and their cost is $C(t\text{-}s, t_p)$: being s any instant we integrate over the interval 0--t.
It is clear that the optimum interval for the preventive replacement depends on t, the duration of the interval 0--t, over which we want to optimise, and the "cost ratio" c_0/c_1.
The optimum value t^*_p, as found in the literature on preventive maintenance, is the solution of

$$h(t^*_p)MTTF(t^*_p) = c_1/(c_1\text{-}c_0) + (c_0/(c_1\text{-}c_0))\ R(t^*_p)/F(t^*_p) \qquad (19)$$

which optimise the ratio $C(t,t_p)/t$, that, for $t \to \infty$, does not depend on t. [steady state]
This is not satisfactory, because it does not take into account properly of the probability theory, and it is not said over which period 0--t we want to optimise. The foundations for finding the solution of the integral equation for a finite time span t is found using "Integral Theory of Reliability".

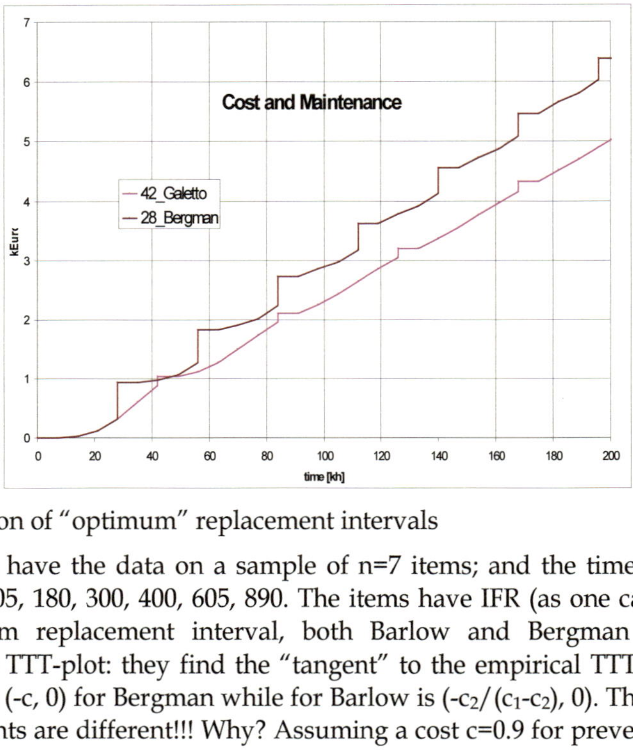

Fig. 23. Comparison of "optimum" replacement intervals

Let's suppose we have the data on a sample of n=7 items; and the time to failure (in the sample) are 60, 105, 180, 300, 400, 605, 890. The items have IFR (as one can easily find). To find the optimum replacement interval, both Barlow and Bergman use a graphical procedure on the TTT-plot: they find the "tangent" to the empirical TTT-plot and passing through the point (-c, 0) for Bergman while for Barlow is $(-c_2/(c_1\text{-}c_2), 0)$. The procedure is the same, but the points are different!!! Why? Assuming a cost c=0.9 for preventive replacement and 1 for failure, Bergman finds $t^*_p = 27.9$
On the contrary, optimising the integral equation (with η and β estimated from the data), F. Galetto finds, over an interval 0--200, as optimum interval $t^*_p = 42$. The graph in fig. 23 shows easily that $t^*_p = 42$ is better than $t^*_p = 28$ (approximating 27.9); the optimum interval depends on the interval 0--t: rarely $t=\infty$ is a good choice! [fig.1, 5, 32, 33, 34, 35]
So we see that for more than 40 years we had the theory to solve various reliability problems.
The same ideas can be used to solve a problem given in example 14.1, pag. 345, of the book *Practical Reliability Engineering*, Wiley & Sons (1997). There it is written:

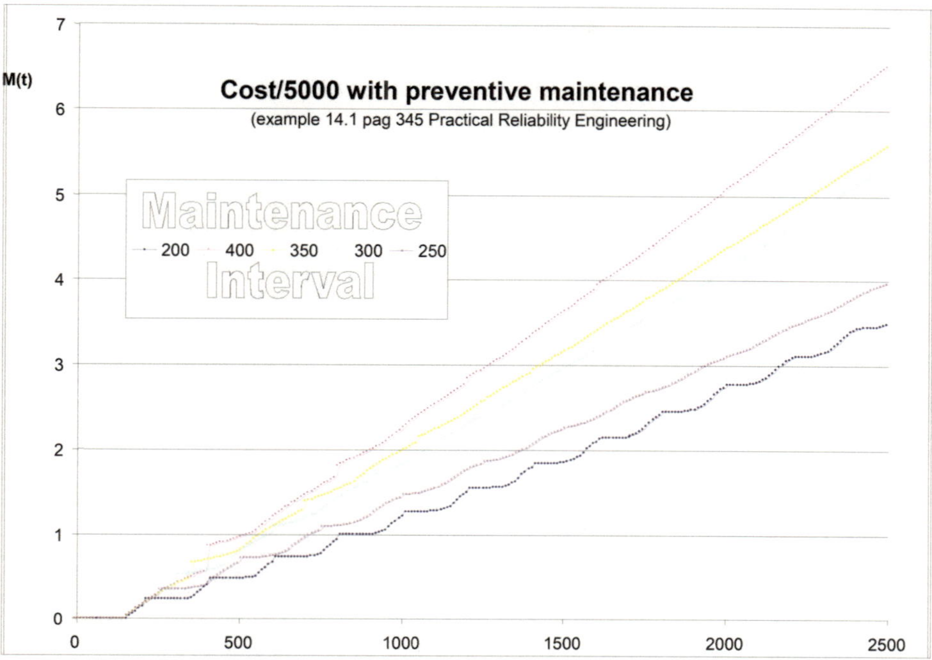

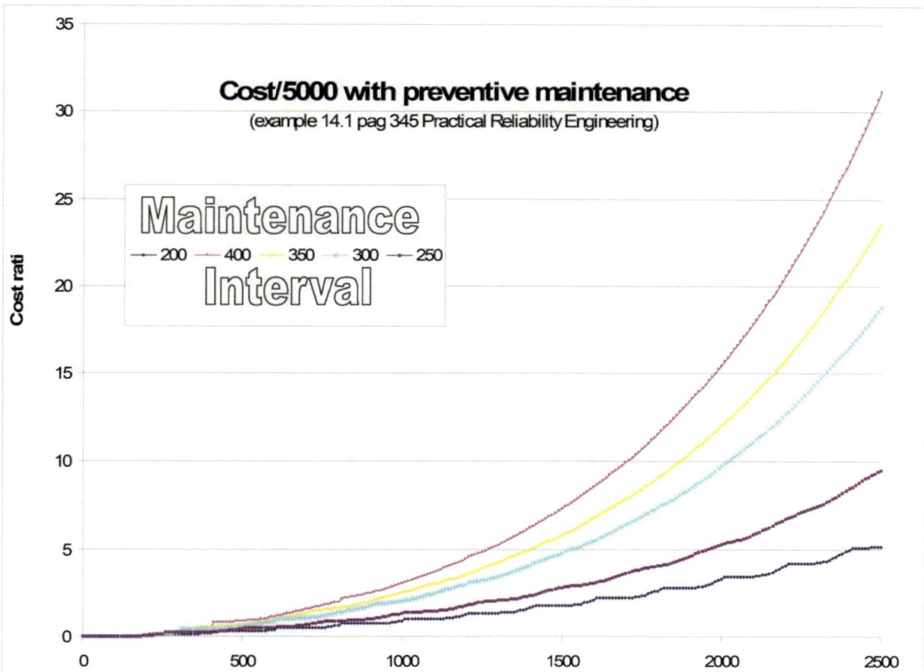

Fig. 24. Costs of preventive maintenance

"A flexible cable on a robot assembly line has a time-to-failure distribution which is Weibull, with γ=150 h, β=1.7, η=300 h. If a failure occurs whilst in use the cost of stopping the line and replacing the cable is \$5000. The cost of replacement during scheduled maintenance is \$500. If the line runs for 5000 hours a year and scheduled maintenance takes place every week (100 hours), what would be the annual expected cost replacement at one-weekly or two-weekly intervals?"

The solution provided in the book, for 5000 h, is

interval (h)	*100*	*200*	*400*
cost/5000	*5.00*	*3.66*	*7.75*

therefore 200 h interval is considered the best.

Actually it is better to replace every 150 h: no failures and only preventive replacements. We made a digression to preventive maintenance problems because their analogy with inventory management; the table shows it

$M_0(t, t_p)$	Mean number of preventive replacement		Mean number of orders
$M_1(t, t_p)$	Mean number of failures		Mean number of Stokouts
c_0	cost of preventive replacement	A	cost of orders
c_1	cost of one failure	p	cost of a Stockout

It is apparent that Reliability Integral Theory will help us in dealing with inventory management.

6. 6th step: the case of random demand with "NONconstant" demand rate and NOT steady state of the stochastic process

We assume the following hypotheses: 1) ***delivery takes a constant Lead Time L, after the order***, 2) any order incurs a fixed order cost, A, 3) there is no interaction between different products, 4) *demand is random*, 6) *demand rate is NOT constant at every instant of time*.
In the five steps before we considered the process in its steady state, i.e. after a long time [$t\to\infty$]; now we consider the case of finite time t, as done for preventive maintenance.
Letting again $P_i(t)$=P[process in the state i, at time t], be the probability that process in the state i, at time t, we can depict the system with the following transition diagram for the case R=2 and Q=4.

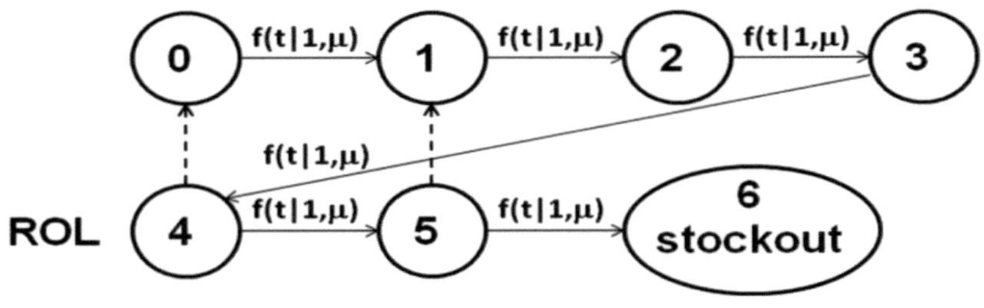

Fig. 25. System inventory states (random demand, variable rate); case Q=4, R=2 [Factory Physics]

The equations are now integral equations, as in the Reliability Integral Theory; the integral equations have the same structure, whatever is the analytic form of the density f(t|1,μ), that we write simply f(t); let g(s) be the probability density of the time to replenishment (so dealing with random Lead Time). Following the Galetto's Reliability Integral Theory ideas we can write, being $R_i(t\text{-}s)$ the probability of no stockout [service level] if the system enters state i, at time s, and

$$\bar{F}(t)=1-F(t) \qquad \bar{G}(t)=1-G(t) \qquad \bar{W}(t)=\bar{F}(t)\bar{G}(t) \tag{20}$$

$$\begin{aligned} R_0(t)&=1-F(t)+\int_0^t f(s)R_1(t-s)ds \qquad & R_1(t)&=1-F(t)+\int_0^t f(s)R_2(t-s)ds \\ R_2(t)&=1-F(t)+\int_0^t f(s)R_3(t-s)ds \qquad & R_3(t)&=1-F(t)+\int_0^t f(s)R_4(t-s)ds \\ R_4(t)&=\bar{F}(t)\bar{G}(t)+\int_0^t f(s)\bar{G}(s)R_4(t)+\int_0^t g(s)\bar{F}(s)R_0(t) \qquad & R_5(t)&=\bar{F}(t)\bar{G}(t) \end{aligned} \tag{21}$$

This can be written in matrix form as

$$R(t)=\bar{W}(t)+\int_0^t B(s)R(t-s)ds \tag{22}$$

where $b_{i,k}(s)ds$ is the matrix of probability transition from state i to state k, in the interval s---s+ds.
The Service Level S(t), i.e. no stockout for the interval 0------t, is $R_0(t)$. The probability $P_i(t)$ of being in state i, at time t, is $P_i(t)=R_i(t)-R_{i+1}(t)$.
The integral of $R_i(t)$, from 0 to ∞, provides the Mean Time To STockOut $MTTSTO_i$, when the system begins in state i.
The instantaneous Inventory Level I(s), for any time s of the interval 0------t, and random Lead Time (for replenishment) is $I(s)=\sum_0^5 (R+Q-i)P_i(s)$ with cost of Inventory, for the interval 0------t $I(t)=h\int_0^t I(s,L)ds$. Since the probabilities $P_i(t)\to 0$, as $t\to\infty$, because it is certain that a stockout happens, $I(\infty)=h\int_0^\infty I(s,L)ds$ is a finite quantity.
Putting all together we have the relationship that provides the cost C(t, L) of the system; the cost rate, usually used in books, is here C(t, L)/t; it is in the following figure 26. If we compute the cost Mean Cost To STockOut $MCTSTO_0$, from state 0 to the state of stockout, the cost rate is $g=MCTSTO_0/MTTSTO_0$. [compare this with the findings in RCM...]
This result is valid for any distribution of the time to sell product, from exponential, to Erlang, to ..., ...
As we can see, for the distribution f(t|1,μ) considered before, the cost rate increases and, after 12 months decreases. The cost rate is lower in the case Q=4 and R=2, while the service is better for Q=2 and R=4, as we found with the steady state analysis.

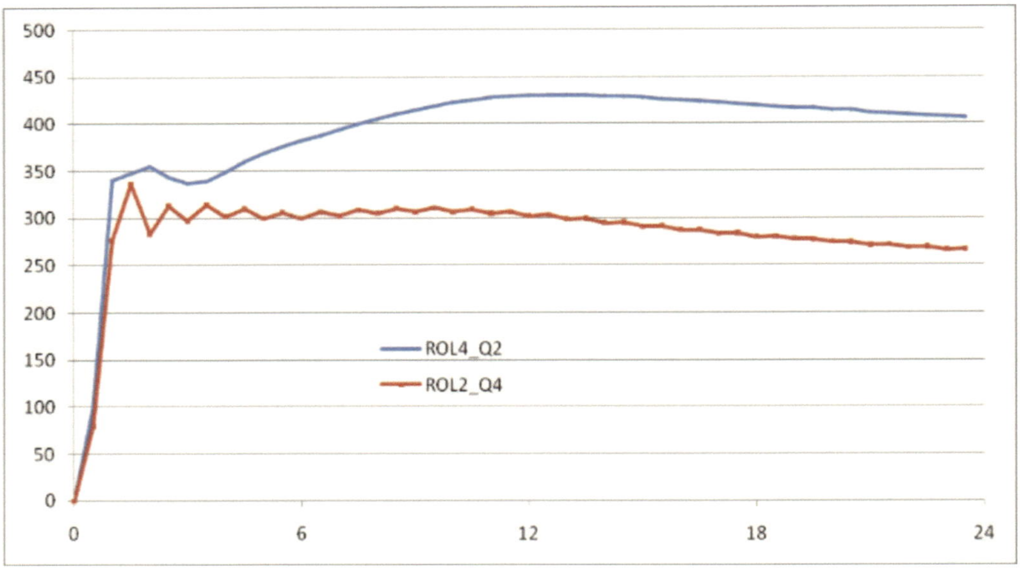

Fig. 26. Cost rate of two inventory systems (random demand at variable rate): Q=4, R=2 vs Q=2, R=4 [Factory Physics]

R=	4	2
Q=	2	4
Cost rate ($/year) at 6 months	**381.54**	**299.29**
Service Level at 6 months	**0.914**	**0.691**

If the service level 0.69, due to the consequences of downtime, is not adequate, we have to choose...
It is therefore very important the interval in which we want optimise. [fig. 1, 32-35]
This subject has been pointed out many times by F. Galetto, in relation with the Preventive Maintenance. We showed it because it has an amazing similarity with inventory management.
The best solution for the cost rate is Q=4 and R=2, while for the service level is Q=2 and R=4 (as before).
We end this paragraph by noting that F. Galetto ideas considered here for the "lost sales" model, or "type 1 Service" model, **as can be found in books and papers**, whose cost involved are (being λ the rate of demand, always considered as constant !!!!):

- $A\lambda/Q$, the "average" order cost per year
- $(1-F_{LT}(R)p\lambda/Q$, the cost of stockout [p is the cost per stockout, in euro] $F_{LT}(R)$ is the CD of demand during the lead time LT, **generally ASSUMED as Normally distributed in books and papers**
- $h(R+Q/2-\lambda LT)$, "average" inventory cost per year

are much more suitable for the analysis of practical problems.
The promise of books and papers, "If stockouts are permitted and lead time is LT > 0, *if demand is random, the formula to be minimised is the*

average cost rate = $A\lambda/Q + h(R + Q/2 - \lambda LT) + (1 - F_{LT}(R))p\lambda/Q$ (where R is the trigger quantity for launching the order Q, p is the penalty for stockouts and $F_{LT}(d)$ is the probability distribution of the demand d, during the lead time LT". actually is based on an inconsistent formula, because it is founded on an **intuitive [not proved] extension** of the formula for <<"constant" demand, no stockouts permitted and lead time zero>>.

Notice that this formula is the same as that in case of "everything known" and constant!!!!!!!!!!!!.

No scientific proof of the formula is ever provided!!! <u>Understanding that the formula is wrong is very easy.</u>

The probability of stockout depends on the competition of two stochastic processes: the demand versus the replenishment. The replenishment density g(t) is not present in any formula you can find **<u>in books and papers</u>**.

One can make a Gedanken Experiment, using the Bernoulli's Theorem (equation of motion in hydrodynamics) to guess: let's consider a physical system of three water containers with the same base area, as in the figure 27; the water flows from the discharge tube of the middle container; when the water level of the middle container falls below R level, the pump is triggered and the water flows (from the lower container) into the upper container till the level Q is achieved: at this time the water is immediately dropped into the middle container. IF this happens before the 0 level in the middle container is reached, the probability of water "stockout" is zero! One needs many cycles to experience water "stockout"!!!! [depending on the random factors, pump delivery and discharge tube, in order to take into account the random demand and the random replenishment time]

The formula average cost rate = $A\lambda/Q + h(R + Q/2 - \lambda LT) + (1 - F_{LT}(R))p\lambda/Q$ does not "agree" with figure 27, and therefore is wrong: you can get all that using F. Galetto ideas, as given in his books and papers. [Brandimarte 2004]

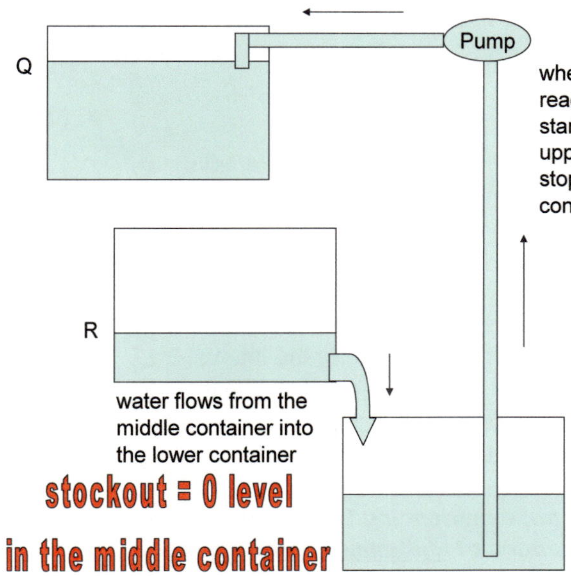

Fig. 27. the water tanks

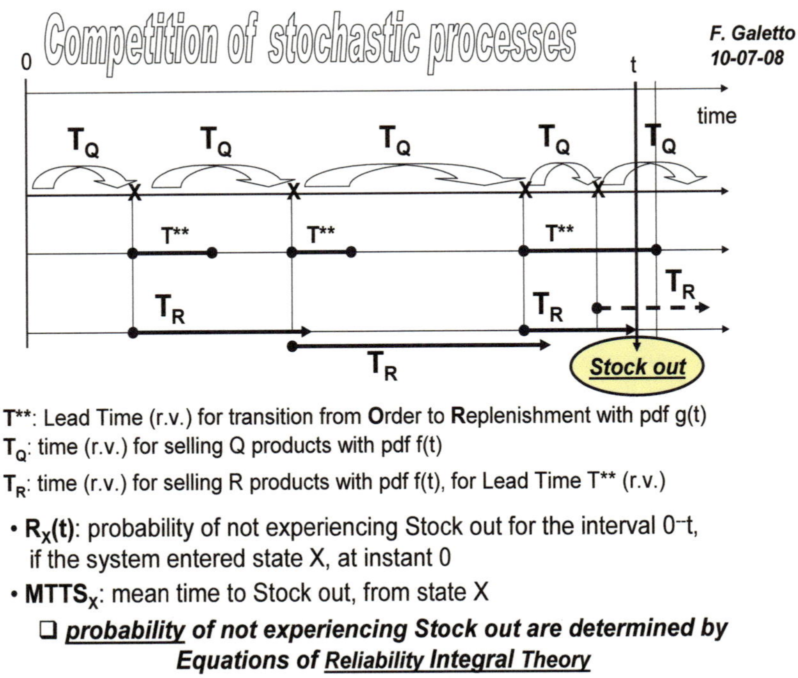

Fig. 28. the competition of the two stochastic processes, selling and replenishment

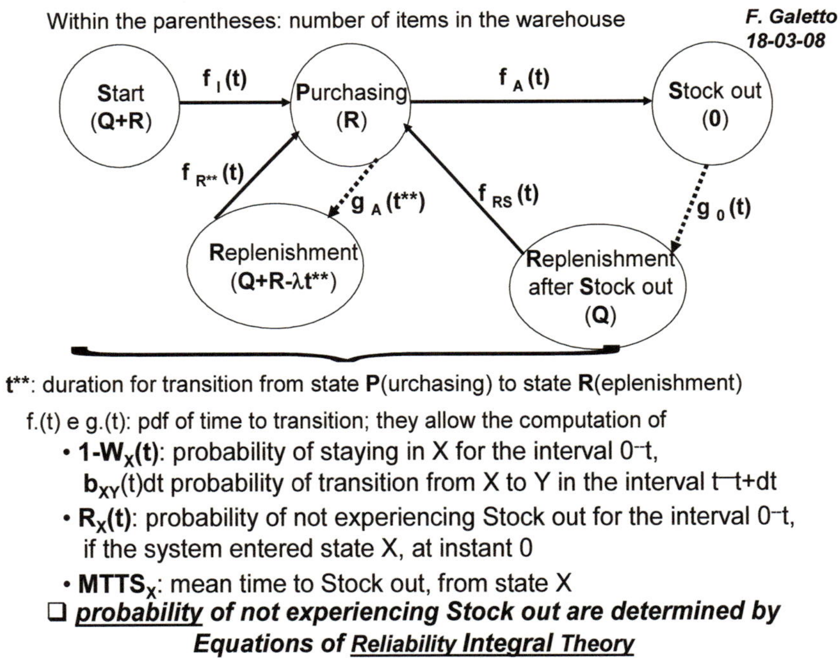

Fig. 29. Transitions between the inventory system due to selling and replenishment competition (stochastic processes)

7. Some others cases found in documents

Let's consider <u>several examples, with wrong solutions, from various sources.</u>
For **example** Brandimarte and Zotteri, in their book, found Q=111, R=143 and type 1 Service level=95.73%, using the following data: A=50, h=2, p=500, Normal Distribution during LT=6 months, with pdf $N(\mu,\sigma)=N(100, 25)$. They say

> We can find the optimal solution $Q^* = 111$ e $R^* = 143$ with a type I service level $F(R) = 95.73\%$ by simply iterating the above process.

Using the same data, and the right ideas (as sketched in fig. 27), F. Galetto finds Q=80, R=92 and type 1 Service level=95.73%: ***<u>lower costs for the</u>*** **same** ***<u>service level</u>*, in the steady state**!!!! This result comes from the right formulae.
If we consider a finite horizon, and the density $f(t\,|\,1, \mu)$, the system faces stockout if $T_R < LT$; if, on the contrary, if $T_R > LT$, then the inventory, expired the time LT, raises its quantity by Q, and a new cycle starts. [see Fig. 27]
The findings, for the three methods, are [Lead time assumed constant]:

Method	*Formula of the books*	*$g=MCTSTO_0/MTTSTO_0$*	*using $f(t\,|\,1, \mu)$*
Q and R	**1**: Q=100, R=141	**2**: Q=100, R=133	**3**: Q=100, R=121
cost (6 months)	603,6	567,8	492,50

The scientific method provides "*<u>Lower costs for the</u>* same *<u>service level</u>*"!! Many other examples could be provided. <u>How many students, all over the world, are learning wrong methods and will take wrong decisions?</u>

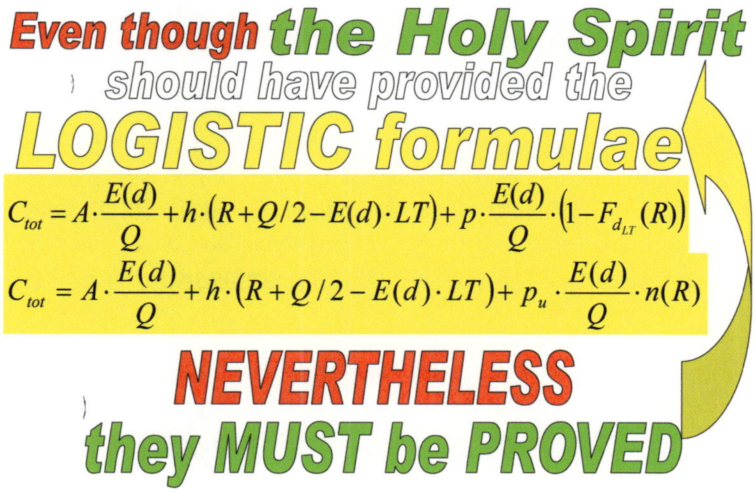

Fig. 30. Logistics and Holy Spirit

A **further example** is taken from the Politecnico di Milano course, they say "*Buyers Product Company distributes an item known as a Tie Bar, which is U-bolt used on truck equipment. The monthly demand is 11 with standard deviation 3.1.*", and they find Q=11, R=19 and type I Service level=94.8%, using the following data: A=10, h=0.022, p=69, Normal Distribution

during LT=1.5 months, with pdf N(μ, σ). They use a different formula of the one used by Brandimarte and Zotteri, and by Hoop and Spearman but they, as well, do not consider the "pump" of fig. 27. Using the same data, and the right ideas (as sketched in fig. 27), F. Galetto finds Q=6, R=23 and type I Service level=98.2%: ***lower costs for*** **better** ***service level***!!!! This result comes from the right formulae.
As a another **example**, A. Caridi, in his book, provides an example where *The weekly demand is Normal distributed with mean 50 and standard deviation 5.*"; he finds Q=294, R=177 and Service level=99.9%, using the following data: A=30, h=1.8, p=525.4, Normal Distribution during LT=3 weeks, with pdf N(μ, σ). He uses a different formula of the one used by Brandimarte and Zotteri, and by Hoop and Spearman but he, as well, does not consider the "pump" of fig. 27. Using the same data and the right ideas (as sketched in fig. 27), F. Galetto finds Q=190, R=133 and Service level=99.91%: ***lower costs for*** **the same** ***service level***!!!! This result comes from the right formulae.
As a **last example** Law and Kelton, in their book Simulation Modelling and Analysis, say "*Consider a company which sells a single product and would like to decide how many items to have in inventory for each of the n months. The times between demands are IID exponential random variable with a mean of 0.1 month. The sizes of the demands D are IID random variables (independent of when the demands occur) with probability P(D=1)=P(D=4)=1/6 P(D=2)=P(D=3)=1/3. At the beginning of each month, the company reviews the inventory level and decides how many items to order from its supplier.*" They compare in example 9.2 two inventory policies: (Q=40, R=20) and (Q=80, R=20) carrying out 10 + 10 simulations, and find that the second policy is better. They do not compute the Service level. F. Galetto makes a comparison (only for comparison purpose), using the following data: A=32, h=1, p=100, Normal Distribution during LT: the result is opposite, the first one is better; moreover there is a policy (Q=5, R=6) much better than both!!! This finding was so peculiar that F. Galetto decided to read thoroughly the book and found in example 9.4 the comparison of 5 alternative policies: (Q, R)= (40, 20), (80, 20), (60, 40), (100, 40), (100, 60): Law and Kelton "selected policy 2, (Q=80, R=20) as being the lowest-cost configuration". F. Galetto finds that also doubling all the cost involved, the policy (Q=5, R=6) is much better than all the previous policies!!! That sounded still strange and F. Galetto went on: he found this statement in example 12.1 "… it appears that the smaller values of both Q and R would be preferable, since lower monthly costs are desired": therefore it is rather surprising that, just few pages before, Law and Kelton chose the policy (Q=80, R=20) as better than (Q=40, R=20). Law and Kelton used simulations, but they, as well, do not consider the "pump".
How many students, all over the world, are learning wrong methods and will take wrong decisions?
These examples show very clearly Deming statements:

> "*The result is that hundreds of people are learning what is wrong. .... I make this statement on the basis of experience, seeing every day the devastating effects of incompetent teaching and faulty applications.*" "*It is a hazard to copy*", "*It is necessary to understand the theory of what one wishes to do or to make.*"

It is important to notice that **you do not need the right formula to understand that a wrong formula is wrong**: an example is the following "*The General Triangle is used for practical applications of trigonometry in determining distances that cannot be measured directly. Such a problem may be solved by making the required distance one side of a triangle, measuring other sides or angles of the triangle, and then applying the Carnot Theorem (cosine law): if α, β, γ are the three angles of a triangle, and a, b, c the respective opposite sides, it may be proved that* $a^2=b^2+c^2-2bc\cos\alpha$

[Carnot Theorem (cosine law)]. You need a lot of ingenuity to solve the problem if you know only the Pythagorean Theorem, which states that the square of the hypotenuse of a right triangle is equal to the sum of the squares of the other two sides. Anyway you do not need the knowledge of the Carnot Theorem (cosine law) to understand that it wrong to apply the Pythagorean Theorem to General Triangles".

Any formula that does not consider the fig. 27 is wrong! How many professors do not use "pump" in their optimisation?

The statement of the Nobel prize M. Gell-Mann is relevant: *"Once that such a misunderstanding has taken place in the publication, it tends to become perpetual, because the various authors simply copy one each other."*....>> {"The Quark and the Jaguar: Adventures in the Simple and the Complex" [W. Freeman and Company, N. Y., 1994]}[fig.1, 5, 32 -35]

8. Reliability centred maintenance and spare parts management

The ideas we presented in the paragraph "*6th step: the case of random demand with "NONconstant" demand rate and NOT steady state of the stochastic process*" can be used for the fields of Reliability Centred Maintenance and Spare Parts Management.

They were presented by F. Galetto in the paper "*A general model for system cost-effectiveness*" at a joint conference of EOQC&IAQ 1975 [European Organisation for Quality Control & International Academy for Quality], in Venice (Italy).

At that time F. Galetto used a Time Homogeneous Markov Process, as we did previously for constant demand rate (exponential distribution).

Let's indicate with λ_{ik} the transition rate from state i to state k, p_{ik} the steady transition probability from state i to state k, m_i the mean time that the system stays in state i before making a transition, $e_{ik}(0, s)$ the earning [or a cost] of the system due the transition from state i to state k for the interval 0--s, $d_{ik}(s)$ the earning [or a cost] of the system due the transition from state i to state k at the instant s, $v_i(t)$ the total expected profit [or cost] of the system for the interval 0--t, if it starts in state i at time 0. If the system makes its 1st transition out of the state i before the instant t it earns a profit

$$\sum_{k=0}^{N} \lambda_{ik} \int_0^t e^{-\lambda_i s}[e_{ik}(0,s) + d_{ik}(s) + v_k(t-s)]ds$$

If the system makes its 1st transition out of the state i after the instant t it earns a profit

$$\sum_{k=0}^{N} p_{ik} e^{-\lambda_i t} e_{ik}(0,t)$$

Putting all together we have the system of integral equations [notice the similarity with what done before for reliability]

$$v_i(t) = \sum_{k=0}^{N} p_{ik} e^{-\lambda_i t} e_{ik}(0,t) + \sum_{k=0}^{N} \lambda_{ik} \int_0^t e^{-\lambda_i s}[e_{ik}(0,s) + d_{ik}(s) + v_k(t-s)]ds \qquad (23)$$

When $t \to \infty$, there is an asymptotic solution $v_i(t)=v_i + gt$, where g is the gain rate; finding the steady state probability of being in state i, φ_i, and r_i, the reward for each entrance into state i, F. Galetto proved that

$$g = \sum_{i=0}^{N} (r_i / m_i)\varphi_i \tag{24}$$

For the use of this formula we have to allow the system to enter the "down states" and return to "up states".
Letting $\Phi_{ij}(t)$ the transition probability for the transition i $\rightarrow$ j, when t $\rightarrow \infty$, we can put the system in an equivalent vector and matrix form (for a number of states such that inverse matrix exists)

$$\vec{v}(t) = [I - P]^{-1}\vec{r} + \Phi(t)[I - P]^{-1}\vec{r} \tag{25}$$

The vector $\vec{r} = \sum_{k=0}^{N} \lambda_{ik} \int_0^{\infty} e^{-\lambda_i s}[e_{ik}(0,s) + d_{ik}(s)]ds$ is a constant vector.

Constant transition rates are not necessary, as shown by F. Galetto in the paper "*CLAUDIA (Cost Life Analysis)*", *21st EOQC Conf.*, Varna (Bulgaria); we indicate with $b_{ik}(s)ds$ the instantaneous transition probability from state i to state k in the interval s--s+ds, p_{ik} the steady transition probability from state i to state k, 1-$W_i(t)$ the probability that the system stays in state i for the interval 0--t. We have

$$v_i(t) = \sum_{k=0}^{N} p_{ik}\overline{W}_i(t)e_{ik}(0,t) + \sum_{k=0}^{N}\int_0^t b_{ik}(s)[e_{ik}(0,s) + d_{ik}(s) + v_k(t-s)]ds \tag{26}$$

and again $\vec{v}(t) = [I - P]^{-1}\vec{r} + \Phi(t)[I - P]^{-1}\vec{r}$ (for a number of states such that inverse matrix exists), and the vector $\vec{r}$ suitably defined.
If we partition the states in two sets, the up states [where the system performs as it must] and the down states [where the system does not perform as it should], we can partition the vectors and the matrices accordingly.

$$\vec{v}(t) = \begin{bmatrix} \vec{v}_1(t) \\ \vec{v}_2(t) \end{bmatrix} = \begin{bmatrix} I_{11} - P_{11} & P_{12} \\ P_{21} & I_{22} - P_{22} \end{bmatrix}^{-1} \begin{bmatrix} \vec{r}_1 \\ \vec{r}_2 \end{bmatrix} + \begin{bmatrix} \Phi_{11}(t) & \Phi_{12}(t) \\ \Phi_{21}(t) & \Phi_{22}(t) \end{bmatrix} \begin{bmatrix} I_{11} - P_{11} & P_{12} \\ P_{21} & I_{22} - P_{22} \end{bmatrix}^{-1} \begin{bmatrix} \vec{r}_1 \\ \vec{r}_2 \end{bmatrix} \tag{27}$$

F. Galetto proved that the steady state system availability A_{SS} = MUT/(MUT+MDT) = MUT/MTBF where the Mean Up Time is the dot product of the two vectors zα*MTTF and the Mean Down Time is zβ*MTTR.
Letting t $\rightarrow \infty$, the limit of the vector $v_1(t)$ is the vector SEPUF, System Expected Profit Until Failure and the limit of the vector $v_2(t)$ is the vector SEPUR, System Expected Profit Until Repair (inverse matrices DO exist!)

$$\vec{v}_1(t \rightarrow \infty) = SEPUF = [I_{11} - P_{11}]^{-1}\vec{r}_1 \qquad \vec{v}_2(t \rightarrow \infty) = SEPUR = [I_{22} - P_{22}]^{-1}\vec{r}_2 \tag{28}$$

Using the same probability vectors zα and zβ we can compute the system UEG, Up Expected Gain, UEG=zα*SEPUF and the system DEG, Down Expected Gain, DEG=zβ*SEPUR; the system CEG, Cycle Expected Gain is CEG=DEG+UEG and finally the gain rate g=CEG/MTBF.
Let's now derive the famous Wilson lot-size formula, in a very general context; we assume only that, if different types of distributions are used, they have the same mean m, the mean

time to sell one product; the "time to sell a new unit (time between demands)" is a random variable "identically" [but not exponentially] distributed and we indicate the probability density of the time between transitions as f(t) [related to the "rate" $\lambda(t)$, with cumulative distribution F(t)]; its mean is m. We compute the gain rate g. When $t \to \infty$, the steady state probability of being in state i, $\varphi_i = 1/Q$ and r_i the reward for each entrance into state i, are r_0=A+ Qhm and r_i=(Q-i)hm; therefore, after some algebra $g = [A/m + hQ(Q+1)/2]/Q$. We can depict, again, the system as before

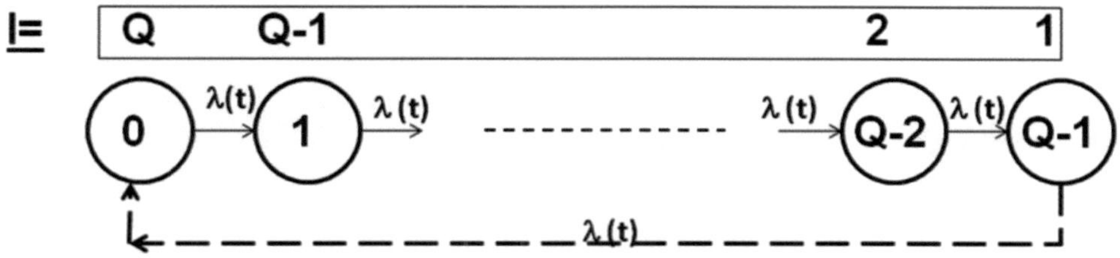

Fig. 31. System inventory states, with random demand and variable demand rate; state i means i products dispatched

8. Conclusion

We presented some cases where professors were completely failing to comply with the ideas of the Standard ISO 9001:2008, in the **1st** place, NOT preventing the generation of wrong methods, in the **2nd** place, NOT realising that methods were wrong (nonconformities), in the **3rd** place, spreading around nonconformities (wrong methods), in the **4th** place, NOT taking the needed corrective actions for the nonconformities (wrong methods), in the **5th** place, punishing people who realised that those methods were wrong!!!!
Since Universities MUST prepare ***flexible graduates*** who can think integratively, with **their own mind**, prevent and solve problems, be life-long learners using their intelligence and intellectual honesty, Universities **must** teach future managers to be Intellectually Honest and to act in a scientific way. To get that professors must understand that "*Quality of methods for Quality is important*": some methods are really wrong. [Galetto 1989, Vienna]
If the people mentioned here (also the ones that I do not know [referees are unknown to me]) are willing to find me wrong and prove that they are right, I am ready to meet all of them together, and to have a profound discussion.
If they accept the challenge, they MUST remember that "***Many wrongs don't make a right***".
Will they accept? Only God knows it ...
"*A prophet is not without honour, but in his own country, and among his own kin, and in his own house.*"(ST Mark)
Unfortunately professors and referees do not believe in the ideas of Deming, and therefore

> ***The result is that hundreds of people are learning what is wrong. .... I make this statement on the basis of experience, seeing every day the devastating effects of incompetent teaching and faulty applications.***

Papers with errors are not scientific, even though the authors say: "*We thank the referees and the editor for careful reading and helpful comments that improved our paper.*"
There are too many people, wrong-headed waffling about Quality, who do not take corrective actions when I signal them their nonconformities:

... they fly into rages and they continue teaching wrongly ...

Why there are so many professionals, wrong-headed waffling about Quality and related methods, and with very little knowledge of Reliability, Design of Experiments, Statistics, Quality Management, Mathematics, Logic, …?
If we want to achieve QUALITY, MANAGERS (now students) NEED TO BE EDUCATED ON QUALITY εQ_{GE}^{IO} by Quality Professors, EDUCATED on Quality. (fig. 32 and 33)

I could, at last, paraphrase ST John *"And there are also many other things, the which, if they should be written everyone, I suppose that even the world itself could not contain the books that should be written."*
Will someone want to see the truth? ***Only God knows that ...***
The personal conclusion is left to the Intellectually Honest reader to whom is offered the **Quality Tetralogy**: Prevent, Experiment, Improve, Plan, SCIENTIFICALLY to avoid disquality, to eliminate disquality, to achieve Quality, to assure Quality, using Intellectual Honesty, as shown in the figure 34 (also fig. 35 for items, with fig. 32 and 33).
Quality Tetralogy is much better than ISO 9004:2008 because Quality Tetralogy takes into account explicitly the need for scientific behaviour either of people or of organisations that really want to make Quality. Moreover it shows clearly that prevention is very important for Quality, where Good Management is strongly related to Good Knowledge for Business Excellence. [fig.1, 5, 32, 33, 34, 35]
Brain is the most important asset: let's not forget it, *IF we want that our students be better that their professors.* [fig.1, 5, 32, 33, 34, 35]
Disquality Vicious Circle MUST be avoided, in all Companies and Universities.

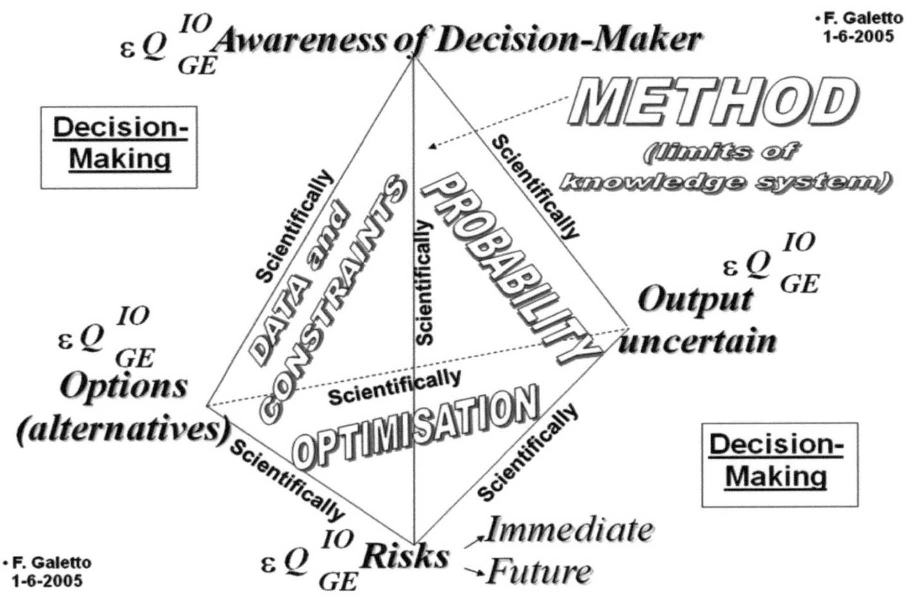

Fig. 32. The Decision-making Tetrahedron

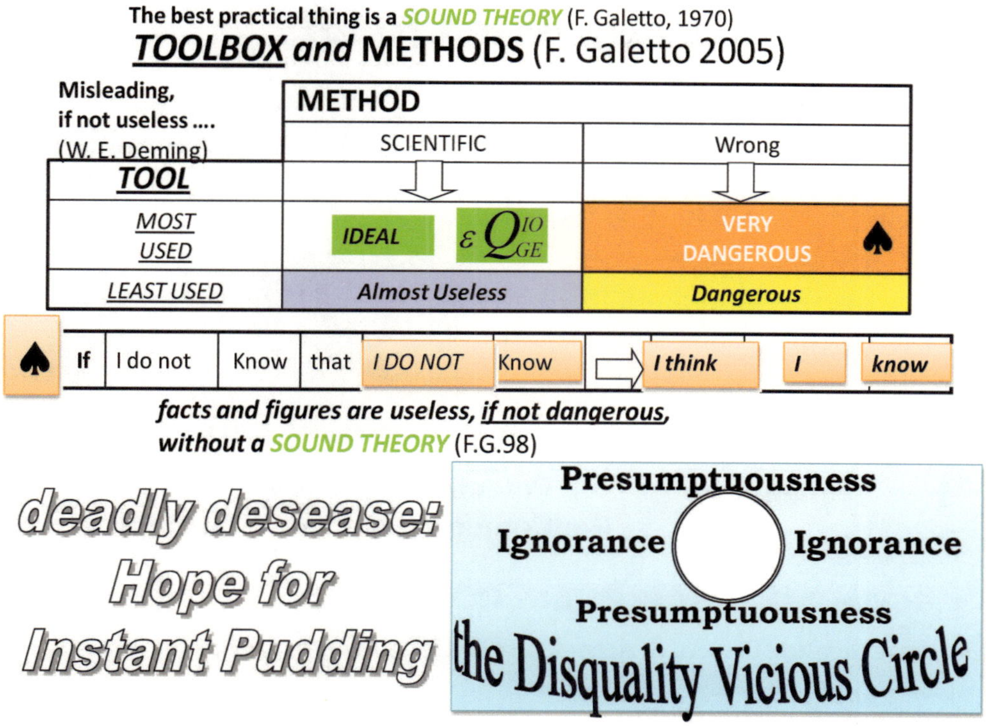

Fig. 33. The Disquality vicious circle and Methods

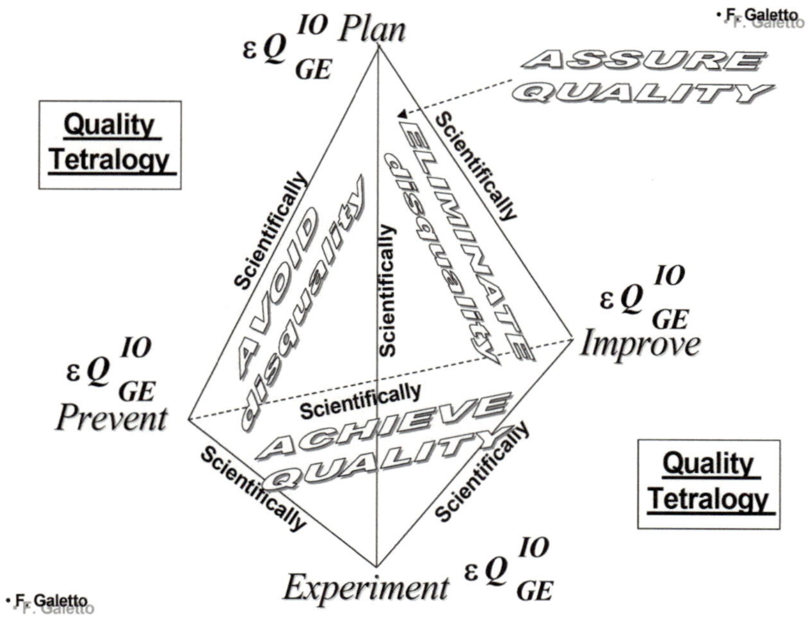

Fig. 34. Quality Tetralogy

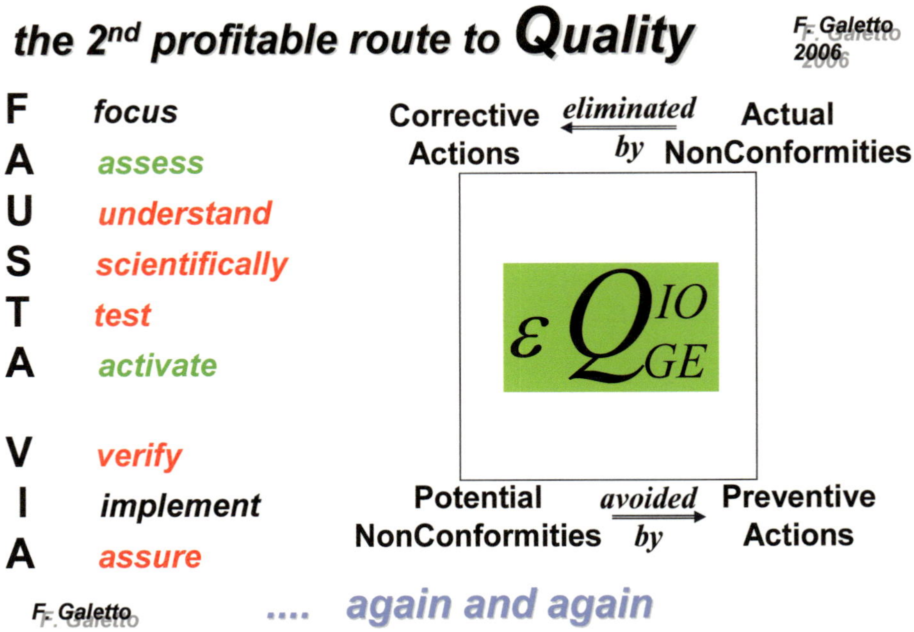

Fig. 35. Preventive and Corrective Actions, and FAUSTA VIA

9. Acknowledgements

The author acknowledges the support offered by QuASAR (via A. Moro 8, 20090 Buccinasco, Italy).

10. References

Quality Engineering

Franceschini F., Rossetto S., (1998) On line Service Quality Control: the Qualitometro Method, *Quality Engineering, 633-643*

Franceschini F., Romano D., (1998) Control Charts for linguistic variables: a method based on the use of linguistic quantifiers, *Int. J. Of Production Research, n° 16 1999, 3791-3801*

Franceschini F., Rossetto S. (1999-2000) Service Qualimetrics: the Qualitometro II Method, *Quality Engineering, 13-20*

Lin C., Hong C., Lai J., (1997) Improvement of a dimensional measurement process using Taguchi robust designs, *Quality Engineering, 561-573*

Schaub D., MONTGOMERY D.C., (1997) Using experimental design to optimize the stereolithography process, *Quality Engineering,* 575-585

Yager, R., (1981) A new methodology for ordinal multiobjective decision based on fuzzy sets, *Decision Sciences*, Vol. 12, 589-600

Yager, R., Filev, D., (1994) *Essentials of Fuzzy Modeling and Control*, Wiley

Zadeh, L., desoer, c., (1963) *Linear System Theory: The State Space Approach*, McGraw-Hill

Zadeh, L., (1965) Fuzzy Sets, *Information and Control*, VIII, 338-56

Zadeh, L., (1976) Linguistic variable and application to approximate reasoning, *Information Science*

Galetto, F. (2006) The Pentalogy, part 1, *Quality Engineering*, NOT submitted

Quality and Reliability Engineering International

Bisgard S., (2005) Innovation, ENBIS and the Importance of Practice in the Development of Statistics, *Quality and Reliability Engineering International*

BERGMAN B., (1977) Some graphical methods for maintenance planning, *Reliability & Maintainability Symposium*, Philadelphia.

Bergman B., (1978?) Total time on test plotting for failure data analyses, *SAAB-SCANIA*

Brandimarte, P., Zotteri G. (2004) *Logistica di distribuzione*, CLUT

Di Bucchianico A., Mooiweer G., Moonen E, (2005) Monitoring infrequent failures of high-volume production processes, *Quality and Reliability Engineering International*

Montgomery D.C. (1996), *Introduction to Statistical Quality Control*, Wiley & Sons (wrong definition of the term "Quality", and many other drawbacks)

O' Connor P.D.T. (1997), *Practical Reliability Engineering*, Wiley & Sons (many, many drawbacks)

Hopp W, J , Spearman M, L *Factory Physics* (2nd ed.), McGraw-Hill Higher Education

Yin G.Z., Jillie D.W. (1987), Orthogonal Design for Process Optimisation and its Application in Plasma Etching, *Solid State Technology*, (may 87)

Galetto, F. (2006) The Pentalogy, part 2, *Quality and Reliability Engineering International*, NOT submitted

International Journal on Quality and Reliability Management

Barlow R., E., DAVIS B:(1978) Total time on test plots, *24th Army Design of Experiments Conf.*, Madison

Barlow R., E., (1978) Analysis of retrospective failure data using computer graphics, *Reliability & Maintainability Symposium*

Erto P. (1982), New practical Bayes estimator for Weibull, *IEEE Trans. Reliability, R-31*

Erto P., RAPONE M. (1984) Non-informative and practical bayesian confidence bounds for reliable life in the Weibull model, *Reliability Engineering* 7, pp. 181-191

Franceschini F. (2002) Learning curves and p-charts for a preliminary estimation of asymptotic performances of a manufacturing process, *Total Quality Management*, Vol. 13, No. 1, 5-12

Franceschini F., Rupil a. (1999) Rating scales and prioritization in QFD, *International Journal on Quality and Reliability Management, 85-97*

Konda R., Rajurkar K.P., Bishu R., Guha A., Parson M. (1999) Design of experiments to study and optimize process performance, *Int. Journal of Quality&Reliability Management*, Vol. 16, No. 1, 56-61

Levi, R., Lombardo, A. (1997) *Nuove frontiere nella programmazione degli esperimenti*, Convegno SIS

Un-known, Inventory Policy Decisions [*doc. used at Milan Politecnico, in the Course of Logistics*]

Galetto, F. (2006) The Pentalogy, part 3, *International Journal on Quality and Reliability Management*, NOT submitted

Quality Progress

aNderson-cook, c., (2005) How to choose the appropriate design, *Quality Progress* (October)

Barone S, Erto P, Lanzotti A (2001), Beyond robust design methodologies: an elementary example of synergy between statistics and advanced engineering design, *SIS Sperimentare per la Qualità*, Turin February 2001

Byrne D, Taguchi, S. (1987), Taguchi's Approach to Parameter Design, *Quality Progress* (December)

Fijiu Antony, Fijiu Antony F. (2001) Teaching the Taguchi method to industrial engineers, *vol. 50, 141-149*, MCB University Press

Law A., Kelton D. (1982) *Simulation Modeling and Analysis*, McGraw-Hill

Nelson L. S., (1994) A control chart for parts-per-million nonconforming items, *Journal of Quality Technology*

Okes, D., (2005) Corral your organization's knowledge, *Quality Progress* (October)

PARK, S. (1996), *Robust Design and Analysis for Quality Engineering*, Chapman & Hall, London

Sarin S. (1997), Teaching Taguchi's Approach to Parameter Design, *Quality Progress* (May)

Silver E., Pyke D., Petersen R. (1998) *Inventory management and Production Planning and Scheduling*, Wiley & Sons

Galetto, F. (2006) The Pentalogy, part 4, *Quality Progress*, NOT submitted

Statistical Methods & Applications (Journal of the Italian Statistical Society)

Caridi A. *Tecniche organizzative e decisionali per la gestione aziendale*, Levrotto & Bella, Torino

Caridi A. *Metodologie per la gestione operativa delle imprese*, Levrotto & Bella, Torino

Giovagnoli, A., Romano, D. (2001) Sperimentazione nella produzione del software: alcune implicazioni sui disegni, *S.Co.2001*, Bressanone, Cleup Editrice

Giovagnoli, A., Romano, D. (2004) Optimal experiments in the presence of a learning effect: a problem suggested by software production, *Statistical Methods & Applications, vol. 13*

Galetto, F. (2006) The Pentalogy, part 5, *Statistical Methods & Applications*, NOT submitted

Palo Alto Psychology Group (on Transactional Analysis)

Berne E. *A che gioco giochiamo* (*Games people play*), Bompiani, Milano

Fisch R., watzlawick p., weakland j. *CHANGE Sulla formazione e la soluzione dei problemi* (*CHANGE On the principles of problem formation and problem solution*), Astrolabio, Roma

James M., Jongeward D., *Nati per vincere* (*Born to win*), Edizioni Paoline, Milano

Watzlawick P. *La realtà della realtà* (*The reality of reality*), Astrolabio, Roma

Watzlawick P., Beavin J., Jacson D. *Pragmatica della comunicazione umana* (*Pragmatics of human communication*), Astrolabio, Roma

Miscellaneous

Deming W.E. (1986), *Out of the crisis*, Cambridge Press

Deming, W.E. (1997), *The new economics for industry, government, education*, Cambridge Press

Feynmann R. (1965), *The Character of Physical Law*, British Broadcasting Corporation

Galetto F. (1975) A general model for system cost-effectiveness, *EOQC & IAQ Joint Conf.*

Galetto F. (1977) SARA (System Availability and Reliability Analysis), *Reliability & Maintainability Symposium*, Philadelphia.

Galetto F. (1977) CLAUDIA (Cost Life Analysis), *21st EOQC Conf.*, Varna

Galetto, F. (1987) Are Bayes' Methods really better?, *IASTED Conf. on Reliability and Quality Control*, Paris

Galetto, F. (1988) Comment on: "New practical Bayes estimator for Weibull distribution", *IEEE Transactions on. Reliability, R-37, NO. 5*
Galetto, F. (1989) Quality of methods for quality is important, *EOQC Conference*, Vienna
Galetto F. (1995) *Affidabilità, Volume 1: Teoria e Metodi di Calcolo*, CLEUP, Padova.
Galetto F. (1995) *Affidabilità, Volume 2: Prove di affidabilità*, CLEUP, Padova.
Galetto F. (1997) We need Quality of Managers, *Quality 97 6th Int. Conf.*, Ostrava, Czech Republic
Galetto, F. (1997) *Qualità. Alcuni metodi statistici da Manager*, CUSL, Torino
Galetto F. (1998) Quality Education on Quality for Future Managers, *1st Conference on TQM for Higher Education Institutions*, Toulon, France
Galetto F. (1999) GIQA, the Golden Integral Quality Approach: from Management of Quality to Quality of Management, *Total Quality Management*, Vol. 10, No. 1
Galetto, F. (1999) Quality Function Deployment, Some Managerial Concerns, *AITEM99*, Brescia
Galetto, F. (1999) Quality Education on Quality Management *2nd Conf. on TQM for HEI*, Verona
Galetto F. (2000) *Qualità. Alcuni metodi statistici da Manager*, CLUT, Torino
Galetto, F. (2000) Quality Education for Professors teaching Quality to Future Managers *3rd Conference on TQM for HEI*, Derby, UK
Galetto, F. (2001) Looking for Quality in "quality books", *4th Conference on TQM for HEI*, Mons, Belgium
Galetto, F. (2002) Fuzzy Logic, Quality and Control Charts, *2nd ICME2002 Conference.*, Ischia, Italy
Galetto, F. (2002) Analysis of "new" control charts for Quality assessment, *5th Conf. on TQM for HEI*, Lisbon, Portugal
Galetto, F. (2002) Quality decisions and ISO 9000:2000 Principles, *6thAMST 99*, Udine, Italy
Galetto, F. (2003) Quality and "quality magazines", *6th Conf. on TQM for HEI*, Oviedo, Spain
Galetto F. (2004) *Gestione Manageriale della Affidabilità: Teoria e Metodi*, CLUT, Torino
Galetto F. (2005) Metodi fuzzy di Yager e Teoria dei Reticoli, *CLADAG 2005*, Parma, Italy
Galetto, F. (2005) Reliability analysis in product development, *AMST 2005*, Udine, Italy
Galetto, F. (2005) Quality and "Statistics Packages", *8th Conf. on TQM for HEI*, Palermo, Italy
Galetto, F. (2006) Quality Education and "quality papers", *IPSI 2006 Marbella*, Marbella, Spain
Galetto, F. (2006) Fuzzy Logic and Quality Control: a scientific analysis, *IPSI 2006 Amalfi*, Amalfi, Italy
Galetto, F. (2006) Does "Peer Review" assure Quality of papers and Education?, *9th Conf. on TQM for HEI*, Paisley, UK
Galetto, F. (2006) Quality Education versus "Peer Review", *IPSI 2006 Montenegro*, Montenegro
Galileo Galilei (1623) *Saggiatore*
Galileo Galilei (1632) *Dialogo sopra i due massimi sistemi del mondo, Tolemaico e Copernicano* (*Dialogue on the Two Chief World Systems*)
Jay A. *Management and Machiavelli*, The Guernsey Press Co., Channel Islands
Kuhn T. (1969) *The structure of Scientific Revolutions*, The University of Chicago
Luce R., Raiffa H. (1957) *Games and decisions*, Wiley & Sons
Pistone G., Wynn H. P. (1996) Generalised confounding with Groebner bases, *Biometrica 83 (1)*

Shewhart W.A. (1931), *Economic Control of Quality of Manufactured Products*, Van Nostrand
Shewhart W.A. (1936), *Statistical Method from the Viewpoint of Quality Control*, Washington
Taguchi G. (1987), *System of experimental design, Volume One*, ASI (American Supplier Institute)
Taguchi G. (1987), *System of experimental design, Volume Two*, ASI (American Supplier Institute)

Biography

Fausto GALETTO was born in Sanguinetto (Verona, Italy, 1942). He received an Electronics Engineering degree and a Mathematics degree from Bologna University in 1967 and 1973 respectively. Since 1992 he has been Professor of "Industrial Quality Management" at Politecnico of Turin.
From 1998 to 2001 he has been Chairman of the Working Committee "AICQ-Università" (Quality and University) of the Italian Association for Quality, taking care of Quality in Courses about Quality in Universities. He has written three books and more than 170 papers on Reliability, Quality Management and Quality Methods (DOE, Applied Statistics, Testing, Process Control, ...). He was formerly Reliability Engineer with CGE (General Electric, 2 years) From 1975 to 1982 he was Reliability Manager with Fiat Auto. Then he was Director of the Quality Dept, (comprising the Reliability, Production Quality Control, and After Sales Depts.) with Philco Italiana for 3 years. Since 1985 he has been Director of the Quality/Reliability Dept. at Iveco-Fiat, for 5 years. Since 1990 he has been Quality Management consultant. Since 1980 he has been Lecturer with the Italian Organisation for Quality Control (AICQ) and with COREP. Co-ordinator of: Reliability Working Group of CUNA (until 1989), Scientific and Technical Committee of QUALITAL (1989), Vice-Chairman of Automotive Sec. of AICQ (85-90)
It seems he is one of the very few who take care of "Quality of Quality Methods used for making Quality".

APPENDIX: Excerpts from ISO Standards. Quality, nonconformities, preventive actions and corrective actions

In the author's opinion, the first step to Quality achievement is to define *logically* and *correctly* what Quality is; in order to provide a practical and managerial definition, since 1985 F. Galetto was proposing the following one:
Quality is the set of characteristics of a system that makes it able to
satisfy the *NEEDS* of the Customer, of the User and of the Society.
This definition highlights the importance of the ***needs*** of the three actors: **the Customer, the User and the Society.**
Prevention is the fundamental idea present: you possibly satisfy the needs only by **preventing the occurrence** of any problem against the needs. Teachers must teach that to *"present"* students (*future* Managers). In order to teach Quality to students, professors have to understand what Quality entails. "Peer Reviewers" should consider the needs of the readers: papers with wrong ideas, errors, false statements, … do satisfy the NEEDS?
The basic ideas for Quality are the following: any serious organisation that finds a nonconformity, must analyse it and **take corrective actions**.
Are acting that way Universities, professors, "Peer Reviewers", magazines, journals, …?

Anybody should have to behave like stated in the Standard ISO 9001:2000. Unfortunately, referees generally are not "Quality experts" and do not know the *ISO 9001:2008, Quality management systems – Requirements;* **any Good Quality Manager knows very well that making Quality involves prevention of potential nonconformities and correction of actual nonconformities (problems)** [while many professors and referees do not]:

ISO 9001:2000, Quality management systems - Requirements

8.3 Control of nonconforming product

The organization shall ensure that product that does not conform to product requirements is identified and controlled to prevent its unintended use or delivery. The controls and related responsibilities and authorities for dealing with nonconforming product shall be defined in a documented procedure.

The organization shall deal with nonconforming product by one or more of the following ways:

a. by taking action to eliminate the detected nonconformity,

b. by authorizing the use, release or acceptance con concession by a relevant authority and, where applicable, by the customer;

c. taking action to preclude its original use or application.

Records of the nature of nonconformities and any subsequent actions taken, including le concessions obtained., shall be maintained (see 4.2.4)

When nonconforming product is corrected, it shall subject to re-verification to demonstrate conformity to requirements.

When nonconforming product is detected after delivery or use, the organization shall take action appropriate to the effects, or potential effects, of the nonconformity.

8.4 Analysis of data

The organisation shall determine, collect and analyse appropriate data to demonstrate the suitability and, effectiveness of the quality management system and to evaluate where continual improvement of the effectiveness of the quality management system can be made. This shall include data generated as a result of monitoring and measurement and from other relevant sources.

The analysis of data shall provide information relating to

a. customer satisfaction (see 8.2.1),

b. conformity to product requirements (see 7.2.1),

c. characteristics and trends of processes and products including opportunities for preventive action, and

d. suppliers.

....

8.5 Improvement

8.5.1 Continual Improvement

The organization shall continually improve the effectiveness of the quality management system, though the use quality policy, quality objectives, audit results, analysis of data, corrective and preventive actions and management review.

8.5.2 Corrective action

The organization shall take action to eliminate the cause of nonconformities in order to prevent recurrence. The corrective actions shall be appropriate to the effects of the nonconformities encountered.

A documented procedure shall be established to define requirements for

a. *reviewing nonconformities (including customer complaints),*
b. *determining the cause of nonconformities,*
c. *evaluating the need for action to ensure that nonconformities do not recur,*
d. *determining and implementing the action needed,*
e. *records of the results of action taken (see 4.2.4) and,*
f. *reviewing corrective action taken.*

8.5.3 ***Preventive action***

The organization shall determine action to eliminate the causes of potential nonconformities in order to prevent occurrence. Preventive actions shall be appropriate to the effects of potential problems.

A documented procedure shall be established to define requirements for
a. *determining potential nonconformities and their causes,*
b. *evaluating the need for action to prevent occurrence of nonconformities,*
c. *records of the results of action taken (see 4.2.4) and,*
d. *reviewing preventive action taken.*

Particularly important is noting that the principle ***g) Factual approach to decision making:*** *"Effective decisions are based on the analysis of data and information."* of the ISO Standards **9004:2000** still does not care of Quality of Quality Methods. Professionals do the same. They do not consider the need for "Quality Decision" in Decision Making. From that it is apparent that ***facts and figures are useless, if not dangerous, without a sound theory***. (F. Galetto), or better, using Deming's own words "**Management need to grow-up their knowledge because experience alone, without theory, teaches nothing what to do to make Quality".**
Unfortunately many organisations do not comply with the Decision Making Tetrahedron (figure 29) in their decision making: in my 40 years experience I saw many time wrong decisions, based on wrong methods.

11

Face Recognition under Varying Illumination

Lian Zhichao and Er Meng Joo
Nanyang Technological University
Singapore

1. Introduction

Face Recognition by a robot or machine is one of the challenging research topics in the recent years. It has become an active research area which crosscuts several disciplines such as image processing, pattern recognition, computer vision, neural networks and robotics. For many applications, the performances of face recognition systems in controlled environments have achieved a satisfactory level. However, there are still some challenging issues to address in face recognition under uncontrolled conditions. The variation in illumination is one of the main challenging problems that a practical face recognition system needs to deal with. It has been proven that in face recognition, differences caused by illumination variations are more significant than differences between individuals (Adini et al., 1997). Various methods have been proposed to solve the problem. These methods can be classified into three categories, named face and illumination modeling, illumination invariant feature extraction and preprocessing and normalization. In this chapter, an extensive and state-of-the-art study of existing approaches to handle illumination variations is presented. Several latest and representative approaches of each category are presented in detail, as well as the comparisons between them. Moreover, to deal with complex environment where illumination variations are coupled with other problems such as pose and expression variations, a good feature representation of human face should not only be illumination invariant, but also robust enough against pose and expression variations. Local binary pattern (LBP) is such a local texture descriptor. In this chapter, a detailed study of the LBP and its several important extensions is carried out, as well as its various combinations with other techniques to handle illumination invariant face recognition under a complex environment. By generalizing different strategies in handling illumination variations and evaluating their performances, several promising directions for future research have been suggested.

This chapter is organized as follows. Several famous methods of face and illumination modeling are introduced in Section 2. In Section 3, latest and representative approaches of illumination invariant feature extraction are presented in detail. More attentions are paid on quotient-image-based methods. In Section 4, the normalization methods on discarding low frequency coefficients in various transformed domains are introduced with details. In Section 5, a detailed introduction of the LBP and its several important extensions is presented, as well as its various combinations with other face recognition techniques. In Section 6, comparisons between different methods and discussion of their advantages and disadvantages are presented. Finally, several promising directions as the conclusions are drawn in Section 7.

2. Face and illumination modelling

Here, two kinds of modeling methods named face modeling and illumination modeling will be introduced. Regarding face modeling, because illumination variations are mainly caused by three-dimension structures of human faces, researchers have attempted to construct a general 3D human face model in order to fit different illumination and pose conditions. One straight way is to use specific sensors to obtain 3D images representing 3D shape of human face. A range image, a shaded model and a wire-frame mesh are common alternatives representations of 3D face data. Several detailed surveys on this area can be referred to Bowyer et al. (2006) and Chang et al. (2005). Another way is to map a 2D image onto a 3D model and the 3D model with texture is used to produce a set of synthetic 2D images, with the purpose of calculating the similarity of two 2D images on the 3D model. The most representative method is the 3D morphable model proposed by Blanz & Vetter (2003) which describes the shape and texture of a human face under the variations such as poses and illuminations. The model is learned from a set of textured 3D scans of heads and all parameters are estimated by maximum a posteriori estimator. In this framework, faces are represented by model parameters of 3D shape and texture. High computational load is one of the disadvantages for this kind of methods.
For illumination variation modeling, researchers have attempted to construct images under different illumination conditions. Modeling of face images can be based on a statistical model or a physical model. For statistical modeling, no assumptions concerning the surface is needed. The principal component analysis (PCA) (Turk & Pentland, 1991) and linear discriminant analysis (LDA) (Etemad & Chellappa, 1997; Belhumeur et al., 1997) can be classified to the statistical modeling. In physical modeling, the model is based on the assumption of certain surface reflectance properties, such as Lambertian surface (Zou et al., 2007). The famous Illumination Cone, 9D linear subspace and nine point lights all belong to the illumination variation modeling.
In (Belhumeur & Kriegman 1998), an illumination model illumination cone is proposed for the first time. The authors proved that the set of n-pixel images of a convex object with a Lambertian reflectance function, under an arbitrary number of point light sources at infinity, formed a convex polyhedral cone in IR^n named as illumination cone (Belhumeur & Kriegman 1998). If there are k point light sources at infinity, the image X of the illuminated object can be modeled as

$$X = \sum_{i=1}^{k} \max(B_{S_i}, 0) \tag{1}$$

where S_i is a single light source whose magnitude $|S_i|$ represents the intensity of the source and the unit normal $S_i/|S_i|$ represents the direction, B is a convex object with surface normals and albedo. Any image in the illumination cone can be determined as a convex combination of extreme rays (images) given by

$$X_{ij} = \max(B_{S_{ij}}, 0) \tag{2}$$

where $S_{ij} = b_i \times b_j$ are rows of B with $i \neq j$. The paper proved that the dimension of this illumination cone equaled the number of distinct surface normals. Furthermore, the illumination cone is proved that it can be constructed from as few as three images. In addition, the set of n-pixel images of an object of any shape and with a more general reflectance function, seen under all possible illumination conditions, still forms a convex cone in IR^n. The paper also extends these results to colour images. Based on the illumination cone model, Georghiades et al. (2001) presented a generative appearance-based method for recognizing human faces under variations in lighting and viewpoint. Their method exploits the illumination cone model and uses a small number of training images of each face taken with different lighting directions to reconstruct the shape and albedo of the face. As a result, this reconstruction can be used to render images of the face under novel poses and illumination conditions. The pose space is then sampled, and for each pose the corresponding illumination cone is approximated by a low-dimensional linear subspace whose basis vectors are estimated using the generative model.

Basri and Jacobs (2003) showed that a simple 9D linear subspace could capture the set of images of Lambertian objects under distant, isotropic lighting. Moreover, they proved that the 9D linear space could be directly computed from a model, as low-degree polynomial functions of its scaled surface normals. Spherical harmonics is used to represent lighting and the effects of Lambertian materials are considered as the analog of a convolution. The results help them to construct algorithms for object recognition based on linear methods as well as algorithms that use convex optimization to enforce non-negative lighting functions.

Lee et al. (2005) showed that linear superpositions of images acquired under a few directional sources are likely to be sufficient and effective for modeling the effect of illumination on human face. More specifically, the subspace obtained by taking k images of an object under several point light source directions with k typically ranging from 5 to 9, is an effective representation for recognition under a wide range of lighting conditions. Because the subspace is constructed directly from real images, the proposed methods has the following advantages, 1)potentially complex steps can be avoided such as 3D model of surface reconstruction; 2) large numbers of training images are not required to physically construct complex light conditions.

In addition to the assumption that the human face is Lambertian object, another main drawback of these illumination modeling methods is that several images are required for modeling.

3. Illumination invariant feature extraction

The purpose of these approaches is to extract facial features that are robust against illumination variations. The common representations include edge map, image intensity derivatives and Gabor-like filtering image (Adini et al., 1997). However, the recognition experiment on a face database with lighting variation indicated that none of these representations was sufficient by itself to overcome the image variation due to the change of illumination direction (Zou et al., 2007).

Recently, quotient-image-based methods are reported to be a simple and efficient solution to illumination variances and have become one active research direction. Quotient Image (QI) (Amnon & Tammy, 2001) is defined as image ratio between a test image and linear combinations of three unknown independent illumination images. The quotient image depends only on the relative surface texture information and is free of illumination. However, the performance of QI depends on the bootstrap database.

Without the bootstrap database and known lighting conditions, Wang et al. (2004a; 2004b) proposed Self-Quotient Image (SQI) to solve the illumination variation problem. The salient feature of the method is to estimate luminance using the image smoothed up by a weighted Gaussian filter. The SQI is defined as

$$Q=\frac{I}{\hat{I}}=\frac{I}{F*I} \tag{3}$$

where $\hat{I}$ is the smoothed version of I, F is the smoothing kernel, and the division is point-wise as in the original quotient image. A detailed analysis is presented to prove that the self-quotient image is robust against illumination variation under: 1) the regions without shadow and with small surface normal variation and 2) the shadow regions. However, the method is still illumination dependent in the regions without shadows but with large surface normal variation. Another advantage of the SQI is that although the analysis is carried out based on Lambertian model of single illumination point, it is also effective of other types of illumination model such as a linear combination of several illumination sources. Furthermore, the SQI does not need an alignment procedure compared to other quotient methods.

Inspired by the SQI, Chen et al. (2005; 2006) developed Logarithmic Total Variation (LTV) model and Total Variation Quotient Image (TVQI) model. The proposed methods employ the TV-L image decomposition model because the TV-L is multiscale but intensity-independent decomposition and has easy parameter selection compared to other TV-based models. The TV-L decomposes the input image *I* into two parts, naming one with large-scale features *u* and the other with small-scale features *v*, as the following formula

$$u=aremin_u \int_\Omega |\nabla u|+\lambda|\log(I)-u|\,dx \tag{4}$$

$$v=\log(I)-u \tag{5}$$

Because the logarithm of the input image *I* can be modeled as

$$\mathrm{Log}I(x,y)=\log\rho(x,y)+\log S \tag{6}$$

Where $\log\rho(x,y)$ is the logarithm function of the albedo and $\log S$ is related to the illumination. In the LTV, we can simply estimated $\log\rho(x,y)$ and $\log S$ as

$$u \approx \log(S') \tag{7}$$

and

$$v \approx \log(\rho') \tag{8}$$

As $\log\rho(x,y)$ is the intrinsic feature which is robust against illumination variations, only small-scale features *v* will be used for recognition. The TVQI is one variation of the LTV model. Without the logarithm transform, the original image *I* is directly divided by *u* which is as the same as that in the LTV. The only difference between them is that the log operator removes noise from the image more and hence improves the performance. The model has better edge-preserving ability and simpler parameter selection and promising results have been achieved. However, it is very time consuming because it needs to find an optimal solution to decomposition step by step.

In Morphological Quotient Image (MQI) proposed by He et al. (2007), morphology operation is employed to smooth up the image and obtain luminance estimation. In the proposed method, closing operator is employed for the illumination estimation. Closing operator is a nonlinear filter, and it is carried out by Dilation operator followed by Erosion operator. The author claims that it can remove small-scale features and retain large-scale features so that it is less destructive of the original boundary shape of foreground (He et al., 2007). Considering the effect of singularity noise, the author also proposed a method based on local maximum and minimum to remove the singularity noise before the closing operator. The method is modeled as

$$\text{Denoise}(I(i,j))=\begin{cases}\max_{(n,m)\in \text{neighbor}(i,j)}(I(m,n)), & \forall(m,n)\in \text{neighbor}(i,j), I(i,j) > I(m,n)\\ \min_{(n,m)\in \text{neighbor}(i,j)}(I(m,n)), & \forall(m,n)\in \text{neighbor}(i,j), I(i,j) < I(m,n)\\ I(i,j), & \text{otherwise}\end{cases} \quad (9)$$

where neighbor(i,j) is the 8-neighbor set of point (i, j). As most of the quotient methods, the size of closing operation is a key parameter for the performance. The paper had a detailed discussion on this parameter and presented a method named "dynamic morphological quotient image (DMQI)" based on the following formula:

$$\text{Dclose}(i,j)=\begin{cases}\text{Close}^{l}(i,j), & \text{Close}^{l}(i,j) > \alpha\text{Close}^{S}(i,j)\\ \text{Close}^{m}(i,j), & \text{Close}^{S}(i,j) \geq \text{Close}^{l}(i,j) \geq \beta\text{Close}^{S}(i,j)\\ \text{Close}^{S}(i,j), & \text{Close}^{S}(i,j) > \alpha\text{Close}^{l}(i,j)\end{cases} \quad (10)$$

where α and β are the threshold parameters while $\alpha > \beta > 1.0$ l, m, and n are three different sizes while $l>m>s>1$. The basic idea is to choose suitable size by the comparison of the closing operator of different sizes. The details can be referred to (He et al., 2007). The proposed methods obtain superior performances compared to the SQI but close to the LTV. In fact, the DMQI transfers the problem of selecting the size to the threshold. It is still a problem to determine the appropriate values. Furthermore, the DQMI will increase computational burden because of searching an appropriate size.

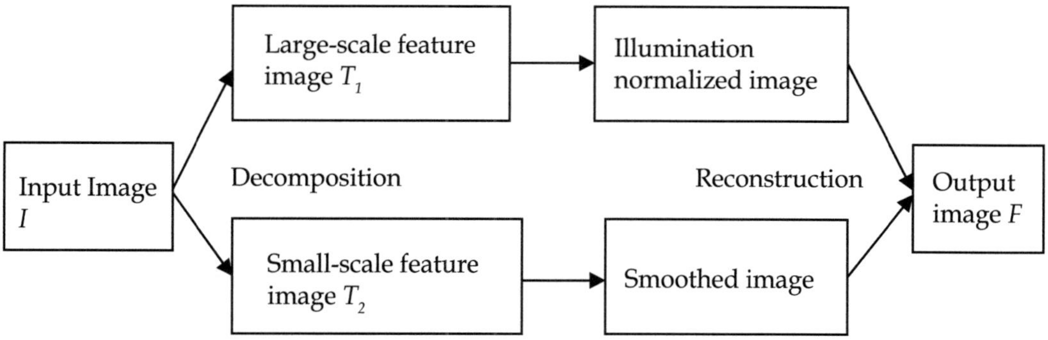

Fig. 1. Framework of the proposed method

In (Xie et al., 2008), an illumination compensation frame similar to the LTV was proposed, as shown in Fig. 1. In the frame, the image I is decomposed into two parts: small-scale and large-scale similar to the LTV. Normalization is performed in large-scale features images T_1 rather than the entire image while small-scale features image T_2 should be smoothed up. After that, an image F combining the normalized large-scale image and the smoothed small-scale image, instead of only using small-scale features in the LTV, will be used for recognition. In the smoothing, a 3×3 mask is employed for convolution if the gray value of the center point in the convolution region is larger than an empirical threshold, and each image is convolved twice. For the normalization on large-scale image, two different methods, the DCT (Chen et al., 2006) and the non-point light quotient image (NPL-QI), are separately applied to large-scale image. The experimental results on the CMU PIE and Yale B as well as the Extended Yale B database show that the proposed framework outperforms existing methods.

In addition to the quotient-image-based methods, local binary pattern (LBP) is another attractive representation of facial features. Local descriptors of human faces have gained attentions due to their robustness against the variations of pose and expression. The LBP operator is one of the best local texture descriptors. Besides the robustness against pose and expression variations as common texture features, the LBP is also robust to monotonic gray-level variations caused by illumination variations. The details of the LBP and several important extensions of the operator will be introduced in the following section, as well as its various combinations with other techniques to handle illumination invariant face recognition under a complex environment.

4. Pre-processing and normalization

In this kind of approaches, face images under illumination variations are preprocessed so that images under normal lighting can be obtained. Further recognition will be performed based on the normalized images. Histogram Equalization (Gonzales & Woods, 1992) is the most commonly used method. By performing histogram equalization, the histogram of pixel intensities in the resulting images is flat. Therefore improved performances can be achieved after histogram equalization. Adaptive histogram equalization (Pizer & Amburn, 1987), region-based histogram equalization (Shan et al., 2003), and block-based histogram equalization (Xie & Lam, 2005) are several important variants of the HE and obtain good performances.

Recently, the methods on discarding low frequency coefficients in various transformed domains are reported to be simple and efficient solutions to tackle illumination variations and have become one active research direction. In (Chen et al., 2006), the image gray value level $f(x,y)$ is assumed to be proportional to the product of the reflectance $r(x,y)$ and the illumination $e(x,y)$ i.e.,

$$f(x,y) = r(x,y) \cdot e(x,y) \tag{11}$$

The reflectance is a stable characteristic of facial features. The goal is to recover the reflectance of faces under illumination variations. After logarithm transform, we have

$$\log f(x,y) = \log r(x,y).\ \log e(x,y) \tag{12}$$

In a face image, illumination usually changes slowly compared with the reflectance except some casting shadows and specularities on the face. As a result, illumination variations mainly lie in the low-frequency band. Therefore, we can remove the low frequency part to reduce illumination variation. In (Chen et al., 2006), the low frequency DCT coefficients are set to zero to eliminate illumination variations. Normally, the 2D DCT is defined as follows:

$$A(u,v) = \sum_{x=0}^{M-1} \sum_{y=0}^{N-1} \alpha(u)\alpha(v) f(x,y) \cos[\pi(2x+1)u / 2M] \cos[\pi(2y+1)v / 2N] \tag{13}$$

and the inverse transform is defined as

$$f(x,y)=\sum_{x=0}^{M-1}\sum_{y=0}^{N-1}\alpha(u)\alpha(v)A(x,y)\cos[\pi(2x+1)u/2M]\cos[\pi(2y+1)v/2N] \quad (14)$$

where $\alpha(u)=\begin{cases}1/\sqrt{M},u=0\\2/\sqrt{M},u=1,2,...,M-1\end{cases}$ and $\alpha(v)=\begin{cases}1/\sqrt{N},v=0\\2/\sqrt{N},u=1,2,...,N-1\end{cases}$

Following (14), after setting the DCT coefficients to zero, we have

$$f'(x,y)=\sum_{u=0}^{M-1}\sum_{v=0}^{N-1}E(u,v)-\sum_{i=1}^{n}E(u_i,v_i) \quad (15)$$

where $E(u,v)=\alpha(u)\alpha(v)A(u,v)\cos[\pi(2x+1)u/2M]\cos[(2y+1)v/2N]$ and n is the number of discarded DCT coefficients. Because illumination variations mainly lie in the low-frequency band, the term $E(u,v)$ can be approximately considered as the illumination $\log e(x,y)$. By comparing (12) and (15), we can see that $f'(x,y)$ obtained by (15) is the expected reflectance part in (12).

Therefore, zeroing the low frequency DCT coefficients in the logarithm domain can eliminate the effects of illumination variation and obtain the reflectance, which can be used in further illumination invariant recognition task. The method does not require multiple images to be trained and good experimental results both in the Yale Face database B and the CMU database are obtained.

Based on Chen's idea, Vishwakarma et al. (2007) proposed to rescale low-frequency DCT coefficients to lower values instead of zeroing them in Chen's. In (Vishwakarma et al., 2007), the first 20 low frequency DCT coefficients are divided by a constant 50, and the AC component is then increased by 10%. Although they presented some comparisons of figures to demonstrate the effect of the proposed method compared to the original DCT method, there is no experimental result to prove the effect of the proposed method for recognition task. Besides, it is difficult to choose the value of rescale parameter only by experiences. Perez and Castillo (2008) also proposed a similar method which applied Genetic Algorithms to search appropriate weights to rescale low-frequency DCT coefficients. Two different strategies of selecting the weights are compared. One is to choose a weight for each DCT coefficient and the other is to divide the DCT coefficients into small squares, and choose a weight for each square. The latter strategy reduces the computational cost because fewer weights are required to choose. However, the GA still takes a large computational burden and the obtained weights depend on the training figures.

As mentioned in the last section, the local binary patterns (LBP) operator is one of the best local texture descriptors. Because of its robustness against pose and expression variations as well as monotonic gray-level variations caused by illumination variations, Heydi et al. (2008) presented a new combination way of using the DCT and LBP for illumination normalization. Images are divided into blocks and the DCT is applied in each block. After that, the LBP is used to represent facial features because the LBP can represent well facial structures when variations in lights are monotonic. The experimental results demonstrate the proposed method can achieve good performances when several training samples per person are used. However, in the case where only one frontal image per person is used for training, which is common in some practical applications, the performance cannot be satisfactory especially in the cases with larger illumination variations.

Besides the DCT, discrete wavelet transform (DWT) is another common method in face recognition. There are several similarities between the DCT and the DWT: 1) They both transform the data into frequency domain; 2) As data dimension reduction methods, they are both independent of training data compared to the PCA. Because of these similarities, there are also several studies on illumination invariant recognition based on the DWT. Similar to the idea in (Chen et al., 2006), a method on discarding low frequency coefficients of the DWT instead of the DCT was proposed (Nie et al., 2008). Face images are transformed from spatial domain to logarithm domain and 2-dimension wavelet transform is calculated by the algorithm. Then coefficients of low-low subband image in n-th wavelet decomposition are discarded for face illumination compensation in logarithm domain. The experimental results prove that the proposed method outperforms the DCT and the quotient images. The kind of wavelet function and how many levels of the DWT need to carry out are the key factors for the performance of the proposed method. Different from the method in (Nie et al., 2008), Han et al. (2008) proposed that the coefficients in low-high, high-low and high-high subband images were also contributed to the effect of illumination variation besides the low-low subband images in n-th level. Based on the assumption, a homomorphic filtering is applied to separate the illumination component from the low-high, high-low, and high-high subband images in all scale levels. A high-pass Butterworth filter is used as the homomorphic filter. The proposed method obtained promising results on the Yale B and CMU PIE databases.

Different from the above methods, Gu et al. (2008) modified the face model (2) into

$$F'(m,n) = G(m,n) \cdot F(m,n) + B(m,n) \tag{16}$$

where $F'(m,n)$ is the gray level of the point under the illumination $G(m,n)$, $F(m,n)$ is the original face image, and $B(m,n)$ is the background noise which is assumed to change slowly. In (Gu et al., 2008), the background noise is estimated and eliminated by multi-level wavelet decomposition followed by spline interpolation. After that, the effect of illumination is removed by the similar multi-level wavelet decomposition in the logarithm domain. Experimental results on Yale B face database show that the proposed method achieves superior performance compared to the others. However, by comparing the results of the proposed method and the DCT, we find the result of the proposed method is worse than that of the DCT. Hence, the proposed method is not as effective as the DCT for illumination invariant recognition. The novelty of the proposed method is that the light variation in an image can be modeled as multiplicative noise and additive noise, instead of only the multiplicative term in (11), which may be instructive in modeling the face under illumination variations in future.

5. Illumination invariant face recognition under complex environment

In fact, there is seldom the case in practical applications that only illumination variations exist. Illumination variations are always coupled with pose and expression variations in practical environments. To deal with such complex environment, an ideal feature representation of human face should not only be illumination invariant, but also robust enough against pose and expression variations. Local descriptors of human faces have gained attentions due to their robustness against the variations of pose and expression. The local binary patterns (LBP) operator is one of the best local texture descriptors. The operator

has been successfully applied to face detection, face recognition and facial expression analysis. In this section, we will present a detailed introduction of the LBP and several important extensions of the operator, as well as its various combinations with other techniques to handle illumination invariant face recognition under a complex environment.
The original LBP operator was proposed for texture analysis by Ojala et al. (1996). The main idea in LBP is to compare the gray value of central point with the gray values of other points in the neighborhood, and set a binary value to each point based on the comparison. After that, a binary string is transformed to a decimal label as shown in the following equation

$$LBP_{P,R}(x,y)=\sum_{i=0}^{P-1}s(g_i-g_c)2^i \quad (17)$$

Where $LBP_{P,R}(x,y)$ is the decimal label of point (x, y), P is the number of sampling points, R is the radius of the patch, g_c is the gray level of central point (x, y), g_i is the gray level of neighborhood sampling point around central point (x, y) and

$$s(x)=\begin{cases}1, x>0\\ 0, x\le 0\end{cases}. \quad (18)$$

A histogram of the decimal label is calculated and can be used as a texture feature. The histogram can be defined as

$$H_i=\sum_{x,y}I\{LBP_{P,R}(x,y)=i\}, i=0,...n-1 \quad (19)$$

Where n is the number of different labels produced by the LBP operator and

$$I\{A\}=\begin{cases}1, \ A \ is \ ture\\ 0, \ A \ isfalse\end{cases} \quad (20)$$

Later, the operator is extended to use circular neighborhoods. The values of pixels are bilinearly interpolated when the point is not in the center of a pixel. Furthermore, a local binary pattern is called uniform if it contains at most two bitwise transitions from 0 to 1 or vice verse when the binary string is considered circular (Ojala et al., 2002). For example, 11111111, 11110000 and 00111100 are uniform patterns. The authors noticed that the uniform patterns accounted for most of all patterns. Therefore, in many applications all non-uniform patterns are classified into a single pattern and more attentions are paid in uniform patterns.
In (Hadid et al., 2004; Ahonen et al., 2004), LBP based methods were presented to deal with face detection and recognition for the first time, and achieved good performance. After an image was divided into non-overlapped blocks, a LBP operator was applied to each block and a histogram of different labels was calculated for each block. All the histograms of each block were concatenated to an entire histogram to build a global description of the image. The salient features of the LBP description are that the description contains three levels information: the labels for the histogram contain information about the patterns on a pixel-level, the labels are summed over a small region to produce information on a regional level and an entire histogram concatenated by regional histograms presents a global description of the image (Ahonen et al., 2004). Because of the features, the LBP operator is considered as one of the best local texture descriptors. Besides the robustness against pose and expression variations as common texture features, the LBP is also robust to monotonic gray-level

variations caused by illumination variations. It is evident that different regions on the face have different discriminative capacities. Therefore, different regions are assigned different weights in similarity measurement. In (Hadid et al., 2004), with the purpose of dealing with face detection and recognition in low-resolution images, the LBP operator was applied in two-level hierarchies, regions and the whole image. In the first level, LBP histograms were extracted from the whole image as a coarse feature representation. Then, a finer histogram, extracted from smaller but overlapped regions, was used to carry out face detection and recognition further.

In (Jin et al., 2004), the author pointed out that the original LBP missed the local structure under some certain circumstance because the central point was only taken as a threshold. In order to obtain all the patterns in a small patch such as 3*3, the mean value of the patch was taken as a threshold instead of the gray level of the central point. Because the central point provides more information in most cases, a largest weight is set to it as following equation

$$LBP_{P,R}(x,y)=\sum_{i=0}^{P-1} s(g_i-m)2^i + s(g_c-m)2^P \tag{21}$$

Where

$$m=\frac{1}{P+1}\left(\sum_{i=0}^{P-1} g_i + g_c\right) \tag{22}$$

and other variables are the same as defined in (17). Although the proposed extension obtains good result, the uniform pattern argument cannot apply in the extension. In (Tan & Triggs, 2010), a local ternary pattern (LTP), another important extension of original LBP is proposed. The most important difference between the LTP and LBP is that the LTP use 3-valued codes instead 2-valued codes in the LBP. A width parameter t is proposed in the following equation instead of (18)

$$s(i)=\begin{cases} 1, i \geq t \\ 0, |i| < t \\ -1, i \leq -t \end{cases} \tag{23}$$

Because of the extension, the LTP is more discriminant and less sensitive to noise. To apply the uniform pattern in the LTP, a coding scheme that split each ternary pattern into its positive and negative halves is also proposed in (Tan & Triggs, 2010). The resulted halves can be treated as two separated LBPs and used for further recognition task.

From another point of view, the LBP can be considered as the descriptor of the first derivation information in local patch of the image. However they only reflect the orientation of local variation and could not present the velocity of local variation. In order to solve the problem, Huang et al. (2004) proposed to apply the LBP to Sobel gradient-filtered image instead of original image. Jabid et al. (2010) proposed local directional pattern which was obtained by computing the edge response value in all eight direction at each pixel position and generating a code from the relative strength magnitude. The local directional pattern is more robust against noise and non-monotonic illumination changes. Moreover, a high-order local pattern descriptor, local derivative pattern (LDP), was proposed by Zhang et al. (2010). LDP is a general framework which describes high-order local derivative direction variations instead of only the first derivation information in the LBP. Based on the experimental results, the third-

order LDP can capture more detailed discriminative information than the second-order LDP and the LBP. The details of the LDP can be referred to (Zhang et al., 2010).
The experimental results in (Ahonen et al., 2006) proved that the LBP outperformed other texture descriptors and several existing methods for face recognition under illumination variations. However, the LBP is still not robust enough against larger illumination variations in practical applications. Several other techniques are proposed to combine with the LBP to tackle face recognition under complex variations. In addition to the DCT as mentioned in the last section, Gabor wavelets are also promising candidates for combination. The LBP is good at coding fine details of facial appearance and texture, while Gabor features provide a coarse representation of face shape and appearance. In (Zhang et al., 2005), a local Gabor binary pattern histogram sequence (LGBPHS) method was proposed in which Gabor wavelet filters were used as a preprocessing stage for LBP feature extraction. The LBP was applied in different Gabor wavelets filtered image instead of the original images and only Gabor magnitude pictures were used because Gabor phase information were considered sensitive to position variations. To overcome the problem, Xie et al. (2010) proposed a novel framework to fuse LBP features of Gabor magnitude and phase images. A local Gabor XOR patterns (LGXP) was developed whose basic idea was that two phases were considered to reflect similar local features if two phases belonged to the same interval. Furthermore, the paper presented two methods to combine local patterns of Gabor magnitude and phase, feature-level and score-level. In the feature-level, two different local pattern histograms were simply concatenated into one histogram and the resulting histogram was used for measuring similarity. In the score-level, two different kinds of histograms were used to compute similarities respectively and then two similarity scores were fused together based on a weighted sum rule.

6. Comparisons and discussions

In this section, we will compare different methods and discuss their advantages and disadvantages. To evaluate the performances of different methods under varying lighting conditions without other variances, there are three popular databases, the Yale B, Extended Yale B and CMU PIE database. In the Yale Face database B, there are 64 different illumination conditions for nine poses per person (Georghiades et al., 2001). To study the performances of methods under different light directions, the images are divided into 5 subsets based on the angle between the lighting direction and the camera axis. The Extended Yale B database consists 16128 images of 28 subjects with the same condition as the Original Yale B (Lee et al., 2005). In the CMU PIE, there are altogether 68 subjects with pose, illumination and expression variations (Sim et al., 2003). Because we are concerned with the illumination variation problem, only 21 frontal face images per person under different illumination conditions are chosen, totally 1421 images.
The performances of several representative approaches of each category are shown in Table 1. The results are directly referred from their papers since they are based on the same database. It can be seen that several methods achieved satisfactory performance. However, each technique still has its own drawbacks. High computational load is one of the main disadvantages for face modeling. For illumination modeling methods, most of them require several training images. Besides, as mentioned before, physical illumination modeling generally is based on the assumption that the surface of the object is Lambertian, which is not consistent with the real human face. Regarding the illumination invariant features, most

of them even the QI-based methods are still not robust enough against larger illumination variation. The LTV and TVQI obtain the best performances among all the mentioned methods. However, they are very time consuming because they needs to find an optimal solution to decompose face images step by step. Compared to QI-based methods, the methods on discarding low frequency coefficients in various transformed domains are easier to implement and usually have lower computational costs because QI-based methods need to estimate albedo point by point. The performances of the methods discarding low frequency coefficients are also good but still not satisfactory as QI-based methods. In fact, illumination variations and facial features cannot be perfectly separated based on frequency components, because some facial features also lie in the low-frequency part as illumination variations. Therefore, some facial information will be lost when low-frequency coefficients are discarded. Furthermore, the performance of illumination normalization methods generally depends on the choices of parameters, most of which are determined only by experience and cannot be suitable for different cases.

Methods	Error Rate (%)						
	Yale B			Yale B+Extended Yale B			CMU
	Subset3	Subset4	Subset5	Subset3	Subset4	Subset5	
Without any methods	10.8	51.4	77.4	n/a	n/a	n/a	43.0
Eigenface	25.8	75.7	n/a	n/a	n/a	n/a	n/a
Eigenface w/o 1st 3	19.2	66.4	n/a	n/a	n/a	n/a	n/a
Linear Space	0	15.0	n/a	n/a	n/a	n/a	n/a
Cones-attached	0	8.6	n/a	n/a	n/a	n/a	n/a
Cones-cast	0	0	n/a	n/a	n/a	n/a	n/a
9PL	0	2.8	n/a	n/a	n/a	n/a	1.9
QI	38.1	65.9	76.7	n/a	n/a	n/a	n/a
QIR	0	9.4	21.2	n/a	n/a	n/a	n/a
SQI	0	3.6	2.1	n/a	n/a	n/a	n/a
MQI	0	0	2.1	n/a	n/a	n/a	n/a
LTV	0	0	0	20.6	23.9	21.7	0
TVQI	0	0	0	n/a	n/a	n/a	0
RLS(LOG-DCT)	n/a	n/a	n/a	12.9	12.4	15.2	0
Histogram Equalization	9.2	54.2	41.1	62.3	78.7	89.9	47.8
DCT	0	0.18	1.71	16.4	14.5	16.2	0.36
LocalDCT+LBP	10.12	15.33	17.29	n/a	n/a	n/a	n/a
DWT	0	0	0.53	n/a	n/a	n/a	n/a

Table 1. Performance comparisons of different methods under only illumination variances

In addition to the above drawbacks of each category, there are some other issues. Firstly, the experiments of most of the methods are based on aligned images whose important points are manually marked. The sensitivity of the methods to misalignment is seldom studied except some SQI-based methods. Secondly, the common experimental databases are not very promising because of the small size and limited illumination variations. For instance, the Yale B database only contains 10 subjects and the CMU PIE database contains limited illumination variations. When the database is larger and contains more illumination variations, the outstanding performances of existing methods may not be sure. The LTV achieves excellent performance in (Chen et al., 2006) when the Yale B database is used. While the Extended Yale B database containing more subjects (28) is used as the test database in (Xie et al., 2008), the performance drops significantly as shown in Table 1.
To evaluate the performances of methods under a complex environment where illumination variances coupled with other variances, FERET is the most popular database which contains 1196 subjects with expression, lighting and aging variations. In addition to the gallery set fa, there are four probe sets, fb (1195 images with expression variations), fc (194 images with illumination variations), dup I (722 images with aging variations) and dup II (234 images with larger aging variations). The performances of common methods, the LBP and several extensions and combinations of the LBP are shown in Table 2. The results are directly referred from their papers since they are based on the same database.

Methods	Error Rate (%)			
	FERET			
	fb	fc	Dup I	Dup II
Fisherface	6	27	45	69
PCA, MahCosine	15	35	56	78
Bayesian, MAP	18	63	48	68
LBP, non-weighted	7	49	39	50
LBP, weighted	3	21	34	36
Local Directional Pattern	3	18	28	31
3-order Local Derivative Pattern on gray-level images	10	13	38	40
3-order Local Derivative Pattern on Gabor feature images	2	1	20	20
LGBPHS non-weighted	6	3	32	47
LGBPHS weighted	2	3	26	29
LGXP	2	0	18	17
Fusing LGBP_mag+LGXP	1	1	6	7

Table 2. performance comparisons of different method under multiple variances

By comparing experimental results on table 2, we can easily find that the performance of most LBP-based method can outperform other methods under expression, illumination and aging variations. However, considering the performances of LBP-based methods in the probe set fc with illumination variation, we can easily find that quotient-image-based methods outperform most of LBP-based methods. But it still can be an effective and promising research direction because of its robustness against other variations such as aging and expression variations. There is seldom the case in practical applications that only illumination variations exist. Illumination variations are always coupled with other variations in practical environments. Furthermore, after the combination with Gabor features such as the weighted LGBPHS, LGXP and fusing method of LGBP and LGXP, the performances of LBP-based methods obtain significant improvements and even achieve comparable level with quotient-image-based methods under illumination variations. Hence, the LBP can be employed to carry out face recognition in a complex practical environment, combined with other recognition techniques such as Gabor wavelets.

7. Conclusions

In summary, the modeling approach is the fundamental way to handle illumination variations, but it always takes heavy computational burden and high requirement for the number of training samples. For illumination invariant feature, the quotient-image-based method is a promising direction. The LBP is also an attractive area which can tackle illumination variation coupled with other variations such as pose and expression. For normalization methods, the methods on discarding low-frequency coefficients are simple but effective way to solve the illumination variation problem. However, a more accurate model needs to be studied instead of simply discarding low-frequency coefficients. In a real complex condition, the LBP combined with other techniques such as Gabor wavelets is an easier and more promising way to deal with illumination variances coupled with other variances.

8. References

Adini, Y.; Moses, Y. & Ullman, S. (1997). Face recognition: the problem of compensating for changes in illumination direction, *IEEE Trans. on Pattern Analysis and Machine Intelligence*, Vol. 19, No. 7, 721-732, ISSN: 0162-8828.

Ahonen, T.; Hadid, A. & Pietikainen M. (2004). Face recognition with local binary patterns, *Proceedings of 8th European Conf. Computer Vision*, pp. 469-481, ISBN: 978-3-540-21984-2, May 2004, Prague, Czech Republic.

Ahonen, T.; Hadid, A. & Pietikainen M. (2006). Face description with local binary patterns: application to face recognition, *IEEE Trans. on Pattern Analysis and Machine Intelligence*, Vol. 28, No. 12, 2037-2040, ISSN: 0162-8828.

Amnon, S. & Tammy R.R. (2001). The quotient image: class-based re-rendering and recognition with varying illuminations, *IEEE Trans. Pattern Analysis and Machine Intelligence*, Vol. 23, No. 2, 129-139, ISSN: 0162-8828.

Basri, R. & Jacobs, D.W. (2003). Lambertian reflectance and linear subspaces, *IEEE Trans. Pattern Analysis and Machine Intelligence*, Vol. 25, No. 2, 218-233, ISSN: 0162-8828.

Belhumeur, P.N.; Hespanha, J.P. & Kriegman, D.J. (1997). Eigenfaces vs. fisherfaces: recognition using class specific linear projection, *IEEE Trans. Pattern Analysis and Machine Intelligence*, Vol. 20, No. 7, 711-720, ISSN: 0162 -8828.

Belhumeur, P. & Kriegman, D. (1998). What is the set of images of an object under all possible illumination conditions, *International Journal of Computer Vision*, Vol. 28, No. 3, 245-260, ISSN: 1573-1405 (electronic version).

Blanz, V. & Vetter, T. (2003). Face recognition based on fitting a 3D morphable model, *IEEE Trans. on Pattern Analysis and Machine Intelligence*, Vol. 25, No. 9, 1063-1073, ISSN: 0162-8828.

Bowyer, K.W.; Chang, K. & Flynn, P. (2006). A survey of approaches and challenges in 3d and multi-modal 3d+2d face recognition. *Computer Vision and Image Understanding*, Vol. 101, No. 1, 1-15, ISSN: 1077-3142.

Chang, K.; Bowyer, K.W. & Flynn, P.J. (2005). An evaluation of multimodal 2d+3d face biometrics. *IEEE Trans. on Pattern Analysis and Machine Intelligence*, Vol. 27, No. 4, 619-624, ISSN: 0162-8828.

Chen, W.; Er, M.J. & Wu, S. (2006). Illumination compensation and normalization for robust face recognition using discrete cosine transform in logarithm domain, *IEEE Trans. on Systems, Man, and Cybernetics, Part B: Cybernetics*, Vol. 36, No. 2, 458-466, ISSN: 1083-4419.

Chen, T.; Yin, W.; Zhou, X.S.; Comaniciu, D. & Huang, T.S. (2005). Illumination normalization for face recognition and uneven background correction using total variation based image models, *Proceedings of the IEEE Conference on CVPR*, pp. 532-539, ISBN: 0-7695-2372-2, June 2005, San Diego, USA.

Chen, T.; Yin, W.; Zhou, X.S.; Comaniciu, D. & Huang, T.S. (2006). Total variation models for variable lighting face recognition, *IEEE Trans. Pattern Analysis and Machine Intelligence*, Vol. 28, No. 9, 1519-1524, ISSN: 0162-8828.

Etemad, K. & Chellappa, R. (1997). Discriminant analysis for recognition of human face images, *Journal of the Optical Society of America A*, Vol. 14, No. 8, 1724-1733, ISSN: 1520-8532 (online).

Georghiades, A.S.; Belhumeur, P.N. & Kriegman, D.J. (2001). From Few to Many: Illumination Cone Models for Face Recognition under Variable Lighting and Pose, *IEEE Trans. Pattern Analysis and Machine Intelligence*, Vol. 23, No. 6, 643-660, ISSN: 0162-8828.

Gonzales, R.C. & Woods, R.E. (1992). *Digital Image Processing, second ed.*, Prentice Hall, ISBN-10: 0201180758, Upper Saddle River.

Gong, W.G.; Yang, L.P.; Gu, X.H. & Li, W.H. (2008). Illumination compensation based on multi-level wavelet decomposition for face recognition, *Optics and Precision Engineering*, Vol. 16, No. 8, 1459-1464, ISSN: 1004-924X.

Hadid, A.; Pietikainen, M. & Ahonen T. (2004). A discriminative feature space for detecting and recognizing faces, *Proceedings of the IEEE Conference on CVPR*, pp. 797-804, ISBN: 0-7695-2158-4, June 2004, Washington DC, USA.

Han, H.; Shan, S.G.; Chen, X.L. & Gao, W. (2008). Illumination transfer using homomorphic wavelet filtering and its application to light-insensitive face recognition, *Proceedings of the International Conf. on Automatic Face and Gesture Recognition*, pp. 1-6, ISBN: 978-1-4244-2153-4, Sep. 2008, Amsterdam, Nethelands.

He, X.G.; Tian, J.; Wu, L.F.; Zhang, Y.Y. & Yang, X. (2007). Illumination normalization with morphological quotient image, *Journal of Software*, Vol. 18, No. 9, 2318-2325, ISSN: 1796-217X.

Heydi, M.V; Edel, G.R. & Yadira, C.M. (2008). A new combination of local appearance based methods for face recognition under varying lighting conditions, *Proceedings of the 13th Iberoamerican congress on Pattern Recognition: Progress in Pattern Recognition, Image Analysis and Applications*, pp. 535-542, ISBN: 978-3-540-85919-2, Sep. 2008, Havana, Cuba.

Huang, X.; Li, S.Z. & Wang, Y. (2004). Shape Localization based on statistical method using extended local binary pattern, *Proceedings of International Conference on Image and Graphics*, pp. 184-187, ISBN: 0-7695-2244-0, Dec. 2004, Hong Kong, China.

Jabid, T.; Kabir, M.H. & Chae, O. (2010). Local Directional Pattern (LDP) for face recognition, *Proceedings of 2010 Digest of Technical Papers International Conference on Consumer Electronics*, pp. 329-330, ISBN: 978-1-4244-4314-7, Jan. 2010, Las Vegas, NV, USA.

Jin, H.; Liu, Q.; Lu, H. & Tong, X. (2004). Face detection using improved LBP under bayesian framework, *Proceedings of International Conference on Image and Graphics*, pp. 306-309, ISBN: 0-7695-2244-0, Dec. 2004, Hong Kong, China.

Lee, K.C.; Ho, J. & Kriegman, D. (2005). Acquiring Linear Subspaces for Face Recognition under Variable Lighting, *IEEE Trans. Pattern Analysis and Machine Intelligence*, Vol. 27, No. 5, 684-698, ISSN: 0162-8828.

Nie, X.F.; Tan, Z.F. & Guo, J. (2008). Face illumination compensation based on wavelet transform, *Optics and Precision Engineering*, Vol. 16, No. 1, 150-155, ISSN: 1004-924X.

Ojala, T.; Pietikainen, M. & Harwood, D. (1996). A comparative study of texture measures with classification based on feature distributions, *Pattern Recognition*, Vol. 29, No. 1, 51-59, ISSN: 0031-3203.

Ojala, T.; Pietikainen, M. & Maenpaa, T. (2002). Multiresolution gray-scale and rotation invariant texture classification with local binary patterns, *IEEE Trans. on Pattern Analysis and Machine Intelligence*, Vol. 24, No. 7, 971-987, ISSN: 0162 -8828.

Perez, C.A. & Castillo, L.E. (2008). Genetic improvements in illumination compensation by the discrete cosine transform and local normalization for face recognition, *Proceedings of SPIE - The International Society for Optical Engineering, International Symposium on Optomechatronic Technologies*, pp. 1-8, ISSN:0277-786X (print), Nov. 2008, San Diego, CA, USA.

Pizer, S.M. & Amburn, E.P. (1987). Adaptive histogram equalization and its variations, *Comput. Vis. Graph. Image Process*, Vol. 39, No. 3, 355–368, ISSN: 0734-189X.

Shan, S.; Gao, W.; Cao, B. & Zhao, D. (2003). Illumination normalization for robust face recognition against varying lighting conditions, *Proceedings of the IEEE workshop on Analysis and Modelling of Faces and Gestures*, pp. 157-164, ISBN: 0-7695-2010-3, Oct. 2003, Nice.

Sim, T.; Baker S. & Bsat M. (2003). The CMU pose, illumination, and expression database, *IEEE Trans. on Pattern Analysis and Machine Intelligence,* Vol. 25, No. 12, 1615-1618, ISSN: 0162-8828.

Tan, X. & Triggs, B. (2010). Enhanced local texture feature sets for face recognition under difficult lighting conditions, *IEEE Trans. on Image Processing*, Vol. 19, No. 6, 1635-1650, ISSN: 1057-7149.

Turk, M. & Pentland, A. (1991). Eigenfaces for recognition, *Jounal of Cognitive Neuroscience*, Vol. 3, No. 1, 71-86, ISSN: 1530-8898 (online).

Vishwakarma, V.P.; Pandey, S. & Gupta, M.N. (2007). A novel approach for face recognition using DCT coefficients re-scaling for illumination normalization, *Proceedings of International Conference on Advanced Computing and Communications*, pp. 535-539, ISBN: 0-7695-3059-1, Dec. 2007, Guwahati, Assam.

Wang, H.; Li, S.Z.; Wang, Y. & Zhang, J. (2004a). Self quotient image for face recognition, *Proceedings of International Conference on Image Processing*, pp. 1397-1400, ISBN: 0-7803-8554-3, Oct. 2004, Singapore.

Wang, H.; Li, S.Z. & Wang, Y. (2004b). Generalized quotient image, *Proceedings of the IEEE Conference on CVPR*, pp. 498-505, ISBN: 0-7695-2158-4, June 2004, Washington DC, USA.

Xie, X. & Lam, K.-M. (2005). Face recognition under varying illumination based on a 2D face shape model, *Pattern Recognition*, Vol. 38, No. 2, 221-230, ISSN: 0031 -3203.

Xie, S.; Shan, S.; Chen, X. & Chen, J. (2010). Fusing local patterns of gabor magnitude and phase for face recognition, *IEEE Trans. on Image Processing*, Vol. 19, No. 5, 1349-1361, ISSN: 1057-7149.

Xie, X.; Zheng, W.; Lai, J. & Yuen, P. (2008). Face illumination normalization on large and small scale features, *Proceedings of 26th IEEE Conference on CVPR*, pp. 1-8, ISBN: 978-1-4244-2242-5, June 2008, Anchorage, AK.

Zhang, B.; Gao, Y.; Zhao, S. & Liu, J. (2010). Local derivative pattern versus local binary pattern: Face recognition with high-order local pattern descriptor, *IEEE Trans. on Image Processing*, Vol. 19, No. 2, 533-544, ISSN: 1057 -7149.

Zhang, W.; Shan, S.; Gao, W.; Chen, X. & Zhang, H. (2005). Local gabor binary pattern histogram sequence (LGBPHS): a novel non-statistical model for face representation and recognition, *Proceedings of IEEE Int'l Conf. Computer Vision*, pp. 786-791, ISBN: 0-7695-2334-X, Oct. 2005, Beijing, China.

Zou, X.; Kittler J. & Messer K. (2007). Illumination invariant face recognition: a survey, *Proceedings of IEEE Conference on Biometrics: Theory, Applications and Systems*, pp. 1-8, ISBN: 978-1-4244-1596-0, Sept. 2007, Crystal City, VA.

12

Recent Advances in Synthetic Aperture Radar Enhancement and Information Extraction

Dušan Gleich and Žarko Čučej
University in Maribor, Faculty of Electrical Engineering and Computer Science, Maribor Slovenia

1. Introduction

Synthetic Aperture Radar (SAR) systems are all-weather, night and day, imaging systems. Automatic interpretation of information in SAR images is very difficult because SAR images are affected by a noise-like characteristic called *speckle* that arises from an imaging device and strongly data and makes automatic image interpretation very difficult. The speckle noise in SAR images can be removed using an image restoration technique called despeckling. The goal of despeckling is to remove speckle-noise from SAR images and to preserve all image's textural features. The statistical modeling of SAR images has been intensively investigated over recent years. In statistical image processing an image can be viewed as the realization of a joint probability density function. Since joint probability functions have analytical forms and few unknown parameters usually, the efficiency of the denoising algorithm depends on how well the chosen model approximates real data.

The wavelet Daubechies (1992) based despeckling algorithms are proposed in Dai et al. (2004), Argenti et al. (2006), Foucher et al. (2001). The second-generation wavelets like Contourlet Chuna et al. (2006) have appeared over the past few years. Despeckling using Contourlet transform Li et al. (2006) and Bandelet Sveinsson & Benediktsson (2007) transforms show superior despeckling results for SAR images compared with the wavelet based methods. Model based despeckling mainly depends on the chosen models. Bayesian methods have been commonly used as denoising methods, where the prior, posterior and evidence probability density functions are modeled. The image and noise models in the wavelet domain are well-defined using the results in Argenti et al. (2006), Gleich & Datcu (2007) and the noise free image is estimated using a MAP estimate. The speckle noise in the SAR images is considered as a multiplicative noise Walessa & Datcu (2000), and can be also presented as a signal-dependent additive noise Argenti et al. (2006). The log transformed image is modeled using zero location Cauchy and zero-mean Gaussian distributions in order to develop minimum means absolute error estimator, and maximum a posteriori estimator. This paper presents the state-of the art methods for information extraction and their comparison in efficiency of despeckling and information extraction. This paper presents three methods for despeckling and information extraction. The first method is wavelet-based despeckling and information extraction method using the General Gauss-Markov Random Field (GGMRF) and Bayesian inference of first and second order. The second and third methods use the GMRF and Auto-binomial model with the Bayesian inference of first and second order. The despeckling performance is compared and the texture parameters estimation is presented.

2. Synthetic Aperture Radar System

The Synthetic Aperture Radar systems are all weather, day and night monitoring systems, which use the electromagnetic radiation for image retrieval. SAR is one of the most advanced engineering inventions systems in the last decade. Specific radar systems are imaging radars, such as side looking SAR and SAR. Practical restriction to the length of the antenna resulted in very coarse resolution in the flight direction. Using a fixed antenna, illuminating a strip or swath to the sensor's ground track, resulted in the concept of stripping mapping. Modern phased-array antennas are able to perform even more sophisticated data collections strategies, as ScanSAR, spotlight SAR, but the strip map mode is the most applied mode on current satellites [1]. The concept of using frequency (phase) information in the radar signal's along-track spectrum to discriminate two scatters within the antenna beam goes back to 1951 (Carl Wiley). The key factor is coherent radar,, where the phase and amplitude are received and preserved for later processing., but long antenna was required. The early SAR systems were based on optical processing of the measured echoed signal using the Fresnel approximation for image formation and are known as range-Doppler Imaging or polar format processing. The experience on airborne SAR systems in 60's and 70's culminated in L-band SAR system Seasat, a satellite launched in June 1978, primarily for ocean studies, the live time was 100 days, but the imaginary was spectacular, highlighting if geologic information and ocean topography information. Since 1981 Shuttle missions carried SAR systems. The first instrument was the Shuttle Imaging radar SIR laboratory and operated for 2.5 days. An improved version of SIRA orbited the Earth in 1984 and was able to steer the antenna mechanically to enable different angels. Cosmos 1870 was the first S-band SAR satellite of former Soviet Union, launched in 1987 and orbited at a height of 270 km and operated for 2 years, ALMAZ-1 was the second satellite launched in 1991 and operated for 1.5 years. First European Remote Sensing Satellite ERS-1 was operational in 1991 and operated until March 2000. Japan started space-borne SAR program in 1992 with JERS in 1992, SIR-C/X-SAR was developed by JPL, DLR and ASI operated with C, L and X band. Canadian Space Agency lunched Radarsat in 1995. A SRTM (Shuttle Radar Topography mission) was carried out between 11 and 23 February 2000. In last decade many other satellites with SAR were lunched: Radarsat-2, ENVISAT, TerraSAR-X, Tandem-X, ALOS, Cosmo-Skymed, SAR lupe and forth coming constellation of Sentinel satellites.

2.1 Principles of SAR

The central idea of SAR processing is based upon matched filtering of the received signal in both the range and azimuth directions. Matched filtering is possible because the acquired SAR data are modulated in these directions with appropriate phase functions. The modulation in range is provided by the phase encoding of transmitted pulse, while the modulation in azimuth is created by the motion in the signal. The point targets are arrayed in a Cartesian type Coordinate system space defined by range, azimuth, and altitude as analogs of x, y and z directions. The altitude direction is omitted in the two-dimensional simulation. The platform in this simulation is an antenna attached to a plane traveling at an orbital velocity, along the azimuth direction and at the midpoint in the flight, the distance to the target equals the range of closest approach or minimum range to target. As an satellite platform is used in the simulation, the curvature of the earth is considered negligible and the orbital velocity is approximately equal to the platform velocity. The transmitted radar signal, $x(t)$, is assumed to be a chirp pulse (linearly frequency modulated signal) given by

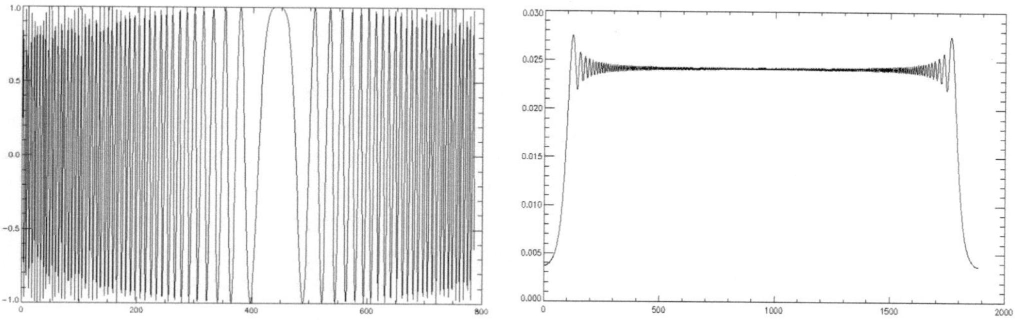

Fig. 1. Chirp signal (left) and its Fourier transform (right).

$$rec\left(\frac{t}{T_r}\right)cos(2\pi f_0 + \pi K_r t^2) \tag{1}$$

where $f_0 = 9.63GHz$, pulse duration $T_r = 25\mu s$, (frequency bandwidth of the chirp=300MHz), K_r is range of the FM rate, measured $MHz/\mu s$. The chirp signal in time domain and its impulse response and its Fourier transform are shown in Fig. 1.
The transmitted radar signal as a cosine with a linearly ramping up frequency over a transmit duration followed by a null receive duration. The transmit window is called the pulse envelope, and defines the duration of the transmission. During the receive duration, the antenna waits to receive reflected radar signals from the targets contained in a one-dimensional range slice echo as function of quick time. One over the combined transmit and receive duration is called the pulse repetition frequency, PRF, and defines the amount of pulses transmitted per second.
The chirp signal is complex and has a complex envelope $g(t)$

$$x(t) = g(t)\exp(j2\pi f_0 \tau) \tag{2}$$

Let a point scatterer has a dimension, smaller then the wavelength $\lambda = c/\nu_0$ be located at a distance R - range away from the radar. The radar platform has a velocity v. The point is seen at the elevation angle and azimuth angle from the antenna main pointing direction. The received echo is proportional to the transmitted wave and delayed by the round-trip delay $2R/c$. In the receiver the echo signal is coherently demodulated, i.e. carrier frequency is removed, resulting echo signal of the point scatterer. The phase term depends on R, governs the interference of echoes from different scatterers. The shape of the pulse envelope $g(\tau)$ determines the range resolution of the radar, it is the ability of radar to distinguish two scatterers at slightly different ranges. $g(\tau) = sinc(\tau B)$. The achievable range resolution defined as half power width of $g(\tau)$.

$$R = 0.885\frac{c}{2B_0} \tag{3}$$

The chirp functions can be compressed to a sinc function by correlation with a chirp function with the same frequency rate, thus leading to the resolution. This so-called range compression is often the first step in SAR data processing. The only relevant parameter influencing on range resolution is range pulse bandwidth. In range only one pulse was considered for explanation. As the sensor advances along its path, subsequent pulses are transmitted and received by radar. The pulses are transmitted every 1/PRF (pulse repartition frequency). The target is illuminated by many pulses. The strength of each pulse varies, primarily because of the azimuth beam pattern. The signal strength decreases until target lies in the first null of the pattern beam. The energy in outside the main beam contributes to the azimuth ambiguities in the processed image. The received signal has the same waveform as transmitted signal, but it is much weaker and has a frequency shift governed by the relative speed of the sensor and the scatterer. If the distance between target and antenna is decreasing, the frequency of the received signal decreases. This effect is called SAR Doppler frequency. The received signal from the target consists of several parameters, which depicts azimuth chirp and range migration effect. The received signal consists of (i) amplitude range dependence and the elevation antenna pattern, (ii) part which reflects 2-way antenna pattern of the sensor, which represents the synthetic aperture length and is proportional to range r0, (iii) echo signal envelope and its position in fast time, (iv) the factor, which translates the range trajectory of the point scatterer into a phase history, it is called azimuth chirp and its frequency is given by

$$f_D = \frac{1}{2\pi}\frac{d}{dt}\phi(t-t_0) = -\frac{2}{\lambda}\frac{v^2}{r_0}(t-t_0) \tag{4}$$

It is also called Doppler frequency. The Doppler frequency at the beam center is Doppler Centroid f_{DC}

$$f_{DC} = f_D(t-t_c) = FMt_c \tag{5}$$

Where FM is frequency modulation rate of the azimuth chirp. The FM rate is always negative.

$$FM = -\frac{2}{\lambda}\frac{v^2}{r_0} \tag{6}$$

The azimuth resolution is given by

$$A = \frac{0.866v\cos\theta}{f_{DC}} \approx \frac{L}{2} \tag{7}$$

The azimuth resolution is independent of range, velocity or wavelength. The actual resolution is a function of how much of the bandwidth is processed and the combined shape of the beam pattern and the weighting function. The received and demodulated radar signal is referred to as the SAR signal space as it is still in its raw form and the two-dimensional image of the magnitude of the two-dimensional imaginary signal would not allow recognition of targets.

2.2 Range Migration algorithm

The range Doppler algorithm (RDA) was developed in 1976-1978 for processing SEASAT SAR data. Later it was used to digitally process space borne SAR image in 1978 and it is still the most widely used algorithm today. RDA operates in range and azimuth frequency domain, but it has the simplicity of one-dimensional operations. The reflected energy from areas on the earth's surface in the same range but in different azimuth, are located on the same azimuth frequency. So, when this frequency is adjusted, the whole target areas with the same frequency (which means in the same range) are adjusted. RDA uses the large difference in time scale of range and azimuth data and approximately separates processing in these two directions using Range Cell Migration Correction (RCMC). RCMC is the most important part of this algorithm. RCMC is performed in range frequency and azimuth frequency domain. Since, azimuth frequency is affected by Doppler Effect and azimuth frequency is bonded with Doppler frequency, it is called Range Doppler Algorithm. RDA can be implemented in three different ways. But they all have similar steps and their difference is only in Secondary Range Compression (SRC). The main steps of RDA are: 1- Range compression 2- Azimuth FFT (transform to range Doppler domain) 3- RCMC 4- Azimuth filtering 5- Inverse FFT (return to range azimuth time domain) 6- Image formation. Range compression is implemented using matched filter. The filter is generated by taking the complex conjugate if the FFT of the zero padded pulse replica, where the zeros are added to the end of the replica array. The output of the range matched filter is the inverse transform between range Fourier transformed raw data and the frequency domain matched filter. Each azimuth signal is Fourier transformed via an azimuth FFT and RCMC is performed before azimuth matched filtering in the range-Doppler domain. After azimuth matched filtering of each signal and azimuth inverse fast Fourier transforms (IFFTs), the final target image is obtained.

Fig. 2 shows, real and imaginary part of the received signal, The simulated raw data and its real part and phase are shown in Fig. 3. Fig.4 shows the process of range compression with RCMC and its phase.

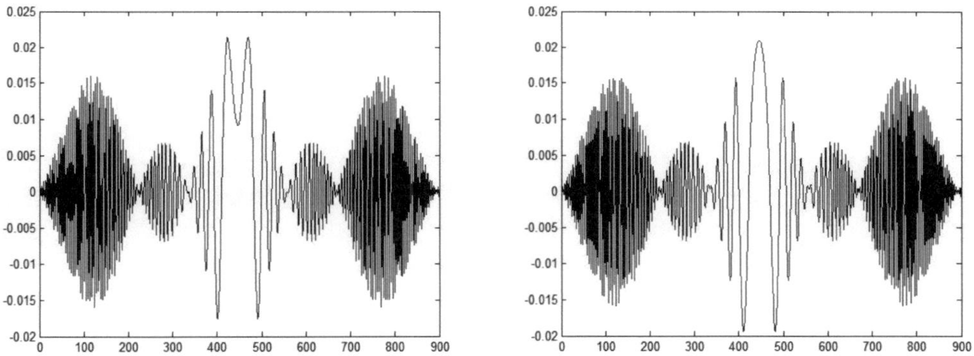

Fig. 2. Real and imaginary part of the received signal.

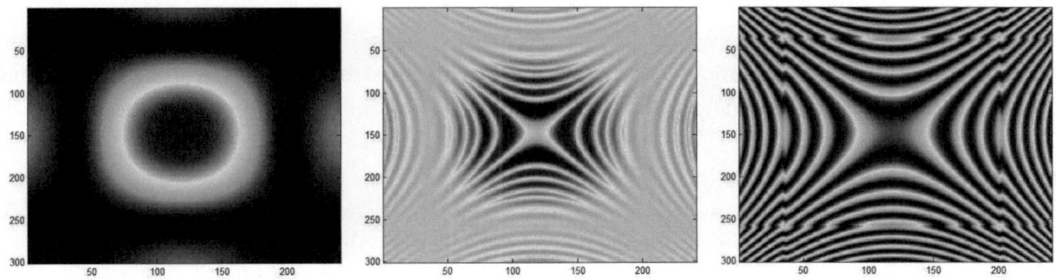

Fig. 3. Simulated SAR raw data: amplitude (left), real part (middle)and phase (right)

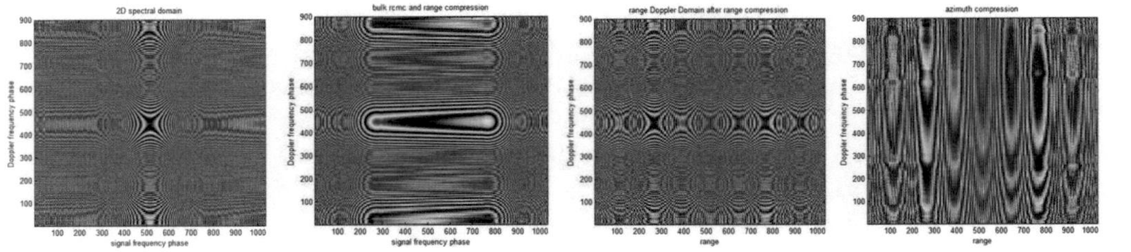

Fig. 4. Phase of spectra in range direction. RCMC. Phase of spectra after range compression. Phase of spectra in azimuth direction.

3. Image and speckle models

SAR images are affected by a noise-like characteristic called speckle that affects all coherent imaging systems and, therefore, can be observed in laser, acoustic and radar images. Basically, this usually disturbing effect is caused by random interferences, either constructive or destructive, between the electromagnetic waves which are reflected from different scatterers present in the imaged area. SAR images appear to be affected by a granular and rather strong noise named speckle. Speckle becomes visible only in the detected amplitude or intensity signal. The complex signal by itself is distorted by thermal noise and signal processing induced effects only. As a consequence of the speckle phenomenon, the interpretation of detected SAR images is highly disturbed and cannot be done with standard tools developed for non-coherent imagery. Magnitude and phase of the scatterers are statistically independent, allowing to obtain the received signal by a simple summation of the individual contributions. Interactions between scatterers are neglected. The phase of the scatterers is uniformly distributed between 0 and 2π, i.e. speckle is assumed to be fully developed.

3.1 SAR image statistics

The SAR image is a complex image, where the real and imaginary part have Gaussian distribution, with zero mean and its real and theoretical distributions are shown in Fig. 5(a) and 5(b). The amplitude of the SAR image is obtained using the absolute value and can be modeled using Gamma distribution

$$p(x) = 2\left(\frac{x}{\mu}\right)^{2L-1} \frac{L^L}{\mu\Gamma(L)} \exp\left(-L\left(\frac{x}{\mu}\right)^2\right) \tag{8}$$

where L represents equivalent number of looks $L = \mu^2/\sigma^2$, μ and σ^2 represent the mean value and variance of the image, respectively. Histograms of amplitude, phase, real and imaginary part of the SAR image are shown in Figs. 5(c)-5(d), respectively.

3.2 Markov random fields

Bayesian data analysis is well suited to image interpretation in combination with appropriate prior models for the noiseless scene. The quality of the estimate, however, depends largely on the employed model and its ability to describe the image content. In this context, Markov and Gibbs random fields (MRFs and GRFs) play an important role, since

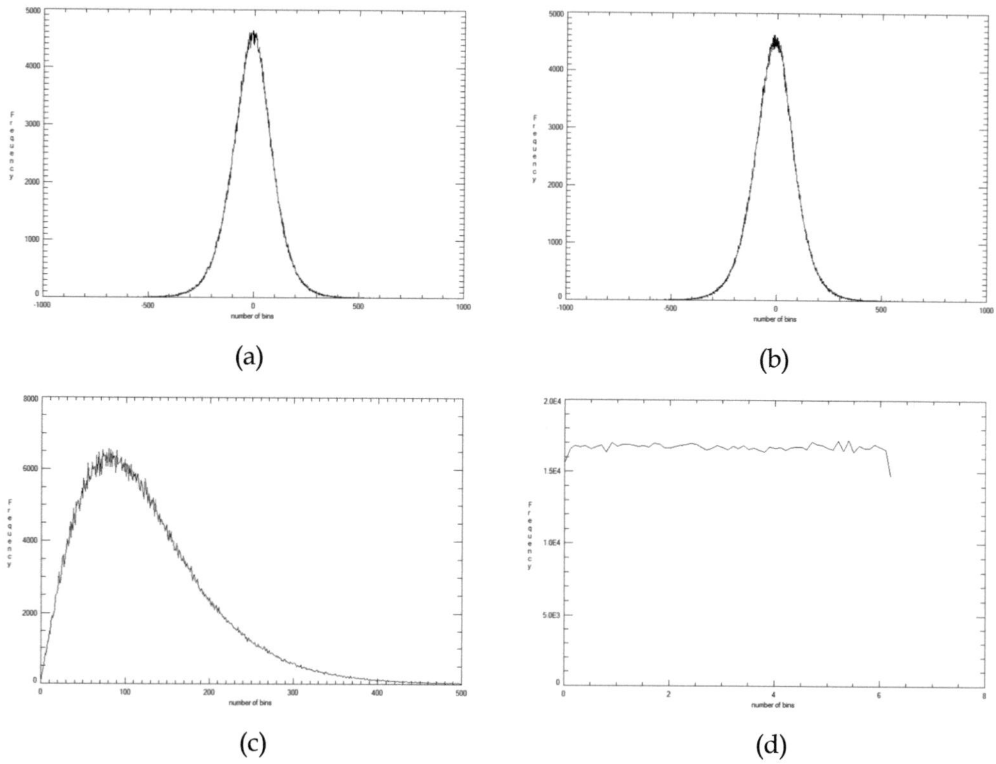

Fig. 5. Histograms of (a) real part, (b) imaginary part, (c) amplitude, (d) phase

they are able to statistically describe correlations, or even more generally, any kind of statistical dependence between neighboring pixels. Furthermore, they are easily applicable within the Bayesian framework. Originating from statistical physics, where they have been used for the study of phase transitions, they are now widely employed to model two-dimensional lattices, such as image data. In the beginning, the use of Markov models in image processing was limited due to the constraint of causality, but after a solution to this problem had been found, they quickly became one of the standard image processing tools.
The information of digital images is not only encapsulated in gray-values of individual pixels. More than that, images are usually composed of different regions and features with similar statistical properties, such as textures, lines and contours. As of this, several independently considered pixels usually are not significant to describe all information of a certain image region, but become important by their relations and interactions with pixels in a neighborhood. The characteristics of these local interactions between pixels, defining different regions of an image, can be modeled by a Markovian formalism, which is suitable for the envisaged framework of Bayesian data analysis. The MRF model characterize the spatial statistical dependency of 2-D data by symmetric set called neighbor set. The expression $\sum_{r\in\zeta_s} \theta_r(x_{s+r} + x_{s-r})$ represents the sum of all the distinct cliques of neighboring pixels at a specific subband. For the first order model of MRF, a sum is performed over horizontal and vertical neighboring pixels. The neighbor set for a first model order is defined as ζ= {(0,1), (0,–1)(1,0), (–1,0)} and for a second model order ζ= {(0,1), (0,–1)(1,0),

(−1,0), (1,1), (−1,−1), (1,−1), (−1,1)}. The MRF model is defined for symmetric neighbor set, therefore, if $r \in \zeta_s$ then $-r \notin \zeta_s$ and ζ is defined as $\zeta = (r : r \in \zeta_s)$ [$(-r : r \in \zeta_s)$. MRF can be described by potential functions working on a local neighborhood due to the Gibbs-Markov equivalence. In principle, there are no restrictions to the contents of these potential functions. The potentials attached to different cliques do not even have to be stationary but can vary throughout the image. For the problem of image restoration or information extraction, however, a certain number of "standard" potential functions exist.
Local interactions can be described by potentials V_c for different cliques c. These potentials are a function of the gray-values of the pixels belonging to a clique. Hence, the global energy of the whole image can be written as the sum over all potentials

$$U(x) = \sum_{c \in C} V_c(x) \tag{9}$$

In the same way, the local energy at pixel xi

$$U(x_i) = \sum_{c \in C, i \in C} V_c(x_i) \tag{10}$$

which is the sum of the potentials over all cliques that include pixel x_i. As a result, the local statistical interactions of pixels within an image can be described by an appropriate set of potential functions V_c and a corresponding clique system C.

3.3 Gauss-Markov model

Gauss-Markov model is defined by the local energy function

$$U_i(x_i) = \frac{(x_i - \mu_i)^2}{2\sigma^2}, \mu_i = \sum_{k,j \in C} \theta_{k,l}(x_{k,l} + x'_{k,l}) \tag{11}$$

Parameter $\theta_{k,l}$ represents the model vector parameter. The neighborhood configuration is encapsulated in a weighted sum over all neighboring pixels resulting in a prediction μ_i for the center pixel. Assuming some distortion of the prediction μ_i by additive Gaussian noise N_i of zero mean and variance σ^2 the corresponding conditional pdf of Gauss-Markov random fields can be written in a closed form as

$$p(x) = \frac{1}{\sqrt{2\pi\sigma^2}} \exp - \frac{(x_i - \mu_i)^2}{2\sigma^2} \tag{12}$$

which corresponds to a linear auto-regressive process with $xi = \mu_i + n_i$, where n_i is a realization of N_i.

3.4 Auto-binomial model

An autobinomial distribution is given by

$$p(x) = \binom{G}{x} \rho^x (1-\rho)^{G-x}, \rho = \frac{1}{1+\exp(-\eta)}, \eta = a + \sum_{r \in C} \frac{b_r(x_r + x'_r)}{G} \tag{13}$$

where $\boldsymbol{\theta} = a, b_{11}, b_{12}, b_{21}, b_{22}, \ldots$ represents avto-binomial model (ABM) parameters and G the maximal value in the image. A value a parameterizes the pdf of x without spatial

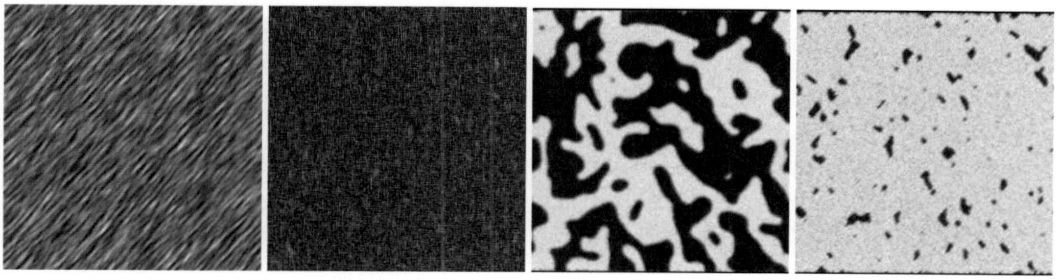

(a) (b) (c) (d)

Fig. 6. (a)-(b) Generated textures using GMRF. (c)-(d) Generated textures using ABM.

interactions. The number of parameters b_{ij} depends on the model order. Figs. 6(a)-6(d) show textures generated using the GMRF model and the auto-binomial model. The auto-binomial model generates more blob-like textures, while the GMRF model produces more natural and not very sharp textures.

4. Bayesian statistical modeling

Noise-free image models and noise models should be defined in order to remove noise from SAR image using Bayesian inference. The marginal distribution of wavelet subbands is well approximated by generalized Gaussian distribution. It is assumed that the image model in the wavelet domain is well approximated using general Gaussian distribution, and the noise distribution is non-stationary Gaussian noise with zero mean and locally varying variance, which is estimated from a given spatial neighborhood. We assume that the speckle noise in the wavelet domain can be approximated well using Gaussian distribution. The first level of Bayesian inference is $p(\boldsymbol{x} \mid \boldsymbol{y},\boldsymbol{\theta}) = \frac{p(\boldsymbol{y} \mid \boldsymbol{x},\boldsymbol{\theta})p(\boldsymbol{x} \mid \boldsymbol{\theta})}{p(\boldsymbol{y} \mid \boldsymbol{\theta})}$ where $\boldsymbol{y}$ is a noisy image, $\boldsymbol{x}$ is a noise-free image, $\boldsymbol{\theta}$ represents the model's parameter, $p(\boldsymbol{y} \mid \boldsymbol{x}, \boldsymbol{\theta})$ denotes the conditional pdf of $\boldsymbol{y}$ over $\boldsymbol{x}$ and its so-called ***likelihood*** pdf, $p(\boldsymbol{x} \mid \boldsymbol{\theta})$ denotes ***prior*** pdf and $p(\boldsymbol{y} \mid \boldsymbol{\theta})$ represents ***evidence*** pdf. The $p(\boldsymbol{y} \mid \boldsymbol{\theta})$ pdf does not play a role in the maximization over $\boldsymbol{x}$ and, therefore, the Maximum A Posteriori (MAP) estimator is given by $\hat{x}(y) = \text{argmax}_x\, p(\boldsymbol{y} \mid \boldsymbol{x}, \boldsymbol{\theta})p(\boldsymbol{x} \mid \boldsymbol{\theta})$ where ***likelihood*** and ***prior*** pdf's should be defined. The MAP estimator is an optimal estimator and minimizes the cost function.

5. Maximum a posteriori despeckling using Gauss-Markov Random Field

Model based despeckling using Gauss-Markov Random Field (GMRF) model, a maximum a posteriori (MAP) estimation and evidence maximization framework was proposed in Walessa & Datcu (2000). It uses the Bayesian approach using the first level of Bayesian inference to obtain the maximum a posteriori (MAP) estimate of despeckled image. This method uses gamma pdf (8) as likelihood $p(y \mid x, \theta)$ and as prior $p(x \mid \theta)$ a GMRF (12), which models and preserves textures within the image. The MAP estimate is obtained by maximizing a product $p(y \mid x, \theta)p(x \mid \theta)$. is given by

$$x^4 - x^3 \sum_{j \in n} \theta_j x_j + 2L\sigma^2 x^2 - 2L\sigma^2 y^2 = 0. \tag{14}$$

The equation is solved analytically for variable x. The solution represents the approximated noise-free coefficients, which depends on texture parameter $\boldsymbol{\theta}$. The parameter estimation $\boldsymbol{\theta}$ is determined using the second level of Bayesian inference using evidence maximization. Due to the complexity of the integral it can not be computed analytically. The evidence integral consists of mutually independent process. Multidimensional probability density function is approximated by a multivariate Gaussian probability density function with Hessian matrix $\mathbf{H}$, which is centered on the maximum of a posteriori pdf. Approximation of the evidence $p(\mathbf{y} \mid \boldsymbol{\theta})$ is given by

$$p(\mathbf{y} \mid \boldsymbol{\theta}) = \int p(\mathbf{y} \mid \mathbf{x}, \boldsymbol{\theta}) p(\mathbf{x} \mid \boldsymbol{\theta}) dx \approx \frac{(2\pi)^{\frac{m}{2}}}{\sqrt{|\mathbf{H}|}} \prod_{i=1}^{m} p(y_i \mid x_{i_{MAP}}) p(x_{i_{MAP}} \mid \boldsymbol{\theta}) \tag{15}$$

where x_{iMAP} is the MAP estimate of x_i obtained using the fixed parameter vector $\boldsymbol{\theta}$ and $\mathbf{H}$ is the Hessian matrix. In order to obtain the highest evidence the set of chosen parameter $\boldsymbol{\theta}$ changes iteratively. H denotes Hessian matrix, which is the square matrix of the second order partial derivatives of a univariate function given by

$$H = -\nabla\nabla \sum_{s=1}^{N\times N} \log(p(y_s \mid x_s) p(x_s \mid \theta)) \tag{16}$$

where index s denotes the index in the 2D lattice.

$$\begin{aligned} \log p(y \mid \theta) &\approx 0.5 \log(2\pi^{(N\times N)/2} / \sqrt{H}) + \sum_{s=1}^{N\times N} \log p(y_s \mid x_{s_{MAP}}) + \log p(x_{s_{MAP}} \mid x_{s_\eta}, \theta) \\ &\approx \sum_{s=1}^{N\times N} (0.5(N\times N)\log 2\pi - \log h_{ii}) + \log p(y_s \mid x_{s_{MAP}}) + \log p(x_{s_{MAP}} \mid x_{s_\eta}, \theta)) \end{aligned} \tag{17}$$

$$\begin{aligned} \log p(y \mid \theta) = \sum_{s=1}^{N\times N} \Bigg[& 0.5(N\times N)\log 2\pi - \log h_{ii}) + \log\left(2\left(\frac{y_s}{x_s}\right)^{2L-1} \frac{L^L}{x_s \Gamma(L)} \exp - L\left(\frac{y_s}{x_s}\right)^2\right) \\ & + \log\left(\frac{1}{\sqrt{2\pi\sigma^2}} \exp - \frac{(x_i - \mu_i)^2}{2\sigma^2}\right)\Bigg] \end{aligned} \tag{18}$$

$$h_{ii} \approx \left(6L\frac{y_s^2}{x_s^4} - \frac{2L}{x_s^2} + \frac{1}{\sigma^2}\left(1 + |\boldsymbol{\theta}|^2\right)\right) \tag{19}$$

where h_{ii} are the main diagonal elements of the Hessian matrix H. The second derivate can be computed analytically. The final approximation is given by $|H| \approx \prod_{i=1}^{N} h_{ii}$.

The parameter $\boldsymbol{\theta}$ requires sequential computation of the MAP estimate and its evidence $p(y \mid \theta)$. In the first step the MAP estimate is computed using initial parameter $\boldsymbol{\theta}$. For those MAP estimates within window size of $N \times N$ the evidence is computed. One parameter θ_i is changed and the evidence is computed. If the evidence is increased, new estimate is kept, and second parameter θ_{i+1} is changed and the evidence is computed. If the evidence decreases the parameter θ_i is unchanged. All parameters θ_i are changed until the evidence is growing. When the evidence is not changing any more, $\boldsymbol{\theta}$ represents the final solution.

6. Maximum a Posteriori despeckling using Auto-binomial Model (MAP-ABM)

A Maximum a Posteriori despeckling using Auto-binomial Model method Hebar et al. (2009) is also based on the Bayesian approach. The likelihood probability is modeled using the Gamma distribution (8) and an auto-binomial model (13) is used as a prior pdf. The auto-binomial model is discrete function, therefore, the differential is introduced to solve the MAP estimation numerically. The MAP estimate is given by

$$\frac{\Delta}{\Delta x_i}\log p(x_i \mid y_i) = \frac{\Delta}{\Delta x_i}\log\left[2\left(\frac{y_i}{x_i}\right)^{2L-1}\frac{L^L}{x_i\Gamma(L)}\exp\left(-L\left(\frac{y_i}{x_i}\right)^2\right)\right] + \frac{\Delta}{\Delta x_i}\log\left[\binom{G}{x_i}\rho^{x_i}(1-\rho)^{G-x_i}\right] \quad (20)$$

The first expression can be solved analytically. However, the second expression which represents the Auto-binomial model is solving subtracting log $p((x_i + 1) \mid \theta_i)$ – log $p(x_i \mid \theta_i)$ numerically. The result is given by the zeros of

$$-2L\frac{y_i}{x_i} + 2L\frac{y_i^2}{x_i^3} + \log\left(\frac{G-x_i}{x_i+1}\right) + \log\left(\frac{\rho}{1-\rho}\right) \quad (21)$$

The MAP estimate was found using Brent's method algorithm for numerical solution of roots. In the second level of Bayesian inference, the evidence maximization was adapted to logarithm form using the Auto-binomial model. The parameter ρ in (20) depends on model parameter θ, defined in (13). The parameter $\boldsymbol{\theta}$ define ABM and it is determined using the evidence maximization approach. The evidence is given by

$$\begin{aligned}\log p(y \mid \theta) = \sum_{s=1}^{N\times N}&\Big[0.5(N\times N)\log 2\pi - \log h_{ii}\Big) \\ &+\log\left(2\left(\frac{y_s}{x_s}\right)^{2L-1}\frac{L^L}{x_s\Gamma(L)}\exp\left(-L\left(\frac{y_s}{x_s}\right)^2\right)\right) \\ &+\log\left(\binom{G}{x_s}\rho_s^{x_s}(1-\rho_s)^{G-x_s}\right)\Big]\end{aligned} \quad (22)$$

$$h_{ii} \approx \sum_{s=1}^{N\times N}\left(\frac{2L}{x_s^2} - 6L\frac{y_s^2}{x_s^4} - \frac{1}{G-x_s} - \frac{1}{x_s+1}\right) \quad (23)$$

The evidence maximization is very similar to the algorithm MAP-ABM. The texture parameters are changed in order to increase the evidence. The evidence shows how good the model fits to the original data. The synthetic generated data are fitted to the original data.

7. Maksimum a posteriori despeckling using generalized Gaussian-Markov Random field model

The wavelet subbands represents coarse to fine representation of the image in the terms of frequencies and spatial orientation. The reader is pointed to the literature for details regarding the wavelet transform Daubechies (1992), Chan (1995), Chui (1992). The decomposition is implemented using high and low pass filters, therefore the subbands at the high scale represents subbands with high frequencies and subbands at the low scale represents subbands with low frequencies. The time-frequency analysis can be easily done using the properties of subband decomposition. The subbands, in general, have Generalized Gaussian distribution and zero mean. The despeckling and information extraction using Bayesian inference, therefore, require models based on Gaussian distribution. The speckle within the wavelet domain is approximated using the Gaussian distribution and an image model can be approximated by the Generalized Gaussian distribution. Information extraction using GMRF can be extended using the generalized GMRF. The prior pdf $p(x)$, which has the form of a Generalized Gaussian Markov Random Field (GGMRF), is given by

$$p(x_s \mid \theta) = \frac{\nu\eta(\nu,\sigma_x)}{2\Gamma(1/\nu)} \exp\left(-\left[\eta(\nu,\sigma_x)\left|x_s - \sum_{r\in\zeta_s}\theta_r(x_{s+r} + x_{s-r})\right|\right]^{\nu}\right) \quad (24)$$

Let σ_x and $\boldsymbol{\theta}$ define the GGMRF with a neighbor set ζ_s. The parameter ν represents the shape parameters of the GGMRF. The MAP estimate using GGMRF prior and the Gaussian likelihood is given by

$$-\nu\eta(\nu,\sigma_x)\left[\eta(\nu,\sigma_x)\left|x_s - \sum_{r\in\zeta_s}\theta_r(x_{s+r} + x_{s-r})\right|\right]^{\nu-1} \frac{y_s - x_s}{\sigma_n^2} = 0. \quad (25)$$

The variance σ_x of a noise-free image and variance of speckle noise σ_n are estimated using the results of Foucher et al. (2001):

$$\sigma_n^2 = \psi_j \mu_x^2 C_F^2 (1 + C_x^2), \quad C_x^2 = \frac{C_{Wy}^2 - \psi_j C_F^2}{\psi_j (1 + C_F^2)} \quad (26)$$

where $\mu_x = E[x]$ and C_x^2 is the normalized standard deviation of noisy wavelet coefficient is $C_{Wy} = \sigma_{Wy}/\mu_y$ and the normalized standard deviation of noise $C_F = \sqrt{1/L}$ for intensity images (where L is the number of looks) and $C_F = \sqrt{(4/\pi - 1)/L}$ for intensity images. The parameter ψ_j is defined as a product of the high pass g_k and low pass h_k filter coefficients used at j-th level of wavelet decomposition $\psi_j = \left(\sum_k h_k^2\right)^2 \left(\sum_k k_k^2\right)^{2(j-1)}$. Finally, the noise variance is given by:

$$\sigma_n^2 = \frac{C_F^2(\psi_j \mu_y^2 + \sigma_{Wy}^2)}{1 + C_F^2} \quad (27)$$

where $\mu_y = E[y]$. The estimate for σ_n is used for all values of parameter ν. The texture parameter θ of GGMRF was estimated using minimum mean square estimate.

μ = 127.94	MAP-GMRF	MAP-ABM	MAP-GGMRF
MSE	264.34	259.31	245.45
Mean	127.84	127.86	127.89
ENL	651	539	826
Speckle	3.15	3.18	3.15
Mean($y/\hat{x}$)	0.97	0.95	0.94

Table 1. Filter Evaluation for Synthetic test images.

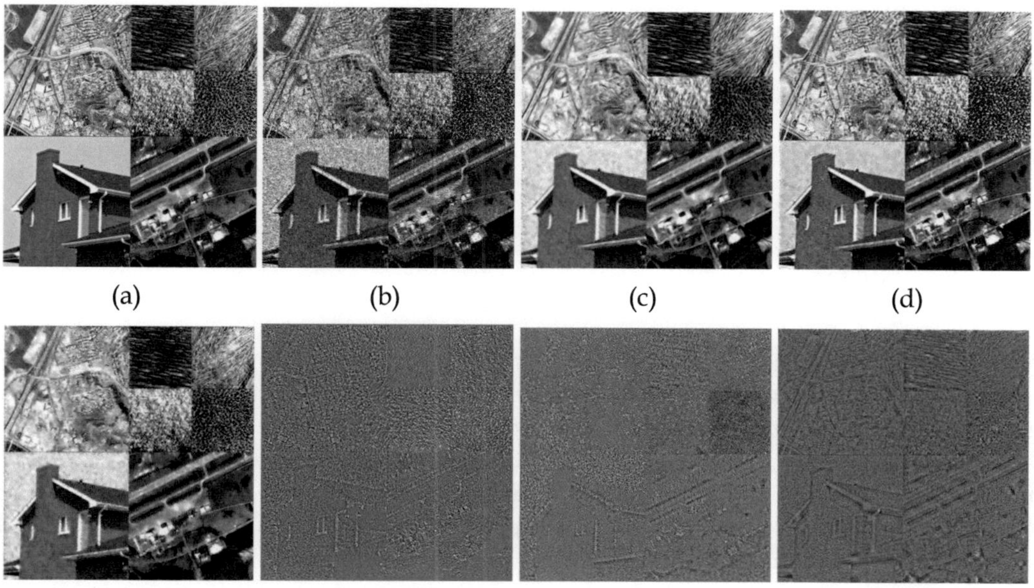

(a) (b) (c) (d)

(e) (f) (g) (h)

Fig. 7. (a)Original mosaic image. (b) Speckled mosaic. (c) Despeckled obtained with MAPGMRF. (d) Despeckled obtained with MAP-ABM. (e) Despeckled obtained with wavelet MAP-GGMRF. (f) Ratio image obtained with the MAP-GMRF. (g) Ratio image obtained with the MAP-ABM (h) Ratio image obtained with the wavelet MAP-GGMRF.

8. Experimental results

This section presents the efficiency of the proposed methods using objective and subjective criteria. The synthetic image, shown in Fig. 7(a), which is affected by a simulated multiplicative speckle is shown in Fig. 7(b). The MAP-GMRF and the MAP-ABM methods operate within the image domain and use the same model parameters. The window size is 15×15 the MRF order is 2 for all experiments and the step size is 1. The reconstructed image obtained with the MAP-GMRF, MAP-ABM and the MAP-GGMRF algorithms are shown in Figs. 7(c)- 7(e), respectively. The mean square error (MSE), mean of the reconstructed image, ENL of the reconstructed image, ENL of the ratio images and mean of the ratio images are reported in Table 1. The best results in the objective measurements gives the wavelet based methods, which uses the GGMRF model and is followed by the MAP-ABM and the MAP-MBD methods. All methods well reserve the mean of the reconstructed image and from the ENL results can be concluded that the MAP-GGMRF method gives the most smoothes

(a) (b) (c) (d)

Fig. 8. (a)Original image of Cairo, Egypt (©DLR). (b) MAP-MBD despeckled (c) MAP-ABM despeckled. (d) MAP-GGMRF despeckled.

μ = 190.4	MAP-GMRF	MAP-ABM	MAP-GGMRF
Mean 190.6	190.2	190.3	
ENL	90	96	118
Speckle	4.15	4.18	4.15
Mean($y/\hat{x}$)	0.99	0.98	0.99

Table 2. Filter Evaluation for Synthetic test images.

reconstructed image and the MAP-ABM gives the most sharpest image. The ratio images shown in Figs. 7(f)-7(h), which represent the speckle, because speckle is multiplicative $y = xn$ and the ratio images represents $y/x = n$. The speckle in Table 1 represents the ENL of ratio images and should be around 3, because original images were affected by speckle with 3 ENL. All methods well estimate the speckle. The mean of speckle should be 1 and all presented methods well estimate the speckle.

Presented methods were tested using the real SAR image of Cairo, Egyipt, provided by the TerraSAR-X satellite. The resolution is 1.1 m in azimuth and 0.86 m in range. It was acquired using 300 MHz chirp. The original image is shown in Fig. 8(a) and despeckled using GMRF, ABM and GGMRF models on Figs. 8(b)-8(d). The MAP-ABM method gives very good results using, because structures are good modeled, speckle well removed and the mean of the reconstructed image is preserved well, as reported in Table 2. The MAP-GMRF method well estimates speckle, but introduces GMRF based structures, which appear, as inability of the model to adapt to the real textures. The MAP-GGMRF well remove speckle and models

(a) (b) (c)

Fig. 9. (a)Ratio image obtained with the MAP-GMRF. (b) Ratio image obtained with the MAPABM(c) Ratio image obtained with the wavelet MAP-GGMRF.

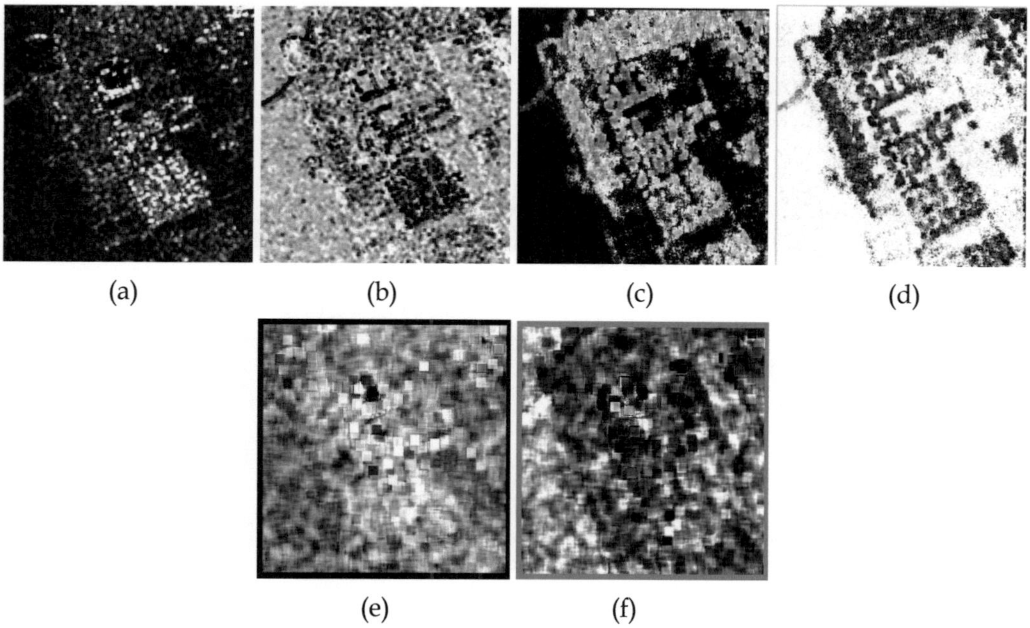

Fig. 10. Horizontal (HH) and vertical (VV) textural parameters (a)HH, MAP-GMRF. (b) VV, MAP-GMRF. (c) HH, MAP-ABM. (d) VV, MAP-GMRF. (d) HH, MAP-GGMRF. (e) VV, MAPGGMRF.

textures in the real-SAR image. Figs. 9(a)-9(c) show the ratio images of real SAR images. The speckle is well estimated with all presented methods.

The MRF based methods are able to extract features parameters. In this case the texture can be extracted using texture models. The texture parameters obtained with the GMRF, ABM and GGMRF models are shown in Figs. 10(a)-10(f), where the horizontal and vertical cliques are shown. The ABM model well models homogeneous and heterogeneous regions, as well it separates different kind of textures, as show the ABM's texture parameters on Figs. 10(c)-10(d). The GMRF model is not as efficient as the ABM model in modeling real textures, but it is still able to model homogeneous and heterogeneous regions and the parameters estimated with the GMRF model are shown in Figs. 10(a)-10(b). The wavelet based method has difficulties in modeling textures. This can be the consequence of the linear model used for the texture parameter estimation. The texture parameters obtained with the GGMRF model are shown in Fig. 10(e)-10(f).

The computational efficiency of the proposed methods were tested on real SAR image with 1024 ×1024 pixels and the execution times were 414, 560 and 103 seconds for MAP-GMRF, MAP-ABM and MAP-GGMRF methods.

9. Conclusion

Presented methods in this paper are based on Markov Random Fields. The efficiency of two methods, which work within the image domain and the wavelet based method is compared. The wavelet-based method gives good results in the objective measurements on simulated data, well preforms in the terms of despeckling, but its ability of information extraction in very poor. The ABM in GMRF based methods well despeckles the real and simulated data and the ABM gives very good results using real SAR data. The ABM has better ability to separate blob-like textures, which occur in the real SAR images for city areas. The GMRF model is more appropriate for the natural textures.

10. References

Argenti, F., Bianchi, T. & Alparone, L. (2006). Multiresolution map despeckling of sar images based on locally adaptive generalized gaussian pdf modeling, *IEEE Transaction on Image Processing* 15: 3385–3399.

Arulampalan, S., M, Maskell, S., N., G. & Clap, T. (2002). A tutorial on particle filters for online nonlinear/non-gaussian bayesian tracking, *IEEE Transaction on Signal Processing* 50: 174–188.

Chan, Y. T. (1995). *Wavelet Basics,* Kulwer Academic Publishers, Norwell, Massachussetta, USA.

Chui, C. K. (1992). *Wavelets: A Tutorial in Theory and Applications,* Academic Press, San Diego, USA.

Chuna, A. L. d., Zhou, J. & Do, M. N. (2006). The nonsubsampled contourlet transform: Theory, design,and application, *IEEE Transaction on Image Processing* 15: 3089–3101.

Dai, M., Peng, C., Chan, A. & Loguinov, D. (2004). Multiresolution map despeckling of sar images based on locally adaptive generalized gaussian pdf modeling, *IEEE Transaction on Geoscience and Remote Sensing* 42: 1642–1648.

Daubechies, I. (1992). *Ten Lectures onWavelets,* Society for industrial and applied mathematics, Philadelphia, Pennsylvania.

Foucher, S., Benie, G. B. & Boucher, J.-M. (2001). Multiscale map filtering of sar images, *IEEE Tran. Image Processing* 10(1): 49–60.

Gleich, D. & Datcu, M. (2007).Wavelet-based despeckling of SAR images using Gauss-Markov random fields, *IEEE Transaction on Geoscience and Remote Sensing* 45(12): 4127–4143.

Hebar, M., Gleich, D. & Cucej, Z. (2009). Autobinomial model for sar image despeckling and information extraction, *IEEE Transaction on Geoscience and Remote Sensing* 47(8): 2818– 2835.

Li, Y.-q., He, M.-y. & Gang, X.-f. (2006). Ieee conference on signal processing, *A New Adaptive Algorithm for Despeckling of SAR images Based on Contourlet Transform.*

Sivia, D. S. (1996). *Data Analysis: A Bayesian Tutorial,* Oxford, U.K., Clarendon.

Sveinsson, J. R. & Benediktsson, J. A. (2007). Ieee international conference on geoscience and remote sensing, *Speckle Reduction of SAR Images in the Bandelet Domain.*

Walessa, M. & Datcu, M. (2000). Model-based despeckling and information extraction from sar images, *IEEE Transaction on Geoscience and Remote Sensing* 38: 2258–2269.

13

Non Invasive Estimating of Cattle Live Weight Using Thermal Imaging

Denis Stajnko, Peter Vindiš, Marjan Janžekovič and Maksimiljan Brus
University of Maribor, Faculty of Agriculture and Life Sciences, Pivola 10, 2311 Hoče, Slovenia

1. Introduction

The body mass is one of highly important indicators of the development of the young cattle, therefore it is essential to follow it up. Only the animals with sufficient body frame and with well muscled top - quality body parts can be successfully fattened to high body mass. To obtain the highest precision in measuring of cattle weight gain, weighing should take place repeatedly in the period prior to slaughter.

Methods for assessing growth by the weighing of animals are an important factor in monitoring production capacity of cattle according to their inheritance capacity, food conversion, average daily gain and carcass yield all of which subsequently affect the output of the herd. The most reliable information about the body mass of cattle can be obtained by weighing the animals. Accurate data on the body mass are obtained by weighing with the use of various weighing devices, such as the spring weighing devices or more modern electronic weighing devices. Since in most cases, weighing is done manually the process often needs at least two stockmen, and takes 3 to 5 minutes per bull. In addition, the procedure is stressful for the whole herd, and from an ergonomic point of view, unsatisfactory (Brandl & Jørgensen, 1996).

However, the raisers did not have available weighing devices frequently and the animals cannot be often weighed, thus the individual body parts are measured alternatively. Usually, measuring of the whither size suffices, because the body frame, size and length are in positive relation to intensity and capacity of meat production. However, the information acquired is less accurate than the one obtained by the weighing. The differences are affected by the breed type, satiety of the animal, manner of feeding and even tightness of the tape during measuring (Kogel & Utz, 1988). It is also known, as much as the calves deviate from the optimal body development, the establishing of the body mass deviates. Thus, in order to calculate the body mass more accurately, it is necessary to consider also the trunk length in addition to the whither size.

In the following chapters the comparison between the manual and automated electronic weighing systems is going to be presented firstly, which clearly shows the most important advantages of the modern systems. Then, the non invasive, indirect weight determination from the dimensions of the animal, measured by an image-processing model will be presented and explained that can be used for automatic and precise estimation of body dimensions from images of live animals and for predicting the body weight of individual cattle.

2. Manual weighing

Manual weighing represents the oldest and simplest method for assessing the body mass of live animal, which served for centuries precise enough for commercial use. Nowadays weighing on balance is still important method for measuring the growth of animals and estimating the fodder conversions, because the device is cheap and easy to handle. However, whenever using manual balance in progeny test of bulls sires a farmer must first insure a fattening barn for each manual weighing, where a particular number of animals are placed together into the group boxes. The groups are usually formed according to the body mass so the animals remained together until the end of the growing. Normally a plan of several weighing is scheduled, starting from housing till slaughtering in 60 days interval. For each weighing the animal must be moved from the group box on the weighing device, which is very stressful for the cattle as well as the stablemen. The simplest manual weighing device is shown in Fig. 1, which is calibrated manually once the cattle stand calmly on it. After the balance is set correctly, the stablemen can read the weight.

Fig. 1. Common weighing of cattle on the scale

The next generation of balances represents the electronic weighing device, which contrary to manual devices is calibrated automatically and can read the body weight autonomously as well. A sample of automatic electronic device EC 2000 is shown in the Fig. 2. As seen, during the weighing the load bars must be installed under the platform on a firm, level surface and prevent platform movement. Then the load bar cables are connected to the indicator to ensure that they would not be walked on, chewed by animals or squashed in any way.

Once the cattle is standing on the weighing scale additional measurements of the trunk, length, the chest size, the withers height and the croup height can be measured as well. The height of the withers, the croup height, the body length, the croup length, the chest width, the haunch width and the chest depth are usually done by means of Lydtin's rod (Fig. 3).

The beginning and the end of certain body dimension are taken by two foldable arms, which can be moved vertically on the rod. However, for measuring of animals the stableman must apply additional devices as the 117 cm long hollow Lydtin's rod, measuring tape - meter and the compasses (Fig. 3 left). The measuring tape is a 2.00 cm long scale made of linen or metal and serve to measure the chest size. Unfortunately, there are certain differences between the body masses stated by individual authors. The compasses are metallic and ensure measuring of up to 60 cm length (Kräußlich, 1994; Cepon et al., 2006).

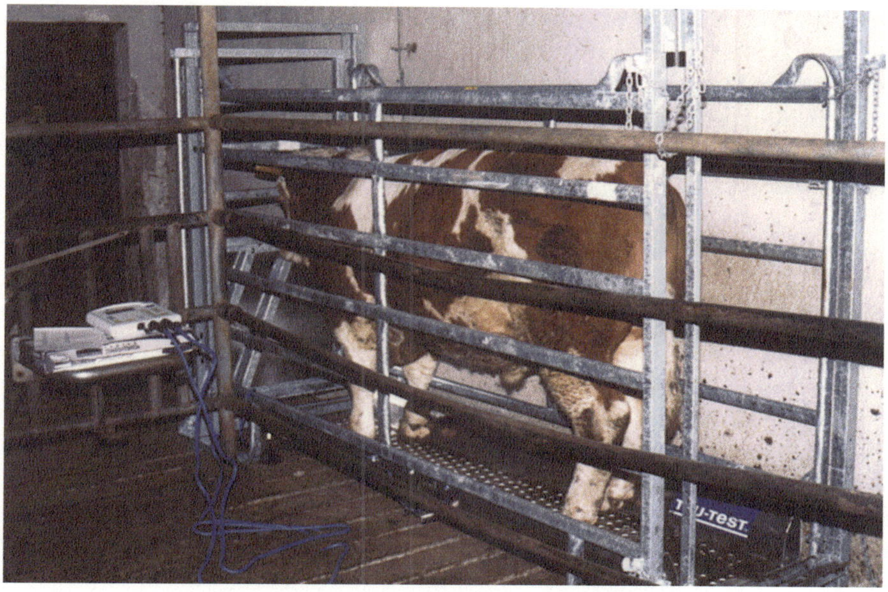

Fig. 2. A cattle standing on the electronic weighing device EC 2000

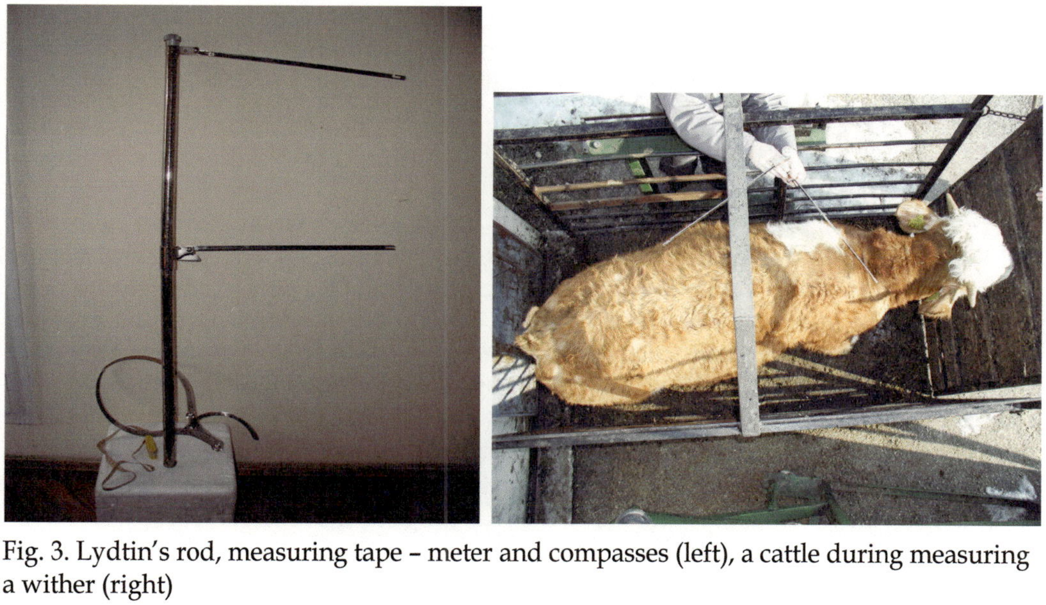

Fig. 3. Lydtin's rod, measuring tape - meter and compasses (left), a cattle during measuring a wither (right)

3. Automatic weighing

Automatic weighting systems have been intensively researched for pigs, sheep and poultry, however in cattle production only weighting of dairy cows is reported by Cveticanin & Wendl (2004) and Pastell et al., (2006). Different automatic weighing systems have been intensively researched in cattle as well as dairy production.
The sophisticated radio frequency identification system was found to be a highly effective tool for documenting bunk attendance, feeding behaviour and weighing of animals on the scale in cattle production, whenever animals were equipped with two separate RF transponders (Schwartzkopf-Genswein et al., 2002).
There is a worldwide movement towards automation in cattle husbandry, with the objective of fully automating every process from feeding to milking. Automatic milking has become a common practice in dairy production and, at the end of the year 2003, about 2200 farms worldwide used a milking robot (Rousing et al., 2004). Milking robots offer a unique possibility for the dynamic measurement of body weight. For example, it is highly probable that hoof problems can easily be noted by separately measuring the load on each leg. Dairy farming is developing into full automated production system in which scientists want to automate every single process from feeding to milking in order to reduce production costs and maximise milk yield. Dynamic weighing of cattle represents an important segment of this system. Weighing in motion without stopping the animal's movement after it leaves the milking parlour is of interest due to continuity of the milking process and smaller variations of body weight when measured at the same time of the day. The forces to the ground during the cow's passage are recorded on walk-through weighers (Rousing et al., 2004).
Cveticanin & Wendl (2004) designed the fuzzy-logic dynamic weighing system for dairy cows based on a mathematical model for simulating a cow's walk, which calculates the body weight with an average error of less than 2 %. The simplified two- legged system measures the force to the ground produced by a cow's feet when the animal is crossing the scale. Depending on walking speed and force, a body weight is calculated and compared with the database.
Pastell et al. (2006) described another automatic weighing system made from four strain gauge balance devices installed in a milking robot. The computer program was able to measure the average weight, the weight variation of each leg and the total weight with 90 % accuracy. From many different models, two might be suggested for monitoring of young sires.

3.1 The GrowSafe™ system

The GrowSafe™ (Fig. 4) system consisted of two antennas, each embedded in a rubberized mat lining the outer wall of the 30 m feedbunks, passive transponders (Texas Instruments Inc., Dallas, TX) encased in plastic ear tags (Allflex, Dallas, TX), a data-logging reader panel connected to the antennae, and a computer to which data were uploaded and analysed (Gibb & McAllister, 1999; Schwartzkopf-Genswein et al., 1999). The antennae emitted a 130 kHz electromagnetic field, and detected the transponders borne by the cattle whenever they came within 50 cm of the feedbunk.
This system can identify and record bunk attendance at the bunk of an unlimited number of animals simultaneously. The reader panel logs the presence of each transponder every 6 s for as long as the transponders are within the read range of the antenna. These data can be use to derive the bunk visit frequency and duration. For the purpose of summarizing the transponder data, different meal criterion can be selected. According to Gibb & McAllister

(1999) a 300 s meal criterion is most suitable, since it is based on visual observation and validation work carried out by (Schwartzkopf-Genswein et al., 2002) and is the same as that reported by Sowell et al. (1998) for beef cattle.

Passive radio transponder data is possible to be collected on all the animals for 24 h per day throughout the growing period. The computer on which the data are storied must be checked every week to ensure that all cells are read when the animals' transponders are held next to the cell.

Every time an animal visits the water trough GrowSafe Beef™ measures weight and drinking behaviour, so the graph can be plotted illustrating the number of visits hourly at each GrowSafe Beef™ drinking position over a three day period.

Fig. 4. GrowSafe Beef™ weighing system

At least two other system similar to the GrowSafe Beef™ system are known from the literature. First, Cveticanin & Wendl (2004) designed the fuzzy-logic dynamic weighting system of dairy cow based on the mathematical model for simulating cow walk, which calculates the body weight with the absolute average error less than 2 %. The simplified two legged system measures the force to the ground when the animal is crossing the scale and generate a curve, which is compared with the database. Pastell et al. (2006) described another automatic weighing system made from four strain gauge balances equipment installed into a milking robot. The computer program was able to measure the average weight, the weight variation of each leg and total weight with 90 % accuracy.

4. Weight determination using body measurements

Since weighting of older cattle represents a dangerous job for the stableman, the significant correlation between live weight and dimensions of the cattle has led many authors to study the possibility of estimating body weight from the dimensions of the cattle. Heinrichs et al. (1992) indicated that the linear regression of body weight on heart girth had the highest R^2, followed by hip width, body length and wither height. Although all measurements are highly correlated, addition of the second body measure contributes a little predictive benefit in the estimation of Holstein heifers' body weight. Also Wilson et al. (1997) detected the addition of heart girth as a second measurement to the wither height as the most important contribution for estimating the body weight of Holstein veal calves.

Enevoldsen & Kristensen (1997) evaluated the use of wither height, hip height and width to predict the body weight. Seven regression models were developed based on indicators, which are relatively simple to obtain precisely because the anatomical locations are easy to identify.

Also Willeke & Dürsch (2002) detected high significant correlation in hip height, heart girth and weight also for the Simmental heifers suggested the third order polynomial equation as the most fitting.

The chest size as a basis for the determination of the body mass of living cattle is increased close behind the shoulder-bones. During this measuring the animal must stand with the legs placed parallel and the head should be kept normally (Fig. 1). Each time after the measurement is taken, the body mass is read according to the table. However, it must be kept into account that the determination of the body mass on the basis of the chest size is only approximate.

5. Determining dimensions by image analysis

Computer-controlled systems for the remote monitoring of livestock have the potential to increase production efficiency and improve animal health and welfare. Examples of potential applications for image analysis based systems in pig husbandry were suggested by Schofeld (2003) and include recording of animal weight, growth rate, quality and conformation, control of diet, monitoring behavioural vices and providing management decision support. Schofeld (1993) describes how remote monitoring systems have the greatest value where continuous observation of intermittent events is essential, and where data collection is tedious and labour intensive, e.g. monitoring weight gain, feeding behaviour and breeding processes including heat detection and farrowing.

A visual image analysis (VIA) system can provide continuous automatic collection of size and shape data in pigs. Thus, it serves as an accurate means of for reflecting pig live mass and for tracking changes in the pig size over time periods that are sufficiently short for commercial use (White et al., 2004).

In order to apply image analysis to the weighing of bulls, the determination of animal body dimensions from images must be possible. Prior to using the image processing, a prediction function was established using the relationship between body dimensions from acquired images and the live weight of the specific cattle breed. Since the image is only a 2-D plain projection of the animal, the loss of one dimension limits the application of such a system to measuring vertical and horizontal dimensions. Therefore, the prediction functions should be precise enough to obtain valid information and can be similar to those described in the previous chapter only when the hip height and wither height are included in the polynomial equations.

According to Schaefer & Tong (1998), the thermal expression of warm-blooded animals is highly correlated with various tissue composition characteristics of specific animals, which involve the relative proportions and total quantities of different types of tissue in the animal. Therefore infrared thermal images taken of liveanimals are suggested for detecting and inspecting the body composition noninvasively.

Kmet et al. (2000) studied the application of image processing for slaughter value analysis on the basis of three images (above, left and rear) captured from 15-month-old, live

Simmental bulls. Live weight was found to be highly correlated with a stepwise linear regression model based on the animal shoulder width, lumbar protuberance in the body width, upper body area and rear thigh area.
In the next chapter we are going to present the results of original approach for determining the body dimensions and estimating the body mass of cattle via thermal camera and image analysis developed by Stajnko et al. (2008), which was based on the data collected from May 2006 to June 2008 at the Faculty's experimental farm in Rogoza.

6. Image analysis procedure

As opposed to common RGB visual techniques, thermography is based on sensing an object's own heat radiation. This enables evaluation of different characteristics of observed objects with the use of visual cameras. The authors have found few references concerning application of thermal imaging for determining plant parts, counting fruit, vegetable, seedlings or selecting weeds from plants and background. In our experiment the examined cattle were captured from the side by the AGEMA 570 (Flir Systems™) thermal camera with an image resolution of 320x240 pixels. The emissivity of the object was set to 0.98 and the temperature resolution was better than 0.5°C, which enables precise detection of body heat in any environmental condition. The measurements were performed using cold concrete wall surroundings, which enabled a temperature difference and therefore a sharp edge between the animal and the background on the capture images.
The uncertainty of body edge measurements depends on the image resolution and the position of animal in relation to the camera. Therefore, for holding the distance between the camera and the object constant for all measurements, the animals were guided through a narrow corridor, which also prevented the animal from moving perpendicular to the camera. When the animal was walking through the corridor, we were waiting until it stood in an appropriate position on the image frame. Such procedure was possible because the animals were not aware of being captured by the thermal camera.

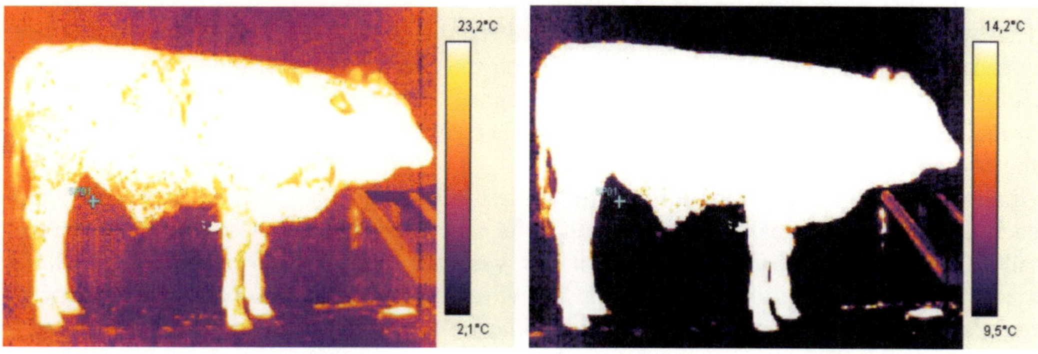

Fig. 5. Sample thermal images at 320x240 pixel resolution showing a 280 kg cattle before (left) and after temperature adjustment (right)

Since a thermal camera supports only its own IMG image format, each series of images was first converted into a BMP format prior to further image processing. As seen from Fig. 5, during this process, contrasts between the cattle body and the background was extended by adjusting the temperature scale on each series of thermal images according to the average body and surroundings temperature.

The algorithm for determination of animal's measures will be illustrated with one sample of a cattle image (Fig. 5), chosen to be representative for demonstrating the results of the procedure. As seen from the BMP image, the thermal camera was able to separate the cattle from the surroundings accurately, so any additional image separation was not required. Prior to every set of measurements a Lydtin's stick was captured on the image together with the animal. It was applied for the pixel/unit calibration as it ensured enough temperature gradient to the cattle body, which was required for the automatic image processing. Because the thermal image was relatively small for precise measurements, all calculations were conducted on the subpixel level, which increased the accuracy significantly.

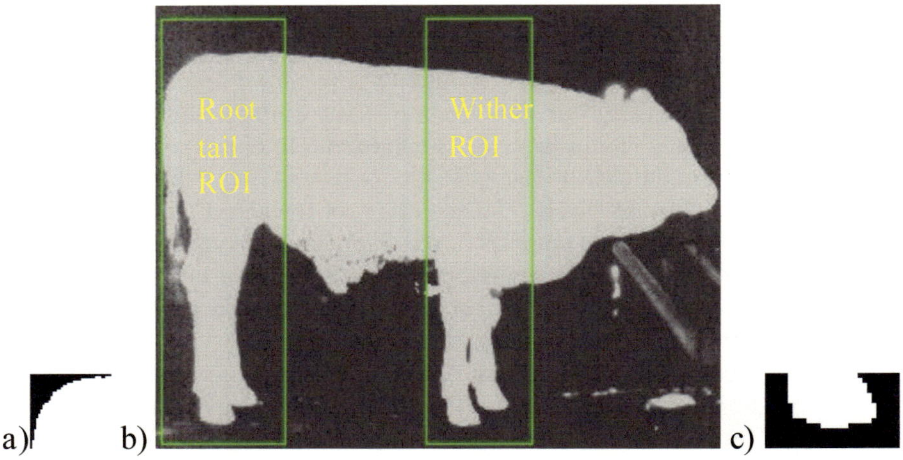

Fig. 6. Root tail mask (a) and front hoof mask (c) for locating a starting point of the coordinate system on each of two ROIs (green line) on the 8-bit image (b)

6.1 ROIs and templates

The measurements were based on the idea of fixing the root tail (Fig. 6a) and front hoof templates (Fig. 6c) on each image and adjusting the coordinate system accordingly, so that different positions of the animal did not influence the measurements. To prevent finding unreal positions, locating the root tail was limited to the root tail ROI and the front roof to the wither ROI, respectively.

As shown on the Fig. 6, a root tail ROI and wither ROI image were defined uniformly on the each image. Thus, a mask image containing the sample of root tail was applied on the root tail ROI in the first stage. Once the root tail was located on the ROI, the new coordinate system was fixed to animal root tail (Fig. 7b), whereby the bottom left corner of the root tail template was given the coordinates (0.0). Similar procedure was also applied for locating of front hoof mask (Fig. 6c) on the wither ROI (Fig. 7d).

6.2 Locate hip procedure

Before determining the hip height (*Hh*), the hip (*HipY*) had to be found on the boundary, whereby the *HipY* was assumed as a small saddle point on the boundary. Therefore for describing and locating it a second order polynomial mathematical model was developed (Fig. 8 - red line), which fit the boundary quite well (Fig. 8 - blue line). However, by calculating the first derivate of *Y* points not one extreme was detected, thus for the selection of saddle points the following relational and logical operations were additionally carried out:

$$\text{HipY} \quad y'_{(i)}=0 \text{ and } y''_{(i-1)} > 0 \text{ and } y''_{(i+1)} < 0 \tag{1}$$

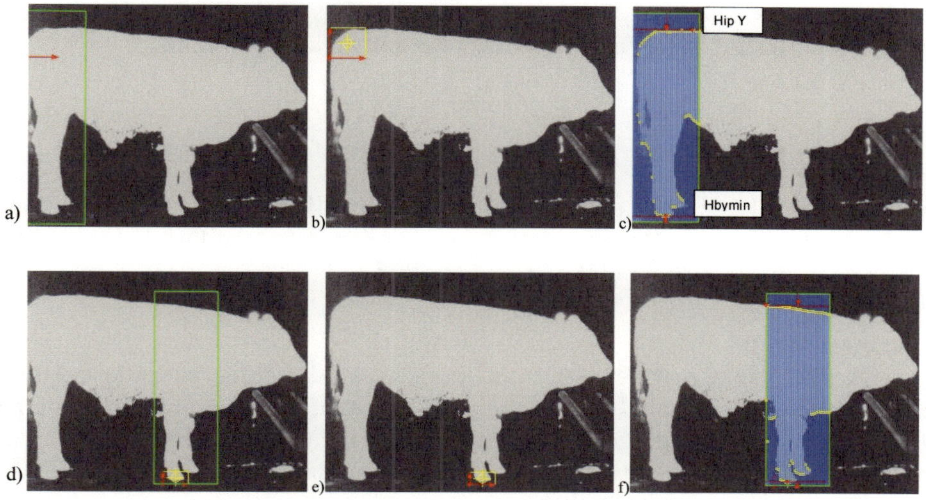

Fig. 7. Image processing to obtain the body dimensions; a) root tail ROI, b) fixing new root coordinate, c) hip height measurement, d) wither ROI, e) fixing front hoof coordinates, f)wither height measurement.

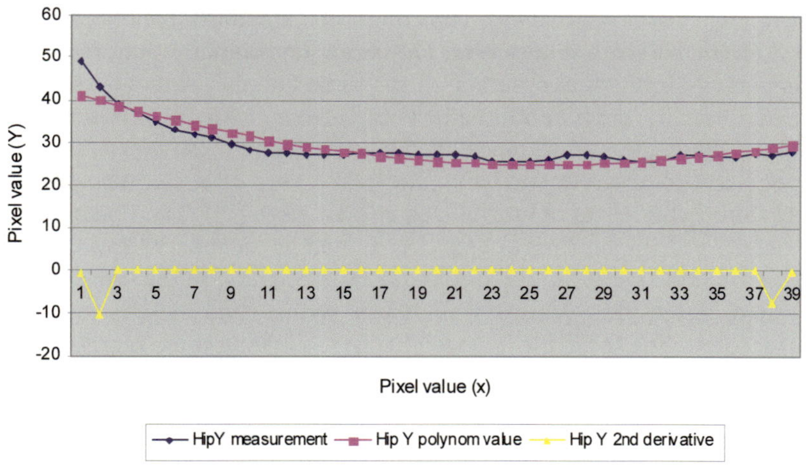

Fig. 8. A second-polynomial mathematical model (red) for detecting the hip on the boundary layer (white).

6.3 Procedure for measuring hip

As seen from the Fig. 7c, the hip height (*Hh*) was defined as a vertical distance between the *HipY* and the bottom part of the back hoof (Hby_{min}), which had to be located from the root tail ROI.

6.4 Locate wither procedure

Before determination of the wither height (*Wh*), the wither point (*WitY*) was found on the upper part of the boundary layer first. A wither was assumed to be a local maximum point inside the wither ROI. Therefore another polynomial mathematical model was developed, which fit the real wither accurately. After processing the first derivate of *Y* points on such model, the minimum extreme points were calculated (yellow line) and compared to measured data according to the following relational and logical operations:

$$Wy_{max} \quad y'_{(i)}=0 \text{ and } y_{(i-1)} < y_{(i)} < y_{(i+1)} \tag{2}$$

6.5 Measure wither

A wither was defined as a vertical distance between wither (*WitY*) and the most bottom part of the front hoof (Hfy_{min}) on the boundary layer. As seen from the Fig. 7f, this point was assumed to be the most bottom point of the wither ROI.

6.6 Calculating weight

On the basis of the eight-year data set, three models for calculating the cattle weight were developed, which include main body characteristics of each animal of the given Simmental herd. Since, in the period of progeny test all cattle were in fact sons of eight cattle sire lines, the herd was genetically relative unique. Thus, the applied data served excellently for evaluating our group of experimental animals.

As already reported by Enevoldsen & Kristensen (1997) and Heinrichs et al. (1992) measurement of heart-girth (chest circumference) was commonly used to estimate dairy heifer body weight from previously derived equations or tables. However, many experiments showed that variability of heart girth measurements depended significantly from the weighing classes (42–590 kg). Thus measured standard deviations can varied from 2.19 cm to 2.74 cm within one observer. However, repeatability between two heart-girth measurements by an individual observer on the same animal using a blind heart girth tape was >0.99. additionally correlation coefficients between two measurements by different observers using blind measuring tapes on the same animal also were >0.99, with 99% of total differences due to observer and heifer, indicating very little random variation.

Based on previous experiences of Enevoldsen & Kristensen (1997) and Heinrichs et al. (1992) the wither height and the hip height was determined as most significant body dimensions for estimating the cattle body weight also in our experiment with thermal camera and image analysis system. From this reason we choose wither and height measures as most convenient for estimating the cattle live weight. The following three regression models were chosen to be investigated:

$$\text{(BW 1) } Bw = -1072.47+12.47*Wh \qquad R^2=0.89 \ (p<0.01) \tag{3}$$

$$\text{(BW 2) } Bw = -1277.40+13.50*Rh \qquad R^2=0.93 \ (p<0.01) \tag{4}$$

$$\text{(BW 3) } Bw = -1236.50+3.01*Wh+10.301*Rh \qquad R^2=0.93 \ (p<0.01) \tag{5}$$

Various commercial programs for performing the above described procedure exist. For our research the IMAQ Vision 7.1. and Labview 7.0. from National Instruments® were used in our research. Statistical analyses of results obtained manually and by thermal imaging were performed using SPSS Package Program 13.0.

7. Accuracy of the thermal image procedure

The summary statistics for means, standard deviations and coefficient of variation for whither height and hip height of the experimental Simmental cattle at different age of animals are presented in the Table 1. In the Table 2 the mean cattle weight estimation is represented on the basis of three regression models BW 1, BW 2 and BW3, respectively which clearly show that the body weight of animals was better predicted with all models from the middle period of testing than at the first two measurements.
Also Wilson et al. (1992) reported better results for week 16 than week 8 and 4, whenever testing the Holstein veal calves for the period of 14 weeks. Thus, it was suggested for the future experiments to take BW 3 model with the wither height and hip height input parameters as most accurate for estimating weight of young cattle at the average age of 139 days.
At the second weighting (day 207) all three models overestimated the BW most however, the BW 1 model most closely fit the measured data. For all successive weightings the BW was estimated equally with all models, while for the last measurement at day 449, the SD for BW 1 was slightly higher than for the other two. Although the BW 1 resulted in the smallest absolute difference from the weighted BW again, it is seen from the SD values that additional body dimensions need to be introduced into future models for this particular age of animals.

AGE	Wh_m			Wh_e			Hh_m			Hh_t		
(days)	$\bar{x}$	SD	CV	$\bar{x}$	SD	CV	$\bar{x}$	SD	CV	$\bar{x}$	SD	CV
139	102	3.54	3.47	102	5.81	5.70	109	3.21	2.94	109	6.04	5.54
207	107	4.83	4.51	112	4.12	3.68	115	3.57	3.10	120	2.74	2.28
261	116	3.23	2.78	120	3.73	3.11	122	3.22	2.64	126	3.28	2.60
317	122	2.92	2.39	125	3.91	3.13	129	2.3	1.78	129	3.09	2.40
380	129	3.19	2.47	128	3.12	2.44	133	3.06	2.30	134	2.92	2.18
401	128	4.01	3.13	130	2.45	1.88	135	3.71	2.75	135	2.34	1.73
449	133	3.27	2.46	132	1.92	1.45	138	3.21	2.33	137	1.50	1.09
R^2	0.7479*						0.7554**					

** - $p<0.01$, Wh_m wither height manually, Wh_e wither height estimated, Hh_m hip height manually, Hh_e hip height estimated

Table 1. Mean wither height (Wh) and hip height (Hh) of Simmental cattle measured manually and estimated with thermal camera at different ages (n=24)

The established correlation coefficients for estimating the body weight on the basis of our three models are very close to results of Enevoldsen & Kristensen (1997) on Danish Frisien and Jersey cows, whereby the established R^2 varied between 0.80 and 0.89. Moreover, the results of our linear regression models correspond very well with the linear models developed by Wilson et al. (1997) for measuring the body weight of special-fed Holstein veal calves, the established R^2 was 0.73 for the wither height and 0.89 for the hip height, respectively. Knowing that several hundred animals were manually measured in both experiments, the thermography and image analysis procedure is feasible and an equivalent method sufficient for predicting the body weight on live animals.

Furthermore, when comparing the results of our experiment with Heinrichs et al. (1992), who on a much bigger sample of experimental heifers, undoubtedly established better correlations for hip height (R^2=0.95), for wither height (R^2=0.94) and for both dimensions together (R^2=0.98), the indirect estimating of body weight from images still represents an accurate procedure to be evaluated also in other breeds and fodder conditions.
The high correlation indicates that all three models applied in the research estimated the cattle weight accurately during the whole observing period, although a little difference between all of them appeared at a specific age of cattle.

AGE	BWm (kg)		BW 1 (kg)			BW 2 (kg)			BW 3 (kg)		
days	$\bar{x}$	SD	$\bar{x}$	SD	Index BW1/ BWm	$\bar{x}$	SD	Index BW2/ BWm	$\bar{x}$	SD	Index BW3/ BWm
139	181	31,19	193	72,42	110	190	81,58	105	189	79,48	104
207	254	38,78	318	51,27	125	346	37,01	136	339	39,56	133
261	356	46,98	420	46,53	118	424	44,27	119	423	44,27	119
317	450	35,9	481	48,66	107	470	41,68	104	473	42,76	105
380	498	26,68	522	38,91	105	527	39,37	106	527	39,28	106
401	528	51,15	551	30,57	104	550	31,54	104	551	30,93	104
449	594	30,29	573	23,94	96	568	20,27	96	570	20,75	96
R^2			0,796**			0,792**			0,798**		

** - p<0,01
BWm body weight manually
BW 1 estimated body weight with model 1
BW 2 estimated body weight with model 2
BW 3 estimated body weight with model 3

Table 2. Mean body weight of experimental Simmental cattle measured manually and estimated with three models at different ages (n=24).

The high regression statistics indicate that all models applied in the research estimated the bull weight accurately across the whole observing period, although the BW2 models with Hh as the input parameter appeared to be more precise. The system was proven to facilitate fast, frequent investigation of bulls even in the growing pens without painful stress for the whole herd. However, for extended on-line application in the open field, introduction of the specific BW2 models is preferable to BW1. Thus, for measuring the Wh, a steadier posture of the animal during image capture is required, which is relatively difficult to achieve. This procedure proved to be particularly difficult with young bulls till day 340 since these animals were rather wild in the pens and during measuring on the scales. However, additional optimising of the chosen parameters measured by the thermal camera could even improve predictions of the live weight of young animals.
The system was proved to enable a faster investigation of cattle frequently even in the growing pens without painful stress for the whole herd. However, for wider on-line application in the open field, the introduction of the simplest BW 1 with the Hh is preferred, since the measuring of Wh requires better positioning of the animal during capture with the camera, which is relatively difficult to achieve. This procedure was shown particularly

difficult with young cattle until day 340 that were still very wild in the pens and during measuring on the scales.

8. Acknowledgement

The authors acknowledge the vital contributions made by the following colleagues: Marko Ocepek, who was responsible for the manual measurements, Petra Eker the head of the stable and stableman Aleš Pauman, who were always willing to help during the measurements on the scale.

9. References

Brandl, N. & Jørgensen, E. (1996). Determination of live weight of pigs from dimensions measured using image analysis. Computers and electronics in agriculture. 15., 52-72, ISSN 0168-1699

Cepon, M.; Klopcic, M., Potocnik, K., Zgur, S. & Dovc, P. (2006). Technical rules and description of methods for measuring and calculating production and other properties and methods for predicting genetic values for pure breed reproductive cattle in Slovenia, Biotechnical Faculty, Zootechnical department, Domžale.

Cveticanin, D. & Wendl, G. (2004). Dynamic weighing of dairy cows: using a lumped-parameter model of cow walk. *Comput. Electron. Agric.*, 44., 63–69, ISSN 0168-1699

de Haer, L.C.M. & Merks, J.W.M. (1992). Patterns of daily food intake in growing pigs. *Anim. Prod.*, 54., 95–104, ISSN 0003-3561

de Koning K. & Rodenburg, J. (2004). Automatic milking: state of the art in Europe and North America. In: *Automatic Milking*. A Better Understanding, Meijering A; Hogeveen H; deKoning C. J. A. M., (Ed.), 27–41, Wageningen Academic Publishers, ISSN 0168-1699, Wageningen

Enevoldsen, C. & Kristensen, T. (1997). Estimation of Body Weight from Body size measurements and body condition scores in dairy cows. *Journal of Dairy Science*, 80., 9., 1988-1995, ISSN 0022-0302

Gibb, D.J. & McAllister, T.A. (1999). The impacts of feed intake and feeding behaviour of cattle on feedlot and feedbunk management, *Proceedings of the 20th Western Nutrition Conference on Marketing to the 21st Century*, pp. 101–116

Heinrichs, A.J.; Rogers, G.W. & Copper, J.B. (1992). Predicting body weight and wither height in Holstein using body measurements. *Journal of Dairy Science*, 75., 12., 3546-3581, ISSN 0022-0302

Kmet, J.; Sakowski, T., Huba, J., Peskovicova, D., Chrenek, J. & Polak, P. (2000). Application of video image analysis in the slaughter value estimation of live Simmental bulls. *Archiv für Tierzucht*, 43., 4., 411-416, ISSN 0003-9438

Kogel, S. & Utz, J. (1988). Wie gut eigenen sich Fleckviehbullen fur Gebrauchskreuzungen. *Tierzuchter*, 40., 385-388, ISSN 0040-7364

Kräußlich, H. (1994). *Tierzuchtungslehre*. Verlag Eugen Ulmer, ISBN 3-8001-4371-2, Stuttgart

Pastell, M.; Takko, H., Gröhn, H., Hautala, M., Poikalainen, V., Praks, J., Veermäe, I., Kujala, M. & Ahokas, J. (2006). Assessing cows' welfare: weighing the cow in a milking robot. *Biosyst. Eng.*, 93., 1., 81–87, ISSN 1537-5110

Rousing, T.; Bonde, M., Badsberg, J.H. & Sørensen, J.T. (2004). Stepping and kicking behaviour during milking in relation to response in human-animal interaction test and clinical health in loose housed dairy cows. *Livest. Prod. Sci.*, 88., 1–8, ISSN 0301-6226

Schaefer, A.L. & Tong, A.K. (1998). Process for determining a tissue composition characteristic of an animal. Patent number PCT/CA1998/000209

Schofeld, C. P. (1993). Image analysis for non-intrusive weight and activity monitoring of live pigs. In: *Proceedings of the 4th International Symposium on Livestock Environment*, pp. 503-510, ISBN 0929355415,University of Warwick, England, ASAE Publication

Schwartzkopf-Genswein, K.S.; Atwood, S. & McAllister, T.A. (2002). Relationships between bunk attendance, intake and performance of steers and heifers on varying feeding regimes. *Appl. Anim. Behav. Sci.*, 76., 3., 179–188, ISSN 0168-1591

Sowell, B.F.; Bowman, J.G.P, Branine M.E. & Hubbard, M.E. (1998). Radio frequency technology to measure feeding behavior and health of feedlot steers. *Appl. Anim. Behav. Sci.*, 59., 277–284, ISSN 0168-1591

Stajnko, D.; Brus, M. & Hočevar, M. (2008). Estimation of bull live weight through thermo graphically measured body dimensions *Computers and Electronics in Agriculture*, 61., 2., May 2008, 233-240, ISSN 0168-1699

White, R.P.; Schofield, C.P., Green, D.M., Parsons, D.J. & Whittemore, C.T. (2004). The effectiveness of a Visual Image Analysis (VIA) system for monitoring the performance of growing/finishing pigs. *Anim. Sci.*, 78, 409–418, ISSN 1357-7298

Willeke, H. & Dürsch, T. (2002). Prediction of the body weight of Simmental heifers using heart girth measurements. *Archiv für Tierzucht*, 45., 1., 23-28, ISSN 0003-9438

Wilson, L.L.; Egan, C.L. & Terosky, T.L. (1997). Body measurements and body weights of special-fed Holstein Veal Calves. *Journal of Dairy Science*, 80., 11., 3077-3082, ISSN 0022-0302

Group Tracking Algorithm for Crowded Scene

Mohd Rizal Arshad and Umair Soori
Underwater Robotics Research Group (URRG), Universiti Sains Malaysia
Malaysia

1. Introduction

Automatic visual monitoring systems gain more significance as the enhancement of high speed processors that are able to execute the prolonged algorithm efficiently. Video surveillance monitoring systems are typically applied to study human behavior in a crowded situation. It is used to observe posture, movement, trajectories and the interaction between people. For this purpose CCD cameras are installed at many crowded places. Most researchers' work however is focused on the people classification and the recognition of activities. Human identification is important because of a need of surveillance in the crowded scenes. Group motion tracking is applied to monitor the Groups of People (GOP) as single entities in the global flow rather than monitoring each person individually. It has been studied on the basis of dynamic movement and the surrounding of crowd density which will affect the speed of an individual/group. Large crowd flow perhaps causes deadly accidents if large numbers of GOP smash into each other in narrow passageways, streets or bridges. The system must identify multiple GOP within their global flow according to their Spatio-temporal characteristics. Figure 1 illustrates the density of large crowd flow. The Religious and Sport activities are the application examples. According to Crowd Dynamics Ltd, (Crowd Dynamics Ltd) in the year of 2006, 363 pilgrims lost their lives while performing the Hajj. There are a number of readily available wide area surveillance systems but most of the systems are not suitable for high density crowd monitoring. For safety surveillance of large crowd, there should be a system which can detect and track unstable GOP by careful monitoring of crowd and display results in real-time scenario. And, with the results being displayed in real-time, it will certainly assist the system's operator to make better decision.

(a) (b) (c) (d)

Fig. 1. Examples of large crowd flow, (a) New York City Marathon (b) Stoning stage in Makkah (c) Dense Traffic and (d) Fish Schooling

The literature on large crowd flow has got a less coverage from researchers. In the case of large crowd flow scenarios, such as huge flow of peoples as in religious ceremonies or in sport activates, where the flow of crowd have so many individuals or small numbers of groups. On this, commonly used processing techniques cannot be utilized for such uncertain conditions. Dense or huge crowded scenes have so many individuals and groups that pose considerably constraints on these current pre-processing techniques. Ali and Shah (2007) describes crowd flow segmentation.

The basic concept which they have used is the Lagrangian particle dynamics to uncover the spatial organization of the flow field generated by crowd flow. Their work is focussed on the crowd flow segmentation, rather than detection and tracking groups of people in a large crowd flow. Their technique is an off-line technique. They generated one mean field from sequence of images to perform the analysis.

The main objective of this research work is to develop an efficient monitoring system which can detect and track GOP within a huge crowd, with accurate and computationally efficient manner. A high density crowd flow may exhibits some basic properties of fluid flow. Techniques available in fluid mechanics can be applied to study the flow properties of GOP moving in a large crowd. Previously, crowd flow has been treated as fluid flow to study crowd behavior. The majority of research done in Computational Fluid Dynamics CFD is Eulerian and Lagrangian analysis. Eulerian analyses examine fixed points in space in a fluid flow, while Lagrangian analyses examine individual particles paths. Technically, global large crowd flow has many similar characteristics as the fluid flow. When coherent structures are studied in terms of its quantities as a consequence of crowd flow trajectories, they are named as Lagrangian Coherent Structures or LCS. The LCS separates the flow of distinct behavior by managing the boundaries where flow field experiencing the different dynamics. This flow boundary in unsteady flows was introduced in a series of papers by Haller (Haller (2001), Haller (2005a) and Haller (2005b)) the boundaries are referred as Lagrangian coherent structures (LCS). New method to evaluate LCS is Finite-Time Lyapunov Exponent field (FTLE) was developed by Shadden (Shadden *et al.* (2005, Shadden (2006)). Davies *et al.* (1995) presents the image processing techniques for monitoring crowd behavior. Another idea is to treat the crowd flow as a fluid dynamic, the crowd turbulence is used to study the physics of crowd disasters (Helbing *et al.* 2007). The density of crowd is an important isotropic quantity that appears to determine the probability of a deadly accident. The crowd flow contains two types of tragedies that is trampling and crushing of pedestrians (Lee and Roger 2005) Trampling occurs when pedestrians are in motion. Crushing usually occur when a moving crowd have a contact with a stationary crowd. The crowd motion organization phenomena such as the directional separation, lane formation, direction towards bottlenecks and stop-and-go type of flow also creates critical conditions. (Helbing *et al.* 2007b).

In crowded scenarios, the focus is on detecting and tracking groups in a global flow rather than in studying individual motion. In this circumstance, Lagrangian Coherent Structure is the most appropriate method. Lagrangian Coherent Structure or LCS is frequently used in fluid mechanics applications in order to distinguish the fluid flow and its associated characteristics. The basic inspiration to used LCS on crowd flow is to treat a flow as a single entity globally, and to track the unstable groups inside the flow. LCS can be computed in different ways, but Finite Time Lyapunov Exponent or FTLE field is the chosen approach (Shadden 2006) since it gives maximum stretching of the nearby particles.

2. Theoretical background

2.1 Lagrangian Coherent Structures LCS

The idea of Lagrangian coherent structures (LCS) stems from dynamical systems which have been extensively used in fluid dynamics analysis. LCS has also been used in the analysis of phase space of systems on the velocity vector field. Coherent motion is defined as a region at which at least one essential flow variable shows important correlation with another variable over a range of space and time Shadden (Shadden *et al.* 2005, Shadden 2006).

When coherent structures are studied in terms of its quantities as a consequence of crowd flow trajectories, they are named as Lagrangian Coherent Structures (LCS). The LCS is defined as ridges in the FTLE field. Ridges are the boundaries between the flows of distinct dynamics. The boundary can be determined by tracking flow particles and searching for the material lines that are named *separatrices*. It has effectively been utilized to partition the flow regions for different dynamics. The technical definition of LCS states that where the gradient of the FTLE field is normal to the eigenvector with the minimum eigenvalue of the Hessian matrix, a scalar field is formed that is the LCS Shadden (2006). The LCS is an invented boundary through which the amount of two or more fluids cannot pass to each other. All the particles within the divided region have similar behavior, known as coherent behavior.

In the case of time dependent systems, the crowd flow can be classified as stable and unstable manifolds of hyperbolic fixed points as coherent structures. But typically, one uses the notion of coherent structures in the context of more general flows. Modeling of a dynamical system in a LCS scene gives boundaries in the spatiotemporal separating region. This organization dynamically separates the distinct behavior in the crowd flow which is unseen in the velocity vector field. The boundaries of flow region can be determined by tracking the flow particles during advection which will indicate the material lines. Thus, flow regions with different characteristics would be highlighted. This flow boundary in unsteady flows was introduced in a series of papers by Haller (Haller 2001, Haller 2005a and Haller 2005b). These boundaries are referred to as Lagrangian Coherent Structures (LCS).

A vector field can be represented as a set of LCS. This LCS has sub regions in which each region contains similar behavior with respect to the crowd flow. The LCS reflects the large scale analysis of a vector field since they are based on the integration of trajectories. At each point in space, the LCS measures the rate of separation of neighboring particle and its trajectories. The LCS of unsteady fields usually distorts and shifts over time, but it still can be recognized. In fluid dynamics, LCS boundaries are the higher ridges of Finite Time Lyapunov Exponent Fields. This ridge refers to material surfaces that get advected with the crowd flow and move towards regions where the flow is separated in positive or negative time. The flow is separated along these boundaries surfaces.

The Lyapunov exponent measures the behavior of the flow particles in a dynamical system. It quantifies the exponential rate of convergence or divergence between particles of the neighboring trajectories in a global sense. A positive exponent involves divergence, and a negative one means convergence. Therefore, a system with positive exponents has positive information in that trajectories that are initially close together move at a distance over time. The more positive the exponent, the faster they separate. In the same way for negative exponents, the trajectories move together with each other. A system with both positive and negative Lyapunov exponents is said to be chaotic.

2.2 Finite-Time Lyapunov Exponent field (FTLE)

A new method to evaluate LCS is Finite-Time Lyapunov Exponent field (FTLE) was developed by Shadden (Shadden *et al.* 2005, Shadden 2006). The LCS can be calculated in various ways. One of these methods is based on the FTLE field. It evaluates a value that corresponds to how quickly two imaginary particles would separate from each other as the flow progresses. It measures the maximum linearized growth rate of the distance perturbation between the nearby flow particles over the time interval to its trajectories. In other words, it measures the rate at which two neighboring particles diverge from each other at a given location and time interval. The FTLE differentiates the amount of flow particle stretching about the trajectory over time. It is defined by the local maxima of the FTLE field which specifies regions with distinct dynamics in the flow Haller (2001).

Let us suppose that the flow field experienced distinct dynamics in two or more different regions of the same flow. Within each sub region, FTLE contains a coherent motion in the flow that is all the particles inside each region contain a similar behavior which is indicated by the Eigenvalue of λ_{max} (Δ) close to zero. The boundary of two flow region contains different dynamics in which particles at these boundaries encloses as incoherent behavior. This condition creates higher Eigenvalue which rises as boundaries in FTLE field. The maximum stretching of particles is given by the square root of the largest eigenvalue. As the stretching is produced by velocity vector field, it would increase exponentially with the time series. The logarithm of the resulting value is computed and additionally normalized by the absolute advection time $|T|$. This leads to the explanation of the FTLE field. The notation (formulation) of the FTLE will be defined in section 2.3.

The FTLE indicates sections in the flow with different dynamics due to flow particle pairs straddling the edges of the boundary that separate them. This is also to indicate that they are faster than other arbitrary flow particle pairs. Area of maximum material stretching generates local maxima of the velocity field that may specify either local maximal stretching or local maximal shear. Trajectories of the flow particles can be integrated in negative or positive time. This is similar to the scalar parameters in a flow gathering in the coherent structures which can be achieved from the flow vector field. Consequently, FTLE can be calculated by integrating trajectories in backward time ($T < 0$). The ridges in the FTLE field indicate attracting material lines or attracting Lagrangian coherent structures (attracting LCS) Shadden (2006).Integrating trajectories in forward time ($T > 0$) produce FTLE ridges that spot the location of distinct flow as material lines, or repelling Lagrangian coherent structures (repelling LCS).

These positive-time and negative-time LCS are defined as the boundary between qualitatively different regions in the flow. The integration time can be increased or decreased depending on the amount of feature required from the computation. In addition, the location of the ridge indicating the boundary of the dissimilar flow of crowd does not change.

2.3 Formulation of FTLE

Let the open set $D \subset \mathbb{R}^2$ be the domain of the flow of crowd under study. Given a time dependent velocity field $\mathbf{v}(\mathbf{x},t)$ defined on D. Categorize a trajectory of $x(t;t_0,x_0)$ which is starting at point $\mathbf{x}_0 \in D$ at time t_0 to be the solution of

$$\begin{cases} \dot{\mathbf{x}}(t;t_0,\mathbf{x}_0) = \mathbf{v}(\mathbf{x}(t;t_0,\mathbf{x}_0),t), \\ \mathbf{x}(t_0;t_0,\mathbf{x}_0) = \mathbf{x}_0 \end{cases} \tag{1}$$

The velocity field $\mathbf{v}(\mathbf{x},t)$ is satisfying the continuity assumptions C^0 in time and C^2 in space, where C^0 assumption is responsible for smoothness of the flow field. A trajectory of a particle $\mathbf{x}(t;t_0,\mathbf{x}_0)$ depends on the initial position, x_0, and the initial time, t_0, to its final position at time T. From velocity field $\mathbf{v}(\mathbf{x},t)$ and its continuity assumptions, it follows that trajectory $\mathbf{x}(t;t_0,\mathbf{x}_0)$ is C^1 in time and C^3 in space. The solution of the dynamic system, as defined in equation (1), is viewed as a map from their position x_0 at time t_0 to their position at time t. This is referred to as a *flow map,* and denoted by $\phi_{t_0}^{t}$, and it satisfies equation (2)

$$\phi_{t_0}^{t} : D \to D : \mathbf{x}_0 \mapsto \phi_{t_0}^{t}(\mathbf{x}_0) = \mathbf{x}(t;t_0,\mathbf{x}_0) \tag{2}$$

Furthermore, flow map $\phi_{t_0}^{t}$ satisfies the following properties as shown in equation (3) and (4)

$$\phi_{t_0}^{t}(\mathbf{x}) = \mathbf{x}, \tag{3}$$

$$\phi_{t_0}^{t+s}(\mathbf{x}) = \phi_{s}^{t+s}(\phi_{t_0}^{s}(\mathbf{x})) = \phi_{s}^{t+s}(\phi_{t_0}^{t}(\mathbf{x})) \tag{4}$$

here s defined as a arbitrary constant, but fixed $s \in \mathbb{R}$ (Theorem 3.1, [1]). Now, after a time interval T passes, advection of particles moves from $\phi_{t_0}^{t}$ to $\phi_{t_0}^{t_0+T}$ to calculate the amount of stretching to its trajectory, consider the evolution of the perturbed point illustrated in equation (5)

$$\mathbf{y} = \mathbf{x} + \delta\mathbf{x}(0) \tag{5}$$

Where $\delta\mathbf{x}(0)$ is infinitesimal and arbitrarily oriented. After a time interval T, this perturbation becomes Equation (6)

$$\delta\mathbf{x}(t_0+T) = \phi_{t_0}^{t_0+T}(\mathbf{y}) - \phi_{t_0}^{t_0+T}(\mathbf{x}) = \frac{d\phi_{t_0}^{t_0+T}(\mathbf{x})}{d\mathbf{x}}\delta\mathbf{x}(0) + O(\|\delta\mathbf{x}(0)\|^2) \tag{6}$$

Since $\delta\mathbf{x}(t_0)$ is infinitesimal, the method can assume that the $O(\|\delta\mathbf{x}(t_0)\|^2)$ term is negligible, from which the growth of linearized perturbations are obtained. The magnitude of the perturbation is shown in Equation (7)

$$\|\delta\mathbf{x}(t_0+T)\| = \sqrt{\left\langle \delta\mathbf{x}(t_0), \frac{d\phi_{t_0}^{t_0+T}(\mathbf{x})}{d\mathbf{x}}^{*} \frac{d\phi_{t_0}^{t_0+T}(\mathbf{x})}{d\mathbf{x}} \delta\mathbf{x}(t_0) \right\rangle} \tag{7}$$

where * denotes the transpose of matrix of the matrix, while $\frac{d\phi_{t_0}^{t_0+T}(\mathbf{x})}{d\mathbf{x}}$ is the spatial gradient of the flow map.

$$\Delta = \frac{d\phi_{t_0}^{t_0+T}(\mathbf{x})}{d\mathbf{x}}^{*} \frac{d\phi_{t_0}^{t_0+T}(\mathbf{x})}{d\mathbf{x}} \tag{8}$$

In equation (8) Δ is a *finite-time* version of the Cauchy Green deformation tensor. Maximum separation of advected particles initially located at $\mathbf{x}_0$ t_0 when $\delta\mathbf{x}(0)$ is aligned with the eigenvector which is associated with the maximum eigenvalue of Δ, shown in Equation (9)

$$\max_{\delta\mathbf{x}(0)} \|\delta\mathbf{x}(T)\| = \sqrt{\lambda_{\max}(\Delta)}\ \|\overline{\delta\mathbf{x}}(0)\| \tag{9}$$

Now introducing the finite-time Lyapunov exponent (FTLE) $\sigma_t^T(\mathbf{x})$ in Equation (10)

$$\sigma_{t_0}^T(\mathbf{x}) = \frac{1}{|T|} \ln \sqrt{\lambda_{\max}(\Delta)} \tag{10}$$

Equation (10) is of Finite-time Lyapunov exponent (FTLE) with a finite integration time *T*, which is related to point $\mathbf{x}_0 \in D$ at time t_0. This technical and mathematical explanation of FTLE field with respect to eigenvalue is first given by Shadden [2005, 2006]. The FTLE can be described as the flow region experiences distinct dynamics in two or more different areas of the same flow. Within this each region, we have a coherent motion in the flow i.e. all the particles inside each region contain similar behavior which is indicated by the eigenvalue of $\lambda_{\max}(\Delta)$ close to zero. While at the boundary of two regions, having different dynamics, particles at these boundaries having an incoherent behavior, creates higher eigenvalue which are rise as boundaries in FTLE field. The absolute value |T| is used instead of T in Equation (10) for the reason that FTLE can be calculated for T > 0 and T < 0. The material line is called a repelling LCS when (T>0) over the time interval in forward time. On the other hand the material line is called an attracting LCS (T < 0) over the interval in backward time. Repelling and attracting LCS reveals stable and unstable manifolds of a dynamic system.

2.4 Eigenvector parallelism method

Eigenvalues play an important role in conditions where the matrix is a transformation from one vector space onto itself. Systems of linear ordinary differential equations are the primary examples. The values can correspond to frequencies of vibration, or critical values of stability parameters, or energy levels of atoms it has been discussed in more detail by Moler, C. (2008). As mentioned earlier, LCS can be defined as ridges on the flow field where particles show incoherent behavior. This phenomenon can be explained by the existence of higher eigenvalues at certain region of the flow field. These boundaries separate two regions, and are known as separatrices. Moreover the method requires an approach to extract the information from FTLE field, and identify the precise unstable GOP with respect to its surroundings.

In recent years, valuable developments have been made in image segmentation. Several algorithms have been proposed in which Normalized cut algorithm, is one of the method used for image segmentation first proposed by Shi and Malik (2000). This Normalized cut algorithm is also applicable to perform segmentation on the boundaries of FTLE field. One weakness of this algorithm is that, it process at high computational time to produce results. But in this application, the prime goal is to make the algorithm efficient enough to execute in real-time in real world scenarios. This requires fast running algorithm. In order to overcome this problem generalized eigenvalue is utilized to measure vector parallelism, named this phenomenon as Eigenvector Parallelism. This technique calculates eigenvalue divergence on the FTLE boundaries to identify/segment the exact unstable GOP with respect to their global flow. Consequently, it will differentiate the unstable or hazardous GOP's boundaries from its flow boundaries with a low computational time.

2.5 Formulation of Eigenvector Parallelism Method

In Eigenvector Parallelism Method, the technique first correlates the two constitutive mean flow fields RM_u^{u+T} and holds the peak-mean value denoted as PM_u^{u+T} of the vector field F_u^{u+T}. The characteristic Equation of eigenvalues and eigenvectors is given as:

$$\boldsymbol{A}\boldsymbol{x} = \lambda \boldsymbol{x} \tag{11}$$

In Equation (11), λ is an *eigenvalue,* $\boldsymbol{x}$ is an *eigenvector* and the pair (λ, $\boldsymbol{x}$) is called an *eigenpair* for matrix $\boldsymbol{A}$. All eigenvalues and eigenvectors satisfy the Equation (11) for a given matrix, $\boldsymbol{A}$. The generalized eigenvalue is used in this application to determine eigenvalues between PM_u^{u+T} and VR_u^{u+T}. The nontrivial solutions of generalized eigenvalue can be written as

$$\boldsymbol{A}\boldsymbol{x} = \lambda \boldsymbol{B}\boldsymbol{x} \tag{12}$$

In Equation (12), $\boldsymbol{A}$ *and B* are matrices and λ is a scalar eigenvalue. The values of λ satisfy the equation is the generalized eigenvalues and the corresponding values of x are the generalized eigenvectors.

$$\boldsymbol{PM_u^{u+T}}\, \boldsymbol{x} = \lambda\, \boldsymbol{VR_u^{u+T}}\, \boldsymbol{x} \tag{13}$$

Equation (13) corresponds to the peak-mean value and the vector's position where the boundaries arise.

$$(\boldsymbol{VR_u^{u+T}})^{-1}\, (\boldsymbol{PM_u^{u+T}} - \boldsymbol{VR_u^{u+T}}\lambda)\, \boldsymbol{x} = 0 \tag{14}$$

Equation (14) is the simply form of Equation (13). It is a common form of generalized eigenvalue problem.

$$det\, [\, (\boldsymbol{VR_u^{u+T}})^{-1}\, (\boldsymbol{PM_u^{u+T}} - \boldsymbol{VR_u^{u+T}}\lambda)\,] = 0 \tag{15}$$

Equation (15) reveals the Eigenvector Parallelism method. It finds the largest generalized eigenvalue between PM_u^{u+T} and VR_u^{u+T}. If λ, eigenvalue, is greater than high-threshold or less than low-threshold indicates unstable flow whereas if λ lies between the high and low thresholds it indicates the stable flow.

3. Implementation

This section is focused on the implementation of LCS. It requires optical flow which estimates the flow vectors field of the crowd. This flow vectors need filtered data for fine LCS implementation. Advection of particles is calculated by numerical integration method (Forth-order Runge-Kutta-Fehlberg). Flow map is used to map the advection of flow particles. Further on proposed method eigenvector parallelism is applied on the FTLE boundaries to identify the unstable flow. Figure 2 represents a brief overview of the methodology of the system. Steps of implementation process have been briefly described below:

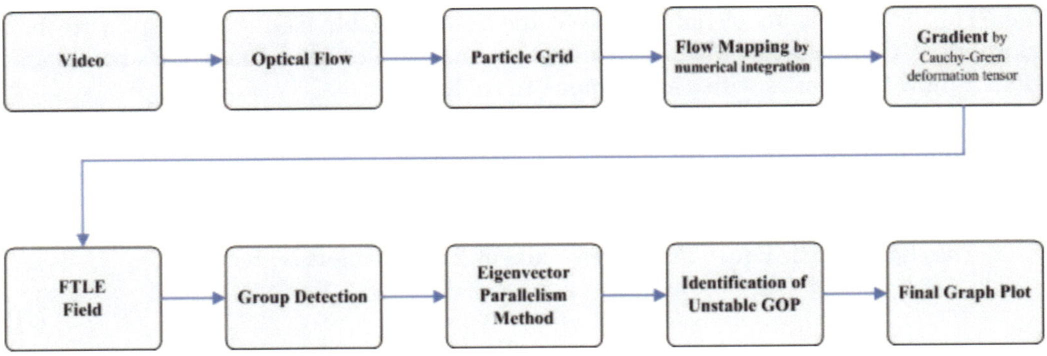

Fig. 2. Conceptual flow chart of the algorithm.

3.1 Optical flow

The input prerequisite for FTLE analysis is the velocity vector field. Optical flow, Lucas-Kanade (Lucas & Kanade 1981) technique is used. This is a two frame differential method to estimate motion in a moving object. This method aims to calculate the motion between two image frames which are taken at times t and $t + 1$ at every pixel location. This method is also frequently known as the differential methods, since it is based on local Taylor series approximations of the image signal. It also uses partial derivatives with respect to the spatial and temporal coordinates.

The term optic flow refers to visual phenomenon that has apparent visual motion that can be experienced as an object move through the world. There is a directly mathematical relationship between the magnitudes of the optical flow. If the speed of motion is doubled, the optic flow will also be double. The optical flow also depends on the angle between the direction of view and the moving objects. Advantages of the optical flow algorithm include that it yields a high density of flow vectors. That is, if the flow information missing in inner parts of homogeneous objects is filled-in from the motion boundaries

3.2 Smoothing of data

Data smoothing is an important process which contributes to simplify the LCS implementation. It is based on Noise Filtering and Mean value. Figure 3 shows the block diagram of data smoothing process. It is very useful technique which exposes the clear picture of obtained results from optical flow. The optical flow field of crowd motion carries

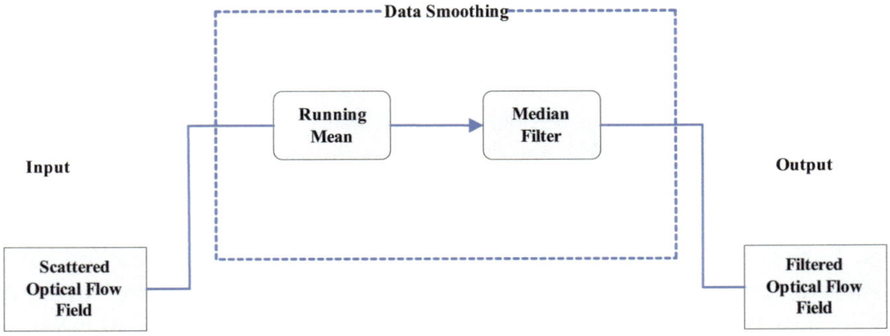

Fig. 3. Block diagram of data smoothing process.

scattered resulting vectors. This is shown in Figures 4 where it is observed that flow vectors of dense crowd have scattered direction and magnitude which is unable to define distinct group behaviors. Data smoothing helps to expose different groups present in the crowd flow by noise reduction and mean flow field.

The task for noise reduction is performed by median filtering, which is a non-linear spatial signal enhancement technique. While mean flow field is calculated by taking mean in time series or running mean. It is commonly defined as the continuing calculation. The degree of smoothness can be controlled by adjustment of the neighborhood range or the fitting weights. F_u denoted as optical flow field under observation and its running mean as RM_u, here u represents the number of frame in real time video sequence. Running means is programmed in this methodology to reset after a few frames, so that FTLE field can exactly identify the true position of the unstable group.

3.3 Advection of particles

In order to detect and track the movement of the flow of crowd, the system launched a Cartesian grid of particles. This movement is known as the advection of particles. These particles are placed on the running mean RM_u of flow field F_u, where particles have certain (constant) distance between them. Initially, particle position is $\mathbf{x}_0$, at time t. As time T passes, flow of crowd change its position therefore, the optical flow field becomes F_u^{u+T} and its running mean RM_u^{u+T}. The final position of particle turn out to be to $\mathbf{x}(t+T;t,\mathbf{x}_0)$. Each particle advection is computed with a forth-order Runge-Kutta-Fehlberg algorithm.

3.3.1 Forth-Order Runge-Kutta-Fehlberg

The Runge–Kutta method is an important tool. It is used to perform the approximation of solutions of ordinary differential equations. There are different types of Runge–Kutta methods, classified by how many points are used within each time step. The method applied in the FTLE computation is the 4th Order Runge–Kutta method. This is the most often used method of the Runge-Kutta family. It extends the idea of the mid-point method by using the information.

The fourth order Runge-Kutta algorithm requires four gradient or "k" terms (as given in equation 16), which can calculate from following equations (17), (18), (19) and (20)

$$y_{n+1} = y_n + \frac{1}{6}(k_1 + 2k_2 + 2k_3 + k_4) \tag{16}$$

$$k_1 = f(y_n, t_n)\Delta t \tag{17}$$

$$k_2 = f(y_n + \frac{k_1}{2}, t_n + \frac{\Delta t}{2})\Delta t \tag{18}$$

$$k_3 = f(y_n + \frac{k_2}{2}, t_n + \frac{\Delta t}{2})\Delta t \tag{19}$$

$$k_4 = f(y_n + k_3, t_n + \Delta t)\Delta t \tag{20}$$

Where k1, k2, k3 and k4 are the gradient of fourth-order Runge-Kutta algorithm. This advection of particles is mapped by flow map. Figure 5 demonstrate the Cartesian grid of particles.

(a)

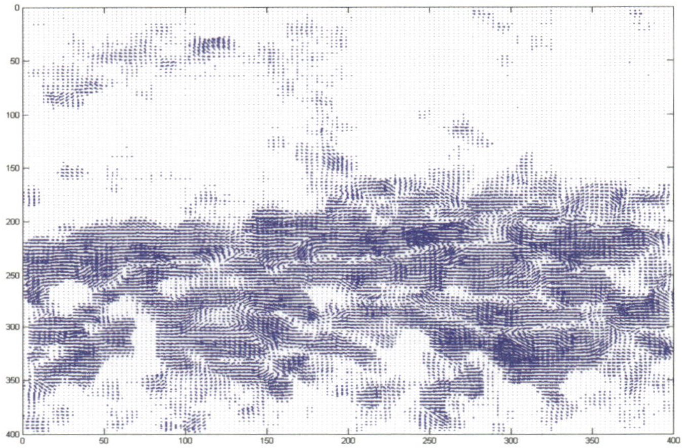

(b)

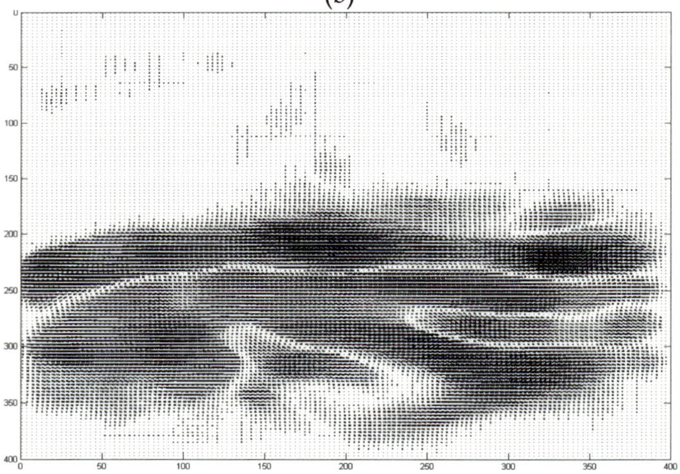

(c)

Fig. 4. The of optical flow result. (a) Video frame of the scene. (b) Optical flow field. (c) Running mean and filtered optical flow field.

For a clear illustration of particle advection, consider the two nearby flow particles, as shown in Figure 5. Initially, at position $\mathbf{x}_0$ $\mathbf{y}_0$, these two arbitrary flow particles are at the sides of the boundary where the dynamical change occurs. As the flow progress to time interval ***T***, these particles quickly separate and diverge from each other. As a result, a boundary is formed. This boundary is referred to as ridges in the FTLE field.

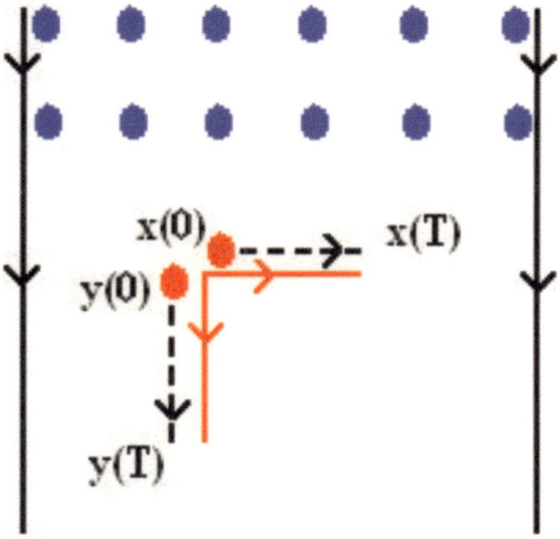

Fig. 5. Two flow particles (red in color) diverge from each other, as a result boundary formed (red in color). While blue circles represents as a grid of particles

3.4 Flow mapping

The flow map is used to map flow particles from its initial position at time *t*, to their final position at time *(t+T)*. Consequently flow map ϕ_x, ϕ_y tracks the positions of *x* and *y* particles respectively, due to the flow field generated by the movement of crowd. Note that the method reset the running mean after few frames in order to get the exact information of moving objects. In this formulation, the time interval *T* represents the next frame in a real-time video sequence. Figure 6 shows the illustration of flow mapping.

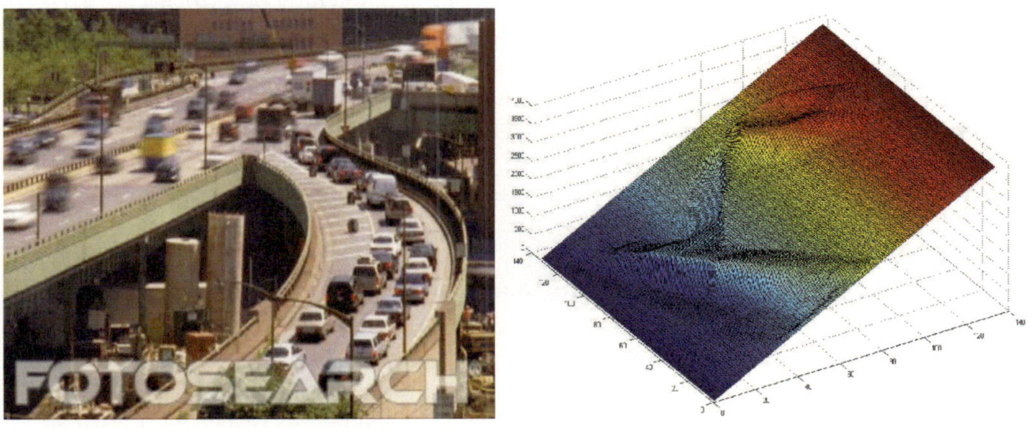

Fig. 6. Illustration of flow mapping. (a) Video frame of the scene. (b) Flow mapping results.

3.5 FTLE field

In order to obtain the FTLE field, the gradient of the flow map has to be calculated. $\frac{d\phi_x}{dx}, \frac{d\phi_x}{dy}, \frac{d\phi_y}{dx}$ and $\frac{d\phi_y}{dy}$ are refer to as spatial gradients. Gradient of flow map can be calculated by Equation (21)

$$\frac{d\phi_t^T}{dt} = \begin{bmatrix} \frac{d\phi_x}{dx} & \frac{d\phi_x}{dy} \\ \frac{d\phi_y}{dx} & \frac{d\phi_y}{dy} \end{bmatrix} \tag{21}$$

$$\frac{d\phi_t^T}{dt}\Big|_{(x_{i,j}(t),y_{i,j}(t))} = \begin{bmatrix} \frac{x_{i+1,j}(t+T)-x_{i-1,j}(t+T)}{x_{i+1,j}(t)-x_{i-1,j}(t)} & \frac{x_{i,j+1}(t+T)-x_{i,j-1}(t+T)}{y_{i,j+1}(t)-y_{i,j-1}(t)} \\ \frac{y_{i+1,j}(t+T)-y_{i-1,j}(t+T)}{x_{i+1,j}(t)-x_{i-1,j}(t)} & \frac{y_{i,j+1}(t+T)-y_{i,j-1}(t+T)}{y_{i,j+1}(t)-y_{i,j-1}(t)} \end{bmatrix} \tag{22}$$

Equation (21) is the extended form of Equation (22) in which finite derivatives with values at the neighboring grid points are used where *(i, j)* denotes position of the point in the FTLE computational grid. This phenomenon was first explained by Shadden (2006). The initial position of grid particles is found to be $x_{i,j}(t), y_{i,j}(t)$. After time T passes, the particles on grid get advected to $x_{i,j}(t+T), y_{i,j}(t+T)$. Figure 7 demonstrate the spatial gradients of the flow map.

Finally, the formulation is ready to be used in calculating the FTLE field in Equation (10). The FTLE returns the edges which are ridges where the crowd flow displays distinct behavior.

Finite-time Lyapunov exponents (FTLE) measure flow particle stretching as it moves with the crowd flow for a given time T. The FTLE field is computed by advection of each sample point $\mathbf{x}_0 \in D$ at time t_0 with the flow for time T. This will result in a flow map ϕ_x, which maps a sample point x_0 to its advected position. The maximum stretching of particles can be computed from the gradient of the flow map. Maximum stretching of particles are given by the eigenvector that belongs to the square root to the largest eigenvalue.

Positive and negative integration time intervals can be used to determine forward and backward time FTLE fields, to create the repelling and attracting LCS. Particle grid is used to determine the region of the flow, where the LCS is located at the appropriate integration time, T. A denser grid for higher spatial resolution calculation will require higher computational cost. Figure 8 show the FTLE results on the running frames.

3.6 Eigenvector parallelism method

This peak-mean value, PM_u^{u+T}, represents the majority vector behavior in the flow field. Note that the method is computing the peak-mean value after every integration length $|T|$, after every frame, in order to update the peak-mean position. Peak-mean value contains the global flow characteristic. It is the dominant flow, and inside it, small GOPs are also propagating. Figure 9 reveal the peak-mean values calculated on its respected flow. It shows the robustness of calculated peak-mean values position wise.

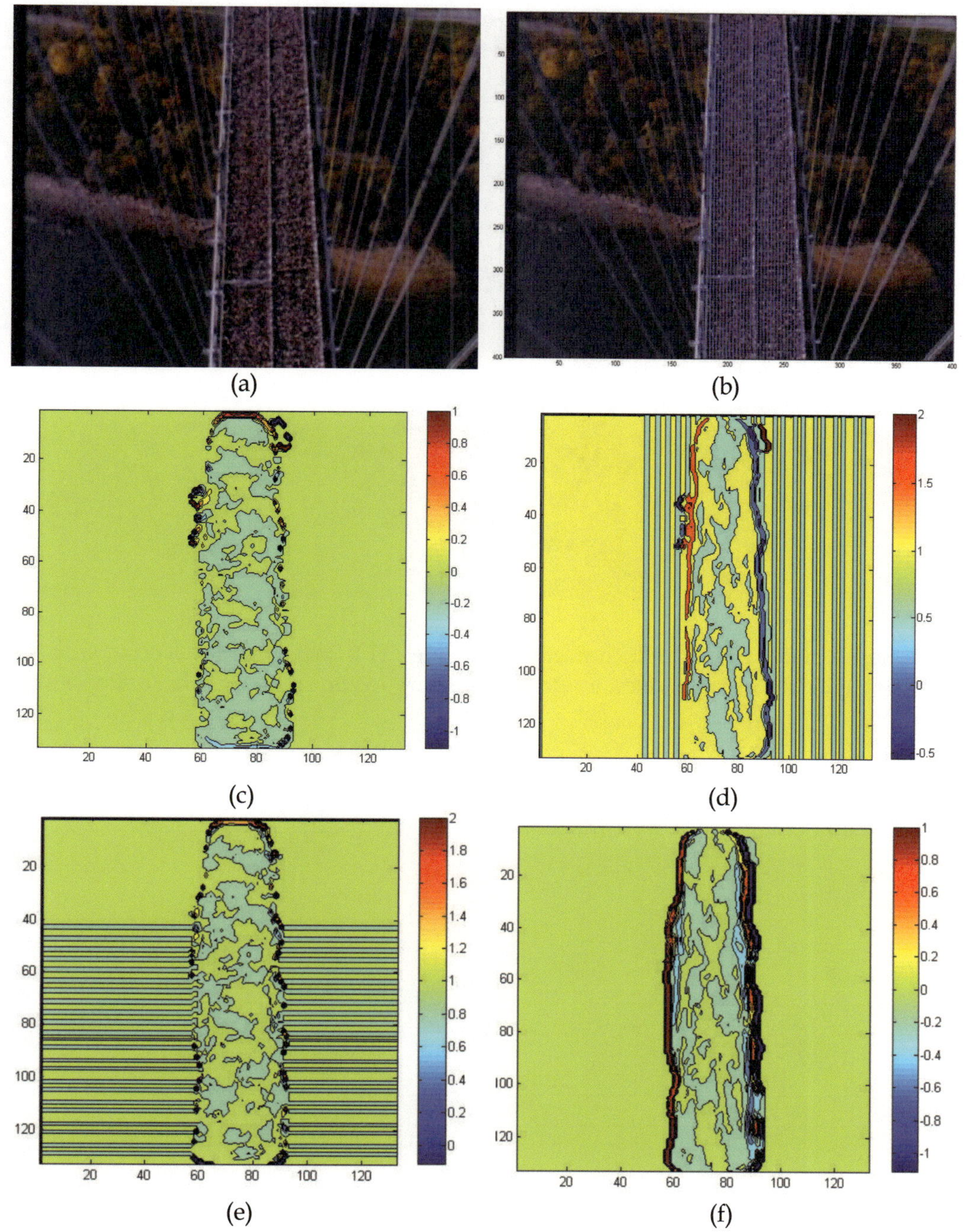

Fig. 7. Result of (a) original video frame. (b) Optical flow field. (c) Gradient of the flow map with respect to $\frac{d\phi_x}{dx}$ (d) Gradient of the flow map with respect to $\frac{d\phi_x}{dy}$ (e) Gradient of the flow map with respect to $\frac{d\phi_y}{dx}$ (f) Gradient of the flow map with respect to $\frac{d\phi_y}{dy}$

(a)

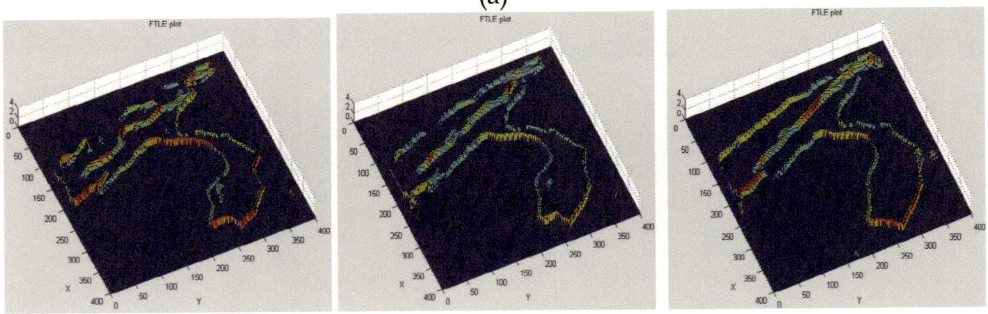

(b)

Fig. 8. Result of (a) original video frames (b) Running FTLE field, boundaries occur where flow having incoherent dynamics, inside the boundary region all particles have similar fate

Fig. 9. The Peak-Mean value zoomed in window of sequence shown in figure 4, red vector represents Peak-Mean value.

The system calculates the eigenvector divergence by computing the eigenvalue between PM_u^{u+T} and on the vectors at same position where the boundary or ridges occur in the FTLE field. This shows significant results in which, the boundaries of FTLE field having incoherent behavior with respect to global flow signify as higher eigenvalue as compared to

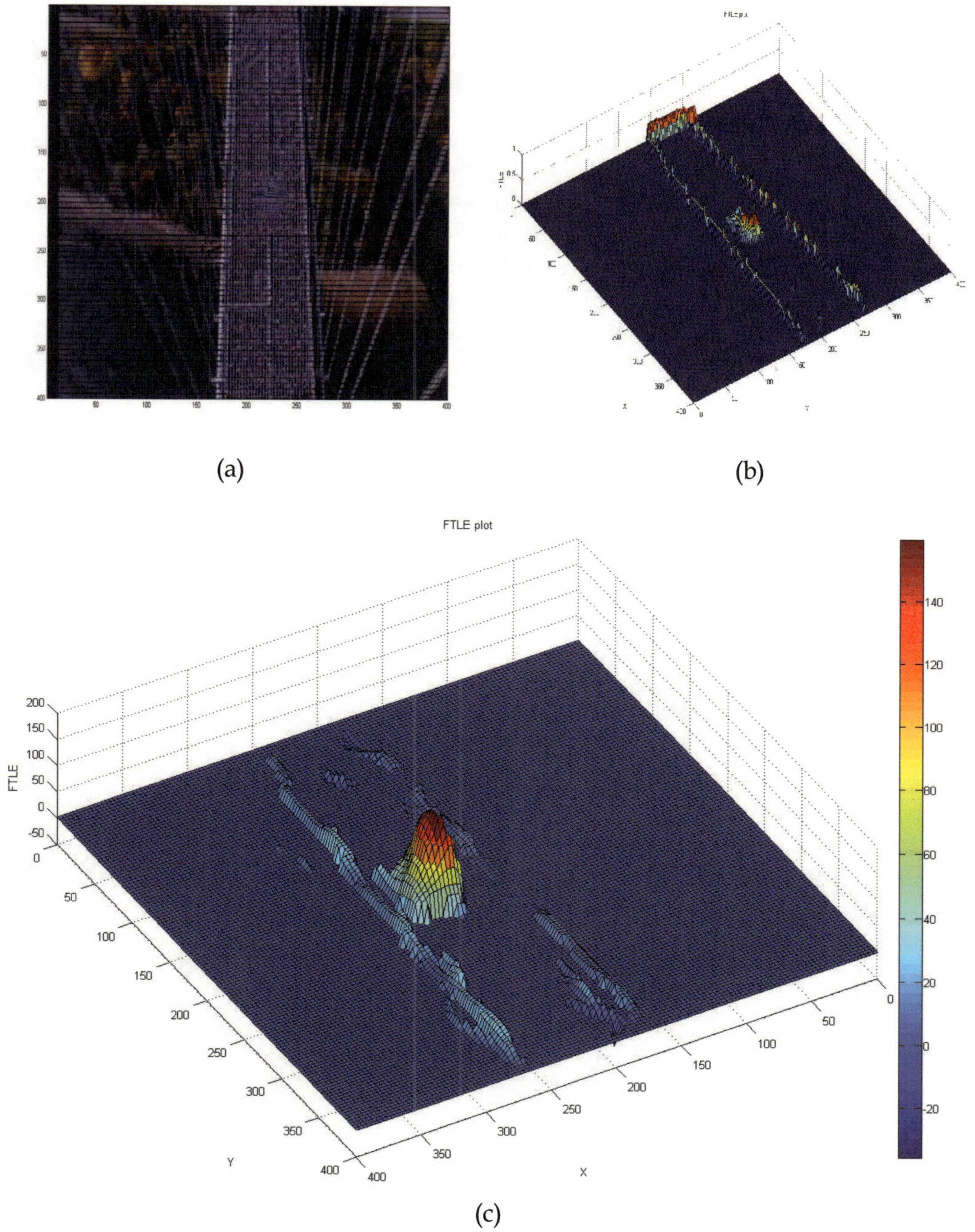

Fig. 10. The eigenvector parallelism method result. (a) Mean field of sequence New York City marathon with synthetic instability which is highlighted by red box. (b) FTLE field of the sequence, where in middle there is another boundary shows the unstable GOP. (c) Eigenvector parallelism method result, where unstable GOP identify by higher eigenvalue.

the entire flow FTLE boundaries eigenvalue. This occurs because vectors at the boundaries of FTLE field of unstable GOP have distinct behaviors. Whereas, PM_u^{u+T} contains the majority behavior in the global flow. When the system computes the eigenvalue between PM_u^{u+T} and the vectors position at boundaries of FTLE field, as a result the stable flow boundaries shows approximately similar characteristic as the peak-mean value. Therefore, the eigenvalue minimize these boundaries, showing evidence of the analogous flow. In other case, unstable GOP boundaries are detected by the FTLE field owing to different dynamics. Vectors at these boundaries give higher eigenvalue when they are computed with PM_u^{u+T}. Figure 10 shows the results of Eigenvector Parallelism Method where unstable GOP is detected as higher eigenvalue.

This approach has been tested by changing the direction of unstable GOP on self introduced instability video sequences, and subsequently, observing the imperative results. As the incoherent or unstable GOP changes its flow direction with respect to the global flow, eigenvalue will be increased. Greater the change in direction of flow vector, higher will be the eigenvalue. It will increase until the vectors aligned at the opposite direction as compare to the peak-mean value. In such case where vectors are aligned in opposite directions, a negative eigenvalues in obtained showing unstable GOP. Figure 11 elucidates the negative eigenvalue of GOP, where GOP contains opposite direction with respect to entire flow.

3.6.1 Identification of unstable groups

Unstable GOP has dissimilar dynamical behavior and LCS is used to track their boundaries. For the convergence of the detected unstable groups, the technique employed a simple scheme to study the neighboring flow. Let the boundary box of detected unstable group under action denoted by $B_{k,l}$, where k, l is its dimensions. At this instance, patch of box $R_{k',l'}$ is launched on the $B_{k,l}$, such that size of k', l' is determined by a ratio. It can be obtained by taking a ratio between the image frames to the detected object. The resulting ratio will be an integer which will increase the dimension of k', l' up to a certain fold. The size of $R_{k',l'}$ is determined by this ratio which is minimizing the computational cost. However different patch size gives different computational cost. A comparison of computational cost is shown in Table 1. In this example, similar detected object is used, in which different ratios are tested in order to calculate the computational costs.

Ratio	20	40	60
Time (sec)	0.0469	0.0625	0.0938

Table 1. Comparison of computational cost at different ratios.

Note here that if k', l' go out to the image boundary, then the method reinstate that side of k',l' to the image frame. The maximum limit of k',l' turn out to be the image frame boundary. The typical example of patch demonstrated in Figure 12(a). This patch contains the information of the neighboring behavior of the vectors in a flow as shown in Figure 12(b). If the patch demonstrates a change in a behavior with respect to the global flow then it reveals that the unstable group exists. However in other case if patch demonstrates the similar behavior with respect to global flow it means that there is no such unstable group exists. Afterwards, the detected boundary box $B_{k,l}$ either detected as instability or merge with the global flow.

(a)

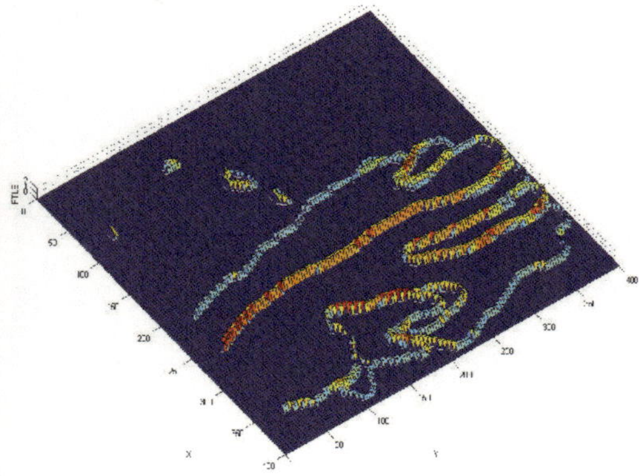

(b)

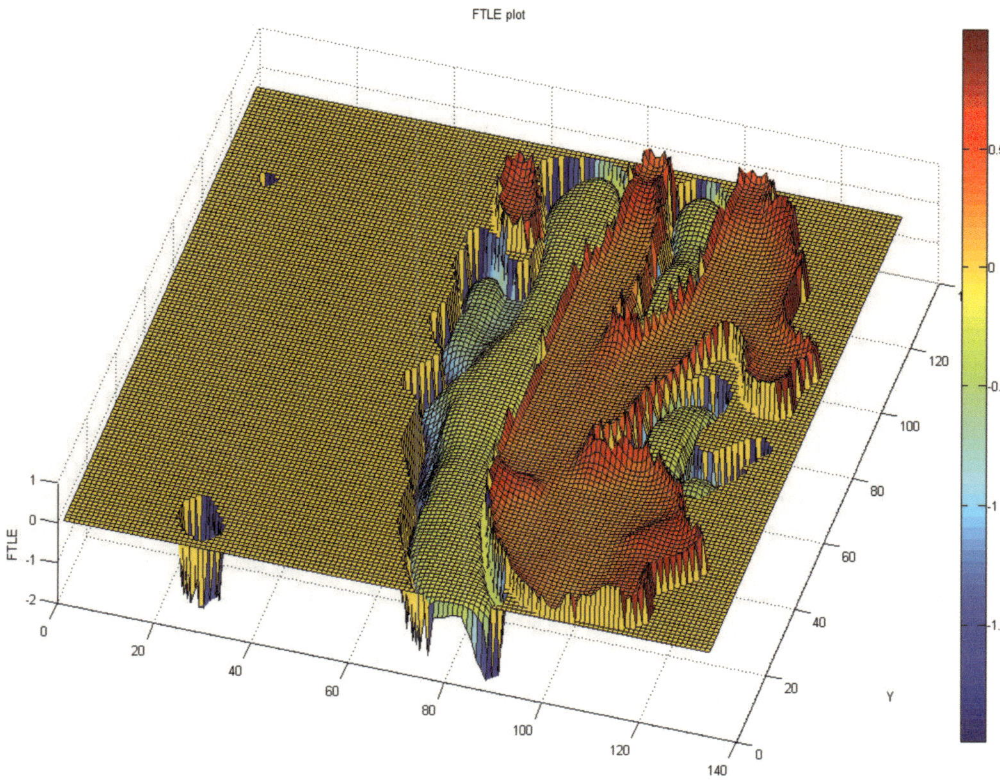

(c)

Fig. 11. The eigenvector parallelism method result (a) Mean field of sequence extracted from the National Geographic documentary, titled 'Inside Mecca' where two GOP propagates inside the big group against the direction, highlighted by red box (b) FTLE field of the sequence (c) Result shows GOP against the direction encloses by less than zero eigenvalue

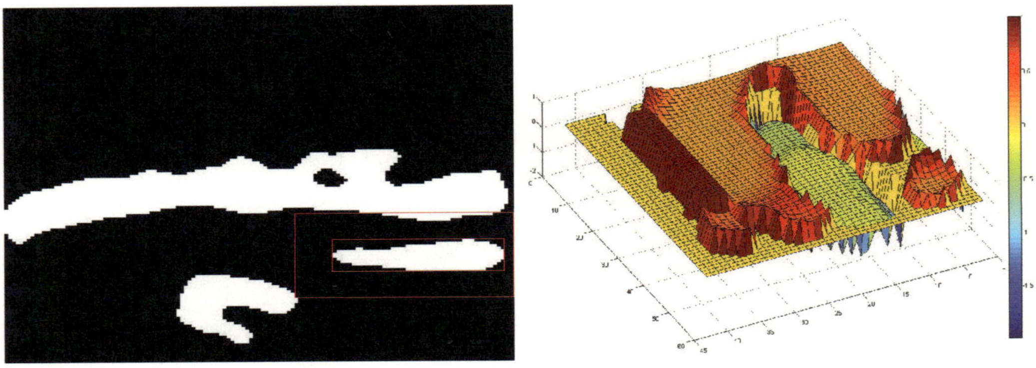

(a) (b)

Fig. 12. The result of identification of exact unstable groups. (a) Detected unstable GOP blob and its patch. (b) Patch contains the neighboring behavior of detected unstable GOP.

4. Results and discussion

Group motion detection is a significant tool to study the GOP behavior in a crowded environment. We have utilized LCS to examine GOP in a large gathering. We have tested the algorithm using a range of videos taken from Ali and Shah (2007). This consists of high density crowded scene including videos during Hajj, New York City Marathon and traffic scenes.

4.1 Group detection

In the sequence entitled 'Inside Makkah', as shown in Figure 11(a), a dense and random crowd flow is observed. In this video scene, the direction of global flow is from left to right, three GOP can been seen moving against the direction of the global flow which is detected by Eigenvector Parallelism Method as shown in Figure 11(c). It is noted that two GOP are having hazardous motion dynamics with respect to surrounding crowd because they are disturbing the global flow. It can computed by using method explain in Section 3.6. The third GOP is not hazardous despite having different direction because they are moving independently without propagating inside the moving crowd. Figure 13(a) is the watershed plot used for clear visualization of unstable GOP. Similarly Figure 13(b) is the watershed plot of video sequence shown in Figure 10. Now a comparison of obtained results has been performed with well known methods i.e. K-Mean on optical flow *(u,v)* field. It is necessary to mention here, that numbers of segments are pre-defined to run this method. Figure 13(c) displays result of K-Mean method which is unable to detect unstable GOP present in the scene although, number of segments has been increased up to 12 in this case. Figure 13(d) shows resulting flow segments of the same video sequence which is under discussion, but this result is obtained from Ali and Shah (2007). Figure 13(d) shows segmentation of crowd according to flow. It is unable to track small groups present at the bottom of the video frame having distinct dynamics. Their method identified the flow (at bottom flow) as single flow and represented it as a single segment. It is because there focus is on flow segmentation not on the tracking of GOP. In contrast, our method detected the flow pattern of crowd as well as tracking small GOP having distinct dynamics with respect to surrounding flow.

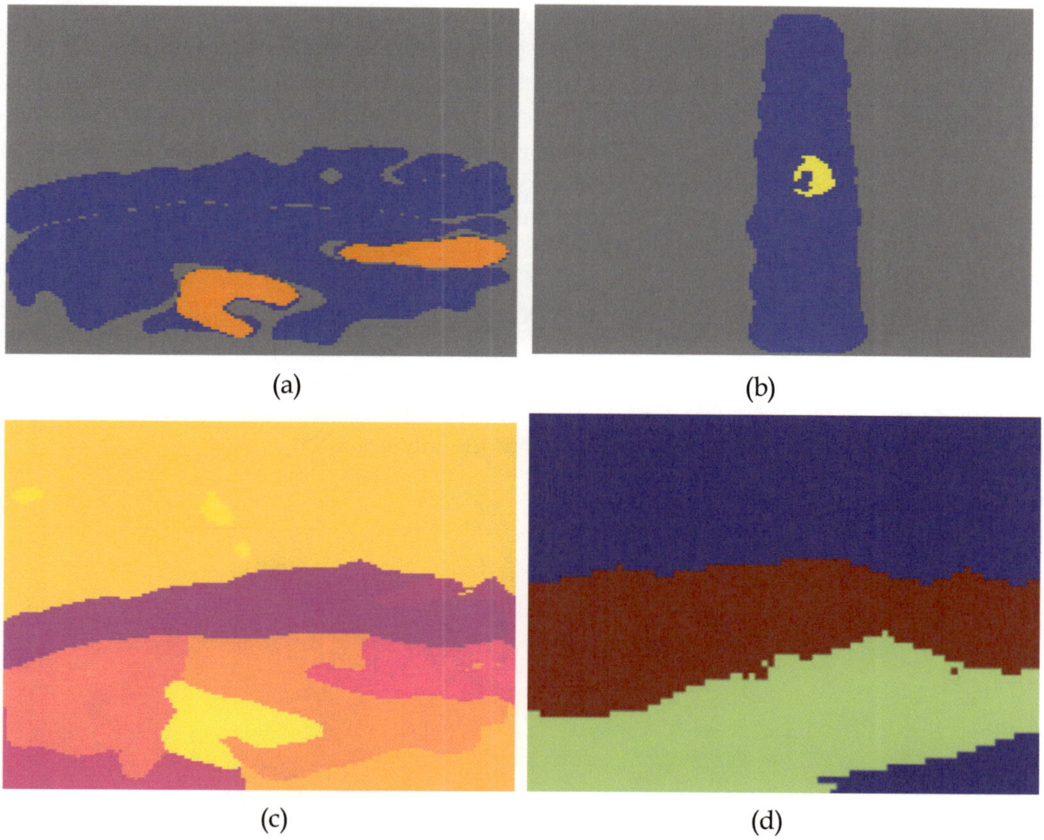

Fig. 13. Eigenvector Parallelism Method result and Comparison. (a) Watershed plot of video sequence, titled "Inside-Makkah", where unstable GOP is detected (in orange). (b) Watershed plot of video sequence New York City Marathon, where unstable GOP is detected. (c) Comparison plot with respect to K-Mean algorithm. (d) Flow segmentation result of video sequence as shown in Figure 11, result is obtained from Ali and Shah (2007).

The next result which is discussed here is shown in sequence Figure 1(b). The approach is tested on a video sequence of hurling stones at Jamarat Bridge. This video represented a highly important area where large crowd of people gather to perform a similar task. In the past, most of the deadly incidents occur at Jamarat Bridge due to collision of people in high density crowd. Detection and tracking of GOP having unstable dynamics are challenging task in this video sequence, since the flow pattern is quite complex and density of crowd is very high. The proposed method is able to work and produce results in such a highly dense crowd. The direction of global flow in this scene is from right to left. Few GOP are detected and tracked having different direction. The result of Eigenvector Parallelism Method is displayed in Figure 14(b).

Figure 14(c) is the watershed plot used for clear visualization of unstable GOP. The result was then compared with K-Mean methods. In this case K-Mean is unable to segment the crowd flow exactly, due to complexity and density of the scene. In Figure 14(c) three hazardous groups are highlighted below vacuum region (at the bottom) while two GOP are present above vacuum region. While K-Mean method could only detects two GOP at the bottom out of three while merged the upper groups with the global flow as shown in Figure 14(d). This shows the robustness of the proposed Eigenvector Parallelism Method.

4.2 Test set

The video sequence of New York City Marathon already used in Figure 10, in which artificial instability was generated by Ali and Shah (2007). In this sequence unstable GOP had different direction with respect to the global flow but GOP was static throughout the video. Now a moving GOP is introduced in the video sequence shown in Figure 15(a), the direction of mobile GOP is from left to right which is changing its position in every incoming frame. This continuous change in position makes the GOP a challenging object to track.

This is mathematically described as, Pt = (offset x + fr) + offset y. Where *Pt* is referred as position of patch (i.e. unstable GOP), *fr* is number of frame sequence which can be defined as *fr*= 1, 2, 3….n and *offset* is value where patch is initially launched.

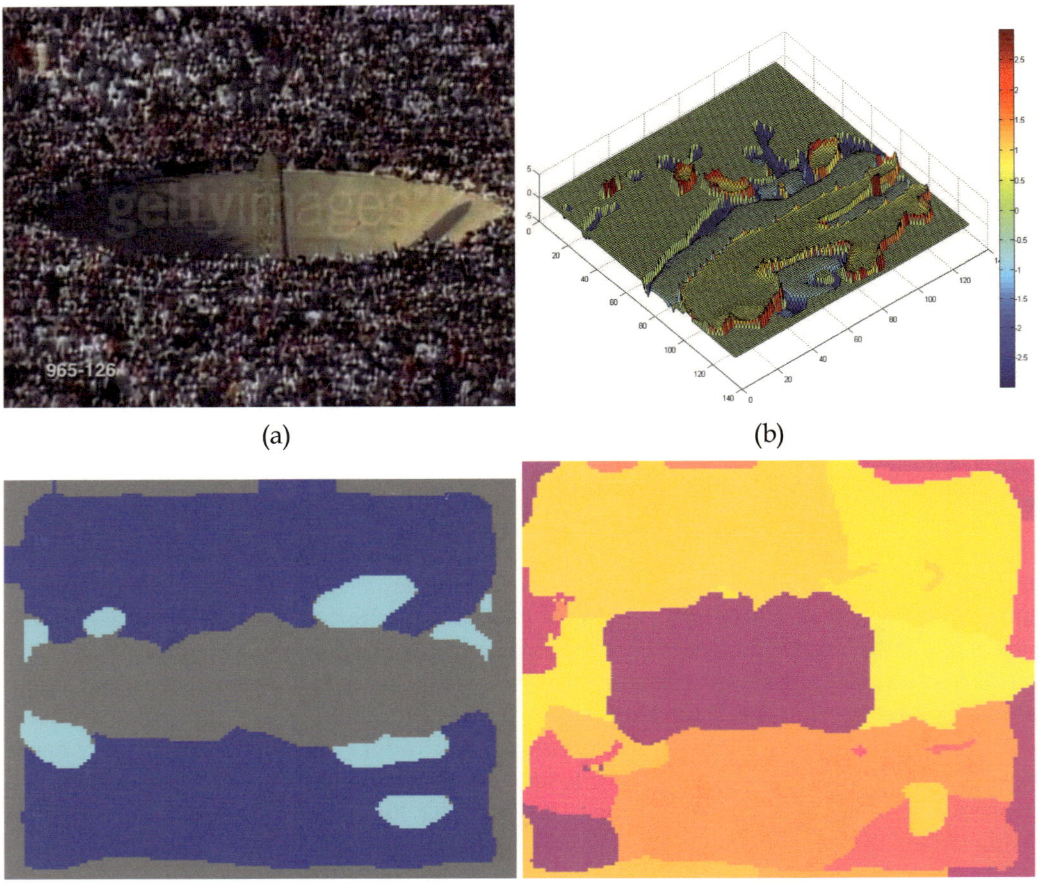

(a) (b)

(c) (d)

Fig. 14. Group detection result (a) Video frame of the sequence as shown in Figure 1(b). (b) FTLE field plot. (c) Watershed plot of the stable flow. (d) Comparison plot with respect to KMean algorithm

Now as a result of applying proposed algorithm, a mobile FTLE field is obtained, since GOP is changing its position continuously, ridges of unstable GOP boundary is also changing in correspondence. This is demonstrated in a series of resulting images as shown in Figure 15(b). These results validate the employment of technique on real time scenario and the algorithm is based on the frame wise calculation, the LCS is computed at every single frame rather than being computed on one mean field only. It is important to note that Running Mean in this methodology is programmed to reset after a few frames, so that FTLE field can exactly identify the true position of the unstable group. A significant result is shown in Figure 15(c).

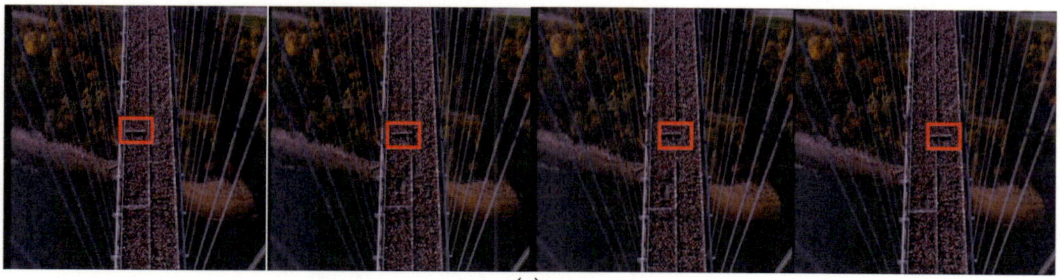

(a)

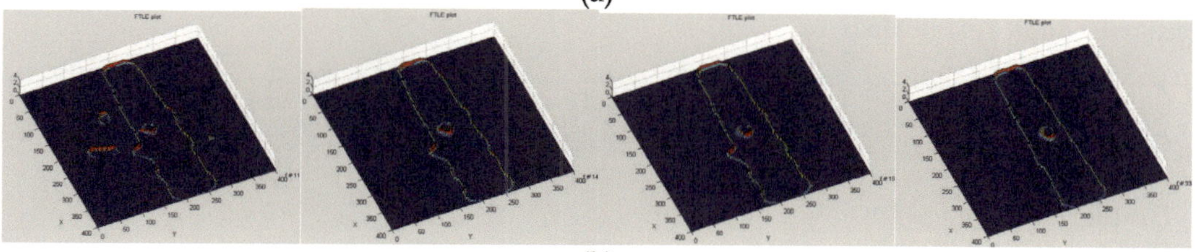

(b)

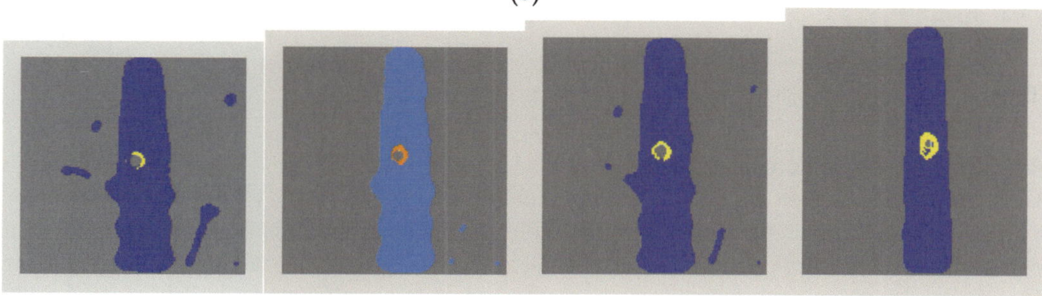

(c)

Fg. 15. The real-time detection result. (a) Video frames of the synthetic instability, where GOP changing its position (in Red). (b) The FTLE field of frames. (c) Watershed plot, real-time detection of moving GOP (in yellow)

4.3 Algorithm computational time

The robustness of the work depends on the fast running algorithm that will run efficiently, in order to do real-time analysis. To apply the Lagrangian technique on the image sequences requires few numbers of frames in reading memory. These frames become the integration length |T| for the algorithm. This requirement indicates that Lagrangian methodology is only applicable for off-line analysis. The solution of off-line analysis problem is solved by

MatLab™ M-file and pre-system Simulink™ interface, both simultaneously worked together. Simulink model worked as pre-system, consist of reading frames from data acquisition box and data smoothing. While the M-file worked as post-system, contains of all the methodology of Lagrangian technique. This project is applicable for frame wise analysis rather than estimate one mean field from the integration length $|T|$. In this formulation, the integration length $|T|$ represents the next frame in real-time videos. The algorithm was implemented, and all analyses have been conducted on a 3 GHz core2duo Pentium IV computer, executing Windows XP. The processing time for a single frame, size of 400x400 RGB image, is approximately 0.5 second that is 2 frames per second. This technique has assumed that the group motion is a slow performing motion because people moving in a large crowded scene. However, the execution time can be increased up to 5 frames per second by reducing the image size. Nevertheless, this will cause a loss of spatial image information.
In general Lagrangian sense, taking a denser particle grid will give higher spatial resolutions, which will lead to a higher computation time. If longer time integration is used, more of the boundaries will be exposed. Since flow particles were observed for longer time period consequently more boundaries will be exposed. This methodology cannot make use of longer time integration due to the computational cost restriction. Table 2 shows the computational cost of sub-systems for different sub-methods. Table 2 is computed on the sequence title "Inside Makkah".

Sub Methods	Mix	Min	Mean	Mode
Optical Flow	0.1073	0.0604	0.0804	0.076
Flow Map	0.0313	0.0156	0.0292	0.0313
Gradient and FTLE	0.3125	0.2656	0.2877	0.2813
Eigenvector Parallelism	0.1719	0.1406	0.1481	0.1406
Patch and Plot	0.0625	0.0313	0.0511	0.0469
Total	0.6855	0.5135	0.5965	0.5761

Table 2. Summary of the system by processing time (in seconds)

4.4 Comparison of computational time

LCS boundaries notify the distinct characteristic of crowd flow, whilst the eigenvector parallelism method characterizes the unstable group in their global flow. Figure 16 is a comparison graph plot between two methods, i.e. Normalize Cut algorithm and Eigenvector Parallelism method, computational-time wise. It can be observed, if the algorithm is executed with eigenvector parallelism method, it requires lower computational cost. In fact, three times lower as compared to Multi-scale Normalize Cut algorithm. Note at this instant, this technique is not proposing any comparative method of Normalize Cut algorithm. Eigenvector parallelism method has only used to classify the GOP having distinct characteristics on the boundary of the FTLE field.

5. Conclusion

This chapter provides a general framework for group motion detection and tracking in real-time crowded scenarios by using Lagrangian based approach. The main objective of this research is to detect and track Groups of People (GOP) that may create a calamity due to

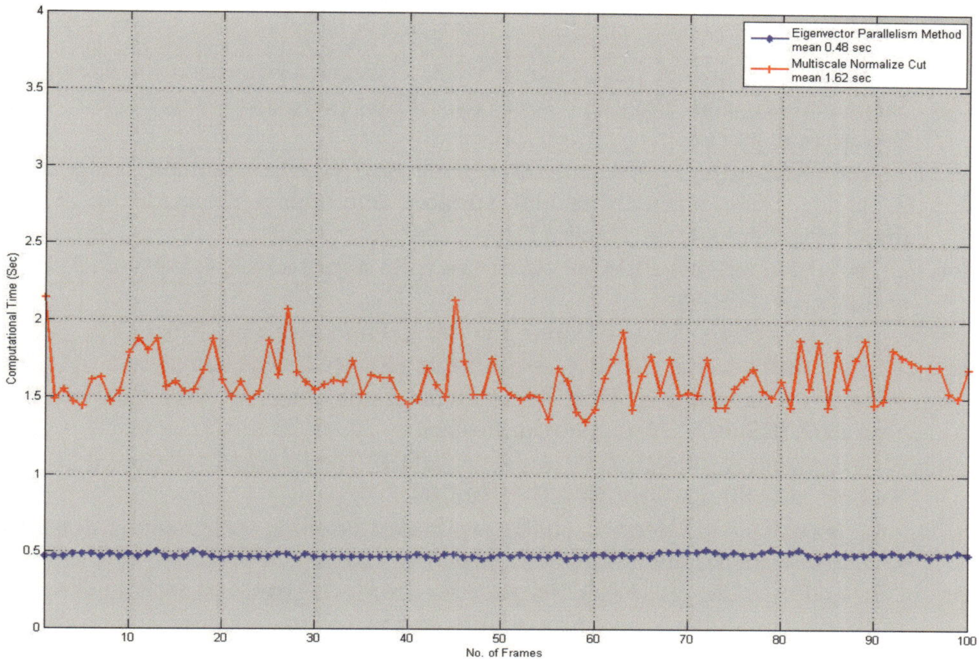

Fig. 16. Comparison graph plot between two methods, Normalize Cut algorithm and Eigenvector Parallelism method (sequence of New York City Marathon with synthetic instability)

their unstable motion. This objective has been achieved by employing a Lagrangian Coherent structure (LCS). The motivation for using LCS method came from the field of fluid mechanics which is able to reveal the spatial organization of the flow field created by the crowd flow. The Finite Time Lyapunov Exponent (FTLE) Field is one of the most appropriate approaches to obtain the LCS. It measures the maximum divergence between two particles as the flow progresses. At first the optical flow was used to give the flow field on which the system launched a particle grid for tracking the advection of crowd flow. These advected of particles are mapped by flow mapping on which spatial gradient is computed. Finally Finite-time Lyapunov Exponent (FTLE) field is computed on this gradient of flow map. The FTLE field restores the boundaries where the crowd flow experiences the dynamic change. On these boundaries, the system employed a new method of eigenvector parallelism in order to identify the precise unstable groups that are propagating in the global flow.

One of the common requirements of the motion detection algorithms in computer vision is the perspective views of camera. In this approach for detection of GOP in a crowded scene, the flow of crowd must be visualized from certain height for the visibility of the spatial organization of the flow. The variability of the image captured will also produce significant noise source to the overall analysis. In this case, stationary camera is used to minimize the capture noise factor. The developed monitoring system successfully tracks a range of objects, which can easily be used for actual monitoring requirements. The method suggested is very robust and can be adapted to various crowded scenarios such as traffic flow and fish schooling, where thousands of objects are involved.

6. References

Ali, S., and Shah, M. (2007) A Lagrangian Particle Dynamics Approach for Crowd Flow Segmentation and Stability Analysis. IEEE Computer Vision and Pattern Recognition, pp. 1-6

Crowd Dynamics Ltd, http://www.crowddynamics.com/Disasters/jamarat_bridge.htm

Haller, G. (2001) Distinguished material surfaces and coherent structures in three-dimensional fluid flows. Physica D. pp. 248-277.

Haller, G. (2005a) Lagrangian coherent structures from approximate velocity data. Physics of fluids, pp. 1851-1861

Haller, G. (2005b) An objective definition of a vortex. J. Fluid Mech. pp. 525, 1-26.

Helbing, D. Johansson, A. HE Habib Z. Al-Abideen. (2007a) Crowd turbulence: the physics of crowd disasters. The Fifth International Conference on Nonlinear Mechanics June 2007. (ICNM-V) Shanghai, pp. 967-969.

Helbing, D. Johansson, A. and H. Z. Al-Abideen. (2007b) The Dynamics of Crowd Disasters: An Empirical Study. Phys. Rev. E 75, 046109.

LEE Ris S. C. and HUGHES Roger L. (2005) Exploring trampling and crushing in a crowd. Journal of transportation engineering vol. 131, no.8, pp. 575-582.

Lucas, B. D. and Kanade, T. (1981) An iterative image registration technique with an application to stereo vision, Proceedings of imaging understanding workshop, pp. 121-130.

Shadden, S.C. Lekien, F. and Marsden, J. E. (2005) Definition and properties of Lagrangian coherent structures from finite-time Lyapunov exponents in two-dimensional aperiodic flows. Physica D. pp. 271-304.

Shadden, S. C. (2006) A dynamical systems approach to unsteady systems. PhD thesis, California Institute of Technology, USA

Shi, J. and Malik, J. (2000) Normalized cuts and image segmentation. IEEE Transactions on Pattern Analysis and Machine Intelligence, pp. 888-905

15

Development of Fuzzy Neural Networks: Current Framework and Trends

Fan Liu and Meng Joo Er
Nanyang Technological University
Singapore

1. Introduction

Fuzzy systems have been demonstrated their ability to solve different kinds of problems in classification, modeling control and in a considerable number of industry applications. It has been shown as a powerful methodology for dealing with imprecision and nonlinearity efficiently (Wang, 1994). However, one of the shortcomings of fuzzy logic is the lack of learning and adaptation capabilities. As we know, neural network (NN) is one of the important technologies towards realizing artificial intelligence and machine learning. Many types of neural networks with different learning algorithms have been designed and developed (Deng et al., 2002; Levin & Narendra, 1996; Narendra &Parathasarathy, 1998). Recently, there is an increasing interest to hybridize the approximate reasoning method of fuzzy systems with the learning capabilities of neural networks and evolutionary algorithms. Fuzzy neural network (FNN) system is one of the most successful and visible directions of that effort.

FNNs as hybrid systems have been proven to be able to reap the benefits of fuzzy logic and neural networks. In these hybrid systems, standard neural networks are designed to approximate a fuzzy inference system through the structure of neural networks while the parameters of the fuzzy system are modified by means of learning algorithms used in neural networks. One purpose of developing hybrid fuzzy neural networks is to create self-adaptive fuzzy rules for online identification of a singleton or Takagi-Sugeno-kang (TSK) type fuzzy model (Takagi & Sugeno, 1985) of a nonlinear time-varying complex system. The twin issues associated with a fuzzy system are 1) parameter estimation which involves determining parameters of premises and consequences and 2) structure identification which involves partitioning the input space and determining the number of fuzzy rules for a specific performance. FNN systems have been found to be very effective and of widespread use in several fields.

In recent years, the idea of self-organization has been introduced in hybrid systems to create adaptive models. Some adaptive approaches also have been introduced in FNNs whereby not only the weights but also the structure can be self-adaptive during the learning process (Er & Wu, 2002; Huang et al., 2004; Jang, 1993; Juang &Lin, 1998; Leng et al., 2004; Lin &Lee, 1996; Qiao & Wang, 2008).

The technology of FNNs combines the profound learning capability of neural networks with the mechanism of explicit and easily interpretable knowledge presentation provided by fuzzy logic. In a word, FNN is able to represent meaningful real-world concepts in comprehensive knowledge bases. The typical approach of designing an FNN system is to build standard neural networks first, and then incorporate fuzzy logic in the structure of neural networks. The key idea is as follows: Assuming that some particular membership functions have been defined, we begin with a fixed number of rules by resorting to either trial-and-error methods or expert knowledge. Next, the parameters are modified by learning algorithm such as backpropagation (BP) algorithm (Siddique & Tokhi, 2001). The BP is a gradient descent search algorithm. It is based on minimization of the total mean squared error between the actual output and the desired output. This error is used to guide the search of the BP algorithm in the weight space. The BP is widely used in many applications in that it is not necessary to determine the exact structure and parameters of neural networks in advance. However, the problem of the BP algorithm is that it is often trapped in local minima and the learning speed is very slow in searching for global minimum of the search space. The speed and robustness of the BP algorithm are sensitive to several parameters of the algorithm and the best parameters vary from problems to problems. Therefore, many adjustment methods have been developed, notably evolutionary algorithms such as genetic algorithms (GAs) or particle swarm optimization (PSO). By working with a population of solutions, the GA can seek many local minima, and thus increase the likelihood of finding global minimum. This advantage of GA can be applied to neural networks to optimize the topology and parameters of weights. The key point is to employ an evolutionary learning process to automate the designing of the knowledge base, which can be considered as an optimization or search problem. The GA is used to optimize the parameters of neural networks (Seng et al., 1999; Siddique & Tokhi, 2001; Zhou & Er, 2008) or identify the optimal structure of neural networks (Chen et al., 1999; Tang et al., 1995,). Moreover, the adaptation of neural network parameters can be performed by different methods such as orthogonal least square (OLS) (Chen et al.,1991), recursive least square (RLS) (Leng et al., 2004), linear least square (LLS) (Er & Wu, 2002), extended Kalman filter (EKF) (Kadirkamanathan & Niranjan, 1993; Er et al., 2010) and so on.

The objective of this chapter is to develop FNNs by hybrid learning techniques so that these systems can be used for online identification, model and control nonlinear and time-varying complex systems. In this chapter, we propose two kinds of self-organizing FNN that attempt to combine fuzzy logic with neural network and apply these learning algorithms to solve several well-known benchmark problems such as static function and linear and nonlinear function approximation, Mackey-Glass time-series prediction and real-world benchmark regression prediction and so on.

The chapter is organized as follows. The general frame of self-organizing FNN is described in Section 2. The first learning algorithm combined FNN with EKF is presented in Section 3. It is simple and effective and is able to generate a FNN with high accuracy and compact structure. Furthermore, a novel neuron pruning algorithm based on optimal brain surgeon (OBS) for self-organizing FNN is described in Section 4 in detail. Simulation studies on several well-known benchmark problems and comparisons with other learning algorithms have been conducted in each section. The summary of FNN associated with conclusions and future work are discussed in Section 5.

2. General frame of self-organizing FNNs

The self-organizing fuzzy neural network system primarily implements TSK or TS type (Sugeno & Kang, 1988) fuzzy model. The general architecture is depicted in Fig. 1. This five-layer self-organizing FNN implements a TSK type fuzzy system. Without loss of generality, we consider a multi-input-single-output (MISO) fuzzy model with input vector $X=(x_1,x_2,\ldots,x_r)$ and output variable y.

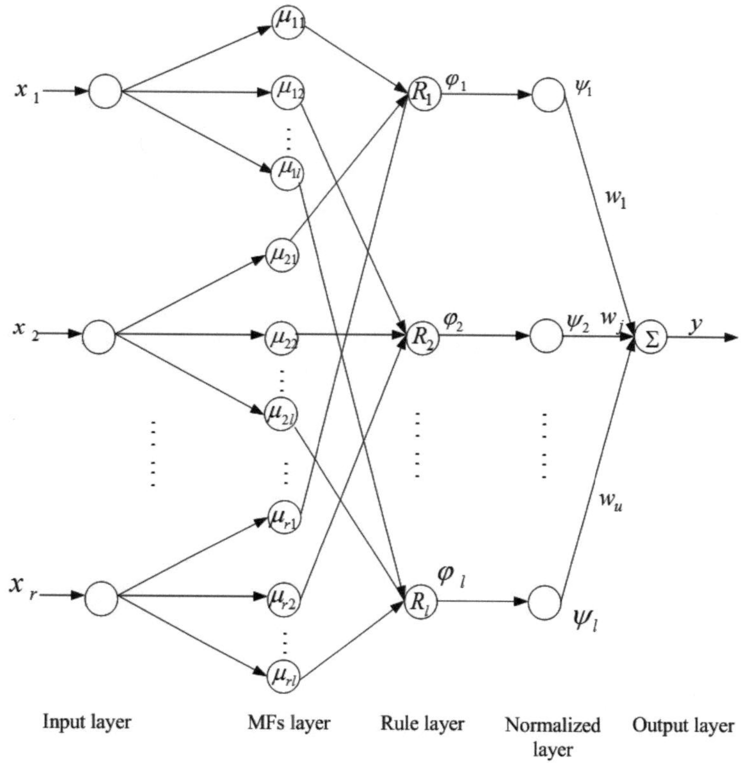

Fig. 1. General architecture of FNNs.

Layer 1 is an input layer and transmits values of input linguistic variable $x_i(i=1,2,\cdots r)$ to layer 2 directly, where r is the number of input variables. Each input variable x_i has l membership functions (MFs) $\mu_{ij}(i=1,2,\cdots r, j=1,2,\cdots,l)$ as shown in layer 2. The MFs can be triangular function (G. Leng et al., 2009) or Gaussian function (Wu and Er, 2004) or other functions. In this chapter, we choose Gaussian functions given by

$$\mu_{ij}(x_i)=\exp\left(-\frac{(x_i-c_{ij})^2}{\sigma_{ij}^2}\right) \quad i=1,2,\cdots,r, j=1,2,\cdots,l \tag{1}$$

where μ_{ij} is the jth membership function of the ith input variable x_i, c_{ij} and σ_{ij} are the center and width of the jth membership function with respect to the ith neuron, respectively. Layer 3 is the rule layer. Each node in this layer represents a possible IF-part of fuzzy rules. If the T-norm operator used to compute each rule's firing strength is multiplication, the output of the jth rule $R_j(j=1,2,\cdots l)$ is

$$\varphi_j(x_1,x_2,\ldots,x_r)=\exp\left(-\sum_{i=1}^{r}\frac{(x_i-c_{ij})^2}{\sigma_{ij}^2}\right) \quad j=1,2,\ldots,l\,. \tag{2}$$

Layer 4 is the normalized layer. The number of neurons in this layer is equal to that of layer 3. The output of the *jth* neuron in this layer is

$$\psi_j = \frac{\varphi_j}{\sum_{i=1}^{l} \varphi_i}, \quad j = 1,2,\cdots,l \tag{3}$$

Layer 5 is output layer and each node represents an output linguistic variable. The output of this layer is the weighted summation of incoming signals given by

$$y(x_1 \cdots x_r) = \sum_{j=1}^{l} w_j \psi_j \tag{4}$$

where y is the output variable and w_j is the THEN-part or connection weight of the *jth* rule. For the TSK model, weights are the polynomials of the input variables

$$w_j = A_j \cdot B = a_{j0} + a_{j1}x_1 + \cdots a_{jr}x_r \tag{5}$$

where $A_j=[\alpha_{j0}\alpha_{j1}\ldots\alpha_{jr}]$ is the weight vector of input variables in *jth* rule and B=$[1x_1\ldots x_r]$ is a column vector.
Suppose the *nth* data pair is arriving, and u RBF units are generated for the n training data pairs. The overall output of the FNN is

$$\mathrm{Y} = \mathrm{W}\Psi \tag{6}$$

where for the TSK model, W and Ψ are given by

$$W = [a_{10}a_{20} \cdots a_{u0} \; a_{11}a_{21} \cdots a_{u1} \; a_{r1}a_{r2} \cdots a_{ur}] \tag{7}$$

$$\Psi = \begin{bmatrix} \psi_{11} & \cdots & \psi_{1n} \\ \vdots & \vdots & \vdots \\ \psi_{u1} & \cdots & \psi_{un} \\ \psi_{11}x_{11} & \cdots & \psi_{1n}x_{1n} \\ \vdots & \vdots & \vdots \\ \psi_{u1}x_{11} & \cdots & \psi_{un}x_{1n} \\ \vdots & \vdots & \vdots \\ \psi_{11}x_{r1} & \cdots & \psi_{1n}x_{rn} \\ \vdots & \vdots & \vdots \\ \psi_{u1}x_{r1} & \cdots & \psi_{un}x_{rn} \end{bmatrix} \tag{8}$$

where ψ_{ij} is the output of the *ith* neuron in the normalized layer when *jth* training data arrives.

3. Self-constructing Fuzzy Neural Networks with Extended Kalman Filter (SFNNEKF)

In this section, a self-constructing fuzzy neural network employing extended Kalman filter (SFNNEKF) is designed and developed. The learning algorithm based on EKF is simple and effective and is able to generate a FNN with a high accuracy and compact structure. The proposed algorithm comprises of three parts: (1) criteria of rule generation; (2) pruning technology and (3) adjustment of free parameters. The EKF algorithm is used to adjust the free parameters of the SFNNEKF. The performance of the SFNNEKF is compared with other learning algorithms in the tasks of function approximation, nonlinear system identification and time-series prediction. Simulation studies and comparisons with other algorithms demonstrate that a more compact structure with high performance can be achieved by the proposed algorithm.

3.1 Learning algorithm of SFNNEKF

3.1.1 Error Reduction Ratio (ERR)

Suppose that for n observations, the FNN has generated uRBF neurons. The output matrix of the hidden layer is given by (8) then (6) can be written as

$$T = \Phi W + E \tag{9}$$

where $T \in R^n$ is the desired output vector and E is the error vector, $\Phi = \Psi^T$ can be rewritten as follows:

$$\Phi = KA \tag{10}$$

where K is a $n \times u$ matrix with orthogonal columns and A is a $u \times u$ upper triangular matrix. Substituting (10) into (9), we obtain

$$T = KAW + E = KG + E \tag{11}$$

The orthogonal lease squares solution G is given by $G = (K^T K)^{-1} K^T T$ or equivalently

$$g_i = \frac{k_i^T T}{k_i^T k_i} \quad 1 \le i \le u \tag{12}$$

An error reduction ratio (ERR) due to k_i as defined in (Shen et al., 1991) is given by

$$err_i = \frac{g_i{}^2 k_i^T k_i}{T^T T} \quad 1 \le i \le u \tag{13}$$

Substituting (12) into (13) yields

$$err_i = \frac{(k_i^T T)^2}{k_i^T k_i T^T T} \quad 1 \le i \le u \tag{14}$$

The ERR offers a simple and effective way of seeking a subset of significant regressors. In this chapter, we use it as a growing criterion to evaluate the network generalization capability. We define

$$\eta = \sum_{i=1}^{u} err_i \tag{15}$$

If $\eta < k_{err}$, where k_{err} is a prespecified threshold, the FNN needs more hidden nodes to achieve good generalization performance and a neuron will be added to the network. Otherwise, no neurons will be added.

3.1.2 Criteria of growing neurons

For the ith observation(P_i,t_i), calculate the output error of the SFNNEKF, e_i, the distance $d_i(j)$ and the ERR as follows:

$$\|e_i\| = \|t_i - y_i\| \tag{16}$$

$$d_i(j) = \left\|P_i - C_j\right\|, j = 1,\cdots,u \tag{17}$$

$$\eta = \sum_{i=1}^{u} err_i \tag{18}$$

If

$$\|e_i\| > k_e, d_{\min} > k_d \; and \; \eta < k_{err} \tag{19}$$

where $d_{\min} = \arg\min(d_i(j))$, $j = 1,2,\cdots,u$, k_e, k_d are two predetermined parameters which are chosen as follows:

$$k_e = \max[e_{\max} \times \beta^i, e_{\min}] \quad 0 < \beta < 1 \tag{20}$$

$$k_d = \max[d_{\max} \times \gamma^i, d_{\min}] \quad 0 < \gamma < 1, \tag{21}$$

a new neuron is added to the SFNNEKF network and the center, width and the output layer weight for the newly generated neuron are set as follows:

$$C_i = P_i \tag{22}$$

$$w_i = e_i \tag{23}$$

$$\sigma_i = k \times d_{\min} \tag{24}$$

where k is an overlap factor that determines the overlap of responses of the RBF units.

3.1.3 Criteria of pruning neurons

To facilitate the following discussion, we rewrite the output matrix of the hidden layer, as follows:

$$\Phi = \begin{bmatrix} p_{11} & \cdots & p_{u1} \\ \vdots & \vdots & \vdots \\ p_{1n} & \cdots & p_{un} \end{bmatrix} \tag{25}$$

In order to evaluate the contribution of each hidden neuron to the network output, the root mean square error (RMSE) of each hidden node is calculated as follows:

$$h_i = \sqrt{\phi_i^T \phi_i / n}, i = 1,\cdots,u \tag{26}$$

where $\phi_i = [p_{i1},\cdots,p_{in}]^T$ is the column vector of matrix Φ. If $h_i < k_{rmse}$ where k_{rmse} is a prespecified threshold, the ith hidden neuron is inactive and should be deleted.

3.1.4 Adjustment of weights

When no neurons are added or pruned from the network, the network parameter vector W_{EKF} is adjusted using the EKF method (Kadirkamanathan & Niranjan, 1993)

$$W_{EKF}(n) = W_{EKF}(n-1) + e_n k_n \tag{27}$$

where $W_{EKF} = [w_1, C_1^T, \sigma_1, \cdots, w_u, C_u^T, \sigma_u]$ is the network parameter vector and k_n is the Kalman gain vector given by

$$k_n = [R_n + a_n^T P_{n-1} a_n]^{-1} P_{n-1} a_n \tag{28}$$

Here, a_n is the gradient vector and has the following form

$$\begin{aligned} a_n = [&\psi_1(X_n), \psi_1(X_n)(2w_1\sigma_1)(X_n - C_1)^T, \\ &\psi_1(X_n)(2w_1\sigma_1^3)\|X_n - C_1\|^2, \cdots, \\ &\psi_u(X_n), \psi_u(X_n)(2w_u\sigma_u)(X_n - C_u)^T, \\ &\psi_u(X_n)(2w_u\sigma_u^3)\|X_n - C_u\|^2]^T \end{aligned} \tag{29}$$

where R_n is the variance of the measurement noise and P_n is the error covariance matrix which is updated by

$$P_n = [I - k_n a_n^T] P_{n-1} + QI \tag{30}$$

where Q is a scalar that determines the allowed random step in the direction of gradient vector and I is the identity matrix. When a new neuron is allocated, the dimensionality of the P_n increases to

$$P_n = \begin{pmatrix} P_{n-1} & 0 \\ 0 & P_0 I \end{pmatrix} \tag{31}$$

where P_0 is an estimate of uncertainties in the initial values assigned to the parameters.

3.2 Simulation results

3.2.1 Function approximation

First, a very popular function, Hermite polynomial, is used to evaluate the performance of the proposed SFNNEKF. The function is given by

$$f(x) = 1.1(1 - x + 2x^2)\exp(-\frac{x^2}{2}) \tag{32}$$

Parameters of the SFNNEKF are set as follows: $d_{\max} = 1$, $d_{\min} = 0.2$, $e_{\max} = 0.8$, $e_{\min} = 0.01$, $k_{err} = 0.99$, $k_{rmse} = 0.005$, $k = 0.5$, $\beta = 0.97$, $\gamma = 0.97$, $P_0 = 1.1$ and $Q = 0.01$. A total of 200 training samples are randomly chosen from the interval [−4, 4] for all the methods. Fig. 1 shows the growth of hidden neurons and Fig. 2 shows the RMSE with respect to the training samples. A comparison of structure and performance with MRAN (Lu et al., 1997) and DFNN (Er & Wu, 2002) is summarized in Table 1. It can be seen that the DFNN algorithm achieves the best RMSE performance in this case, but it needs more training time, because the TSK model makes the DFNN network structure more complicated. The SFNNEKF algorithm can obtain almost the same RMSE performance as the DFNN with faster learning speed and it has better performance than the MRAN algorithm in terms of training time and RMSE.

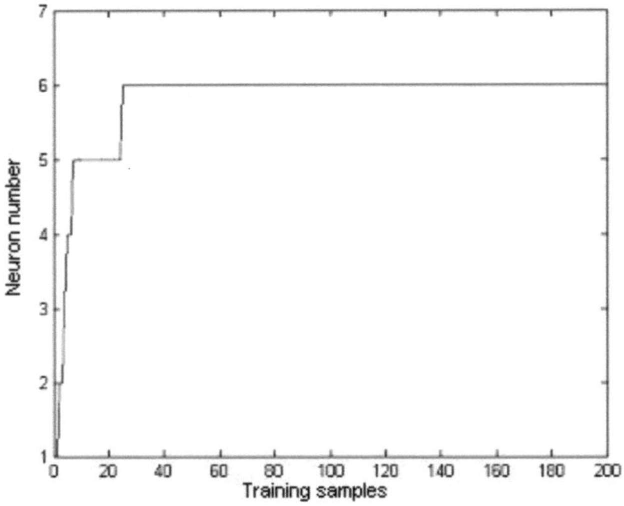

Fig. 1. Growth of neurons

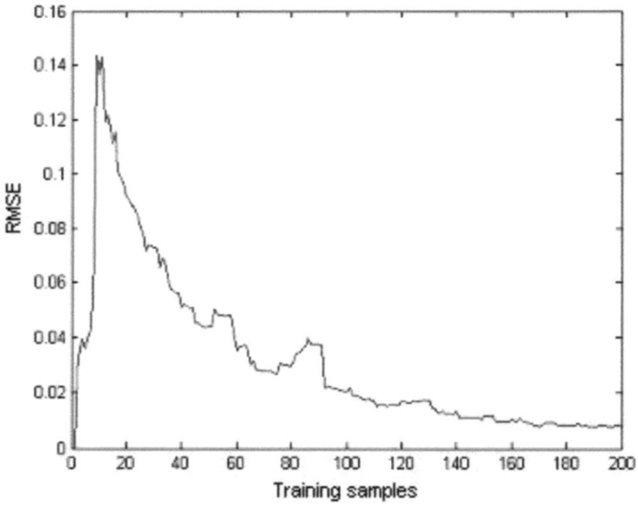

Fig. 2. RMSE during training

Algorithm	Number of neurons	RMSE	Training time(s)
SFNNEKF	6	0.0078	0.38
DFNN	6	0.0052	2.97
MRAN	7	0.0376	0.53

Table 1. Comparison of structure and performance of different algorithms (Example 3.2.1)

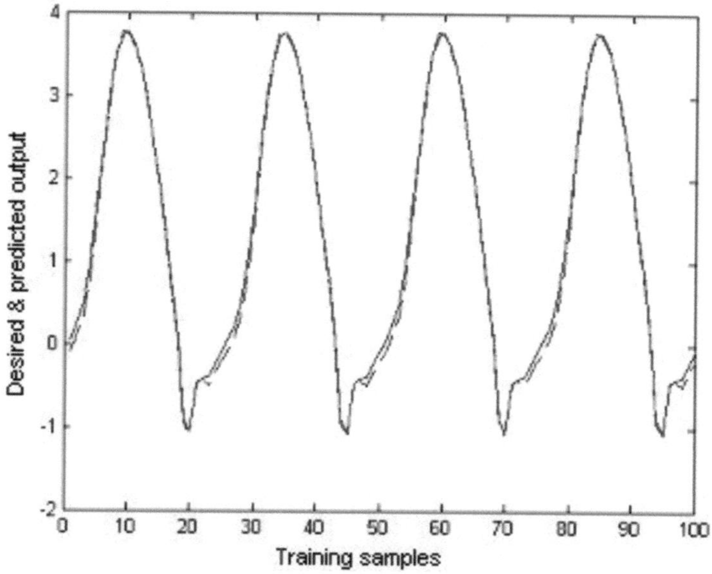

Fig. 3. Identification result: Desired (-) and Identified (---)

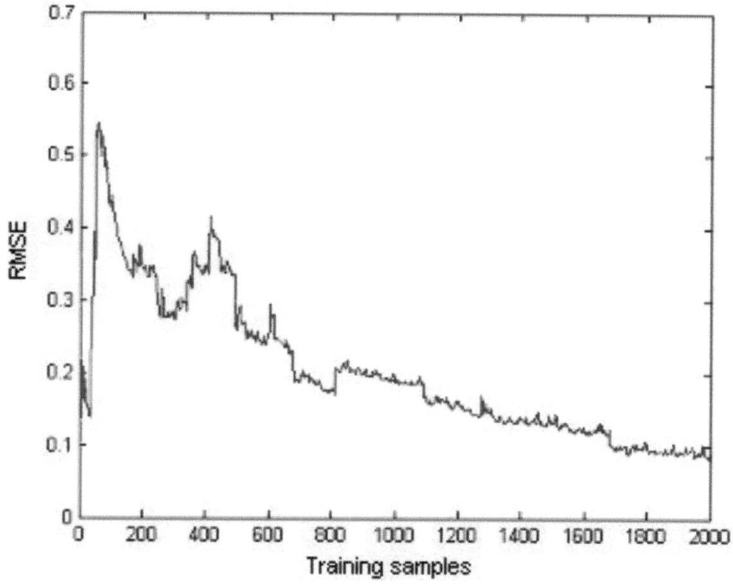

Fig. 4. RMSE during training

3.2.2 Nonlinear plant identification

The plant be identified is described by the second-order difference equation (Narendra & Parathasarathy, 1990)

$$y(t+1) = f[y(t), y(t-1)] + u(t) \tag{33}$$

where

$$f[y(t),y(t-1)]=\frac{y(t)y(t-1)[y(t)+2.5]}{1+y^2(t)+y^2(t-1)} \tag{34}$$

Parameters of the SFNNEKF are set as follows:
$d_{\max}=1$, $d_{\min}=0.2$, $e_{\max}=0.8$, $e_{\min}=0.01$, $k_{err}=0.96$, $k_{rmse}=0.005$, $k=0.5$, $\beta=0.97$, $\gamma=0.97$, $P_0=1.1$, and $Q=0.01$.
The input $u(k)$ is assumed to be independent identically distributed (i.i.d) random signal uniformly distributed in the interval [−2, 2] and a total of 2000 samples are randomly chosen for the training process. After this, the sinusoidal input signal $u(t)=\sin(2\pi t/25)$ is used to test identified model. Fig. 3 depicts the identified results using the SFNNEKF algorithm. In order to observe the result clearly, only the first 100 samples are shown in Fig. 3. Here, the solid-line curve is the desired plant output and the dash-line curve is for the identified model output. It can be seen that the SFNNEKF algorithm can identify the plant very well. The RMSE for training samples is shown in Fig. 4. The SFNNEKF algorithm generated a total of 15 neurons at the end of the training process. Table 2 shows a comparison of structure and performance of different algorithms. It is clear that the SFNNEKF algorithm can achieve a satisfactory RMSE performance with a simple network structure. Although the RMSE of the DFNN algorithm is 0.056, it needs more neurons (i.e. complicated network structure) to realize it. For the training speed, the SFNNEKF algorithm is the fastest method in all the three sequential learning algorithms. As a whole, the SFNNEKF algorithm demonstrates superior performance than the DFNN and MRAN algorithms in terms of networks complexity and training time.

Algorithm	Number of neurons	RMSE	Training time (s)
SFNNEKF	15	0.087	30.25
DFNN	26	0.056	608.51
MRAN	40	0.1525	69.79

Table 2. Comparison of structure and performance of different algorithms (Example 3.2.2)

3.2.3 Mackey-Glass time-series prediction

The Mackey-Glass time-series prediction is a benchmark problem which has been considered by a number of researchers (Lu et al., 1997; Wu & Er, 2000; Cho &Wang, 1996; Juang & Tin, 1998; Kadirkamanathan & Niranjan, 1993). The time series in our simulation is generated by

$$x(t+1)=(1-a)x(t)+\frac{bx(t-\tau)}{1+x^{10}(t-\tau)} \tag{35}$$

for a=0.1, b=0.2 and τ=17. A sampled version of the series is obtained by the above equation. The prediction model is given by

$$x(t+p)=f[x(t),x(t-\Delta t),x(t-2\Delta t),x(t-3\Delta t)] \tag{36}$$

For the purpose of training and testing, 6000 samples are generated between t=0 and t=6000 from (33) with initial conditions $x(t)$=0 for t<0 and $x(0)$=1.2. Hence, these data are used for preparing for the input and output pairs in the (34).

Suppose p=6, Δt=6, select first 500 sample pairs between $118 \le t \le 617$ as training data. Parameters of the SFNNEKF are set as follows:

$d_{\max}=1$, $d_{\min}=0.18$, $e_{\max}=1.1$, $e_{\min}=0.02$, $k_{err}=1.2$, $k_{rmse}=0.00025$, $k=0.5$, $\beta=0.95$, $\gamma=0.98$, $P_0=1.1$, and $Q=0.01$

The results for n=500, p=6 are shown in Fig. 5 and Fig. 6.

Figures illustrate the simulation results of the SFNNEKF in the case that p is 6 and the number of rules is 34. It indicates that the SFNNEKF possesses remarkable generalization capability. If we selected p=50 and Δt=6, for the convenience of comparison, the generalization capability is evaluated by the normalized root mean squared error (NRMSE) or the non-dimensional error index (NDEI), which is defined as the RMSE divided by the standard deviation of the target series (Platt, 1991). Generalization comparisons between the SFNNEKF, DFNN (Er & Wu, 2002), RAN (Platt, 1991) RANEKF (Kadirkamanathan & Niranjan, 1993), and MRAN (Lu et al., 1997) is listed in table 3. It is shown that SFNNEKF can obtain better performance even it has generated more rules than DFNN. However, the SFNNEKF shows superiority compared with the RAN and RANEKF algorithms in terms of the performance of the NRMSE, which measures the average prediction performance. The final value of the NRMSE is 0.0327 for SFNNEKF with 41 rules compares with 0.071 for the RAN and 0.056 for the RANEKF.

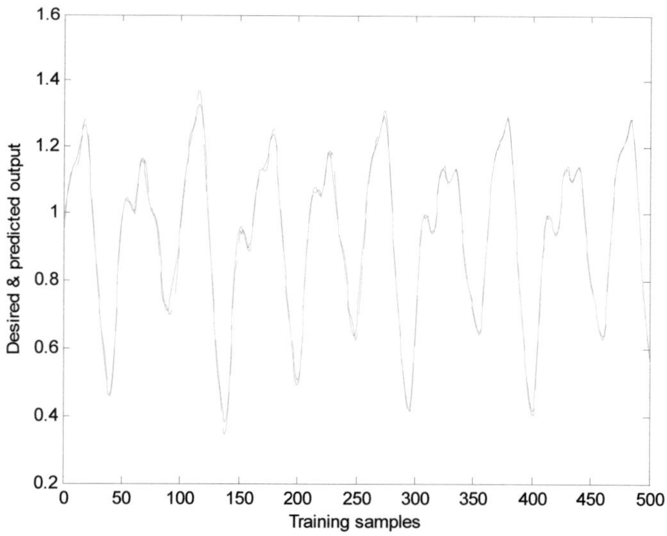

Fig. 5. Mackey-Glass time series from 642 to 1141 and six-step

Algorithm	Pattern length	Number of rules	NRMSE
SFNNEKF	2000	41	0.0327
DFNN	2000	25	0.0544
RAN	5000	50	0.071
RANEKF	5000	56	0.056
MRAN	5000	28	a

[a] The generalization error is measured by weighted prediction error (WPE) (example 3.2.3)

Table 3. Generalization comparison between SFNNEKF, DFNN, RAN, RANEKF and MRAN

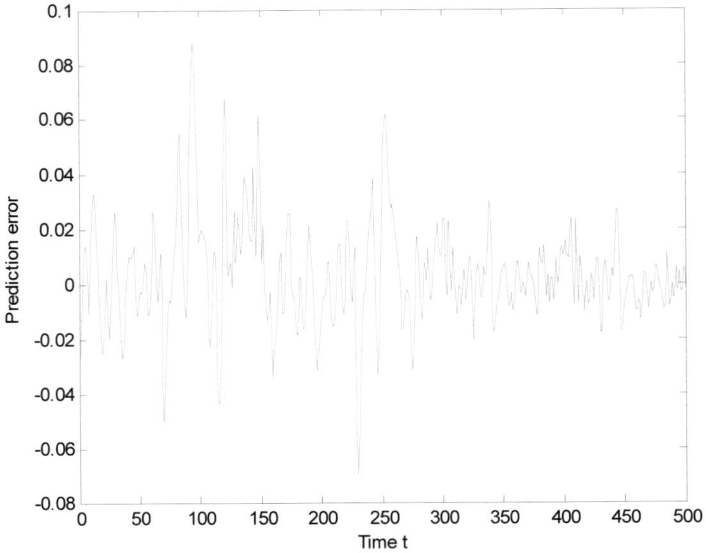

Fig. 6. Prediction error

3.3 Conclusions

A new self-constructing fuzzy neural network has been proposed in this part. The basic idea of the proposed approach is to construct a self-constructing fuzzy neural network based on criteria of generating and pruning neurons. The EKF algorithm has been used to adapt the consequent parameters when a hidden unit is not added. The superior performance of the SFNNEKF over some other learning algorithms has been demonstrated in three examples in this part. Simulation results show that a more effective fuzzy neural network with high accuracy and compact structure can be self-constructed by the proposed SFNNEKF algorithm.

4. A neuron pruning algorithm based on optimal brain surgeon for self-organizing fuzzy neural networks with parsimonious structure

In this section, a novel learning algorithm for creating a self-organizing FNN to implement TSK type fuzzy models is proposed. The optimal brain surgeon (OBS) (Hassibi & Stork, 1993) is employed as a neuron pruning mechanism to remove unimportant neurons directly during the training procedure. Distinguished from other pruning strategies based on the OBS, there is no need to calculate the inverse matrix of Hessian, we simplify the calculation by using LLS method to obtain the Hessian matrix. To acquire precision model, the LLS method is performed to obtain the consequent parameters of the network. The proposed algorithm has a parsimonious structure and is generated with high accuracy. The effectiveness of the proposed algorithm is demonstrated in several well-known benchmark problems such as static function approximation, two-input nonlinear function approximation and real-world non-uniform benchmark regression problems. Simulation studies are compared with other existing published algorithms. The results indicate that the proposed algorithm can provide comparable approximation and generalization performance with a more compact structure and higher accuracy.

4.1 Learning algorithm of the FNN

The learning procedure of the proposed self-organizing FNN comprises two stages. In the first stage, the structure of the FNN is generated based on the growth criteria and the proposed OBS-based pruning method. In the second stage, parameters of newly created neurons are assigned and consequent parameters of all existing neurons will be updated by the LLS method.

4.1.1 Structure design of the FNN

To determine the proper number of neurons or fuzzy rules of FNNs, we adopt two growth criteria to generate neurons. In order to obtain a compact structure, the OBS algorithm (Hassibi & Stork, 1993) is employed as a pruning criterion. An initial structure of the FNN is first constructed and the importance of each hidden neuron or fuzzy rule is evaluated by the OBS algorithm, the least important neuron will be deleted if the performance of the entire network is accepted after deleting this unimportant neuron. This procedure will repeat until the desired accuracy can be satisfied. We will describe the learning algorithm in detail in the sequel.
The learning stage is based on a data set composed by n input-output pairs:

$$P = \{(X_k, t_k\} = \{(x_{k1}, x_{k2}, \cdots, x_{kr}), t_k\}, k = 1, 2\cdots, n. \tag{37}$$

When the kth observation (X_t,t_k) arrives, the overall FNN output of the existing structure using (2)-(4) is denoted by y_k, the system error can be defined by (16)
If

$$\|e_k\| > k_e \tag{38}$$

where k_e is a predefined error tolerance, a new fuzzy rule should be considered if other criteria of generation have been satisfied simultaneously. The term k_e decays during the learning process as follows

$$k_e = \begin{cases} e_{\max} & 1 < i < n/3 \\ \max[e_{\max} \times \beta^i, e_{\min}], & n/3 \le i \le 2n/3 \\ e_{\min} & 2n < i \le n \end{cases} \tag{39}$$

where $e_{\max}$ is the maximum error chosen, $e_{\min}$ is the desired accuracy of the FNN output and $\beta \in (0,1)$is a convergence constant.
The second growth criterion is the accommodation criterion. It can be described as follows: when the kth observation (X_t,t_k) arrives, calculate the distance d_{kj} between the observation X_k and the center C_j of the u existing neurons, i.e.

$$\|d_{kj}\| = \|X_k - C_j\|, k = 1, 2, \cdots, n, j = 1, 2, \cdots, u, \tag{40}$$

the minimum distance between the kth observation and the nearest center is described as

$$d_{\min} = \arg\min(d_{kj}), k = 1, 2, \cdots, n, j = 1, 2\cdots, u. \tag{41}$$

If

$$d_{\min} > k_d \tag{42}$$

where k_d is determined by (21).
Here, d_{max} is the largest length of the input space, d_{min} is the smallest length of interest and $\gamma \in (0,1)$ is the decay constant. If these two growth criteria are satisfied simultaneously, a new hidden neuron will be generated.
When growth procedure is complete, a pruning algorithm is employed to optimize the structure of the FNN to obtain a compact network structure. For this algorithm, we use the OBS as a pruning strategy. The OBS algorithm uses the second-order derivative information of the error function to find the unimportant neuron to get a tradeoff between the network complexity and good performance of entire network. The basic idea of the OBS algorithm is described as follows. Firstly, we assume that the pruning algorithm is used after the training process has converged or is fully trained. It means that the network reaches a local minimum of the error surface. The functional Taylor series of the cost function E with respect to parameters w is given by

$$\Delta E = \left(\frac{\partial E}{\partial w}\right)^T \cdot \Delta w + \frac{1}{2}\Delta w^T \cdot \frac{\partial^2 E}{\partial w^2} \cdot \Delta w + O(\|\Delta w\|^3) \tag{43}$$

where $H = \frac{\partial^2 E}{\partial w^2}$ is the Hessian matrix which contains all second-order derivative information. For a network trained to a local minimum in error,

$$\left(\frac{\partial E}{\partial w}\right)^T \cdot \Delta w = 0 \tag{44}$$

and we also ignore the third and all higher order terms. The goal is to set one of the parameters w_q to zero to minimize the increase in error given by (41). Eliminating w_q can be expressed as

$$\Delta w_q + w_q = 0 . \tag{45}$$

Then the optimal model of OBS can be formulated as an optimization problem as follows

$$\begin{aligned} \min \quad & \frac{1}{2}\Delta w^T H \Delta w \\ s.t. \quad & I_q^T \Delta w + w_q = 0 \end{aligned} \tag{46}$$

where I_q is the unt vector in parameter space corresponding to parameter w_q.
Solving the constrained problem using the Lagrangian method

$$L = \frac{1}{2}\Delta w^T H \Delta w + \lambda(I_q^T \Delta w + w_q) \tag{47}$$

where λ is a Lagrange undetermined multiplier. After taking functional derivatives, employ the constraints and obtain resulting change in error are

$$\Delta w = -\frac{w_q}{[H^{-1}]_{qq}} H^{-1} \cdot I_q \tag{48}$$

$$L = \frac{1}{2} \frac{w_q^2}{[H^{-1}]_{qq}} \tag{49}$$

where H^{-1} is the inverse of the Hessian matrix H and $[H^{-1}]_{qq}$ is the qth element of H^{-1}.

Note that the OBS algorithm needs to calculate the inverse of the Hessian matrix. In fact, for very small dimension of the Hessian matrix, its inverse can be obtained by standard matrix methods while inverting a matrix of hundreds or thousands of terms seems computationally intractable. For our algorithm, we use the LLS method to avoid calculating the inverse of the Hessian matrix. The cost function used in our algorithm is defined as the training error $E_t(\Theta)$

$$E_t(\Theta) = \frac{1}{2} \sum_{k=1}^{n} [t(k) - \phi^T(k)\Theta]^2 \tag{50}$$

where $\Theta = W^T$ is the parameter vector, $t(k)$ is the desired output of the FNN and $\phi^T(k) = [\phi_1(k)\, \phi_2(k) \cdots \phi_{u\times(r+1)}(k)]$, $k = 1,2\cdots,n$.

The functional Taylor series of the cost function of the FNN with respect to parameter vector Θ is

$$\Delta E_t(\Theta) = \left(\frac{\partial E_t(\Theta)}{\partial \Theta}\right)^T \cdot \Delta\Theta + \frac{1}{2}\Delta\Theta^T \cdot \frac{\partial^2 E_t(\Theta)}{\partial \Theta^2} \cdot \Delta\Theta + O(\|\Delta\Theta\|^3) \tag{51}$$

where $H = \frac{\partial^2 E_t(\Theta)}{\partial \Theta^2}$ is the Hessian matrix. For a network trained to a local minimum in error,

$$\left(\frac{\partial E_t(\Theta)}{\partial \Theta}\right)^T \cdot \Delta\Theta = 0 \tag{52}$$

and the third and all higher order terms are ignored. Then (49) can be rewritten as

$$\Delta E_t(\Theta) \approx \frac{1}{2}\Delta\Theta^T \cdot \frac{\partial^2 E_t(\Theta)}{\partial \Theta^2} \cdot \Delta\Theta = \frac{1}{2}\Delta\Theta^T H \Delta\Theta \tag{53}$$

In the following part, we will discuss how to use the Hessian matrix H to measure the increase in cost function $E_t(\Theta)$ due to deleting some parameters and then present the pruning algorithm. From (11) and (53) the Hessian matrix can be rewritten as

$$H = \frac{\partial^2 E_t(\Theta)}{\partial \Theta^2} = \Phi^T \Phi \tag{54}$$

After obtaining the Hessian matrix H, we can calculate the increase in cost function $E_t(\Theta)$ due to a change in parameters Θ. Since deleting the ith parameter in Θ is equivalent to setting the value of the corresponding parameter to zero, then the change in $E_t(\Theta)$ due to the removal of a subset G of parameters is

$$\Delta E_t(\Theta) \approx \frac{1}{2}\Delta\Theta_G^T H \Delta\Theta_G \tag{55}$$

where

$$[\Delta\Theta]_i = \begin{cases} [\Theta]_i & if\ i \in G \\ 0 & if\ i \notin G \end{cases} \tag{56}$$

where $[\Theta]_i$ denotes *ith* element of Θ.

After all, the importance of each hidden neuron or fuzzy rule can be evaluated by the change in cost function or training squared error $\Delta E_t(\Theta)$, the smaller the value of the change in the cost function, the less important is the neuron. Based on these descriptions, the proposed OBS-based pruning algorithm can be summarized as follows

1. Calculate the output of the existing FNN after growing all coming data.
2. According (50, calculate the RMSE for training, $E_t(\Theta)$.
3. Compute the Hessian matrix H according to (54).
4. Evaluate the importance of each hidden neuron in the network: $\Delta E_t(\Theta_i) = \frac{1}{2}\Delta\Theta_i^T H \Delta\Theta_i$ for $i = 1,2\cdots,M$ where M is the number of parameters.
5. Define the tolerance limit of the change in the training for the RMSE as λE_{RMSE}, where $\lambda$is a predefined constant and $0<\lambda<1$.
6. Define the expected RMSE for training as k_{RMSE}. In general, k_{RMSE} is a very small positive value.
7. Find the smallest value of change in cost function

$$[\Delta E_{t\min}, ind_{\min}] = \min_i \Delta E_t(\Theta_i), i = 1,2,\cdots,M \tag{57}$$

   where $\Delta E_{t\min}$ denotes the smallest value of $\Delta E_t(\Theta)$ and $ind_{\min}$ denotes the index of the smallest value.
8. Calculate the RMSE after deleting the least importance hidden neuron E_{RMSE}^D, choose $E^D = \max(\lambda E_{RMSE}, k_{RMSE})$, if $E_{RMSE}^D < E^D$, remove this neuron, and go to step 7) for the second least important neuron, and so on. Otherwise, do not remove any neurons and proceed to the weight adjustment stage.

Therefore, the structure (number of hidden neurons or fuzzy rules) of FNN is obtained based on the growth and pruning criteria.

4.1.2 Update of parameters and weight adjustment

After the network structure is established, the network enters the second stage: parameters of newly created neurons are assigned and the consequent parameters of all existing neurons will be updated by the simple but efficient LLS method.

For the first observation (X_1,t_1) arrives, since there are no hidden neurons at the beginning, some initializations are conducted. Parameters of the first neuron are assigned as follows

$$C_1 = X_1 \tag{58}$$

$$\sigma_1 = width0 \tag{59}$$

$$w_1 = t_1 \tag{60}$$

where C_1 and σ_1 is the center and width of the first neuron respectively, and w_1 is the connective weight of the first neuron.
The objective of weight adjustment is as follows

$$Y = W\Psi \tag{61}$$

$$\tilde{E} = \|T - Y\| \tag{62}$$

We try to find an optimal weight vector $W^* \in R^{u\times(r+1)}$ such that the error energy $\tilde{E}^T\tilde{E}$ is minimized. By using the LLS method, we can find the optimal W^* is in the form of

$$W^* = T\Psi^+ = T(\Psi^T\Psi)^{-1}\Psi^T \tag{63}$$

Since the structure of our FNN is very compact after structure learning process, the dimension of W and Ψ is small, the LLS method provides a computationally simple and efficient weight adjustment process.

4.2 Illustrative examples

In this section, the effectiveness of the proposed algorithm is demonstrated in three kinds of well-known benchmark examples: static function approximation, two-input nonlinear approximation and real-world non-uniform benchmark regression problems (Boston housing, auto-mpg and abalone) (Frank & Asuncion, 2010). The simulation results are also compared with other algorithms such as the OLS (Chen et al., 1991), RAN (Platt, 1991), RANEKF (Kadirkamanathan & Niranjan, 1993), MRAN (Lu et al., 1997), GAP-RBF(Huang et al., 2004), OS-ELM (Liang et al., 2006) GDFNN (Wu et al., 2001), SOFNN (Leng et al., 2005), FAOS-PFNN(Wang et al., 2009).

4.2.1 Static function approximation

The first example is on static function approximation. The underlying function to be approximated is a three-input nonlinear function *f(x,y,z)* which is widely used to verify the effectiveness of proposed algorithms of Khayat et al., 2009; Wu et al., 2001; Qiao & Wang, 2008; Chen et al., 1991.

$$f(x,y,z) = (1 + x^{0.5} + y^{-1} + z^{-1.5})^2 \tag{64}$$

A total of 216 uniformly training data are randomly sampled from the input ranges $[1,6]\times[1,6]\times[1,6]$ and the corresponding target data. Another 125 uniformly testing data are randomly selected from the same operating range to check the generalization of the proposed FNN. The parameters are selected as follows: $e_{\max} = 5$, $e_{\min} = 0.8$, $d_{\max} = 0.83$, $d_{\min} = 0.47$, $\beta = 0.97$, $\gamma = 0.99$, $\lambda = 0.8$, $width0 = 2$ and $k_{RMSE} = 0.3$.
To be in conformity with other learning algorithms, the same performance index, termed average percentage errors (APE) is used

$$APE = \frac{1}{n}\sum_{k=1}^{n}\frac{|t(k) - y(k)|}{|t(k)|}\times 100\% \tag{65}$$

where n is the number of data pairs, *t(k)* and *y(k)* are the *kth* desired output and actual output of the FNN, respectively.

Simulation results are shown in Fig. 7, where we see that a four-hidden-neuron structure is generated. The RMSE curving of training data with 216 epochs is shown in Fig. 8. The input variables x,y and z define four membership functions respectively. As we can see from the resulting figures, the trained network obtains a high precision and the RMSE is also confined to a very small value.

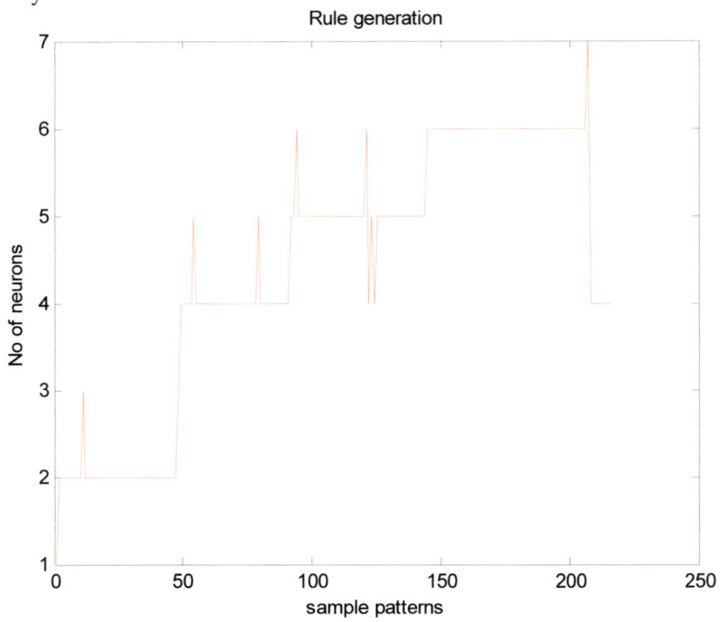

Fig. 7. Growth of fuzzy rules

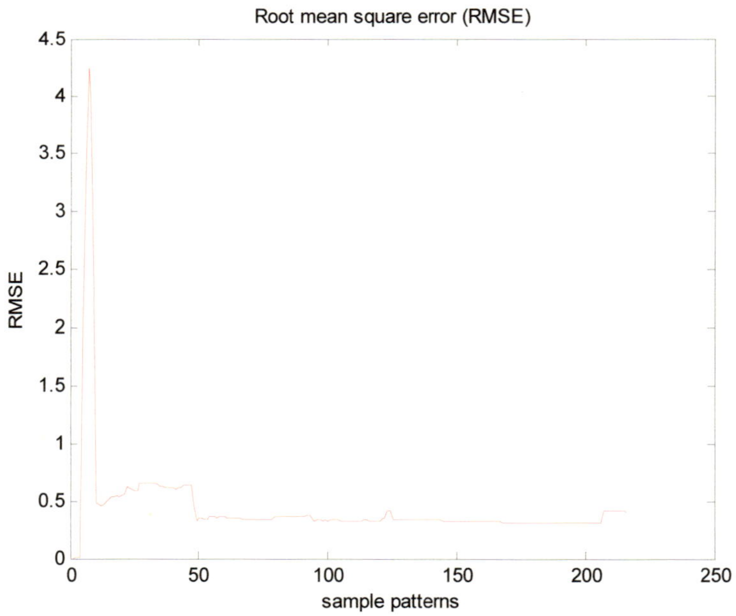

Fig. 8. Root mean squared error (RMSE) during training

Model	APE_{trn} %	APE_{chk} %	Parameter number	Training set size	Testing set size
OLS	2.43	2.56	66	216	125
GDFNN	2.11	1.54	64	216	125
SOFNN	1.1380	1.1244	60	216	125
The proposed algorithm	2.76	1.55	40	216	125

Table 4. Comparisons of the Proposed Algorithm with Other Methods (Static Function Approximation) (example 4.2.1)

Comparative studies of the proposed algorithm with other published works, such as the OLS (Chen et al., 1991), GDFNN (Wu et al., 2001) and SOFNN (Leng et al., 2005) are shown in Table 4. APE_{trn} % and APE_{chk} % are APE of training data and testing data, respectively. As it can be seen from Table 4, the proposed algorithm has the least number of parameters which means that it achieves the most compact structure compared with other algorithms while the approximation performance is worse than that of the SOFNN and GDFNN and nearly the same as that of the OLS. It should be noted that the proposed algorithm has a satisfactory generalization performance as its APE of testing is only 1.55 which is less than OLS and almost the same as that of the GDFNN. In brief, the proposed algorithm achieves the most parsimonious structure with good accuracy.

4.2.2 Two-input nonlinear sinc function

This example is used to demonstrate the performance of the proposed algorithm in noisy and noise-free environments. This function is also used in Leng et al., 2004 and Leng et al., 2009. It is defined as follows

$$z = \sin c(x,y) = \frac{\sin(x)\sin(y)}{xy}, x \in [-10,10], y \in [-10,10] \tag{66}$$

A total of 121 two-input data without noise and the corresponding target data are chosen as training data. Another set of uniformly sampled 121 input-target data are selected as testing data. The training parameters are selected as follows: $e_{\max} = 1.1$, $e_{\min} = 0.02$, $d_{\max} = 2$, $d_{\min} = 0.2$, $\beta = 0.9$, $\gamma = 0.97$, $\lambda = 0.8$, $width0 = 2$ and $k_{RMSE} = 0.005$.
A total of 5 hidden neurons (i.e. fuzzy rules) FNN is generated. The number of membership functions associated inputs x and y is five. When the training data is without noise, the RMSE for training is 0.0073 whilst the RMSE for testing is 0.0057. In order to determine the affect of noise, the training data are mixed with Gaussian white noise sequences which have zero mean and different variances as shown in Table 5.

Variances σ^2	NUMBER OF Neurons	NUMBER OF MFS	RMSE for training	RMSE for testing
$\sigma = 0$	5	5,5	0.0073	0.0057
$\sigma = 0.01$	5	5,5	0.0072	0.0056
$\sigma = 0.05$	6	6,6	0.0061	0.0048
$\sigma = 0.1$	7	7,7	0.0063	0.0050

Table 5. Performance of two-input sinc function with noise (example 4.2.2)

It can be observed from Table 5, the number of hidden neurons increases with the level of noise. That is because more neurons will be required to filter the noise. Both the RMSE for training and testing are small values though the data mixed with high level of noise. It means that the proposed algorithm is robust even when the training data is perturbed by noise. It demonstrates that our algorithm is suitable for noisy environment.

4.2.3 Boston housing prediction

The Boston housing prediction problem is to predict the median value of owner-occupied homes in suburbs of Boston. The database has 506 observations and each observation consists of 13 inputs (12 continuous inputs and one binary-valued input) and one continuous output (median value of owner-occupied homes). The 13 inputs and the output are normalized to the range [0, 1]. For this problem, 481 training data and 25 testing data are randomly generated from the Boston housing data set in each trial of simulation studies. The training parameters are selected as follows: $e_{\max}=5$, $e_{\min}=0.8$, $d_{\max}=0.83$, $d_{\min}=0.47$, $\beta=0.99$, $\gamma=0.99$, $\lambda=0.8$, $width0=2$ and $k_{RMSE}=0.05$. Performance comparisons with other algorithms are shown in Table 6.

Model	NUMBER OF Neurons	RMSE FOR Training	RMSE for testing	Training set size	Testing set size
RAN	18.8	0.3449	0.3432	481	25
RANEKF	19.98	0.1328	0.1437	481	25
MRAN	13.58	0.1440	0.1356	481	25
GAP-RBF	3.5	0.1507	0.1418	481	25
The proposed algorithm	2	0.0916	0.0583	481	25

Table 6. Comparisons of the proposed algorithm with other methods (Boston housing)

As observed from Table 6, the proposed algorithm obtains the smallest RMSE for training and testing, which means that the approximation and generalization performance is better than that of other learning algorithms. It is highlighted that the average number of hidden neurons generated by the system is only 2, which is less than that of other learning algorithms. Therefore, the proposed algorithm has the most compact structure of all the learning algorithms. In other words, our algorithm needs the least number of neurons to conduct the Boston housing prediction with comparable accuracy simultaneously.

4.2.4 Auto-mpg prediction

The auto-mpg problem is to predict the fuel consumption (miles per gallon) of different models of cars based on the displacement, horsepower, weight and acceleration of cars. A total of 392 observations are collected for the prediction problem. Each observation consists of seven inputs (four continuous inputs: displacement, horsepower, weight, acceleration, and three discrete inputs: cylinders, model year and origin) and one continuous output (the fuel consumption). For simplicity, the seven input attributes and one output have been normalized to the range [0, 1]. A total of 320 training data and 72 testing data are randomly chosen from the auto-mpg data set in each trial of simulation studies. The training parameters are selected as the previous Boston housing problem except the expected RMSE for training set is as k_{RMSF}=0.008. Performance comparisons among RAN (Platt, 1991),

RANEKF (Kadirkamanathan & Niranjan, 1993), MRAN (Lu et al., 1997), GAP-RBF (Huang et al., 2004), OS-ELM (Liang et al., 2006), FAOS-PFNN (Wang et al., 2009) and our proposed algorithm are presented in Table 7. It can be seen that the RMSE for testing our algorithm is the smallest among these learning algorithms while the RMSE for training is less than other algorithms except the FAOS-PFNN. It can be summarized that our proposed algorithm has the best generalization ability of all the learning algorithms though the approximation performance is a little worse than the FAOS-PFNN. Moreover, the number of fuzzy rules of our algorithm is only 2 and is less than other algorithms so that it has the most parsimonious structure among these learning algorithms. In brief, the overall performance of our algorithm is superior to other algorithms.

Model	NUMBER OF Neurons	RMSE FOR Training	RMSE for testing	Training set size	Testing set size
RAN	4.44	0.2923	0.3080	320	72
RANEKF	5.14	0.1088	0.1387	320	72
MRAN	4.46	0.1086	0.1376	320	72
GAP-RBF	3.12	0.1144	0.1404	320	72
FAOS-PFNN	2.9	0.0321	0.0775	320	72
OS-ELM	25	0.0696	0.0759	320	72
The proposed algorithm	2	0.0646	0.0513	320	72

Table 7. Comparisons of the proposed algorithm with other methods (Auto-mpg)

4.2.5 Abalone age prediction

The abalone problem has 4177 cases predicting the age of abalone from physical measurements. Each observation consists of 8 continuous inputs and 1 integral output. Similar to the age-auto prediction problem, the 8 inputs and 1 output are normalized to the range [1, 0]. A total of 3000 training data and 1177 testing data are randomly generated from the abalone data set in each trial of simulation studies. The training parameters are set as the same of the previous Boston housing problem.

Tab le 8 presents the performance comparisons of our algorithm with other learning algorithms. It is clear from the table that the RMSE for testing the proposed algorithm is the smallest of all algorithms. It means that our algorithm has the best generalization performance and obtained the smallest network size.

Model	NUMBER OF Neurons	RMSE FOR Training	RMSE for testing	Training set size	Testing set size
RAN	345.58	0.0931	0.0978	3000	1177
RANEKF	409	0.0738	0.0794	3000	1177
MRAN	87.571	0.0836	0.0837	3000	1177
GAP-RBF	23.62	0.0963	0.0972	3000	1177
FAOS-PFNN	4.54	0.0311	0.0807	3000	1177
OS-ELM	25	0.0761	0.0770	3000	1177
The proposed algorithm	2	0.0746	0.0735	3000	1177

Table 8. Comparisons of the proposed algorithm with other methods (Abalone)

4.3 Discussions

In this part a novel learning algorithm for creating a self-organizing fuzzy neural network (FNN) to implement the TSK type fuzzy model with a parsimonious structure was proposed. The OBS is employed as a pruning algorithm to remove unimportant neurons directly during the training process. Apart from other pruning strategies based on the OBS, there is no need to calculate the inverse matrix of Hessian; we simplify the calculation by using the LLS method to obtain the Hessian matrix.

The effectiveness of the proposed algorithm has been demonstrated in four well-known benchmark problems: namely static function approximation, nonlinear dynamic system identification, two-input nonlinear function and real-world non-uniform benchmark problems. Moreover, performance comparisons with other learning algorithms have also been presented in this part. The results indicate that the proposed algorithm can provide comparable approximation and generalization performance with a more compact parsimonious structure and higher accuracy.

5. Conclusions and future work

In this chapter, the development of fuzzy neural networks has been reviewed and the main issues for designing fuzzy neural networks including growing and pruning criteria and different adjustment methods of consequent parameters have been discussed. The general frame of fuzzy neural networks based on radial basis function neural networks has been described in Section 2. Two self-organization FNNs have been developed. For the first FNN, the SFNNEKF algorithm employs ERR as a generation condition in constructing the network which makes the growth of neurons smooth and fast. The EKF algorithm has been used to adjust free parameters of the FNN to achieve an optimal solution. Simulation results show that a more effective fuzzy neural network with high accuracy and compact structure can be self-constructed by the proposed SFNNEKF algorithm. For the second FNN, it is composed of two stages: the structure identification stage and the parameter adjustment stage. The structure identification consists of constructive and pruning procedures. An initial structure starts with no hidden neurons or fuzzy rule sets and grows neurons based on the criteria of neuron generation. Then the OBS is employed as a pruning strategy to further optimal the obtained initial structure. At last, the well-known LLS method is adopted to tune the free parameters in the parameter adjustment stage for sequentially arriving training data pairs. Simulation studies are compared with other algorithms. The simulation results indicate that the proposed algorithm can provide comparable approximation and generalization performance with a more compact structure and higher accuracy.

In a word, fuzzy neural networks are hybrid systems that combine the advantages of fuzzy logic and neural networks, there existed many kinds of FNN developed by researchers. Recently, the idea of self-organizing has been introduced in FNN. The purpose is to develop self-organizing fuzzy neural network systems to approximate fuzzy inference through the structure of neural networks to create adaptive models, mainly for approximate linear and nonlinear and time-varying systems. FNNs have been widely used in many fields. For our future work, studies will focus on the structure learning since appropriate number of fuzzy rules or find proper network architecture and developing optimal parameter adjustment methods.

6. References

Chen, S.; Cowan, C. F. N. & Grant, P. M. (1991). Orthogonal least squares learning algorithm for radial basis function network, *IEEE Transactions on Neural Networks*, vol. 2, pp. 302-309

Chen, S.; Wu, Y. & Luk, B. L.(1999). Combined genetic algorithm optimization and regularized orthogonal least squares learning for radial basis function networks, *IEEE Trans. Neural Networks*, vol. 10, no. 5, pp. 1239-1243

Cho, K. B. & Wang, B. H.(1996). Radial basis function based adaptive fuzzy systems and their applications to system identification and prediction, *Fuzzy Sets and Systems*, vol. 83, no. 3, pp. 325-339

Deng, J.; Sundararajan, N. & Saratchandran, P.(2002). Communication channel equalization using complex -valued minimal radial basis function neural networks, *IEEE Transactions on Neural Networks*, vol.13, no. 3, pp. 687- 696

Er, M. J. & Wu, S. Q. (2002) A fast learning algorithm for parsimonious fuzzy neural systems, *Fuzzy Sets and Systems*, vol. 126, pp. 337-351

Er, M. J.; Liu, F & Li, M. B. (2010). Self-constructing fuzzy neural networks with extended Kalman filter, *International Journal of Fuzzy Systems*, vol. 12, no. 1, pp. 66-72

Frank, A. & Asuncion, A. (2010), UCI Machine Learning Repository [http://archive.ics.uci.edu/ml], Irvine, CA: University of California, School of Information and Computer Science

Hassibi, B. & Stork, D. G.(1993). Second order derivatives for network pruning: optimal brain surgeon, in: *Advances in Neural Information Processing Systems*, Morgan Kaufman, San Mateo, CA, pp. 164-171

Huang, G. B.; Saratchandran, P. & Sundararajan, N.(2004). An efficient sequential learning algorithm for growing and pruning (GAP-RBF) networks, *IEEE Transactions on Systems, Man and Cybernetics, Part B: Cybernetics*, vol. 34, pp. 2284-2292

Jang, J. S. R. (1993). ANFIS: Adaptive-Network-Based Fuzzy Inference System, *IEEE Transactions on Systems, Man, and Cybernetics*, vol. 23, no. 3, pp. 665-684

Juang, C. F. & Lin, C. T.(1998). An on-line self-constructing neural fuzzy inference network and its applications, *IEEE Trans. Fuzzy Syst.* 6 pp.12–32

Kadirkamanathan, V & Niranjan, M.(1993). A function estimation approach to sequential learning with neural networks, *Neural Computation*, vol. 5, no. 6, pp. 954-975

Khayat, O.; Ebadzadeh, M. M.; Shahdoosti, H. R.; Rajaei R. & hajehnasiri, I. K.(2009). A novel hybrid algorithm for creating self-organizing fuzzy neural networks, *Neurocomputing*, 73(1-3) pp. 517-524

Leng, G.; Prasad, G. & McGinnity, T. M.(2004). An on-line algorithm for creating self-organizing fuzzy neural networks, *Neural Networks*, vol. 17, pp. 1477-1493

Leng, G.; McGinnity, T.M. & Prasad, G.(2005). An approach for on-line extraction of fuzzy rules using a self-organizing fuzzy neural network, *Fuzzy Sets and Syst.* 150, pp.211-243.

Leng, G.; Zeng, X. J. & Keane, J. A .(2009). A hybrid learning algorithm with a similarity-based pruning strategy for self-adaptive neuro-fuzzy systems, *Applied Softing Computing*, 9, pp. 1354-1366

Levin, A.U.& Narendra, K. S. (1996). Control of nonlinear dynamical system using neural networks-part II: Observability, identification, and control, *IEEE Transactions on Neural Networks*, vol. 7, no. 1, pp. 30-42

Liang, N. Y.; Huang, G. B.; Saratchandran, P. & Sundararajan, N.(2006). A fast and accurate online sequential learning algorithm for feedforward networks, *IEEE Trans. Neural Networks* 17, pp.1411-1423

Lin, C. T. & Lee, C. S. G.(1996). *Neural Fuzzy Systems: a Neural-Fuzzy Synergism to Intelligent Systems*, Englewood Cliffs, NJ: Prentice-Hall

Lu, Y.; Sundararajan, N. & Saratchandran, P.(1997). A sequential learning scheme for function approximation using minimal radial basis function neural networks, *Neural Computation*, vol. 9, no. 2, pp. 461-478

Narendra, K. S. & Parathasarathy, K. (1990). Identification and control of dynamic systems using neural networks, *IEEE Transactions on Neural Networks*, vol. 1, no. 1, pp. 4-27

Platt, J. (1991). A resource-allocating network for function interpolation, *Neural Computation*, vol. 3, no. 2, pp. 213-225

Qiao, J. F. & Wang, H. D.(2008). A self-organizing fuzzy neural network and its applications to function approximation and forecast modeling, *Neurocomputing*, 71, pp. 564-569

Seng, T. L.; Khalid, M. B. & Yusof, R.(1999). Tuning of a neuro-fuzzy controller by genetic algorithm, *IEEE Trans. Syst., Man, Cyhern. B, Cybern.*, vol. 9, no. 2, pp. 226-236

Siddique, M. N. H. & Tokhi, M. O. (2001). Training Neural Networks: Backpropagation vs Genetic Algorithms, *Proceeding of the International Joint Conference on Neural Networks* 4, pp. 2673-2678

Sugeno, M. & Kang, G. T.(1988). Structure identification of fuzzy model, *Fuzzy Sets and Systems*, 28, pp. 15-33

Takagi, T. & Sugeno, M. (1985). Fuzzy identification of systems and its applications to modeling and control, *IEEE Transactions on Sytems, Man, and Cybernetics* 15 pp. 116-132

Tang, K. S.; Chan, C. Y.; Man, K. F.; & Kwong, S. (1995). Genetic Structure for NN Topology and Weights Optimization, *IEE Conference Publication*, No. 414, pp.250-255

Wang, L.X. (1994). *Adaptive Fuzzy Systems and Control: Design and Stability Analysis*, Englewood Cliffs, NJ: Prentice-Hall

Wang, N.; Er, M. J. & Meng, X. Y. (2009). A fast and accurate online self-organizing scheme for parsimonious fuzzy neural networks, *Neurocomputing*, 72, pp. 3818-3829

Wu S. Q. & Er, M. J.(2000). Dynamic fuzzy neural networks - a novel approach to function approximation, *IEEE Transactions on Systems, Man and Cybernetics, Part B: Cybernetics*, vol. 30, no. 2, pp. 358-364

Wu, S. Q.; Er, M. J. & Gao, Y. (2001). A fast approach for automatic generation of fuzzy rules by generalized dynamic fuzzy neural networks, *IEEE Trans. Fuzzy Syst.* 9 pp. 578-594.

Zhou, Y. & Er, M. J. (2008). An evolutionary approach toward dynamic self-generated fuzzy inference systems, *IEEE Transactions on system, man and cybernetics, part b: cybernetics*, vol. 38, no. 4, pp. 963-969

16

EMC Aspect as Important Parameter of New Technologies

Irena Kováčová and Dobroslav Kováč
Technical University of Košice
Slovak Republic

1. Introduction

Equipment disturbances and errors have become more serious as a consequence of the growth of the electronic circuit complexity. According to new technical legislation and also economic consequences, the electromagnetic compatibility (EMC) concept of all products must be strictly observed (Montrose & Nakauchi, 2004). It must start with the specification of the equipment performance and end with the equipment installation procedures. The importance of the electromagnetic compatibility (EMC) of all electrical products has grown rapidly during the last decade. The environment is increasingly polluted with electromagnetic energy. The interference output into the surroundings is doubled every three years, and covers a large frequency range.

2. EMC couplings

The EMC concept is defined as competence of functional coexistence of electrical and also biological devices or systems at the same time and in such a way that even though they are located in the common electromagnetic environs, there is no relevant influencing factor of their normal functionality (Vaculíková & Vaculík, 1998). Devices can but don't need to have the mutual dependence. On the one hand the systems must be robust against the other systems influences, but on the other hand they must not affect adversely the normal functionality of other devices (Fig. 1). On one side, interferences are deliberately or involuntarily produced. The place of their origin is called interference source. On the other side, devices can be hindered in their function by such interferences. Those objects are called interference objects.

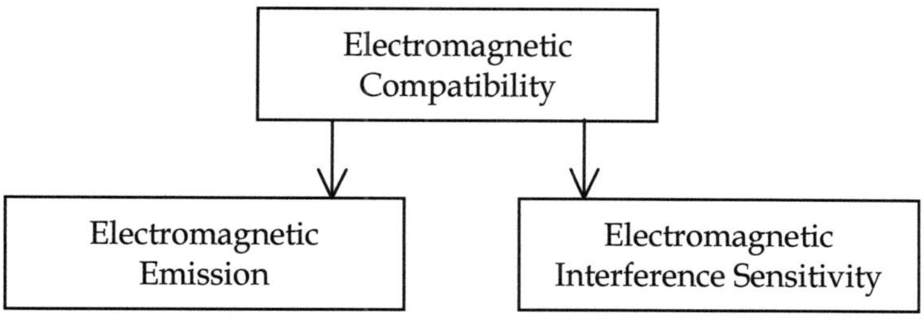

Fig. 1. Division of EMC into key aspects

Each system utilized in practice is exposed to disturbing effects generated by the various sources such as, for example, power switches, contactor tapes, relays, arc furnaces, high frequency heating, commutator motors, and power semiconductor converters, etc, see Fig. 2.

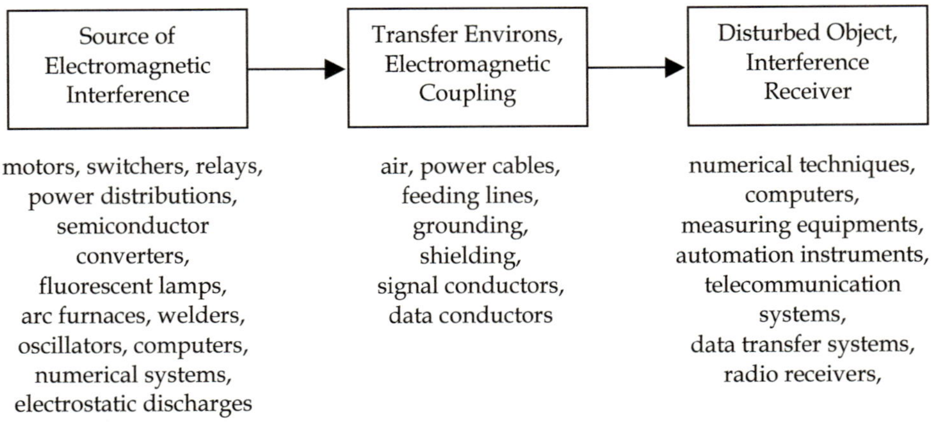

Fig. 2. Basic chain of EMC and examples of individual section types

Noise surrounding influences, which are manifested by unfavorable linkages, interference noises, resonant and transient states, can cause not only incorrect equipment functionality, but also its destruction in extreme cases. The interference source can be for instance a power semiconductor converter or motor. Interference is produced in the interference source getting into electronics in undesirable ways and is due to various effects distorting signals. Transmission can be direct, for example by galvanic coupling between interference source and interference sink. Interference can be spread through air or via ducts, or coupled inductively or capacitively into signal lines. Mutual electromagnetic coupling of individual electrical equipments can be realized by several ways as shown in Fig. 3.

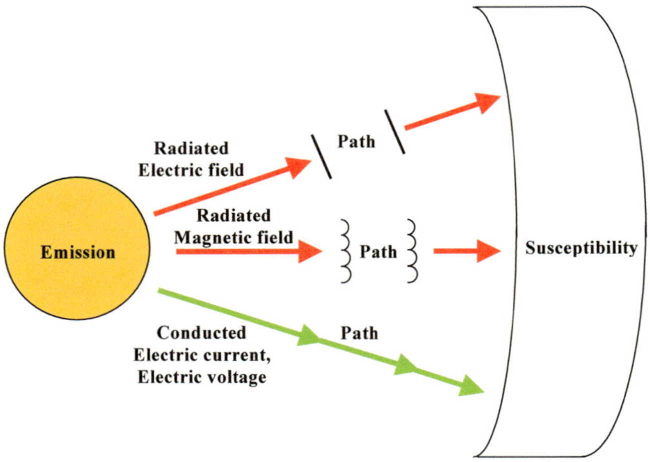

Fig. 3. Ways of mutual electromagnetic coupling

From the viewpoint of the theoretical analysis it is evident that the radiated energy transfer between individual investigated equipments is done by the following ways: inductive coupling, capacitive coupling, galvanic coupling, electromagnetic coupling.

3. Inductive coupling

Inductive coupling is typical for two and more galvanically separated electric loops at the moment when the smaller one is driven by a time variable current creating the corresponding time-variable magnetic field (Kůs, 2002). In such case their mutual intercircuit effect is expressed as a function of the slope of the current increase or decrease, circuit environmental magnetic property as well as circuit geometric dimensions.
To predict the intercircuit inductive coupling, our focus will be on two electric loops l_1 and l_2 with currents i_1 and i_2. We will try to determine the effect of loop l_1 on loop l_2 (Fig. 4).

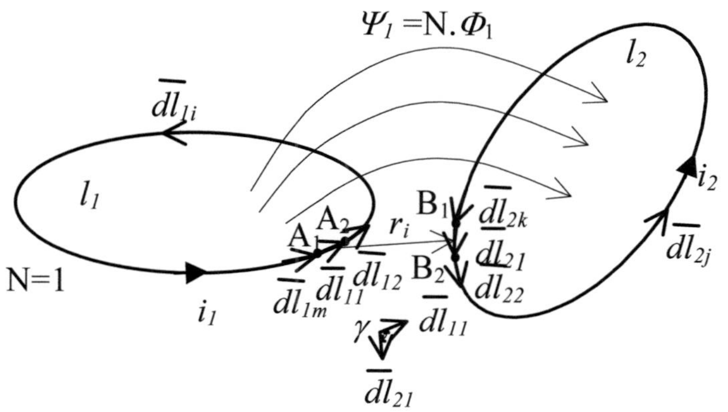

Fig. 4. Investigated loops

According to the Maxwell's equation for a quasi-stationary magnetic field

$$rot\,\overline{E} = -\frac{\partial \overline{B}}{\partial t} \quad \text{and following its integral form} \quad \int_S rot\,\overline{E}.d\overline{S} = -\int_S \frac{\partial \overline{B}}{\partial t}.d\overline{S} = -\frac{\partial}{\partial t}\int_S \overline{B}.d\overline{S} \tag{1}$$

and after applying the Stoke's theorem, we obtain the equation for the induced voltage

$$u_{i2} = -\mathrm{N}.\frac{\partial \phi_1}{\partial t} = -\frac{\partial \psi_1}{\partial t} = -M\frac{\partial i_1}{\partial t} \tag{2}$$

where M is the coefficient of the mutual inductance. For the magnetic flux Φ_1 the equation

$$\phi_1 = \oint_{l_2} \overline{A}_2.d\overline{l}_2 \tag{3}$$

is valid, where $\overline{A}_2$ is the vector of the magnetic field potential created by the current i_1. We can calculate the value of this vector by the following equation:

$$\overline{A}_2 = \frac{\mu.i_1}{4\pi}\oint_{l_1}\frac{d\overline{l}_1}{r_{12}}\,. \tag{4}$$

After substituting the last equation with the equation valid for the magnetic flux ϕ_1 and then for induced voltage u_{i2}, the next relations are obtained:

$$\phi_1 = \oint_{l_2} \left[\frac{\mu . i_1}{4\pi} \oint_{l_1} \frac{d\bar{l_1}}{r_{12}} \right] . d\bar{l_2} = \frac{\mu . i_1}{4\pi} \oint_{l_1} \oint_{l_2} \frac{d\bar{l_1} . d\bar{l_2}}{r_{12}} \tag{5}$$

$$u_{i2} = - \frac{\partial \left(\frac{\mu . i_1}{4\pi} \oint_{l_1} \oint_{l_2} \frac{d\bar{l_1} . d\bar{l_2}}{r_{12}} \right)}{\partial t} = - \frac{\left(\frac{\mu}{4\pi} \oint_{l_1} \oint_{l_2} \frac{d\bar{l_1} . d\bar{l_2}}{r_{12}} \right) \partial i_1}{\partial t} = -M \frac{\partial i_1}{\partial t} . \tag{6}$$

For the practical use, it is more advantageous to express the induced voltage in the form of a differentials:

$$u_i = - \frac{di}{dt} . \sum_{i=1}^{m} \sum_{j=1}^{k} \frac{\mu}{4\pi} \frac{dl_{1i} . dl_{2j} . \cos \gamma_{dlij}}{r_{ij}} \tag{7}$$

If we know the geometrical dimensions of the investigated loops (Fig. 5) and want to determine their mutual inductive coupling then we can use the next equation (8) for the induced voltage. It is based on the 3D Cartesian coordinate system.

$$u_i = - \frac{di}{dt} . \sum_{i=1}^{m} \sum_{j=1}^{k} \frac{\mu}{4\pi} \frac{(\mathbf{A}_{x2i} - \mathbf{A}_{x1i}).(\mathbf{B}_{x2j} - \mathbf{B}_{x1j}) + (\mathbf{A}_{y2i} - \mathbf{A}_{y1i}).(\mathbf{B}_{y2j} - \mathbf{B}_{y1j}) + (\mathbf{A}_{z2i} - \mathbf{A}_{z1i}).(\mathbf{B}_{z2j} - \mathbf{B}_{z1j})}{\sqrt{\left(\left(\mathbf{B}_{x1j} + \frac{|\mathbf{B}_{x2j} - \mathbf{B}_{x1j}|}{2} \right) - \left(\mathbf{A}_{x1i} + \frac{|\mathbf{A}_{x2i} - \mathbf{A}_{x1i}|}{2} \right) \right)^2 + \left(\left(\mathbf{B}_{y1j} + \frac{|\mathbf{B}_{y2j} - \mathbf{B}_{y1j}|}{2} \right) - \left(\mathbf{A}_{y1i} + \frac{|\mathbf{A}_{y2i} - \mathbf{A}_{y1i}|}{2} \right) \right)^2 + \left(\left(\mathbf{B}_{z1j} + \frac{|\mathbf{B}_{z2j} - \mathbf{B}_{z1j}|}{2} \right) - \left(\mathbf{A}_{z1i} + \frac{|\mathbf{A}_{z2i} - \mathbf{A}_{z1i}|}{2} \right) \right)^2}} \tag{8}$$

For a global solution of the inductive coupling part of the EMC problem, inside the overall electric power system, it is necessary to analyze the circuit globally focusing on mutual intercircuit inductance coupling. The result is the following integral-differential system of equations:

$$\begin{aligned} u_{cc1} &= R_{c1} . i_1 + L_{c1} . \frac{di_1}{dt} + \frac{1}{C_{c1}} \int i_1 . dt + \sum_{\substack{j=1 \\ j \neq 1}}^{k} u_{ij} \\ &\vdots \\ u_{cck} &= R_{ck} . i_k + L_{ck} . \frac{di_k}{dt} + \frac{1}{C_{ck}} \int i_k . dt + \sum_{\substack{j=1 \\ j \neq k}}^{k} u_{ij} \end{aligned} \tag{9}$$

For this purpose it is very suitable to explore the existing simulation programs such as for example the PSPICE program utilized worldwide.

In the next part, we will try to determine the effect of the one-quadrant impulse converter on the sensing circuit as shown Fig. 5. The circuit dimensions are a = 0.2 m, b = 0.3 m, c = 0.1 m, d = 0.05 m, e = 0.005m. The radius of the copper wires is R = 0.0006 m and the relative permitivity of the circuit environment is μ_r = 0.991. Electrical parameters of the simulation circuit are R_Z = 11.66 Ω, L_Z = 400 μH, R = 10 Ω, R_G = 100 Ω and U_{CC} = 70V. The IGBT transistor Q was switched on at the frequency 10 kHz and the switch on/off ratio was 0.5.

The inductance of the first and second loops are given as

$$L_1 = L_{e1} + L_{i1} = \frac{\mu_0 b}{\pi} \ln \frac{a - R}{R} + \frac{\mu_0 a}{\pi} \ln \frac{b - R}{R} + \frac{\mu . 2 . (a + b)}{8\pi} = 1.294 \ \mu H \tag{10}$$

$$L_2 = L_{e2} + L_{i2} = \frac{\mu_0 c}{\pi}\ln\frac{d-R}{R} + \frac{\mu_0 d}{\pi}\ln\frac{c-R}{R} + \frac{\mu.2.(c+d)}{8\pi} = 0.294\ \mu H \tag{11}$$

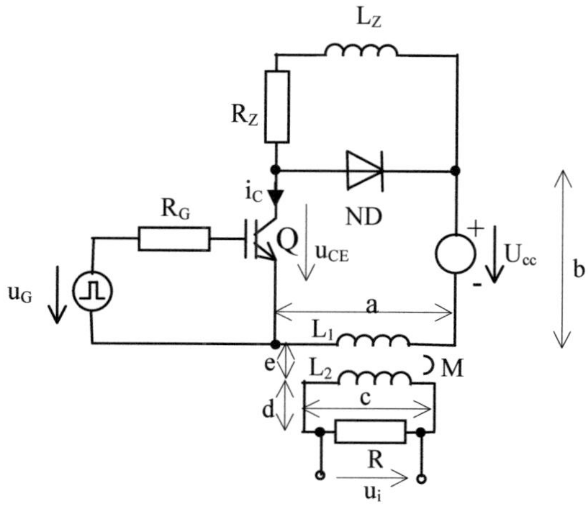

Fig. 5. Investigated circuit

The mutual inductance M calculated from the above mentioned equation is M = 477.4 nH. The magnetic coupling coefficient k is given as

$$k = \frac{M}{\sqrt{L_1 + L_2}} = 0.774 \tag{12}$$

Simulation results are shown in Fig. 6. Results obtained with measurements are shown in Fig. 7 and switching details in Fig. 8.

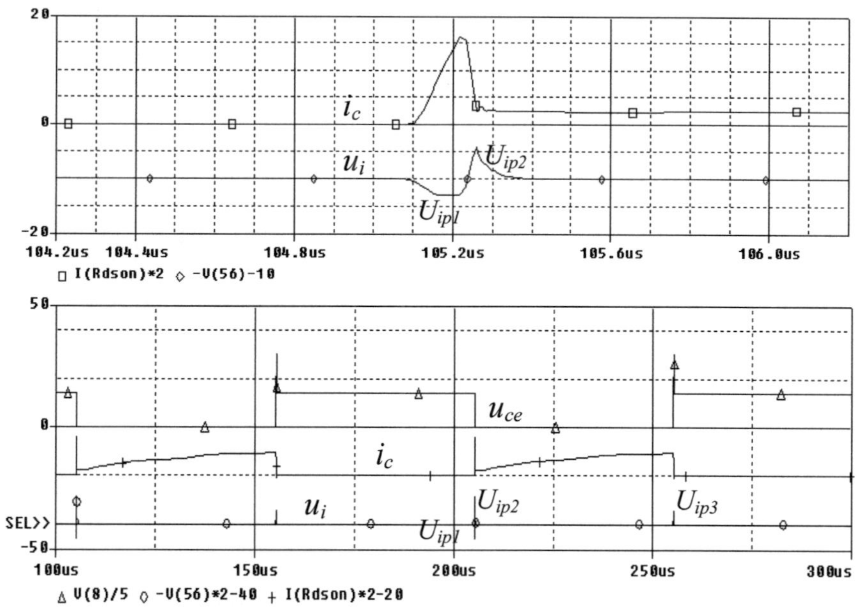

Fig. 6. Simulation results

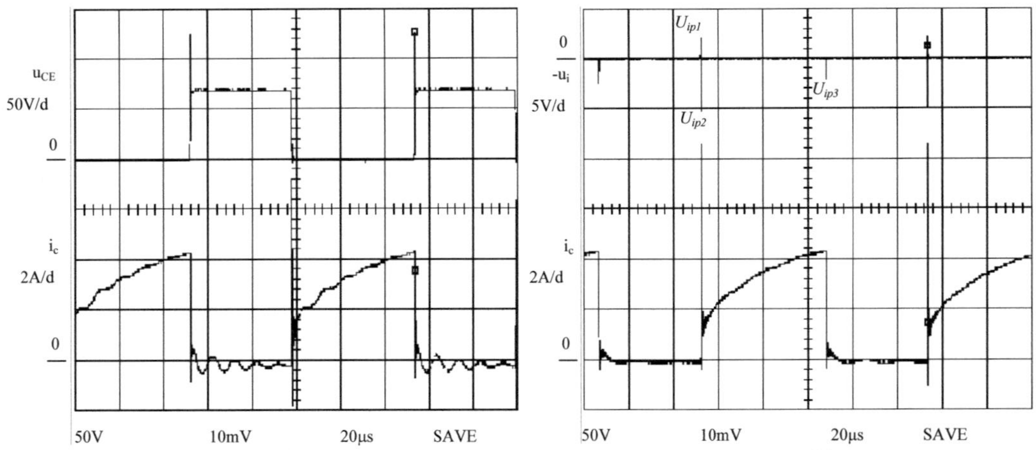

a) b)

Fig. 7. Measured courses a) voltage u_{CE} and current i_C; b) voltage $-u_i$ and current i_C

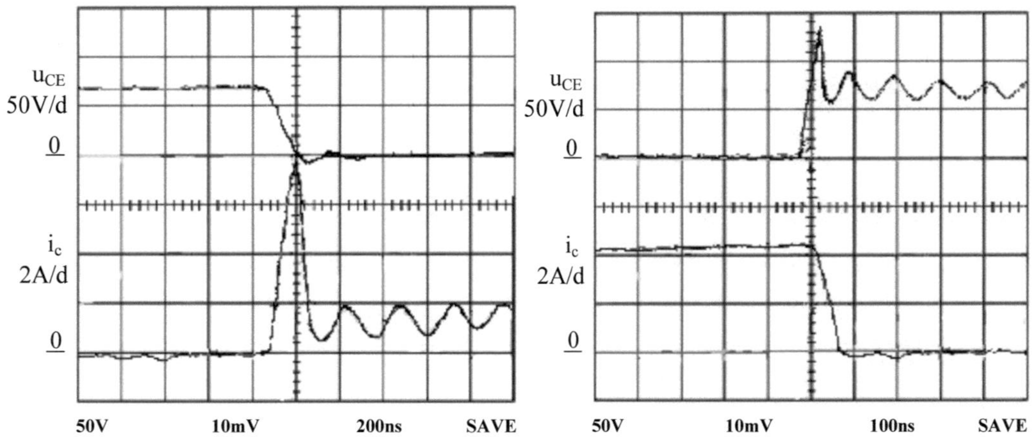

a) b)

Fig. 8. Details of voltage u_{CE} and current i_C a) switching on state; b) switching off state

A comparison of the simulated and measured results shows that peaks of transistor current *ic* have the same values, i.e. 8.4 A, in both cases. The same values, i.e. 4.4 A, have both the simulated and measured transistor current at the moment when transistor is switched off. There is a small difference only between the simulated and measured curves of the transistor voltage u_{CE}. The overvoltage generated at the transistor switching off reaches the value of 150 V for the simulated result. However, the corresponding overvoltage has only the value of 130 V for the measured result. Peaks of the simulated and measured induced voltages have the same values of U_{i1} = -2.2 V, U_{i2} = 5.02 V, U_{i1} = 2.1 V. This means that such method is acceptable for inductive coupling investigation of the EMC problem.

4. Capacitive coupling

The capacitive coupling is typical for galvanically separated circuit nodes among which the mutual influence is represented by electric field strength $\overline{E}$. Its distribution is given by the potential at the particular nodes, geometry of the system and dielectric properties of materials and media involved (Fig. 9).

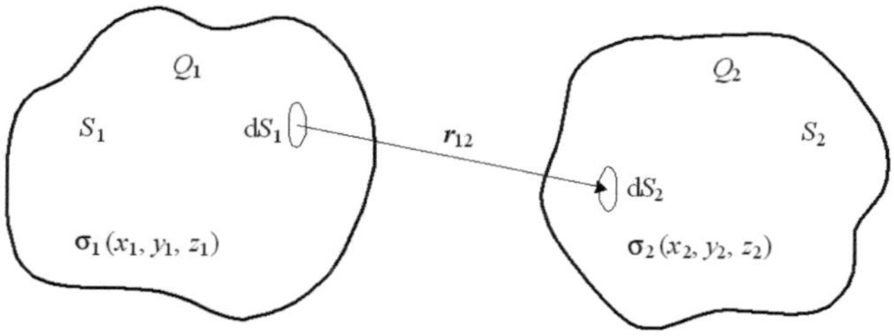

Fig. 9. Capacitive coupling

For the predictive investigation of the capacitive couplings we will start from the well-known Maxwell equation modified for electrostatic field

$$\mathrm{rot}\,\overline{E} = 0. \tag{13}$$

The vector of electric field strength generated by the first electrode at any external point $\overline{r}_0$ is

$$\overline{E}_1 = \frac{1}{4\pi\varepsilon_0}\int_{S_1}\frac{\overline{r}_{10}}{r_{10}^3}.\sigma_1 dS, \tag{14}$$

where S_1 is electrode surface and σ_1 is its surface density calculated by ratio $\sigma_1 = Q_1/S_1$. The total vector $\overline{E}$ at point $\overline{r}_0$ of the system is then given as the sum of vectors $\overline{E}_1$ and $\overline{E}_2$ induced by both charged surfaces. The value of voltage between the electrodes follows from equation

$$U_{12} = \varphi_1 - \varphi_2 = \int_1^2(\overline{E}_1 + \overline{E}_2).d\overline{r}_{12} = \frac{1}{4\pi\varepsilon_0}\int_1^2\left(\int_{S_1}\frac{\overline{r}_{10}}{r_{10}^3}.\sigma_1 dS + \int_{S_2}\frac{\overline{r}_{20}}{r_{20}^3}.\sigma_2 dS\right)d\overline{r}_{12} \tag{15}$$

where r_{12} is the distance between two elementary parts of the surfaces dS_1 and dS_2. If we suppose that $Q_1 = Q$ and $Q_2 = -Q$, then the capacitance of the system may be expressed by equation

$$C_{12} = Q / U_{12} \tag{16}$$

Often the engineers must determine the mutual parasitic capacitance of two wires of general geometry, as is shown in Fig. 10. In such cases the analytical expression for the resultant capacitance is either very complicated or does not exist at all and the only way how to find its value is to use an appropriate numerical procedure. But its application often requires introduction of suitable simplifying assumptions.

Consider an arrangement of two massive conductors with homogeneous charges Q and $-Q$. Both conductors are of cylindrical shape whose radii are R_1 and R_2, respectively, while their lengths are l_1 and l_2. Let us divide them into thin slices whose thicknesses are in turn Δl_{1i}, $i = 1, m$ and $\Delta l_{2j}\, j = 1, n$, so that $l_1 = \sum_{i=1}^{m}\Delta l_{1i}$, $l_2 = \sum_{j=1}^{n}\Delta l_{2j}$.

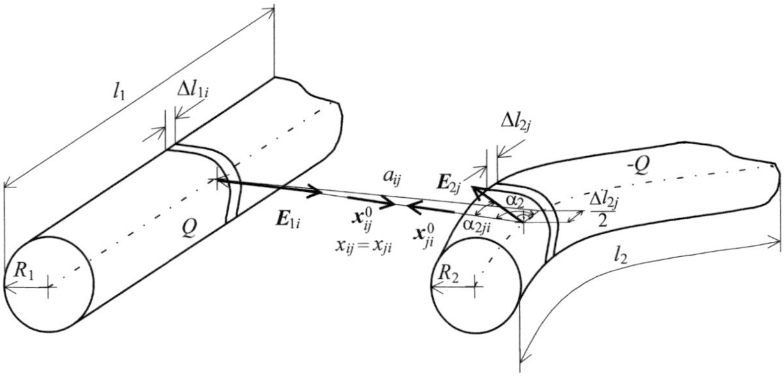

Fig. 10. Capacitive coupling

The potential of the second conductor can be expressed by formula

$$\varphi_2 = \sum_{j=1}^{n}\sum_{i=1}^{m}\left(\int_{R_2}^{\infty} \overline{E}_{2j}.d\overline{x}_{ji} + \int_{x_{ij}-R_2}^{\infty} \overline{E}_{1i}.d\overline{x}_{ij}\right) = \sum_{j=1}^{n}\sum_{i=1}^{m}\left(\int_{R_2}^{\infty} \frac{-Q.\overline{x}^0_{ji}}{2\pi\varepsilon\Delta l_{2j}x}.d\overline{x}_{ji} + \int_{x_{ij}-R_2}^{\infty} \frac{Q.\overline{x}^0_{ij}}{2\pi\varepsilon\Delta l_{1i}x}.d\overline{x}_{ij}\right) =$$
$$= \frac{Q}{2\pi\varepsilon}\sum_{j=1}^{n}\sum_{i=1}^{m}\left(\frac{\ln R_2}{\Delta l_{2j}}\cos\alpha_{E_{2j}x^0_{ji}} - \frac{\ln\left(x_{ij}-R_2\right)}{\Delta l_{1i}}\cos\alpha_{E_{1i}x^0_{ij}}\right). \tag{17}$$

However for correct calculation we have to take only such members of i series for which is valid fact that its vectors $\overline{E}_{1i}$ and $d\overline{x}_{ij}$ are collinear, so only such which fulfill the condition

$$\cos\alpha_{E_{1i}x^0_{ij}} = \cos\alpha_{1ij} = 1 \tag{18}$$

The expression $\cos\alpha_{E_{2j}x^0_{ji}} = \cos\alpha_{2ji}$ is possible to derive from Fig. 10. as final equation:

$$\cos\alpha_{2ji} = \sqrt{1-\left(\frac{x^2_{ij}+0.25\Delta l_{2j}{}^2 - a^2_{ij}}{x_{ij}.\Delta l_{2j}}\right)^2} \tag{19}$$

Analogously, it is possible to obtain the potential of the first conductor.
The voltage between both conductors is

$$U_{12} = \varphi_1 - \varphi_2 = \frac{Q}{2\pi\varepsilon}\sum_{i=1}^{m}\sum_{j=1}^{n}\left(\frac{\cos\alpha_{E_{1i}x^0_{ij}}}{\Delta l_{1i}}.\ln\frac{\left(x_{ij}-R_2\right)}{R_1} + \frac{\cos\alpha_{E_{2j}x^0_{ji}}}{\Delta l_{2j}}.\ln\frac{\left(x_{ji}-R_1\right)}{R_2}\right). \tag{20}$$

Now it is possible to express the value of parasitic capacitance using the formula

$$C_{12} = \frac{2\pi\varepsilon}{\sum_{i=1}^{m}\sum_{j=1}^{n}\left(\frac{\cos\alpha_{E_{1i}x^0_{ij}}}{\Delta l_{1i}}.\ln\frac{\left(x_{ij}-R_2\right)}{R_1} + \frac{\cos\alpha_{E_{2j}x^0_{ji}}}{\Delta l_{2j}}.\ln\frac{\left(x_{ji}-R_1\right)}{R_2}\right)}. \tag{21}$$

The verification of correctness of the obtained results can be carried out by simulation and measurements. For this purpose, it is possible to use the connection of a DC impulse converter shown in Fig. 11.

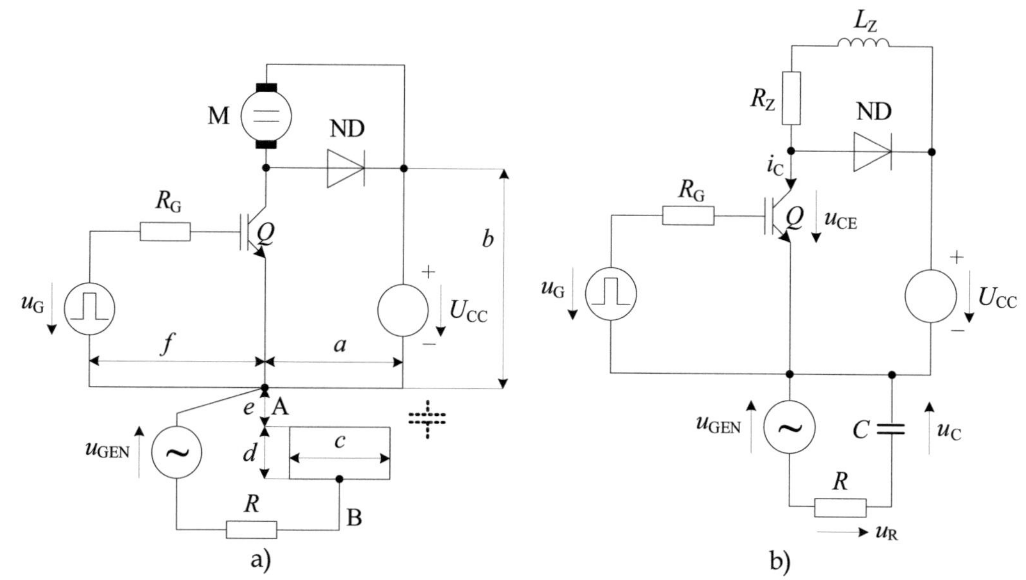

Fig. 11. Investigated circuit a) measured; b) simulated

Now we will determine the value of the parasitic capacitance between the node A of impulse converter and node B of the sense loop. The ambient dielectric is air. The geometrical dimensions of the investigated circuits are $a = f = 0.2$ m, $b = 0.3$ m, $c = 0.1$ m, $d = 0.05$ m, $e = 0.00135$ m. The conductors are made of copper, with radius $R = 0.0006$ m. From the above parameters and figure Fig. 12 it is possible to calculate the individual partial parasitic capacitances

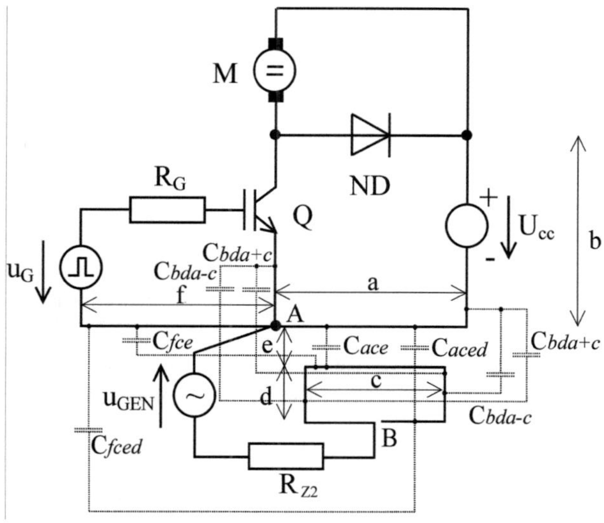

Fig. 12. Detailed expression of main parasitic capacitancies

Based on equation (21) and Fig. 12 the individual circuit capacitances are C_{ace} = 16.629 pF, C_{aced} = 0.8306 pF, C_{fce} = 0.6391 pF, C_{fced} = 0.6314 pF, $C_{bda\text{-}c}$ = 0.3989 pF, C_{bda+c} = 0.3658 pF, $C = C_{ace} + C_{aced} + C_{fce} + C_{fced} + 2\,C_{bda\text{-}c} + 2\,C_{bda+c}$ = 20.26 pF.
Now, it is possible to realize the simulation analysis in the PSPICE program. The connection of the simulated circuit is shown in Fig. 11. The parameters of the individual elements are U_{CC} = 70 V, R_Z = 11.66 Ω, L_Z = 400 μH, R_{Z2} = 1 MΩ, $u_{GEN} = 2\sin(\omega t)$ V. The simulation results for frequencies f = 10 kHz and f = 50 kHz are depicted in Fig. 13.

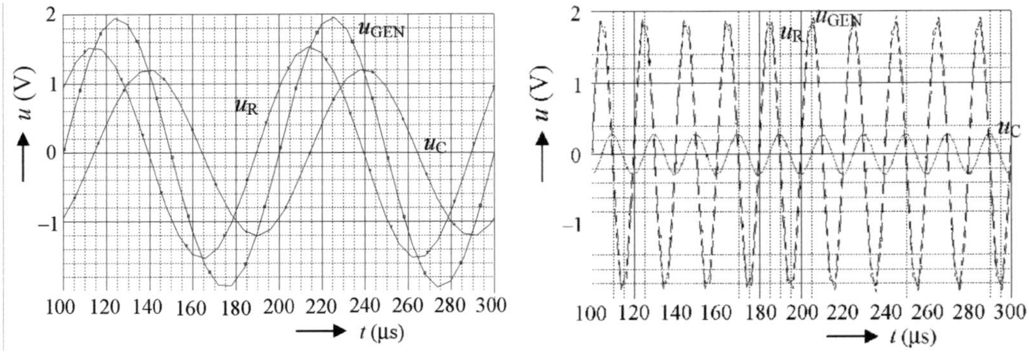

Fig. 13. Simulation results for frequency a) f = 10 kHz; b) f = 50 kHz

The measured values of u_{CE}, u_{GEN}, and u_C are shown in Fig. 14.
The comparison of the simulated and measured results shows that the results are identical. This coincidence leads to the conclusion that the derived analytical formula for parasitic capacitance is correct.
The presented analysis indicates that not only the high current switching frequencies have the main influence on the EMC of the converter, but also their switch-off state with small parasitic resonant load current is equally important.
Although such converter capacitances seem to be negligible, the above analysis shows that they may be of crucial influence. One case occurs when the switching frequency is high, another when the node belongs to the circuit with high impedance. This is obvious for the capacitive coupling between CMOS integrated circuits and power converter circuit, when the EMC aspects can be vital for correct operation of the equipment (Clayton, 1992).

5. Galvanic coupling

The problem of galvanic coupling deals with individual electric equipment or their part's interconnections in such a way, that minimum one or (in some cases as for example feeding net) more common conductors, interconnecting these equipments and so mutual influence is generated.
The working frequencies and the length of common conductor must be taken always into account. In all cases of the galvanic coupling, the fact that electrical components are not ideal and so they are containing certain parasitic capacitances, inductances and real resistances, is valid. Due to higher working frequency of currents flowed by the common conductors, they must be taken as circuits with distributed parameters, during the process of predictive result galvanic coupling investigation. If the working frequencies will be lower, then the interconnecting circuits can be taken as circuits with concentrated parameters.

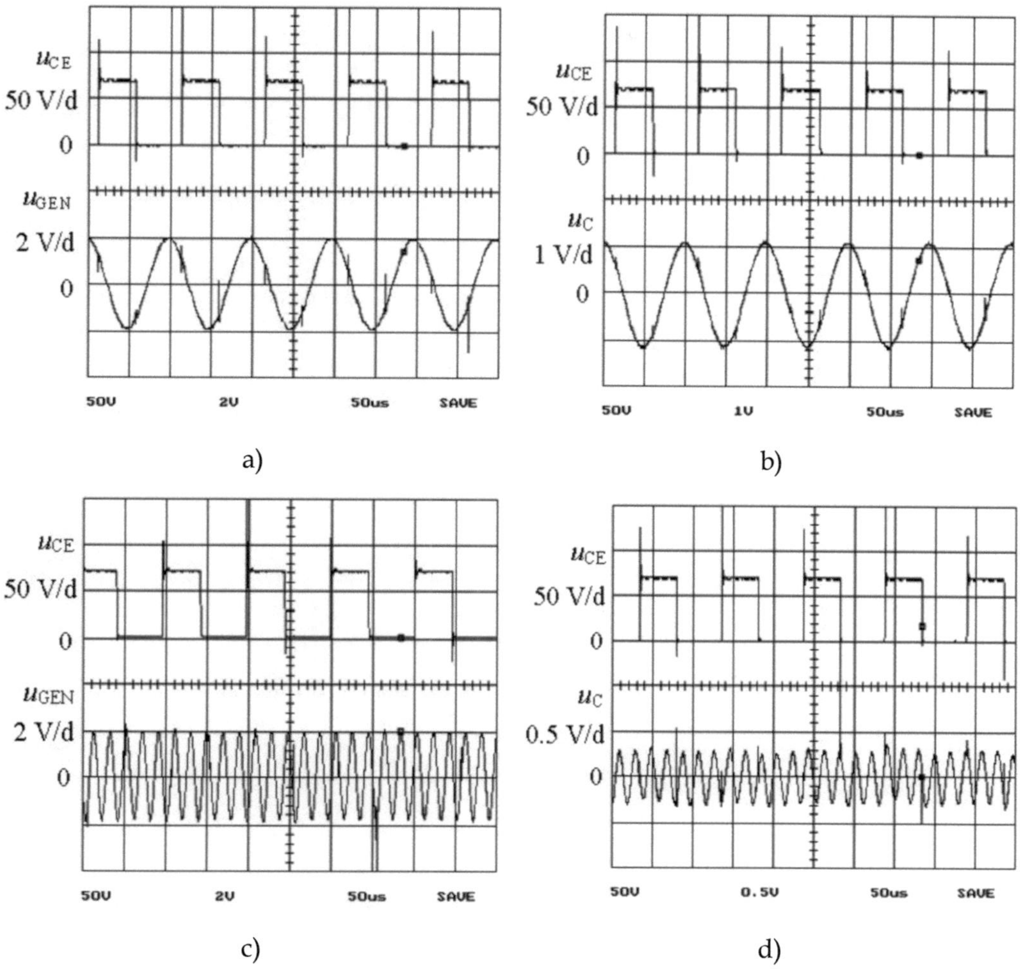

Fig. 14. Measured voltages a) u_{CE} and u_{GEN}; b) u_{CE} and u_C for frequency $f = 10$ kHz; c) u_{CE} and u_{GEN}; d) u_{CE} and u_C for frequency $f = 50$ kHz

5.1 Solution for the low frequencies and concentrated parameters

Minimum two or more electric circuits, which are mutually galvanically interconnected by one common conductor with its length l, represent a type of galvanic coupling. Due to low frequency operation it is possible to define the common conductor electrical parameters by concentrated parameters of its resistance R and inductance L. If we suppose in the next step, that the conductor will be made of copper, so the voltage drop on its resistance R will be much smaller in comparison with the voltage drop across its inductance L, which is caused by the time depending change of current. So, for the simplified analysis of the problem the conductor resistance will be neglected in the following. The schematic representation of the described problem is shown in the following figure Fig. 15.

The mathematical description of the situation in the investigated circuit (Fig. 15. a) is then given by the next system of integral-differential equations (if the load created by serial connection of R_1, L_1 and C_1 components is supposed):

$$
\begin{aligned}
u_1 - u_L - u_2 &= u_1 - L.\frac{di_3}{dt} - \left(R_1.i_1 + L_1.\frac{di_1}{dt} + \frac{1}{C_1}.\int i_1.dt \right) = 0 \\
u_{1'} - u_L - u_{2'} &= u_{1'} - L.\frac{di_3}{dt} - \left(R_{1'}.i_{1'} + L_{1'}.\frac{di_{1'}}{dt} + \frac{1}{C_{1'}}.\int i_{1'}.dt \right) = 0 \\
u_{1^k} - u_L - u_{2^k} &= u_{1^k} - L.\frac{di_3}{dt} - \left(R_{1^k}.i_{1^k} + L_{1^k}.\frac{di_{1^k}}{dt} + \frac{1}{C_{1^k}}.\int i_{1^k}.dt \right) = 0 \\
i_3 &= i_1 + i_{1'} + \sum_{k=''}^{n} i_{1^k}
\end{aligned}
\qquad (22)
$$

where n is the number of all different loops, contained in the same common conductor. In the case of great number of loops, the analytic investigation of galvanic coupling influence on individual electric circuits is relatively complicated, so it is possible to utilize the available computer numerical simulation programs.

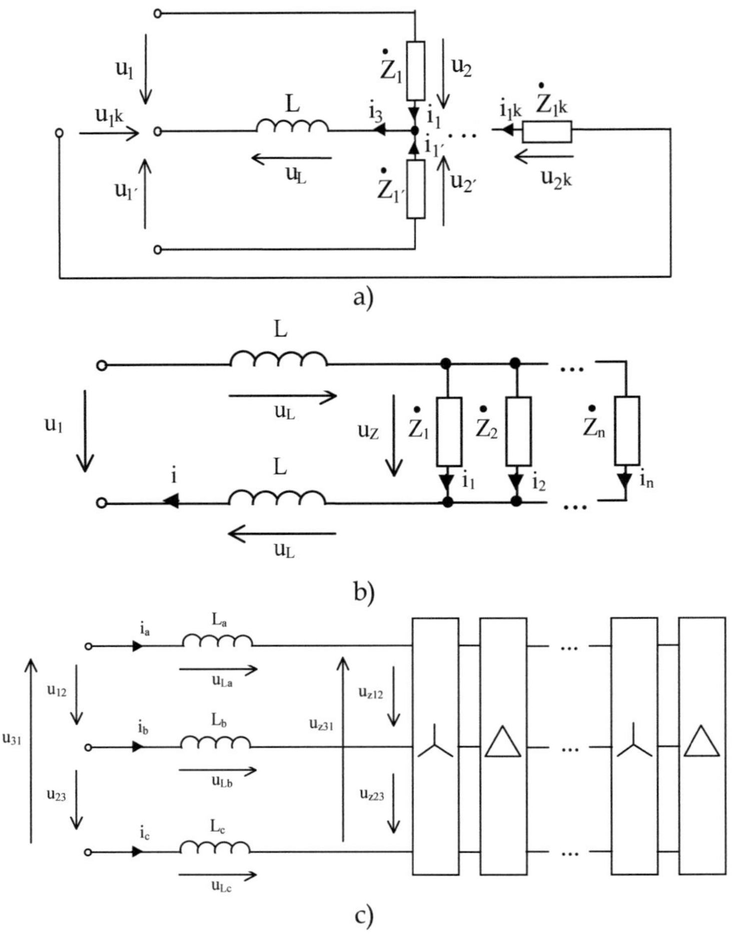

Fig. 15. The schematic representation of the circuit interconnections by a) one common conductor; b) two conductors; c) several common conductors

The multiple interconnection of electrical or electronics circuits realized by two common conductors is typical especially for one phase or DC feeding conductors, as it is shown in figure Fig. 15. b. Due to existence of both the incoming conductor inductances L, the total circuit inductance is double. The mutual galvanic coupling is generated at the moment of the optional loop's impedance change. The impedance can be changed up, or down. This situation is typical for the impulse converter circuits, but it is clear that such case occurs also in all other circuits, which use the switching parts.
The interconnection of many electrical or electronic circuits, by several common conductors, is typical for three phase feeding net, as it is shown in figure Fig. 15. c. In case, where four conductors will do those circuits interconnections and also if one of them is a neutral wire, the problem will be the same as the problem of three individual circuits, connected together by only one common conductor. This problem was already described. The circuit can be described by system of equations expressed by a complex vector as:

$$\begin{aligned} \overline{U}_{12} &= j\omega L\overline{I}_1 + (R_1 + j\omega L_1 - j\frac{1}{\omega C_1}).\overline{I}_1 - (R_2 + j\omega L_2 - j\frac{1}{\omega C_2}).\overline{I}_2 - j\omega L\overline{I}_2 \\ \overline{U}_{23} &= j\omega L\overline{I}_2 + (R_2 + j\omega L_2 - j\frac{1}{\omega C_2}).\overline{I}_2 - (R_3 + j\omega L_3 - j\frac{1}{\omega C_3}).\overline{I}_3 - j\omega L\overline{I}_3 \\ & \overline{I}_1 + \overline{I}_2 + \overline{I}_3 = 0 \end{aligned} \tag{23}$$

In the following step, we will try to obtain imagination about the galvanic coupling existence of only two interacting circuits. For the simplification of the analytic investigation it is suitable to suppose, that pure resistors create the loads in both the galvanic connected circuits and that the circuits are in steady states and they are supplied from DC voltage sources as it is shown in figure Fig. 16.
Consider the jump change of supplying voltage from value $U_{1'}$ to zero supposed in lower circuit and no change of supplying voltage or load in the upper circuit. The time dependence description of the voltage u_2 can be obtained by equation

$$u_2 = U_1 - u_L = U_1 - L.\frac{di_3}{dt} = U_1 + U_{1'}.\frac{R_1}{(R_1 + R_{1'})}.e^{-\frac{R_1 R_{1'}}{L(R_1+R_{1'})}.t} \tag{24}$$

From the obtained relation it is clear, that the first circuit load voltage is changed about value $(U_{1'}.R_1)/(R_1+R_{1'})$ due to existence of the change inside the circuit, which is galvanically connected with the previous one. No working activity of the first circuit was done and so its switch on steady state remains. In dependence on the load resistor values ratio the voltage drop can be within the open interval $(0,U_{1'})$.
If the supply voltage switching on state inside the second circuit will be investigated, the information about the voltage load u_2 could be obtained by the similar method.

$$u_2 = U_1 - u_L = U_1 - L.\frac{di_3}{dt} = U_1 - U_{1'}.\frac{R_1}{(R_1 + R_{1'})}.e^{-\frac{R_1 R_{1'}}{L(R_1+R_{1'})}.t} \tag{25}$$

It is evident, that the load voltage value inside the first circuit, can be changed about the voltage drop within the open interval $(-U_{1'},0)$, again in dependence on load resistor values ratio.

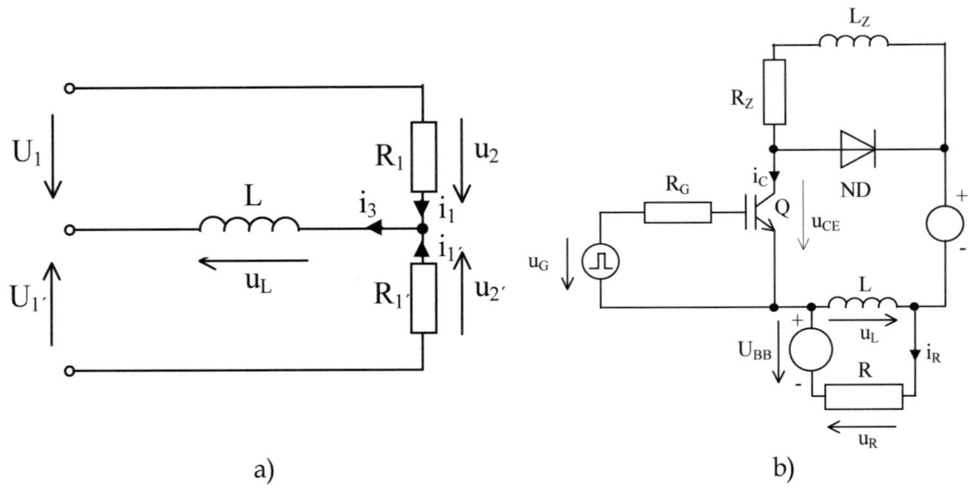

Fig. 16. Electrical scheme of a) the investigated; b) the simulated and measured circuit

Generally, the switching process inside the second circuit is reflected through galvanic coupling to the total possible load voltage u_2 change within the interval range ($-U_{1'}$, $U_{1'}$), depending on load values ratio and the sign of derivation of the current flowed via common conductor inductance L.

The computer numerical simulation realized by the PSPICE program helps us to verify the dependencies obtained analytically. Let the common conductor length be l = 0.1 m. The influence of its magnetic field in distance d = 1 m will be taken into account. The radius of copper conductors is R = 0.6 mm and their relative permeability is μ_r = 0.991. Then inductance L = 302 nH. In the next step will suppose, that voltage $u_{1'}$ has a rectangle shape with the amplitude 70 V, duty factor z = 0.5 and switching frequency f = 10 kHz. The other circuit parameters are $R_{1'}$ = 11.66 Ω, U_1 = 5 V, R_1 = 10 kΩ and L = 302 nH. Based on the derived equations and given parameters, we can calculate the voltage u_2 peaks so, that the time in the equations (24) and (25) will be replaced by t = 0. Then we will obtain:

$$u_2(t_{sw\,off}) = U_1 + U_{1'}.\frac{R_1}{(R_1 + R_{1'})} = 5 + 70.\frac{10000}{10011.66} = 74.918 \text{ V} \tag{26}$$

Analogically it is possible to state the voltage peak of u_2 at the moment of the second circuit switch on.

$$u_2(t_{sw\,on}) = U_1 - U_{1'}.\frac{R_1}{(R_1 + R_{1'})} = 5 - 70.\frac{10000}{10011.66} = -64.918 \text{ V} \tag{27}$$

The courses of the input voltages u_1 and $u_{1'}$, the load voltages u_2 and $u_{2'}$ and the voltage u_L are introduced in figure Fig. 17. All data were obtained by computer circuit simulation in the PSPICE program for given circuit parameters. The coincidence of the results obtained analytically as equations derived in the previous parts and by computer numerical simulation is evident, at the first sight.

Let the derived results verification be done by simulation and practical measuring of the power semiconductor converter circuit connected according to the scheme shown in figure Fig. 16b (Tihanyi, 1995). The circuit parameters are: U_{CC} = 70 V, R_Z = 11.66 Ω, L_Z = 400 μH,

L = 302 nH, R = 10 kΩ, U_{BB} = 5 V. The power IGBT transistor is switching with the frequency of 10 kHz and the duty cycle z = 0.5.

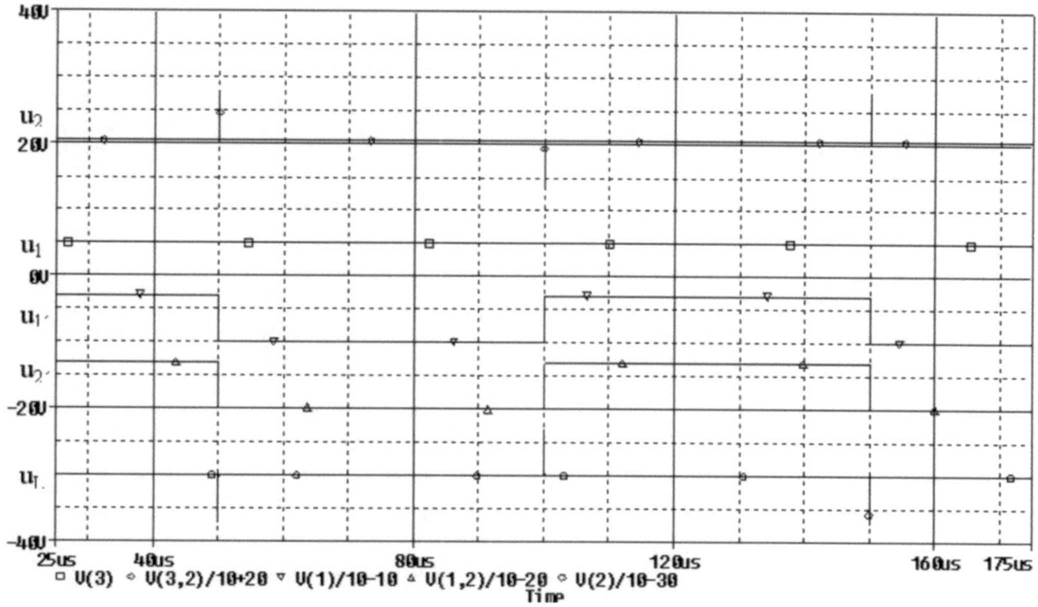

Fig. 17. Results obtained by simulation in the PSPICE program

The courses of the transistor voltage u_{CE}, inductance voltage u_L and resistance R voltage u_R obtained by simulation for the frequency f = 10 kHz are depicted in figure Fig. 18a.

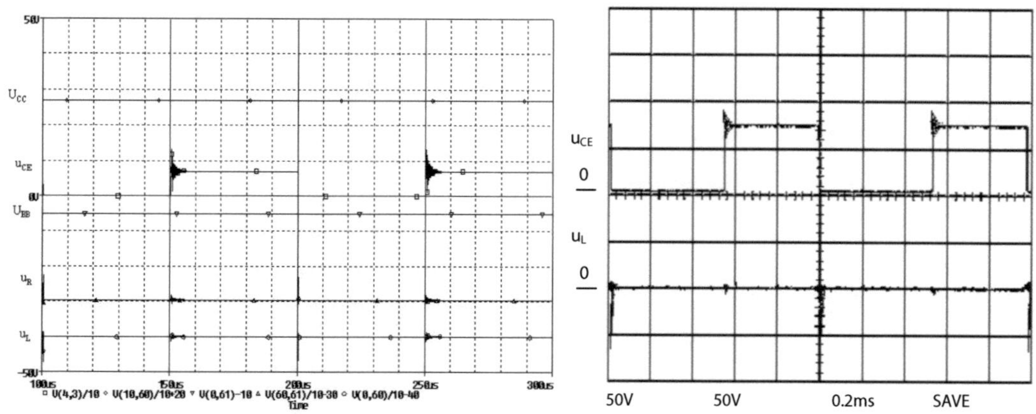

a) b)

Fig. 18. The results obtained by a) simulation in the PSPICE program; b) measurement

In this case the voltage jump does not exist, because the transistor is switching by a finite velocity. On the basis of this fact, the switching inductance voltage drop reaches the values of approximately ±10 V in dependence on the current's rising or falling slope. The most expressive inductance voltage drop appears at the moment of the transistor current falling, caused by the existence of the charge of commutation diode. This time, the current slope is markedly increasing, and so the parasitic inductance voltage drop is increasing too. Comparable results, obtained by the verification measurement, are displayed in figure Fig. 18b. The coincidence with the simulation results is evident.

5.2 Solution for the higher frequencies and distributed parameters

The mutual interconnection of electric circuits by two common conductors with the length l (the length is long or the transferred signal has high frequency) represents the investigation problem of a line with distributed parameters (in the following "long transmission line" or "long line" only). The basic representation of such electric circuit interconnection is drawn in figure Fig. 19.

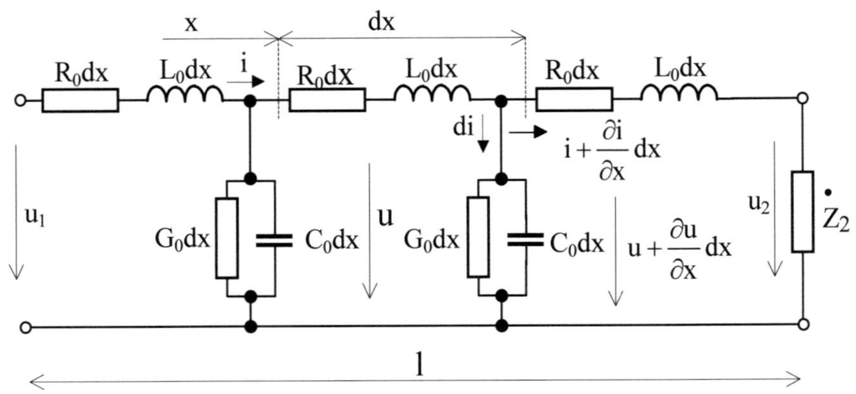

Fig. 19. The equivalent scheme of long transmission line with distributed parameters

It is known from the electric circuit theory that the time dependence investigation of line voltage or current, at optional line position, leads to the system solution of two partial-differential equations.

In that case an input voltage and a current of long transmission line it is possible to describe by time harmonic functions in the form,

$$u = U_m \sin(\omega t + \psi_u) \quad \Rightarrow \bar{U} e^{j\omega t} \tag{28}$$

$$i = I_m \sin(\omega t + \psi_i) \quad \Rightarrow \bar{I} e^{j\omega t} \tag{29}$$

the resulting solution of the given equation system, expressed by complex voltage and current vectors, will be given as:

$$\bar{U} = \bar{U}_1 ch\, \bar{\gamma} x - \bar{Z}_v \bar{I}_1 sh\, \bar{\gamma} x \tag{30}$$

$$\bar{I} = \bar{I}_1 ch\, \bar{\gamma} x - \frac{\bar{U}_1}{\bar{Z}_v} sh\, \bar{\gamma} x \tag{31}$$

where

$$\bar{\gamma} = \beta + j\alpha = \sqrt{(R_0 + j\omega L_0)(G_0 + j\omega C_0)} \tag{32}$$

$$\beta = \sqrt{\frac{1}{2}\left[\sqrt{\left(R_0^2+\omega^2 L_0^2\right)\left(G_0^2+\omega^2 C_0^2\right)}+R_0 G_0-\omega^2 L_0 C_0\right]} \quad (33)$$

$$\alpha = \sqrt{\frac{1}{2}\left[\sqrt{\left(R_0^2+\omega^2 L_0^2\right)\left(G_0^2+\omega^2 C_0^2\right)}-R_0 G_0+\omega^2 L_0 C_0\right]} \quad (34)$$

$$\overline{Z}_v = \sqrt{\frac{\left(R_0+j\omega L_0\right)}{\left(G_0+j\omega C_0\right)}} = Z_v.e^{j\varphi_v} \quad (35)$$

In the field of power electronics a non-harmonic unipolar or bipolar signal is utilized many times for indirect converters. To enable a given problem's mathematical analysis, the non-harmonic signal must be described by the system of harmonic functions.
The expression of the investigated voltage dependence will be done by calculated coefficients of Fourier's series and by the next equation.

$$u(t) = \sum_{k=0}^{\infty}\left(a_k.\cos(k\omega t)+b_k \sin(k\omega t)\right) \quad (36)$$

where: $a_0 = \frac{1}{T}\int_0^T f(\omega t)dt$, $a_k = \frac{2}{T}\int_0^T f(\omega t).cos(k\omega t)dt$, $b_k = \frac{2}{T}\int_0^T f(\omega t).sin(k\omega t)dt$.

For a long line galvanic coupling influence investigation, it is necessary to obtain the time dependence of the voltage at the end of the long transmission line. It is possible to calculate the searched voltage on the basis of an equation expressing the time voltage dependence at an optional position of a long transmission line, which is far-away from the beginning of the line about the distance x so, that this length will be replaced by the line length l and the complex current vector $\overline{I}_1$ will be replaced by the relation $\overline{U}_1 / \overline{Z}_{input}$. Let the feeding voltage have square-wave shape with the amplitude U_1.

$$\overline{U}_2 = \frac{U_1}{2}.\left(\left(e^{(\beta l+j(\alpha l+\varphi_U))}+e^{-(\beta l+j(\alpha l-\varphi_U))}\right)-\frac{a+jb}{c+jd}.\left(e^{(\beta l+j(\alpha l+\varphi_U))}-e^{-(\beta l+j(\alpha l-\varphi_U))}\right)\right) \quad (37)$$

where the expressions a, b, c, d are calculated on the basis of following equations:

$$a = Z_2.e^{\beta l}.\cos(\alpha l+\varphi_{Z2})-Z_2.e^{-\beta l}.\cos(\varphi_{Z2}-\alpha l)+Z_v.e^{\beta l}.\cos(\alpha l+\varphi_{Zv})+Z_v.e^{-\beta l}.\cos(\varphi_{Zv}-\alpha l) \quad (38)$$

$$b = Z_2.e^{\beta l}.\sin(\alpha l+\varphi_{Z2})-Z_2.e^{-\beta l}.\sin(\varphi_{Z2}-\alpha l)+Z_v.e^{\beta l}.\sin(\alpha l+\varphi_{Zv})+Z_v.e^{-\beta l}.\sin(\varphi_{Zv}-\alpha l) \quad (39)$$

$$c = Z_2.e^{\beta l}.\cos(\alpha l+\varphi_{Z2})+Z_2.e^{-\beta l}.\cos(\varphi_{Z2}-\alpha l)+Z_v.e^{\beta l}.\cos(\alpha l+\varphi_{Zv})-Z_v.e^{-\beta l}.\cos(\varphi_{Zv}-\alpha l) \quad (40)$$

$$d = Z_2.e^{\beta l}.\sin(\alpha l+\varphi_{Z2})+Z_2.e^{-\beta l}.\sin(\varphi_{Z2}-\alpha l)+Z_v.e^{\beta l}.\sin(\alpha l+\varphi_{Zv})-Z_v.e^{-\beta l}.\sin(\varphi_{Zv}-\alpha l) \quad (41)$$

The electric circuits interconnection realized by one common conductor with the distributed parameters, is a special case, where more electric circuits are utilizing one common conductor, which is either long or serves for high frequency signal conduction.

The problem analysis will be done for the case of two electric circuits interconnection, the scheme of which is shown in figure Fig. 20. Let the upper circuit be supplied by a DC

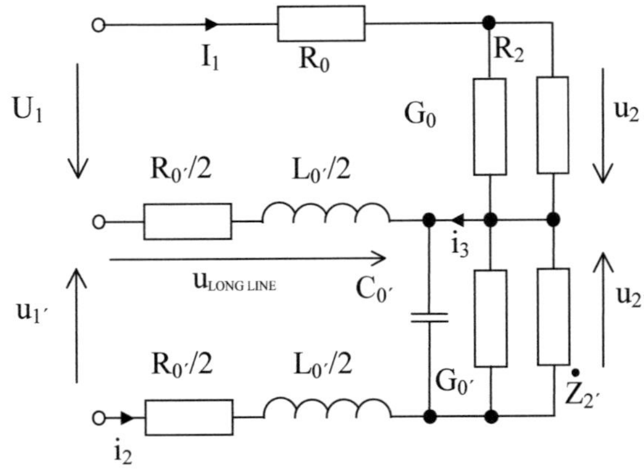

Fig. 20. The scheme of investigated circuit connection

voltage source with the value U_1 = 5 V. As interface conductor the same cable as in the previous case was used, it means a CYSY 4x1.5 mm^2 with the length 15m and with parameters $R_{0'}$ = 0.047 Ω/m, $L_{0'}$ = 343 nH/m, $G_{0'}$ = 33.3 μS/m, $C_{0'}$ = 118 pF/m.
The upper circuit has no signal change. The output voltage u_2 should be reflecting only the voltage drops caused by long line longitudinal resistance and a vertical drop-in. Let the lower circuit be supplied by the same periodical impulse signal $u_{1'}$ as in the case of the previous analysis. It is possible to state the mutual circuit galvanic coupling influence by finding the upper circuit real voltage u_2 course. According to the 2nd Kirchoff's law, we can write the equation for the investigated circuit:

$$u_2 = U_1 - u_{1'} + u_{2'} - R_0.I_1 = U_1 - u_{1'} + u_{2'} - R_0.\frac{U_1}{\frac{R_2.G_0}{R_2 + G_0} + R_0} \tag{42}$$

The analytical form for the voltages $u_{1'}$ and $u_{2'}$ the description can be obtained, from the previous analysis, as equations for input and output voltages of long transmission line. By the substitution of these voltages, the searched relation for time dependence of the voltage u_2 is possible to receive. Any accessible Excel program will do the graphical interpretation of the resulting solution again, figures Fig. 21.
Equally, as in the previous case a multiple verification of correctness can be done by the PSPICE program simulation (Fig. 22) and by practical measurement (Fig. 23).
The coincidence of the obtained results is evident. Small differences concerning the input and output voltage oscillation damping are given by the fact, that for the input and output voltages the infinite Fourier's series were replaced by only the first 40 components in the Excel program.
Very often a symmetrical three-phase load is connected to the inverter impulse output, with the frequency of few tenths of kHz, by the cable with the length within the range 3 up to 20m during the practical use of power semiconductor converters. This case represents the interconnection of two circuits, by a long line with the distributed parameters in the three phases connection.

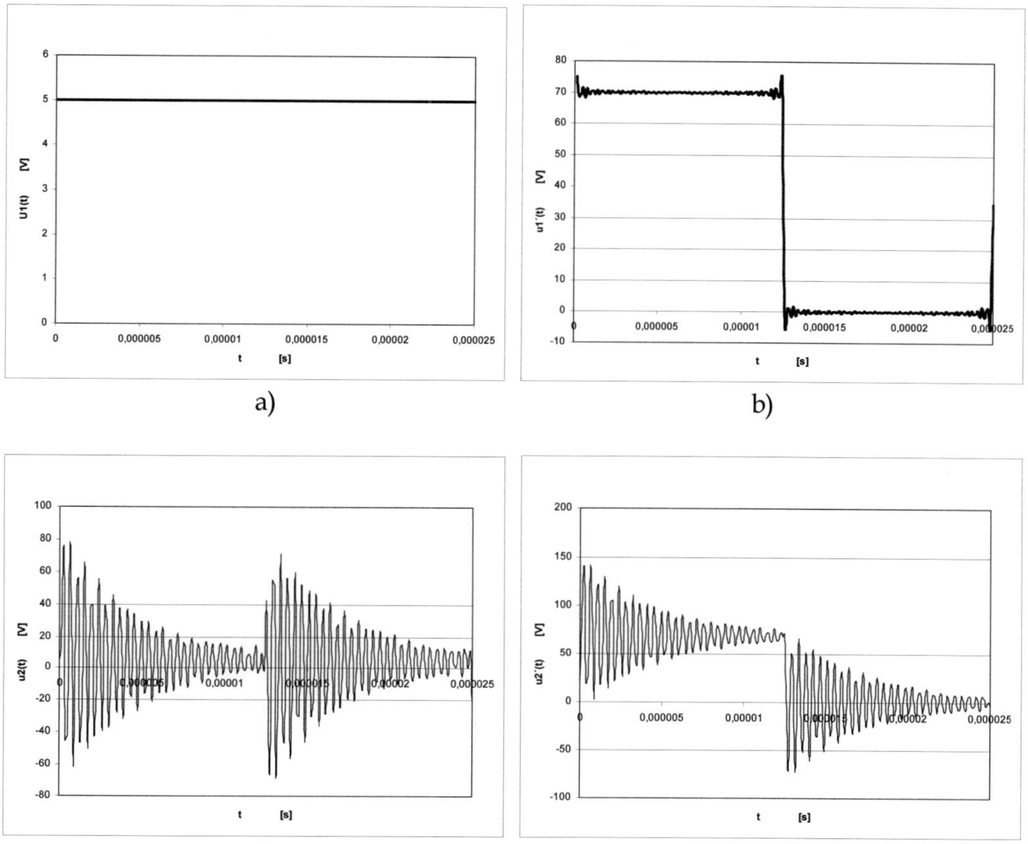

a) b) c) d)

Fig. 21. Theoretical results a) input voltage U_1; b) input voltage $u_{1'}$; c) output voltage u_2; d) output voltage $u_{2'}$

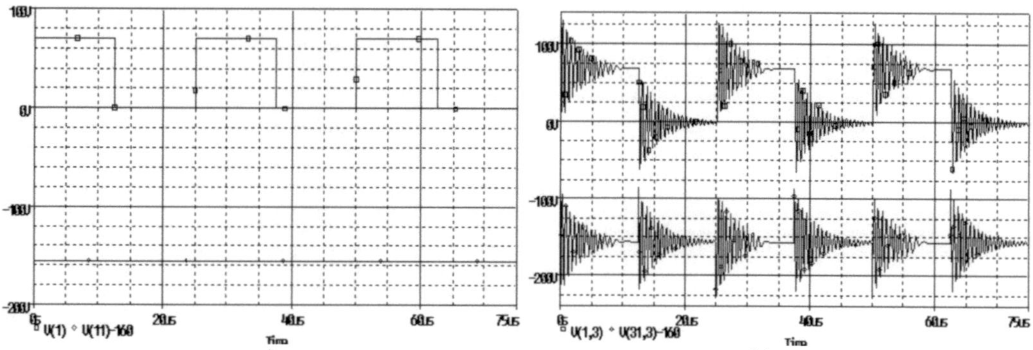

a) b)

Fig. 22. Simulated results a) input voltages $u_{1'}$ and U_1; b) output voltages $u_{2'}$ and u_2

Let the galvanic coupling investigation of such circuit topology be done by a temporal dependence calculation of the voltages $u_{12'}$, $u_{23'}$ and $u_{31'}$ at the end position of a long transmission line. The input long line voltages are graphically depicted in figure Fig. 24.

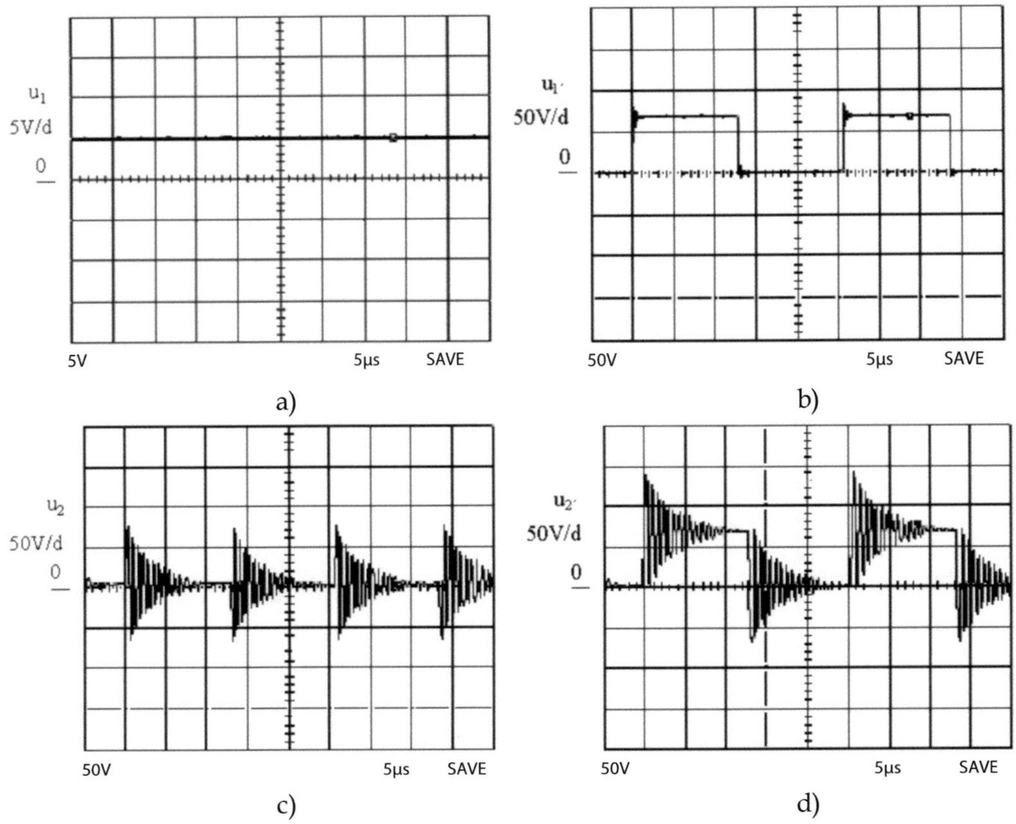

Fig. 23. Measured results a) input voltages u_1; b) input voltages $u_{1'}$; c) output voltage u_2; d) output voltage $u_{2'}$

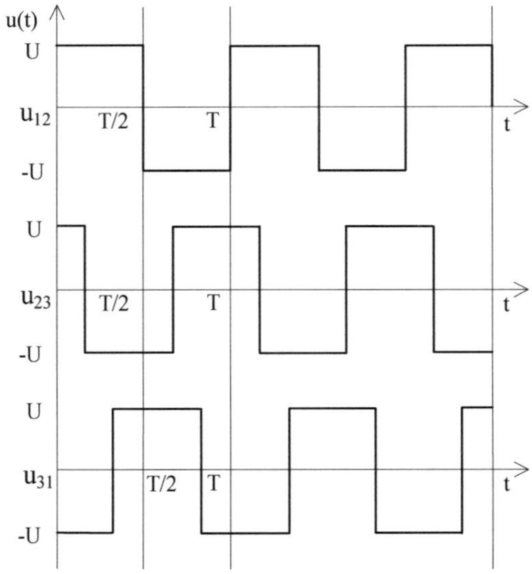

Fig. 24. The input voltages u_{12} , u_{23} and u_{31}

The amplitudes of the input voltages are U = 400 V. The same interconnecting cable was used as in the previous case with the parameters: CYSY 4x1.5 mm^2, with the length 15m, R_0 = 0.047 Ω/m, L_0 = 343 nH/m, G_0 = 33.3 μS/m, C_0 = 118 pF/m. The load is symmetrical, resistive-inductive with parameters R_2 = 10 Ω, L_2 = 1 mH. For the calculation of the output voltages $u_{12'}$, $u_{23'}$ and $u_{31'}$ can be used the relations derived in previous analyses, but it is necessary to express the non-harmonic input feeding voltages of the long transmission line by a harmonic functions. The Fourier's series will be used again.

$$u_{12}(t) = \frac{4U}{\pi} sin(\omega t) + \frac{4U}{3\pi} sin(3\omega t) + \frac{4U}{5\pi} sin(5\omega t) + ... = \sum_{k=0}^{\infty} \frac{4U}{(2k+1)\pi} sin((2k+1)\omega t) \quad (43)$$

$$u_{23}(t) = \frac{4U}{\pi} sin(\omega(t - \frac{T}{3})) + \frac{4U}{3\pi} sin(3\omega(t - \frac{T}{3})) + \frac{4U}{5\pi} sin(5\omega(t - \frac{T}{3})) + ... = \sum_{k=0}^{\infty} \frac{4U}{(2k+1)\pi} sin((2k+1)\omega(t - \frac{T}{3})) \quad (44)$$

$$u_{31}(t) = \frac{4U}{\pi} sin(\omega(t - \frac{2T}{3})) + \frac{4U}{3\pi} sin(3\omega(t - \frac{2T}{3})) + \frac{4U}{5\pi} sin(5\omega(t - \frac{2T}{3})) + ... = \sum_{k=0}^{\infty} \frac{4U}{(2k+1)\pi} sin((2k+1)\omega(t - \frac{2T}{3})) \quad (45)$$

If the calculated relations for the input voltages are substituted by the derived equation (37), which describes the temporal dependence of the voltage at the end of the long line and only the imaginary part of the complex solution will be taken into account, because only this part corresponds to the sinusoidal input voltage, thus we can obtain the relations (46) up to (48).

$$u_{12'}(t) = \sum_{k=0}^{\infty} \frac{2U}{(2k+1)\pi} . (e^{\beta l}.\sin((2k+1)\omega t + \varphi_U + \alpha l) + e^{-\beta l}.\sin((2k+1)\omega t + \varphi_U - \alpha l) - \frac{\sqrt{a^2+b^2}}{\sqrt{c^2+d^2}}.e^{\beta l}.$$
$$.\sin((2k+1)\omega t + \varphi_U + \alpha l + arctg\frac{b}{a} - arctg\frac{d}{c}) + \frac{\sqrt{a^2+b^2}}{\sqrt{c^2+d^2}}.e^{-\beta l}.\sin((2k+1)\omega t + \varphi_U - \alpha l + arctg\frac{b}{a} - arctg\frac{d}{c})) \quad (46)$$

$$u_{23'}(t) = \sum_{k=0}^{\infty} \frac{2U}{(2k+1)\pi} . (e^{\beta l}.\sin((2k+1)\omega(t - \frac{T}{3}) + \varphi_U + \alpha l) + e^{-\beta l}.\sin((2k+1)\omega(t - \frac{T}{3}) + \varphi_U - \alpha l) - \frac{\sqrt{a^2+b^2}}{\sqrt{c^2+d^2}}.e^{\beta l}.$$
$$.\sin((2k+1)\omega(t - \frac{T}{3}) + \varphi_U + \alpha l + arctg\frac{b}{a} - arctg\frac{d}{c}) + \frac{\sqrt{a^2+b^2}}{\sqrt{c^2+d^2}}.e^{-\beta l}.\sin((2k+1)\omega(t - \frac{T}{3}) + \varphi_U - \alpha l + arctg\frac{b}{a} - arctg\frac{d}{c})) \quad (47)$$

$$u_{31'}(t) = \sum_{k=0}^{\infty} \frac{2U}{(2k+1)\pi} . (e^{\beta l}.\sin((2k+1)\omega(t - \frac{2T}{3}) + \varphi_U + \alpha l) + e^{-\beta l}.\sin((2k+1)\omega(t - \frac{2T}{3}) + \varphi_U - \alpha l) - \frac{\sqrt{a^2+b^2}}{\sqrt{c^2+d^2}}.e^{\beta l}.$$
$$.\sin((2k+1)\omega(t - \frac{2T}{3}) + \varphi_U + \alpha l + arctg\frac{b}{a} - arctg\frac{d}{c}) + \frac{\sqrt{a^2+b^2}}{\sqrt{c^2+d^2}}.e^{-\beta l}.\sin((2k+1)\omega(t - \frac{2T}{3}) + \varphi_U - \alpha l + arctg\frac{b}{a} - arctg\frac{d}{c})) \quad (48)$$

During the calculation process, the load impedance value recalculation from star to triangle could not be forgotten, because the temporal curves of interline voltages are searched. The Excel program utilized for the first 40 components of Fourier's series will again do the graphical representation of the obtained results. The respective curves are drawn in Fig. 25. The following figure (Fig. 26) shows the sum of all three inputs and output interlines voltages. From the courses, it is evident, that during such a choice of feeding signal shape, the non-harmonic supply system, containing the expressive amount of 3rd harmonic voltage and its multiples, is generated. In the case of four-conductor circuit interconnection, the loop current, flowing via a neutral wire, is created by the resulting potential of the source node, which is in contradiction to the standard requirements.

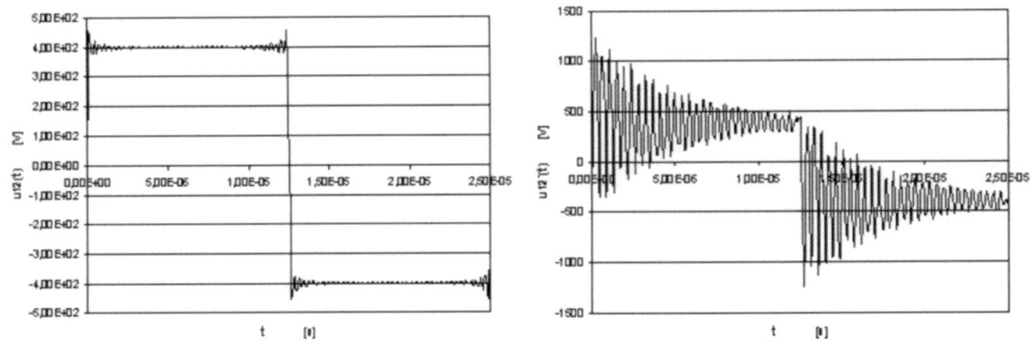

a) b)

Fig. 25. Synthesis of results a) input voltage u_{12}; b) output voltage $u_{12'}$

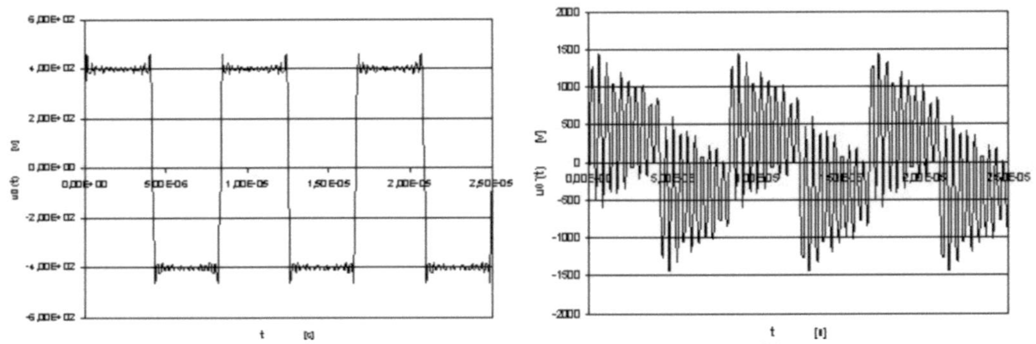

a) b)

Fig. 26. The potential of the a) source node; b) load node

The simulation results are displayed in the following Fig. 27 and measured in the Fig. 28. The coincidence between the courses obtained by analytical calculation, simulation method and by measurement is evident. So we can just suppose, that the derived relations are correct.

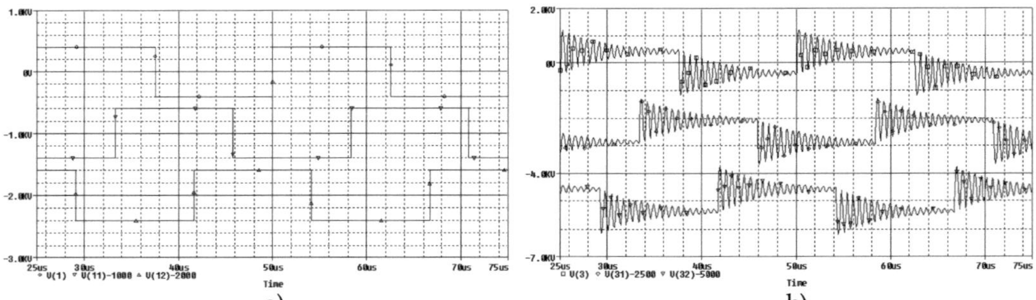

a) b)

Fig. 27. Simulation results of three phase non-harmonic a) input voltages; b) output voltages

6. Electromagnetic coupling

The electromagnetic coupling is typical for galvanically separated electrical circuits, between which the exchange of the electromagnetic energy exists in the form of the radiated and absorbed power.

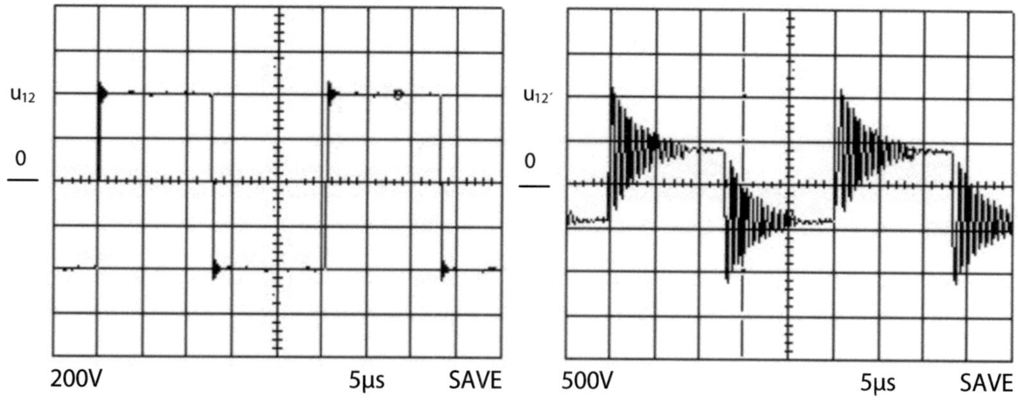

Fig. 28. Measured three phase non-harmonic a) input voltage u_{12}; b) output voltage $u_{12'}$

Let the mutual influence of two separated circuits be investigated. We come out from the first two Maxwell's equations in general form, defined by the vector potential. Let it is suppose, that the energy exchange is done through the air.

$$\overline{E} = -\nabla \varphi - \frac{\partial \overline{A}}{\partial t} \tag{49}$$

$$\overline{B} = \nabla \times \overline{A} \tag{50}$$

The potential φ and magnetic vector potential $\overline{A}$ investigation is leading to the solution of the partial-differential equations of the second order. The volume density of the environ charge is defined by ρ and the current density of conductor surface by $\overline{J}$.

$$\nabla^2 \varphi - \frac{1}{c^2}\frac{\partial^2 \varphi}{\partial t^2} = -\frac{\rho}{\varepsilon_0} \tag{51}$$

$$\nabla^2 \varphi - \frac{1}{c^2}\frac{\partial^2 \varphi}{\partial t^2} = -\frac{\rho}{\varepsilon_0} \tag{52}$$

Also next condition must to fulfilled by the searched solution (c is velocity of light):

$$\nabla . \overline{A} = -\frac{1}{c^2}\frac{\partial \varphi}{\partial t} \tag{53}$$

The relations for potential φ and magnetic vector potential $\overline{A}$ expressed for position 1 in dependence on the source parameters at the point 2 can be obtained by mathematical solving. For simplification of solution it will be supposed, that the length $\overline{l_i}$ of conductor element is so small in comparison with the vector length $\overline{r}_{12} = \overline{r}_i$, that the distances of the beginning and finishing points of conductor element of length, measured from the point 1, are the same. Situation is pictured in Fig. 29. The direction of current density vector $\overline{J}$ is coincident with the direction of unit conductor vector $\overline{l}^0$.

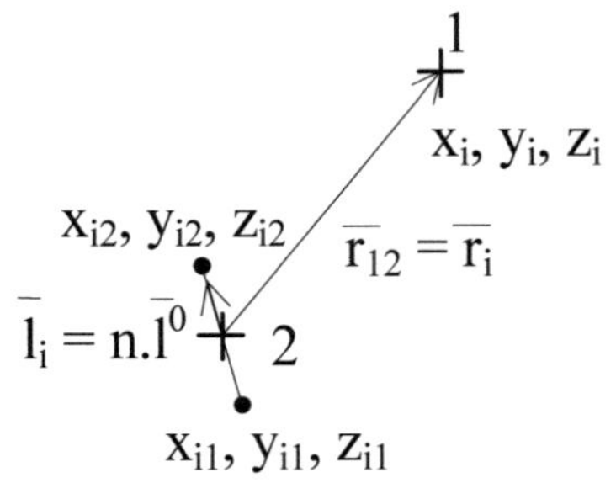

Fig. 29. Investigated point and element of the conductor length

$$\varphi(1,t) = \int \frac{\rho(2,t-\frac{r_{12}}{c})}{4\pi\varepsilon_0 r_{12}} dV_2 \tag{54}$$

$$\bar{A}(1,t) = \int \frac{\bar{J}(2,t-\frac{r_{12}}{c})}{4\pi\varepsilon_0 c^2 r_{12}} dV_2 \tag{55}$$

For the purpose of electrotechnical equipment EMC investigation let it is consider the expression for magnetic vector potential $\bar{A}$ will be related to the elementary radiator represented by the electrical dipole with the dipole moment $\bar{p}$. The variables $\bar{p}'$ and $\bar{p}''$ represent first and second derivation of the dipole moment vector according the time.

$$\bar{p}_i = q\bar{l}_i = \int idt\bar{l}_i \quad \bar{p}_i' = \frac{dq}{dt}\bar{l}_i = i\bar{l}_i \quad \bar{p}_i'' = \frac{di}{dt}\bar{l}_i \tag{56}$$

The optional current course can be expressed by Fourier series as sum of the DC component and k components of individual harmonic functions:

$$i = C_0 + \sum_{k=1}^{n\to\infty} C_k \sin(k\omega t + \psi) = I_0 + \sum_{k=1}^{n\to\infty} I_{mk} \sin(k\omega t + \psi) \tag{57}$$

Dipole moment and its time derivations then have the forms:

$$\bar{p}_i = I_0 t l_i \bar{l}_i^0 - \sum_{k=1}^{n\to\infty} p_k \cos(k\omega\, t + \psi)\bar{l}_i^0 \quad \bar{p}_i' = I_0 l_i \bar{l}_i^0 + \sum_{k=1}^{n\to\infty} k\omega\, p_k \sin(k\omega\, t + \psi)\bar{l}_i^0 \quad \bar{p}_i'' = \sum_{k=1}^{n\to\infty} (k\omega)^2 p_k \cos(k\omega\, t + \psi)\bar{l}_i^0 \tag{58}$$

The next equation describes the magnetic vector potential $\bar{A}_i$ of electric dipole.

$$\bar{A}_i(1,t) = \frac{1}{4\pi\varepsilon_0 c^2} \frac{\bar{p}_i'(t-\frac{r_i}{c})}{r_i} \tag{59}$$

By its substitution into the equation (50) the resulting relation for magnetic intensity vector $\bar{H}_i$ of the electromagnetic field will be obtained. It can be expressed by the components of the 3D Cartesian system:

$$\overline{H}_i = \frac{\overline{B}_i}{\mu} = \frac{\nabla \times \overline{A}_i}{\mu} = \overline{H}_x + \overline{H}_y + \overline{H}_z = \frac{1}{4\pi} \frac{\left[\overline{p}_i^{'} + \left(\frac{r_i}{c} \right) \overline{p}_i^{''} \right]_{t-\frac{r_i}{c}} \times \overline{r}_i}{r_i^3} \tag{60}$$

Electric intensity $\overline{E}_i$ vector calculation, as the second component of electromagnetic field, will be deduced from condition (53). The found solution of the partial-differential equation of the second order for magnetic vector potential $\overline{A}$ must fulfill this condition.

$$\nabla.\overline{A}_i = -\frac{1}{4\pi\varepsilon_0 c^2} \frac{\left(\overline{p}_i^{'}(t-\frac{r_i}{c}) + \left(\frac{r_i}{c} \right) \overline{p}_i^{''}(t-\frac{r_i}{c}) \right) \overline{r}_i}{r_i^3} = -\frac{1}{c^2} \frac{\partial \varphi_i}{\partial t} \tag{61}$$

The time gradient of potential at the investigated place is necessary to express from the above-mentioned equation.

$$\frac{\partial \varphi_i}{\partial t} = \frac{1}{4\pi\varepsilon_0} \frac{\left(\overline{p}_i^{'}(t-\frac{r_i}{c}) + \left(\frac{r_i}{c} \right) \overline{p}_i^{''}(t-\frac{r_i}{c}) \right) \overline{r}_i}{r_i^3} \tag{62}$$

The relation for potential will be received after the integration.

$$\varphi_i = \frac{1}{4\pi\varepsilon_0} \frac{\left(\overline{p}_i(t-\frac{r_i}{c}) + \left(\frac{r_i}{c} \right) \overline{p}_i^{'}(t-\frac{r_i}{c}) \right) \overline{r}_i}{r_i^3} + K \tag{63}$$

Integral constant K expresses a possible existence of the electrostatic field. It should be omitted during the investigation of electromagnetic wave spreading and so the final formula can be simplified.

By substitution of the obtained dependencies for potential φ and magnetic vector potential $\overline{A}$ into the equation (49) and by its modification the searched formula for electric field intensity $\overline{E}$ vector caused by harmonic pulsating dipole can be expressed.

$$\overline{E} = \overline{E}_x + \overline{E}_y + \overline{E}_z = -\frac{1}{4\pi\varepsilon_0 r_i^3} \left[-\overline{p}_i(t-\frac{r_i}{c}) - \left(\frac{r_i}{c} \right) \overline{p}_i^{'}(t-\frac{r_i}{c}) - 3 \frac{\left(\left(\overline{p}_i(t-\frac{r_i}{c}) + \left(\frac{r_i}{c} \right) \overline{p}_i^{'}(t-\frac{r_i}{c}) \right) \overline{r}_i \right) \overline{r}_i}{r_i^2} + \frac{\overline{p}_i^{''}(t-\frac{r_i}{c})}{c^2} \left(r_i^2 - \overline{r}_i \overline{r}_i \right) \right] \tag{64}$$

Note, that above-mentioned condition $l = \sum_{i=1}^{m\to\infty} l_i$ for total length of the investigated current conductor is valid, too.

Let's investigate the EMC from the viewpoint of electromagnetic coupling. For this purpose it is satisfactory to analyze the value of resulting vectors $\overline{E}$ and $\overline{H}$, at the given position, which is created by the superposition of individual vectors $\overline{E}_i$ and $\overline{H}_i$ of power radiated from all devices and their parts situated inside the investigated environs. If the non-harmonic currents supply the circuits of radiated sources, then the superposition method of individual harmonic components of Fourier series needs to be applied for the resulting vectors $\bar{E}$ and $\bar{H}$ searching. It is also necessary to keep in mind that the additional induced voltage is developed inside the individual loops of investigated circuit due to electromagnetic coupling existence. These voltages can affect circuit basic functionality. The equipment EMC investigation thus means the voltage value stating in such a way that the question of circuit functionality can be answered and circuit immunity stated.

$$u_i = u_{imag} + u_{ielec} = -\frac{d\psi}{dt} + \int \bar{E} d\bar{l} = -\frac{d\bar{B}\bar{S}}{dt} + \int \bar{E} d\bar{l} = -\mu_0 S \sum_{i=1}^{m\to\infty} \frac{\Delta H_i}{\Delta t} \cos\alpha_i + \sum_{i=1}^{m\to\infty} E_i l_i \cos\beta_i \qquad (65)$$

Let the correctness verification of derived equations be done by induced voltage oscillograph measurement inside the circuit connected according to Fig. 30. As the source of

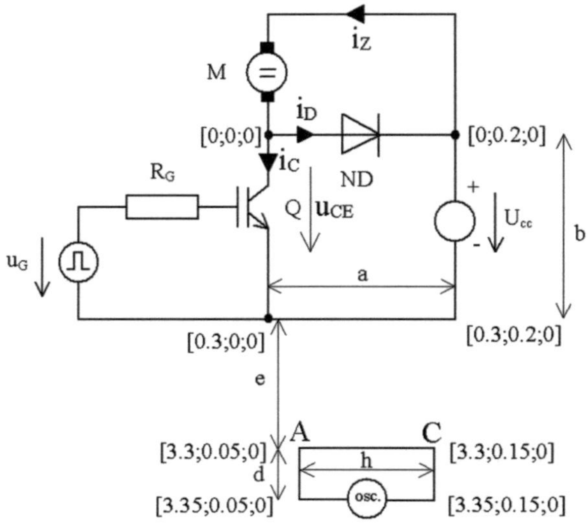

Fig. 30. Investigated circuit scheme.

radiation the one quadrant impulse converter is used with the same working parameters as presented in the previous subchapters. Let the circuit location be on the x, y plane. The co-ordinates of Cartesian coordinate system describe individual key points of connection. On the basis of the results obtained from Fourier and transient analyses offered by PSPICE program the DC and the first nine components of Fourier series can express the courses of all power circuit currents and transistor voltage. The final simulation and measured results are presented in figure Fig. 31.

On the basis of the obtained coefficients let the Excel program do the verification synthesis of transistor current course. The result is introduced in Fig. 32. By comparing courses one can state that due to considering only first nine members of Fourier series the peak transistor current generated by the commutation charge of diode was neglected and also the certain undulation was infiltrated. But otherwise its shape is identical with the real measured current course.

By substituting the individual harmonic amplitudes and phases to the Fourier series one can obtain the analytical form of investigated non-harmonic currents. By their application in the equations (60) and (64) it is possible to receive the searched solution for the electromagnetic

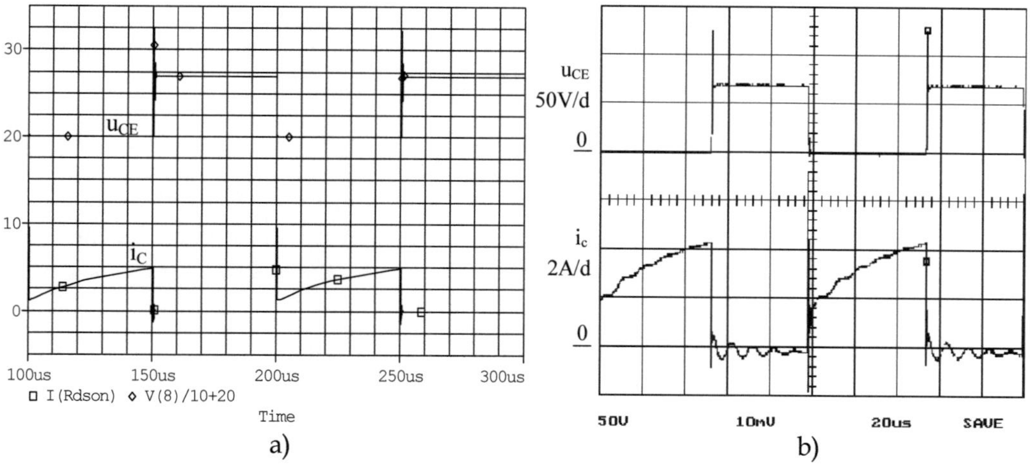

Fig. 31. Transistor voltage and current obtained by a) simulation; b) measurement

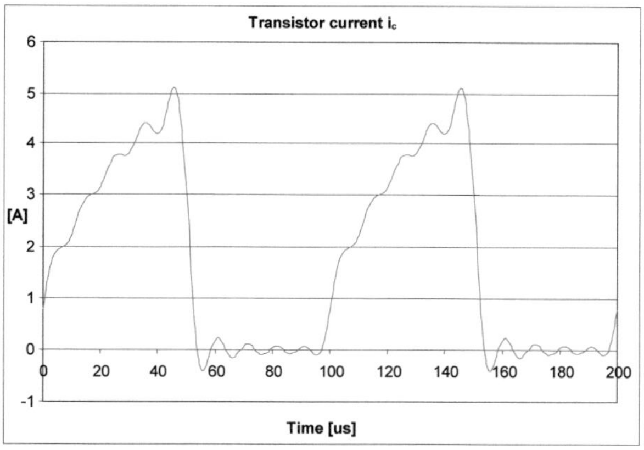

Fig. 32. Transistor current - synthesis by 9 members of Fourier series

wave components. The induced voltage generated by the magnetic component of electromagnetic wave can be stated in such a way that the values of axis components of magnetic intensity vector will be calculated at the position in the centre of impacted loop. If the loop dimensions are omissible towards the length of electromagnetic wave, then the magnetic field intensity inside the loop can be allowed to be constant at the given moment and the induced voltage can be calculated according to the equation:

$$u_{imag} = -\mu_0 S \left[\frac{\sqrt{H_x^2(t+\Delta t) + H_y^2(t+\Delta t) + H_z^2(t+\Delta t)}}{\Delta t} - \frac{\sqrt{H_x^2(t) + H_y^2(t) + H_z^2(t)}}{\Delta t} \right] \tag{66}$$

where S is the surface of impacted loop which represents the impacted electrical circuit.
The induced voltage generated by the electric component of electromagnetic wave can be stated in such a way that the values of axis components of electric intensity vector at the positions A[3.3;0.05;0] and C[3.3;0.15;0] will be found. The induced voltage value then should be calculated on the basis of the well-known relation from the field of theoretical

electrical engineering; however, only if we take into consideration the fact that the moving electromagnetic wave changes its own intensity by the value ΔE_x (or ΔE_y) during its transition time $\Delta t' = d/c$ (or $\Delta t'' = h/c$) along the investigated loop.

$$u_{ielec} = \left(E_{xA}(t+\Delta t') - E_{xA}(t)\right)d + \left(E_{xC}(t+\Delta t') - E_{xC}(t)\right)d + \left(E_{yA}(t+\Delta t'') - E_{yA}(t)\right)h + \left(E_{yC}(t+\Delta t'') - E_{yC}(t)\right)h \quad (67)$$

Resulting induced voltage, calculated as the superposition of its magnetic and electric compounds, does not provide satisfactory graphical representation in analytical form. The numerical method of searching time depending solution and the graphical presentation are more advantageous in this case because the computer programs currently available, for example, the Excel program, allow its application very easily. On the basis of the previous equation calculations, which were done for two periods of basic harmonics, one can obtain the graphical interpretation of resulting induced voltage inside the impacted loop, which is shown in the Fig. 33.

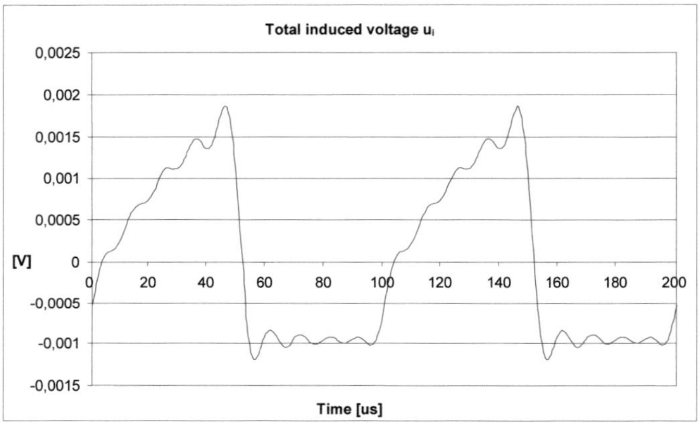

a)

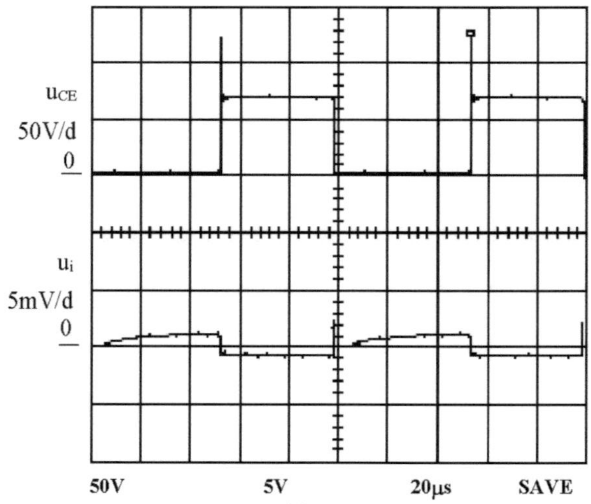

b)

Fig. 33. Total induced voltage u_i inside the investigated loop a) calculated; b) measured

By comparing the simulated and measured results one can find out that positive amplitudes reach approximately the same values 1.8 mV and similarly the negative amplitudes have the values 1 mV. The existing ripple and the absence of short positive voltage impulse with the amplitude 2.5 mV inside the induced voltage course obtained by simulation is caused by considering only the first nine components of Fourier series. Generally it is possible to say that there exists a relatively great coincidence between the simulated and measured results. Thus the correctness of derived equations is confirmed as well as the fact that if higher number of Fourier series components are used the better coincidence of both type results will be obtained. It means that during the electromagnetic coupling investigation, as one part of general EMC investigation, it is necessary to reconsider the compromise between the number of Fourier series components and the required calculation precision.
The above-mentioned simulated and measured results are sufficiently identical with the theoretical results and so they confirm the correctness of derived equations. Such a way they can be used for predictive stating of EMC quality of individual new electrotechnical products (Williams, 2001).
Based on the performed analysis also we can find out that the intensity of electromagnetic coupling is directly proportional to the amount and the time change slope of circuit current, which is radiating the electromagnetic energy. In the same way electromagnetic coupling intensity depends on the length of this circuit. It is also directly proportional to the surface and the length values of disturbed circuit. It is indirectly proportional to the distance between the interference source and the disturbed circuits, to the reflection coefficient and to the permeability and permittivity values of space between the both circuits.

7. Conclusion

The performed analysis enables constructers to improve the EMC parameters of the newly constructed devices not only by expensive testing measurements, but also in advance, by the theoretical analysis and simulation. They can state its supposed and required properties by a predictive method based upon the results introduced in this chapter (Kováčová et al., 2006). The improving of EMC will thus be more comfortable, cheaper, easier and quicker.
All results presented in this chapter has been prepared under the support of Slovak grant projects VEGA No.1/0660/08, KEGA No. 003-003TUKE-4/2010, KEGA No. 3/6386/08, KEGA No. 3/6388/08.

8. References

Clayton, R. P. (1992). *Introduction to electromagnetic compatibility,* John Wiley & Sons, ISBN 0-471-54927-4 , New York, USA

Kováčová, I. ; Kováč, D. & Kaňuch, J. (2006). *EMC from the look of the theory and practice,* BEN Publisher, ISBN 80-7300-202-7, Prague, 2006, Czech Republic

Kůs, V. (2002). *The influence of semiconductor converters on feeding net,* BEN Publisher, ISBN 80-7300-062-8, Prague, Czech Republic

Montrose, M. & Nakauchi, E. (2004). *Testing for EMC Compliance: Approaches and Techniques,* John Wiley & Sons, ISBN 0-471-43308-X, New York, USA

Tihanyi, L. (1995). *Electromagnetic compatibility in power electronics,* IEEE Press, ISBN 0-7803-0416-0, Piscataway,USA

Vaculíková, P. & Vaculík, E. (1998). *Electromagnetic compatibility of electrical engineering systems,* Grada Publisher, ISBN 80-7169-568-8, Prague, Czech Republic
Williams, T. (2001). *EMC for Product Designers,* An imprint of Elsevier Science, ISBN 0-7506-4930-5, Oxford, UK

17

Theoretical Issues in Modeling of Large-Scale Wireless Sensor Networks

Di Ma, Meng Joo Er, Senior Member, IEEE
Intelligent Systems Center, Nanyang Technological University, Research Techno Plaza, Singapore

1. Introduction

In large-scale WSNs (wireless sensor networks), packets of a source node are often transmitted via multi-hop relays to reach their sink nodes. The hop-count, h, of a sink node is related to a particular hop-count originator (namely the source node) and it is defined as the least number of multi-hop relays required to send one packet from the source to the sink in this chapter. A source node can use a simple controlled flooding to set up the hop-counts relative to itself for all other nodes [1]. Let d denote the Euclidean distance between a source and its sink (the source-to-sink distance is denoted as SS-distance in the sequel), various statistical models that characterize the relationships between h and d are some of the fundamental problems in modeling large-scale WSNs. These results can be applied to address many other WSN research issues such as range-free localization, communication protocol design and evaluation, throughput optimization, transmission power control and etc.

Given a WSN whose nodes are distributed randomly according to a two-dimensional homogeneous Poisson point process of density λ, we investigate two statistical relationships between hop-count h and SS-distance d in this chapter. First of all, we propose a method termed CSP (Convolution of Successive Progress) to compute the K-hop connection probability for a two-dimensional network. The K-hop connection probability is defined as the conditional probability that a sink has a hop-count $h = K$ with respect to a source given that the SS-distance is d. Mathematically, the K-hop connection probability is defined as the conditional probability[1] $P(h = K \mid d)$. The CSP method is also extended into three-dimensional networks.

Secondly, based on the results of K-hop connection probability, we also present a method to compute the PDF (probability density function) of the SS-distance d conditioned on hop-count $h = K$, namely the PDF of SS-distance d of all nodes with a hop-count $h = K$. Mathematically, this conditional PDF[2] is denoted as $f(d \mid h = K)$. Simulation studies show that the proposed methods are able to achieve significant error reduction in computing these hop-distance statistics (i.e. the conditional probability/PDF) compared with existing methods.

---

[1] Unless otherwise specified, the conditional probability is referred to $P(h = K \mid d)$ in this paper.

[2] Unless otherwise specified, the conditional PDF is referred to $f(d \mid h = K)$ in this paper.

The rest of the chapter is organized as follows. Section 2 reviews some related works. Section 3 described the system models used in the analysis. The CSP algorithms for both two-dimensional and three-dimensional networks are presented in Section 4. A method of computing the conditional PDF $f(d \mid h = K)$ is then discussed in Section 5. Section 6 presents simulation results and discussions. Finally, Section 7 concludes the chapter.

2. Related works

Evaluation of various statistical models that characterize the relationships between hop-count h and SS-distance d are some of the fundamental problems in modeling large-scale WSNs. In [2], the solution of the conditional PDF $f(d \mid h = K)$ for one-dimensional networks is presented. The authors of [3] and [4] derived the conditional probability $P(h = K \mid d)$ based on the results of [2] for one-dimensional networks. However, only models are provided to the solution of $P(h = K \mid d)$ in two-dimensional networks. In [5], the exact analytical solution of the conditional probability $P(h = K \mid d)$ is derived for $K = 1$ and $K = 2$ in two-dimensional networks. However, probabilities $P(h = K \mid d)$ for $K > 2$ were studied by analytical bounds and extensive simulations. The author of [6] proposed an iterative formulation of $P(h = K \mid d)$. Though not stated explicitly in his paper, its derivation is based on an "independent assumption". This independent assumption is then highlighted in [7]. The analytical solutions proposed in [6] and [7] are the analytical approximations of $P(h = K \mid d)$ and only converges to the true statistics when the node density λ in the network tends to infinity. Due to the complexity of two-dimensional multi-hop percolation process, the authors of [8] proposed a simulation-based attenuated Gaussian approximation to model the conditional PDF $f(d \mid H = K)$. All previously mentioned results are based on the deployment model that nodes are distributed according to a one-dimensional or two-dimensional Poisson process. The author of [9] provided an analytical approximation for the probability of 2-hop connection between two randomly selected nodes in network whose nodes are distributed according to a Gaussian distribution.

Another interesting relationship between hop-count and distance is known as progress per hop. Works related to this are reported in [10] - [13]. The authors of [10] derived a solution for the expected per hop progress in two-dimensional networks. The expected per hop progress problem was also studied in [11] and [12] with different applications in protocol evaluation and localization. The authors of [13] presented an analytic approach to capture statistical bounds on hop-count for a given SS-distance in a greedy routing approach.

The statistical relationships between hop-count and SS-distance can be applied to address many WSN research problems. For example, many range-free WSN localization algorithms employ the principle of hop-count-to-distance transformation to localize nodes. The DV-hop WSN localization algorithm of [14] employs a heuristics approach known as correction factor to estimate the distance between two nodes based on the hop-count between them. Similar methods are also reported in [15] and [16]. The network throughput problem and optimal transmission radii were also studied in [10] based on the analytical expression of expected per hop progress.

3. System model

In this section, we discuss radio channel model, node deployment model and network topology model used in this chapter.

A. Channel model

As in many WSN literatures, we adopt an unit disk channel model (in some literatures, it is also known as lossless model) in this chapter. A source can communicate directly with all nodes within a disk centered at itself with a communication range *r*, but cannot communicate with nodes beyond the disk. The link between a pair of nodes is also assumed to be symmetric, namely, if node A can receive packets from node B directly, then node B also can receive packets from node A directly. The disk model is often used in the theoretical analysis of WSNs. There are other realistic channel models available (such as log-normal shadowing model [17]). These realistic channel models take the random effect of noise, attenuation, shadowing and etc. into consideration. The communication between a pair of nodes is thus characterized by PRR (packet reception rate) or LP (link probability) rather than the absolute SS-distance. In this chapter, since our study is a general analysis of the statistical relationship between hop-count and SS-distance, we adopt the unit disk channel model so that the radio channel can be regarded as lossless, invariant and homogeneous.

B. Deployment model

We assume all nodes with the same communication range *r* are randomly deployed in a plane according to a two-dimensional homogeneous Poisson point process of density λ. Furthermore, we require that all nodes deployed can form a fully-connected network. We make use of the WSN connectivity results presented in [18] to determine suitable values of λ so that all nodes deployed can form a connected network almost surely (probability greater than 0.99).

C. Topology model

Based on the channel and deployment model, we can model the WSN as an undirect graph *G*. A graph $G(V,E)$ consists a set of vertices (nodes) and edges (links), the set of vertices and edges are denoted by *V* and *E* respectively. The shortest network path between vertices i ($i \in V$) and vertices j ($j \in V$) is defined as the path that travels through the minimum number of edges from i to j. Therefore, the number of edges traveled is actually the hop-count between i and j. There are many algorithms proposed in the literature to set up the shortest network path in a WSN. These algorithms are out of the scope of this work. In this chapter, we assume that the network paths and the hop-counts between all node pairs have already been set up in advance.

4. Convolution of Successive Progress

In this section, we propose a method termed CSP (Convolution of Successive Progress) to compute the *K*-hop connection probability in two-dimensional WSNs, i.e. $P(h = K \mid d)$. We then extend the CSP method to compute the *K*-hop connection probability in three-dimensional networks.

A. Problem statement

A formal definition of the *K*-hop connection probability is given in this subsection. Let h and d denote the hop-count and distance between a pair of source and sink. The *K*-hop connection probability is an important hop-distance statistic and it is defined as the probability that the source can reach the sink in *K* number of multi-hop relays given that the

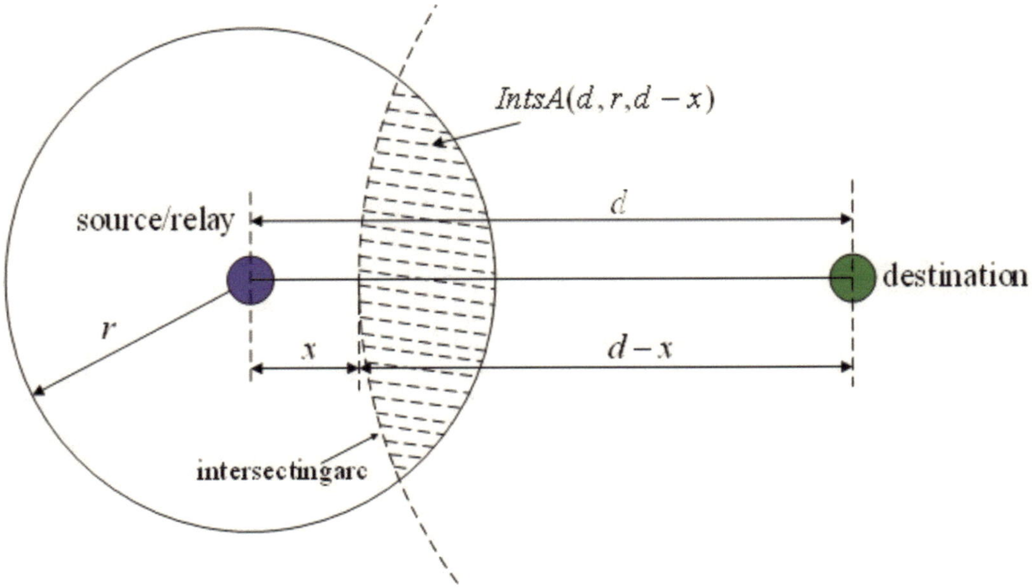

Fig. 1. Maximum progress from the source to the sink. Note that the source node can be a relay node as well. The dotted arc is the intersecting arc.

distance between the source and the sink is d, i.e. $P(h = K \mid d)$. In order to solve for $P(h = K \mid d)$, we construct a multi-hop network path from the source to the sink and computes the distribution of the length of the network path. First of all, we discuss how to compute the PDF of the length for a single hop.

B. Probability density function of maximum progress towards sink

We first introduce a random variable X (small letter x denotes an instance of X) known as maximum progress [10] per communication hop. It is a measure of the maximum progress in Euclidean distance from the source to the sink in one hop relay. Let $A(d_{12}, r_1, r_2)$ represent the intersectional area of two disks given the radii of the disks are r_1 and r_2 respectively and the distance between the centers of the two disks is d_{12}. The analytical form of $A(d_{12}, r_1, r_2)$ is given as follows:

$$A(d_{12},r_1,r_2) = r_1^2 cos^{-1}\left(\frac{d_{12}^2 + r_1^2 - r_2^2}{2d_{12}r_1}\right) + r_2^2 cos^{-1}\left(\frac{d_{12}^2 + r_2^2 - r_1^2}{2d_{12}r_2}\right) - \frac{1}{2}\sqrt{(-d_{12} + r_1 + r_2)(d_{12} + r_1 - r_2)(d_{12} - r_1 + r_2)(d_{12} + r_1 + r_2)} \quad (1)$$

As depicted in Fig. 1, the distance between the source and the sink is d. A circle with a radius $d - x$ centered at the sink intersects with the coverage disk of the source and creates an intersectional region (shaded area). Therefore, nodes falling on the intersecting arc have the same distance $d - x$ to the sink. Furthermore, a node falling on the intersecting arc is selected as the relay node if there are no nodes in the shaded intersection region (the source has no neighboring nodes which has a shorter distance to the sink then the relay node falling on the intersecting arc). The CDF (Cumulative Distribution Function) of X, $F(x)$, can be computed as the probability that there are no nodes in the shaded intersectional region. The CDF and PDF of X are computed as follows:

$$F(x) = P(X \le x) = \exp(-\lambda \cdot A(d,r,d-x)) \tag{2}$$

$$f(x) = \frac{dF(x)}{dx} = -\lambda \exp(-\lambda \cdot A(d,r,d-x)) \frac{d}{dx} A(d,r,d-x) = \psi(\lambda,d,r,x) \tag{3}$$

$$\text{where, } \psi(\lambda,d,r,x) = -\lambda \exp(-\lambda \cdot A(d,r,d-x))(C1 + C2 + C3 + C4) \tag{4}$$

$$C1 = -\frac{r(2d-2x)}{d\left(4 - \frac{(d^2+r^2-(d-x)^2)^2}{d^2r^2}\right)^{\frac{1}{2}}}$$

$$C2 = -2(d-x)cos^{-1}\left(\frac{d^2+(d-x)^2-r^2}{2d(d-x)}\right)$$

$$C3 = \frac{(d-x)^2\left(\frac{2}{d} - \frac{d^2+(d-x)^2-r^2}{d(d-x)^2}\right)}{\left(4 - \frac{(d^2+(d-x)^2-r^2)^2}{d^2(d-x)^2}\right)^{\frac{1}{2}}}$$

$$C4 = \frac{(-d+x)(-r^2-2dx+x^2)}{\sqrt{(-x+r)(2d-x-r)(x+r)(2d-x+r)}}$$

It can be seen from Eq. (3) that the PDF of X, $f(x)$, is parameterized on the node density λ, the source-tosink distance d and the communication range r. Therefore, we use the function $\psi(\lambda, d, r, x)$ given by Eq. (4) to simplify the representation of $f(x)$. Let $r = 10$, the PDF of X for different SS-distance d given that $\lambda = 0.03537$ and $\lambda = 0.08842$ are plotted in Fig. 2 and Fig. 3 respectively. Given a fixed communication range, it can be seen that the shape of the function ψ is largely controlled by its first parameter node density λ and weakly depends on its second parameter SS-distance d. In the later discussion, we shall make use of this property to simplify some computations.

The PDF of maximum progress from the source to the sink is given by $\psi(\lambda, d, r, x)$. The function ψ can also be used for the PDF of maximum progress from a relay node to the sink. Suppose the distance between a relay node and the sink is d_{rs}, the PDF of maximum progress from the relay node to the sink is then given by $\psi(\lambda, d_{rs}, r, x)$. In the later discussion, we use X_i ($i = 0, 1, ...$) to represent the random variable of maximum progress from the hop i relay node ($i = 0$ for the source) to the sink.

C. $K = 1$ and $K = 2$

For $K = 1$, $P(h = 1 | d) = 1$ if $d \le r$ and $P(h = 1 | d) = 0$ otherwise. For $K = 2$, $P(h = 2 | d) = P(d-X_0 < r)$ if $r < d \le 2r$ and $P(H = 2 | d) = 0$ otherwise. Since X_0 is the maximum progress from the source to the sink, $d-X_0$ is the remaining distance to be covered/progressed. Therefore,

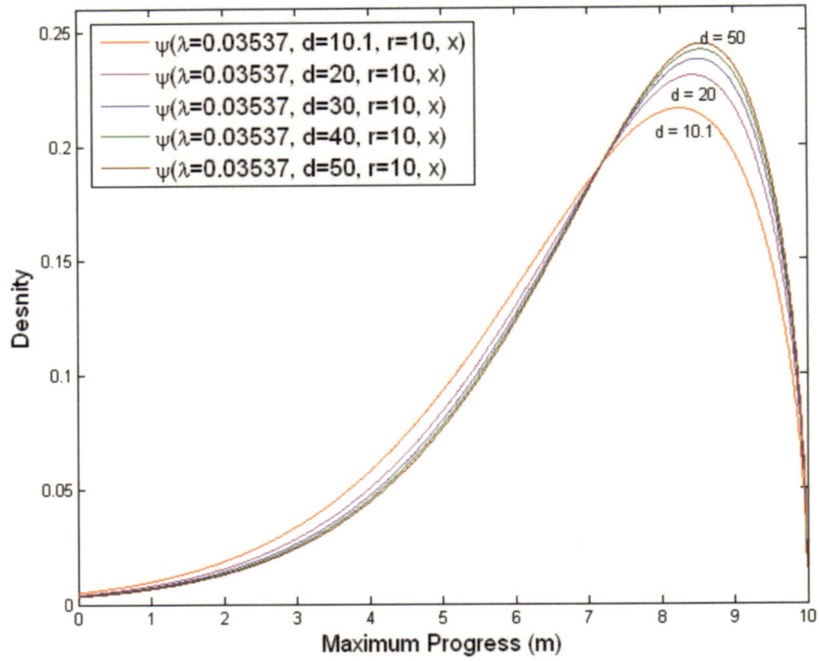

Fig. 2. Probability density function of maximum progress given different SS-distance, λ = 0.03537 and r = 10.

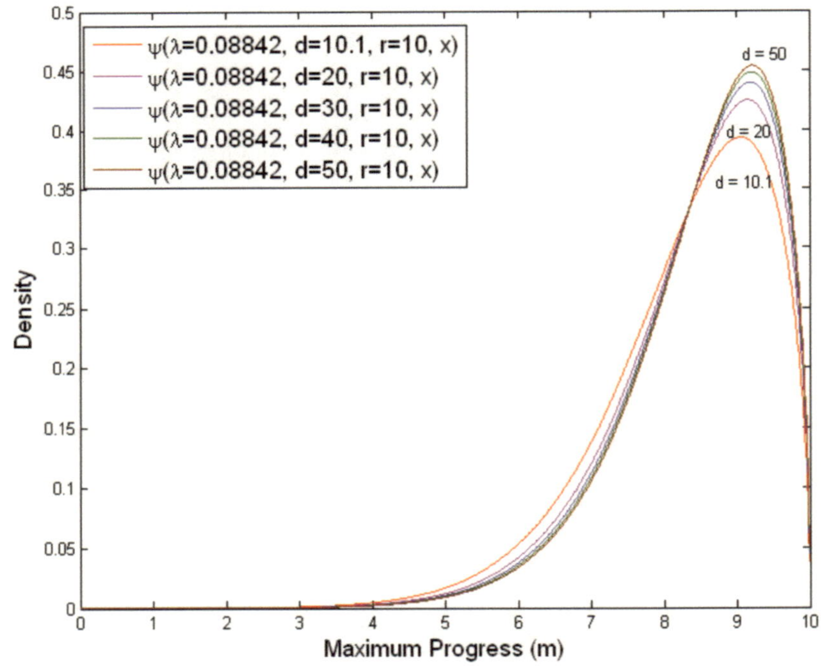

Fig. 3. Probability density function of maximum progress given different SS-distance, λ = 0.08842 and r = 10.

$P(d-X_0 < r)$ is the probability that a hop-1 relay node at the maximum progress from the source to the sink is within the coverage of the sink node. We can show that this approach of formulating $P(h = 2|d)$ yields exactly the same form as the K-hop connection probability given in [7]. In particular, for $r < d \leq 2r$, $P(H = 2|d)$ is given as follow:

$$\begin{aligned} P(h=2\,|\,d) &= P(d-X_0<r)=1-P(X_0\leq d-r) \\ &=1-\exp(-\lambda\cdot A(d,r,d-(d-r)))=1-\exp(-\lambda\cdot A(d,r,r)) \end{aligned} \tag{5}$$

D. $K > 2$

For $K > 2$, the conditional probability $P(h = K|d)$ is computed recursively based on the method of convolution of successive progress. We shall discuss how to compute $P(h = 3|d)$ first.

Starting from the source, after one hop of maximum progress X_0 from the source to the sink, the remaining distance to be progressed is $d - X_0$ and a hop-1 node at the maximum progress becomes the relaying node. From this hop-1 relay node, the maximum progress towards the sink is X_1. Therefore, $P(h = 3|d)$ can be formulated as the product of the probability that a hop-2 relay node at the maximum progress is within the coverage disk of the sink node, and the probability that the sink node's hop-count is neither $h = 1$ nor $h = 2$. Mathematically, it is given as follows:

$$P(h=3\,|\,d)=P(d-X_0-X_1<r)(1-\sum_{i=1}^{2}P(h=i\,|\,d)) \tag{6}$$

Similar to the meaning of $P(d - X_0 < r)$, $P(d - X_0 - X_1 < r)$ is the probability that the hop-2 relay node at the maximum progress is within the coverage disk of the sink node. The PDF of X_0 and X_1 are given by $\psi(\lambda, d, r, x_0)$ and $\psi(\lambda, d-X_0, r, x_1)$ respectively, noting that $d-X_0$ is the RS-distance (distance between the hop-1 relay node and the sink). It can be seen that the PDF of X_1 depends on the random variable X_0. Recall the property that the shape of function ψ is largely controlled by its first parameter λ rather than the second parameter SS-distance/RS-distance, therefore, we assume that X_1 is independent of X_0. Define a new random variable Z_1 as the sum of X_0 and X_1, the PDF of Z_1 can be calculated as follows:

$$f(z_1)=f(x_0)\otimes f(x_1)=\int_0^r f(x_0)f(z_1-x_0)dx_0=\int_0^r \psi(\lambda,d,r,x_0)\psi(\lambda,d-X_0,r,z_1-x_0)dx_0 \tag{7}$$

where $\otimes$ is the convolution operator. Now, $P(d-X_0-X_1< r) = P(d-Z_1< r) = 1-P(Z_1\leq d-r)$. The conditional probability $P(h = 3|d)$ is then computed as follows:

$$\begin{aligned} P(h=3\,|\,d) &=(1-P(Z_1\leq d-r))(1-\sum_{i=1}^{2}P(h=i\,|\,d)) \\ &=(1-\int_0^{d-r} f(z_1)dz_1)(1-\sum_{i=1}^{2}P(h=i\,|\,d)) \\ &=(1-\int_0^{d-r}\int_0^{r}\psi(\lambda,d,r,x_0)\psi(\lambda,d-X_0,r,z_1-x_0)dx_0dz_1)(1-\sum_{i=1}^{2}P(h=i\,|\,d)) \end{aligned} \tag{8}$$

Similarly, for $P(h = 4 | d)$, it can be computed as $P(d - X_0 - X_1 - X_2 < r)(1 - \sum_{i=1}^{3} P(h = i | d))$. In general, for $K > 2$, the conditional probability is given as follow:

$$\begin{aligned} P(h = K | d) &= P(d - X_0 - X_1 ... - X_{K-2} < r)(1 - \sum_{i=1}^{K-1} P(h = i | d)) \\ &= P(d - Z_{K-2} < r)(1 - \sum_{i=1}^{K-1} P(h = i | d)) \\ &= (1 - \int_0^{d-r} f(z_{K-2}) dz_{K-2})(1 - \sum_{i=1}^{K-1} P(h = i | d)) \end{aligned} \tag{9}$$

where, $Z_{K-2} = X_0 + X_1 + X_2 + ... + X_{K-2}$

PDF of $Z_{K-2} : f(z_{K-2}) = f(x_0) \otimes f(x_1) \otimes f(x_2) ... \otimes f(x_{K-2})$

PDF of $X_0 : f(x_0) = \psi(\lambda, d, r, x_0)$

PDF of $X_1 : f(x_1) = \psi(\lambda, d - X_0, r, x_1)$

PDF of $X_2 : f(x_2) = \psi(\lambda, d - X_0 - X_1, r, x_2)$

...

PDF of $X_{K-2} : f(x_{K-2}) = \psi(\lambda, d - X_0 - X_1 ... - X_{K-3}, r, x_{K-2})$

It can be seen that the random variable Z_{K-2} is the progress of the multi-hop network path from the source to the hop $K - 1$ relay node and its PDF can be computed by convolving the PDFs of successive maximum progresses. Therefore, the name CSP which reflects the algorithm's computation methodology is phrased.

E. Extension to three-dimensional networks

The CSP algorithm can be extended to three-dimensional network based on the same intuition of its two-dimensional counterpart. In this case, we assume that nodes with communication range r_{3D} are deployed in a space according to a three-dimensional homogeneous Poisson point process of density λ_{3D}.

1) Probability Density Function of Maximum Progress: We have derived the analytical form of the PDF of maximum progress in two-dimensional networks. In three dimensional networks, the radio coverage of a node is a sphere rather than a disk. Therefore, the intersectional area as shown in Fig. 1 becomes an intersection volume between two spheres. Similarly, let X (small letter x denotes an instance of X) represent the maximum progress from a source to a sink in three-dimensional networks. Let V (d_{12}, r_1, r_2) represent the intersectional volume of two spheres given the radii of the spheres are r_1 and r_2 respectively and the distance between the centers of the two spheres is d_{12}. The analytical form of V (d_{12}, r_1, r_2) is given as follows:

$$V(d_{12}, r_1, r_2) = \frac{\pi(r_1 + r_2 - d)^2 (d^2 + 2d(r_1 + r_2))}{12d}. \tag{10}$$

Visualize the Fig. 1 in three-dimensional space, the distance between the source and the sink is still d. A sphere with a radius $d - x$ centered at the sink intersects with the radio coverage sphere of the source and creates an intersectional volume (visualize the shaded part as a volume). Therefore, nodes falling on the intersecting surface (visualize the dotted intersecting arc as a surface) have the same distance $d-x$ to the sink. Furthermore, a node falling on the intersecting surface is selected as the relay node if there are no nodes in the shaded intersectional volume. The CDF of X, $F(x)$, can be computed as the probability that there are no nodes in the shaded intersectional volume. The CDF and PDF of X are computed as follows:

$$F(x) = P(X \le x) = \exp(-\lambda_{3D} \cdot V(d, r_{3D}, d-x)) \tag{11}$$

$$f(x) = \frac{dF(x)}{dx} = -\lambda_{3D} \exp(-\lambda_{3D} \cdot V(d, r_{3D}, d-x)) \frac{d}{dx} V(d, r_{3D}, d-x) = \psi_{3D}(\lambda_{3D}, d, r_{3D}, x) \tag{12}$$

$$\psi_{3D}(\lambda_{3D}, d, r_{3D}, x) = -\lambda_{3D} \exp(-\lambda_{3D} \cdot V(d, r_{3D}, d-x))(D1 + D2) \tag{13}$$

$$D1 = -\frac{\pi(r_{3D} - x)(d^2 + 2dr_{3D} - 3r_{3D}^2 + 2d(d-x) + 6r_{3D}(d-x) - 3(d-x)^2)}{6d}$$

$$D2 = \frac{\pi(r_{3D} - x)^2(4d - 6r_{3D} - 6x)}{12d}$$

Similarly, we use the function $\psi_{3D}(\lambda_{3D}, d, r_{3D}, x)$ given by Eq. (13) to simplify the representation of the PDF of maximum progress X in three dimensional space. In the following discussion, we use X_i (i = 0, 1, ...) to represent the random variable of maximum progress from the hop i relay node (i = 0 for the source) to the sink in three-dimensional networks.

2) K = 1, 2: Similarly, $P(h = 1 \mid d) = 1$ if $0 < d \le r_{3D}$ and $P(h = 1 \mid d) = 0$ otherwise. For $P(h = 2 \mid d)$, it is given as follows:

$$P(h = 2 \mid d) = \begin{cases} 1 - \exp(-\lambda_{3D} \cdot V(d, r_{3D}, r_{3D})), r_{3D} < d \le 2r_{3D}; & (14) \\ 0, \text{ otherwise.} & (15) \end{cases}$$

where $V(d, r_{3D}, r_{3D}) = \frac{\pi(2r_{3D} - d)^2(d^2 + 4dr_{3D})}{12d}$.

3) $K > 2$: For $K > 2$, the CSP method for computing $P(h = K \mid d)$ in three-dimensional network is exactly the same as Eq. (9) except that the PDF of maximum progress is changed from function to function ψ_{3D} given in Eq. (13).

V. Probability density function of SS-distance conditioned on hop-count

We have proposed a method of computing the K-hop connection probability $P(h = K \mid d)$. In this section, we derive the solution of the PDF of SS-distance d given that hop-count $h = K$ based on the result of K-hop connection probability. Mathematically, this conditional PDF is denoted as $f(d \mid h = K)$.

We have assumed that nodes are deployed according to a Poisson process in the previous sections, therefore, the sensor node deployment region and the SS-distances of all nodes are unbounded. To simplify the analysis in this case, we define a disk shape deployment region of radius R ($R \gg r$). Without loss of generality, we assume that the source node is located at the center of the deployment disk. All other nodes falling inside the deployment disk can be approximated as uniformly distributed in the deployment disk[3]. Since all nodes are distributed in a disk of radius R, the SS-distance d of all nodes satisfy $0 < d \leq R$.

A. Standard approach: computing $f(d \mid h = K)$ using Bayes Theorem

Since we have computed the conditional probability $P(h = K \mid d)$, we can derive the PDF $f(d \mid h = K)$ using Bayes Theorem as follows:

$$f(\mathrm{d} \mid h = K) = \frac{P(h = K \mid \mathrm{d}) f(\mathrm{d})}{P(h = K)} = \frac{P(h = K \mid \mathrm{d}) f(\mathrm{d})}{\int_0^R P(h = K \mid \mathrm{d}) f(\mathrm{d}) d\mathrm{d}} \tag{16}$$

Given that all nodes are distributed uniformly in a disk of radius R and the source node is located at the center of the disk, the PDF of the SS-distance d of all nodes is given as $f(d) = \frac{2\mathrm{d}}{R^2}$. The PDF $f(d \mid h = K)$ can be computed by substituting $f(d)$ and $P(h = K \mid d)$ into Eq. (16). However, computation of $f(d \mid h = K)$ using Bayes Theorem requires that the value of $P(h = K \mid d)$ is known priorly. Furthermore, the conditional probability $P(h = K \mid d)$ is recursively formulated and it depends on the results of $P(h = K' \mid d)$ $(K' < K)$. Therefore, computing $f(d \mid h = K)$ using Bayes Theorem is heavy from a computational point of view. We propose an alternative approximation method to compute $f(d \mid h = K)$ without evaluating $P(h = K \mid d)$ in the first place.

B. Alternative approach: random truncation

Since the SS-distances of all hop-1 nodes are less than r, $f(d \mid h = 1)$ can be derived as a truncated distribution of $f(d)$ as follows:

$$f(d \mid h = 1) = f(d \mid d \leq r) = \frac{1}{F(r)} \cdot \frac{2d}{R^2} = \frac{1}{\int_0^r \frac{2\mathrm{d}}{R^2} d\mathrm{d}} \cdot \frac{2d}{R^2} = \frac{2d}{r^2} \tag{17}$$

where $F(r) = P(d \leq r) = \int_0^r \frac{2\mathrm{d}}{R^2} d\mathrm{d}$. Similarly, the PDF $f\ (d \mid h = 2)$ can also be derived as a truncated distribution of $f(d)$ as $f(d \mid h = 2) = f(d \mid r < d \leq X_0 + r)$. Since $P(h = 2 \mid d) = P(d < X_0 + r)$ if $r < d \leq 2r$. The upper bound on d, $X_0 + r$, is simply the maximum SS-distance of all hop-2 nodes.

Unlike the case of $f(d \mid h = 1)$, the upper truncation $X_0 + r$ itself is random in this case. Define a new random variable Y as $Y = X_0 + r$ and $r \leq Y \leq 2r$. Since the PDF of X_0 is given as $\psi(\lambda, d, r, x_0)$, the PDF of Y is the shifted version of the PDF of X_0 and is given by $f(y) = \psi(\lambda, d, r, y - r)$. Therefore, the PDF $f(d \mid h = 2)$ is computed as follows:

$$f(d \mid h = 2) = f(d \mid r < d \leq X_0 + r) = f(d \mid r < d \leq Y) = \frac{1}{F(X_0 + r) - F(r)} \int_r^{2r} f(d) rect(d, r, y) f(y) dy$$

$$= \frac{1}{F(X_0 + r) - F(r)} \int_r^{2r} \frac{2d}{R^2} \cdot rect(d, r, y) \psi(\lambda, d, r, y - r) dy$$

[3] The number of nodes falling inside a region of fixed area can be approximated as a Poisson random variable given that all nodes are distributed uniformly in a bounded deployment region.

$$\begin{aligned}
&\approx \frac{1}{F(\mathbb{E}[X_0]+r)-F(r)} \int_r^{2r} \frac{2d}{R^2} \cdot rect(d,r,y)\psi(\lambda,d,r,y-r)dy \\
&= \frac{1}{\int_r^{\mathbb{E}[X_0]+r} \frac{2d}{R^2} dd} \int_r^{2r} \frac{2d}{R^2} \cdot rect(d,r,y)\psi(\lambda,d,r,y-r)dy
\end{aligned} \tag{18}$$

where $rect(d, r, y) = 1$ if $r < d \le y$ and $rect(d, r, y) = 0$ otherwise. In Eq. (18), we approximate $F(X_0 + r)$ as $F(\mathbb{E}[X_0] + r)$ in order to simplify the computation.

We can use the same approach to derive the PDF $f(d \mid h = 3)$. The lower truncation of $f(d \mid h = 3)$ is simply the upper truncation of $f(d \mid h = 2)$. The upper truncation of $f(d \mid h = 3)$ is the maximum SS-distance of all hop-3 nodes and is given by X_0+X_1+r. Define a random variable Y_1 as $Y_1 = X_0+X_1+r$ and $r \le Y_1 \le 3r$. As we have computed the PDF of $Z_1 = X_0 + X_1$ in Eq. (7), the PDF of of Y_1 is the shifted version of the PDF of Z_1:

$$f(y_1) = \int_0^r \psi(\lambda,d,r,x_0)\psi(\lambda,d-X_0,r,y_1-r-x_0)dx_0 \tag{19}$$

Therefore, we compute $f(d \mid h = 3)$ as follows:

$$\begin{aligned}
f(d \mid h=3) &= f(d \mid X_0+r<d \le X_0+X_1+r) = f(d \mid Y<d \le Y_1) \\
&= \frac{1}{F(X_0+X_1+r)-F(X_0+r)} \int_r^{3r}\int_r^{2r} f(d)rect(d,y,y_1)f(y)f(y_1)dydy_1 \\
&\approx \frac{1}{F(\mathbb{E}[X_0+X_1]+r)-F(\mathbb{E}[X_0]+r)} \int_r^{3r}\int_r^{2r} \frac{2d}{R^2} rect(d,y,y_1)f(y)f(y_1)dydy_1 \\
&= \frac{1}{\int_{\mathbb{E}[X_0]+r}^{\mathbb{E}[X_0+X_1]+r} \frac{2d}{R^2} dd} \int_r^{3r}\int_r^{2r} \frac{2d}{R^2} rect(d,y,y_1)f(y)f(y_1)dydy_1
\end{aligned} \tag{20}$$

where $f(y)$ and $f(y_1)$ are the PDF of Y and Y_1 respectively. In general, the PDF $f(d \mid h = K)$ for $K > 3$ can be computed as follows:

$$\begin{aligned}
f(d \mid h=K) &= f(d \mid \sum_{i=0}^{K-3} X_i + r < d \le \sum_{i=0}^{K-2} X_i + r) = f(d \mid Y_{K-3} < d \le Y_{K-2}) \\
&= \frac{1}{F(\sum_{i=0}^{K-2} X_i + r) - F(\sum_{i=0}^{K-3} X_i + r)} \int_r^{Kr}\int_r^{(K-1)r} f(d)rect(d,y_{K-3},y_{K-2})f(y_{K-3})f(y_{K-2})dy_{K-3}dy_{K-2} \\
&\approx \frac{1}{F(\mathbb{E}[\sum_{i=0}^{K-2} X_i]+r) - F(\mathbb{E}[\sum_{i=0}^{K-3} X_i]+r)} \int_r^{Kr}\int_r^{(K-1)r} \frac{2d}{R^2} rect(d,y_{K-3},y_{K-2})f(y_{K-3})f(y_{K-2})dy_{K-3}dy_{K-2} \\
&= \frac{1}{\int_{\mathbb{E}[\sum_{i=0}^{K-2} X_i]+r}^{\mathbb{E}[\sum_{i=0}^{K-3} X_i]+r} \frac{2d}{R^2} dd} \int_r^{Kr}\int_r^{(K-1)r} \frac{2d}{R^2} rect(d,y_{K-3},y_{K-2})f(y_{K-3})f(y_{K-2})dy_{K-3}dy_{K-2}
\end{aligned} \tag{21}$$

where, $Y_{K-3} = \sum_{i=0}^{K-3} X_i + r$, PDF of $Y_{K-3} : f(y_{K-3}) = f(\sum_{i=0}^{K-3} x_i + r)$

$Y_{K-2} = \sum_{i=0}^{K-2} X_i + r$,PDF of $Y_{K-2} : f(y_{K-2}) = f(\sum_{i=0}^{K-2} x_i + r)$

$$f(\sum_{i=0}^{K-3} X_i) = f(x) \otimes f(x_1) \otimes f(x_2) ... \otimes f(x_{K-3})$$

$$f(\sum_{i=0}^{K-2} X_i) = f(x) \otimes f(x_1) \otimes f(x_2) ... \otimes f(x_{K-2})$$

6. Simulation studies

In this section, we study the accuracy of the proposed method in computing $P(h = K\,|\,d)$ and $f(d\,|\,h = K)$ through simulation studies. Firstly, we compare the accuracy of the two different methods in computing the conditional probability $P(h = K\,|\,d)$, namely the method proposed in [7] (this method is termed as Independent Assumption Method (IAM) in the sequel) and the CSP algorithm proposed in this chapter. Secondly, we study the accuracy of the proposed method in computing the conditional PDF $f(d\,|\,h = K)$.

A. Simulation settings

For two-dimensional networks, the communication range r is set to 10. We vary the density λ of the network and carry out 1000 independent simulations. The simulated statistics of $P(h = K\,|\,d)$ and $f(d\,|\,h = K)$ are then derived from the simulation data. For the three-dimensional network, all settings are the same except the communication range $r_{3D} = 15$.

B. *K*-hop connection probability *P*(*h* = *K* |*d*)

1) Mean Absolute Error: We adopt the accuracy metric known as MAE (Mean Absolute Error) introduced in [7] as the performance measure. For comparison purpose, we partition the domain of d into M bins. MAE_K is then defined as follows:

$$MAE_K = \frac{1}{M} \sum_{i=1}^{M} |P_a(h = K\,|\,d_i) - P_s(h = K\,|\,d_i)| \tag{22}$$

where $P_a(h = K\,|\,d_i)$ and $P_s(h = K\,|\,d_i)$ are the analytical and the corresponding simulation results of the conditional probability respectively. The index K on MAE indicates the particular value of K-hop considered. Fig. 4 shows the simulation results and the analytical results (computed using IAM) of the conditional probability $P(h = K\,|\,d)$ (K = 2 to 5) for networks with density $\lambda = 0.03537$. We observe that the analytical result of $P(h = 2\,|\,d)$ closely matches the simulation result of $P(h = 2\,|\,d)$. This is expected since the analytical solution of $P(h = 2\,|\,d)$ given in Eq. (5) is exact. However, the analytical results deviate from the simulation results as K increases. It can be observed that the discrepancy becomes significantly large for $P(h = 5\,|\,d)$. On the other hand, Fig. 5 shows the simulation results and the analytical results (computed using the CSP method) of the conditional probability $P(h = K\,|\,d)$ (K = 2 to 5) for networks with density $\lambda = 0.03537$. It is observed that the analytical results closely match the simulation results for all values of K. In fact, even without the MAE metric, it is not difficult to conclude from the observation that computation of $P(h = K\,|\,d)$ based on the CSP method is more accurate than the method of IAM.

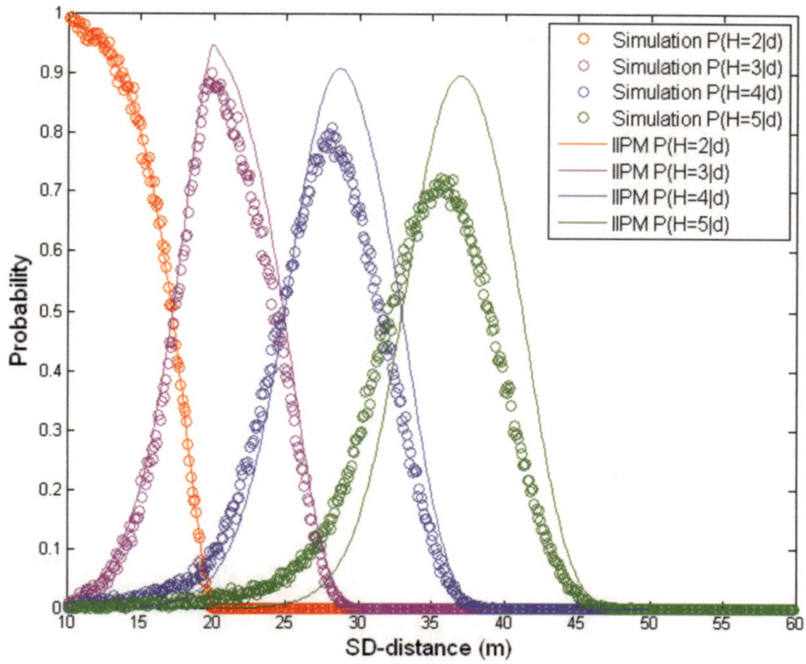

Fig. 4. Simulation results and analytical results (IAM method) of $P(h = K \mid d)$ for $K = 2$ to 5. Network density $\lambda = 0.03537$.

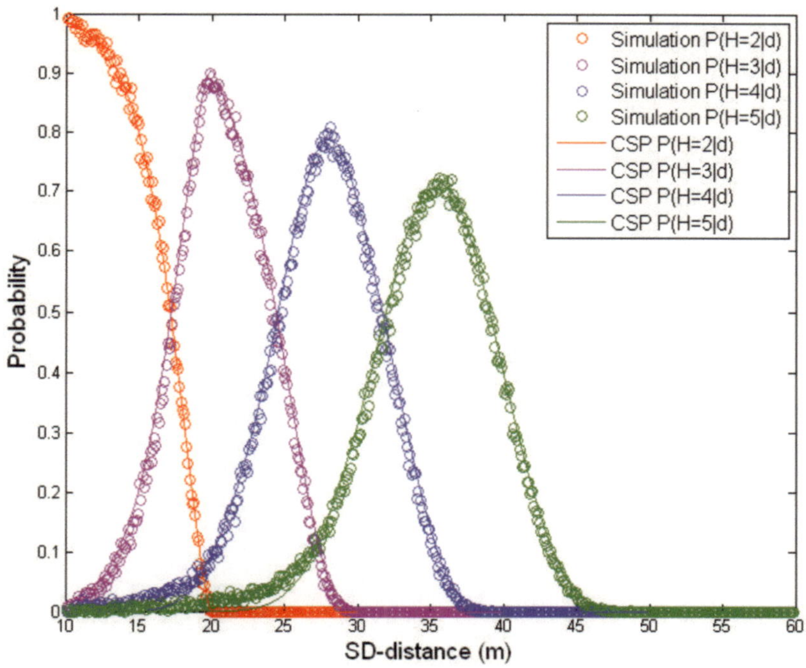

Fig. 5. Simulation results and analytical results (CSP method) of $P(h = K \mid d)$ for $K = 2$ to 5. Network density $\lambda = 0.03537$.

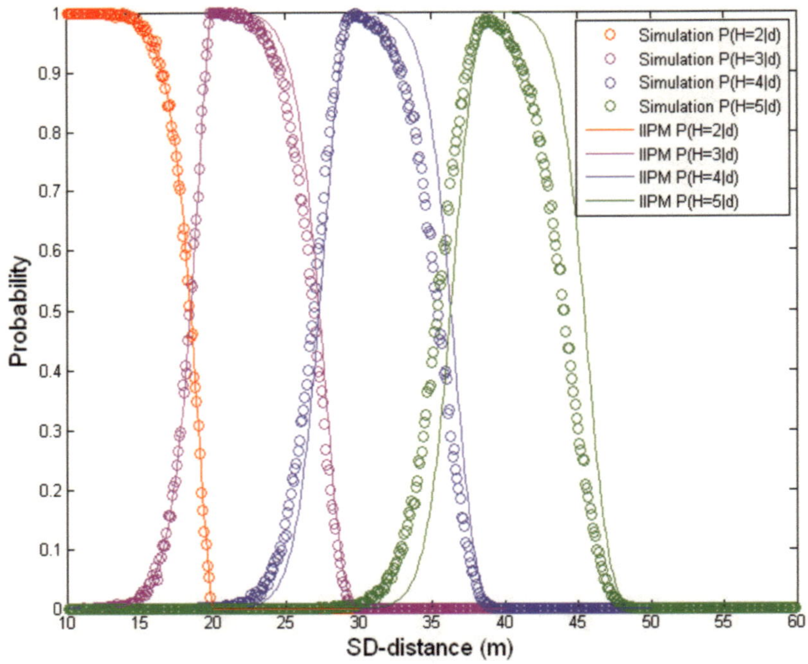

Fig. 6. Simulation results and analytical results (IAM method) of $P(h = K \mid d)$ for $K = 2$ to 5. Network density $\lambda = 0.08842$.

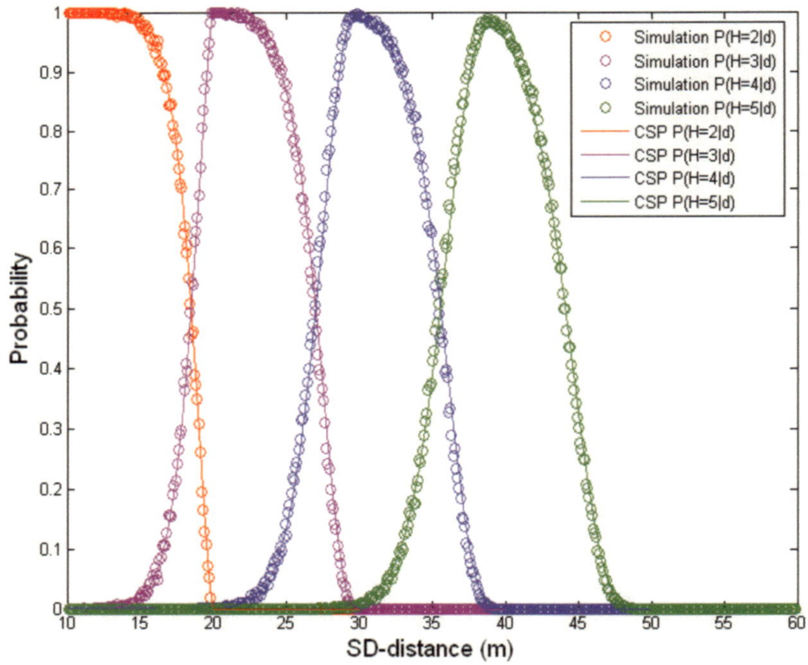

Fig. 7. Simulation results and analytical results (CSP method) of $P(h = K \mid d)$ for $K = 2$ to 5. Network density $\lambda = 0.08842$.

We also plot the analytical results of $P(h = K \mid d)$ for networks with density $\lambda = 0.08842$ based on the method of IAM and the CSP in Fig. 6 and 7 respectively. Simulation results of $P(h = K \mid d)$ are also plotted in each figure. In Fig. 6, we observe that the discrepancy between the analytical results of the method of IAM and the simulation results reduces as compared to the previous case where density $\lambda = 0.03537$. The reason is that the independent assumption of the IAM method only holds when λ tends to infinity. As a consequence, computation of $P(h = K \mid d)$ based on the IAM method becomes more accurate as λ increases. Although the discrepancy is reduced as compared to Fig. 4, the error observed in Fig. 6 is still non-negligible. On the other hand, it can be observed in Fig. 7 that the analytical results of the CSP method concur with the simulation results.

To compare the performance of the IAM and the CSP methods quantitatively, we plot the MAE of both methods against the node density λ in Fig. 8, 9 and 10. Since the analytical solution of $P(h = 2 \mid d)$ is exact, error in computing $P(h = 2 \mid d)$ is due to computer simulation (such as finite steps taken in the numerical integration) rather than methodology. Therefore, we plot $MAE_{K=2}$ in all figures as a benchmark indicator. In Fig. 8, we plot $MAE_{K=3}$ of the IAM and the CSP methods. It is observed that the $MAE_{K=3}$ of the IAM method is much larger than the $MAE_{K=3}$ of the CSP method. Although the $MAE_{K=3}$ of the CSP method is larger than the benchmark indicator $MAE_{K=2}$, it is observed that the $MAE_{K=3}$ approaches the benchmark $MAE_{K=2}$ as the number of nodes increases. Fig. 9 and 10 shows the $MAE_{K=4}$ and $MAE_{K=5}$ of both methods. It is observed that the MAE_K of the CSP method are smaller than the MAE_K of the IAM method for all values of K. For instance, the $MAE_{K=5}$ of the CSP method is about 10 times smaller than the $MAE_{K=5}$ of the IAM method.

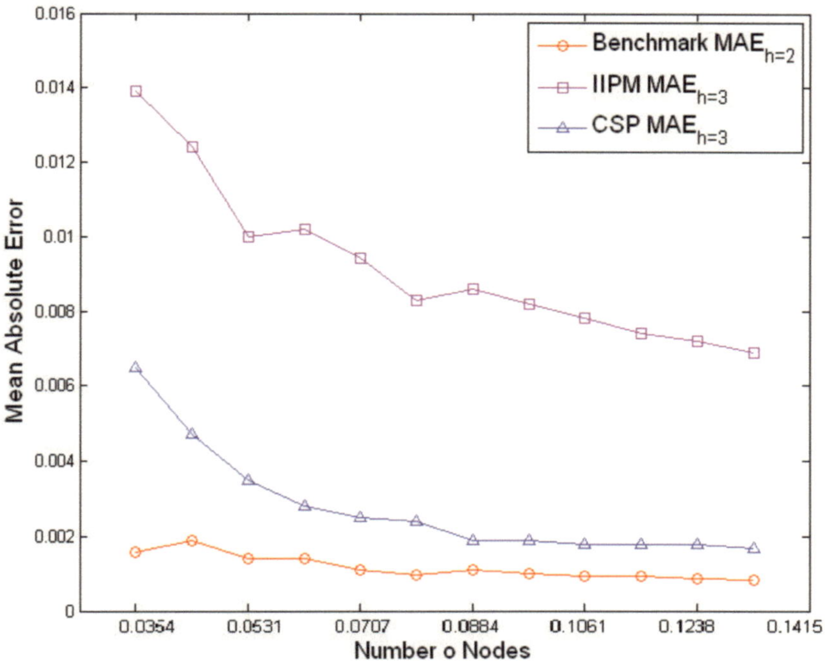

Fig. 8. The $MAE_{K=3}$ of the IAM method and the CSP method against the node density λ. The $MAE_{K=2}$ is plotted as a benchmark indicator.

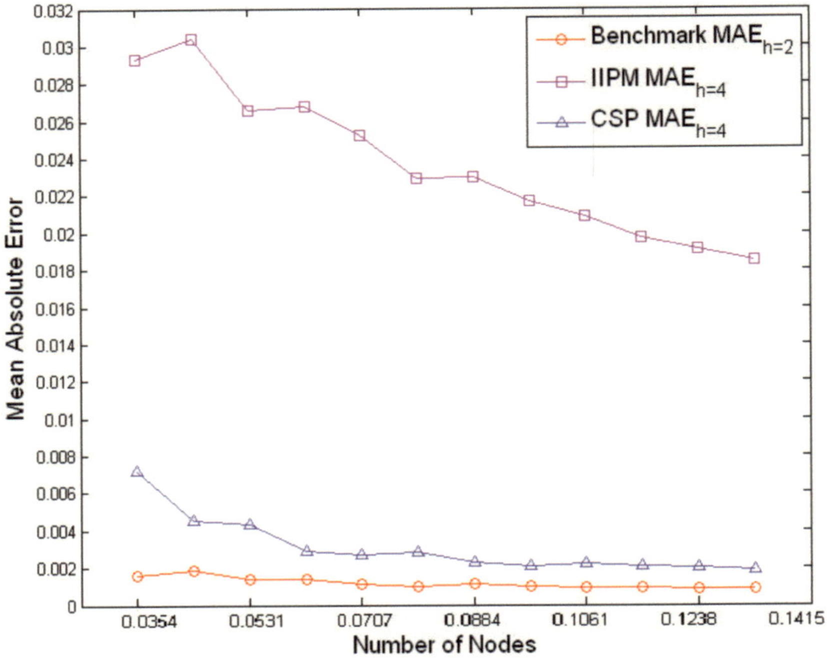

Fig. 9. The $MAE_{K=4}$ of the IAM method and the CSP method against the node density λ. The $MAE_{K=2}$ is plotted as a benchmark indicator.

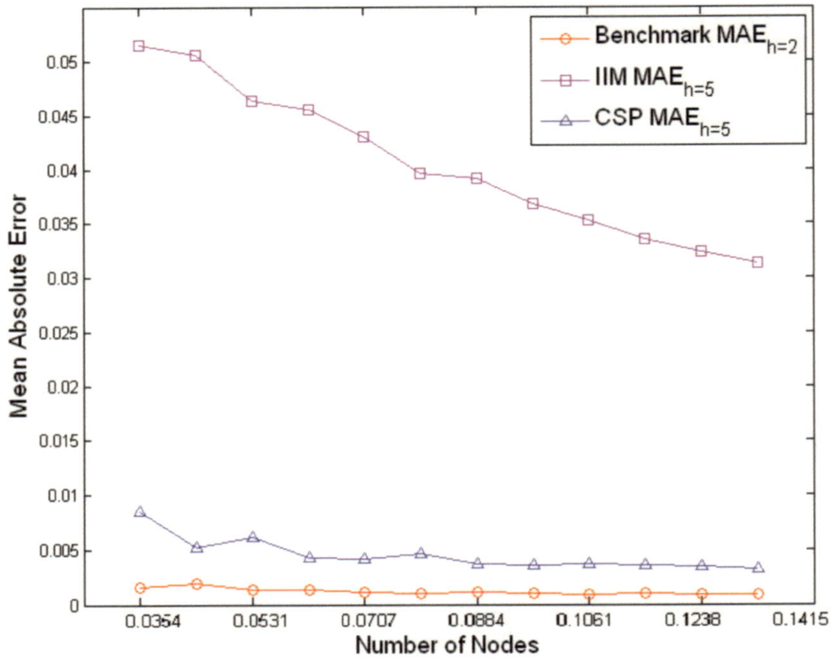

Fig. 10. The $MAE_{K=5}$ of the IAM method and the CSP method against the node density λ. The $MAE_{K=2}$ is plotted as a benchmark indicator.

2) Snowball Effect: Since both IAM and CSP methods are formulated recursively, errors in computing $P(h = K \mid d)$ will propagate to/accumulate in the computation of $P(h = K' \mid d)$ ($K' > K$). We compare this snowball effect of both methods. In Fig. 11, we plot the *MAE* of both methods against hop-count K for three network densities, namely λ = 0.03537, 0.08842 and 0.1326. As shown in the figure, the snowball effect of the IAM method is prominent since the *MAE* of the IAM method increases rapidly as K increases. For the CSP method, although the formulation of the conditional probability is also recursive, the snowball effect is negligible.

3) K-hop Outage Probability: The analytical result of the K-hop connection probability $P(h = K \mid d)$ can be easily extended to the solution of a problem known as K-hop outage probability. The K-hop outage probability is defined as the probability that a sink can be connected to a source in less than or equal to K number of multi-hop relays, given that the SS-distance is d. The K-hop outage probability can be evaluated as the sum of individual K-hop connection probability, i.e. $\sum_{i=1}^{K} P(h = i \mid d)$. Fig. 12 shows the K-hop outage probability plots based on the simulation results and the analytical results for networks of density λ = 0.05305. It can be seen that the analytical result concur with the simulation results.

4) Three-dimensional Network: We have extended the CSP method into three-dimensional networks. To validate the method, we plot the analytical results and simulation results of $P(h = K \mid d)$ for three-dimensional network of density λ = 0.001658 and λ = 0.002210 in Fig. 13 and 14 respectively. It can be observed from the figures that the analytical results concur with the simulation results.

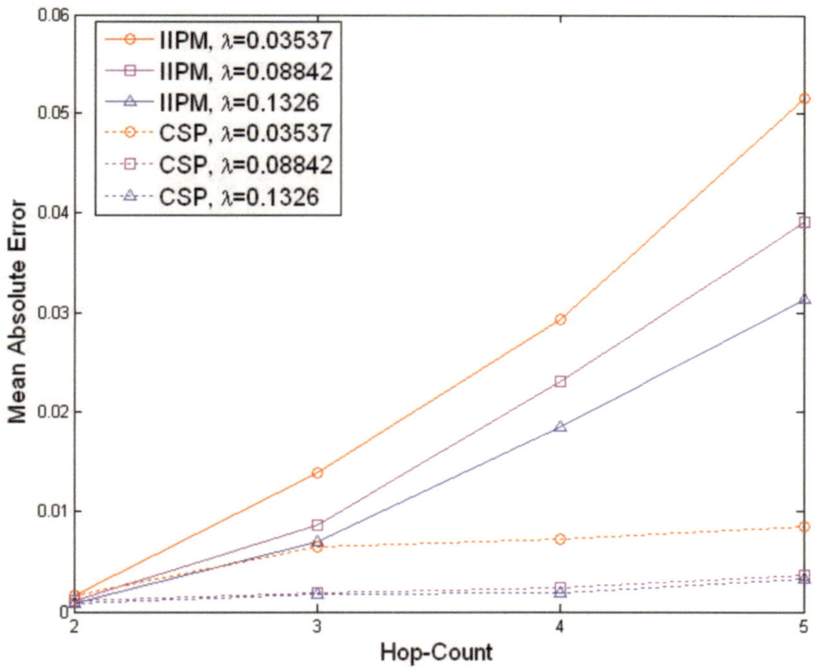

Fig. 11. Illustration of the snowball effect. The MAE of the IAM method increases rapidly as hop-count increases. On the other hand, the MAE of the CSP method does not increase much as hop-count K increases.

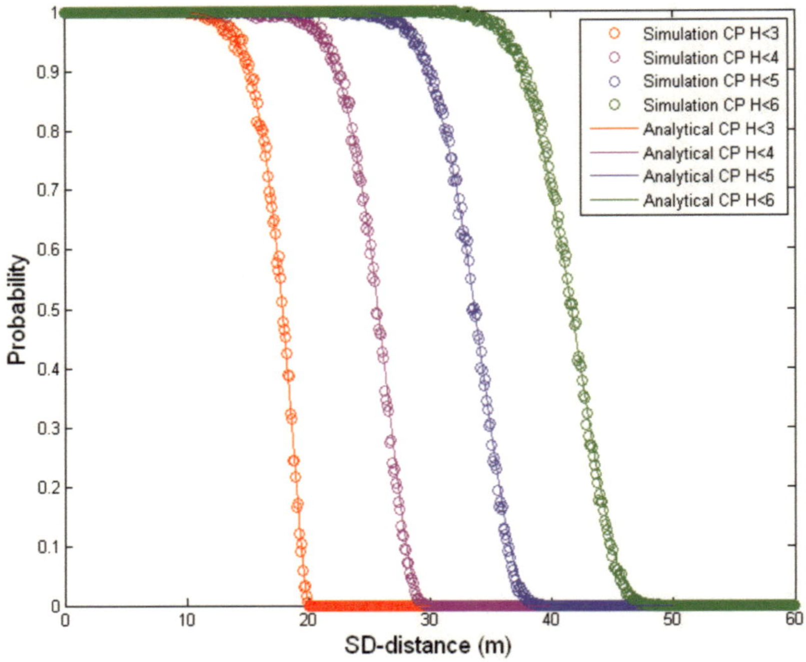

Fig. 12. Illustration of the *K*-hop outage Probability for $K = 2$ to 5, $\lambda = 0.05305$

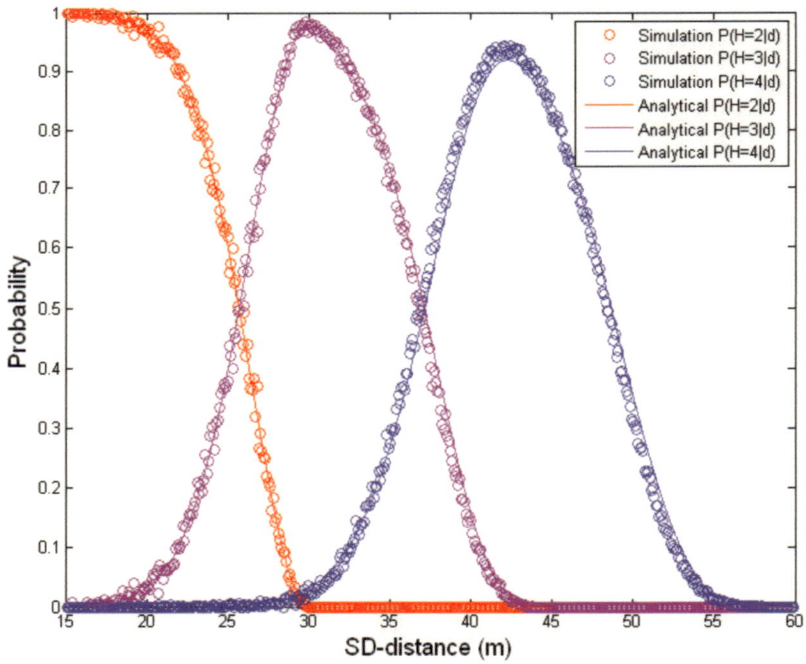

Fig. 13. Comparison of the conditional probability $P(h = K \mid d)$ in three-dimensional network based on the simulation results and the analytical results, $\lambda = 0.001658$.

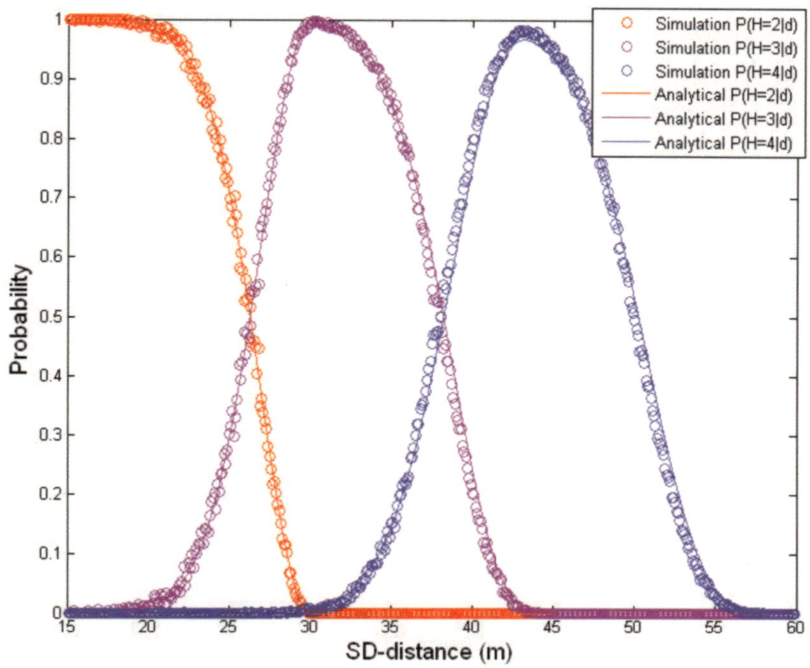

Fig. 14. Comparison of the conditional probability $P(h = K \mid d)$ in three-dimensional network based on the simulation results and the analytical results, $\lambda = 0.002210$.

C. Conditional probability density function *f*(*d* |*H* = *K*)

In this sub-section, we compare the simulation results and the analytical results of the conditional PDF $f(d \mid h = K)$. The simulation results and the analytical results of $f(d \mid h = K)$ ($K = 2$ to 5) are plotted in Fig. 16, 17, 18 and 19 respectively. The density of the network is set to $\lambda = 0.03537$. It is observed that the analytical results match the simulation results very well. Some literatures ([3] and [8]) study the Guassianity of the conditional PDF $f(d \mid h = K)$ by using Skewness and Kurtosis as a measure, and then use Gaussian PDF to fit the simulation data to approximate the conditional PDF $f(d \mid h = K)$. These
heuristic approaches of approximating $f(d \mid h = K)$ require statistical fitting. The method proposed in this chapter, on the other hand, is a general formulation of the conditional PDF $f(d \mid h = K)$. We also plot the simulation results and the analytical results of the PDF $f(d \mid h = K)$ ($K = 2$ to 5) for networks with density $\lambda = 0.08842$ in Fig. 20, 21, 22 and 23 respectively. We observe that the analytical results also match the simulation results very well. Quantitatively, we plot the MAE_K error against the density λ of network in Fig. 15. In this case, MAE_K is defined as follows:

$$MAE_K = \frac{1}{M}\sum_{i=1}^{M} |f_a(d_i \mid h = K) - f_s(d_i \mid h = K)| \tag{23}$$

where $f_a(d \mid h = K)$ and $f_s(d \mid h = K)$ are the analytical and simulation result respectively. As shown in Fig. 15, the MAE is of the order of 10^{-3}. The error is indeed very small.

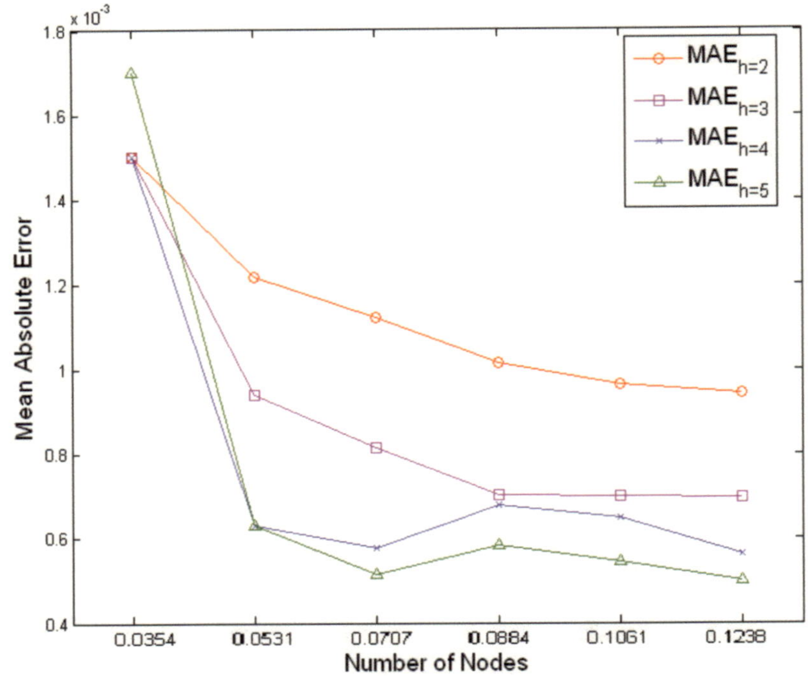

Fig. 15. Mean Absolute Error of the analytical result $f(d \mid h = K)$ against the number of node deployed.

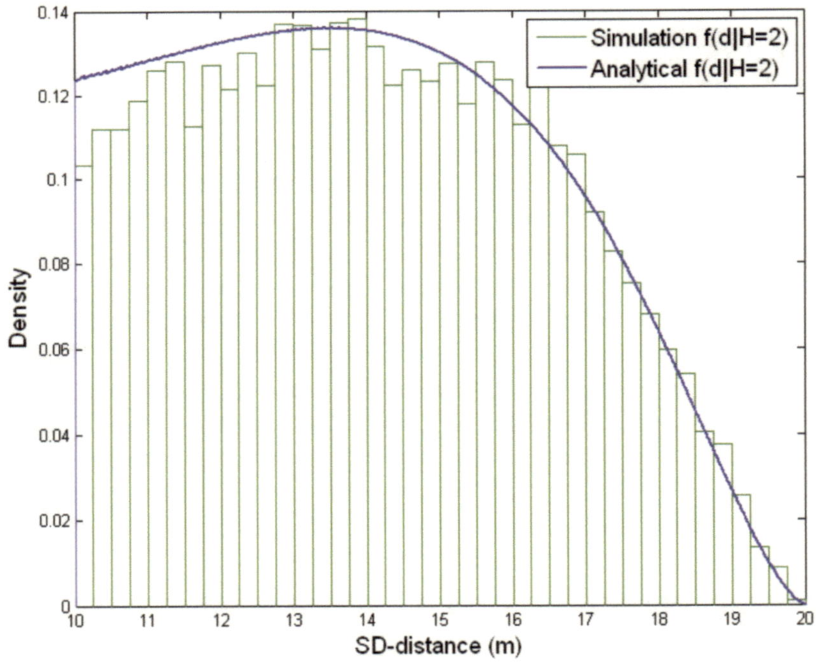

Fig. 16. The conditional pdf $f(d \mid h = 2)$ based on the simulation data (histogram plot) and the analytical result, $\lambda = 0.03537$.

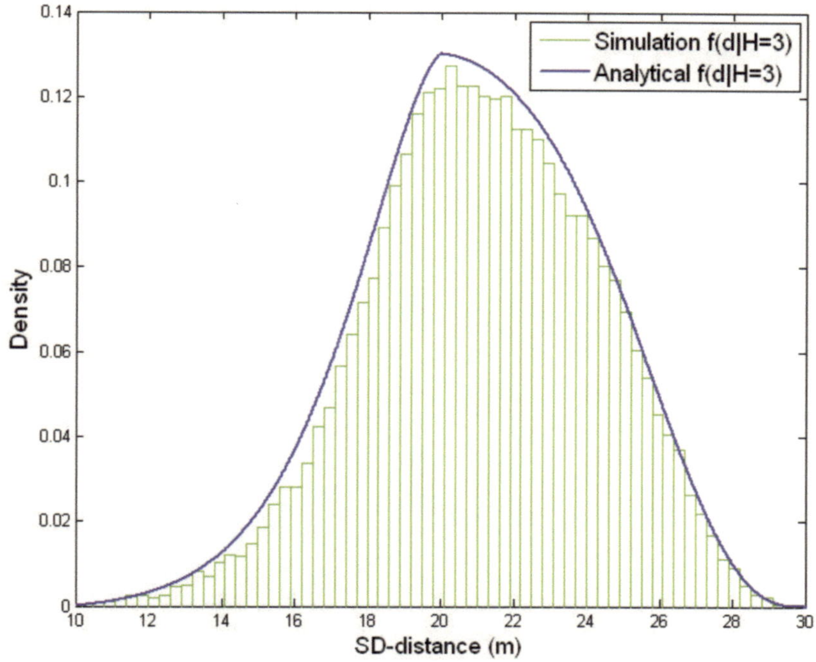

Fig. 17. The conditional pdf $f(d \mid h = 3)$ based on the simulation data (histogram plot) and the analytical result, $\lambda = 0.03537$.

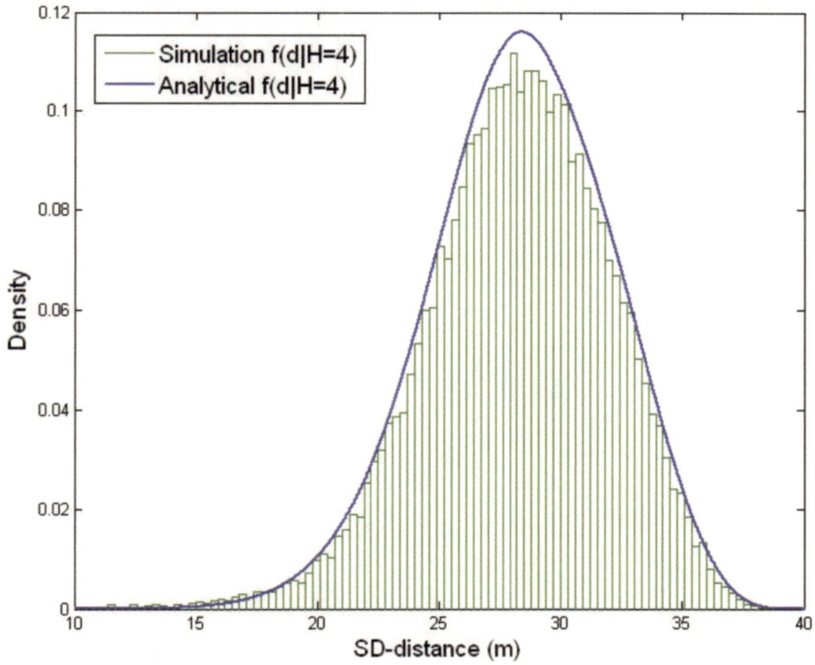

Fig. 18. The conditional pdf $f(d \mid h = 4)$ based on the simulation data (histogram plot) and the analytical result, $\lambda = 0.03537$.

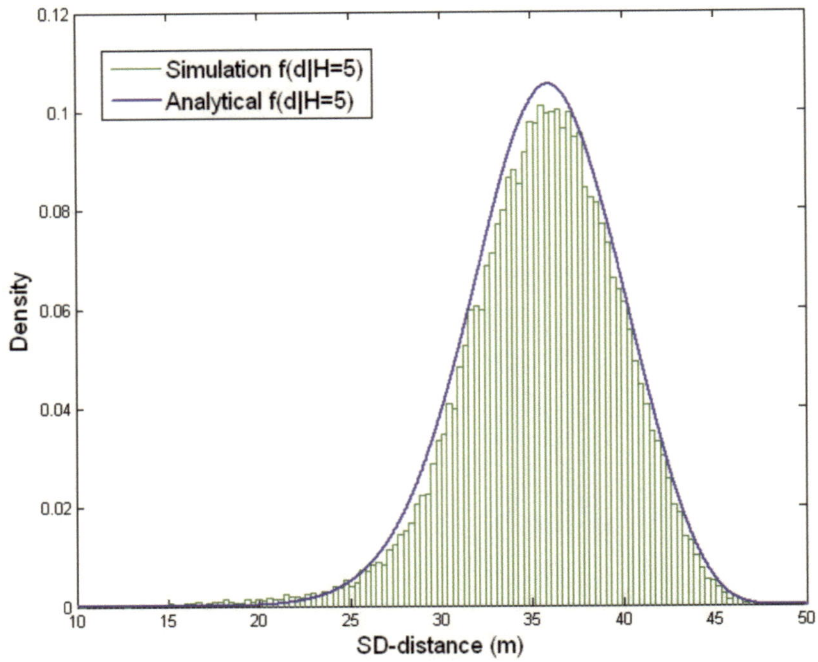

Fig. 19. The conditional pdf $f(d \mid h = 5)$ based on the simulation data (histogram plot) and the analytical result, $\lambda = 0.03537$.

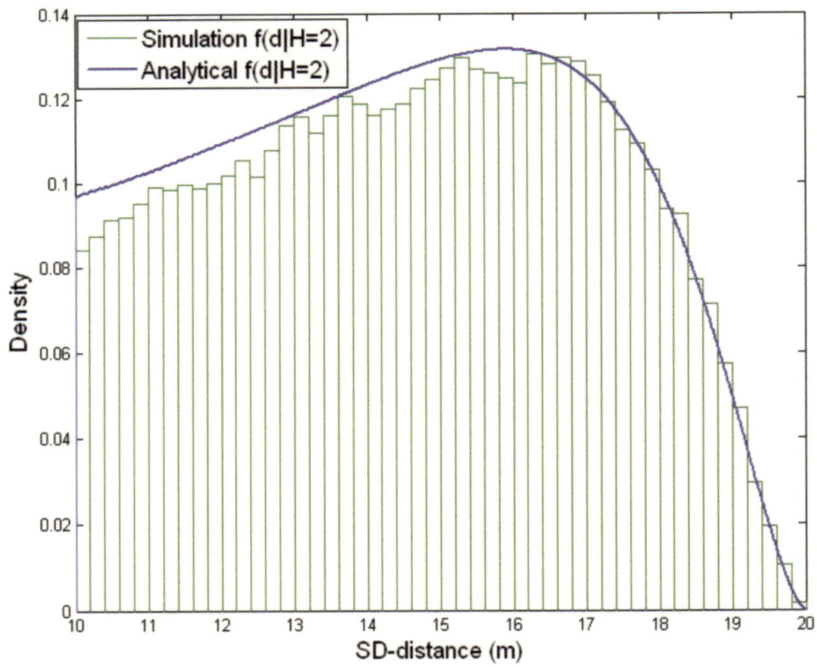

Fig. 20. The conditional pdf $f(d \mid h = 2)$ based on the simulation data (histogram plot) and the analytical result, $\lambda = 0.08842$.

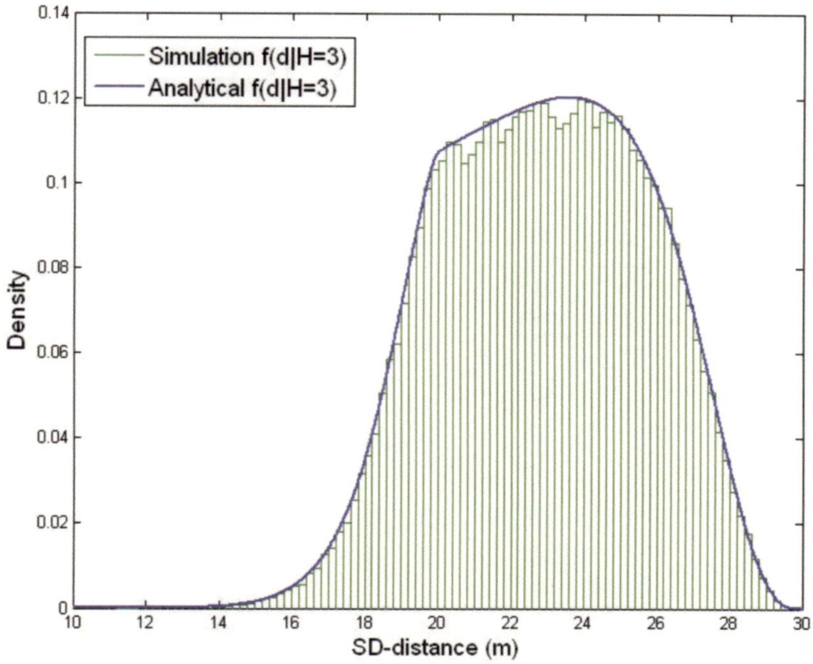

Fig. 21. The conditional pdf $f(d \mid h = 3)$ based on the simulation data (histogram plot) and the analytical result, $\lambda = 0.08842$.

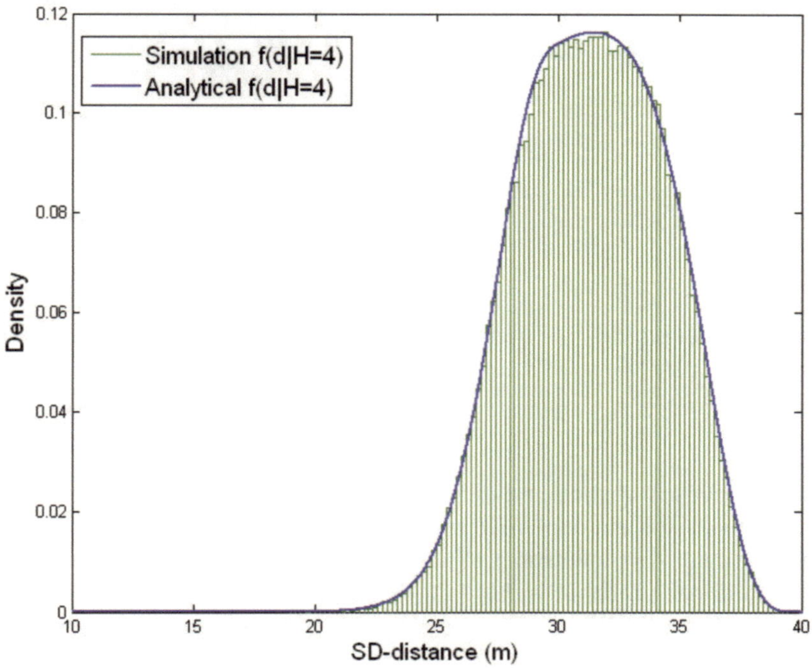

Fig. 22. The conditional pdf $f(d \mid h = 4)$ based on the simulation data (histogram plot) and the analytical result, $\lambda = 0.08842$.

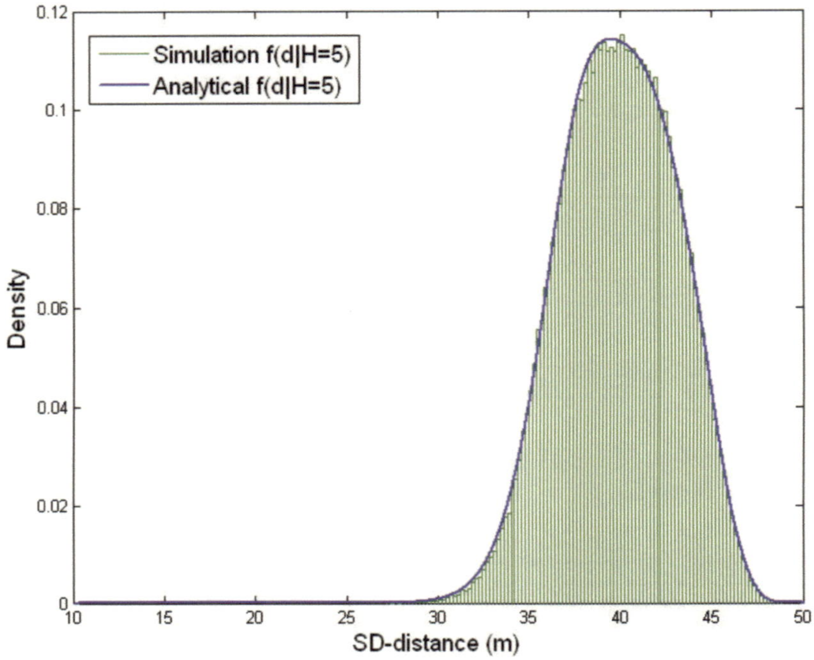

Fig. 23. The conditional pdf $f(d \mid h = 5)$ based on the simulation data (histogram plot) and the analytical result, $\lambda = 0.08842$.

7. Conclusions

Evaluation of various statistical relationships between hop-count and source-to-sink distance are some of the fundamental research problems in large-scale WSNs. In this chapter, we investigate two statistical relationships between hop-count and SS-distance, namely the conditional probability $P(h = K \mid d)$ and the conditional PDF $f(d \mid h = K)$. We propose a method termed CSP to compute $P(h = K \mid d)$ in both two and three-dimensional networks. This method is also extended to compute the conditional PDF $f(d \mid h = K)$.
Simulation results show that significant error reduction in computing the conditional probability and the conditional PDF can be achieved compared with the existing methods.

8. References

[1] B. Wang, C. Fu and H. B. Lim, "Layered diffusion based coverage control in wireless sensor networks," in *IEEE the 32rd Conference on Local Computer Networks (LCN)*, 2007, pp. 504–511.

[2] Y. Cheng and T. G. Robertazzi, "Critical connectivity phenomena in multihop radio models," *IEEE Transactions on Communications*, vol. 37, no. 7, 1989.

[3] S. Vural and E. Ekici, "Probability distribution of multi-hop-distance in one-dimensional sensor networks," *Computer Networks (Elsevier)*, vol. 51, no. 3, pp. 3727–3749, 2007.

[4] S. Dulman, M. Rossi, P. Havinga and M. Zorzi, "On the hop count statistics for randomly deployed wireless sensor networks," *Int. J. Sensor Networks*, vol. 1, 2006.

[5] C. Bettstetter and J. Eberspacher, "Hop distances in homogeneous ad hoc networks," *Vehicular Technology Conference*, vol. 4, pp. 2286 - 2290, 2003.

[6] S. Chandler, "Calculation of number of relay hops required in randomly located radio network," *IEEE Electronic Letter*, vol. 25, no. 24, 1989.

[7] X. Ta, G. Mao and B. D. Anderson, "On the probability of k-hop connection in wireless sensor networks," *IEEE Communication Letters*, vol. 11, no. 9, 2007.

[8] L. Zhao and Q. Liang, "Hop-distance estimation in wireless sensor networks with applications to resources allocation," *EURASIP Journal on Wireless Communication and Networking*, 2007.

[9] L. E. Miller, "Probability of a two-hop connection in a random mobile network," *Proc. 35th Conf. on Information Sciences and Systems*, 2001.

[10] L. Kleinrock and J. Silvester, "Optimum transmission radii for packet radio networks or why six is a magic number," *IEEE National Telecommunications Conference*, 1978.

[11] J. Kuo and W. Liao, "Hop count distribution of multihop paths in wireless networks with arbitrary node density modeling and its applications," *IEEE Transactions on Vehicular Technology*, vol. 56, no. 4, 2007.

[12] Y. Wang, X. Wang, D. Wang and D. P. Agrawal, "Range-free localization using expected hop progress in wireless sensor networks," *IEEE Transactions on Parallel and Distributed Systems*, 2008.

[13] S. De, A. Caruso, T. Chaira and S. Chessa, "Bounds on hop distance in greedy routing approach in wireless ad hoc networks," *International Journal of Wireless and Mobile Computing*, vol. 1, no. 2, 2006.

[14] D. Niculescu and B. Nath, "Ad hoc positioning system (aps)," *Global Telecommunications Conference*, vol. 5, pp. 2926 - 2931, 2001.

[15] S. Y. Wong, J. G. Lim, S. Rao and W. K. Seah, "Density-aware hop-count localization (dhl) in wireless sensor networks with variable density," *Wireless Communications and Networking Conference, IEEE*, vol. 3, pp. 1848 - 1853, March 2005.

[16] S. Yang, J. Yi and H. Cha, "Hcrl: A hop-count-ratio based localization in wireless sensor networks," *IEEE Communications Society Conference on Sensor, Mesh and Ad Hoc Communications and Networks*, pp. 31–40, June 2007.

[17] T. S. Rappaport, *Wireless communications: principles and practice*, Prentice Hall PTR, 1996.

[18] C. Bettstetter, "On the minimum node degree and connectivity of a wireless multihop network," *ACM international symposium on Mobile ad hoc networking and computing,* 2002.

18

Information Technology in Collaborative Networks

Lorenzo Ros-McDonnell and M.Victoria de-la-Fuente-Aragon
Universidad Politecnica de Cartagena
Spain

1. Introduction

The purpose of an information system is to manage data, information and knowledge connected with human activity. Information Systems in Collaborative Networks manage available data and describe conditions and information generated by data integration corresponding to the various stages of products and services in the network, and the actions taken by network staff in order to modify these stages. Starting from the information available, these systems integrate data and, by contrasting them with the experience accumulated in the system's memory, ensure optimum decision-making.

Collaborative Networks Information Systems have not been formally fixed, mainly because of their complexity but also because until very recently an automated data-processing system capable of attempting automation had not existed.

Nowadays the major obstacle to reach an adequate level of automation in collaborative networks information systems is the lack of systematisation. Overcoming this impediment is crucial to allow the development of an electronic network (e-network), which consists of an automated data-processing system trying to achieve computer-aided management of a Collaborative Network Information System.

This chapter presents an analysis and a modelization method for the decision-making process in a collaborative network, as the main target to be developed within the same network. Not only is this a technological change, it is something else. It proves to be the only way to share network knowledge in a co-operative manner, among professionals from several companies, and with different degrees of collaboration expertise. The results of the analysis of this innovative kind of proposed collaborative network process illustrate how collaboration is carried out through the various processes, and demonstrate the perfect way to tackle e-network development.

2. Designing a collaborative network

A simple definition of networks is "a set of actors connected by a set of ties" with actors being "persons, teams, organizations, concepts, etc." (Borgatti & Foster, 2003). Participation in networks has become very important for any organization that strives to achieve a differentiated competitive advantage. Among the wide variety of existing networks, collaborative networks are especially relevant. These have emerged over the last few years as a result of the challenges faced by both the business and scientific worlds, since collaboration has become the key issue to rapidly answer market demands in manufacturing companies, through sharing competence and resources (Camarinha-Matos et al., 2009).

The collaborative network paradigm offers new possibilities for effective and agile organization of future manufacturing systems. In order to be successful in a very competitive and rapidly changing environment, companies need significantly improved competencies in terms of dealing with new business models, strategies, organizational and governance principles, processes and technological capabilities. In this context, collaborative networks show a high potential for value creation through new capabilities to cope with innovation needs, uncertainty, mass customization and fierce competition (Camarinha-Matos & Afsarmanesh, 2005).

A more comprehensive, fine-tuned description is again contributed by Camarinha-Matos and Afsarmanesh (2005); according to them, a collaborative network is constituted by a variety of entities that are largely autonomous, geographically distributed and heterogeneous in terms of their operating environment, culture, social capital and goals.

And yet these entities work together to better achieve compatible goals, using ICT for supporting the development of collaborative business opportunities. As dynamic inter-organizational models, communication mechanisms play a vital role in collaborative networks, alongside coordination as the method to support the exchange of information between interdependent activities or processes and among collaborative enterprises.

In this context, a collaborative network defined as a virtual global manufacturing network, is materialized by a group of dynamic enterprises in constant transformation, with horizontal and vertical connections set up among them and / or with other independent companies -even with competitors. This is turn dismisses the urge to maintain their internal manufacturing resources and manages and shares efficiently those resources available within the network.

2.1 Objectives of a collaborative network

A network knows well what it is doing; from an inter-organizational perspective, what will allow it to correctly define its processes, tasks, activities and ICT tools and mechanisms is not only the psychological processes underlying the behaviour of network actors, but also its evolution in time, its decision-making ability, and its knowledge of what really works (Gösling et al., 2007).

One feature of inter-organizational networks which particularly differentiate them from standard or traditional organizations is the absence of hierarchy. How can appropriation concerns and inter-organisational networks be managed, and how can tasks in networks be coordinated in the absence of pure hierarchy? (Gösling et al., 2007). The question of how to guide the behaviours of their collaboration partners to prevent possible confrontations makes it necessary to define the control mechanisms (outcome control, behavioural control, social control and institutions) and the processes (formal and informal), together with a good information system (ICT) to support them.

Control in collaboration relationships is necessary because it allows ensuring the optimal performance of the collaboration, identifying plans and activities of the actors, and regulating the conduct of factors in the collaboration. (Gösling et al., 2007). The collaboration reflects the achievement of a delicate balance between actors in the network, which will need to be constantly reviewed and renegotiated.

The benefits of collaboration can be pecuniary and non-pecuniary: financial, market access, interaction, sympathy. Actors should have positive expectations in order to have an incentive to start and maintain an inter-organisational relationship. But inefficient collaborative settings, premature termination of a tie, negative expectations about the future value of an inter-organisational relationship, as well as failures of joint efforts and goals can be observed (Gösling et al., 2007).

The key ingredients of alliance success (Bleeke & Ernst, 1995) include flexibility in the management of the tie, building trust with partners, regular communication, constructive management of conflict, continuity of personnel for the inter-organisational tie, managing partner expectations, and so on.

In this sense, relationships inside a collaborative network must be tolerant enough to permit obtaining a permeable organization, allowing simultaneous collaboration with a varied group of participants, all with different features. Organisation of the manufacturing network must be thought of as a permeable, flexible, open and dynamic system, in which relations occurring in the network facilitate the actors' connection and disconnection, their linking up with one or several sub-groups in the network, and the co-existence of participants with varied characteristics.

It can be anticipated that this dynamic system will be defined by low barriers to entry and exit, geographical flexibility, low costs, fast diffusion of technology, high diversification and exceptional economies of scale.

The paradigm of collaborative networks can help companies, namely SMEs, to face these challenges and reach competitive advantage. A company joining efforts with other companies may typically expect to achieve: a larger dimension; access to new markets and new knowledge; sharing of risks and resources; a collaborative environment for innovation, through the combination of synergies, competencies, culture and experiences; and joining of complementary skills and capacities which allow each entity to focus on its core competencies while keeping a high level of agility (Camarinha-Matos, 2009).

2.2 Construction phases of a collaborative network

In the construction of a collaborative network several aspects should be taken into account, such as the cultures of the network and the companies that constitute it, as well as the relationships already formed or to be created in the future among the companies that will constitute this network. The analysis of these factors will mainly allow establishing the various phases through which a network will pass during its construction.

In the design of a collaborative network as a virtual organization for global manufacturing, the cultural differences among the companies that are integrated in it, especially if they are to collaborate robustly, could pose a difficult challenge. Opposed focuses on activities such as, for example, internal communication, the realization of objectives, the professional career system, the structure of power or the relationship employee-superior, etc. may translate into conflicts in terms of task performance, expectations and practices in the collaborative network. For this reason, one could conclude that the organizational culture of the network will have to avoid a high degree of incompatibilities in the cultural practices of its members.

The relationships between the companies that may be comprised in the network generate a society that results in the appearance of a source of information on the reliability and capacity of both its current members and its potential participants. This society represents a dynamic system formed by the previous relationships and the current partners, and evolves in time as new relations and connections are established.

The analysis of the influence of these social networks in the construction of a virtual collaborative network is basic, since in the transactions between companies of a network, relational capital is in many cases more valuable than economic capital (Luo, 2001). The companies participating in a virtual network may face a high risk of opportunistic conducts, due to the unpredictable behaviour of potential partners and the high costs that this would cause if it actually happened. This situation, originated in the lack of information on the reliability of the potential collaborator, whose conduct is a key factor in the success of the alliance, could be a source of uncertainty.

Social integration will enable the companies forming the virtual network to receive information regarding the capacities, aptitudes and necessities of new collaborators to the network, thus increasing reliability in the face of opportunistic conducts. These social relations need time to settle and seed but, once established, they will become a catalyst for managerial relationships inside the network.

Therefore, knowing the map of existing social relationships, besides being helpful when building the network, is fundamental in order to succeed. The virtual network will be closely related with the intensity of the social relationships present in it.

As described above, one of the key factors when constructing the virtual manufacturing network is constructing confidence. There are other key factors, such as transparency, clear-cut power relationships and fulfilment of commitments and obligations. These factors have an obvious influence on the social relations being built in a virtual manufacturing network.

Figure 1 shows the various phases of trust in the relationships between companies inside a collaborative virtual network. Point 1 is the denominated *structural trust* (Madhok, 1995).

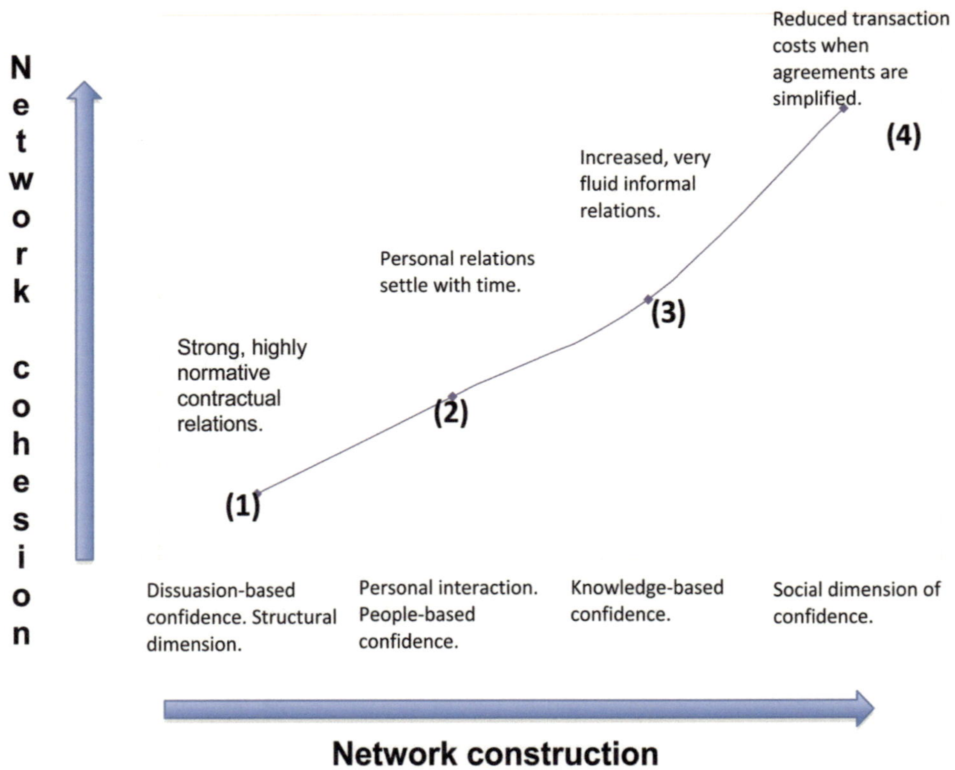

Fig. 1. Relationships between level of trust and degree of virtualization in the network. (Adapted from: Rodriguez-Monroy & Vilana-Arte, 2010)

This level of confidence is based on the tangible aspects of the collaboration. Explicit mechanisms are usual, such as very formal contracts including penalty systems or coercive measures to avoid opportunistic conducts. Although essential in the initial phases, it is not enough in the long run as it is unstable and easily affected by factors such as transparency or keeping commitments and it does not keep in mind the social aspect, relying on the symmetry of contributions.

With time, personal relationships develop and the interactions among persons from different companies generate a higher degree of confidence (point 2). In this phase the relationships in the virtual collaborative network are based on reliance rather than on a formal contract. The foundations of this trust have a cognitive component originated in the experience of previous interactions. This, according to Saphiro et al. (1992), is a kind of knowledge-based confidence, which expands into mutual understanding.

An important aspect of the virtual collaborative network is the directly proportional relationship between the degree of virtualization and the level of confidence attained. The collaborative network under construction will gradually become more and more virtualized, as time passes and honest trust among companies builds up.

In point 3 the actors of the network begin to establish more casual, fluid relationships, and this is what defines a phase of trust based on knowledge, where network processes become smoother and the costs of transactions decrease drastically.

With time, trust becomes a very effective mechanism in the relationships between companies, helping to mitigate the problems generated by strong competition among them, or the organizational complexity of the virtual collaborative network. Trust will also reduce the costs of transaction because it reduces the costs of design and negotiation of the contracts (point 4). This phase is denominated *social trust* (Madhok, 1995).

The conclusions are that confidence is a cultural mechanism in virtual networks which grows slowly with time and, if appropriate measures are taken in order to reduce transaction costs radically, managerial collaboration will flow more effortlessly and knowledge transfer will be eased.

In the development of a collaborative network, basic actions are instigated which facilitate teamwork between companies to quickly progress along the confidence curve:

- Social companies must invest their resources in improving confidence in the early phases of collaboration.
- It is necessary to minimize rotations of personnel so that social relationships have continuity and increase mutual trust.
- Intense collaborations should initially be avoided as the process of construction of social trust requires time.
- Social relationships can be improved by creating value for complementary capacities.

In short, the virtual collaborative network will focus initially on a reduced number of activities and main abilities that will be complementary to those of other partners. When these capacities are mutually appreciated, progress in future developments will strengthen trust and minimize opportunistic conducts.

It must not be forgotten that that one of the reasons for the existence of global production networks is their ability to transfer and utilize knowledge in a more efficient way than by means of external mechanisms of the market.

This type of knowledge constitutes one of the lasting competitive advantages (Gupta & Govindarajan, 2000). It is also a major factor in the managerial differentiation (Trice & Beyer, 1993). Knowledge transfer within the network could help approach cultural practices

(Hofstede et al., 1990). By diluting and expanding these assets in the network, a cultural homogenization process takes place.

Figure 2 shows the cultural mechanisms occurring in the constitution of a network, both before the formalisation (*ex ante*) of collaboration and after it (*ex post*). This is a continuous process where these mechanisms are mutually recognised. These four cultural mechanisms-social integration, knowledge transfer, trust, and cultural similarities among network members, should not be understood as static mechanisms, or independent from the managerial collaboration process. They are dynamic elements that exert mutual and continuous influence during the whole life of the collaboration; they are in constant progress and are capable of reinforcing the relationship. For the network to be a successful one, it is not necessary that all the mechanisms have a strong activity, but rather, that a certain harmony or synchronization exists in them.

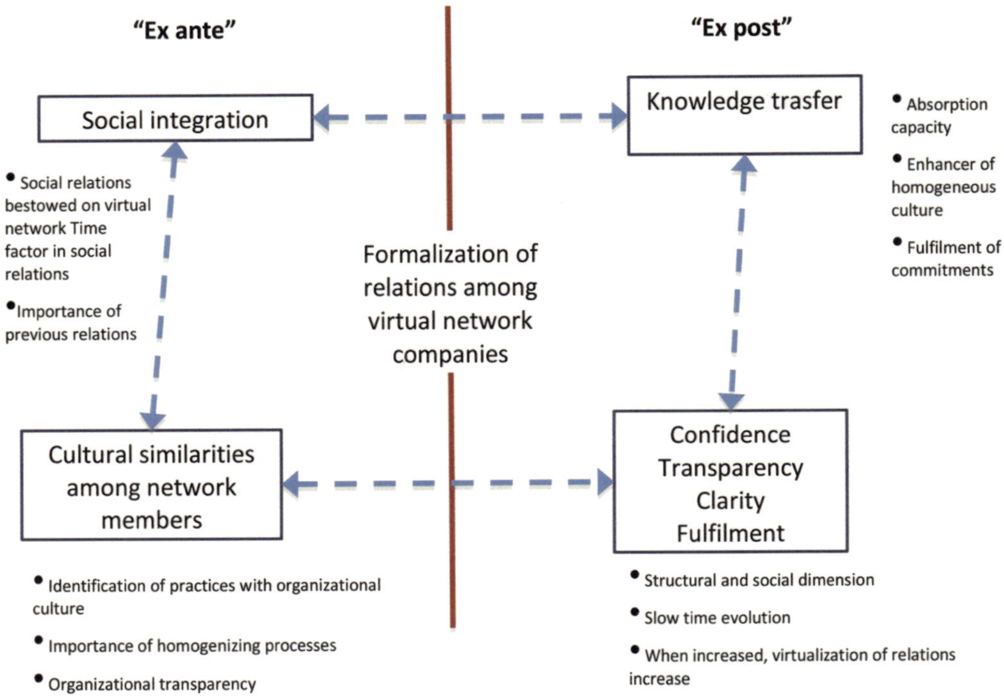

Fig. 2. Cultural mechanisms in the network. (Adapted from: Rodriguez-Monroy & VIlana-Arte, 2010)

3. Information in a collaborative network

Support of collaborative networks modifies the traditional focus of the enterprise information system design. Collaborative networks being open organizations, they require open information systems.

These systems must allow for uncomplicated and fluid communication between the different actors of the network, whether they are inside or outside the perimeter of the organization. This means an opposed approach to the integration view of information system design. The ability to capture and share information between different information systems of various companies is often limited by the diversity of the business processes, organizational units, structures of data and technologies, as well as the difficulty of sharing knowledge between the solutions of the different partners (Vatcharaphun et al. 2010)

3.1 Information flow in a collaborative network

The information flows that have to interact in a collaborative network come from information systems used by independent organizations; this makes it necessary to re-define the concept of interoperability, which should be re-formulated in order to reduce the complexity in the articulation of the problem.

At a strategic level, information flows are determined by communications and messages that respond to the management of common objectives in the collaborative space. They seek control and coordination between the activities of the partners. At an operational level, information resources such as data, technology and software components should be specified up to interface level for each particular information system. These flows should be negotiated with and directed by software components, aligning them with the different process levels of the company. This alignment process of the different levels of the participant companies should not be interpreted as a process of "information system integration". As described in section 2.2 above, trust is a key factor in network building, but there are other factors affecting information flows to a larger extent: transparency and clarity in power relationships. These key factors should be taken into consideration when establishing the information flows of the virtual network, so that they settle down between the appropriate decision-makers of each participant company.

The classical corporate boundaries have recently begun to blur and the value chain is leasing its attributes, and being replaced by a web of fluid and flexible relations, as stated by Camarinha-Matos (2009), In decision-making processes inside a collaborative network, clients are a core asset in terms of value creation; they contribute to increase the operational efficiency of the network by introducing new possibilities and their innovations identify unique competitive advantages.

In the collaborative network, the role of clients is evolving from that of mere consumers of products and services to being "partners" in the process of value creation. As described by Camarinha-Matos (2009)., the paradigm of collaborative networks offers new opportunities in the implementation of agility in production, as well as in other industrial sectors. A collaborative network involves a group of companies or actors in the network, together with another group of clients, supported by an appropriate platform and infrastructure (section 3.1). This platform is basic for the decision-making process (at strategic and / or operational levels), with many of these decisions being agreed among diverse network actors.

Interaction gaps between network actors could pose a serious problem in order to effectively involve other actors: this obstacle should be overcome by network-wide decision-making, as well as by an appropriate operational structure. An example of implementation of a knowledge-based information system for decision-making can be found in Vatcharaphun et al. (2010).

4. Conclusion

Technology improves at an ever-increasing rate, but the speed at which companies adapt their strategies and competencies to develop technological innovations and exploit market opportunities remains limited. While networks provide an option to increase agility through collaborative access to relevant external competencies, we know little about systematically managing such networks (Katzy & Crowston, 2008).

When building or designing a virtual global manufacturing network, cultural differences among the companies integrated in it for intense collaboration are one of the main challenges and must be treated with care. Opposed focuses on activities, such as internal communication, attainment of objectives, professional career, power structure, hierarchical relationships, etc. could cause conflicts in the performance of functions, expectations and practices. The conclusion is that an appropriate dynamization of the network will avoid a high degree of incompatibilities in the cultural practices of each of its members.

In order to build a virtual global manufacturing network, an incremental process must be adhered to, and a reduced number of activities and main abilities that will be complementary to those of other partners must be identified and focused on. When these capacities are mutually appreciated, progress can be made in future developments to reinforce confidence and to minimize opportunistic conducts.

5. References

Benhard R. Katzy & Kevin Crowston (2008). Competency rallyng for technical innovation – the case of the Vituelle Fabrik *Technovation,* 28, pp.679-692, ISSN:0166-4972

Bleeke, J. & Ernst, D. (1995). Is your strategic alliance really a sale? *Harvard Business Review,* 73, pp.97-105, ISSN: 0017-8012

Borgatti, S. & Foster, P. (2003). The network paradigm in organizational research: A review and typology. *Journal of Management,* 29, pp.991-1013, ISSN: 0149-2063.

Camarinha-Matos, L. & Afsarmanesh, H. (2005). Collaborative networks: Anew scientific discipline. *Journal of intelligent manufacturing,* 16, pp.439-452, ISSN: 0956-5515.

Camarinha-Matos, L. (2009). Collaborative networked organizations: Status and trends in manufacturing. *Annual Reviews in Control,* 33, pp.199-208, ISSN: 1367-5788.

Camarinha-Matos, L.; Afsarmanesh, H.; Galeano, N. & Molina, A. (2009). Collaborative networked organizations—Concepts and practice in manufacturing enterprises. *Computers and Industrial Engineering,* 57, pp.46-60, ISSN: 0360-8352.

Gupta, A.K. & Govindarajan, V. (2000). Knowledge flows within multinational corporations. *Strategic Management Journal,* 21, 4, pp. 473-496. ISSN: 1097-0266.

Gösling, T., Oerlemans, L. & Janse, R. (2007). Inside networks. Ed. Edward Elgar Publishing, ISBN: 978-84542-9, Chentelham, UK.

Hofstede, G.; Nevijen, B.; Ohayv, D. & Sanders, G. (1990). Measuring organizational cultures: a qualitative and quantitative study across twenty cases. *Administrative science quarterly,* 35, 2, pp.286-316, ISSN: 0001-8392.

Katzy, B.R. & Crowston, K. (2008). Competency rallying for technical innovation—The case of the Virtuelle Fabrik. *Technovation,* 28, pp.679-692, ISSN: 0166-4972.

Luo, Y. (2001). Antecedents and consequences of personal attachment in cross-cultural cooperative ventures. *Administrative science quarterly,* 46, 2, pp. 177-201, ISSN: 0001-8392.

Madhok, A. (1995). Revisiting multinational firms' tolerance for joint ventures: a trust-based approach. *Journal of International Business Studies,* 26, 1, pp.117-138, ISSN: 0047-2506.

Rodriguez-Monroy, C. & Vilana-Arte, J.R. (2010). Hacia qué cultura sistemática en las redes virtuales de fabricación global. *Dyna Ingeniería e Industria,* 85, 4, pp.294-302, ISSN: 0012-7361.

Saphiro et al. (1992). Definitions of transpersonal psychology. Journal of Transpersonal Psychology, 24, pp.79-98, ISSN: 002-524X

Trice, H.M. & Beyer, J.M. (1993). *The cultures of work organisations.* Ed. Prentice Hall, ISBN: 978-0131914384, Englewood Cliffs, New Jersey.

Vatcharaphun, R., Lorré, J.P., Bénabe, F., & Pingaud, H. (2010). Knowledge-base system for collaborative process specification *Computers in Industry,* 61, pp.161-175, ISSN: 0166-3615

19

Identification of Distributed Parameter Systems, Based on Sensor Networks

Constantin Volosencu
"Politehnica" University of Timisoara
Romania

1. Introduction

The chapter theme results at the crossroads of some major scientific and technical domains: modern intelligent wireless sensor networks, distributed parameter systems, multivariable linear and non-linear estimation techniques, especially using artificial intelligence tools and virtual instrumentation (Tubaishat & Madria, 2003), (Giannakis, 2008), (Kubrulsky & de S. Vincente, 1977), (Volosencu, 2008). And, an important application is fault detection and diagnosis in system monitoring (Chiang et. al., 2001). This modern concept involving may be represented in Fig. 1.

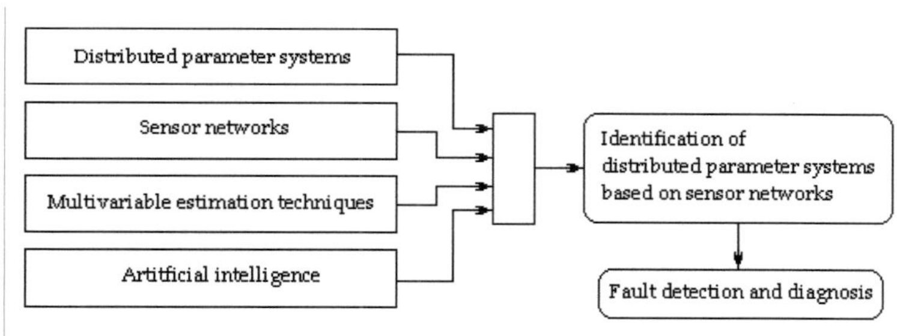

Fig. 1. Topics involving

The domain of system identification may be developed today using the powerful tool represented by the intelligent sensor networks, placed in real distributed parameter systems. Wireless sensor networks (Akyildiz, F. et. al, 2002) may be seen as a collection of numerous sensor nodes, each with sensing (temperature, humidity, sound level, light intensity, magnetism, acceleration etc.) and wireless communication capabilities, providing huge opportunities for monitoring and mathematical modeling of the time-evolution of the physical quantities under investigation. Sensor networks have proved their huge viability in the real world in the last years (Feng et. al. 2002). One of the important problem related to the usage of wireless sensor networks in harsh environments is the identification of the states of the physical variables in the field, based on the measurements provided by the sensors (Novak & Mira, 2003), (Pottie & Kaiser, 2000), (Tong et. al., 2003), (Zhang et al., 2005).

The modern intelligent sensor networks, with hundred and thousands of ad-hoc tiny sensor nodes spread across a geographical area, may be seen as a "distributed sensor, which may

be placed in the field of the distributed parameter systems. The sensor network, as a "distributed sensor", allows the usage of multivariable estimation techniques, in different ways: classical linear methods of modeling or methods based on artificial intelligence for complex non-linear systems. As smart and small devices the modern sensors are capable to be implemented in large distributed parameter systems.
As an example of distributed parameter system with large application in practice the process of heat conduction is presented. Other applications are presented in literature (Rosculet & Craiu, 1979), (Basmadjian, 1999).
The identification techniques (Ucinski, 2004), (Banks & Kunish, 1989), (Sjoberg, et. al., 1997), (Zhu et. al., 2007) are useful for applications ranging from control systems, fault detection and diagnosis, signal processing to time-series analysis.
The artificial intelligence tools (Chairez et al., 2009), (Jassar et. al., 2009) may be used for identification of nonlinear complex systems as the distributed parameter systems are. ANFIS (Roger Jang, 1993), (Depari et. al., 2005), (Hou & Li, 2006), (Mellit et. al., 2007) as a method for non-linear system identification is a powerful tool to estimate future behavior in distributed parameter systems from acquired data obtained using wireless sensor connected in a distributed network placed in the field.
The chapter presents a short survey of some results obtained in the study of using of sensor networks with multivariable estimation techniques for distributed parameter system identification. Sensor network topics, sensor network architectures and sensor network applications are presented. Starting from the measurements collected by the sensor nodes inside an investigated distributed parameter systems, this chapter offers an efficient methodology for identification with linear and non-linear time series. Some estimation algorithms and a method for monitoring distributed parameter systems based on sensor networks and the adaptive-network-based fuzzy inference scheme are presented (Volosencu, 2010). The chapter presents an application of a multivariable auto-regression estimation technique for estimation of heat transfer in space. A case study of temperature flow for a parabolic equation is analysed, based on these approach.
Limited resources in terms of computational power, energy, memory and bandwidth impose heavy constraints on functionality of an effective malfunction detection system. For this reason these algorithms are designed and suitable for execution on the base station level and, by this, it is appropriate even for large-scale sensor networks. Sensor networks have proved their huge viability in the real world, being just a matter of time until this kind of networks will be standardized and used broadly in the field.

2. Sensor networks

Wireless sensor networks are extremely distributed systems having a large number of independent and interconnected sensor nodes, with limited computational and communicative potential. The sensors are deployed for data acquisition purposes on a wide range of locations, sometimes in resource-limited and hostile environments such as disaster areas, seismic zones, ecological contamination sites and other. In this structure data processing is at the sensor level, data transmission is wireless, sensing mechanism is not necessarily power supply is not necessarily wireless.
Sensor network applications include: environmental monitoring, civil infrastructure monitoring, shared resource utilization, tracking, perimeter protection and surveillance. Application are in micro-climates, air quality, soil moisture, animal tracking, energy usage,

office comfort, wireless thermostats, wireless light switches. In techniques they have as applications data acquisition of physical and chemical properties, at various spatial and temporal scales, as in distributed parameter systems, for automatic identification, measurements over long period of time. The sensor networks are deployed for data acquisition purposes on a wide range of locations, in resource-limited and hostile environments such as disaster areas, seismic zones, ecological contamination sites. *All applications are distributed parameter systems.*

The modern sensors are smart, small, lightweight and portable devices, with a communication infrastructure intended to monitor and record specific parameters like temperature, humidity, pressure, wind direction and speed, illumination intensity, vibration intensity, sound intensity, power-line voltage, chemical concentrations and pollutant levels at diverse locations. The sensor number in a network is over hundreds or thousands of ad hoc tiny sensor nodes spread across different area. Thus, the network actively participates in creating a smart environment. They are low cost and low energy devices, realized in nanotechnology. With them we may developed low cost wireless platforms, including integrated radio and microprocessors. The sensors are adequate for autonomous operation in highly dynamic environments as distributed parameter systems. We may add sensors when they fail. They require distributed computation and communication protocols. They assure scalability, where the quality can be traded for system lifetime. They assure Internet connections via satellite. The structure of a modern sensor (Akyildiz, F. et. al, 2002), (Pottie & Kaiser, 2000), (Tubaishat & Madria, 2003) is presented in Fig. 2.

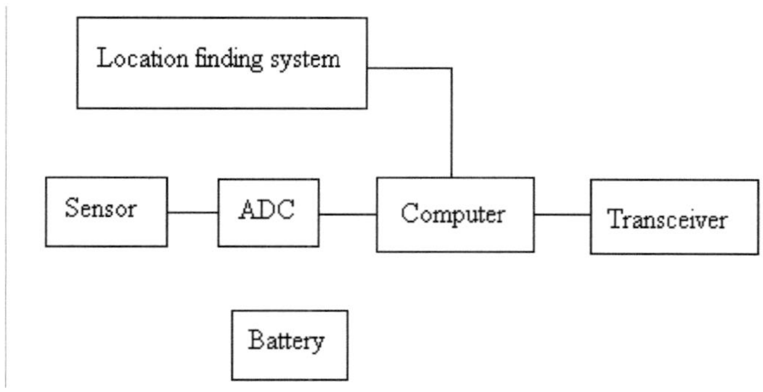

Fig. 2. The structure of a modern sensor

The dimension of such a sensor is comparable with a small coin. The sensors are characterized by: a robust radio technology, cheap and energy efficient processors, lifetime energy source, on-board memory, flexible I/O for various sensors, common highly available components, efficient resource utilization - currently uses 10 μA average, high modularity, flexible open source platform. Some examples of technical data are: 128 KB instruction EEPROM, 4 KB data EEPROM, 512 KB External Flash Memory, radio with 38 K or 19 K baud, at 900MHz, LEDs, μP at 7,3 MHz, JTAG, programming board, ISM Bands: 433-434,8 MHz Europe, power consumption: 16 mA Tx, 9 mA Rx, 2 μA sleep, transmission range: 1m, off the floor 100m range, ground level 10 m range, interface block data to laptop, GPS, cost: $ 95.

Sensor are developed to measure: temperature, humidity, pressure, wind direction and speed, illumination intensity, vibration intensity, sound intensity, acceleration, power-line voltage, chemical concentrations and pollutant levels at diverse locations and others. *All are variables in distributed parameter systems.*

Hundreds or thousands of ad-hoc tiny sensor nodes spread across a geographical area form the basis of a sensor network. Sensor nodes collaborate among themselves to establish a sensing network. The sensor network provides access to information anytime, anywhere, by collecting, processing, analyzing and disseminating data. The network actively participates in creating a smart environment. *Sensor network is working as a distributed sensor.*
The constructive and functional representation of a sensor network is presented in Fig. 3 (Akyildiz, F. et. al, 2002), (Pottie & Kaiser, 2000), (Tubaishat & Madria, 2003).

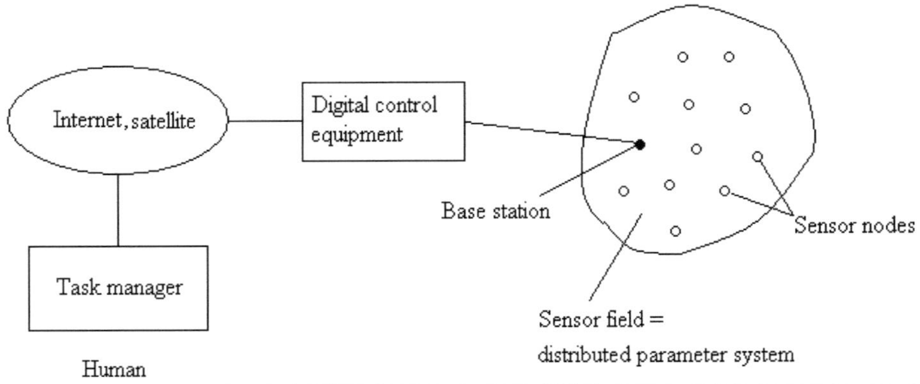

Fig. 3. Sensor network

The sensor networks have different *structures*. The star networks (point-to-point), are networks in which all sensors are transmitting directly with a central data collection point. The mesh networks are networks in which sensors can communicate with each other. In mesh networks sensor nodes can relay messages from other sensor nodes, there is no need for repeaters. Software controls the flow of messages through network with self-configuration. New nodes automatically detected and incorporate. Advantages of the mesh structures are: robustness, easily deployed, no RF site surveys needed, no repeaters needed, easily expanded.
In the field of sensors networks some topics are involved, like: development topics: deployment, localization, synchronization, calibration; wireless communication: wireless radio, characteristics, MAC protocols, link layer techniques, power control; sensor network architecture; networking topics: topology control, data gathering, network monitoring, network coding; data-centric: routing and aggregation, querying and data basis, storage; hardware; software; security. Standards and protocols are imposed for sensor networks development.
Different structure may be uses in practice, for example. The sensor network may be static or mobile. For a static case each sensor node knows its own location, even if they were deployed via aerial scattering or by physical installation. If not, the nodes can obtain their own location through the location process. Moreover, all the sensors passed a one-time authentication procedure done just after their deployment in the field. The sensor nodes are similar in their computational and communication capabilities and power resources to the current generation sensor nodes. Every node has space for storing up to hundreds of bytes of keying materials in order to secure the transfer of information through symmetric cryptography. There is a base station into the network, sometimes called access point, acting as a controller and also as a key server. It is assumed to be a laptop class device and it is

supplied with long-lasting power. An example of a wireless cellular network architecture is presented in Fig. 4.

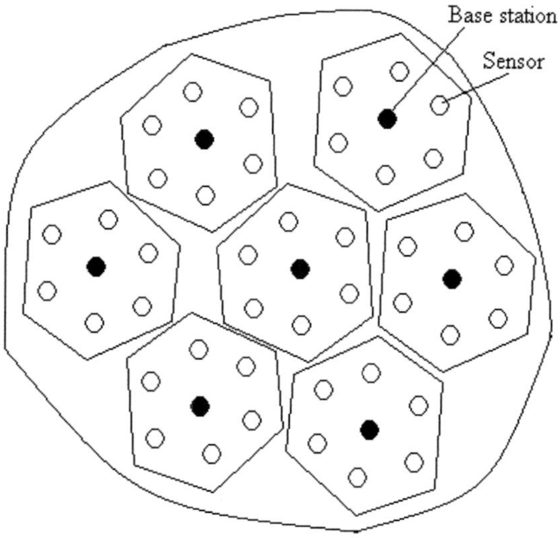

Fig. 4. Cellular network architecture

In this architecture, a number of base stations are already deployed within the field. Each base station forms a cell around itself that covers part of the area. Mobile wireless nodes and other appliances can communicate wirelessly, as long as they are within the area covered by one cell. A versatile architecture is a sensor network with mobile access is presented in Fig. 5.

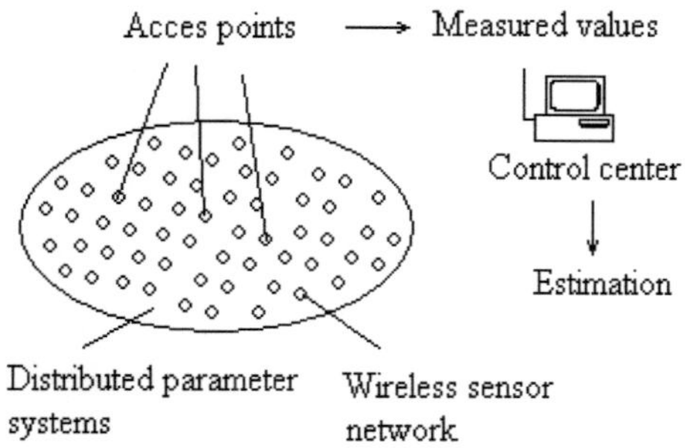

Fig. 5. A sensor network with mobile access

This structure used for large-scale sensor networks. The main difference related to the cellular network architecture is that base stations are considered to be mobile, so each cell has varying boundaries which implies that mobile wireless nodes and other appliances can communicate wirelessly, as long as they are at least within the area covered by the range of the mobile access point. Multiple sensor nodes can detect an event situated in the surrounding area, so redundancy of sensor networks is assured. In the next paragraph we presents some examples of such distribute parameter systems with their mathematical models with partial derivative equations.

The space model of the sensor deployed in the field with the heat sources is presented in Fig. 6.

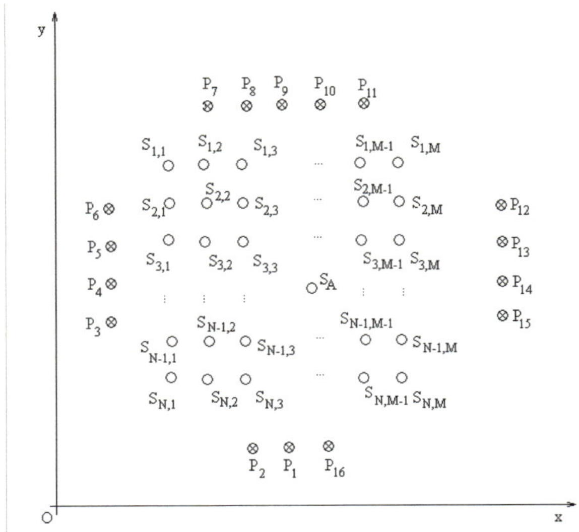

Fig. 6. Sensor deployment

The sensor S_A measures the temperature θ_A in a point in this space. $P_{in}^{j,k}$ is the input power in the point and $P_{out}^{j,k}$ is the output power from the point.
A Crossbow sensor network was used in practice, as it is presented in Fig. 7.

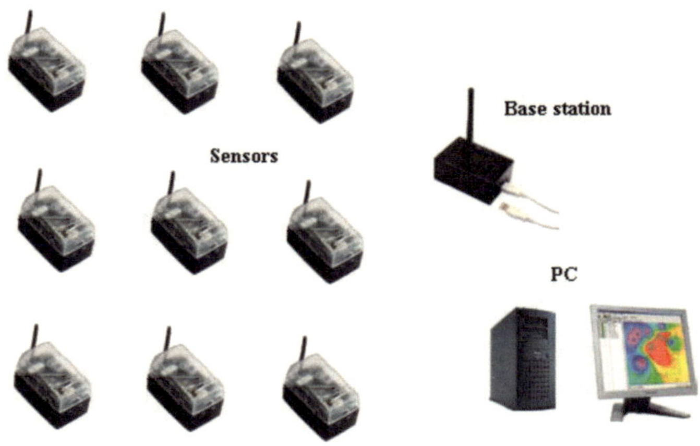

Fig. 7. The sensor network with mobile access

It has the following components: a starter kit, a MICA2 2,4 GHz wireless module, and an MTS320 sensor board. Their nodes are 2 MICAz 2,4 GHz modules, with 2 sensors MTS400, which are measuring temperature, humidity, pressure, ambient light intensity; 1 MICAz 2,4 GHz with 2 sensors MTS310 and 1 module MICAz 2,4 GHz working as a central node when it is connected through the UB port. A gateway MIB520 for node programming and a data acquisition board MDA320 with 8 analogue channels are provided. The network has the following software: MoteView for history sensor network monitoring and real time graphics and MoteWorks for nod programming in MesC language. The user interface allows some facilities, as: administration, searching, connections options and so on.

This modern wireless sensor network has multiple measuring capabilities. So, it can measure temperature, humidity, light intensity or acceleration on 2 axes. For these kind of physical variables the mathematical models are as follows.
For temperature:

$$\frac{\partial \theta}{\partial t} = a\left(\frac{\partial^2 \theta}{\partial x^2} + \frac{\partial^2 \theta}{\partial y^2}\right) + Q(x,y,t) \tag{1}$$

where Q is the time variable source of heating, positioned in space and θ is the temperature.
For light intensity:

$$E(x) = \frac{I}{h^2 + x^2}, \; E = \frac{\Delta\Phi}{\Delta S}, \; \Delta\Phi = I\frac{\Delta S}{r^2} = I.\Delta\alpha \tag{2}$$

where I is the luminous intensity of the light source, at the distance x and high h, as a measure of the source intensity as seen by the eye, E is the luminance at the specific point, defined as a ratio, with $\Delta\Phi$ representing the flux that strikes a tiny area ΔS, calculated considering a spherical surface of radius r, with $\Delta\alpha$ representing the solid angle.
For acceleration:

$$a_x = \frac{dv_x}{dt}, \; a_y = \frac{dv_y}{dt}, v_x = \frac{dx}{dt}, \; v_y = \frac{dy}{dt} \tag{3}$$

where the above notations represents the acceleration a_x, a_y, the speed v_x, v_y and the space x, y on two axis for an object of the mass m, under a force F.
Some characteristics measured for the sensor network are presented in Fig. 8.

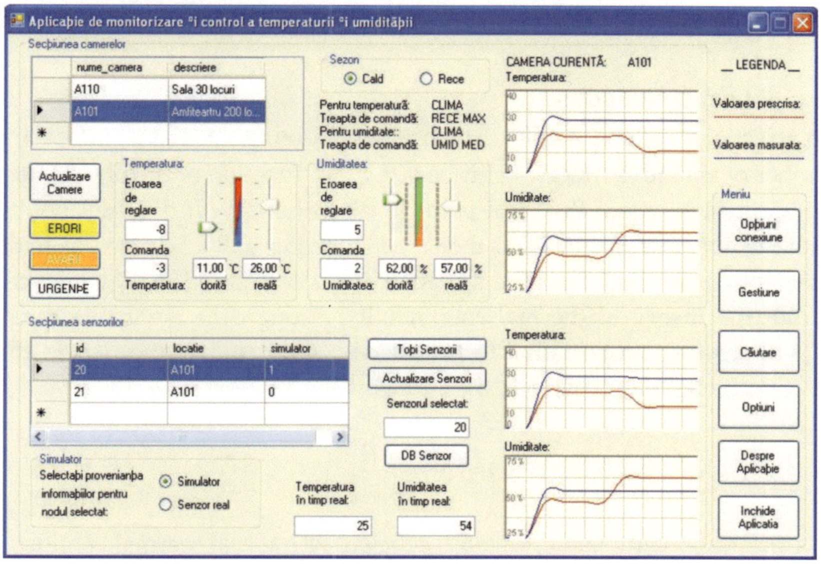

Fig. 8. Temperature aand humidity transient characteristics

Redundancy is an inherent feature of sensor networks that is verified in practice and it is improving important aspects of their functioning (Curiac et. al., 2009).

3. Distributed parameter systems

The distributed parameter systems, opposed to the lumped parameter systems, are systems whose state space is infinite dimensional. An object whose state is heterogeneous has distributed parameters. Such a system is described by partial differential equations. Partial differential equations are used to formulate problems involving functions of several variables, such as the propagation of sound or heat, electrostatics, electrodynamics, fluid, flow, elasticity. Distinct physical phenomena have identical mathematical formulations, and the same underlying dynamic governs them. One of the most important domain of applications of the partial differential equations is the process of heat conduction, with propagation of heat in anisotropic medium: propagation of heat in a porous medium, transference of heat in semi-space compound by two materials submitted to heating, processes of transference of heat between a solid wall and a flow of hot gas, estimation of the temperature field in space with fissured zone having the form of a circular disc. Applications related to electricity domain are: the propagation of electric current in cables, the heating of the electrical contacts. In the field of motion of fluid there are: plane motion of viscous fluids, running of viscous fluids in rectilinear tube, computation of losses of non-stationary heat in subterranean pipe, running of gases in water main. The processes of cooling and drying: cooling of clap, cooling of a sphere, drying of wood pieces, drying in vacuum. Phenomenon of diffusion: diffusion flow in a heavy sphere for chemical reactions happening with finite spit on the sphere surface, the flames diffusion, which appears to the beginning of a tube, repartition density of particles loading by the meteorites. Other applications are: estimation of the ice height covering the snow the arctic seas, motion of underground waters, alloy of heavy fusible particles, investigation of the wave close to the single point of the board of a plane plate, the growing of the gas particles in a fluid, substances combustion, the temperature modification in the air mass. (Rosculet & Craiu, 1979), (Basmadjian, 1999).

3.1 Process of heat conduction

Let it be an object of a volume $V \subset R^3$. The frontier of dominium V is a surface S, formed by a finite number of smooth surfaces. Let it be $\theta(P, t)$ the function of the object's temperature, at the time moment t, where $P \in V$ is a point in the volume V. If different points of object have different temperatures, $\theta(P, t) \neq$ct., then a heat transfer will take place, from the warmer parts to the less warm parts. Let it be a regular surface σ placed in V, which contains the point P. From the theory of thermal conductivity through the $d\sigma$ in the time dt a heat quantity dQ is passing, proportional to the product $d\sigma.dt$ and proportion to the function $\theta(P,t)$ derivative, along the normal n to the surface σ in the point P:

$$dQ = k\left|\frac{\partial \theta(P,t)}{\partial n}\right| dt d\sigma \tag{4}$$

where k is a proportionality factor, called coefficient of internal thermal conductivity of the object. The vector *grad* θ has its direction along the normal at the level surface for θ=ct., in the sense of θ rising.

The law of heat propagation through an object in which there are no heat sources:

$$\gamma\rho\frac{\partial\theta}{\partial t}=\frac{\partial}{\partial x}\left(k\frac{\partial\theta}{\partial x}\right)+\frac{\partial}{\partial y}\left(k\frac{\partial\theta}{\partial y}\right)+\frac{\partial}{\partial z}\left(k\frac{\partial\theta}{\partial z}\right) \tag{5}$$

The heat sources in the object have a distribution given by the function:

$$F(t,P)=F(t,x,y,z) \tag{6}$$

If the object is homogenous $a=\sqrt{k/\gamma/\rho}=ct.$ and the equation (2) is written:

$$\frac{1}{a^2}\frac{\partial\theta}{\partial t}=\frac{\partial}{\partial x}\left(\frac{\partial\theta}{\partial x}\right)+\frac{\partial}{\partial y}\left(\frac{\partial\theta}{\partial y}\right)+\frac{\partial}{\partial z}\left(\frac{\partial\theta}{\partial z}\right) \tag{7}$$

In the case of heat propagation through a bar:

$$\gamma\rho\frac{\partial\theta}{\partial t}=\frac{\partial}{\partial x}\left(k\frac{\partial\theta}{\partial x}\right)+F(t,x) \tag{8}$$

The initial conditions or of the limit conditions have physical significance. The equation

$$\rho\gamma\frac{\partial\theta}{\partial t}=div(k\,grad\,\theta)+F(t,P) \tag{9}$$

does not determine completely the state of the object K. We must take in considerations the initial state of the object, the temperature distribution in the object at the moment t=0:

$$\theta(x,y,z,t)\big|_{t=0}=f(x,y,z) \tag{10}$$

called initial conditions.

3.2 Discrete approximation

We may associate to the equation (5) a system with finite differences. For this purpose the space S is divided into small pieces of dimension l_p:

$$l_p=l/n \tag{11}$$

In each small piece $S_{pi,j}$, i=1,…,n, j=1,…,n of the space S the temperature could be measured at each moment t_k in a characteristic point $P_{i,j}(x_i, y_j)$, of coordinate x_i and y_j. Let it be $\theta_{i,j}^k$ the temperatures in the point $P_{i,j}(x_i, y_j)$ at the moment t_k.

It is a general known method to approximate the derivatives of a variable with small variations. In the equation with partial derivatives there are derivatives of first order, in time, and derivatives of second order in space.

So, theoretically, we may approximate the temperature derivative in time with a small variation in time, with the following relation:

$$\frac{\partial\theta}{\partial t}=\frac{\theta_{i,j}^{k+1}-\theta_{i,j}^{k+1}}{t_{k+1}-t_k} \tag{12}$$

Also, we may approximate the summation of the temperature second derivatives in space, with small variations in space and to obtain the following relations:

$$\frac{\partial^2\theta}{\partial x^2}+\frac{\partial^2\theta}{\partial y^2}=\frac{\theta^i_{i-1,j}-4\theta^i_{i,j}+\theta^i_{i+1,j}+\theta^i_{i,j-1}+\theta^i_{i,j+1}}{l_p^2} \tag{13}$$

We may consider the temperature is measured as samples at equal time intervals with the value

$$h=t_{k+1}-t_k \tag{14}$$

called sample period, in a sampling procedure, with a digital equipment.
Combining the equations (6, 7, 8, 9) in the equation (1) a system with differences results:

$$\theta^{k+1}_{i,j}=\theta^k_{i,j}+\frac{ah}{l_p^2}\left(\theta^k_{i-1,j}+-4\theta^k_{i,j}+\theta^k_{i+1,j}+\theta^k_{i,j-1}+\theta^k_{i,j+1}\right) \tag{15}$$

The sampling period h may be chosen according to different theories for signal sampling. For example, we must choose it without obtaining alias errors at specific frequencies. In practice the sampling period is taken according to the capacity of digital equipment to manipulate data, the time constants of the system, assuring the conditions of stability, controllability and observably for the discrete time model.
An interesting value for h is proposed in (Rosculet & Craiu, 1979) to eliminate the term $\theta_{i,j}^k$:

$$h=\frac{l_p^2}{4a} \tag{16}$$

so:

$$\theta^{k+1}_{i,j}=\frac{1}{4}\left(\theta^k_{i-1,j}+\theta^k_{i+1,j}+\theta^k_{i,j-1}+\theta^k_{i,j+1}\right) \tag{17}$$

The relation (17) gives a discrete approximation of temperature value $\theta_{i,j}^k$ in every characteristic points $P_{i,j}$ of the space S, for i, j =1, …, n, at the every moment t_k, k>1, from the temperature values $\theta_{i-1,j}^{k-1}$, $\theta_{i,j-1}^{k-1}$, $\theta_{i+1,j}^{k-1}$ and $\theta_{i,j+1}^{k}$, at the antecedent moment t_{k-1}, k-1>0, of the adjacent points $P_{i-1,j}$, $P_{i,j-1}$, $P_{i+1,j}$ and $P_{i,j+1}$.
Relations of the approximation error and for stability are given in literature (Rosculet & Craiu, 1979).
The approximation (17) is a linear system with differences of nxn order.
In the discrete model (17) we must take in consideration the position points $P_{iq,jq}$ in the discrete space of the sources $Q_{iq,jq}^k$ at each time moment.
For transversal heat transfer from the surroundings the term transversal heat transfer from the surroundings $q_m(\theta_{ext}-\theta)$ must be added, where q_m is the convective heat transfer coefficient and θ_{ext} is the external temperature. In the discrete model we must take account on each point with a contact with the exterior: $q_m(\theta_{ext\ i,j}^k-\theta_{i,j}^k)$ at each time moment.

3.3 Mathematical models

The distributed parameter systems have general mathematical models in continuous time and space as partial differential equation, of parabolic form, as:

$$\frac{\partial \theta}{\partial t} = c_1 \nabla (c_2 \nabla \theta) + c_3 \theta + Q \tag{18}$$

where the variables $\theta(\zeta, t)$ are depending on time $t \geq 0$ and on space $\zeta \in V$, where ζ is x for one axis, (x, y) for two axis or (x, y, z) for three axis, c_1, c_2 and c_3 are coefficients, which could be also time variant and $Q(\zeta, t)$ is an exterior excitation, variable on time and space.
So, in the general case, an implicit equation may be written:

$$f\left(\frac{\partial \theta}{\partial t}, \frac{\partial \theta}{\partial \zeta}, \frac{\partial^2 \theta}{\partial \zeta^2}, \dots\right) = 0 \tag{19}$$

For the partial differential equations some boundary conditions may be imposed to establish a solution. So, when the variable value of the boundary is specified there are Dirichlet conditions:

$$c_4 \theta = q \tag{20}$$

And, when the variable flux and transfer coefficient are specified there are Neumann conditions:

$$c_5 \nabla \theta + c_6 \theta = 0 \tag{21}$$

In the practical application case studies limits and initial conditions of the equation are imposed:

$$\begin{aligned} &\theta(0,t) = \theta_{\zeta 0},\ t \in [0,T], \theta(\zeta,0) = 0,\ \zeta \in [0,l], \\ &\theta(l,t) = \theta_{\zeta l},\ t \in [0,T] \end{aligned} \tag{22}$$

A system with finite differences may be associated to the equations. For this purpose the space S is divided into small pieces of dimension l_p.
In each small piece S_{pi}, $i=1,\dots,n$ of the space S the variable θ could be measured at each moment t_k, using a sensor from the sensor network, in a characteristic point $P_i(\zeta_i)$, of coordinate ζ_i. Let it be θ_i^k the variable value in the point $P_i(\zeta_i)$ at the moment t_k. It is a general known method to approximate the derivatives of a variable with small variations. In the equation with partial derivatives there are derivatives of first order, in time, and derivatives of first and second order in space.
For the parabolic equation a linear approximate system of derivative equations of first degree may be used:

$$\frac{d\Psi}{dt} = A\Psi + BQ \tag{23}$$

where, this time, ψ is a vector containing the values of the variable $\theta(\zeta, t)$ in different points of the space and at different time moments.
Combining the equations a system of equations with differences results for the parabolic equation:

$$f_p(\theta_i^k, \theta_{i-1}^k, \theta_i^{k+1}, \theta_{i+1}^k) = 0 \tag{24}$$

Taking account of equations (14, 15) it is obvious that several estimation algorithms may be developed as follows, based on the discrete models of the partial derivative equations.

4. Identification techniques

System identification is for building accurate, simplified models of complex systems from noisy time-series data. It provides tools for creating mathematical models of dynamic systems based on observed input/output data. The identification techniques are useful for applications ranging from control system design and signal processing to time-series analysis. Actually, there is a huge amount written on the subject of system identification. But only the experience with real data may help us to understand more. It is important to remember that any estimated model, no matter how good it looks on design, has only picked up a simple reflection of reality. So, in this aspect the sensor network is the powerful tool. The identification techniques are useful for applications ranging from control systems, fault detection and diagnosis, signal processing to time-series analysis. There are identification methods based on parametric model and on nonparametric models. There are identification methods based on parametric model and on nonparametric models. The general system identification block diagram is presented in Fig. 9.

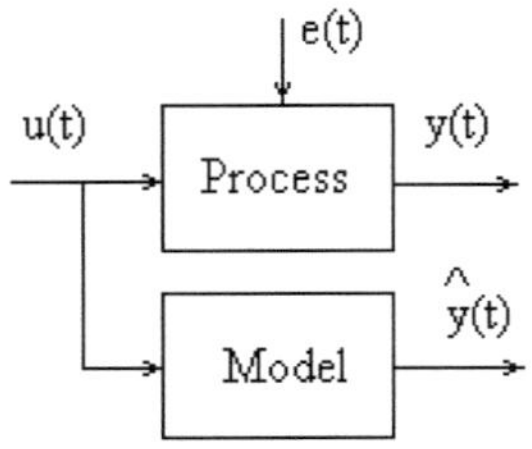

Fig. 9. Identification signals

The signals involved on a process for identification and its model are: the inputs u(t), the errors e(t), the outputs y(t) and the estimated outputs.
A simple estimation of the variable value at the moment t_{k+1} from the values of the adjacent sensors may be done using the above relations and adjacent sensor placed in space. To obtain an identification model for the process in theory and practice there are methods for model identification dedicated to linear or nonlinear systems, or based on artificial intelligence tools as fuzzy logic or neural networks.

4.1 Linear models

For linear systems the most known methods are for the general case with the Box-Jenkins model with some special cases as the ARMAX model – the auto-regression and a moving average of white noise with the simplification of the ARX model. With the ARX model it is possible to predict what the system output - the temperatures in the points of the space will be $\hat{\theta}_{i,j}^{k+1}(t_{k+1})$, based on measurements of the input $Q(x, y, t)$ –the heat generated by an external source and the antecedent and adjacent outputs $\theta_{i-1,j-1}^{k-1}(t_{k-l})$, where l=1,2,...
We may apply this method in all the points of the network, considering the boundary conditions as inputs and the value in the point as an output.

Also, we may use an autoregressive model in an autoregressive predictor. An autoregressive (AR) model may approximate the time evolution of the measured values provided by each sensor. This kind of systems evolves due to its "memory", generating internal dynamics. The AR model definition for temperature in the space is as follows:

$$\hat{\theta}_{i,j}^{k+1}(t_{k+1}) = a_1\hat{\theta}_{i,j}^{k+1}(t_k) + ... + a_n\hat{\theta}_{i,j}^{k+1}(t_{k-n}) + \xi(t) \tag{25}$$

where $\hat{\theta}_{i,j}^{k+1}(t_{k+1})$ is the temperature series under investigation, the series of values measured by the same sensor, a_i are the auto regression coefficients, n is the order of the auto regression and ξ is the noise which is almost always assumed to be a Gaussian white noise. By convention the time series is assumed to be zero mean. If not, another term (a_0) is added in the right member of equation.
The a_i coefficients may be also time-varying:

$$\hat{\theta}_{i,j}^{k+1}(t_{k+1}) = a_1(t)\hat{\theta}_{i,j}^{k+1}(t_k) + ... + a_n(t)\hat{\theta}_{i,j}^{k+1}(t_{k-n}) + \xi(t) \tag{26}$$

Based on the model we may either estimate the coefficients $a_i(t)$ in case that the time series $\theta_{i,j}^{k}(t_k)$, $\theta_{i,j}^{k\text{-}1}(t_{k\text{-}1})$, …, $\theta_{i,j}^{k\text{-}n}(t_{k\text{-}n})$ is known (recursive parameter estimation), either predict future value $\hat{\theta}_{i,j}^{k+1}(t_{k+1})$ in case that $a_i(t)$ coefficients and the past values $\theta_{i,j}^{k}(t_k)$, $\theta_{i,j}^{k\text{-}1}(t_{k\text{-}1})$, …, $\theta_{i,j}^{k\text{-}n}(t_{k\text{-}n})$ are known (AR prediction).

4.2 Adaptive-network-based fuzzy inference

In the tentative of identification of distributed parameter systems using sensor networks and fuzzy logic as a tool of artificial intelligence we must make the following steps: 1. Starting from a primary mathematic model of distributed parameters system - an equation with partial derivatives. 2. Defining system real variables. 3. Choosing of universe of discourse for system variables. 4. Choosing the fuzzy variables for the system and their fuzzy values on the universes of discourse. 5. Choosing the membership function to describe the fuzzy values. 6. Developing the rule base for inference, considering the operator experience working with the distributed parameter system. 7. Choosing the inference method. 8. Choosing the defuzzification method. 9. Developing a fuzzy system to model the distributed parameter system. 10. Comparing the primary mathematic model with the fuzzy model after the simulation and errors determination.
As it was presented above the description of distributed parameter systems is done with mathematical models with real variables u(t, x, y, z), in a 3 dimensional Cartesian coordinate system with the origin (x_o, y_0, z_0), for time t≥0. The equation with partial derivatives is (5). We may do a fuzzy modeling for this system. The variables are defined on the following universe of discourse:

$$\begin{aligned} x \in U_x = [x_0, x_M],\ y \in U_y = [y_0, y_M] \\ z \in U_z = [z_0, z_M],\ v \in U_v = [v_m, v_M] \end{aligned} \tag{27}$$

The fuzzy variables for space are taken the following fuzzy values: ZE, PS, PM, PB, PVB. The system variables, if they have symmetric values face to 0 may take the following fuzzy

values: NB, NM, NS, ZE, PS, PM, PB. Different membership function types may be chosen to define the fuzzy sets of the above fuzzy values, for example triangular and trapezoidal. With these fuzzy values an adequate rule base may be developed. To implement the inference given by the rule base several inference methods could be used, for example max-min or sum-prod. For defuzzification the method of the centre of gravity is commonly used. Placing of sensor network could be done related to the meshes for solving the distributed parameter equation with partial derivatives. Obtaining a fuzzy model we may say that we did system identification based on the fuzzy model.
In the case of estimation based on fuzzy logic the model is a fuzzy system. Such a fuzzy system has the inference from Fig. 10.

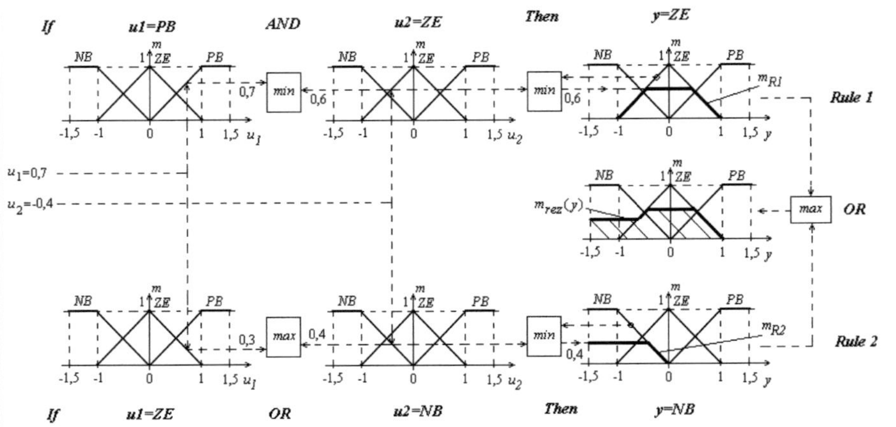

Fig. 10. Fuzzy inference engine

In this structure an input interface of fuzzification transforms the crisp inputs u in fuzzy information A, applied to an inference procedure. The inference is working using a rule base of the fuzzy model. The crisp output y of the fuzzy model is obtained from the fuzzy information B of the inference applying a defuzzification method. The inference is a computational method used in computers to apply the fuzzy reasoning from the rule base. In this inference method the crisp inputs u_1 and u_2 are fuzzified through membership functions assigned to the fuzzy values (NB, ZE, PB) from the rule base. The rule base are computed using fuzzy operations as AND, OR, implemented with minimum or maximum. The output fuzzy set, described by a membership function, is computed with the fuzzy operation OR. These computations are made for all the rules of the rule base. And the result is the fuzzy information B. The output y is the most significant value from the universe of discourse (the definition set of the membership function) of the output membership function.
The same identification algorithms as may be implemented using neuronal networks. In this, case a feedforward neural network, with continuous values, with two hidden layers of neurons, working as multifunction approximation is recommended. The structure of a multilayer neural network with m inputs u_i, i=1,...,m and n outputs y_i, i=1,...,n is presented in Fig. 11.
This neural network has weights for the internal connections w_{ij}^k, and each neuron has is own bias.
The neuron acts like non-linear functions:

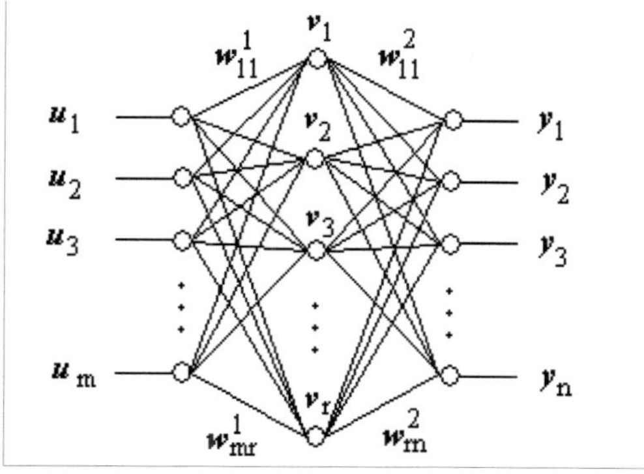

Fig. 11. Neural network structure

$$v_i = f_a\left(\sum_{j=1}^{m} w_{ji}^1 u_j + b_i\right) \tag{28}$$

where f_a is the activation function. Such activation function are the sigmoid th(x) for the neurons from the hidden layers from the interior of the neural network and the linear function $y=x$, for the neurons from the output layer. The neural network transfer function is:

$$\Delta w_{kj} = -\eta \frac{\partial E}{\partial w_{kj}} = \eta \sum_{qi} \delta_i^{2q} w_{ji}^2 S'(h_j^q) u_k^q = \eta \sum_q \delta_j^{1q} u_k^q \tag{29}$$

The neural identification has the block diagram from Fig. 12.

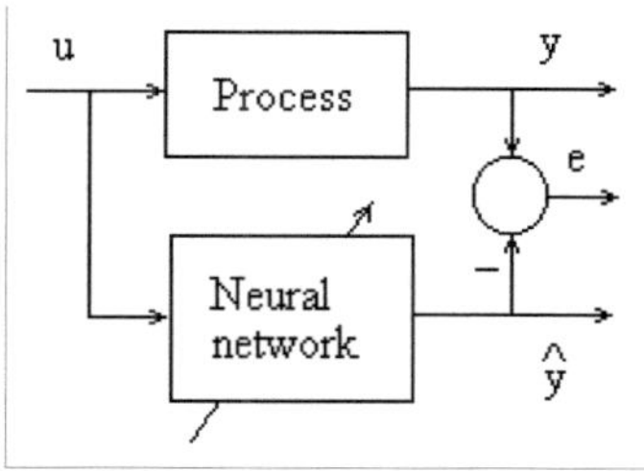

Fig. 12. Direct neural identification

In this case the model is a neural network. The neural model is obtained by training (learning) the neural network with training sets (u_i, y_i), i=1, N, obtained from real measurements from the distributed parameter systems, achieved using sensor networks. A cost function is imposed for training.

$$E(w) = \frac{1}{2} \sum_{qi} (y_i^q - y_i^{qd})^2, \; i = 1,\ldots,p \tag{30}$$

A training method, based on error backpropagation is used. For example the Levenberg Marquard method, using a cvasi-Newton method to minimize the cost function assures the small number of iterations to obtain the appropriate weight and biases values. A rule of weight updating is applied:

$$\Delta w_{kj} = -\eta \frac{\partial E}{\partial w_{kj}} = \eta \sum_{qi} \delta_i^{2q} w_{ji}^2 S'(h_j^q) u_k^q = \eta \sum_{q} \delta_j^{1q} u_k^q \tag{31}$$

As we said above, a supervised learning (by backpropagation) is used to obtain the best values of the unknown weights w and biases b, propagating back through the network the training output error

$$e = y - \hat{y} \tag{32}$$

computing the gradient ΔE.

An example of training error for backpropagation with the Levenberg Marquardt method is presented in Fig. 13.

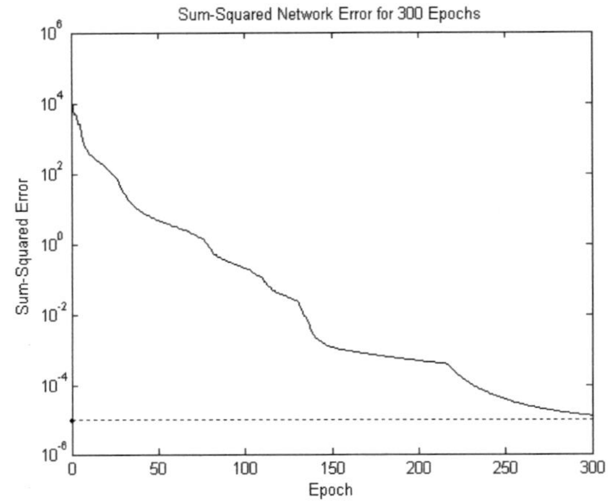

Fig. 13. Traning error

The neural network developed in the neuro-fuzzy modeling frame has the following general structure. If the sum-prod inference is used a neural structure with product between the activation function outputs and weights and summation of the connections signals may be developed. The first layer is the input layer. The second layer represents the input membership or fuzzification layer. The neurons represent fuzzy sets used in the antecedents of fuzzy rules determine the membership degree of the input. The activation function represents the membership functions. The 3rd layer represents the fuzzy rule base layer. Each neuron corresponds to a single fuzzy rule from the rule base. The inference is in this case the sum-prod inference method, the conjunction of the rule antecedents being made with product. The weights of the 3rd and 4th layers are the normalized degree of confidence of the corresponding fuzzy rules. These weights are obtained by training in the learning process. The 4th layer represents the output membership function. The activation function is the output membership function. The 5th layer represents the defuzzification layer, with single output, and the defuzzification method is the center of gravity.

4.3 Algorithms and method

The application is using the following algorithms, obtained from the above general discretization function.

Estimation algorithm 1. It estimates the value of the variable θ_i^{k+1} at the moment t_{k+1}, measuring the values of the variables $\theta_{i-1}^k, \theta_{i+1}^k, \theta_i^k$ at the anterior moment t_k:

$$\theta_i^{k+1} = f_1\left(\theta_{i-1}^k, \theta_{i+1}^k, \theta_i^k\right) \tag{33}$$

This is a multivariable estimation algorithm, based on the adjacent nodes [9].
Estimation algorithm 2. It estimates the value of the variable θ_i^{k+1} at the moment t_{k+1}, measuring the values of the same variable $\theta_i^k, \theta_i^{k-1}, \theta_i^{k-2}, \theta_i^{k-3}$, but at four anterior moments t_k, t_{k-1}, t_{k-2} and t_{k-3}.

$$\theta_i^{k+1} = f_2\left(\theta_i^k, \theta_i^{k-1}, \theta_i^{k-2}, \theta_i^{k-3}\right) \tag{34}$$

4.4 Estimator mechanism

The estimators are linear and also non-linear. All are described by the function $y=f(u_1, u_2, \ldots, u_n)$, using the linear model and the adaptive-network-based fuzzy inference. The general structure is presented in Fig. 14.

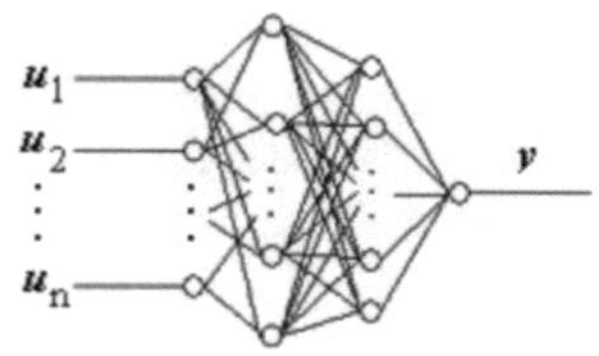

Fig. 14. The estimator input-output general structure

The number of inputs depends on the estimation algorithm, on the specific position in space of the measuring points, on the conditions of determination.
The linear estimation algorithm is obtained with the least square method.
The ANFIS procedure is well known and it may use a hybrid learning algorithm to identify the membership function parameters of the adaptive system.
A combination of least-squares and backpropagation gradient descent methods may be used for training membership function parameters, modeling a given set of input/output data.

4.5 The monitoring structure

The structure of the estimation and decetion system is presented in Fig. 15.

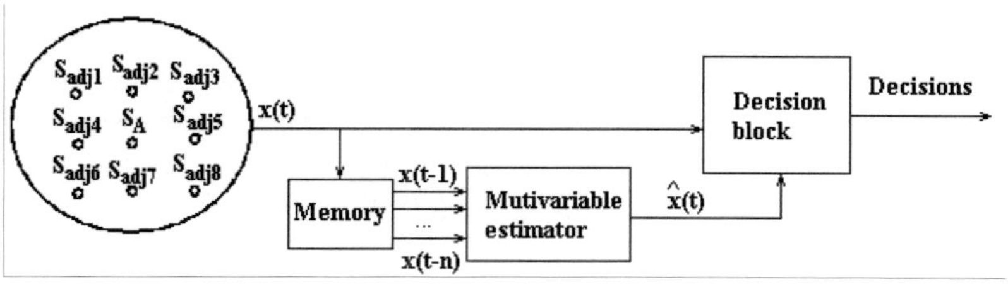

Fig. 15. The monitoring structure

The measured values from sensors are memorized and a multivariable estimation algorithm is applied. Based on the error between the measured and estimated values a decision is taken. The error has the equation:

$$e_A(t) = \left| x_A(t) - \hat{x}_A(t) \right| \tag{35}$$

This procedure has application in fault detection and diagnosis, with example in malicious detection of sensors. Such example is presented.

5. Method for monitoring

The following method is according to the objectives of monitoring of defined distributed parameter system from the practical application in the real world, as heat distribution, wave propagation. These systems have known mathematical model as a partial differential equation as a primary model from physics, with well-defined boundary and initial conditions for the system in practice. These represent the basic knowledge for a reference model from real data observation. The primary physical model must be discretized, to obtain a mathematical model as a multi input - multi output state space model. The unstructured meshes may be generated. The sensors must be placed in the field according to the meshes structured under the form of nodes and triangles. A scenario for practical applications could be chosen and simulated. The simulation and the practical measurements are producing transient regime characteristics. Those transient characteristics are due to the system dynamics in a training process. In steady state we cannot train the neural model. On these transient characteristics, seen as times series, the estimation algorithms may be applied. ANFIS is used to implement the non-linear estimation algorithms. With these algorithms future states of the process may be estimated. Possible fault in the system are chosen and strategies for detection may be developed, to identify and to diagnose them, base on the state estimation. In practice applying the method presumes the following steps: -placing a sensor network in the field of the distributed parameter system; -acquiring data, in time, from the sensor nodes, for the system variables; -using measured data to determine an estimation model based on ANFIS; -using measured data to estimate the future values of the system variables; -imposing an error threshold for the system variables; -comparing the measured data with the estimated values; -if the determined error is greater then the threshold a default occurs; -diagnosing the default, based on estimated data, determining its place in the sensor network and in the distribute parameter system field.
The interpolation techniques may be used for spatial distributed system identification with wireless sensor networks (Volosencu & Curiac, 2009).
Considering the continuous development of the wireless device technology, securing wireless sensor networks became more and more a significant task. One of the important problems that are related to the use of wireless sensor networks in harsh environments is the gap in their security. The strategy on time series predictors based on past and present values obtained from neighboring nodes from this chapter with its estimation algorithms is a basic for discovery of malfunctioning or attacked sensor nodes. Some strategies based on antecedent values provided by each sensor are presented for detecting their malicious activity in (Curiac et. al., 2007), (Curiac et. al., 2009), (Plastoi et. al., 2009).

6. Experimental results

In this chapter a parabolic case study consisting in a heat distribution flux through a plane square surface of dimensions l=1, with Dirichlet boundary conditions as constant temperature on three margins:

$$h_\theta \theta = r \tag{36}$$

with r=0, and a Neuman boundary condition as a flux temperature from a source

$$nk\nabla\theta + q\theta = g \tag{37}$$

where q is the heat transfer coefficient q=0, g=0, h_θ=1.
The heat equation, of a parabolic type, is:

$$\rho C\frac{\partial\theta}{t} = \nabla(k\nabla\theta) + Q + h_\theta(\theta_{ext} - \theta) \tag{38}$$

where ρ is the density of the medium, C is the thermal (heat) capacity, k is the thermal conductivity, coefficient of heat conduction, Q is the heat source, h_θ is the convective heat transfer coefficient, θ_{ext} is the external temperature. Relative values are chosen for the equation parameters: ρC=1, Q=10, k=1.
With the above conditions the equation may be solved using the finite element method. The optimized mean meshes and nodes are presenting in Fig. 16 a). The temperature represented height 3D over the surface analyzed is presented in Fig. 16 b).
The optimal position and the minimum needed number of sensors in a network placed in a distributed parameter system are analysed, based on simulation and practical measurements.
In practice we are using a reduced number of sensors, which is equivalent to a number reduced of nodes and meshes, for example a sensor network with only 13 nodes, placed like in Fig. 17 a). For this case the solution with the finite element method is represented in Fig. 17 b).
The repartition of temperature on isotherms in plane is presented in Fig. 18.
In the application we are choosing the nodes 8, 13, 12 5 and 11 from the Fig. 17 to apply the estimation method. The transient characteristics of the temperature are presented in Fig. 19 for 101 samples.

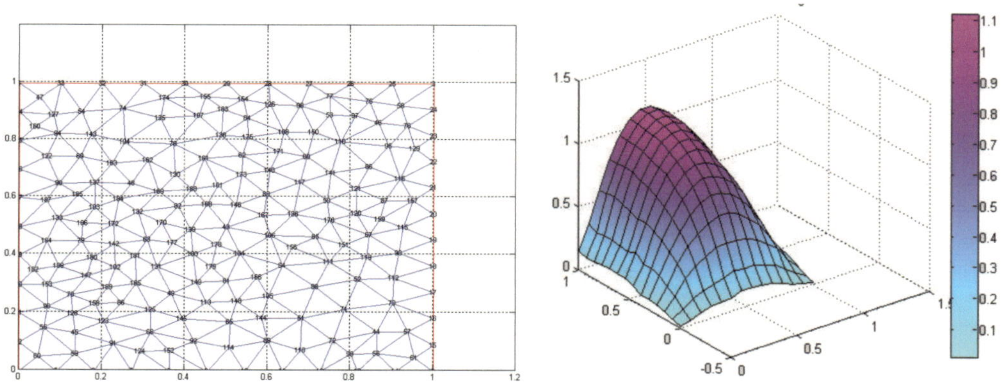

(a) (b)

Fig. 16. The optimized meshes and nodes and temperature

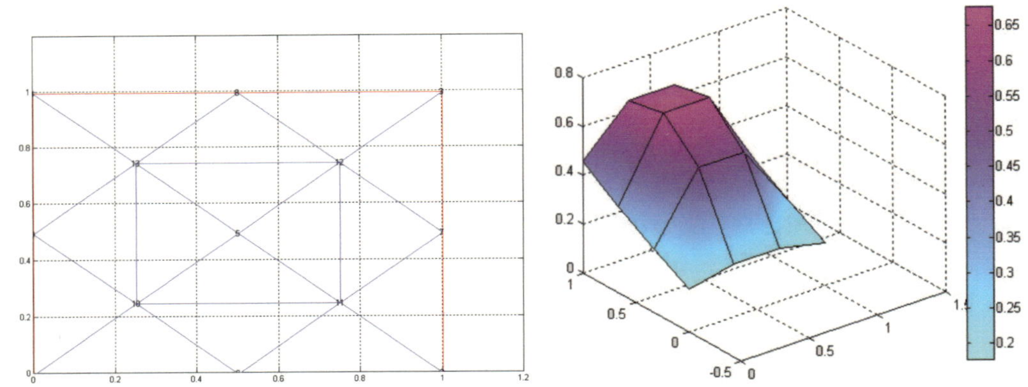

(a) (b)

Fig. 17. Sensor network position in the field and temperature

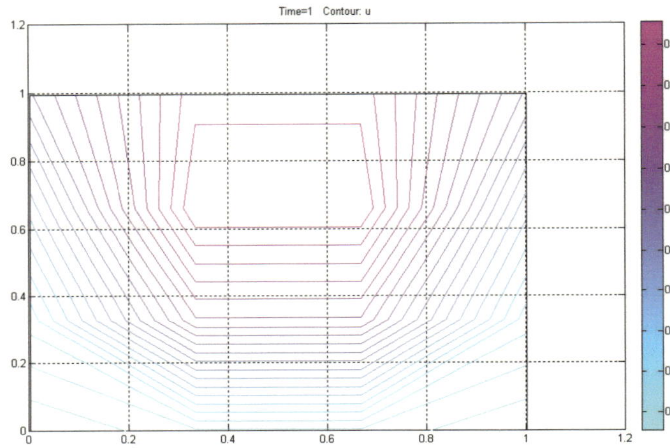

Fig. 18. Temperature in plane

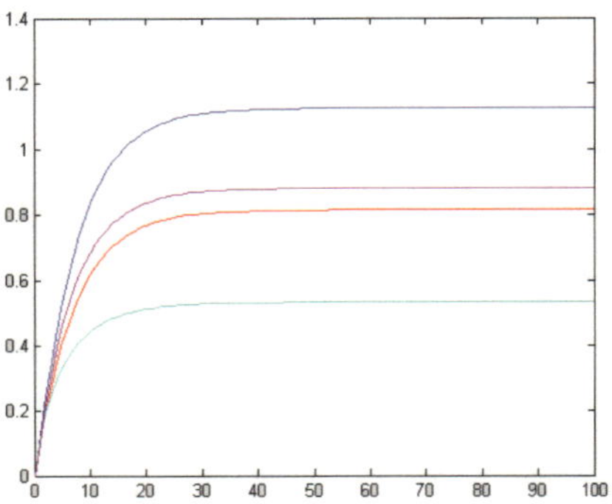

Fig. 19. Temperature transient characteristics

The time period was 1 s and the sampling period was 0,01 s.

In Fig. 19 the temperature for nodes 13 and 12 are the same, because they are on the same isotherms.

We are chosen as an example the node 5 to be the node with the estimated temperature, based on the first recursive algorithm:

$$\theta_5^{k+1} = f(\theta_8^k, \theta_{13}^k, \theta_{12}^k, \theta_{11}^k) \tag{39}$$

And also for the node 5 we will apply the second algorithm, auto-recursive:

$$\theta_5^{k+1} = f(\theta_5^k, \theta_5^{k\text{-}1}, \theta_5^{k\text{-}2}, \theta_5^{k\text{-}3}) \tag{40}$$

The fuzzy inference system structure is presented in Fig. 20.

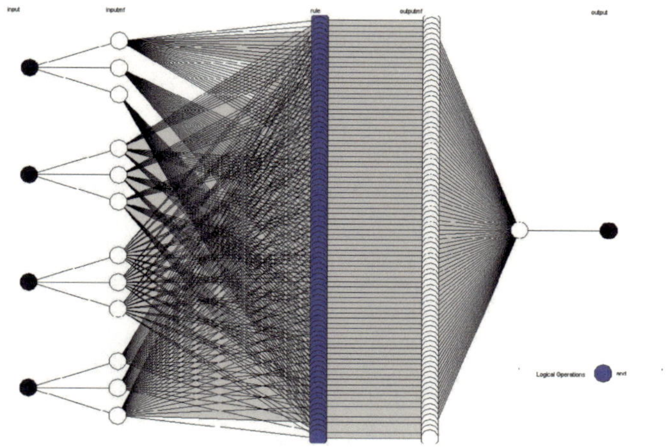

Fig. 20. Fuzzy inference system

The comparison transient characteristics for training and testing output data are presented in Fig. 21.
The average testing error is 2,017.10^{-5}. Number of training epochs is 3.
For the second algorithm the training error was of 0,007, number of epochs 3 and the testing error 0,007.
The fuzzy inference system general structure is the same, but with different parameter values.
The estimated output for the second algorithm is presented in Fig. 22.

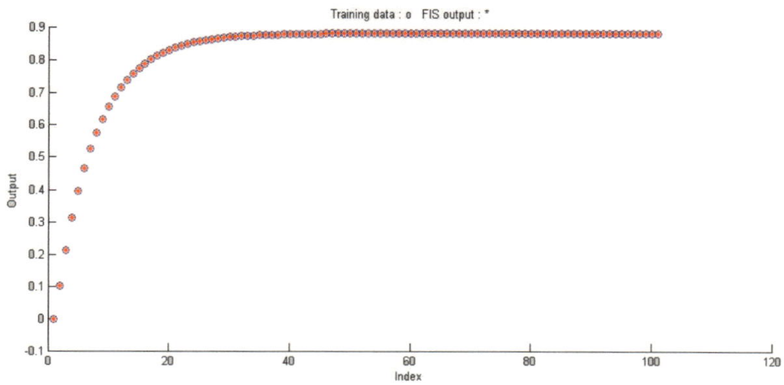

Fig. 21. Comparison between training and testing output

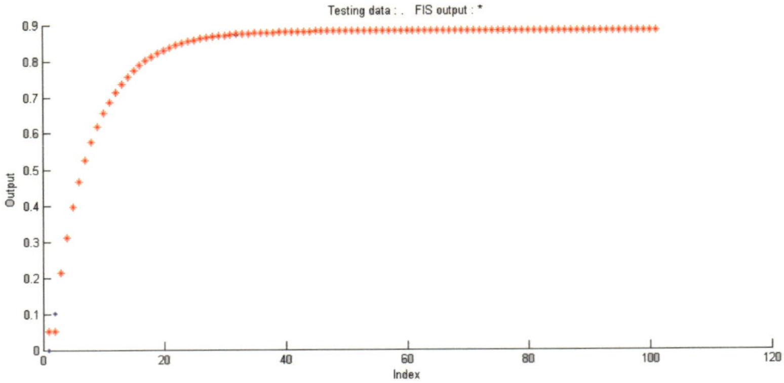

Fig. 22. The estimated output for the second algorithm

Comparing the two algorithms the first one had a better testing error.
Based on the measured values some interpolation may be done. Such an example is presented in Fig. 23.

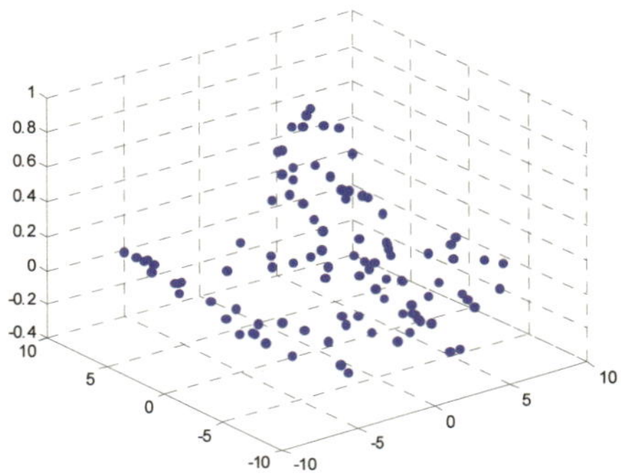

Fig. 23. Interpolation example

If a fault appears at the sensor 5 an error occurs in estimation, like in Fig. 24.
Detection of this error is equivalent to a default at sensor 5, from other point of view in the place of the sensor 5 in the space of the distributed parameter systems and in the heat flow around the sensor 5.

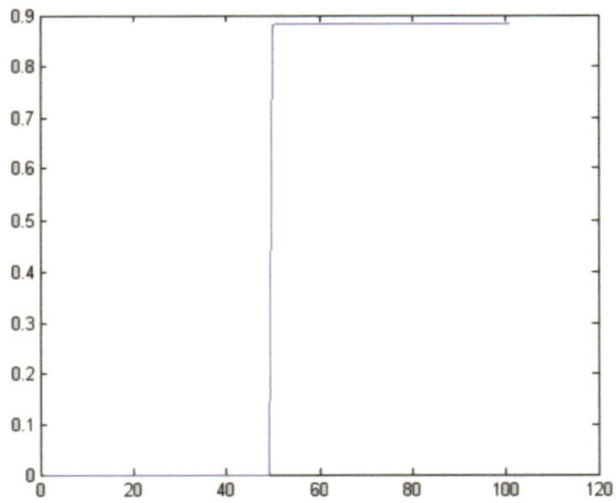

Fig. 24. Error at the fifth node for a fault in the network

For an example of the estimated temperature $\hat{x}_A(t) = \hat{\theta}_A(t)$ for the sensor S_A is presented in Fig. 25, over the original time series $x_A(t)$,

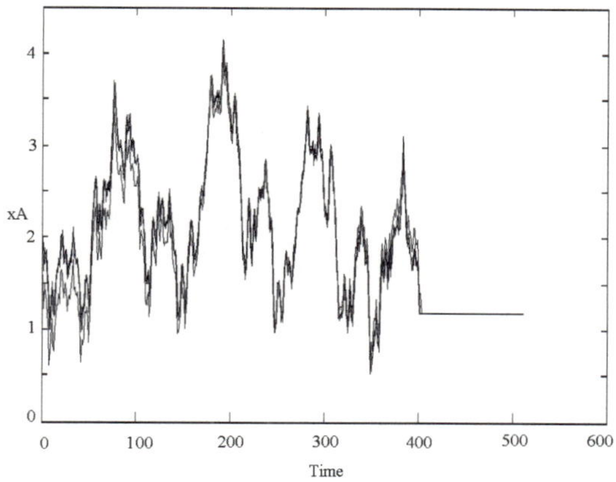

Fig. 25. Sensor value and the estimate

The error $e_A(t) = x_A(t) - \hat{x}_A(t)$ is presented in Fig. 26.

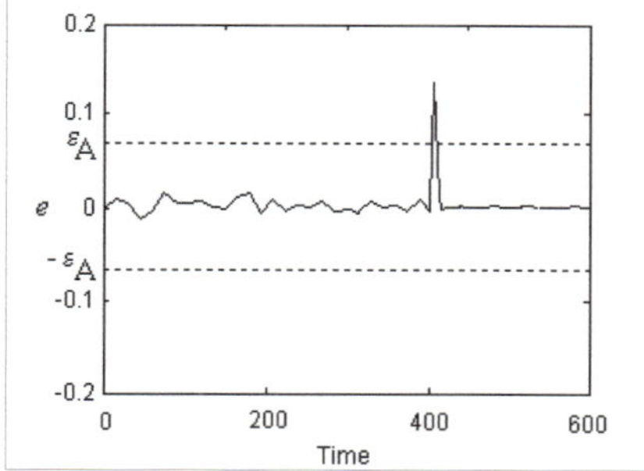

Fig. 26. Sensor error

We may see the error appearance at the time moment 400 s, caused by a fault at the node x_A. The estimated signal follows the real signal after a small delay.
Virtual instrumentation using National Instruments technology was used to implement the monitoring system. The virtual instrument for temperature measurement and estimation is presented in Fig. 27 a). The virtual instrument for temperature estimation error is presented in Fig. 27 b). The sample period was 9 s.

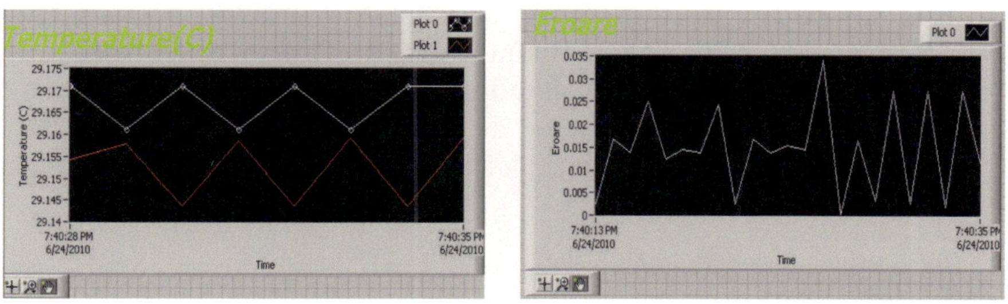

(a) (b)

Fig. 27. (a) Mesured and estimated temperature (b) Estimation error

The validation of results is made based on a quadratic error criterion, which is taken account of all set i=1,…,n of measured data and estimates:

$$J = \sum_{i=1}^{n} e_{Ai}^{2}(t) \tag{41}$$

7. Conclusion

This chapter presents some considerations on time series identification methodology using a wireless sensor network as a complex measurement system. After acquiring the measured values from the area covered by sensor networks, some estimation techniques may be applied. Some auto-regression estimation linear or ANFIS models may be developed. This methodology can be efficiently implemented on sensor network base stations, so there is no need for other hardware resources.

A comparison of different identification methods is presented, in order to use the adaptive-network-based fuzzy inference. Some examples of generated meshes and temperature estimates for different numbers of sensor are presented. The main attention is given to the way of how to chose the number and the positions of the sensor nodes according to the desired accuracy in the identification process.

The chapter presents two algorithms for estimation of state variables in distributed parameter systems of parabolic case. The algorithms are based on non-linear exogenous models with regression and auto-regression. Also, a method for monitoring distributed parameter systems based on these algorithms, sensor networks and ANFIS for non-linear system identification is presented.

The sensor network is seen as a "distributed sensor". The algorithms are based on regression using the values provided by the adjacent nodes of the sensor network and on autoregressive relation with the values from anterior time moments of the same node.

The method described the way how to use all these concepts for fault detection and diagnosis in distributed parameter systems, using the measured values provided by the sensor and the estimated values computed by the ANFIS estimator, calculating an error and detecting the fault based on a decision taken after a threshold comparison. Estimations methods may be applied in the case of discovery of malicious nodes in wireless sensor networks.

A case study for two algorithms are presented for parabolic type. A comparison between the algorithms is made. Good approximations were obtained.

Developing of the algorithms and the method are taken in consideration in the future, in other applications, considering all the capabilities of the sensor nodes to measure physical variables. This approach allows treatment of large and complex systems with many variables by learning and extrapolation. An interesting application could be the monitoring of earth environment at low and high altitudes, based on new types of sensor networks specialized for this purpose.

The implementation was made using virtual instruments of National Instruments technology.

8. Acknowledgement

This work was developed in the frame of PNII-IDEI-PCE-ID923-2009 CNCSIS - UEFISCSU grant.

9. References

Akyildiz, F.; Su, W.; Sankarasubramaniam, Y. & Cayirci, E. (2002). Wireless Sensor Networks: A Survey. *Computer Networks*, 38(4), March, 2002.

Banks, H.T.; & Kunish, K. (1989). Estimation techniques for distributed parameter systems, *Systems & control: foundation & applications*, vol. 1, Note(s): XIII-315.

Basmadjian, D. (1999). *The Art of Modeling in Science and Engineering*, Chapman & Hall, CRC, Boca Raton.

Chairez, I..; Fuentes, R.; Poznyak, A.; Poznyak, T.; Escudero, M. & Viana, L., (2009). Neural network identification of uncertain 2D partial differential equations, *6th International Conference on Electrical Engineering, Computing Science and Automatic Control, CCE*, pp. 1 - 6.

Chiang, L.H.; Russell, E.L. & R.D. Braatz, R.D. (2001). *Fault Detection and Diagnosis in Industrial Systems*, Springer Verlag, London, 2001.

Curiac, D.I.; Volosencu, C.; Doboli, A.; Dranga, O. & Bednarz, T. (2007). Discovery of Malicious Nodes in Wireless Sensor Networks Using Neural Predictors, *WSEAS Transactions on Computer Research*, Issue 1, Vol. 2, Jan. 2007, pp. 38 - 44.

Curiac, D.I.; Volosencu, C.; Pescaru, D.; Jurcă, L. & Doboli, A. (2009). Redundancy and Its Applications in Wireless Sensor Networks: A Survey, *WSEAS Transactions on Computers*, Issue 4, Volume 6, April, 2009, pp. 705-716.

Depari, A.; Flammini, A.; Marioli, D. & Taroni, A. (2005). Application of an ANFIS algorithm to sensor data processing, *IEEE Trans. on Instrumenttaion and Measurement*, Vol. 56, Issue 1, Feb. 2005, pp. 75-79.

Feng, J.; Koushanfar, F. & Potkonjak, M. (2002). System-Architectures for Sensor Networks Issues, Alternatives and Directions, *Proc. of the 2002 IEEE Int. Conf. on Computer Design (ICCD'02)*, Freiburg, 2002, pp.226-231.

Giannakis, G.B. (2008). Distributed Estimation Using Wireless Sensor Networks, *The 12th WSEAS Int. Conf. On Systems*, Heraklion, Crete Island, Greece, 2008.

Hou, Z.X. & Li, H.O. (2006). Nonlinear System Identification Based on Adaptive Neural Fuzzy Inference System, *2006 International Conference on Communications, Circuits and Systems Proceedings*, Vol. 3, 25-28 June 2006, pp. 2067 - 2069.

Jassar, S.; Behan, T.; Zhao, L. & Liao, Z. (2009). The comparison of neural network and hybrid neuro-fuzzy based inferential sensor models for space heating systems, *IEEE International Conference on Systems, Man and Cybernetics, 2009. SMC 2009.* 11-14 Oct. 2009, pp: 4299 - 4303.

Kubrulsky, C.S. & de S. Vincente, M.R. (1977). Distributed parameter system identification. A survey, *International Journal of Control*, Vol. 26, Issue 4, Oct. 1977, pp. 509 - 535.

Mellit, A.; Arab, A.H.; Khorissi, N. & Salhi, H. (2007). An ANFIS-based Forecasting for Solar Radiation Data from Sunshine Duration and Ambient Temperature, *IEEE Power Engineering Society General Meeting*, 24-28 June 2007, pp. 1 - 6.

Novak, R. & Mira, U. (2003). Boundary Estimation in Sensor Networks: Theory and Methods, *Information Processing in Sensor Networks: 2nd Int. Workshop*, IPSN 2003, Palo Alto, CA, 2003.

Plastoi, M.; Banias, O.; Curiac, D.I.; Volosencu, C.; Tudoroiu, R. & Doboli, A. (2009). Integrated System forMalicious Node Discovery and Self-destruction in Wireless Sensor Networks, *Internatioanl Journal on Advances in Networks and Services*, Vol. 2, No. 1, 2009, pp. 241 - 250, ISSN 1942-2644.

Pottie, G.J. & Kaiser, W.J. (2000). Wireless Integrated Network Sensors. *Communications of the ACM*, vol. 43, 2000.

Roger Jang, J.S. (1993). ANFIS: Adaptive Network Based Fuzzy Inference Systems, *IEEE Trans. on Systems, Man, and Cybernetics*, Vol. 23, No. 03, May 1993, pp. 665-685.

Rosculet, M.N. & Craiu, M. (1979). *Ecuatii diferentiale aplicative*, Ed. Academiei RSR, Bucuresti, 1979.

Tong, L.; Zhao, Q. & Adireddy, S. (2003). Sensor Networks with Mobile Agents, *Proceedings IEEE 2003 MILCOM*, Boston, 2003, pp. 688-694.

Tubaishat, M. & Madria, S. (2003). Sensor networks: an overview, *IEEE Potential*, Apr. 2003, Vol. 22, Issue 2, pap. 20- 23.

Ucinski, D. (2004). *Optimal Measurement Methods for Distributed Parameter System Identification*, CRC Press, 2004.

Sjoberg, J., et. all. (1997). Non linear black box modeling in system identification: an unified overview, Automatica, 33, 1997, 1691-1724.

Volosencu, C. (2008). Identification of Distributed Parameter Systems, Based on Sensor Networks and Artificial Intelligence, *WSEAS Transactions on Systems*, Issue 6, Vol. 7, June 2008, pp. 785-801.

Volosencu, C. & Curiac, D.I. (2009). Interpolation Techniques for Spatial Distributed System Identification Using Wireless Sensor Networks, *Recent Advances in Automation& Information, Proceedings of the 10th WSEAS Int. Conf. on Automation & Information (ICAI'09), Prague, March 23-25, 2009,* pp. 383-376.

Volosencu, C. (2010). Algorithms for Estimation in Distributed Parameter Systems Based on Sensor Networks and ANFIS, *WSEAS Transactions on Systems*, Issue 3, Volume 9, March 2010, pp. 283-294, ISSN: 1109-2777.

Zhang H. et all. (2005). Estimation in sensor actuators arrays using reduced order physical models, *4th Int. Symp. Information Processing in Sensor Networks*, Los Angeles, CA, 2005.

Zhu, Y.F.; Tan, H.Z.; Wan, P. & Zhang, Y. (2007). A blind approach to nonlinear system identification, *IET Conference on Wireless, Mobile and Sensor Networks, 2007. (CCWMSN07)*. 12-14 Dec. 2007, pg. 209 – 212.

20

Cognitive Radio: UWB Integration and Related Antenna Design

Mohammed Al-Husseini[1], Karim Y. Kabalan[1], Ali El-Hajj[1] and Christos G. Christodoulou[2]
[1]*American University of Beirut*
[2]*University of New Mexico*
[1]*Lebanon*
[2]*USA*

1. Introduction

The emerging feature-rich and high-data-rate wireless applications have put increasing demand on radio spectrum. The scarcity of spectrum and the inefficiency in its usage, as caused by the current radio spectrum regulations, necessitate the development of new dynamic spectrum allocation policies to better exploit the existing spectrum.

The current spectrum allocation regulations assign specific bands to particular services, and grant licensed band access to licensed users only. Cognitive Radio (CR) will revolutionize the way spectrum is allocated. In a CR network, the intelligent radio part allows unlicensed users (secondary users) to access spectrum bands licensed to primary users, while avoiding interference with them. In this scheme, a secondary user can use spectrum sensing hardware/software to locate spectrum portions with reduced primary user activity or idle spectrum slots, select the best available channel, coordinate access to this channel with other secondary users, and vacate the channel when a primary user needs it. To achieve this, the transceiver in a CR system should have awareness of the radio environment in terms of spectrum usage, power spectral density of transmitted/received signals, and wireless protocol signaling, should be able to adaptively tune system parameters such as transmit power, carrier frequency, and modulation strategy. The transceiver should also be ended with an antenna system that can simultaneously operate over a wide frequency band (sensing) and a chosen narrow band (communication), or operate over an ultra-wide frequency band while possibly blocking signals in a narrow frequency range.

Ultra-wideband (UWB) is a transmission technique that uses pulses with a very short time duration across a very large frequency portion of the spectrum. UWB is different from other radio frequency communication techniques in that it does not use RF carriers, but instead employs modulated high frequency pulses of low power with a duration of less than 1 nanosecond. From the perspective of other communication systems, the UWB transmissions are part of the low power background noise. Therefore UWB promises to enable the usage of licensed spectrum without harmful interference to primary communication systems, and can be used as an enabling technology for implementing CR.

In this chapter, we offer a general overview of Cognitive Radio and dynamic spectrum access, discuss the advantages of using UWB as an enabling technology for CR, and give special attention to the latest research on Antenna Design for CR. The chapter will be organized as follows. Section 2 will discuss the current radio spectrum regulations and spectrum usage, and will focus on the availability of radio spectrum and the efficiency of its use. Section 3 will deal with the concepts of Spectrum Sharing and Dynamic Spectrum Access. Section 4 will investigate the advantages of integrating CR with the UWB technology and the recent research on the topic. Section 5 will review the recent work in antenna design for Cognitive Radio. Finally, a conclusion will be given in Section 6.

2. Current radio spectrum allocations/regulations

Radio spectrum refers to the electromagnetic frequencies between 3 kHz and 300 GHz. Table 1 lists the bands that make up this spectrum. Access to the spectrum is restricted by a radio regulatory regime, which licenses most of it to be exclusively used by traditional communications systems and services. The spectrum allocation regime guarantees that the radio communications systems are protected against interference from other radio systems.

Designation	Frequency	Wavelength
VLF (very low frequency)	3kHz to 30kHz	100km to 10km
LF (low frequency)	30kHz to 300kHz	10km to 1km
MF (medium frequency)	300kHz to 3MHz	1km to 100m
HF (high frequency)	3MHz to 30MHz	100m to 10m
VHF (very high frequency)	30MHz to 300MHz	10m to 1m
UHF (ultra-high frequency)	300MHz to 3GHz	1m to 10cm
SHF (super-high frequency)	3GHz to 30GHz	10cm to 1cm
EHF (extremely high frequency)	30GHz to 300GHz	1cm to 1mm

Table 1. The radio spectrum

Frequency allocation or spectrum allocation refers to licensing parts of the spectrum for exclusive or shared usage, and to declaring other parts as unlicensed or as open spectrum. The process of spectrum allocation is organized by national and international institutions usually called regulators. Internationally, frequency allocation processes are harmonized with the help of the International Telecommunication Union, which is the United Nations agency for information and communications technologies. In Europe, spectrum regulation is the responsibility of the Electronic Communications Committee (ECC) of the European Conference of Post and Telecommunications Administrations (CEPT). In the United Kingdom, the Office of Communications (Ofcom) handles spectrum regulation, whereas in the United States of America, this responsibility is shared between the Federal Communications Commission (FCC) and the National Telecommunications and Information Administration (NTIA). In China and Japan, spectrum allocation is respectively conducted by the Ministry of Information Industry (MII) and the the Ministry of Internal Affairs and Communications (MIC).

Four approaches can differentiate the regulation of radio spectrum (Berlemann & Mangold, 2009). These are 1) the licensed spectrum for exclusive usage, 2) the licensed spectrum for shared usage, 3) the unlicensed spectrum, and 4) the open spectrum.

In the first approach, which FCC calls the exclusive use model, the licensee has exclusive usage rights for a specific spectrum. An example of a spectrum licensed for exclusive usage are the frequency bands sold for use in the Universal Mobile Telecommunication System (UMTS) in Europe.

The second approach (called the command-and-control model by FCC) restricts the licensed spectrum for shared usage to a specific technology. An example of this approach could be the spectrum used for public safety services.

In the unlicensed spectrum approach, which FCC calls the commons model or open access, the spectrum is available to all radio systems operating according to regulated standards. The Industrial, Scientific and Medical (ISM) 2.4 GHz band and the Unlicensed National Information Infrastructure (U-NII) 5-6 GHz bands are examples of unlicensed or license-exempt spectrum.

The fourth and last approach, the open spectrum, allows anyone to access any range of the spectrum without any restriction. Yet, a minimum set of rules from technical standards or etiquettes that are required for sharing spectrum should be respected in this approach.

With the licensed spectrum approaches, spectrum resources could often be wasted. For example, portions of the spectrum could become unused because the communications systems licensed to operate in this spectrum have become more spectrum efficient due to technology advancements, and thus these communications systems can operate in only a percentage of the spectrum initially licensed for that specific service. In another direction, if a service to which spectrum is licensed is not economically successful, its licensed spectrum remains largely unused. Furthermore, the spectrum dedicated to public safety and military radio systems is only occasionally used, which means it is unused most of the times. As a result, large parts of the spectrum are currently used inefficiently. Paradoxically, 90 to 95% of the licensed radio spectrum is not in use at any location at any given time (Berlemann & Mangold, 2009), especially that the current radio regulatory regime is too complex to handle the increasingly dynamic nature of emerging wireless applications. Added to the fact that the demand for additional spectrum is growing fast, even faster than costly technologies like Multiple Input Multiple Output (MIMO) and Space Division Multiple Access (SDMA) can improve spectrum efficiency, the conclusion is that the current spectrum regulations should be fundamentally rethought in order to solve the spectrum scarcity and limited radio resources problems.

Could the solution be in more unlicensed spectrum? There is definitely a strong motivation for more unlicensed spectrum, due to its commercial success and the many different radio communications systems that operate within such spectrum. However, as more parties and technologies utilize unlicensed spectrum, it is becoming more crowded and consequently less available to all. This again necessitates the availability of more spectrum, or more efficient radio systems.

3. Dynamic spectrum access and cognitive radio

The increasing demand for wireless connectivity and current crowding of unlicensed spectra necessitate a new communication paradigm to exploit the existing spectrum in better ways. The current approach for spectrum allocation is based on assigning a specific band to a particular service. This is illustrated by the FCC frequency allocation chart shown in Fig. 1. The spectrum chart contains overlapping allocations in most frequency bands and seems to indicate a high degree of spectrum utilization. However, while the spectral efficiency of some radio systems is continually improving, they are faced with increasing interference that limits network capacity and scalability. The FCC Spectrum Policy Task Force (FCC, 2002) reported vast temporal and geographic variations in the usage of allocated spectrum with utilization ranging from 15 to 85% in the bands below 3 GHz. In the frequency range above 3 GHz the bands are even more poorly utilized. In other words, a large portion of the assigned spectrum is used sporadically, leading to an under utilization of a significant amount of spectrum. This inefficiency arises from the inflexibility of the regulatory and licensing process, which typically assigns the complete rights to a frequency band to a primary user. This approach makes it extremely difficult to recycle these bands once they are allocated, even if these users poorly utilize this valuable resource. A solution to this inefficiency, which has been highly successful in the ISM (2.4 GHz), the U-NII (5–6 GHz), and microwave (57–64 GHz) bands, is to make spectra available on an unlicensed basis. However, in order to obtain spectra for unlicensed operation, new sharing concepts have been introduced to allow use by secondary users under the requirement that they limit their interference to pre-existing primary users.

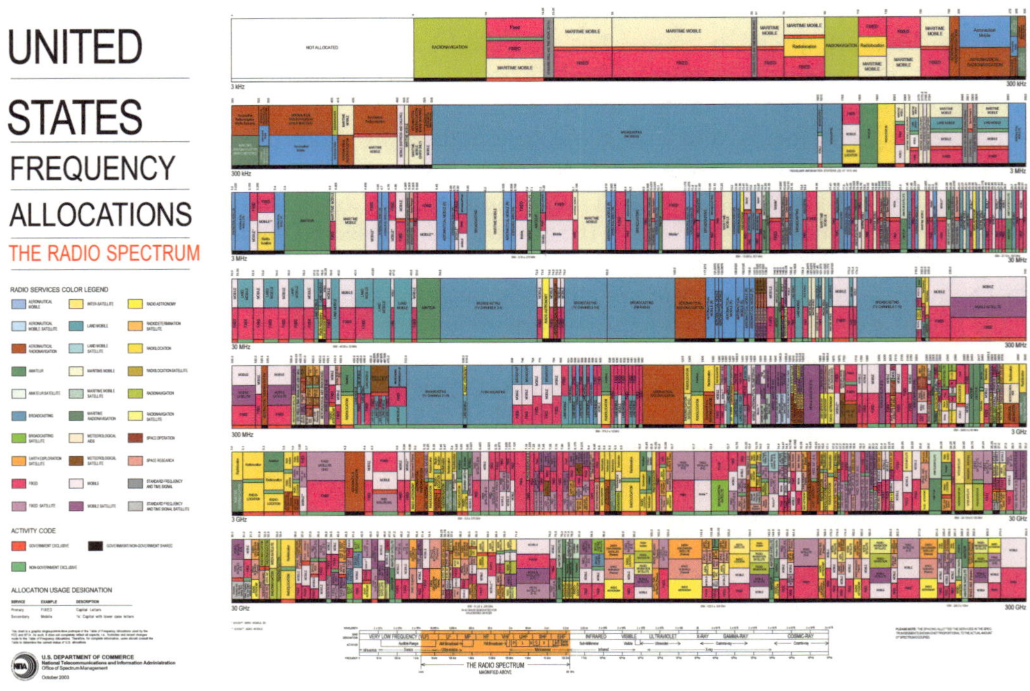

Fig. 1. The US spectrum allocation chart (NTIA, 2003)

Cognitive radio (CR) technology is the key enabling technology which provides the capacity to share the wireless channel with the licensed users in an opportunistic way. CRs are foreseen to be able to provide the high bandwidth to mobile users via heterogeneous wireless architectures and dynamic spectrum access techniques.

In order to share the spectrum with licensed users without interfering with them, and meet the diverse quality of service requirement of applications, each CR user in a CR network must (Chen & Prasad, 2009):

- Determine the portion of spectrum that is available, which is known as Spectrum sensing.
- Select the best available channel, which is called Spectrum decision.
- Coordinate access to this channel with other users, which is known as Spectrum sharing.
- Vacate the channel when a licensed user is detected, which is referred as Spectrum mobility.

To fulfill these functions of spectrum sensing, spectrum decision, spectrum sharing and spectrum mobility, a CR has to be cognitive, reconfigurable and self-organized. An example of the cognitive capability is the CR's ability to sense the spectrum and detect spectrum holes (also called white spaces), which are those frequency bands not used by the licensed users or having limited interference with them. The reconfigurable capability can be summarized by the ability to dynamically choose the suitable operating frequency (frequency agility), and the ability to adapt the modulation/coding schemes and transmit power as needed. The self-organized capability has to do with the possession of a good spectrum management scheme, a good mobility and connection management, and the ability to to support security functions in dynamic environments.

Dynamic spectrum allocation models

Dynamic spectrum access (DSA) represents the opposite direction of the current static spectrum management policy. It is broadly categorized under three models: the dynamic exclusive use model, the open sharing model, and the hierarchical access model. The taxonomy of DSA is illustrated in Fig. 2.

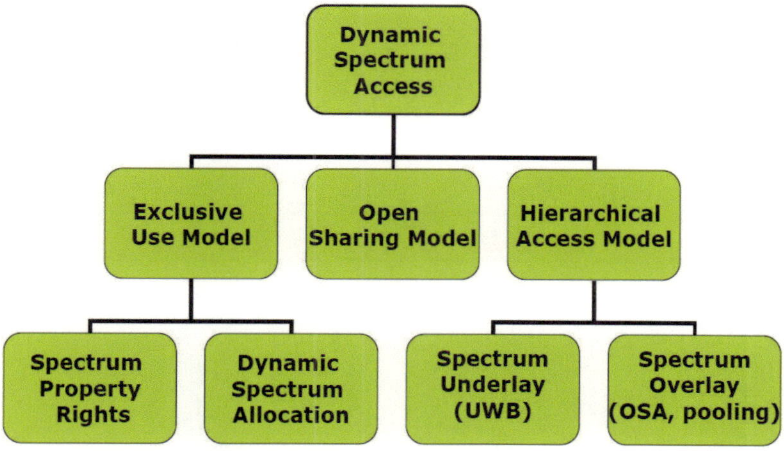

Fig. 2. Dynamic spectrum access models

In the dynamic exclusive use model, the spectrum bands are still licensed to services for exclusive use, as in the current spectrum regulation policy, but flexibility is introduced to improve spectrum efficiency. Two approaches have been proposed under this model: spectrum property rights and dynamic spectrum allocation. The first approach, the spectrum property rights, allows licensees to sell and trade spectrum and to freely choose technology. In the second approach, the dynamic spectrum allocation, the aim is to improve spectrum efficiency through dynamic spectrum assignment by exploiting the spatial and temporal traffic statistics of different services.

The open sharing model employs open sharing among peer users as the basis for managing a spectral region. Supporters of this model rely on the huge success of wireless services operating in the ISM band.

A hierarchical access structure with primary and secondary users is adopted by the third model. Here, the spectrum licensed to primary users is open to secondary users while limiting the interference perceived by primary users. Two approaches to spectrum sharing between primary and secondary users have been considered: spectrum underlay and spectrum overlay.

In the underlay approach, secondary users should operate below the noise floor of primary users, and thus severe constraints are imposed on their transmission power. One way to achieve this is to spread the transmitted signals of secondary users over an ultra-wide frequency band, leading to a short-range high data rate with extremely low transmission power. Assuming that primary users transmit all the time (worst case scenario), this approach does not rely on detection and exploitation of spectrum white space.

The spectrum overlay (also termed opportunistic spectrum access or OSA) approach imposes restrictions on when and where secondary users may transmit rather on their transmission power. In this approach, secondary users avoid higher priority users through the use of spectrum sensing and adaptive allocation. They identify and exploit the spectrum holes defined in space, time, and frequency.

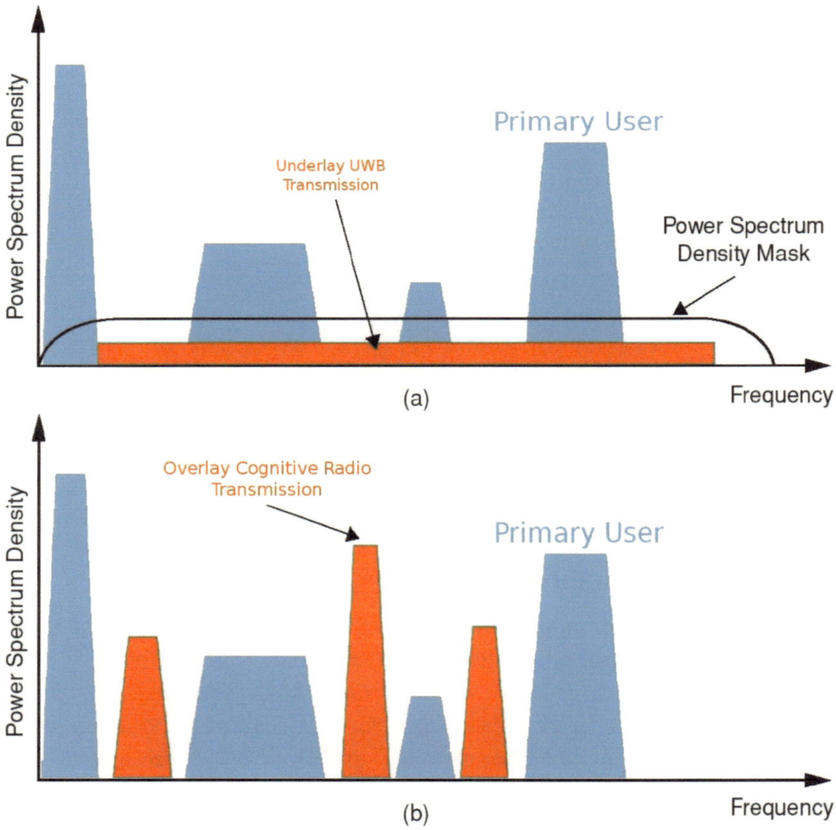

Fig. 3. Underlay (a) and overlay (b) spectrum sharing approaches

The underlay and overlay approaches in the hierarchical model are illustrated in Fig. 3. They can be employed simultaneously for further spectrum efficiency improvement. Furthermore, the hierarchical model is more compatible with current spectrum management policies and legacy wireless systems as compared to the other two models.

4. Ultra-wideband cognitive radio

Ultra-wideband (UWB) is any wireless technology that has a bandwidth greater than 500 MHz or a fractional bandwidth greater than 0.2. Ultra-wideband systems have been attracting an intense attention from both the industry and academic world since FCC allowed the unlicensed usage of UWB in 2002.

UWB is a promising technology for future short- and medium-range high-data-rate wireless communication networks. The most appealing property of UWB is that it is an underlay system, meaning that it can coexist in the same temporal, spatial, and spectral domains with other licensed/unlicensed radios. Other interesting features of UWB include that it has a multi-dimensional flexibility involving adaptable pulse shape, bandwidth, data rate, and transmit power. On top of these, UWB has a low power consumption, and it allows significantly low complexity transceivers leading to a limited system cost. Another very important feature of UWB is providing secure communications. The power spectrum of a UWB transmission is embedded into the noise floor, thus it is very hard to detect. Combined with other higher layer encryption techniques, this feature introduces very secure transmission.

UWB systems are allowed to operate in the 3.1–10.6 GHz band without a license requirement (according to the current FCC regulations in the USA), but under very strict transmission power limits. Both indoors and outdoors, UWB systems are not permitted to transmit more than -42 dBm/MHz in the specified band. This limitation ensures that the UWB systems do not interfere to the licensed operators that use various frequency bands in the UWB frequency range. However, FCC regulations could be revised and regulatory agencies may consider to allow UWB systems to transmit with higher powers and offer more freedom to UWB if UWB is combined with CR to give it the ability to sense the spectrum to ensure the absence of licensed users operation in their target bands.

There are two common technologies for implementing UWB: the Orthogonal Frequency Division Multiplexing based UWB (UWB-OFDM) and the impulse radio based UWB (IR-UWB). IR-UWB is carried out by transmitting extremely short low-power pulses that are on the order of nanoseconds. An advantage of IR-UWB is that it enables to use various types of modulations, including on-off keying (OOK), pulse amplitude modulation (PAM), pulse shape modulation (PSM), pulse interval modulation (PIM), pulse position modulation (PPM), and phase shift keying (PSK).

Time hopping (TH) codes that are specific to each user can be employed by IR-UWB systems for multi-user access. The TH codes, which are specific pseudo-random noise (PN) codes, enable the UWB system to provide access to multiple users conveniently. The multi-user parameters can be adaptively modified according to the change in number of users. To enable more users to communicate, for example, the UWB system can increase the number of chips in each frame at the expense of decreasing each user's data rate. Coherent receivers (such as Rake and correlator receivers) as well as non-coherent ones, such as energy detector and transmitted reference receivers, can be utilized for IR-UWB communications. Along with the flexibility in modulation methods and receiver types, IR-UWB also offers a variety

of options regarding the shapes of the transmitted pulses. IR-UWB systems have an excellent multi-path resolving capability because of the extremely wide frequency band that they occupy. This property makes IR-UWB a precise radar technology as well as a highly accurate ranging and positioning system, in addition to being a communication system.
In OFDM-based UWB, orthogonal subcarriers are employed to modulate the transmitted data. In the current multi-band OFDM planning, which divides the entire UWB band into 14 sub-bands, each subband is considered to be 528 MHz and contains 128 subcarriers. The subcarrier spacing is usually chosen to be less than the channel coherence bandwidth. This makes each subcarrier go through a flat fading channel. As a result, the UWB-OFDM receiver needs a simple equalizer implementation to recover the originally transmitted signal. With UWB-OFDM, it is easy to avoid interference to licensed systems. By simply turning off the subcarriers that overlap with the spectra of the licensed system, a UWB-OFDM transmitter can avoid jamming a licensed signal.

UWB features meeting cognitive radio requirements

Though usually associated with the underlay mode, UWB offers the possibility of also being implemented in the overlay mode (Arslan & Sahin, 2007). The difference between the two modes is the amount of transmitted power. In the underlay mode, UWB has a considerably restricted power, which is spread over a wide frequency band. When a UWB system is operating in the underlay mode, it is quite unlikely that any coexisting licensed system is affected from it. On top of this, underlay UWB can employ various narrowband interference avoidance methods.
In the overlay mode, however, the transmitted power can be much higher. It actually can be increased to a level that is comparable to the power of licensed systems. But this mode is only applicable if two conditions are met: 1) if the UWB transmitter ensures that the targeted spectrum is completely free of signals of other systems, and 2) if the regulations are revised to allow this mode of operation. UWB can also operate in both underlay and overlay modes simultaneously. This can happen by shaping the transmitted signal so as to make part of the spectrum occupied in an underlay mode and some other parts occupied in an overlay mode. Apparently, in any mode of operation, UWB causes negligible interference to other communication systems. This special feature of UWB makes it very tempting for the realization of cognitive radio.
CR should have a high flexibility in determining the spectrum it occupies, because the bands that will be utilized for cognitive communication could vary after each periodic spectrum scan. Flexible spectrum shaping is a part of UWB's nature. In IR-UWB, the occupied spectrum can directly be altered by varying the duration or the form of the short transmitted pulses. In UWB-OFDM, on the other hand, spectrum shaping can be conveniently accomplished by turning some subcarriers on or off according to the spectral conditions.
CR systems are should be able to adjust their data rates according to the available bandwidth, which varies according to the utilization of the bands by the licensed systems. CR systems are also expected to provide a solution for the cases when the available bandwidth is so limited that the communication cannot be continued.
UWB systems are able to make abrupt changes in their throughput. For example, an IR-UWB system can respond to a decrease in available bandwidth by switching to a different wider pulse shape, and can do the opposite if there is more band to use. In UWB-OFDM, the adjustment of the occupied bandwidth is even simpler. The subcarriers that overlap with the newly occupied bands are turned off, and this way the data rate is decreased, or more subcarriers are used to occupy newly available bands, thus increasing the data rate.

Furthermore, UWB provides an exceptional solution regarding the dropped calls. If UWB is performed in overlay mode, and in cases when it becomes impossible to continue the communication, UWB can switch to the underlay mode. Thus, UWB can maintain the communication link even though it is at a low quality since licensed systems are not affected by UWB operated in the underlay mode.

The spectral masks that are imposed by the regulatory agencies (such as the FCC in the USA) are also determinative in spectrum usage in that they set a limit to the transmit power of wireless systems. UWB offers a satisfactory solution to the adaptable transmit power requirement of cognitive radio. Both UWB-OFDM and IR-UWB systems can comply with any set of spectral rules mandated upon the cognitive radio system by adapting their transmit power.

CR networks should be able to provide multi-user access since there will be a number of users willing to make use of the same spectrum opportunities at the same time. CR is also required to be able to modify its multiple access parameters to cope with the changes that may occur in the overall spectrum occupancy, or with the possible fluctuations in the signal quality observed by each user.

From the point of adaptive multiple access, UWB is a proper candidate for CR applications and is very flexible in terms of multiple access. For example, in IR-UWB, the number of users can be determined by modifying the number of chips in a frame. In UWB-OFDM, on the other hand, more users can be allowed to communicate by decreasing the subcarriers assigned to each user.

UWB has information security in its nature. Hence, it can be considered a strong candidate for CR applications in terms of information security. Underlay UWB is a highly secure means of exchanging information. If a UWB system is working in the underlay mode, because of the very low power level, it is impossible for unwanted users to detect even the existence of the UWB signals. Overlay mode UWB, on the other hand, can also be considered a safe communication method. In overlay IR-UWB, multiple accessing is enabled either by time hopping or by direct sequencing. Therefore, receiving a user's information is only possible if the user's time hopping or spreading code is known. UWB-OFDM also provides security by assigning different subcarriers to different users. The level of security can be increased by periodically changing these subcarrier assignments. Apparently, UWB is a secure way of communicating in both its underlay and overlay modes.

UWB communication can be accomplished by employing very low cost transmitters and receivers. The transceiver circuitries required to generate and process UWB signals are inexpensive, and the RF front-end required to send and capture UWB signals are also quite uncomplicated and inexpensive. This property of UWB makes it very attractive for CR, which aims at limited infrastructure and transceiver costs.

Adaptive UWB spectral mask

Fig. 4 depicts the UWB spectrum and the bands for some existing and dedicated narrowband services. UWB signals, which spread over a very wide spectral region at low power levels near the noise floor, will overlap with some of these systems, such as fixed satellite, radio astronomy, and the services operating in the U-NII bands. Despite the very low power level, there have been some concerns that UWB would increase the interference floor and degrade the performances of licensed users.

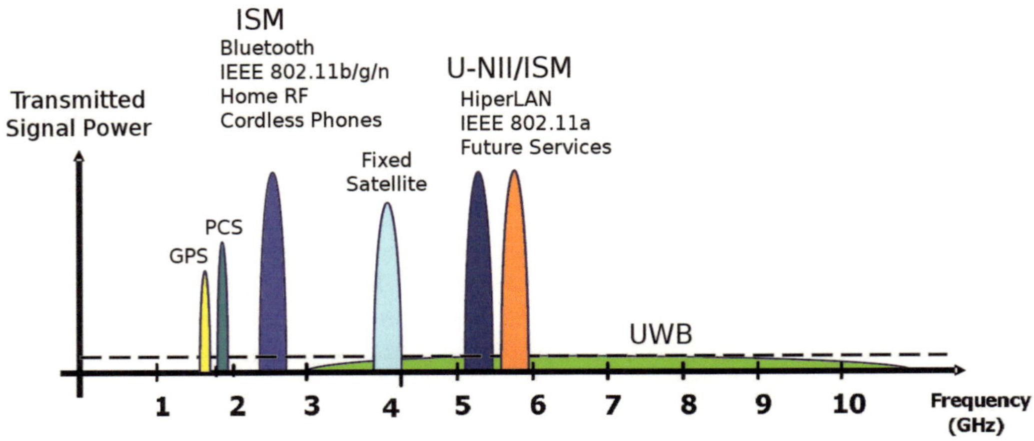

Fig. 4. Narrowband systems and UWB spectrum

A possible solution was discussed by (Zhang et al., 2009). It consists of adapting the UWB pulse to the spectral environment. The UWB pulse can be generated in such a way that its spectral mask exhibits notches in the bands of existing narrow-band wireless services operated in the 3.1-10.6 GHz frequency range. An example of this adaptive pulse is shown in Fig. 5. For this pulse, a limited linear combination of orthogonal pulse wavelets based on prolate spheroidal wave functions (PSWF) and their related auxiliary functions is utilized. The pulse waveform is located in the lower band of 3.1-6.4 GHz, in which several spectral notches (with notch depth of more than 20 dB) are generated, in order to avoid any possible severe interference to the existing narrow-band wireless services, such as radio astronomy, the fixed satellite services, and the 3G wireless communications services.

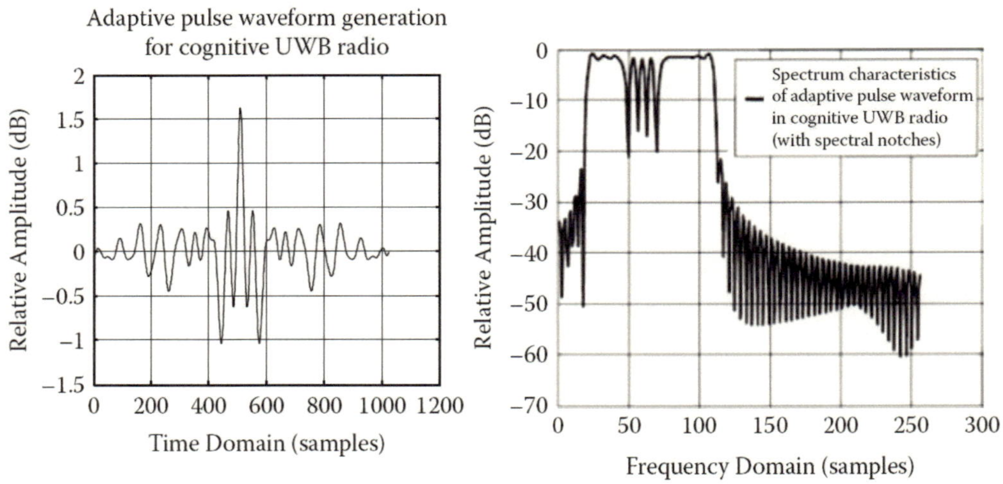

Fig. 5. Adaptive pulse waveform with spectrum-agile characteristics (Zhang et al., 2009)

5. Antennas for cognitive radio

When a CR network implements the opportunistic spectrum access (OSA) approach, secondary users need to identify and use the white space in the spectrum. In this case, the transceiver of the CR device should be ended with an antenna system that can simultaneously sense the channel over a wide frequency range and communicate over a narrow band once the operating frequency is determined.

If UWB is used as the CR enabling technology, UWB antennas can be employed at the transceiver front-end. In the underlay mode, a UWB antenna can be used to transmit/receive the very-low-power pulse. In the overlay mode, the UWB higher-power pulse could be transmitted if the targeted spectrum is completely free of signals of other systems (time white space), or this pulse should be unique and adaptive with spectral notches to avoid strong interference to existing narrow-band wireless services. In both modes, UWB antennas could still be used, however in the overlay mode UWB antennas with controllable frequency notches are more robust.

CR antennas for opportunistic spectrum access

Antennas designed for CR devices operating using the OSA approach are usually dual-port antenna systems with one port used for sensing and the other used for communication. An example of such an antenna is given by (Kelly et al., 2008). This antenna system integrates a UWB antenna (used for sensing) with a narrowband one (used for communication). The UWB antenna, with the ability to sense the spectrum from 3 to 11 GHz, is a coplanar waveguide (CPW) fed wine-glass shape monopole, whereas the other one, with narrowband operation over 5.15 to 5.35 GHz, is a shorted microstrip patch antenna.

The CR antenna system design presented by (Al-Husseini et al., 2010) is comprised of two microstrip-line-fed monopoles sharing a common partial ground. The configuration of the two antennas is shown in Fig. 6. The sensing UWB antenna is based on an egg-shaped patch, obtained by combining a circle and an ellipse at their centers. A small tapered microstrip section is used to match the 50-Ω feed to the input impedance of the patch. The UWB response of the sensing antenna is guaranteed by the design of the patch, the partial ground plane, and the feed matching section. The return loss of the sensing antenna is shown in Fig. 7.

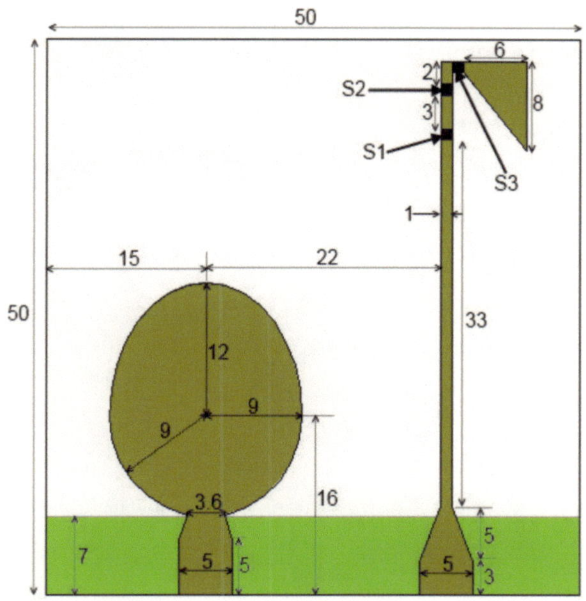

Fig. 6. CR antenna system configuration (Al-Husseini et al., 2010)

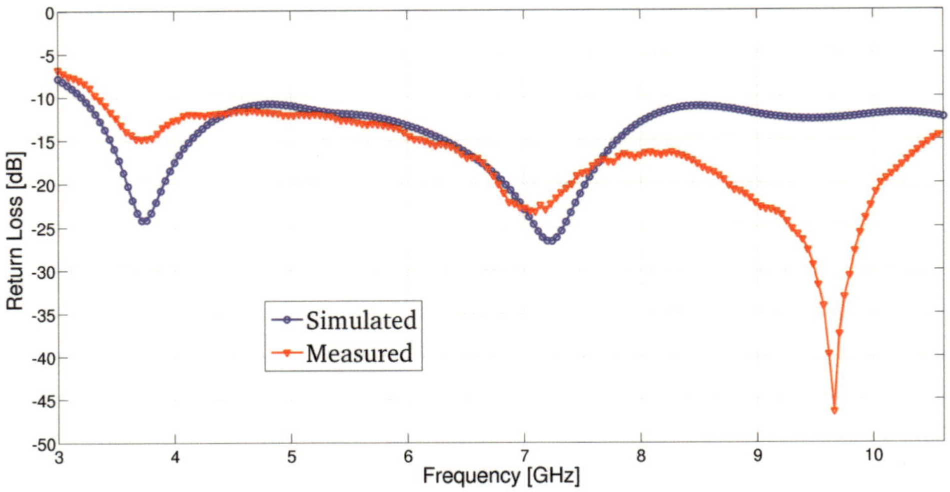

Fig. 7. Return loss of the sensing UWB antenna

The communicating antenna is a combination of a long strip line connected to a 50-Ω feed line via a matching section, and a small triangular conducting part. Two electronic switches are incorporated along the strip line part of the antenna, and a third identical one connects the strip line to the triangular part. By controlling these three switches, the length of the antenna is changed, thus leading to various resonance frequencies in the UWB frequency range. Four switching cases are considered. The resulting measured return loss plots are given in Fig. 8, which shows clear frequency reconfigurability and a coverage of most of the UWB range using only three switches.

The design is simple, low in cost, and easy to fabricate. Both the sensing and communicating antennas have omnidirectional radiation patterns, good peak gain values, and good isolation between their two ports.

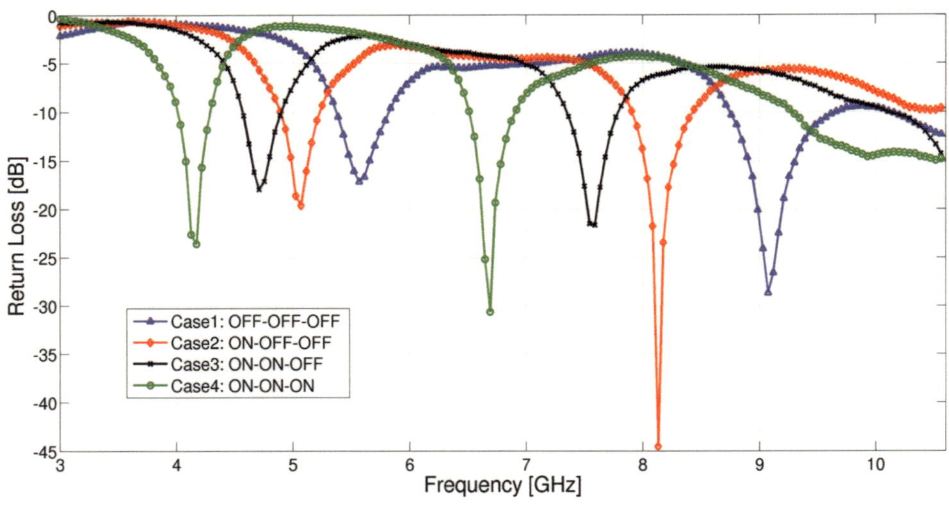

Fig. 8. Measured return loss plots of the communicating antenna

Antennas for UWB-CR

UWB antennas can be used with UWB-enabled CR. The literature is full of research and work pertaining to the design of UWB antennas. (Low et al., 2005) presented a UWB knight's helm shape antenna fabricated on an FR4 board with a double slotted rectangular patch tapered from a 50-Ω feed line, and a partial ground plane flushed with the feed line. Three techniques are applied for good impedance matching over the UWB range: 1) the dual slots on the rectangular patch, 2) the tapered connection between the rectangular patch and the feed line, and 3) a partial ground plane flushed with feed line. Consistent omnidirectional radiation patterns and a small group delay characterize this UWB antenna.
The effect of the ground plane on the performance of UWB antennas is discussed by (Al-Husseini et al., 2009a). Here, two CPW-fed antennas based on the same egg-shaped conductor and same substrate are presented and compared. In the first, the ground plane features a large egg-shaped slot, and in the second, the ground plane is partial and rectangular in shape. The configuration of the two designs is given in Fig. 9. Both designs exhibit UWB response, with Design I offering a larger impedance bandwidth and better omnidirectional radiation pattern but a slightly smaller efficiency.

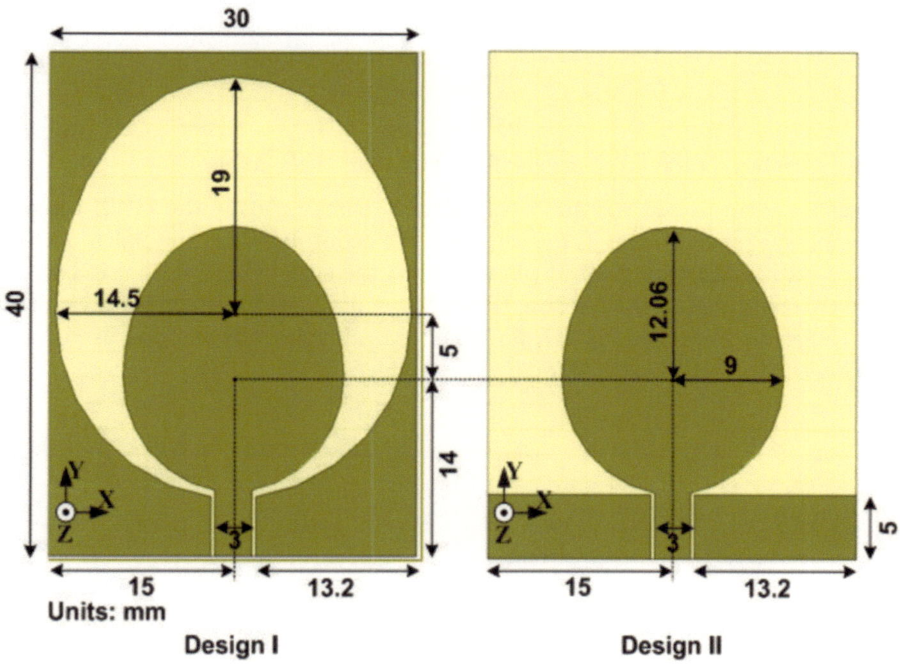

Fig. 9. Configuration of the two UWB designs (Al-Husseini et al., 2009a)

The paper by (Al-Husseini et al., 2009a) presents a low-cost UWB microstrip antenna featuring a microstrip feed line with two 45° bends and a tapered section for size reduction and matching, respectively. The ground plane is partial and comprises a rectangular part and a trapezoidal part. The patch is a half ellipse, where the cut is made along the minor axis. Four slots whose location and size relate to a modified Sierpinski carpet, with the ellipse as the basic shape, are incorporated into the patch. The configuration of this antenna is shown in Fig. 10.

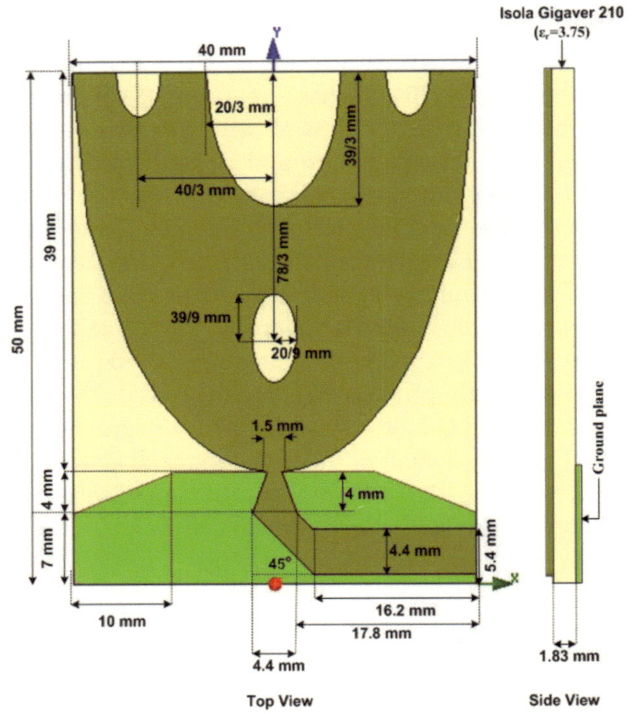

Fig. 10. Configuration of the UWB antenna (Al-Husseini et al., 2009)

Four techniques are applied for good impedance matching over the UWB range: 1) the specially designed patch shape, 2) the tapered connection between the patch and the feed line, 3) the optimized partial ground plane, and 4) the slots whose design is based on the knowledge of fractal shapes. As a result, this antenna has an impedance bandwidth over the 2-11 GHz range, as shown in Fig. 11, and thus can operate in the bands used for UMTS, WLAN, WiMAX, and UWB applications.

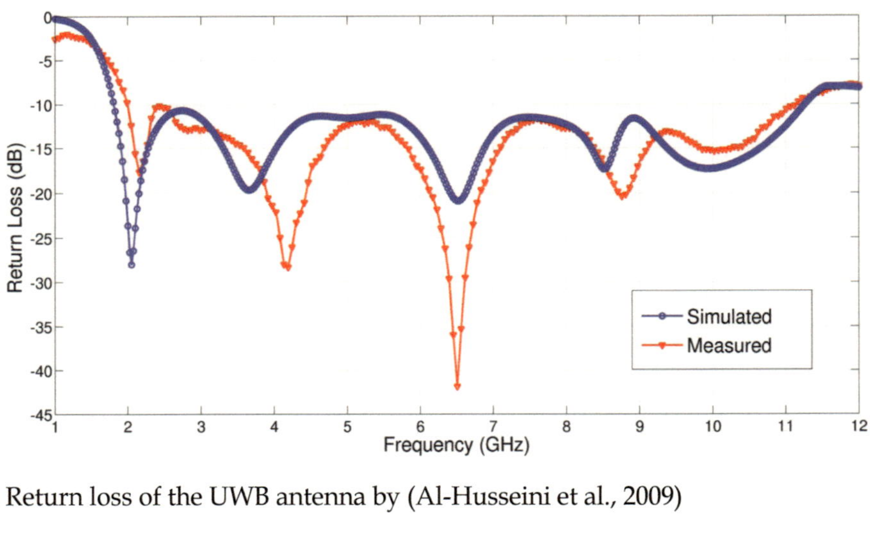

Fig. 11. Return loss of the UWB antenna by (Al-Husseini et al., 2009)

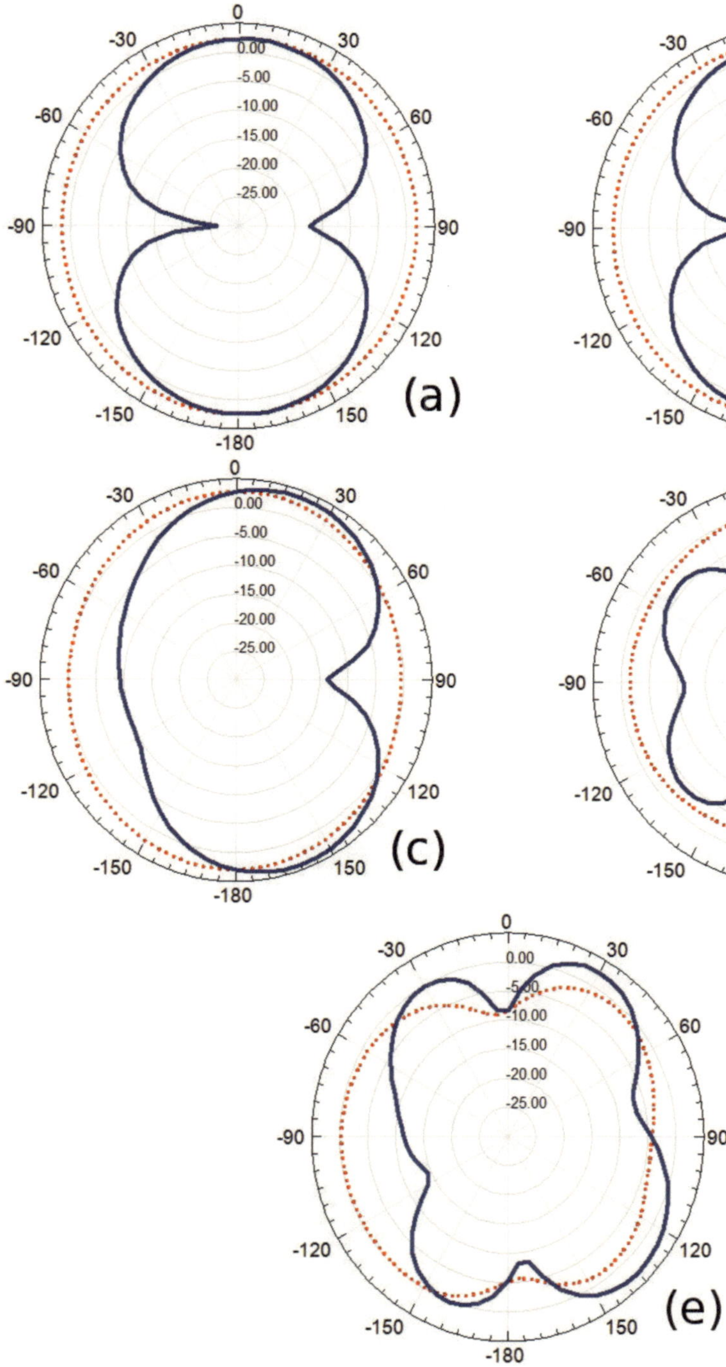

Fig. 12. Patterns in the X - Z plane (dotted line) and Y - Z plane (solid line) for (a) 2.1 GHz, (b) 2.4 GHz, (c) 3.5 GHz, (d) 5.1 GHz, and (e) 7 GHz (Al-Husseini et al., 2009)

Consistent omnidirectional radiation patterns, and good gain and efficiency values characterize this UWB antenna. The radiation patterns are shown in Fig. 12.

In the overlay mode of UWB-enabled CR, UWB antennas with notched bands are tempting. Many UWB antennas with frequency band notches are available in the literature. However, (Al-Husseini et al., 2010a) present a design where the notch is switchable, meaning that it can be turned ON or OFF by controlling an electronic switch. The design makes use of complementary split-ring resonators (CSRRs). A CSRR is etched in the patch of the antenna, and an electronic switch is mounted across its slot. The OFF-state of the switch leaves the corresponding CSRR active, thus causing a band notch. Putting the switch to its ON-state deactivates the resonance of the CSRR and cancels the notch. The configuration of the antenna is illustrated in Fig. 13.
The return loss of the antenna is shown in Fig. 14. The frequency band notch appears when the CSRR is active (switch OFF), and disappears when the CSRR is inactive (switch ON), thus retrieving the UWB response of the antenna. This original UWB response is guaranteed by the design of the original antenna, mainly the use of the partial ground plane and the good matching attained by etching a slit in the ground below the feed.
A variation of this design is obtained by including another CSRR, of a slightly different size, in the patch of the antenna. The combined effect of the two CSRRs leads to a larger and stronger band notch, which still can be canceled by turning both switches (on the two CSRRs) ON. One implication of this variation is the ability to control the width of the notched band.

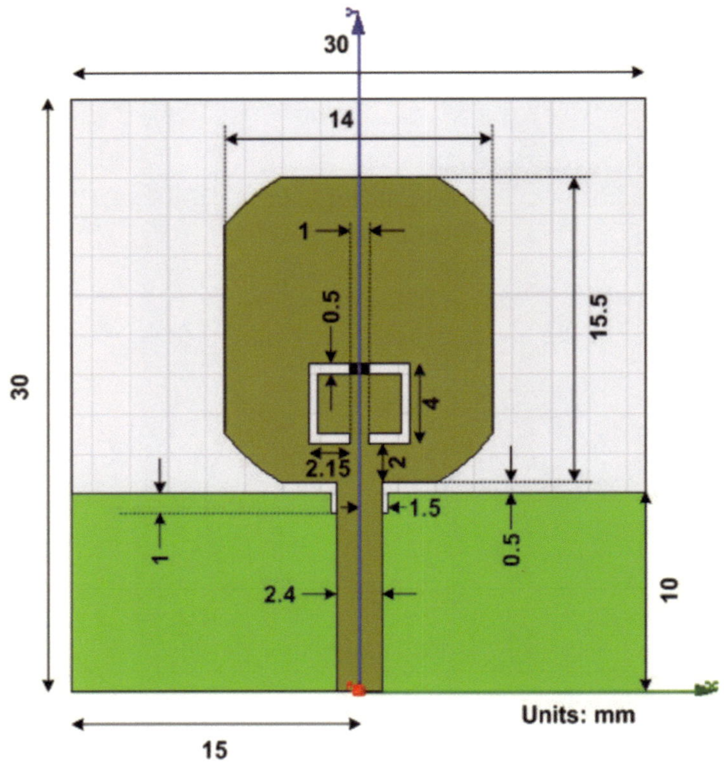

Fig. 13. Configuration of a UWB antenna with switchable band notch (Al-Husseini et al., 2010a)

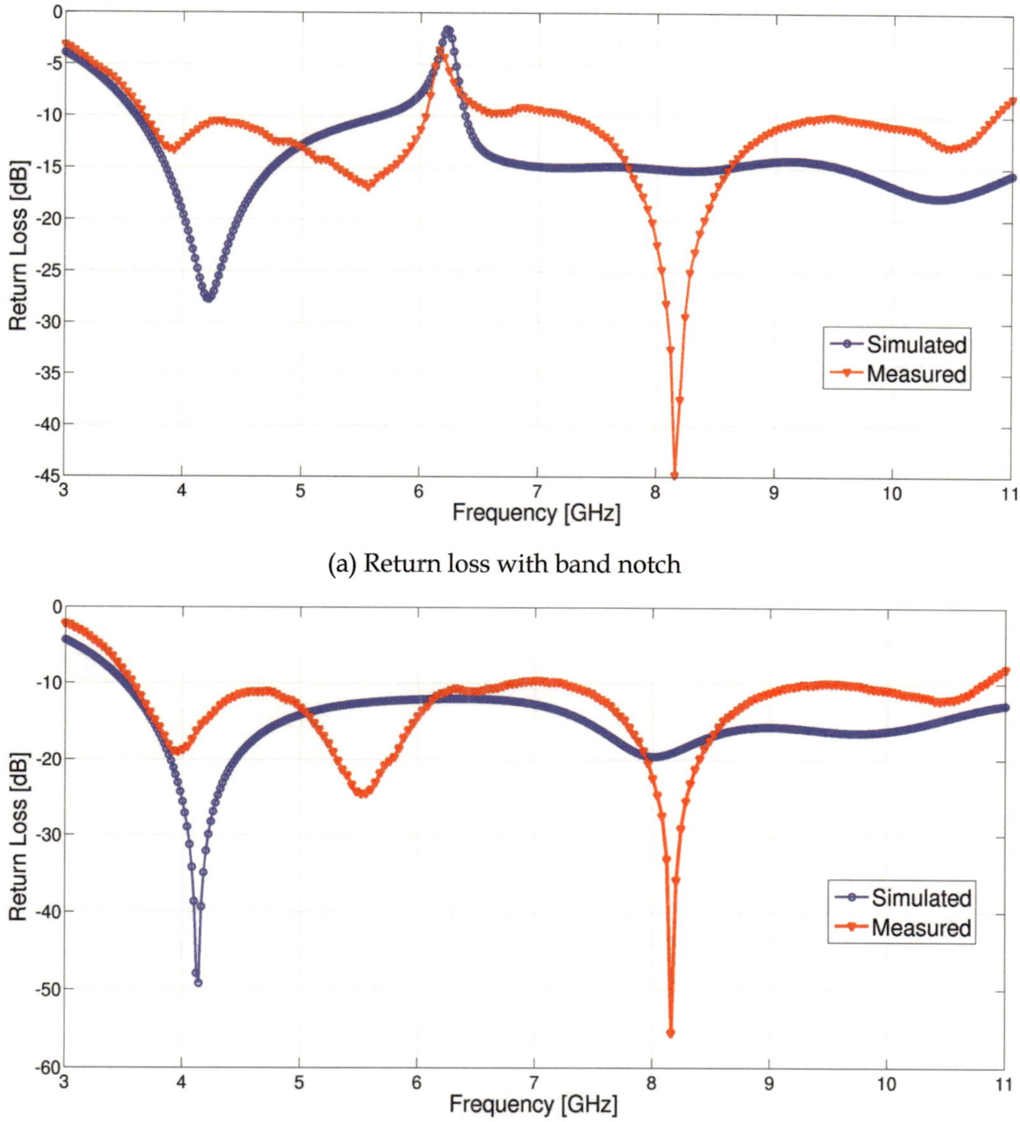

(a) Return loss with band notch

(b) Return loss without band notch

Fig. 14. Notch appears when CSRR is active (switch OFF) and disappears when CSRR is inactive (switch ON) (Al-Husseini et al., 2010a)

6. Conclusion

This chapter has discussed the current spectrum allocation regulations and their shortcomings and has given a general overview of Cognitive Radio and dynamic spectrum access, mainly the exclusive use, the open sharing, and the hierarchical access models of DSA and the difference between the underlay and overlay approaches in the hierarchical access model. The chapter has also discussed the advantages of using UWB as an enabling technology for CR. A major part of the chapter has been a survey of the latest work on antenna design for cognitive radio. Two categories of antennas have been included: antennas that could be used for CR when the OSA approach is implemented, and antennas that could be used for UWB-CR. Further research on both categories of antennas is still under way.

7. References

Al-Husseini, M.; Tawk, Y.; El-Hajj, A. & Kabalan, K.Y. (2009). A low-cost microstrip antenna for 3G/WLAN/WiMAX and UWB applications, *Proceedings of the 2009 international conference on advances in computational tools for engineering applications (ACTEA'09)*, pp. 68–70, ISBN 978-1-4244-3833-4, Jul 2009, Zouk Mosbeh, Lebanon

Al-Husseini, M.; Ramadan, A.; Tawk, Y.; El-Hajj, A. & Kabalan, K.Y. (2009). Design and ground plane consideration of a CPW-fed UWB antenna, *Proceedings of the 2009 international conference on electrical and electronics engineering (ELECO'09)*, pp. II-151–II-153, ISBN 978-1-4244-5106-7, Nov 2009, Bursa, Turkey

Al-Husseini, M.; Tawk, Y.; Christodoulou, C.G.; El-Hajj, A. & Kabalan, K.Y. (2010). A simple dual-port antenna system for cognitive radio applications, *Proceedings of the 2010 international conference on high performance computing and simulation (HPCS'10)*, pp. 549–552, Jun-Jul 2010, Caen, France

Al-Husseini, M.; Costantine, J.; Ramadan, A.; Christodoulou, C.G.; Kabalan, K.Y. & El-Hajj A. (2010). Ultrawideband antennas with switchable band notch using complementary split-ring resonators, *Proceedings of the 2010 international conference on high performance computing and simulation (HPCS'10)*, pp. 560–563, Jun-Jul 2010, Caen, France

Arslan, H. & Sahin, M. (2007). UWB-Based Cognitive Radio Networks, In: *Cognitive Wireless Communication Networks*, Hossain, E. & Bhargava, V.K., (Ed.), 213–230, Springer US, ISBN 978-0-387-68830-5, New York.

Berlemann, L. & Mangold, S. (2009). *Cognitive Radio and Dynamic Spectrum Access*, John Wiley & Sons, ISBN 978-0-470-51167-1, West Sussex, United Kingdom.

Chen, K.-C. & Prasad, R. (2009). *Cognitive Radio Networks*, John Wiley & Sons, ISBN 978-0-470- 69689-7, West Sussex, United Kingdom.

FCC, (2002). *Spectrum Policy Task Force Report*, Tech. Rep. TR 02-155

Kelly, J.R.; Ebrahimi, E.; Hall, P.S.; Gardner, P. & Ghanem, F. (2008). Combined wideband and narrowband antennas for cognitive radio applications, *Proceedings of the 2008 IET seminar on cognitive radio and software defined radios: technologies and techniques*, pp. 1–4, ISBN 978-0-86341-939-3, Sept 2008, London, UK

Low, Z.N.; Cheong, J.H. & Law, C.L. (2005). Low-cost PCB antenna for UWB applications. *IEEE Antennas and Wireless Propagation Letters*, Vol. 4, Aug 2005, 237–239, ISSN 1536 - 1225 NTIA, (2003). *U.S. Frequency Allocation Chart* http://www.ntia.doc.gov/osmhome/allochrt.pdf

Zhang, H.; Zhou, X. & Chen, T. (2009). Ultra-wideband cognitive radio for dynamic spectrum accessing networks, In: *Cognitive Radio Networks*, Xiao, Y. & Hu, F., (Ed.), 353–382, CRC Press, ISBN 978-1-4200-6420-9, Boca Raton, Florida.

21

Methods and Tools for the Temporal Analysis of Avionic Networks

Jean-Luc Scharbarg and Christian Fraboul
Université de Toulouse - IRIT/ENSEEIHT/INPT
France

1. Introduction

Thanks to the Integrated Modular Avionics concept [ARI (1991; 1997)], functions developed for civilian aircraft share computation resources. However, the continual growing number of these functions implies a huge increase in the quantity of data exchanged and thus in the number of connections between functions. Consequently, traditional ARINC 429 buses [ARI (2001)] can't cope with the communication needs of modern aircraft. Indeed, ARINC 429 is a single-emitter bus with limited bandwidth and a huge number of buses would be required. Clearly, this is unacceptable in terms of weight and complexity.

In order to cope with this problem, the AFDX (Avionics Full DupleX Switched Ethernet) [ARI (2002-2005)] was defined and has become the reference communication technology in the context of avionics. AFDX is a full duplex switched Ethernet network to which new mechanisms have been added in order to guarantee the determinism of avionic communications. This determinism has to be proved for certification reasons and an important challenge is to demonstrate that an upper bound can be determined for end-to-end communication delays.

An important assumption is that all the avionics communication needs can be statically described: asynchronous multicast communication flows are identified and quantified. All these flows can be statically mapped on the network of AFDX switches. For a given flow, the end-to-end communication delay of a frame can be described as the sum of transmission delays on links and latencies in switches. Thanks to full duplex links characteristics, no collision can occur on links and transmission delays on links depend solely on bandwidth and frame length. But, as confluent asynchronous flows compete, on each switch output port, highly variable latencies can occur when a frame crosses a switch. Thus it is necessary to analyze these latencies in order to determine the upper bounds on end-to-end communication delays for each flow.

At least three approaches have been proposed in order to compute a worst-case bound for each communication flow of the avionic applications on an AFDX network configuration. They are based on network calculus, trajectories and model checking. Such a worst-case communication delay analysis allows the comparison between the computed upper bounds and the constraints on the communication delays of each flow. Moreover it allows the scaling of the switches memory buffers in order to avoid buffer overflow and frame losses. However, communication delays measured on a real configuration are much lower than the computed upper bound. This is mainly due to the fact that rare events are difficult to observe on a real configuration in a reasonable time.

In order to better understand the real behavior of the AFDX network, a simulation model of the network is proposed as a second step. Such a simulation approach allows the calculation, on the modeled network, of the end-to-end delay for each flow, according to a representative subset of possible scenarios. Thus an end-to-end delay distribution can be obtained for each flow, leading to a better understanding of communication delays. However such an approach cannot be used for certification needs as rare events can be missed by simulation.
This chapter summarizes the assumptions of the AFDX network technology and gives an overview of the different approaches which are used for the temporal analysis of such networks, i.e. the three approaches for the worst-case analysis and the simulation approach for the computation of the distributions of the end to end delays. The approaches are illustrated on a sample configuration and results on a realistic avionic configuration are shown.

2. The end-to-end delay analysis of an AFDX network

This section gives a short overview of an AFDX network and characterizes the end-to-end delay of a flow transmitted on such a network.

2.1 Overview of an AFDX network

The AFDX (Avionics Full DupleX Switched Ethernet) [ARI (2002-2005)] is a switched Ethernet network taking into account avionic constraints. An illustrative example is depicted in figure 1. It is composed of four interconnected switches *S*1 to *S*4. Each switch has no input buffers on input ports and one FIFO buffer for each output port. The inputs and outputs of the network are the *End Systems* (*e*1 to *e*8 in Figure 1). Each end system is connected to exactly one switch port and each switch port is connected to at most one end system. Links between switches are all full duplex.
The end-to-end traffic characterization is made by the definition of *Virtual Links*. As standardized by ARINC 664, Virtual Link (VL) is a concept of virtual communication channel. Thus it is possible to statically define all the flows (VL) which enter the network [ARI (2002-2005)].
End systems exchange Ethernet frames through VLs. Switching a frame from a transmitting to a receiving end system is based on VL. The Virtual Link defines a logical unidirectional connection from one source end system to one or more destination end systems. Coming back to the example in Figure 1, *v*4 is an unicast VL with path {*e*3 - *S*3 - *S*4 - *e*7}, while *v*6 is a multicast VL with paths {*e*1 - *S*1 - *S*2 - *e*6} and {*e*1 - *S*1 - *S*4 - *e*7}.

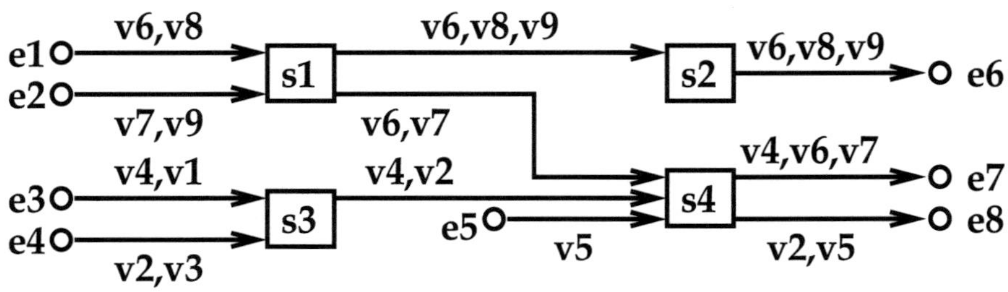

Fig. 1. An illustrative AFDX configuration

The routing is statically defined. Only one end system within the avionics network can be the source of one Virtual Link, (i.e. mono transmitter assumption). A VL v definition also includes the Bandwidth Allocation Gap ($BAG(v)$), the minimum and the maximum frame length ($s_{min}(v)$ and $s_{max}(v)$). $BAG(v)$ is the minimum delay between two consecutive frames of the associated VL (which actually defines a VL as a sporadic flow).
VL parameters ($BAG(v)$, $s_{max}(v)$) compliance is ensured by a shaping unit at end system level and a traffic policing unit at each switch entry port (specificity of AFDX switches, compared to standard Ethernet switches). The delay incurred by the switching fabric is upper bounded by a constant value, i.e. 16 μs.
A realistic AFDX configuration is presented and analyzed in section 7. It includes nearby one thousand VLs. The next paragraph characterizes the end-to-end delay of a VL transmitted on an AFDX network.

2.2 Characterization of the end-to-end delay of a VL

Let's consider a path p_x of a VL v. The end-to-end delay $D(F_v, p_x)$ of a frame F_v transmitted on p_x is defined by

$$D(F_v,p_x) = LD(F_v,p_x) + SD(F_v,p_x) + WD(F_v,p_x) \quad (1)$$

where:

- $LD(F_v, p_x)$ is the transmission delay over the links: thanks to the full duplex characteristic of the AFDX, there are no collisions on the links. Thus, the transmission delay over a link is $t_{byte} \times s(F_v)$ where t_{byte} is the transmission time of one byte and $s(F_v)$ is F_v length. Therefore, considering that all the links have the same bandwidth c (consequently, t_{byte} is the same for all the links),

$$LD(F_v,p_x) = nbl(p_x) \times (t_{byte} \times s(F_v)) \quad (2)$$

  where $nbl(p_x)$ is the number of links in p_x.
- $SD(F_v, p_x)$ is the delay in switches between input and output ports: in the context of this presentation, the delay in a switch from an input port to an output port is considered as a constant td, since the only available information about this delay is a guaranteed upper bound of 16 μs. Thus

$$SD(F_v, p_x) = nbs(p_x) \times td \quad (3)$$

  where $nbs(p_x)$ is the number of switches in p_x.
- $WD(F_v, p_x)$ is the delay in switches and end system output buffers: this delay highly depends on each output port load at the time where F_v reaches it. Thus

$$WD(F_v,p_x) = WD(F_v,p_x,ev) + \sum_{sk \in \Psi_{p_x}} WD(F_v,p_x,sk) \quad (4)$$

  where ev is F_v source end system, Ψ_{p_x} is the set of switches in p_x, $WD(F_v, p_x, ev)$ is the delay in ev output buffer and $WD(F_v, p_x, sk)$ is the delay in sk output port buffer.

Consequently, $D(F_v, p_x)$ can be divided into a fixed part $LD(F_v, p_x) + SD(F_v, p_x)$ and a variable part $WD(F_v, p_x)$. The fixed part can be statically computed since it depends solely on the path p_x, the length of the frame F_v and the bandwidth o the links. The variable part depends on

dynamic characteristics, such as the sequence of frames which are emitted by each VL (the length of each frame) and the offsets between the different VLs, i.e. the emission instant of the first frame of each VL, as it is shown by the following example.
Let's consider the AFDX configuration in figure 2. This configuration includes five unicast VLs $v1...v5$. The parameters of these VLs - their BAGs, frames sizes and paths - are given in table 1. The bandwidth of every link is 100 Mb/s (t_{byte} = 0,08 μs). Figure 3 exhibits three possible scenarios for the transmission of the frames of the five VLs $v1...v5$ on the network in figure 2. The switching delay td is assumed to be null. This means that $SD(Fi, pi) = 0$ for every frame Fi on every path pi. One single BAG of the three considered scenarios is depicted in figure 3. The analysis focuses on the end-to-end delay of the frame F_1 of VL $v1$ (the path is $p1 = e1 - s1 - s3 - e6$). When the length of F_1 is $s_{max}(v1)$ (i.e. 500 bytes), the transmission delay on the links $LD(F1, p1)$ is $3 \times (0{,}08 \times 500) = 120\ \mu s$. When the length of F_1 is $s_{min}(v1)$ (i.e. 300 bytes), this transmission delay $LD(F1, p1)$ is $3 \times (0{,}08 \times 300) = 72\ \mu s$. In figure 3, the frame F_i from VL vi is denoted i.

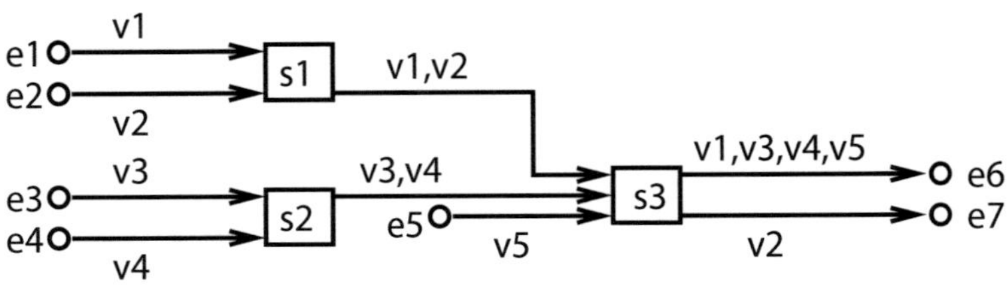

Fig. 2. A sample AFDX configuration

	$BAG(vi)$ (ms)	$s_{min}(vi)$ (byte)	$s_{max}(vi)$ (byte)	path pi
v1	4	300	500	$e1 - s1 - s3 - e6$
v2	4	300	500	$e2 - s1 - s3 - e7$
v3	4	300	500	$e3 - s2 - s3 - e6$
v4	4	300	500	$e4 - s2 - s3 - e6$
v5	4	300	500	$e5 - s3 - e6$

Table 1. Parameters of the sample AFDX configuration

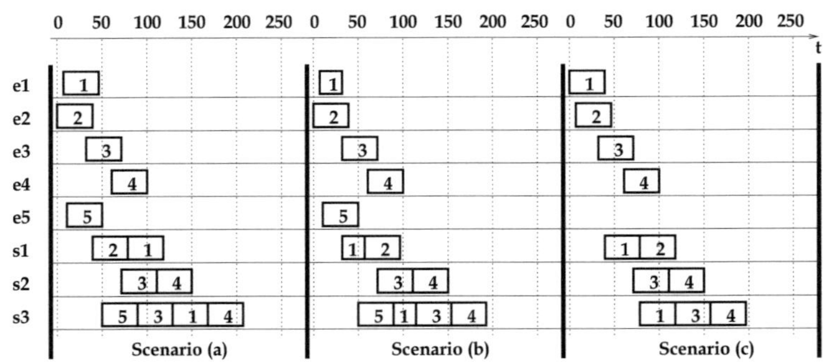

Fig. 3. Three possible scenarios for the sequence of frames

In the scenario **a**, each VL *vi* emits a frame with the maximal length $s_{max}(vi)$. The end-to-end delay of F_1 is 160 μs. It includes the transmission on links (120 μs) and the waiting time in output port buffers (40 μs). Indeed, F_1 waits for frame F_2 in switch *s*1 and it waits for frame F_3 in switch *s*3.
In the scenario **b**, the frames are generated at the same instants as in the scenario **a**, but the length of the frame F_1 of VL *v*1 is now 300 bytes. The end-to-end delay of F_1 is now 107 μs. It includes the transmissions on links (72 μs) and the waiting time in the output port buffer in switch *s*3 (35 μs). The scenarios **a** and **b** show that the length of a given frame can influence its waiting delay in output port buffers.
In the scenario **c**, *v*1, *v*2, *v*3 and *v*4 generate a frame with the maximal possible length (i.e. 500 bytes), while *v*5 does not generate a frame. The instant where the frames from *v*1 and *v*2 are generated are switched in comparison with the two previous scenarios, while these intants are not modified for *v*3 and *v*4. In this scenario **c**, the frame F_1 of *v*1 does not wait in output port buffers. Consequently, its end-to-end delay is 120 μs, i.e. the transmission time on links. This scenario shows that, for a given VL, its offset to the other VLs and the emission or non emission of frames by the other VLs influence its end-to-end delay.
The end-to-end delay analysis of a path p_x of a VL *v* has to take into account all the possible scenarios. This analysis should determine the following characteristics of this end-to-end delay.

- The smallest possible value of the end-to-end delay, which corresponds to the scenarios where the VL *v* emits a frame with minimal length $s_{min}(v)$ which never waits in output ports. This smallest possible value is denoted $D_{min}(v, p_x)$ and it is computed from equations 1, 2 and 3:

$$D_{min}(v, p_x) = nbl_{p_x} \times (t_{byte} \times s_{min}(v)) + nbs_{p_x} \times dt \tag{5}$$

- The highest possible value of the end-to-end delay, which corresponds to the worst case scenario. It is mandatory for the certification of the avionic network. In the general case, finding this worst-case scenario requires an exhaustive analysis of all the possible scenarios. Section 4 presents an approach which implement this exhaustive analysis. Such an exhaustive enumeration is impossible for any realistic configuration, since the number of possible scenarios is huge, due to the number of VLs (around 1000). An alternative solution is the computation of a safe upper bound of the end-to-end delay, based on a modelling of the configuration which over-estimate the traffic and/or underestimate the service offered by the network (pessimistic assumptions). Sections 5 and 6 present two approaches which compute a pessimistic safe upper bound of the end-to-end delay of any VL of an industrial AFDX configuration.
- The distribution of the end-to-end delay between its smallest and its highest possible values. This distribution is valuable when prototyping the whole system. This distribution can be obtained thanks to a simulation approach which is summarized in section 3.

Figure 4 summarizes the characteristics of the end-to-end delay. This delay is always between a minimum and a maximum value. Most of the time, the exact maximum value cannot be computed and it is lower-bounded by the maximum observed value and upper bounded by the computed safe upper bound.

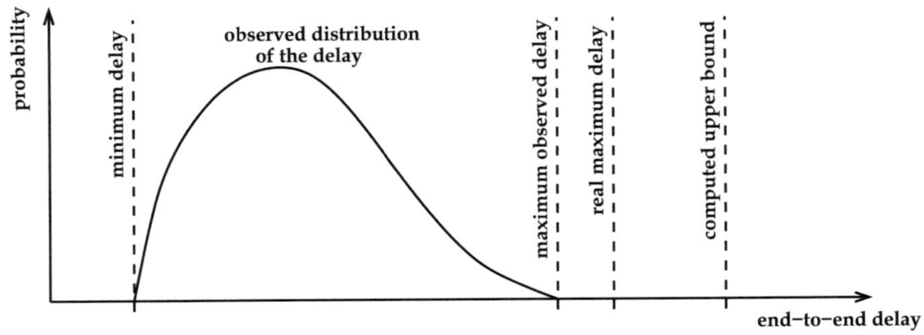

Fig. 4. The end-to-end delay characteristics

3. The simulation approach for the distribution of end-to-end delays

A simulation scenario is characterized by the sequence of frames emitted by each VL and the offsets between the different VLs. It has been previously noted that a typical AFDX network includes around 1000 VLs. Clearly, this leads to a huge set of possible scenarios from which it is difficult to extract a representative subset. The resulting challenge is, for each VL path, to focus on the part of the network that is relevant for this path's end-to-end delay distribution in order to reduce the simulation space. This is a mandatory requirement for the simulation approach. It is fulfilled by means of the VLs taxonomy that is presented in the next section.

3.1 A taxonomy of VLs

The basic idea of the taxonomy is that, given a path *px* of a VL *vx*, the other VLs do not have the same level of influence on it. For example, a *vx* frame can wait for the end of transmission of another frame only if the latter shares at least one output port with *px*. The application of this idea is to focus the simulation on the VLs that influence the end-to-end delay distribution of *vx* frames.

The taxonomy is illustrated considering the unicast VL *vx* in figure 5. Its path *px* is *e*3-*s*3-*s*4-*e*8. The paths or portions of paths of other VLs of this AFDX configuration can be divided into three classes [Charara, Scharbarg & Fraboul (2006)], as depicted in figure 5.

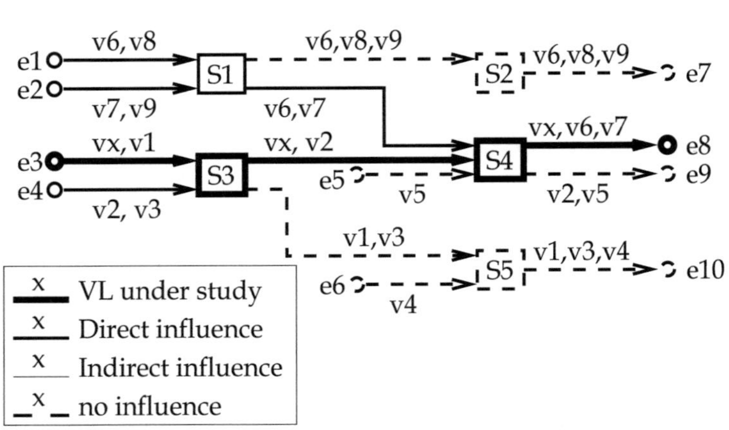

Fig. 5. Taxonomy of VLs

- Class *DI* (Direct Influence) contains all the paths that share at least one output buffer with *px*, truncated after the last output buffer shared with *px*. In figure 5, it contains the whole VL *v7*, path *e1* - *s1* - *s4* - *e8* of *v6* and sub-paths *e3* - *s3* and *e4* - *s3* - *s4* of *v1* and *v2* respectively.
- Class *II* (Indirect Influence) contains all the paths or portions of paths that share no output buffer with *px*, but at least one output buffer with a *DI* or an *I I* path. In figure 5, sub-paths *e1* - *s1* of *v8*, *e2* - *s1* of *v9* and *e4* - *s3* of *v3* are classed as indirect influence portions of VL paths.
- Class *NI* (No influence) contains all the paths or portions of paths that are not in class *DI* or class *II*. It contains all links represented with dashed lines in figure 5.

In this illustrative example containing ten VLs overall, classes *DI* and *II* each contain four and three VLs respectively. Figure 6 shows the partitioning between classes *DI, II* and *NI* for each VL path in a realistic network including 1000 VLs and 6400 paths. The continuous and dashed lines respectively give the number of VLs in class *DI* for each path and the number of VLs in classes *DI* or *II*. In this industrial network, on average, a VL path has 150, 650 and 200 *DI, II* and *NI* VLs respectively.

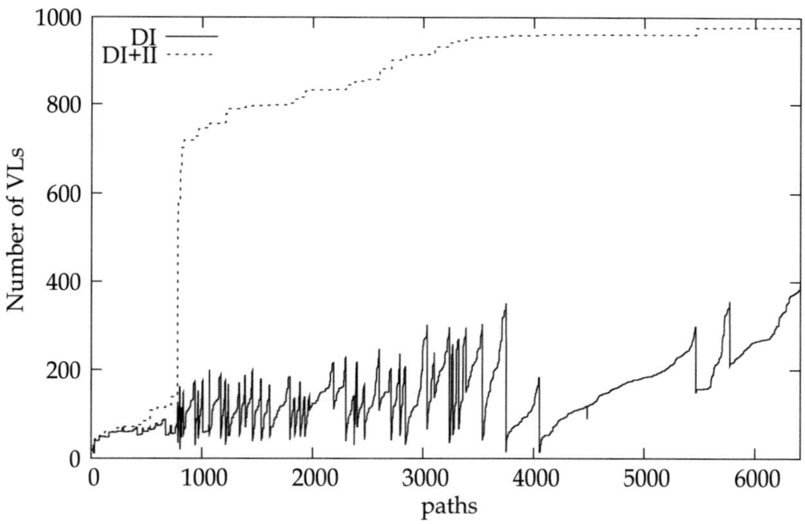

Fig. 6. Industrial configuration taxonomy

Considering this VL classification, VLs in class *NI* clearly have no impact on the end to end delay of their associated path *px*. Thus, VLs in class *NI* will not be considered in the definition of a scenario for a *px* end-to-end delay analysis. For the network analyzed in figure 6, this leads to a drastic reduction of the simulation space for approximately 800 VLs paths (each scenario includes less than 150 VLs instead of nearby 1000). Unfortunately, this reduction is quite poor for the 5600 remaining VLs paths (each scenario includes an average of 800 Vls). In order to obtain a larger reduction of the simulation space, the VL classification has to be exploited more effectively. The main idea concerns VLs in class *II*. They could be ignored in the definition of a scenario for a *px* end-to-end delay analysis provided they have no influence on *px* end-to-end delay distribution. The next section studies the effective influence of VLs in class *II*.

3.2 Effective influence of VLs in class II

The influence of a VL in class *II* on *px* is illustrated with the example depicted in figure 7. It includes one switch *s*1, four end systems *e*1, . . . , *e*4 and three VLs *vx*, *v*1 and *v*2. These three VLs have identical BAGs and frame lengths. Using the taxonomy presented in section 3.1, unicast VL *vx* is directly influenced by *v*1 (class *DI*) and indirectly influenced by *v*2 (class *I I*). Depending on the scenario (phasings for *vx*, *v*1 and *v*2), *v*2 can have an influence on the *vx* end-to-end delay by modifying the *v*1 arrival time at the switch *s*1 output port. The three possible cases are illustrated in figure 8, considering three scenarios. For each of them, figure 8 shows the modification of the *vx* end-to-end delay due to *v*2 frames. For the three scenarios, *v*1 and *v*2 are ready for transmission simultaneously and each *v*2 frame is arbitrarily transmitted before the corresponding *v*1 frame. Thus, the non-transmission of a *v*2 frame advances the arrival time of the corresponding *v*1 frame at the switch *s*1 output port. In scenario *a* in figure 8, this leads to a shorter *vx* end-to-end delay because it allows the *v*1 frame to complete transmission on the *s*1 - *e*3 link before the arrival of the *vx* frame at the *s*1 output port. Conversely, it leads to a longer *vx* end-to-end delay in scenario *b*, because the arrival order of the *vx* and *v*1 frames at the *s*1 output port is inverted and consequently, the *vx* frame has to wait. Finally, the non-transmission has no influence in scenario *c*, because the *vx* frame arrives before the *v*1 one in both cases and as a result never waits.

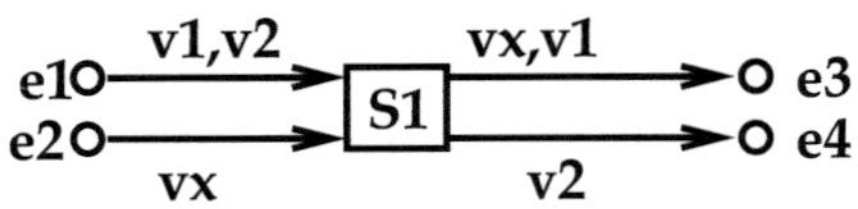

Fig. 7. Example of II Influence

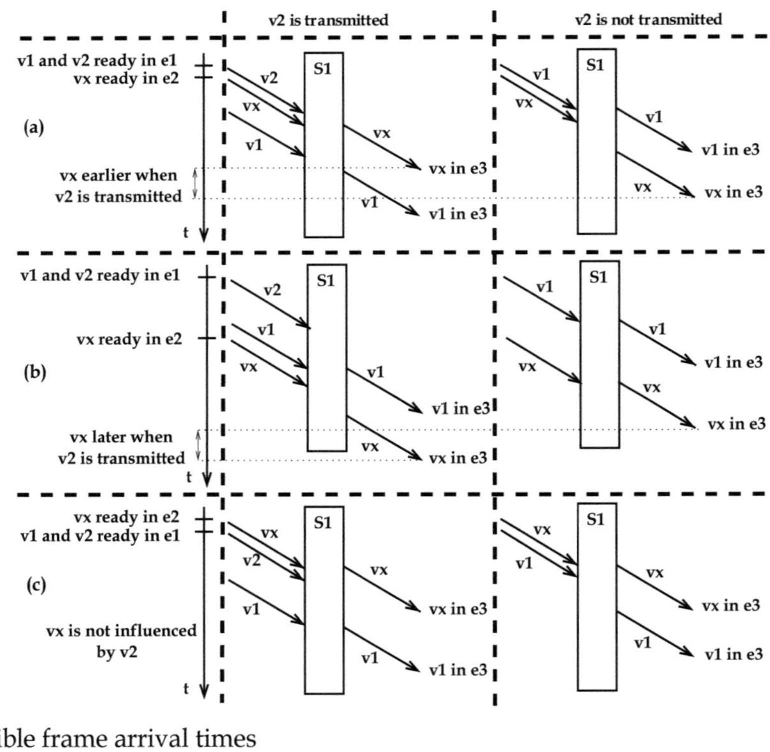

Fig. 8. Possible frame arrival times

Thus, depending on the application scenario, *v*2 frames can shorten, lengthen or have no influence on *vx* end-to-end delays. However, it remains to be seen if VLs in class *II* (e.g. *v*2) modify the end-to-end delay distribution of *px*, their associated VL path.
In order to answer this question, every possible VL path must be examined. The basic idea is to determine, for each VL path, the end-to-end delay distributions considering first, that VLs in class II are present, and second, that they are not present. The goal is to determine whether VLs in class II modify the end-to-end delay distributions (there is at least one VL path for which the two obtained distributions are different) or not (such a VL path does not exist). In the latter case, VLs in class II do not have to be taken into account when determining end-to-end delay distributions.
End-to-end delay distributions are obtained using a simulation approach. The simulation process is detailed in [Scharbarg et al. (2009)]. It considers all the possible kinds of VLs of a typical industrial AFDX configuration. For each considered VL, it compares the distribution of end-to-end delays obtained, first when VLs in class *II* are transmitted, second when VLs in class *II* are not transmitted. The two obtained distributions are the same for all the tested VLs. Thus the conclusion is that VLs in class *II* do not have to be taken into consideration for the computation of *vx* end-to-end delay distribution.
The resulting reduced simulation space makes it possible to determine an experimental probabilistic upper bound for every VL path in a realistic network. The simulation process considers a specific model for each VL path. Since an industrial network configuration includes more than 6000 paths, this leads to a heavy simulation process. A mean of speeding up this process has been presented in [Scharbarg & Fraboul (2007); Scharbarg et al. (2009)]. It consists in building a simplified model for each VL path. Such a model is depicted in Figure 9. It corresponds to a VL path which crosses two switches. The set of componants (switches and end systems) leading to each input port of a switch crossed by the path is modeled by one end system which emits all the VLs crossing this input port. It has been shown in [Scharbarg & Fraboul (2007); Scharbarg et al. (2009)] that this simplification does not modify the computed end-to-end delay distribution.

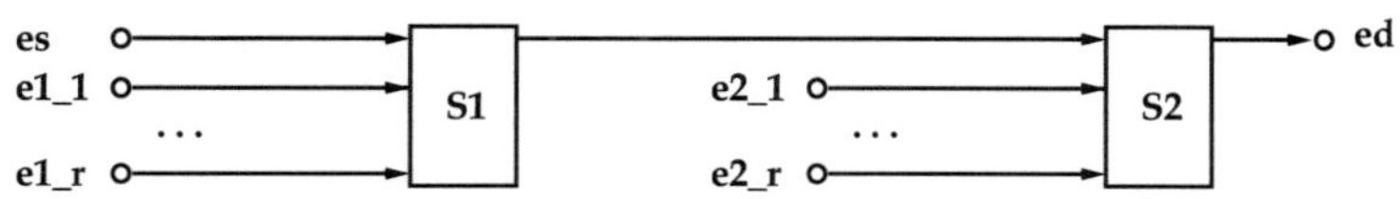

Fig. 9. A generic simulation model

The simplified flow model allows the evaluation of end-to-end delays by queueing network simulation mechanisms. The obtained end-to-end delay distributions give important information for the designer about the real behavior of the applications sharing the AFDX network configuration. Moreover, it provides both an experimental upper bound as well as an estimation of the probability to exceed a given bound.
These experimental upper bounds obtained by simulation are not safe, because simulation mechanisms are unable to efficiently take into account rare events. But safe upper bounds are needed for certification purposes. The next sections present different approaches which allow the computation of such safe upper bounds.

4. The model checking approach for computing exact worst-case delay

The proposed approach is based on a modeling in timed automata. Timed automata have been first proposed in [Alur & Dill (1994)] in order to describe systems behavior with time.

This section first gives a brief overview of timed automata. Then, the modeling of the AFDX network is presented. Finally, the verification process which computes the exact end-to-end delay upper bound is described and applied to the sample configuration in Figure 2.

4.1 Overview of timed automata

A timed automaton is a finite automaton with a set of clocks, *i.e.* real and positive variables increasing uniformly with time. Transitions labels can be:

- a guard, *i.e.* a condition on clock values,
- actions,
- updates, which assign new value to clocks.

The composition of timed automata is obtained by a synchronous product. Each action *a* executed by a first timed automaton corresponds to an action with the same name *a* executed in parallel by a second timed automaton. In other words, a transition which executes the action *a* can be fired only if another transition labeled *a* is possible. The two transitions are performed simultaneously. Thus communication uses the rendez-vous mechanism.

Performing transitions requires no time. Conversely, time can run in nodes. Each node is labeled by an invariant, that is a boolean condition on clocks. The node occupation is dependent of this invariant: the node is occupied if the invariant is true.

Several extensions of timed automata have been proposed. One of these extensions is timed automata with shared integer variables. The principle consists in defining a set of integer variables which are shared by different timed automata. Consequently, the values of these variables can be consulted and updated by the different timed automata [Larsen et al. (1997); Burgueño Arjona (1998)].

A system modelled with timed automata can be verified using a reachability analysis which is performed by model-checking. It consists in encoding each property in terms of the reachability of a given node of one of the automata. So, a property is verified by the reachability of the associated node if and only if this node is reachable from an initial configuration. Reachability is decidable and algorithms exist [Larsen et al. (1997)]. In the general case, reachability analysis is undecidable on timed automata with shared integer variables. In the particular case where the shared variables are represented by nodes of a timed automata, the reachability analysis is decidable.

The approach considered in this paper is based on timed automata with shared integer variables which are represented by nodes of a timed automaton. The modeling of the AFDX with timed automata is now presented.

4.2 The modeling of an AFDX network

The modeling of an AFDX network considers an automaton for each VL and an automaton for each output port of a switch. Figure 10 depicts the timed automaton of a VL with a BAG equal to *period*. This automaton sends a first message $send_i$ ($send_0$ in the example) delayed by a duration between 0 and *period*, and then sends periodically a new message $send_i$ (the period is equal to the BAG of the VL, *i.e. period*). So, this automaton models a periodic VL with an offset between 0 and its BAG.

Figure 11 shows an example of an output port of a switch. Each node of the automaton models a location in the FIFO queue associated to the port. Consequently, the number of nodes of the automaton equals the size of the queue (3 in the example of Figure 11). Each transition from a node $Position_i$ to a node $Position_{i+1}$ of the automaton models the arrival of one frame at the transmit port while each transition from a node $Position_{i+1}$ to a node $Postion_i$ models the end of the transmission from this port. The automaton of the Figure 11 considers two flows (*i.e.* two VLs) received using signals *send*0 and *send*1 and transmitted using signals *send*4 and *send*5, corresponding respectively to *send*0 and *send*1. *delay* is the transmission time of the frame. In the considered example application, all the frames have the same length. *pos*1, *pos*2 and *pos*3 indicate the flows (0 or 1) corresponding to the frames waiting in each position of the queue.

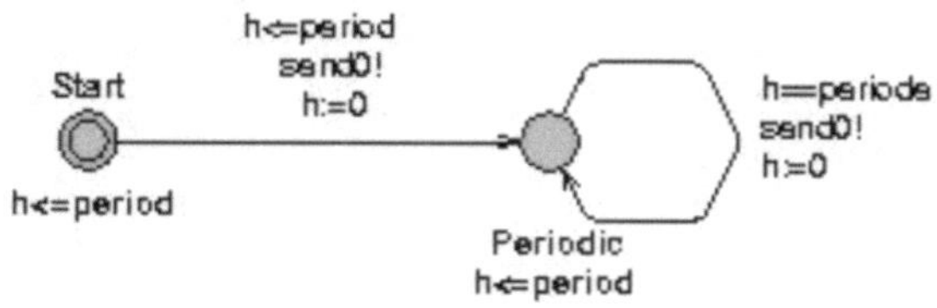

Fig. 10. Automaton of a VL

The global system is obtained by composing the timed automata of the VLs and the outpout ports of the switches. For instance, the network in Figure 2 is composed of 5 VLs and 4 output ports. So, the model is composed of 9 timed automata, as depicted in Figure 12. As an example, VL *v*2 is modelled by the timed automaton *v*2, which sends signal *send*1. This is received by the timed automaton *p1-1* which models the unique output port of the switch *s*1. *v*2 follows the path composed of signals *send*5 and *send*10.

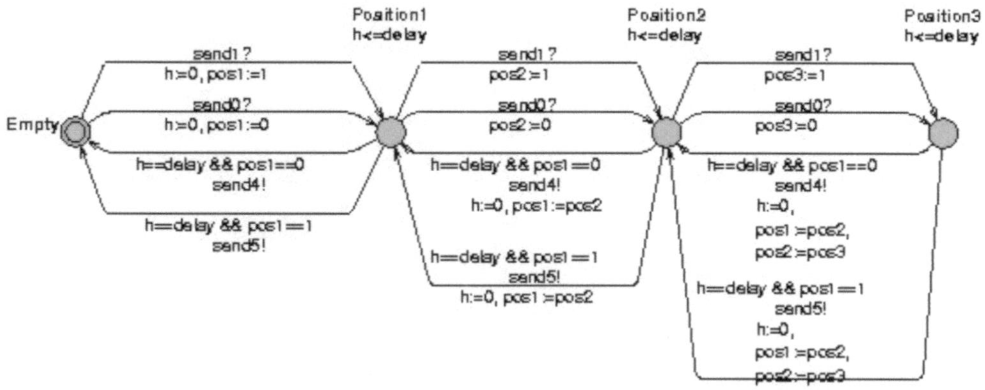

Fig. 11. Automaton of an output port of the switch

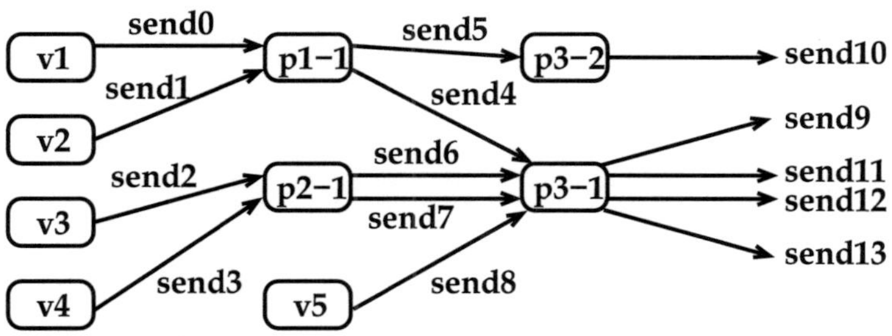

Fig. 12. The global modelled system

4.3 The computation of the exact worst-case end-to-end delay

Using the test automaton method [Burgueño Arjona (1998); Bérard et al. (2001)], the worst case end-to-end delay of each VL is obtained from the model previously described. The test automaton corresponding to the VL $v1$ is depicted in Figure 13. This automaton models the property "delay of $v1$ is less than *bound*". By receiving signal *send*0, it evolves to the node $s2$. Then the signal *send*9 is waited (transmission of $v1$ from the output port of the switch $s3$, see Figure 12). If this signal is not received before the delay of *bound*, the automaton evolves to the node *reject*. This behaviour corresponds to a scenario for which the transmission delay of $v1$ is greater than *bound*. So, the analysis consists in finding the lowest value of *bound* for which the node *reject* is reached. This value is the maximum end-to-end delay.
To verify the property, we use the model-checker *UPPAAL*. The calculation takes less than 1s on a Linux station with a Pentium 4 processor and 2GB of memory size. The exact worst case end-to-end delays obtained for each VLs in the Figure 2 are given in table 2.

VL	Exact worst-case
$v1$	272
$v2$	192
$v3$	272
$v4$	272
$v5$	176

Table 2. EWC end-to-end delays in μs

This approach exhibits the exact worst-case and it is valuable, since it helps to understand the worst-case behaviour of the network. However, it cannot be used for the certification of a realistic network (e.g. the AFDX of the A380), due to the well known combinatorial explosion problem. Therefore, methods which upper bound the end-to-end delay of each flow are used.

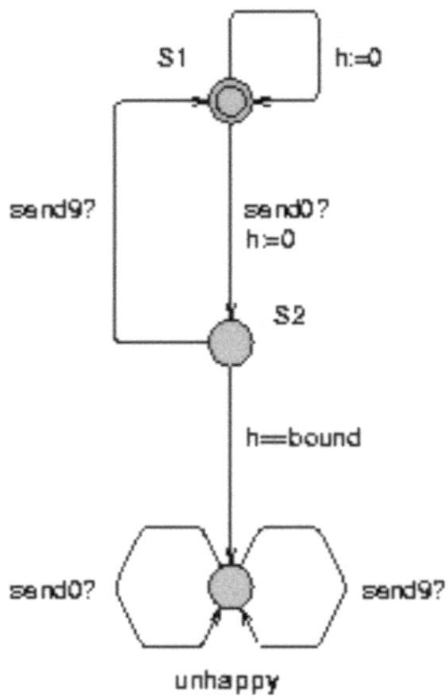

Fig. 13. Test automaton of $v1$

5. AFDX worst-case delay analysis with Network Calculus

Network Calculus [Chang (2000); Le Boudec & Thiran (2001)] has been proposed for the computation of an upper bound for the delay and the jitter of a flow transmitted over a network. It can be used on a set of sporadic flows with no assumption concerning the arrival time of packets.
The basic application of Network Calculus to the AFDX is presented in paragraph 5.1. The improvement of this basic approach in the context of AFDX is described in paragraph 5.2.

5.1 The basic Network Calculus approach for the AFDX

Network Calculus is mathematically based on the (min,+) dioid, for which the convolution $\otimes$ and the deconvolution $\oslash$ are defined as follows:

$$(f \otimes g)(t) = \inf_{0 \le u \le t} \left(f(t-u) + g(u)\right) \quad and \quad (f \oslash g)(t) = \sup_{0 \le u}\left(f(t+u) - g(u)\right) \tag{6}$$

A flow is represented by its cumulative function R, where $R(t)$ is the total number of bits sent up to time t. A flow R is said to have a function α as *arrival curve* if and only if $R \le R \otimes \alpha$. A server has a *service curve* β if and only if for all flow processed by the server, it holds that: $R' \ge R \otimes \beta$, where R is the input flow and R' is the output flow. In that case, $\alpha' = \alpha \oslash \beta$ is an arrival curve for R'.
The delay experienced by a flow R constrained by a service curve α in a node offering a service curve β is bounded by the maximum horizontal difference between curves α and β. This difference is formally defined by:

$$h(\alpha, \beta) = \sup_{s \ge 0}\left(\inf\{\tau \ge 0 \mid \alpha(s) \le \beta(s+\tau)\}\right) \tag{7}$$

Each VL of an AFDX network (a flow) is modeled by a *leaky bucket* $\gamma_{r,b}$, with $b = s_{max}(v)$ and $r = \frac{s_{\max}(v)}{BAG(v)}$. The burst b is the capacity of the bucket and the rate r is the leak rate.
Each output port of an AFDX switch offers a service curve $\beta_{R,T} = R[t - T]^+$. T is the maximal technological latency of the switch, i.e. $16\mu s$. R is the servicing rate (100 Mb/s in our context) and $[x]^+ = max(0, x)$. Thus, in the context of this chapter, the service curve which is offered by each output port is $\beta_{100,16}$.
Figure 14(a) illustrates the delay $h(\alpha,\beta)$ experienced by a flow R constrained by a service curve $\alpha = \gamma_{r,b}$ in an output port of an AFDX switch, provided R is the only flow crossing this output port. The VLs which compete for a given output port are merged into a single flow by summing their respective arrival curves.
The overall computation is illustrated on the small example in Figure 2. Let's consider the VL $v1$. Its arrival curve in S1 is $\alpha_1 = \gamma_{1,4000}$, since $r = \frac{s_{max}(v1)}{BAG(v1)} = \frac{4000}{4000} = 1Mb/s$ and $b = s_{max}(v1) = 4000 bits$. $v1$ shares the output port of $S1$ with $v2$, whose arrival curve in $S1$ is $\alpha_2 = \gamma_{1,4000}$. Consequently, the overall arrival curve for the output port of switch s1 is $\alpha_1 + \alpha_2 = \gamma_{2,8000}$. As previously mentioned, the service curve of this port is $\beta_{100,16}$. Thus, the delay in this output port is bounded by the maximum horizontal difference between $\gamma_{2,8000}$ and $\beta_{100,16}$, which is 96 μs, as depicted in Figure 14(b). It includes the technological latency (16 μs), the

transmission time (40 μs) and the maximum waiting time in the output buffer (40 μs), since each packet of VL $v1$ or $v2$ can be delayed by at most one packet of the other VL.

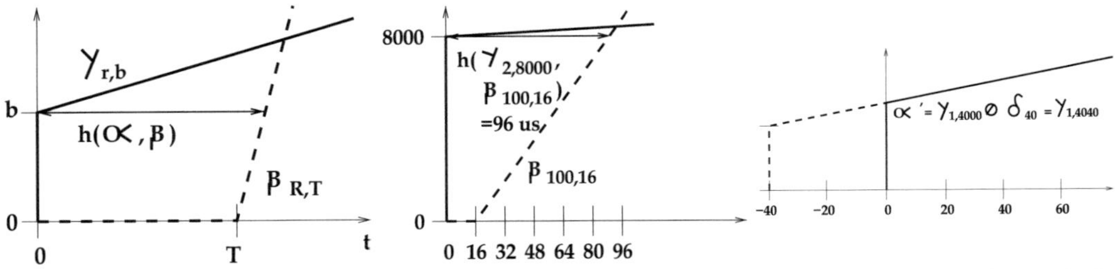

a) The maximum delay $h(\alpha, \beta)$ (b) Output port of switch $S1$ (c) Output curve after switch $S1$ or $S2$

Fig. 14. Curves for network calculus

Then, the computation proceeds to switch $S3$ and it needs the input curves of $v1$, $v3$, $v4$ and $v5$ in $S3$. These input curves are the output curves of the VLs in their previous crossed output port, i.e. $S1$ for $v1$, $S2$ for $v3$ and $v4$, $e5$ for $v5$. In the general case, the output curve α' of the flow is given by: $\alpha' = \alpha \oslash \delta_{jitter}$. α is the input curve of the flow in the port, *jitter* is the maximum jitter encountered by the flow in the port and δ_{jitter} is a guaranteed delay service curve ($\delta_d(t) = 0$ if $t \leq d$, ∞ otherwise). Graphically, it comes down to shift the arrival curve α to the left by the duration of the jitter. The maximum jitter in an output port clearly corresponds to the maximum waiting time in the corresponding buffer. Coming back to $v1$, its maximum jitter when leaving $S1$ is 40 μs, i.e. the maximum waiting time in the output buffer of $S1$. Then, the input curve α'_1 of $v1$ at $S3$ is obtained by shifting α_1 by 40 μs to the left: $\alpha'_1 = \alpha_1 \oslash \delta_{40} = \gamma_{1,4040}$. It is illustrated in Figure 14(c).
Clearly, the input curves of $v3$, $v4$ and $v5$ at $S3$ are respectively $\gamma_{1,4040}$, $\gamma_{1,4040}$ and $\gamma_{1,4000}$. They lead to an overall arrival curve $\gamma_{4,16120}$ in the output port of $S3$. Then, the maximum delay for $v1$ in $S3$ is 177.2 μs, leading to a maximum end-to-end delay of 313.2 μs. It is composed of the transmission delay from $e1$ to $S1$ (40 μs) and the maximum delay computed for $S1$ and $S3$, i.e. 96 μs and 177.2 μs. Column *BNC* in Table 3 summarizes the upper bounds computed with this method for the five VLs of Figure 2.

VL	EWC	BNC	NCG
$v1$	272	313.2	273.6
$v2$	192	192.4	192.4
$v3$	272	313.2	273.6
$v4$	272	313.2	273.6
$v5$	176	217.2	177.6

EWC: exact worst-case (model checking approach)
BNC: basic Network Calculus approach
NCG: Network Calculus approach with grouping

Table 3. Upper end-to-end delays in μs

Results in Table 3 show that, on this small configuration, the basic Calculus approach is pessimistic (more than 40 μs for nearly all the VLs). The next paragraph presents an improvement of the basic Network Calculus approach in the context of AFDX.

5.2 Optimizing the Network Calculus approach with grouping

The pessimism observed in Table 3 is partly due to the fact that the basic Network Calculus approach does not take into account the property that packets of different flows sharing a link cannot be transmitted at the same time on this link (they are serialized). Consequently, the burst considered in the overall input curves of the basic Network Calculus approach can never happen, as soon as at least two flows share the same link. This problem is different from the classical "pay burst only once" case described in [Le Boudec & Thiran (2001)]. Indeed, the objective of "pay burst only once" is to aggregate successive switches in order to give an optimized aggregated service curve. The aggregation of nodes is not possible in our case, since flows can join and leave a path at any switch of the network.

On the example in Figure 2, the input curve of the output port of $S3$ shared by $v1$, $v3$, $v4$ and $v5$ is $\gamma_{4,16120}$. The maximum burst (16120 bits) corresponds to the case where four packets - one for each VL - arrive at the same time in the output port. This is definitely impossible, since $v3$ and $v4$ share the same link. The grouping technique integrates this serialization. It proceeds in two steps. First, the overall arrival curve is computed for each link. It is the minimum between, on the one hand the sum of the arrival curves of all the flows sharing the considered link, on the other hand the curve bounding the burst to the maximum burst among the curves of the different flows sharing the link and the rate to the rate of the link. This first step is illustrated in Figure 15 for a link shared by two flows with arrival curves γ_{r_1,b_1} and γ_{r_2,b_2}. In the second step, the curves obtained for the different links are added. The gain obtained with this technique is due to the reduction of the maximum burst.

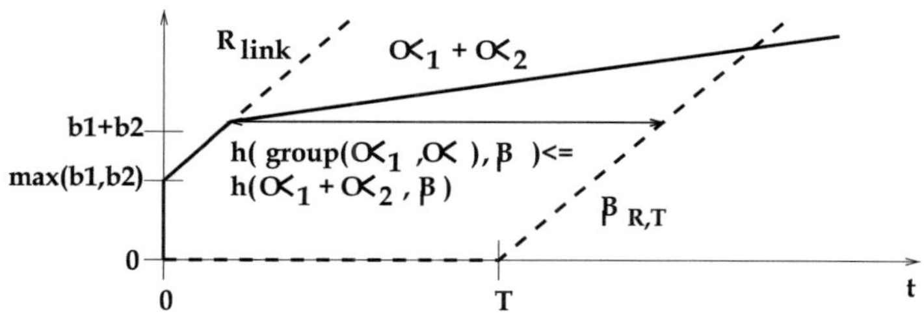

Fig. 15. Grouping flows reduces the maximum delay incurred in an output port

Column NCG in Table 3 gives the upper bounds computed with this technique on the example in Figure 2. Results are clearly improved, compared with the basic Network Calculus approach.

A more recent approach, based on trajectories, has been proposed for the worst-case delay analysis of distributed systems. The next section shows how this approach can be applied and optimized in the context of the AFDX. The main goal is to compare this new approach with the Network Calculus one.

6. AFDX worst-case delay analysis with the Trajectory approach

The Trajectory approach [Martin (2004); Martin & Minet (2006a); Migge (1999)] has been developed to get deterministic upper bounds on end-to-end response time in distributed systems. This approach considers a set of sporadic flows with no assumption concerning the arrival time of packets. The principle of the application of the Trajectory approach to the AFDX has been presented in [Bauer et al. (2009a)]. The improvement of the approach has been proposed in [Bauer et al. (2009b)]. Main features of the Trajectory approach applied to AFDX are summarized and illustrated in Sections 6.1 and 6.2. The proof of the optimization of the Trajectory approach computation is presented in Section 6.3.

6.1 The main features of the Trajectory approach

The approach developed for the analysis of the AFDX considers the results from [Martin & Minet (2006a)]. A distributed system is composed of a set of interconnected processing nodes. Each flow crossing this system follows a static path which is an ordered sequence of nodes. The Trajectory approach assumes, with regards to any flow τ_i following path $\mathcal{P}_i$, that any flow j following path $\mathcal{P}_j$, with $\mathcal{P}_j \neq \mathcal{P}_i$ and $\mathcal{P}_j \cap \mathcal{P}_I \neq \emptyset$, never visits a node of path $\mathcal{P}_i$ after having left this path.

Flows are scheduled with a FIFO algorithm in every visited node. Each flow τ_i has a minimum inter-arrival time between two consecutive packets at ingress node, denoted T_i, a maximum release jitter at the ingress node denoted J_i, an end-to-end deadline D_i that is the maximum end-to-end response time acceptable and a maximum processing time C_i^h on each node N_h, with $N_h \in \mathcal{P}_i$.

The transmission time of any packet on any link between nodes has known lower and upper bounds L_{min} and L_{max} and there are neither collisions nor packet losses on links. The end-to-end response time of a packet is the sum of the times spent in each crossed node and the transmission delays on links. The transmission delays on links are upper bounded by L_{max}. The time spent by a packet m in a node N_h depends on the pending packets in N_h at the arrival time of m in N_h. The problem is then to upper bound the overall time spent in the visited nodes.

The solution proposed by the Trajectory approach is based on the busy period concept. A busy period of level $\mathcal{L}$ is an interval $[t, t')$ such that t and t' are both idle times of level $\mathcal{L}$ and there is no idle time of level $\mathcal{L}$ in (t, t'). An idle time t of level $\mathcal{L}$ is a time such as all packets with priority greater than or equal to $\mathcal{L}$ generated before t have been processed at time t. With FIFO scheduling, no packet from the busy period of level corresponding to the priority of m could have arrived after m on the considered node.

The Trajectory approach considers a packet m from flow τ_i generated at time t. It identifies the busy period and the packets impacting its end-to-end delay on all the nodes visited by m (starting from the last visited node backward to the ingress node). This decomposition enables the computation of the latest starting time of m on its last node. This starting time can be computed recursively and leads to the worst case end-to-end response time of the flow τ_i. This computation will be illustrated in the context of AFDX.

The elements of the system considered in the Trajectory approach are instantiated in the following way in the context of AFDX:

- each node of the system corresponds to an AFDX switch output port, including the output link,
- each link of the system corresponds to the switching fabric,
- each flow corresponds to a VL path.

The assumptions of the Trajectory approach are verified by the AFDX (see Section 2.1). Indeed, switch output ports implement FIFO service discipline. The switching fabric delay is upper bounded by a constant value (16 μs), thus $L = L_{min} = L_{max} = 16\ \mu s$. There are no collisions nor packet loss on AFDX networks. The routing of the VLs is statically defined.

VL parameters match the definition of sporadic flows in the following manner: $T_i = BAG$, $C_i^h = s_{max}/R$, $J_i = 0$. Since all the AFDX ports work at the same rate $R = 100Mb/s$, $C_i^h = C_i = s_{max}/R$ for every node h in the network.

6.2 Illustration on a sample AFDX configuration

Let us consider the sample AFDX configuration depicted in Figure 2. Figure 16(a) shows an arbitrary scheduling of the packets, which are identified by their VL numbers (e.g. packet 3 is a packet from VL $v3$). The scheduling in Figure 16(a) focuses on packet 3. The arrival time of a packet m in a node N_h is denoted $a_m^{N_h}$. Time origin is arbitrarily chosen as the arrival time of packet 3 in node $e3$. The processing time of a packet in a node is 40 μs. It corresponds to the transmission time of the packet on a link. The delay between the end of the processing of a packet by a node and its arrival in the next node corresponds to the 16 μs switch factory delay. Due to the FIFO policy, packet 3 is delayed by packet 4 in $S2$. In node $S3$, packet 5 is delayed by packet 1 and delays packet 4, which delays packet 3.

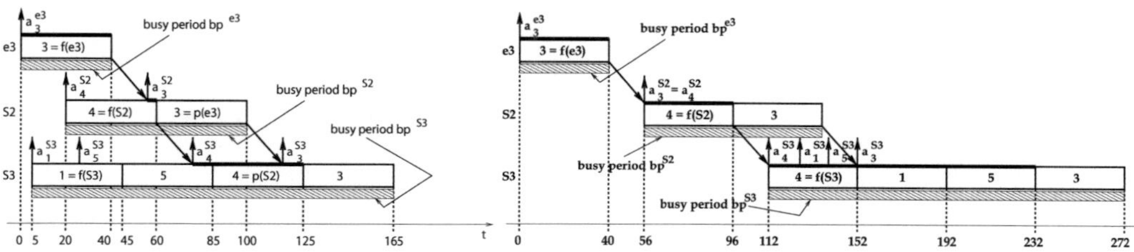

(a) An arbitrary scheduling of packets (b) Latest starting time of packet 3

Fig. 16. Two possible scheduling of packets

Packet 3 from VL $v3$ crosses three busy periods (bp^{e3}, bp^{S2}, and bp^{S3}) on its trajectory, corresponding to the three nodes $N_1 = e3$, $N_2 = S2$ and $N_3 = S3$. Let $f(N_i)$ be the first packet which is processed in the busy period bp^{N_i} during which packet 3 is processed. Considering the scheduling in Figure 16(a), we have $f(e3) = 3$, $f(S2) = 4$ and $f(S3) = 1$. As flows do not necessarily follow the same path in the network, it is possible that packet $f(N_i)$ does not come from the same previous node N_{i-1} as packet 3. This case occurs in node $S2$, where packet 4 comes from node $e4$. It also occurs in node $S3$, where packet 1 comes from node $S1$. Therefore, $p(N_{i-1})$ is defined as the first packet which is processed in bp^{N_i} and comes from node N_{i-1}. Considering the scheduling in Figure 16(a), we have $p(e3) = 3$ and $p(S2) = 4$.

The starting time of packet 3 in node $S3$ is obtained by adding parts of the three busy periods bp^{e3}, bp^{S2}, and bp^{S3} to the delays between the nodes, i.e. 2×16 μs. From [Martin & Minet (2006a)], the part of the busy period bp^{N_i} which has to be added is the processing time of packets between $f(N_i)$ and $p(N_i)$ minus the time elapsed between the arrivals of $f(N_i)$ and $p(N_{i-1})$, i.e. $a_{p(N_{i-1})}^{N_i} - a_{f(N_i)}^{N_i}$. On the example in Figure 16(a), the parts which have to be considered are the transmission of packet 3 in node $e3$, the time elapsed between the arrival of packet 3 and the end of processing of packet 4 in node $S2$, the time elapsed between the arrival of packet 4 and the end of processing of packet 5 in node $S3$. These parts are shown by thick lines on top of the packets in Figure 16(a). The starting time of packet 3 in node $S3$ on the example in Figure 16(a) is 125 μs.

It has been shown [Martin & Minet (2006a)] that the latest starting time of a packet m in its last node is reached when $(a^{N_i}_{p(N_{i-1})} - a^{N_i}_{f(N_i)}) = 0$ for every node N_i on the path of m. It comes to postpone the arrival time of every packet joining the path of m in the node N_i in order to maximize the waiting time of m in N_i.

The result of this postponing on the example in Figure 16(a) is illustrated in Figure 16(b). The arrival time of packet 4 at node $S2$ is postponed to the arrival time of packet 3 at node $S2$. In node $S3$, packets 1 and 5 have been postponed in order to arrive between packet 4 and 3. Then, the worst case end-to-end delay of a packet is obtained by adding its latest starting time on its last visited node and its processing time in this last node. For packet 3 in Figure 16(b), this worst case end-to-end delay is 232 + 40 = 272 μs. More precisely, this delay includes the transmission times of packet 3 on node $e3$, packet 4 on node $S2$ and packets 4, 1, 5 and 3 on node $S3$. On this example, it can be seen that packets 3 and 4 are counted twice. Actually, it has been shown [Martin & Minet (2006a)] that exactly one packet has to be counted twice in each node, except the slowest one. In the context of the AFDX, all the nodes work at the same speed. Thus, the slowest node is arbitrarily chosen as the last one. In the example in Figure 16(b), packet 3 and 4 are respectively counted twice in nodes $e3$ and $S2$. Packet 3 is the longest one transmitted in nodes $e3$ and $S2$, while packet 4 is the longest one transmitted in node $S2$ and $S3$.

In the context of an AFDX network, it is not always possible to find a scheduling which cancels the term $(a^{N_i}_{p(N_{i-1})} - a^{N_i}_{f(N_i)})$ for every node N_i, as proposed in [Martin & Minet (2006a)]. Let us consider VL $v5$ of the example depicted in Figure 2. bp^{S3} is the busy period of level corresponding to the priority of packet 5. In order to maximize the delay of packet 5 in bp^{S3}, the arrival time of packets 3 and 4 in $S3$ have to be as large as possible, but not larger than the arrival time of packet 5 in node $S3$, because of the FIFO scheduling policy:

$$a_3^{S3} \leq a_5^{S3} \text{ and } a_4^{S3} \leq a_5^{S3} \quad (8)$$

Since the two packets come from the same link, they are already serialized:

$$\left| a_3^{S3} - a_4^{S3} \right| \geq C = 40 \mu s \quad (9)$$

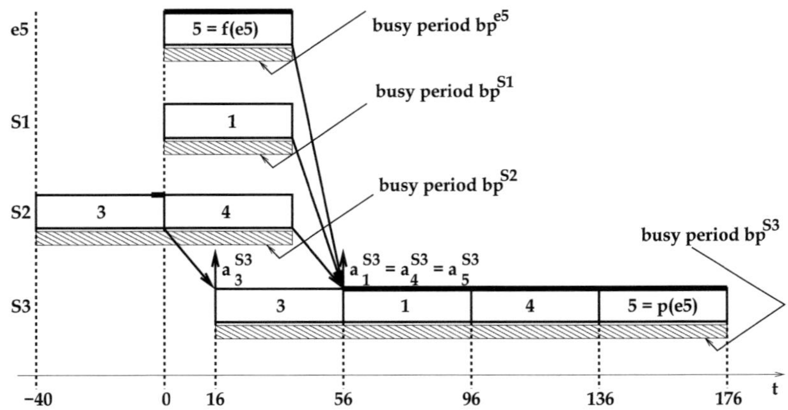

Fig. 17. Latest starting time of VL $v5$

Without loss of generality, let us consider that packet 3 arrives before packet 4. From (8) and (9), we have:

$$a_4^{S3} = a_5^{S3} \text{ and } a_3^{S3} = a_5^{S3} - 40\ \mu s \tag{10}$$

The resulting worst-case scheduling is depicted in Figure 17. $p(e5)$ is packet 5 and f(S3) is packet 3. From (10), we have $(a_{p(e5)}^{S3} - a_{f(S3)}^{S3}) \geq 40\ \mu s$ for any possible scheduling. Thus, considering that $(a_{p(N_{i-1})}^{N_i} - a_{f(N_i)}^{N_i}) = 0$ for every node N_i is a pessimistic assumption in the context of the AFDX.

The next section presents the implementation of the Trajectory approach.

6.3 Optimization of the Trajectory approach computation

The computation of the worst-case end-to-end delay a packet of a flow τ_i has been formalized in [Martin & Minet (2006a)]. In our context, all the nodes work at the same rate and the jitter in each emitting node is null. Thus, the worst case end-to-end response time of any flow τ_i is bounded by:

$$R_i = \max_{t \geq 0}\left(W_{i,t}^{last_i} + C_i - t\right) \tag{11}$$

$last_i$ is the last visited node of flow τ_i and $W_{i,t}^{last_i}$ is a bound on the latest starting time of a packet m generated at time t on its last visited node. The definition of $W_{i,t}^{last_i}$ given in [Martin & Minet (2006a)] becomes:

$$W_{i,t}^{last_i} =$$

$$\sum_{\substack{j \in [1,n] \\ j \neq i \\ \mathcal{P}_j \cap \mathcal{P}_i \neq \varnothing}} \left(1 + \left\lfloor \frac{t + A_{i,j}}{T_j} \right\rfloor\right) \cdot C_j \tag{11}$$

$$+ \left(1 + \left\lfloor \frac{t}{T_i} \right\rfloor\right) \cdot C_i \tag{12}$$

$$+ \sum_{\substack{h \in \mathcal{P}_i \\ h \neq last_i}} \left(\max_{\substack{j \in [1,n] \\ h \in \mathcal{P}_j}} \{C_j\} \right) \tag{13}$$

$$+ (|\mathcal{P}_i| - 1) \cdot L_{max} \tag{14}$$

$$- \sum_{\substack{N_h \in \mathcal{P}_i \\ N_h \neq first_i}} (\Delta_{N_h}) \tag{15}$$

$$-C_i \tag{16}$$

Where

$$\Delta_{N_h} = a^{N_h}_{p(N_{h-1})} - a^{N_h}_{f(N_h)} \tag{17}$$

Term (11) corresponds to the processing time of packets from every flow τ_i crossing the flow τ_i and transmitted in the same busy period as m. $A_{i,j}$ integrates the maximum jitter of packets from τ_i and τ_j on their first shared output port.

Term (12) is the processing time, on one node, of the packets of the flow τ_j which are transmitted in the same busy period as m.

Term (13) is the processing time of the longest packet for each node of path $\mathcal{P}_i$, except the last one. It represents the packets which have to be counted twice, as explained before.

Term (14) corresponds to the sum of switching delay.

Term (15) sums for each node N_h in $\mathcal{P}_i$ the duration between the beginning of the busy period and the arrival of the first packet coming from the preceding node in $\mathcal{P}_i$, i.e. N_{h-1}. This term is null in the context of [Martin & Minet (2006a)].

C_i is subtracted, because $W^{last_i}_{i,t}$ is the latest starting time and not the ending time of the packet from τ_i on its last node.

Solving $R_i = \max(W^{last_i}_{i,t} + C_i - t)$ comes to find the maximum vertical deviation between the function $t \mapsto W^{last_i}_{i,t} + C_i$ and the identity function $t \mapsto t$.

The optimization of this computation in the context of the AFDX concerns Term (15). Indeed, it has been shown in Section 6.2 that, for some VLs, there exists no scheduling leading to $\Delta_{N_h} = 0, \forall N_h \in \mathcal{P}_i$.

In the following, we describe the computation of a lower bound on $\Delta_{N_h} \forall N_h \in \mathcal{P}_i$ and we prove its correctness.

The value of Δ_{N_h} is illustrated in Figure 18.

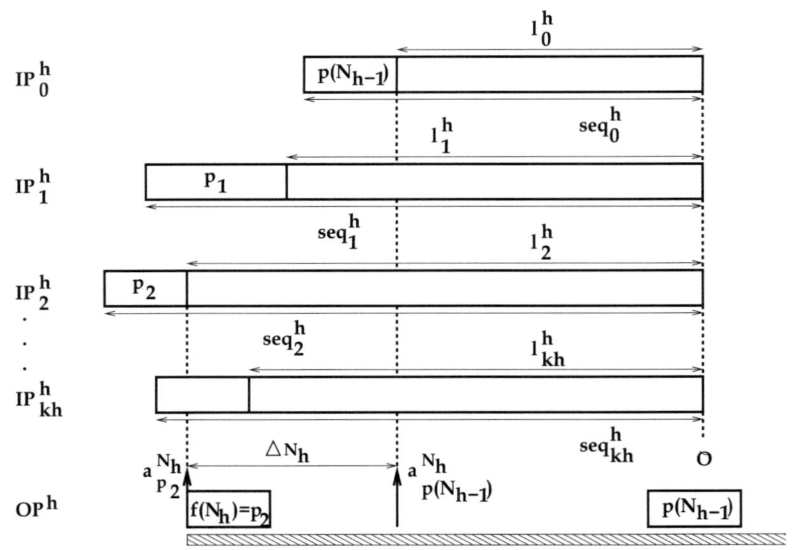

Fig. 18. Illustration of Δ_{N_h}

The packet m of flow τ_i under study is sent on the output link OP^h in a busy period bp^{N_h}. The packets which compose bp^{N_h} are determined thanks to terms (11) and (12). These packets are grouped by input link. IP_0^h is the input link of τ_i, while $IP_x^h(1 \le x \le k_h)$ are the other input links. Sequence $seq_x^h(0 \le x \le k_h)$ contains the packets of bp^{N_h} coming form IP_x^h. In order to maximize the delay of packet m in node N_h, each sequence $seq_x^h(1 \le x \le k_h)$ is postponed so that it finishes at the same time as sequence seq_0^h. This finishing time is denoted θ in Figure 18. This construction is a generalization of the Trajectory approach presented in [Martin & Minet (2006a)]: instead of postponing individually each packet, sequences of already serialized packets are postponed. As defined in (17), Δ_{N_h} is the delay between the earliest arrival of a packet of bp^{N_h} (i.e. the beginning of bp^{N_h}) and the arrival of the first packet of bp^{N_h} coming from IP_0^h. In Figure 18, Δ_{N_h} is the difference between the arrival of $p2$ and the arrival of $p(N_{h-1})$.

The latest starting time of m in its last node is maximized when $\sum_{\substack{N_h \in \mathcal{P} \\ N_h \neq first_{i\,i}}} \left(\Delta_{N_h}\right)$ is minimized. It comes to determine the lower bound of each term Δ_{N_h} of the sum.

From (17), it is obvious that the minimum value of Δ_{N_h} is obtained by minimizing $a_{p(N_{h-1})}^{N_h}$ and maximizing $a_{f(N_h)}^{N_h}$.

Let us define $l_x^h(0 \le x \le k_h)$ as the duration of sequence seq_x^h without its first packet. Then, we have:

$$a_{f(N_h)}^{N_h} = \theta - \max_{1 \le x \le k_h} l_x^h \quad and \quad a_{p(N_{h-1})}^{N_h} = \theta - l_0^h \tag{18}$$

Consequently, minimizing $a_{p(N_{h-1})}^{N_h}$ comes to maximize l_0^h. It is obtained when the smallest packet of sequence seq_0^h is transmitted at the beginning of seq_0^h.

Similarly, maximizing $a_{f(N_h)}^{N_h}$ comes to minimize each l_x^h for $1 \le x \le k_h$. It is obtained when the largest packet of sequence seq_x^h is transmitted at the beginning of seq_x^h, for $1 \le x \le k_h$.

To summarize, Δ_{N_h} is lower bounded by the maximum of 0 and:

$$\max_{1 \le x \le k_h}\left(\min\left(l_x^h\right)\right) - \max\left(l_0^h\right) \tag{19}$$

7. Analysis of a realistic configuration

The realistic AFDX network considered in this chapter is composed of two redundant networks [Charara, Scharbarg, Ermont & Fraboul (2006)]. Each network includes 123 end systems, 8 switches, 964 Virtual Links and 6412 VL paths (due to VL multicast characteristics). The left part in Table 4 gives the dispatching of VLs among BAGs. It can be seen that BAGs are harmonic between 2 and 128. The right part in Table 4 gives the dispatching of VLs among frame lengths, considering the maximum length s_{max}. The majority of VLs consider short frames. Table 5 shows the number of VL paths per length (i.e. the number of crossed switches).

BAG (ms)	Number of VL
2	20
4	40
8	78
16	142
32	229
64	220
128	255

Frame length (bytes)	Number of VL
0-150	561
151-300	202
301-600	114
601-900	57
901-1200	12
1201-1500	35
> 1500	3

Table 4. BAGs and frame lengths

Nb of crossed switches	Number of paths
1	1797
2	2787
3	1537
4	291

Table 5. VL paths lengths

The temporal analysis of this realistic configuration has been conducted. Table 6 summarizes the results obtained by the safe upper bound computation. As previously mentioned, the model checking approach cannot be applied on such large scale configurations. Both the Network Calculus and the Trajectory approaches have been implemented using Python programming language. Upper bounds of the end-to-end delays for each VL path of the realistic configuration have been computed with this tool. This computation takes less than two minutes for any approach on a Pentium 4 processor running at 2.8 GHz. Table 6 gives for both approaches the average upper bounds among all the VLs of the configuration, as well as the minimum and the maximum upper bounds. The obtained upper bounds are slightly tighter with the trajectory approach.

	Network calculus	Trajectories
Minimum	0.386 *ms*	0.293 *ms*
Average	4.532 *ms*	4.247 *ms*
Maximum	13.194 *ms*	12.949 *ms*

Table 6. Safe upper bounds on the industrial configuration

The end-to-end delay distributions have been computed for the VLs of the realistic configuration, thanks to a home made tool implementing the simulation approach presented in Section 3. Table 7 gives the results obtained for five VL paths. Table 7 gives, for each VL path, the BAG, the minimum and the maximum frame sizes, the number of crossed switches (hops) and the load in each output port. For instance, vl_4 crosses three switches. It shares its end system output port with 5 other VLs. Similarly, vl_4 shares the output port of its first crossed switch with 79 VLs and the output ports of the two consecutive ones with 34 and 49 VLs.

	Characteristics					Delay			
	BAG	s_{min}	s_{max}	Hops	Load	Min	Upper bound		
							Simu	NC	Traj
vl_1	128	263	263	1	8, 6	0.058	0.162	0.364	0.463
vl_2	8	84	467	1	5, 46	0.090	0.248	1.171	1.017
vl_3	64	91	91	1	8, 135	0.030	0.351	3.944	3.554
vl_4	8	84	467	3	5, 79, 34, 49	0.197	0.603	4.752	4.683
vl_5	128	107	107	4	17, 85, 96, 71, 46	0.106	0.759	7.610	7.727

Table 7. Analysis of five typical VLs

Table 7 gives the lower and upper delays observed by simulation for each VL (columns *Min* and *Simu*) and the safe upper bounds computed by the network calculus and trajectory approaches (columns *NC* and *Traj*). For each VL, the lower delay observed by simulation corresponds to the minimum possible value of the delay. The delay distributions for vl_1 and vl_4 are depicted in figures 19(a) and 19(b). It appears that the delay distribution is close to the minimum possible value of the delay and far from the the safe upper bound computed by either the network calculus or the trajectory approach. This is mainly due to the fact that the AFDX network is lightly loaded. Thus, the probability that several frames reach the same output port at the same time is very low.

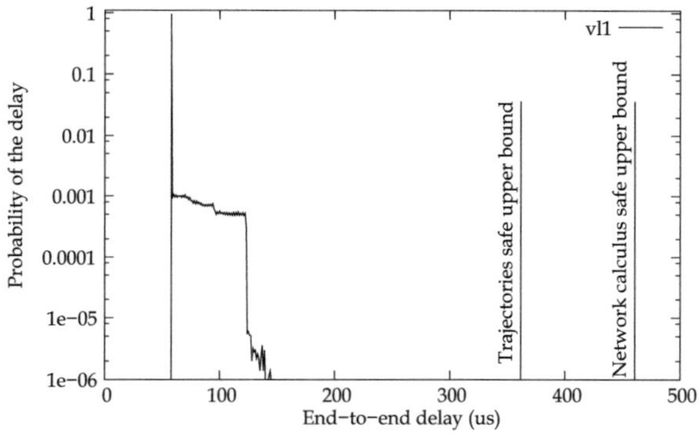

(a) Delay analysis of vl_1

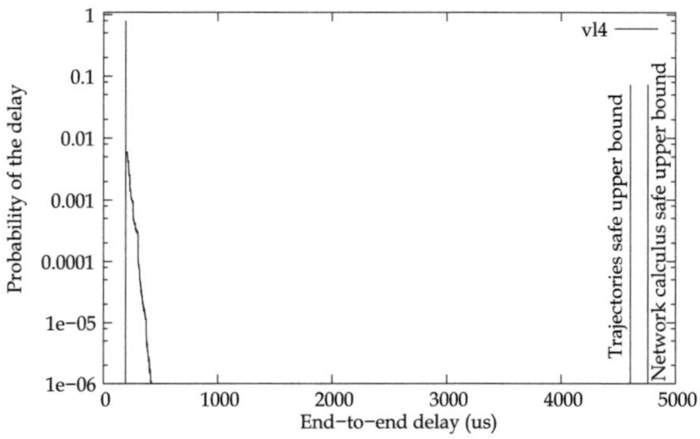

(b) Delay analysis of vl_4

Fig. 19. Delay analysis of two VLs

8. Conclusion

This chapter gives an overview of the temporal analysis of switched Ethernet avionic networks. Today, three approaches exist for the computation of a safe upper bound of the end-to-end delay of each flow transmitted on the avionic network. The first approach is based on model checking and allows the computation of the exact worst-case delay of each flow, but it is limited to small configurations, due to the combinatory explosion problem. The two other approaches are based on trajectories and network calculus and allow the computation of a safe upper bound of the end-to-end delay, which is most of the time larger than the exact worst-case, due to the pessimistic assumptions made by the two approaches. Nevertheless, these two approaches can be applied to industrial configurations. The computation of a safe upper bound is complemented by the evaluation of the end-to-end delay distribution, thanks to a simulation approach.

The worst-case analysis approaches presented in this paper consider a set of sporadic flows with no assumption concerning the arrival time of packets. This does not take into account the scheduling of the flows which are emitted by the same component. This scheduling could be integrated in the modeling by the mean of assumptions on the relative arrival time of packets, as it has been done in the automotive context [Grenier et al. (2008)]. The integration of this scheduling in the modeling of flows should distribute temporally the transmission of packets and very likely reduce the waiting time of packets in output buffers. Moreover, the sporadic characteristic of avionics flows could be taken into account with the help of a probabilistic modeling, as it has been proposed for the a periodic traffic in the automotive context [Khan et al. (2009)]. This leads to a probabilistic analysis of the worst case delay of flows. Such an analysis has been proposed [Scharbarg et al. (2009)], based on a stochastic Network Calculus approach [Vojnović & Le Boudec (2002; 2003)].

For future aircraft, the addition of other type of flows (audio, video, best-effort, . . .) on the AFDX network is envisioned. These different flows have different timing constraints and criticity levels. Thus, it is necessary to differentiate them and the FIFO policy on switch output ports is not suitable. Thus, it is necessary to consider other service disciplines, such as static priority queueing or weighted fair queueing [Parekh & Gallager (1993)]. The introduction of static priority queueing in the stochastic Network Calculus approach has been presented in [Ridouard et al. (2008)]. The Trajectory approach is promising for handling heterogeneous flows needing QoS aware servicing policies at switches level [Martin & Minet (2006a;b)].

9. References

Alur, R. & Dill, D. L. (1994). Theory of Timed Automata, *Theoritical Computer Science* 126(2): 183–235.

ARI (1991). ARINC 651, Aeronautical Radio Inc. ARINC specification 651. Design Guidance for Integrated Modular Avionics., *Technical report*, Aeronotical Radio Inc.

ARI (1997). ARINC 653, Aeronautical Radio Inc. ARINC specification 653. Avionic application Software Standard Interface., *Technical report*, Aeronotical Radio Inc.

ARI (2001). ARINC 429, Aeronautical Radio Inc. ARINC specification 429. Digital Information Transfer System (DITS) parts 1,2,3., *Technical report*, Aeronotical Radio Inc.

ARI (2002-2005). ARINC Specification 664: Aircraft Data Network, Parts 1,2,7, *Technical report*, Aeronotical Radio Inc.

Bauer, H., Scharbarg, J.-L. & Fraboul, C. (2009a). Applying and optimizing trajectory approach for performance evaluation of afdx avionics network, *Proceedings of the 21th ECRTS WiP section*, Dublin, pp. 57,60. http://gerfaut83.free.fr/article/Bauer-Scharbarg-Fraboul.pdf.

Bauer, H., Scharbarg, J.-L.&Fraboul, C. (2009b). Applying trajectory approach to afdx avionics network, *Proc. of the 14th International Conference on Emerging Technologies and Factory Automation*, IEEE, Mallorca, pp. 1–8.

Bérard, B., Bidoit, M., Finkel, A., Laroussinie, F., Petit, A., Petrucci, L. & Schnoebelen, Ph. (2001). *Systems and Software Verification. Model-Checking Techniques and Tools*, Springer.

Burgueño Arjona, A. (1998). *Vérification et synthèse de systèmes temporisés par des méthodes d'observation et d'analyse paramétrique*, PhD thesis, Ecole Nationale Supérieur de l'Aéronautique et de l'Espace, Toulouse, France.

Chang, C.-S. (2000). *Performance Guarantees in Communication Networks*, Springer-Verlag, London, UK. isbn = {1852332263}.

Charara, H., Scharbarg, J.-L., Ermont, J. & Fraboul, C. (2006). Methods for bounding end-to-end delays on an AFDX network, *Proceedings of the 18th ECRTS*, Dresden, Germany, pp. 193–202.

Charara, H., Scharbarg, J.-L. & Fraboul, C. (2006). Focusing simulation for end-to-end delays analysis on a switched Ethernet, *Proceedings of the WiP session of RTSS*, Rio de Janeiro, Brasil.

Grenier, M., Havet, L. & Navet, N. (2008). Scheduling messages with offsets on Controller Area Network: a major performance boost, *in* N. Navet & F. c. Simonot-Lion (eds), *The automotive embedded systems handbook*, Taylor and Francis, chapter 14.

Khan, D., Navet, N., Bavoux, B. & Migge, J. (2009). Aperiodic traffic in response time analysis with adjustable safety level, *Proc. of the 14th International Conference on Emerging Technologies and Factory Automation*, IEEE, Palma de Mallorca, Spain.

Larsen, K. G., Pettersson, P. & Yi, W. (1997). UPPAAL in a Nutshell, *International Journal on Software Tools for Technology Transfer* 1(1–2): 134–152.

Le Boudec, J.-Y. & Thiran, P. (2001). *Network Calculus: A Theory of Deterministic Queuing Systems for the Internet*, Vol. 2050 of *Lecture Notes in Computer Science*, Springer-Verlag. ISBN: 3-540-42184-X.

Martin, S. (2004). *Maîtrise de la dimension temporelle de la qualité de service dans les réseaux*, PhD thesis, Université Paris XII.

Martin, S. & Minet, P. (2006a). Schedulability analysis of flows scheduled with fifo: application to the expedited forwarding class, *20th International parallel and distributed processing symposium*, Rhodes Island, Greece.

Martin, S. & Minet, P. (2006b). Worst case end-to-end response times of flows scheduled with fp/fifo, *5th IEEE International Conference on Networking*, Mauritius.

Migge, J. (1999). *L'ordonnancement sous contraintes temps-réel: un modèle à base de trajectoires*, PhD thesis, INRIA, Sophia Antipolis France.

Parekh, A. & Gallager, R. (1993). A generalised processor sharing approach to flow control in integrated services networks: the single-node case, *IEEE/ACM transactions on networking* 1(3): 344–357.

Ridouard, F., Scharbarg, J.-L. & Fraboul, C. (2008). Probabilistic upper bounds for heterogeneous flows using a static priority queueing on an AFDX network, *Proc. of the 13th International Conference on Emerging Technologies and Factory Automation*, IEEE, Hambourg, pp. 1220–1227.

Scharbarg, J.-L. & Fraboul, C. (2007). A generic simulation model for end-to-end delays evaluation on an avionics switched Ethernet, *Proc. of the 7th International Conference on Fieldbuses and networks in industrial and embedded systems*, IFAC, Toulouse, France.

Scharbarg, J.-L., Ridouard, F. & Fraboul, C. (2009). A probabilistic analysis of end-to-end delays on an AFDX network, *IEEE transactions on industrial informatics* 5(1).

Vojnović, M. & Le Boudec, J. (2002). Stochastic analysis of some expedited forwarding networks, *in Proceedings of Infocom, New-York*.

Vojnović, M. & Le Boudec, J. (2003). Bounds for independent regulated inputs multiplexed in a service curve network element, *IEEE Trans. on Communications* 51(5).